Health Psychology

Contents

Contents

Contributors

Dr Paul Bennett
School of Psychology
University of Wales College of Cardiff
PO Box 901
Cardiff CF1 3YG, UK

Ms Nicola Bradbury
Joint Service Development Project
Monyhull Hospital
Monyhull Hall Road
Kings Norton
Birmingham B30 3QB, UK

Ms Annabel Broome
Aspen House
3, High Street
Sydling St. Nicholas
Dorchester
Dorset DT2 9PB, UK

Professor Tom Cox
World Health Organisation
Department of Psychology
University of Nottingham
Nottingham NG7 2RD, UK

Mrs Louise Earll
Department of Health Psychology
Gloucestershire Royal Hospital
Great Western Road,
Gloucester GL1 3NN, UK

Ms Aleda Erskine
Department of Psychology
Royal Northern Hospital
Holloway Road
London N7 6LD UK

Dr Myra Hunter
Unit of Psychology
Guy's Hospital Medical School
St Thomas Street
London SE1 9RS, UK

Dr Simon Jakes
District Psychology Service
Michael Tetley Hall
Sandhurst Road
Tunbridge Wells
Kent TN2 3JS, UK

Mr Peter James
Department of Psychology
North Tyneside Health Care
Preston Hospital
Tyne and Wear NE2 0LR, UK

Mr Bernard Kat
County Hospital
Durham DH1 4ST, UK

Dr John Kincey
Department of Clinical Psychology
Gaskell House
Manchester Royal Infirmary
Swinton Grove
Manchester M13 0EU, UK

Mr Bob Lewin
Astley Ainslie Hospital
Canaan Lane
Edinburgh EH9, UK

Professor Philip Ley
18, Freeman Avenue
Castle Hill
New South Wales
Australia 2154

Dr Sue Llewelyn
Department of Psychiatry
University of Edinburgh
Royal Edinburgh Hospital
Morningside
Edinburgh EH10 5HF, UK

Mr Clive Long
Psychology Department
St. Andrew's Hospital
Billing Road
Northampton NN1 5DG, UK

Dr Theresa M. Marteau
Psychology and Genetics Research Group
United Medical and Dental Schools of Guy's
and St. Thomas's, Guy's Campus
London Bridge
London SE1 9RT, UK

Mr Keith Nichols
Department of Psychology
Washington Singer Laboratories
University of Exeter
Devon EX4 4QG, UK

Dr Sheila Payne
Department of Psychology
University of Southampton
Highfield
Southampton SO9 5NH, UK

Dr Phil Richardson
Dept. of Academic Psychiatry
St. Thomas Hospital
Lambeth Palace Road
London SE1 7EH, UK

Dr Elizabeth Robinson
School of Psychology
University of Birmingham
Edgbaston
Birmingham B15 2TT, UK

Dr Lorraine Sherr
Department of Public Health
Royal Free Hospital School of Medicine
Rowland Hill
London NW3 9PF, UK

Dr Richard Shillitoe
Department of Clinical Psychology
Airedale General Hospital
Skipton Road
Steeton
Keighley
West Yorkshire BD20 6TD, UK

Ms Nicola Whitehead
Clinical Psychology Service
Cross Street Health Centre,
Dudley
West Midlands DY1 1RN, UK

Mr Stephen Wilkinson
Royal Midland Counties Hospital
Tachbrook Road
Leamington Spa
Warwickshire CV31 3EQ, UK

Ms Amanda C. de C. Williams
Department of Psychology
Royal Northern Hospital
Holloway Road
London N7 6LD, UK

Ms Christine Wilson
Midlands Centre for Spinal Injuries
Robert Jones and Agnes Hunt Orthopaedic
Hospital
Oswestry
Shropshire, UK

Introduction

This is the second edition of *Health Psychology: Processes and Applications*. The first edition was published in 1989 because of the growing awareness of the importance of psychological processes in the experience of health and health care. At that time there was no easily available text which provided a thorough introduction to, and overview of, psychology as applied to both processes and particular applications to different medical specialties. Health psychology has, however, developed considerably since the first edition was published. Professionals are becoming increasingly aware of the contribution of psychology in an enormous variety of areas, and health psychologists themselves have grown in confidence and number. The first edition of this volume probably played some part in these developments as, since 1989, *Health Psychology* has become a well-tried text for training and updating health care professionals, as well as for teaching both undergraduates and postgraduates.

A number of changes have prompted us to produce an updated edition of this book. For instance, behavioural medicine is now included in all basic medical training, so that medical students are made aware of the relevance of psychological issues in health care from the very start. Also, health psychology is being routinely included in many professional training courses, such as clinical psychology, speech therapy, dietetics and nursing. In addition, the public is becoming more demanding of the care they receive, with the Patients' Charter helping them to articulate their own needs and dissatisfactions with health services.

It is changes such as these which have encouraged us to produce this second edition. Authors have also had the opportunity to update their chapters in the light of recent developments in their particular specialties, and the editors have also included discussion of some of the growing demands in health care, for example in the field of HIV and AIDS. In addition, we are delighted to be able to include three new chapters, one on the provision of health care by Bernard Kat, and a new chapter on psychology as applied to cardiac care by Bob Lewin. We have also added a new chapter on stress, by Tom Cox, which has allowed an exploration of theoretical models of stress and coping in greater depth, and brings particular insights from the growing area of occupational health psychology. Because of the changing scene in health care, chapters have been updated to a greater or lesser extent, depending on the field, and a number of chapters from the first edition have not been included, either because of overlap or because the topics are covered adequately elsewhere.

As previously, the book is divided into two sections. Part 1 looks at the general psychological processes that are relevant across many health care settings. Issues such as attitudes to health, stress, communication between medical staff and patients, institutional management of illness, and problems with delivering sensitive psychological care are central to understanding the importance of psychology in health care. Part 2 concerns a sample of the particular fields in which psychology has been able to make a significant contribution. Our choice is inevitably selective. There are numerous areas in which psychology could play an important role but which we have not been able to include, for reasons of space or because other texts exist, or because the applications are still at a very early stage of development. For example, psychological aspects of dental care, ophthalmology and radiotherapy are growing areas, but to include all possible areas would dilute the quality or increase the length and weight of the book to the point where no-one would attempt to lift it, let alone read it! Our central concern is to demonstrate clearly how psychology can operate in a number of particular fields, using the insights and methods described in the first part of the book. The reader is strongly recommended to read the first part before consulting the second part about specific applications. The second part is, to an extent, illustrative of the processes and theories which are introduced in the first part, as applied to specific medical specialities.

Background to health psychology

The developing interest in health psychology over the last decade or so, from both professionals and patients, has been prompted by a number of significant catalysts, although mind–body interplay has long been recognized. Nevertheless, the extent to which psychological impact has been recognized and has influenced medical practice has varied throughout time. On some occasions the psychological contribution has been seen as less important than the somatic contribution; at other times (as at present) there are upsurges in emphasis on the psychological component.

The following list attempts to identify and summarize significant current catalysts of this trend towards emphasizing psychological factors:

- The identification of epidemiological and social factors that relate certain behaviours to increased risks of serious disease.

- An increase in chronic disease as a proportion of total illness suffered.
- Higher costs of health care and the need to contain demand.
- A public interest in alternative, self-care and self-control methods of health care.
- The growth in psychological research and effective psychological therapy.
- Significant developments in psychosomatic research, leading to the identification of psychosocial factors in the vulnerability to, and maintenance of, health problems.
- Dissatisfaction with medical care and an increasing awareness of iatrogenic problems.

Broadly speaking, it is these factors that have increased the concentration of efforts in health psychology. These efforts have been focused on the three processes, which largely reflect a medical, service perspective of illness, and mesh into prevailing structures and models:

- The aetiology of health problems.
- The concurrence of psychological processes with medical problems.
- The development and refinement of specific psychological techniques for medical problems.

These processes have been variously covered in many recent titles relating to health psychology (Rachman, Vols 1, 2 and 3, 1977, 1980, 1984; Bakal, 1979; Stone *et al.*, 1979; Surwitt *et al.*, 1982; Mechanic, 1983; Nichols, 1993), to which the reader can refer for more general information.

This volume is an attempt to give health care practitioners the chance to utilize recent findings on psychological aspects of health care. In some chapters this will simply focus on a general review of the pertinent background literature; in others it is possible to take a further step into applied studies and case material. The differences reflect the maturity of work in the different specialties.

There are many reasons for the differences in depth of research and application, and not all professionals reading this book and possibly wishing to adopt a different conceptual framework and different style of work, will find it easy. It would be irresponsible to suggest that such change is easy, and the following paragraphs attempt to clarify some of the blocks that might be expected.

Although it is clearly simplistic to suppose that all health care professionals hold consistent views on medicine – encapsulated in the biomedical model of health – it does appear that this is the predominant model taught in medical schools, and it may explain some of the conflicts that arise when practitioners, attempting to introduce psychosocially oriented management, find themselves in conflict with traditional practice. This conflict can arise for a number of reasons.

First, the biomedical model appears to promote passivity in the patient and a guarding of expertise by the care-giver. The psychosocial model attempts to encourage active participation by the sufferer, and a sharing of responsibility and decision-making that challenges these traditional roles. Of course, this also has implications for the sharing of information and ownership of responsibility for actions, such as high-risk health behaviours like smoking.

Secondly there are different attitudes to success and outcome. The biomedical model attempts to cure, and measures success by the absence of disease. The psychosocial model sees 'healthiness' as a continuum. The latter model has some advantage to the chronically ill person, for whom 'coping' is the best possible outcome if they cannot expect to be 'cured'.

Since the medical profession has been so powerful in the delivery of health care, it is not surprising to discover that the main developments in health psychology have been in those areas of particular interest to the power-holders, and not necessarily of major interest to the behavioural scientist.

The major developments of importance to the behavioural scientist which seem to offer a wide range of potential to the general public can be listed as follows, and reflect the research emphasis of more recent years:

- The interplay of **personality, stress** and **vulnerability,** e.g. the effects of stress on the immune system and the way this affects responses to infection.
- The identification of **behavioural risk factors** relating to chronic life-threatening illness, e.g. smoking and cardiovascular disorders; sexual behaviour.
- The development of **self-management studies,** e.g. pain management programmes.
- Clearer understanding of the **process of health care,** for example
  - care seeking
  - communications
  - compliance.
- The development of **psychological techniques** for medical problems, e.g. relaxation, biofeedback and stress management.
- Identifying **psychological reactions** that relate to medical problems, for example grief or denial.
- **Health promotion**. The development of **explanatory** models and processes relating to health behaviour, e.g. health belief model, self-efficacy, attribution theory, Health Locus of Control, the theory of reasoned action.

Broome (1986) and Marteau and Johnson (1987) recommend that applications in health promotion and health psychology are not simply developed as useful techniques but are clearly related to psychological explanatory theory, such as those mentioned above. Hence we hope that readers will read Part 2 of this volume in the context of the material presented in Part 1.

References

Bakal, D.A. (1979) *Psychology and Medicine*, Tavistock Publications, London.

Broome, A.K. (1986) Psychological Explanation and Health Promotion Proceedings of the BPS Annual Conference, *Bulletin of the British Psychological Society*, 39, A35.

Marteau, T.M. and Johnson, M. (1987) Health psychology: the danger of neglecting psychological models. *Bulletin of the British Psychological Society*, 40, 82–5.

Mechanic, D. (1983) *Handbook of Health, Health Care and the Health Professions*, Free Association Press, New York.

Nichols, K.A. (1993) *Psychological Care in Physical Illness*, Croom Helm, London.

Rachman, S.J. (1977, 1980, 1984) *Contributions to Medical Psychology, vols 1, 2 and 3*, Pergamon Press, New York and Oxford.

Stone, G. C., Cohen, F. and Adler, N.E. (1979) *Health Psychology – A Handbook*, Jossey Bass.

Surwitt, R.S. Williams, R.B., Steptoe, A. and Biersner, R. (1982) *Behavioural Treatment of Disease*, Plenum Press, New York.

Part One

Processes

Chapter one

Health beliefs and attributions

Theresa M. Marteau

Introduction

The beliefs and attributions that people hold can influence their health in one of two main ways: first, by affecting their behaviour, such as attendance at a screening programme; the food they eat; whether they take prescribed medication; and secondly, more directly by affecting a physiological system, such as the immune or cardiovascular systems. These two modes of influence are not mutually exclusive. A patient's health may also be influenced by the beliefs and attributions of health professionals. These may affect patient outcomes in one of two ways: first, by affecting staff decisions about which medical procedures or treatments to use, and secondly by influencing patients' cognitions. Although there is general agreement among psychologists that health beliefs and attributions are important in explaining and predicting health behaviours and health outcomes, there is less agreement about which beliefs and attributions are important, and how much of the variance in outcomes they predict.

Drawing upon various theoretical approaches, the relationship between the cognitions of both patients and staff and health behaviour and health outcomes will be critically reviewed. The implications of these findings for health promotion, disease prevention and maximizing the effectiveness of treatment as well as staff training will be discussed.

Patients' beliefs and attributions: cognitions and behaviour

Many different beliefs and attributions have been considered as precursors to health-related behaviours. General as well as health-specific cognitions, derived from various theoretical models, have been used to predict behaviour in the face of a health threat as well as in response to an illness or its treatment. Although there is some overlap in the cognitions invoked by these different models, this section will be organized according to the theories that currently predominate in this field.

Expectancy-value models

Many cognitive models of behaviour are based upon an expectancy-value approach to motivation which asserts that individuals are motivated to maximize gains and minimize losses. Behavioural choice and persistence are a function of the expected success of the behaviour in attaining a goal and the value of that goal. Three models based on this approach are described below.

Social learning theory

Rotter's social learning theory posits that: 'the potential for a behaviour to occur in any specific psychological situation is a function of the expectancy that the behaviour will lead to a particular reinforcement in that situation and the value of that outcome' (Rotter, 1954, p. 102). Of these two social learning theory constructs, expectancy has received the most attention. One generalized expectancy in particular – locus of control – has been the focus of much work. Locus of control is the generalized expectancy about whether one's own behaviour or forces external to oneself control reinforcements. Starting with Rotter's scale, measuring generalized expectancies on one dimension (Rotter, 1966), locus of control has been expanded to include three orthogonal dimensions: internality, powerful others and chance (Levenson, 1973).

Locus of control can be measured as a general expectancy (as in the original locus of control scale) or an expectancy specific to a particular situation. Strickland (1978) suggests that in a novel or ambiguous situation an individual's behaviour is predictable from generalized expectancies. These diminish in importance the more experience the person has in a situation. Then situation-specific expectancies become important. Several locus of control scales have been developed to measure expectancies about different health-related situations, including health (Wallston, Wallston and DeVellis, 1978; Lau and Ware, 1981), fetal health (Labs and Wurtele, 1986), dental health (Carnahan, 1979) and diabetes (Bradley *et al.*, 1984).

The concept of health as a value has been neglected in health research (Lau, Hartman and Ware, 1986): it is frequently assumed that the value placed on health is uniformly high. The most common method of measuring health value is based on Rokeach's (1973) terminal values ranking test, for which respondents are asked to assess the value of health relative to such items as a comfortable life, world peace, happiness and health. Other measures of value include a short four-item Likert scale developed by Lau, Hartman and Ware (1986) which measures absolute values of health as opposed to the relative value provided by the use of Rokeach's measure.

Health-related behaviour

Certain health-related behaviours reduce morbidity and mortality (Breslow and Enstrom, 1980). Using both or just one of the social learning constructs, there have been attempts to predict various health-related behaviours, including eating and drinking in moderation, brushing and flossing teeth, attending for health checks, breast self-examination, exercise, getting enough sleep, wearing seat belts and seeking health-relevant information.

Kristiansen (1985) found that total scores on seven health-preventive behaviours were predicted from a high value on health, world peace and a low value on an exciting life, explaining 32% of the variance in direct risk scores. These results illustrate the importance of assessing other values as well as health in predicting health-related behaviours. Lau, Hartman and Ware (1986) found that neither an internal locus of control nor a high value on health considered alone were predictive of breast self-examination (BSE). However, when considered in combination, a positive correlation was found: women who perceived their own health to be within their control, or did not believe in chance controlling their health, and who placed a high value on health, were significantly more likely to perform BSE. In predicting information seeking, Wallston, Maides and Wallston (1976) found that people who valued their health highly and who had an internal locus of control were willing to read more hypertension-related information than subjects who, despite valuing health highly, had an external locus of control.

In a review of several studies examining the relationship between locus of control and health-related behaviours, Wallston and Wallston (1982) concluded (p. 77): '... research correlating health locus of control beliefs with measures of behaviours carried out to maintain or enhance health has produced few significant relationships'. Most of the studies included in their review, however, did not include a measure of health value. A belief that one's own health is controllable, either by oneself or others, together with a high value on health, is more likely to be associated with engaging in health-promoting behaviours than believing one's health is uncontrollable and placing a low value on health. More consistent findings are evident when both expectations and value attached to the outcome are considered than either alone.

Response to treatment

Many studies have attempted to predict a wide range of adherence behaviours, such as dietary compliance (Wallston and McLeod, 1979) and medication compliance among those with hypertension (Lewis, Morisky and Flynn, 1978); dietary control in renal patients (Levin and Schulz, 1980); behavioural management of diabetes (Schlenk and Hart, 1984); and a variety of health-related behaviours of people with epilepsy (DeVellis, *et al.*, 1980).

As well as influencing patients' decisions about whether to follow a recommended treatment regimen, perceived control over an illness may also influence patients' choice when offered a range of possible treatments. When offered a choice of three treatment approaches for diabetes (an insulin pump; intensified conventional treatment; or continuation with current regimen of once- or twice-daily injections), patient choice was influenced by perceived control over their diabetes. Patients who chose the insulin pumps perceived less personal control over their diabetes and attributed significantly more control to doctors, compared to patients choosing any other treatment option (Bradley *et al.*, 1987).

The reinforcement value of undertaking any recommended course of action in the face of illness has rarely been studied (an exception being perhaps when operationalized as benefits and barriers in the Health Belief Model), but is assumed to be high. Based on studies of well

people, as reviewed above, this assumption is perhaps not founded. The predictive power of expectancies of control over outcome may be increased if the value of the outcome is considered as well.

A second version of social learning theory places self-efficacy in a key role. Self-efficacy is the expectation that one is sufficiently competent to perform a behaviour. It is one of two cognitions used in Bandura's social learning theory to predict behaviour, the other being outcome expectancy: the expectation that a behaviour will lead to a particular outcome. Self-efficacy is also incorporated into protection motivation theory (Rippetoe and Rogers, 1987) and the theory of planned behaviour (Ajzen, 1988). Self-efficacy has been found to predict a variety of behaviours, both health-related and other (for review, see Bandura, 1991).

Self-efficacy predicts both intentions and behaviour for a range of health-promoting and disease-preventing behaviours, including flossing of teeth, engaging in safe sex practices, practising breast self-examination and the initiation and maintenance of exercise behaviour (for review, see Schwartzer, 1992). Although the amount of variance in intentions and behaviour accounted for by self-efficacy varies across studies, some studies report accounting for large amounts. For example, in a Dutch study of smoking in adolescents, Kok and colleagues (1990) accounted for 44% of the variance in intention and 50% of the variance in reported behaviour. Self-efficacy can also be used to predict changes in behaviour, with post-treatment self-efficacy being a better predictor of maintaining behaviour change than self-efficacy assessed before treatment (for review, see Schwartzer, 1992).

Response to illness

The recovery of cardiovascular functioning in postcoronary patients is enhanced by self-perceptions of coping resources (Taylor *et al.*, 1985). Patients with rheumatoid arthritis were treated with a cognitive–behavioural programme that resulted in the enhancement of perceived self-efficacy, reduced pain and joint inflammation (O'Leary *et al.*, 1988). Following self-efficacy training, compliance with medical regimens was improved in patients with chronic obstructive pulmonary diseases (Kaplan, Atkins and Reinsch, 1984). Recent research therefore suggests that the power of cognitive models to predict behaviour may be significantly enhanced by the inclusion of a measure of self-efficacy.

Fishbein's theory of reasoned action

This theory is based on the assumption that most human behaviour is under voluntary control and hence is largely guided by intention. Intention is determined both by the individual's attitude towards performing the behaviour and by their subjective norms, i.e. their perception of the degree to which significant others think performing the behaviour is important (Fishbein and Ajzen, 1975). The attitude component is the product of the beliefs (expectations) that performing a specific behaviour will lead to a certain consequence, and the individual's valuation of that consequence (i.e. how good or bad such an outcome would be). The subjective normative component of the model also incorporates an expectancy and value component. It is the product of the expectation that significant others will consider the performance of the behaviour important, and the value of that person's approval. This theory thus considers both the individual's attitude towards a behaviour and the influence of the social environment as important predictors of behavioural intention. The relative contribution of the two components of the model will depend in part upon the behaviour in question.

The theory of reasoned action was extended by Ajzen (1988) to include an additional variable, perceived behavioural control. The similarity between this variable and self-efficacy has been noted by several researchers (Kok *et al.*, 1990; Schwarzer, 1992).

Health-related behaviour

Although Fishbein's model has been used to predict a wide range of behaviours, the study of health-related behaviours has been limited. There has been some research showing the utility of the model in predicting smoking and giving up smoking (Fishbein, 1982); breast-versus bottle-feeding (Manstead, Profitt and Smart, 1983); and the use of contraception (Davidson and Jacquard, 1975). The possible relevance of this theory to the adoption of safe-sex practices in the face of the threat of AIDS is suggested by the results of a recent study. Although Fishbein's model was not used to guide this study, the belief that peers were changing their habits was consistently related to the use of safer sexual practices. It was unrelated to knowledge of AIDS, perceived risk or perceived efficacy of safer sexual behaviour (Joseph *et al.*, 1987).

Response to treatment

Socially mediated factors were found to be more important than specific attitudinal factors in predicting dietary intentions among patients with diabetes (Shenkel *et al.*, 1985–6). Patients consistently intended to comply with their diet according to their expectations of significant others and the value of their approval, but their own attitudes towards following the diet were not significantly associated with intention.

While this model of behaviour has been successful in predicting significant amounts of variance in behavioural intention, it has not been used much to date in the health field, perhaps because the development of appropriate measures is too time-consuming (Wallston and Wallston, 1984). New beliefs have to be assessed for each behaviour and population. A further possible factor inhibiting its wider use concerns the nature of psychology research conducted in the applied setting of health care. Research is not always guided by psychological theory (Marteau and Johnston, 1987), and frequently the research is not conducted by psychologists. This in part may account for the relative neglect of a potentially powerful, but less accessible, model (the theory of reasoned action) and the popularity of models which are perhaps less powerful but have higher face validity, such as the health belief model.

The health belief model

The health belief model (HBM), unlike the two previous theories, was developed specifically to explain and predict behaviour in health contexts (Becker, 1974). Although originally developed to predict preventive health behaviours, the model has also been used to predict the behaviour of both acutely and chronically ill patients. The likelihood of an individual undertaking a particular action is seen as a function of the individual's perceptions of their susceptibility to the illness, the seriousness of the illness, and the potential benefits and costs involved in undertaking the particular action. Cues to action, which may be internal (such as the perception of a symptom) or external (such as a health education message), will determine whether a behaviour is performed. However, the precise way in which the variables combine to predict behaviour is unclear. Stone (1979) suggests that the health belief model makes relative rather than quantitative predictions. Although most researchers combine the variables in a linear fashion, Wallston and Wallston (1984) suggest that implicit in the theory is a multiplicative model.

Health-related behaviour

The HBM has most frequently been used in studies of the uptake of numerous health-promoting behaviours, such as participation in screening programmes for raised blood pressure, cervical cancer and genetic abnormalities;

uptake of inoculations; and the adoption of risk-reducing behaviours such as exercise regimens, giving up smoking, reducing alcohol consumption and altering dietary behaviours. In a review of 24 studies examining preventive health behaviours, Janz and Becker (1984) reported that the strongest predictors were perceived barriers to the behaviour and perceived susceptibility to the condition in question. They conclude that data published during the decade prior to their review provide substantial support for the usefulness of the health belief model as a framework for understanding individuals' health-related decision-making.

Response to treatment

The health belief model has been used particularly to examine the extent to which people follow advice in, for example, treatments for diabetes, hypertension and renal disease. In a review of 19 such studies, perceived barriers and benefits were found to be the most powerful dimensions, followed by perceived severity of the condition (Becker and Rosenstock, 1984).

While there has been much research guided by the health belief model, the model and the research have not been without their critics. The main criticisms concern the conceptualization of the model, the operationalization of its constructs, and its predictive power. These are discussed in more detail later in this chapter.

Attribution theory

Attribution theory is concerned with the way people explain events (Kelley and Michela, 1980). It deals with causes that individuals infer from outcomes that have occurred in the past. By contrast, social learning theory deals with expectancies about the future. However, the distinction between perceived control over events and attributions for causes may be blurred in some research (Wallston *et al.*, 1987). The distinction between attributions of causes of past events and perceived control over a future situation has been made by Brickman and colleagues (Brickman *et al.*, 1982), who treat judgements about the cause of a problem as separate from judgements about solutions to the problem. Hence in a health-related context attributions concerning the origin of an illness will not necessarily be the same as attributions concerning its treatment or course.

Health-related behaviour

Although general attribution research has focused on the attributions people make for their own and others' behaviour (Jones and Nisbett, 1971; Kelley and Michela, 1980; Hewstone, 1983), there has been relatively little work specifically on attributions concerning health-related behaviours. Several researchers have documented the explanations of well people for the causes of illness and health. Based on unstructured interviews with 80 French people concerning their ideas about health and illness, Herzlich (1973) suggested that, whereas health was seen as something within the individual, illness was seen as an encroachment upon the way of life, particularly life in an urban environment. Individual factors such as heredity were seen as necessary but not sufficient to cause illness. Farr (1977) has suggested, however, that the questions in this study were asked in a way that encouraged respondents to attribute health to internal factors and illness to external factors. None the less, other studies using different methods have also found this pattern of attributions (Marby, 1964; Blaxter, 1979).

The studies above have been concerned with documenting explanations for illness and health, but have not been concerned with the relationship between these explanations and the individual's behaviour. There is some evidence that attributions concerning the cause of an illness or its prevention may antecede health-preventive behaviours. In a prospective study attempting to predict attendance at a clinic to screen for high blood pressure, King (1982) found that people were more likely to attend if they perceived the cause of the condition to be external but controllable. Attributions concerning failures to stop smoking were related to smokers' expectations of succeeding at giving up smoking. In accord with predictions from Wiener's (1979) attribution model of achievement motivation, smokers who attributed other smokers' failure to stop smoking to stable (as opposed to unstable) factors, had lower expectations of giving up smoking themselves (Eiser *et al.*, 1985). Overall, a higher expectation of success was associated with giving up smoking. A study by Sonne and Janoff (1982) illustrates how attributions concerning weight loss may contribute to programme effectiveness. Overweight participants were given one of two weight-loss programmes: one emphasized self-control, the other external control by the therapist. Both programmes were equally effective during the treatment period, but at follow-up the self-control group had maintained more progress. Weight loss during the 11 week follow-up period was predicted by participants' attributions for improvement, measured immediately after the treatment programme.

Response to treatment

Research on attributions in the context of an illness has focused more on the emotional than the behavioural consequences of a particular attribution. Attribution theory maintains that a sudden threat or change in the environment provokes people to search for reasons for that threat or change, in order to understand, predict and control it (Kelley, 1967). This phenomenon seems to be very common in the face of illness (e.g. Bard and Dyk, 1956; Chodoff, Friedman and Hamburg, 1964; Taylor, Lichtman and Wood, 1984). Since attributions are thought to enable individuals to feel in control of their environment, attributions made to the self may be more adaptive than external attributions. Studies of various groups, including cancer patients, mothers of acutely ill children, children with diabetes, rape and accident victims, suggest, however, that self-blame is not always associated with a positive adaptation (for review, see Tennen, Affleck and Gershmann, 1986).

It has been suggested that self-blame encompasses two very different sets of attributions: behavioural self-blame, i.e. attribution to one's own (modifiable) behaviour, and characterological self-blame, i.e. attribution to stable aspects of oneself (Janoff-Bulman, 1979). Several studies now support the view that when self-blame is associated with perceived control over recurrence or recovery, it may lead to a more positive adaptation (Timko and Janoff-Bulman, 1985; Tennen, Affleck and Gershmann, 1986; Affleck et al., 1987). In health-related contexts the distinction between attributions for the cause of the problem and attributions for its course is important. Although no particular attribution for the cause of the cancer was associated with better adjustment among women with breast cancer, believing that they and others could now control the cancer was associated with good adjustment (Taylor, Lichtman and Wood, 1984).

Attributions may be related to specific as well as global-outcome measures of adaptation. For example, in a study of patients with diabetes, diabetic control in some was predicted from their explanations for factors affecting control: patients who attributed less of the variance in their control to their own efforts had better diabetic control (Bradley et al., 1987). However, there were no measures in this study of patients' behavioural management of their diabetes, so it is not known how these attributions may have influenced diabetic control, whether via a behavioural or a psychophsiological pathway. One study that considered both the emotional and behavioural consequences of attributions is a study of victims of industrial accidents

(Brewin, 1984a). Return to work was related to patients' moral evaluations of their actions: the more negative the evaluation, the quicker the return to work. This was interpreted as an example of the effect of guilt on attempts to make restitution. Upon return to work, victims who felt more causally responsible for their minor accidents reported feeling less tense and anxious and more alert and active.

As in studies considering the relationship between other beliefs and health outcomes, it is also important that the mechanism for any reported relationship is considered for theoretical as well as practical reasons.

Patients' beliefs and attributions: cognitions and health outcomes

In the previous section the relationship between patients' cognitions and various health-related behaviours was outlined. Beliefs and attributions may also influence a person's health or recovery from illness by their direct influence upon a physiological system. Hitherto, studies of the effect of patients' cognitions on their health have explicitly or implicitly been concerned with the relationship between cognitions and behaviour. The relationship between cognitions and physiological state has less often been addressed.

Although explanatory style seems to predict depression and achievement, its ability to predict general health has only recently been investigated. The way an individual habitually explains causal events appears to be reliably associated with health, both in the short and the long term.

There is a relationship between immune system functioning and vulnerability to disease. To predict individual differences in the functioning of the immune system, it is necessary to consider a number of psychological variables (Levy and Wise, 1987). McClelland and Jemmott (1980) found coping effectiveness to be more important than other psychological variables in predisposition to illness. Coping and the cognitive factors underlying it may moderate the relationship between stress and immune system changes. Antoni (1987) suggests that a hormonal assessment of coping style and effectiveness would make a useful contribution to the psychoimmunology literature.

Using a sample of 172 students, Peterson (1986) tested the ability of explanatory style to predict physical illness. Subjects completed a version of the Attributional Style Questionnaire containing 24 hypothetical bad events. Illness 4 weeks later was predicted from a composite of two of the three attributional dimensions: stability and globality (hopelessness). Kamen and Seligman (1987) report on a study concerned with predictability of health in the long term from explanatory style. They found that having a pessimistic outlook (i.e. explaining the causes of bad events in internal, stable and global terms) in early adult life was reliably associated with poor health in middle and late adulthood.

As well as being a risk factor for poor health in both the short and the long term, Seligman and Peterson (Kamen and Seligman, 1987) have found some evidence to suggest that pessimism is related to mortality. Using extracts from sports pages for the first half of this century, they categorized quotes from members of the baseball Hall of Fame in terms of explanatory style. An optimistic explanatory style for positive and negative events was positively correlated with longevity.

That explanatory style may affect health by affecting the immune system is currently under study by various groups. Seligman's group find some evidence that pessimism may bring about immunosuppression. One index of immune function is the T-helper cell/T-suppressor cell ratio (T4/T8). Proper functioning of the immune system requires that these two subpopulations of T lymphocytes are balanced, a low ratio indicating immunosuppression. Preliminary results indicate that individuals with a pessimistic explanatory style had significantly lower T4/T8 ratios than those with an optimistic style. In addition, explanatory style reliably predicted the T4/T8 ratio over and above the influence of prior health and current health.

Attempts to change people's beliefs about causes of events, increasing an individual's sense of personal responsibility and control, have produced long-term improvements in objective health (Rodin and Langer, 1977) and enhanced immune competence, an effect which persisted at a 1-month follow-up (Kiecolt-Glaser et al., 1985).

Many anecdotal reports suggest that an individual's cognitions may affect the course of a disease (Levy and Wise, 1987). More recently, methods for assessing the function of the immune system have become available so that controlled studies are now possible in this field. Important relationships between psychosocial and immunological factors and disease course have been demonstrated in AIDS, arthritis, asthma and herpes, as well as some cancers. For example, Greer, Morris and Pettingale (1979) carried out a prospective study of 69 women who underwent a simple mastectomy for early breast cancer. The results showed a significant relationship between reactions to the diagnosis and 5-year follow-up: 75% of the women who reacted to the diagnosis with denial and a fighting spirit were alive with no recurrence at follow-up, whereas only 35% of the women who showed stoic acceptance and helplessness/hopelessness had a favorable outcome. Thus, responding to breast cancer with helplessness, hopelessness and stoic acceptance may have a deleterious effect upon the ability to combat the disease.

Staff beliefs and attributions

Whereas the beliefs of patients will influence their behaviour and health outcomes, more of the variance in outcome is explained by considering the health beliefs and attributions of health professionals as well. The cognitions of health professionals may affect patient outcomes, first by affecting clinical decisions about the use of any medical or surgical interventions, and secondly by influencing patients' decisions regarding any health-related behaviours.

The cognitions of health professionals have not been the focus of much research. One reason why psychologists may have neglected the cognitions of health professionals is that they implicitly accept that their behaviour is based on medical knowledge, an empirically derived set of shared beliefs (Johnston and Marteau, 1987). Thus their beliefs and behaviour are assumed to be independent of context. Variations are thought to arise from a lack, or a conscious disregarding, of knowledge (Marteau and Johnston, 1987). Eisenberg (1986) argues that there is much variation in the practice of doctors because much medical knowledge is ambiguous and few services are absolutely necessary. Factors influencing practice may include beliefs and attitudes of health professionals, which can be shown to vary in keeping with various psychological models of behaviour.

Staff cognitions and behaviour

Staff vary in their approaches to patients and diseases, in ways that are not fully explained by variations in medical knowledge. Various researchers have reported that health professionals' beliefs about illness and its management vary along the dimensions proposed by the health belief model. Marteau and Baum (1984), for example, reported differences between two groups of hospital-based physicians in the perceived seriousness of diabetes, vulnerability of patients to the complications of the disease, and the perceived benefits of treatment. Paediatricians considered diabetes in childhood as significantly less serious than did

general physicians, and the risk of complications and death due to the disease as significantly lower. Paediatricians believed less strongly in the effectiveness of lowered blood glucose levels to reduce the likelihood of the development of complications. These beliefs were related to behaviour, since the two groups of doctors had different goals of treatment for the children in their care.

Doctors' belief in the effectiveness of an intervention was found to be associated with patient health outcomes (Weinberger, Cohen and Mazzuca, 1984). Patients were more likely to achieve near-normal blood glucose levels if they were treated by doctors who believed more strongly in the benefit of strict blood glucose control in reducing the likelihood of diabetic complications. Doctors' knowledge of diabetes was unrelated to their patients' diabetic control. The authors suggest that physicians' knowledge at best affects performance in the clinical situation through its effects upon beliefs in the efficacy of a particular action. Marteau and Baum's results further suggest that beliefs may determine the precise form of action, namely the type of glycaemic control that would be targeted and accepted. Beliefs in the effectiveness of a procedure have been shown to be associated not only with treatment goals and patient outcomes, but also with the performance of a procedure. Nurses who were skilled in performing basic life support perceived resuscitation procedures to be more effective than did the less skilled (Wynne *et al.*, 1987).

The attributions that staff make in explaining events can affect their approach to treatment. Attribution theory predicts that more help will be given when dependency is attributed to factors such as lack of ability on the victim's part (internal but uncontrollable), than when it is attributed to a lack of effort on the victim's part (internal and controllable) (Ickes and Kidd, 1976). Brewin (1984b), for example, found that attributions made by preclinical medical students influenced their willingness to prescribe psychotropic medication. If patients' life events were attributed to uncontrollable rather than controllable causes, the students were more likely to consider psychotropic medication an appropriate form of treatment. Although suggestive, this study needs repeating with a sample of qualified practising clinicians.

That attributions of health professionals may influence their attitudes towards patients was evident in a study of nurses' and doctors' attitudes towards patients with the same conditions but with different behavioural histories. Across five conditions, patients who had engaged in a relevant preventive behaviour, such as not smoking in those with lung cancer, were seen as more compliant, more likely to be concerned about their condition and more enjoyable to work with than those with the same condition but who had not engaged in relevant behaviour. (Marteau and Riordan, 1992).

Staff cognitions and patient cognitions

As well as influencing the health outcomes of patients by determining the choice of treatment, staff cognitions may also influence health outcomes by influencing patient cognitions and hence patient behaviour.

The doctor–patient relationship is one based on at least three different forms of 'social power': legitimate power, which depends on the target's acceptance of role obligations to follow the agent's instructions or advice; expert power, arising from the agent being seen by the target as having superior knowledge and ability; and informational power, which depends on the persuasiveness of the information conveyed by the agent (French and Raven, 1959; Eiser, 1986). On the basis of this power, health professionals may influence patients' cognitions and behaviour. The extent to which patients are influenced by health professionals may depend upon the extent to which they ascribe

any of the types of power to the health professional.

Health professionals may influence the beliefs, attributions and behaviour of patients by giving them information, and through expressing their beliefs about the patient's health and the best way to overcome a particular health problem. The extent to which a patient may take the advice will depend on many factors, including how much of the advice is remembered and understood, as well as how satisfied the patient is with the consultation (Ley, 1982). Although much is written about the high rates of non-compliance among patients (i.e. patients not adhering to the advice of health professionals), with a frequent mean estimate of 50%, the reverse side of this coin is that 50% of patients *are* influenced by the advice of health professionals. Hence, health professionals' beliefs about a disease and its management are a large factor in influencing patients' approaches to the management of illnesses.

The way in which information is presented to patients may influence their decisions regarding the uptake of a recommended action. Most normative and descriptive models of decision-making postulate that decisions are influenced by the probability of an outcome as well as the value of that outcome. Prospect theory (Kahneman and Tversky, 1979) suggests that these decisions are further influenced by the manner in which these probabilities are presented. For example, when asked whether they would consider surgery under various probabilities of success for their hypothetical lung cancer, students, patients and physicians were more likely to choose surgery when the possible outcome was presented as the probability of surviving as opposed to the probability of dying (McNeil *et al.*, 1982). There is also some evidence to suggest that the advice doctors give patients is also influenced by a framing effect. Medical students were more likely to recommend surgery to patients when they had been given information concerning survival in a positive frame than when the same information had been framed negatively (Marteau, 1989).

As well as influencing patients' cognitions directly, staff cognitions may differentially affect patients according to patients' cognitions. By considering staff cognitions in conjunction with those of patients, it is evident that patients and doctors neither always hold the same beliefs about a disease (Marteau and Baum, 1984; Marteau and Johnston, 1986a), nor goals of treatment (Marteau *et al.*, 1987), nor explanations for the course of a disease (House, Pendleton and Parker, 1986; Gamsu and Bradley, 1987). For example, physicians and patients were found to differ in their attributions concerning compliance with a recommended diet (House, Pendleton and Parker, 1986). Whereas physicians overwhelmingly perceived motivational problems as the reason for diabetic patients' non-compliance, patients themselves saw this as largely due to environmental and physiological factors, and hence outside their control.

Whether obstetricians and patients had compatible views of pregnancy was found to affect the course of labour (Rosengren, 1961). Further evidence supporting the role of attribution congruence between patient and doctor in influencing patient outcomes was found in a study examining consultations of patients with diabetes (Gillespie and Bradley, 1988). When the doctor was instructed to negotiate and agree with the patient on the causes of any problems discussed, there was a tendency, although it failed to reach statistical significance, for such patients to have better diabetic control when assessed 6 weeks after the consultation. Patient satisfaction with the consultation was unrelated to attribution congruence. As only one doctor (as well as 54 patients) took part in this study, further work is needed to determine the generalizability of these results.

Summary

The postulated relationships between the cognitions of patients and health professionals, health behaviour and health outcomes described above are depicted in Fig. 1.1. Patients' cognitions may influence health outcomes indirectly by influencing health-related behaviours (A), and directly by influencing physiological systems (B). Cognitions of health professionals will influence their own

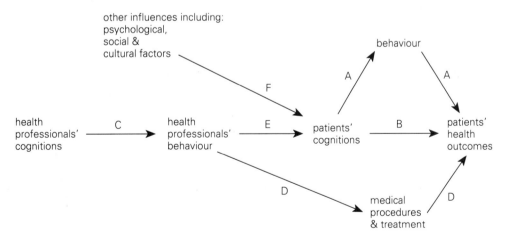

FIGURE 1.1 Postulated relationship between patients' and health professionals' cognitions, patients' and health professionals' behaviour and patients' outcomes.

behaviour (C), which in turn may influence patients' health outcomes directly by determining how the health professional manages a disease (D), and more indirectly by influencing the cognitions of the patient (E). Patients' cognitions are also influenced by other factors, including beliefs about their health status (F). This diagram inevitably misrepresents the dynamic nature of the relationships between cognitions, behaviour and health. However, it does depict some of the relationships and the main ways in which their links have been studied.

Critique of cognitive approaches to health behaviour and health outcomes

Cognitive models have provided the theoretical underpinning to many studies concerned with identifying the factors that mediate differential health outcomes, but the results have been equivocal and none of the individual differences studied has consistently predicted health and illness behaviours (Turk, Rudy and Salovey, 1986). There are at least two possible explanations for why cognitive models tend to account for small amounts of variance in health outcomes: first, although the theories are valid they have been inadequately tested, and secondly, the theories themselves are not valid.

Currently used theories have perhaps not been tested adequately in at least three ways. First, many different measures have been used to operationalize the same construct, with frequently little acknowledgement as to reliability and validity (Marteau, 1987). Secondly, although a theory may have been used to guide cognition selection, the data collected are not always analysed in accord with theoretical predictions. For example, in the majority of studies using the multidimensional health locus of control scale (Wallston, Wallston and DeVellis, 1978), scores on each of the three dimensions are considered separately, and covariation is sought between scores on a dimension and a dependent variable. Wallston and Wallston (1982), however, have proposed that patterns of scores are used to describe each person's overall locus of control. They propose eight different patterns of health locus of control expectancies, based on whether an individual is relatively high or low on each of the three dimensions. A typological use of this scale has been little explored. Finally, a theory may have been conceptualized incorrectly by researchers. Although there has been much interest in the application of attribution and attributional theories to clinical practice, recent reviews find mixed empirical support for attributional hypotheses and have generally cautioned against overenthusiasm for these new ideas (Coyne and Gotlib, 1983; Brewin, 1985). Brewin and Antaki (1987) have argued that this stems from most researchers taking subjects' explanations solely as a reflection of the perceived causal relationships between a set of variables. Ordinary explanation has at least three other functions: labelling, moral evaluation and self-presentation. Brewin and Antaki argue that the term 'attribution' has been used indiscriminately to include all functions.

The second main set of explanations for why value-expectancy models and attribution theory account for small amounts of variance in outcome is that they are the wrong theories from which to derive cognitions to predict health behaviour and outcomes. Several lines of argument have been put forward challenging the validity of theories currently used in this area. Some have argued that the models have been too static, as a result of which they fail to capture the different processes involved in the performance of health-related behaviours. The different processes involved when people confront a health threat are addressed in two recent models: the precaution adoption process (Winstein, 1988) and the health action process approach (Schwartzer, 1992).

In Weinstein's model, people are considered to be more or less likely to undertake a health-related behaviour according to the presence or absence of certain beliefs. It is a developmental model, positing that the first stage in undertaking a behaviour is knowing about the existence of a health threat. The second stage is reached when people believe that someone in their social environment is vulnerable to a health threat. The third stage concerns the belief that the individual is personally vulnerable.

In the health action process approach, Schwartzer draws a distinction between the decision-making or motivation stage and the action or maintenance stage. In the motivation phase an individual forms an intention about whether to behave in a certain way. This is influenced by outcome expectancies and perceptions of the health threat. The action phase determines how hard people try to perform a particular behaviour.

Others have argued that the theories used are not appropriate because they are not health specific. Silver and Wortman (1980) argue that theoretical concepts, such as causal attribution, perceived control and social comparison, are borrowed from studies of college students and applied to the behaviour of patients without first assessing whether the theoretical concept is appropriate to the setting or tap the same concept in the new setting. Leventhal and Nerenz (1985) reject the prevalent theories in this area as not representing how the patient conceptualizes or represents illness threats. They reject the health belief model because it is based upon the assumption that people react to illness in terms of perceived seriousness and vulnerability. Rather, they suggest that people's knowledge is more concrete, situationally specific and more categorical than probabilistic. Social learning theory is rejected for similar reasons.

Leventhal's thesis is that: 'individuals feel motivated to engage in health-protective actions when they notice concrete body symptoms or sensations that could be interpreted as warning signs of future or current disease threats' (Leventhal and Nerenz, 1985). To test

this hypothesis, open-ended questions are used to allow the patient to define attributes relevant to his or her representation of the illness, followed by structured probes to explore in depth the patient's perceptions of the causes, mechanisms and consequences of an illness (Meyer, Leventhal and Gutmann, 1985). Using this approach, Leventhal and Nerenz (1985) propose four core dimensions that go to make up people's implicit model of illness: identity – what the disease is; consequences – short- and long-term; time line – temporal course; and cause. Turk and colleagues (1986), working with a similar perspective, produced four other dimensions: seriousness, personal responsibility, controllability and changeability. It is perhaps too soon to comment on the possible advantages of this approach over other theoretical approaches.

Yet others have argued that cognitive approaches to explaining and predicting health behaviours and outcomes have not proved very powerful because their application has been too individualistic. The need to consider a wider perspective is underlined by Winett (1985), who argues that unless broader environmental influences and constraints upon behaviour are considered, there is a danger that health psychology will become a health psychology of the detached individual, without regard to the social, economic and environmental context.

In a review of anthropological, sociological and psychological literatures, Landrine and Klonoff (1992) conclude that models in health psychology have largely neglected culture, which may account for some of the negative results from studies. For example, they suggest that the relatively poor predictive validity of the multidimensional health locus of control scale and the attributional style questionnaire may be due to the dimensions of health schemas that they assess. They do not, for example, permit distinctions between beliefs that one's health is controlled by family, witches, gods or doctors, and yet these different attributions may well predict differences in health-related behaviours and outcomes.

A further line of attack against these models concerns their cognitive perspective. Sampson (1981) criticizes cognitivism for, among other things, its relativistic denial of a reality or a truth, giving primacy to the individual knower and subjective determinants of behaviour. Similarly, Cartwright (1979) argues that social behaviour depends on more than individual cognitive determinants, and that the traditional social psychological remedies for social problems, namely, to change beliefs and attitudes, are most often ineffective because cognitions are only one of the many proximal determinants of behaviour.

Practical implications and applications

The preceding review and critique pinpoint some of the main approaches that have been taken to look at the relationships between cognitions, behaviour and outcome in a health context, as well as providing some possible explanations for why a cognitive perspective has not proved more fruitful thus far. While much of the work conducted in this area has been descriptive and undertaken primarily for research purposes, the findings have various possible practical applications.

Health education campaigns frequently revolve around changing beliefs by giving information or changing attitudes by providing a different image of a behaviour. However, basic psychological research, such as determining the readability of information (Sherr, 1987) or the relative influence of attitudes towards the behaviour and subjective norms, is not always carried out or indeed acted upon by those responsible for health education programmes (for review, see Kirscht, 1983).

Although various cognitions have been found to explain and predict numerous health behaviours and outcomes, there has been less

research into attempting to change outcomes by changing cognitions. If changing cognitions does not produce a change in behaviour, it does not necessarily follow that cognitions are not causally related to behaviour. Rather, it demonstrates how factors other than cognitions need to be considered in altering behaviour. Whereas some studies report that changing cognitions influences behaviour (Haefner and Kirscht, 1970) and outcomes (Kaman and Seligman, 1987), others report behavioural change by focusing on the target behaviour itself (Cummings *et al.* 1981; Marteau and Johnston, 1986b). More controlled intervention studies are required to determine the circumstances in which cognitive changes affect behavioural change.

In acknowledging the role of patient and staff cognitions in behaviour and health outcomes, staff need to be taught about psychological models of behaviour and how these apply to the behaviour of both patients and health professionals. In attempting to explain the behaviour of patients without a background in behavioural sciences, health professionals tend to invoke, albeit implicitly, an 'educational model of behaviour', based on the assumption that behaviour is determined primarily by medical knowledge: by giving people more information, their behaviour will accord more with the wishes of the health professional (Marteau and Johnston, 1986a). The core assumptions of such a model of patient health-related behaviours are not supported by results of empirical studies. Furthermore, they rest on a view of human behaviour that is untenable in the light of contemporary psychology.

Staff training at both pre- and post-qualification level could incorporate various models of behaviour, including the cognitive–behavioural ones. With such a framework staff may be able to conceptualize patient behaviour differently, as well as how to influence it. Similarly, by extending such models to encompass the behaviour of health professionals, staff may begin to appreciate some of the psychological factors impinging upon their own behaviour in professional settings, and perhaps to consider ways of altering it where appropriate.

Conclusions

That there is a relationship between health beliefs, attributions and behaviour and health outcomes, is established. Which cognitions are relevant, in which circumstances and how strong the relationship is, is less certain. Thus far, only small amounts of variance in health care tend to be accounted for. By ascertaining the validity of the models used it is likely that more of the variance can be account for. The validity of models is likely to be improved by having a less narrow interpretation of currently available models as well as by developing new models in health care settings. By expanding models to encompass health professionals' and patients' cognitions, as well as the situation, future research using a cognitive perspective is likely to bear more fruit.

References

Affleck, G., Tennen, H., Croog, S. and Levine, S. (1987) Causal attribution, perceived control, and recovery from a heart attack. *Journal of Social and Clinical Psychology*, 5, 356–64.

Antoni, M.H. (1987) Neuroendocrine influences in psychoimmunology and neoplasia: a review. *Psychology and Health*, 1, 3–24.

Ajzen, I. (1988) *Attitudes, Personality and Behavior*, Open University Press, Milton Keynes.

Bandura, A. (1991) Self-efficacy mechanism in physiological activation and health-promoting behaviour, in: *Neurobiology of Learning, Emotion and Affect*, (ed J. Madden), Raven Press, New York, pp. 229–70.

Bard, M. and Dyk, R.B. (1956) The psychodynamic significance of beliefs regarding the cause of serious illness. *Psychoanalytic Review*, 43, 146–62.

Becker, M.H. (ed) (1974) The health belief model and personal health behaviour. *Health Education Monographs*, 2, 324–508.

Becker, M.H. and Rosenstock, I.M. (1984) Compliance with medical advice, in: *Health Care and Human Behaviour*, (eds A. Steptoe and A. Mathews), Academic Press, London, pp. 175–208.

Blaxter, M. (1979) Concepts of causality: lay and medical models, in *Research in Psychology and Medicine*, vol. II, (eds D.J. Oborne, M.M. Gruneberg and J.R. Eiser) Academic Press, London, pp. 154–61.

Bradley, C., Brewin, C.R., Gamsu, D.S. and Moses, J.L. (1984) Development of scales to measure perceived control of diabetes mellitus and diabetes-related health beliefs. *Diabetic Medicine*, 1, 213–18.

Bradley, C., Gamsu, D.S., Moses, J.L. *et al.* (1987) The use of diabetes-specific perceived control and health belief measures to predict treatment choice and efficacy in a feasibility study of continuous subcutaneous insulin infusion pumps. *Psychology and Health*, 1, 133–46.

Breslow, L. and Enstrom, J.E. (1980) Persistence of health habits and their relationship to mortality. *Preventive Medicine*, 9, 469–83.

Brewin, C.R. (1984a) Attributions for industrial accidents: their relationship to rehabilitation outcomes. *Journal of Social and Clinical Psychology*, 2, 156–64.

Brewin, C.R. (1984b) Perceived controllability of life events and willingness to prescribe psychotropic drugs. *British Journal of Social Psychology*, 23, 285–7.

Brewin, C.R. (1985) Depression and causal attributions: what is their relation? *Psychological Bulletin*, 98, 297–309.

Brewin, C.R. and Antaki, C. (1987) An analysis of ordinary explanations in clinical attribution research. *Journal of Social and Clinical Psychology*, 5, 79–98.

Brickman, P., Rabinowitz, V.C., Karuza, J. *et al.* (1982) Models of helping and coping. *American Psychologist*, 37, 368–84.

Bulman, R. and Wortman, C.B. (1977) Attributions of blame and coping in the 'real world': severe accident victims react to their lot. *Journal of Personality and Social Psychology*, 35, 351–63.

Carnahan, T.M. (1979) The development and validation of the multidimensional dental locus of control scales. Unpublished doctoral dissertation, State University of New York, Buffalo.

Cartwright, D. (1979) Contemporary social psychology in historical context. *Social Psychology Quarterly*, 42, 82–93.

Chodoff, P., Friedman, P.B. and Hamburg, D.A. (1964) Stress, defenses and coping behavior: observations in parents of children with malignant disease. *American Journal of Psychiatry*, 120, 743–9.

Coyne, J.C. and Gotlib, I.H. (1983) The role of cognition in depression: a critical appraisal. *Psychological Bulletin*, 94, 472–505.

Cummings, K.M., Becker, M.H., Kirscht, J.P. and Levin, N.W. (1981) Intervention strategies to improve compliance with medical regimens by ambulatory hemodialysis patients. *Journal of Behavioural Medicine*, 4, 111–27.

Davidson, A.R. and Jaccard, J.J. (1975) Population psychology: a new look at an old problem. *Journal of Personality and Social Psychology*, 31, 1073–82.

DeVellis, R.F., DeVellis, B.M., Wallston, B.S. and Wallston, K.A. (1980) Epilepsy and learned helplessness. *Basic and Applied Social Psychology*, 1, 241–53.

Eisenberg, J.M. (1986) *Doctors' Decisions and the Cost of Medical Care*, Michigan, Health Administration Press.

Eiser, J.R., (1986) *Social Psychology: Attitudes, Cognitions and Social Behaviour*, Cambridge University Press, Cambridge.

Eiser, J.R., van der Plight, J., Raw, M. and Sutton, S.R. (1985) Trying to stop smoking: effects of perceived addiction, attributions for failure, and expectancy for success. *Journal of Behavioural Medicine*, 8, 321–41.

Farr, R.M. (1977) Heider, Harre, and Herzlich on health and illness: some observations on the structure of 'representations collectives'. *European Journal of Social Psychology*, 7, 491–504.

Fishbein, M (1982) Social psychological analysis of smoking behaviour, in *Social Psychology and Behavioural Medicine*, (ed J.R. Eiser) John Wiley and Sons, Chichester, pp. 179–97.

Fishbein, M. and Ajzen, I. (1975) *Belief, Attitude, Intention and Behavior: an Introduction to Theory and Research*, Addison-Wesley, Reading, Massachusetts.

French, K. and Raven, B.H. (1959) The bases of social power, in *Studies in Social Power* (ed D. Cartwright), Institute for Social Research, Ann Arbor, Michigan, pp. 150–67.

Gamsu, D.S. and Bradley, C. (1987) Clinical staff's attributions about diabetes: scale developments and staff vs patient comparisons. *Current Psychological Research and Reviews*, 6, 69–78.

Gillespie, C.R. and Bradley, C. (1988) Causal attributions of doctor and patients in a diabetes clinic. *British Journal of Clinical Psychology*, 27, 67–76.

Greer, S., Morris, T. and Pettingale, K.W. (1979) Psychological response to breast cancer: effect on outcome. *Lancet*, ii, 785–7.

Haefner, D. and Kirscht, J.P. (1970) Motivational and behavioural effects of modifying health beliefs. *Public Health Report*, 85, 478–84.

Herzlich, C. (1973) *Health and Illness: A Social Psychological Analysis*, Academic Press, London.

Hewstone, M. (ed) (1983) *Attribution Theory: Social and Functional Extensions*, Blackwell, Oxford.

House, W.C., Pendleton, L. and Parker, L. (1986) Patients' versus physicians' attributions of reasons for diabetic patients' noncompliance with diet. *Diabetes Care*, 9, 434.

Ickes, W.J. and Kidd, R.F. (1976) An attributional analysis of helping behaviour, in *New Directions in Attribution Research*, vol.1, (eds J.H. Harvey, W.J. Ickes and R.F. Kidd), Erlbaum Associates, Hillsdale, New Jersey, pp. 311–34.

Janoff-Bulman, R. (1979) Characterological versus behavioral self-blame: inquiries into depression and rape. *Journal of Personality and Social Psychology*, 37, 1798–1809.

Janz, N.K. and Becker, M.H. (1984) The health belief model: a decade later. *Health Education Quarterly*, 11, 1–47.

Johnston, M. and Marteau, T.M. (1987) The health beliefs of the health professionals, in *Clinical Psychology: Research and Developments*, (ed. H. Dent), Croom Helm, London, pp. 126–31.

Jones, E.E. and Nisbett, R.E. (1977) The actor and the observer: divergent perceptions of the causes of behavior, in *Attribution: Perceiving the Causes of Behavior*, (eds E.E. Jones, D.E. Kanouse, H.H. Kelley, R.E. Nisbett, S. Valins and B. Weiner), General Learning Press, Morristown, New Jersey.

Joseph, J.G. Montgomery, S.B., Emmons, C.A. *et al.* (1987) Magnitude and determinants of behavioral risk reduction: longitidinal analysis of a cohort at risk for AIDS. *Psychology and Health*, 1, 73–95.

Kahneman, D. and Tversky, A. (1979) Prospect theory: an analysis of decision under risk. *Econometrica*, 47, 263–91.

Kamen, L.P. and Seligman, M.E.P. (1987) Explanatory style and health. *Current Psychological Research and Reviews*, 6, 207–18.

Kaplan, R.M., Atkins, C.J. and Reinsch, S. (1984) Specific efficacy expectations mediate exercise compliance in patients with COPD. *Health Psychology*, 3, 223–242.

Kelley, H.H. (1967) Attribution theory in social psychology, in *Nebraska Symposium on Motivation*, (ed. D. Levine), University of Nebraska Press, Lincoln, Nebraska.

Kelley, H.H. and Michela, J.L. (1980) Attribution theory and research. *Annual Review of Psychology*, 31, 457–501.

Kiecolt-Glaser, J.K., Glaser, R., Williger, E. *et al.* (1985) Psychosocial enhancement of immunocompetence in a geriatric population. *Health Psychology*, 4, 25–41.

King, J.B. (1982) The impact of patients' perceptions of high blood pressure on attendance at screening: an attributional extension of the health belief model. *Social Science and Medicine*, 16, 1079–92.

Kirscht, J.P. (1983) Preventive health behavior: a review of research and issues. *Health Psychology*, 2, 277–302.

Kok, G., De Vries, H., Mudde, A.N. and Strecher, V.J. (1990) Planned health education and the role of self-efficacy: Dutch research. *Health Education Research*, 5.

Kristiansen, C.M. (1985) Value correlates of preventive health behavior. *Journal of Personality and Social Psychology*, **49**, 748–58.

Labs, S.M. and Wurtele, S.K. (1986) Fetal health locus of control scale: development and validation. *Journal of Consulting and Clinical Psychology*, **54**, 814–19.

Landrine, H. and Klonoff, E.A. (1992). Culture and health-related schemas: a review and proposal for interdisciplinary integration. *Health Psychology*, **11**, 267–76.

Lau, R.R. and Ware, J.E. (1981) The conceptualisation and measurement of a multidimensional health-specific locus of control scale. *Medical Care*, **19**, 1147–58.

Lau, R.R. Hartman, K.A. and Ware, J.E. (1986) Health as a value: methodological and theoretical considerations. *Health Psychology*, **5**, 25–43.

Levenson, H. (1973) Multidimensional locus of control in psychiatric patients. *Journal of Consulting and Clinical Psychology*, **41**, 397–404.

Leventhal, H. and Nerenz, D. (1985) The assessment of illness cognition, in *Measurement Strategies in Health Psychology*, (ed P. Karoly), Wiley and Sons, New York, pp. 517–54.

Levin, A. and Schulz, M.A. (1980) Multidimensional health locus of control and compliance in low and high participation hemodialysis. Unpublished Msc thesis, University of Wisconsin, Madison.

Levy, S.M. and Wise, B.D. (1987) Psychosocial risk factors, natural immunity, and cancer progression: implications for intervention. *Current Psychological Research and Reviews*, **6**, 229–43.

Lewis, F.M., Morisky, D.E. and Flynn, B.S. (1978) A test of construct validity of health locus of control: effects of self-reported compliance for hypertensive patients. *Health Education Monographs*, **6**, 138–48.

Ley, P. (1982) Satisfaction, compliance, and communication. *British Journal of Clinical Psychology*, **21**, 241–54.

McClelland, D.C. and Jemmott, J.B. (1980) Power motivation, stress and physical illness. *Journal of Human Stress*, **6**, 6–15.

McNeil, B.J., Pauker, S.G., Sox, H.C. and Tversky, A. (1982) On the elicitation of preferences for alternative therapies. *New England Journal of Medicine*, **306**, 1259–62.

Manstead, A.S.R., Proffitt, C. and Smart, J.L. (1983) Predicting and understanding mothers' infant-feeding intentions and behavior: testing theory of reasoned action. *Journal of Personality and Social Psychology*, **44**, 657–71.

Marby, J.H. (1964) Lay concepts of etiology, *Journal of Chronic Diseases*, **17**, 371–86.

Marteau, T.M. (1987) Health related beliefs, attitudes and attributions: issues in measurement. *Proceedings of the Health Psychology Section, British Psychological Society*, pp. 32–7.

Marteau, T.M. (1989) Framing of information: its influence upon decisions of doctors and patients. *British Journal of Social Psychology*, **28**, 89–94.

Marteau, T.M. and Baum, J.D. (1984) Doctors' views on diabetes. *Archives of Diseases of Childhood*, **59**, 566–70.

Marteau, T.M. and Johnston, M. (1986a) Determinants of beliefs about illness: a study of parents of children with diabetes, asthma, epilepsy, and no chronic illness. *Journal of Psychosomatic Research*, **30**, 673–83.

Marteau, T.M. and Johnston, M. (1986b) Doctors taking blood from children: a suitable case for treatment? *British Journal of Clinical Psychology*, **25**, 159–60.

Marteau, T.M. and Johnston, M. (1987) Health psychology: the danger of neglecting psychological models. *Bulletin of the British Psychological Society*, **40**, 82–5.

Marteau, T.M. and Riordan, D.C. (1992) Staff attitudes to patients: the influence of causal attributions for illness. *British Journal of Clinical Psychology*, **31**, 107–110.

Marteau, T.M., Johnston, M., Baum, J.D. and Bloch, S. (1987) Goals of treatment in diabetes: a comparison of doctors and parents of children with diabetes. *Journal of Behavioural Medicine*, **10**, 33–48.

Meyer, D., Leventhal, H. and Gutmann, M. (1985) Common-sense models of illness: the example of hypertension. *Health Psychology*, **4**, 115–35.

O'Leary, A., Shoor, S., Lorig, K. and Holman, H.R. (1988). A cognitive-behavioral treatment for rheumatoid arthritis. *Health Psychology*, **7**, 527–42.

Peterson, C. (1986) Explanatory style as a risk factor for illness. Unpublished manuscript, University of Michigan.

Rippetoe, P.A. and Rogers, R.W. (1987) Effects on components of protection motivation theory on adaptive and maladaptive coping with a health threat. *Journal of Personality and Social Psychology*, **52**, 596–604.

Rodin, J. and Langer, E.J. (1977) Long-term effects of a control relevant intervention with the institutionalised aged. *Journal of Personality and Social Psychology*, **35**, 897–902.

Rokeach, M. (1973) *The Nature of Human Values*, Free Press, New York.

Rosengren, J. (1961) Some social psychological aspects of delivery room difficulties. *Journal of Nervous and Mental Diseases*, **132**, 515–21.

Rotter, J.B. (1954) *Social Learning and Clinical Psychology*, Prentice-Hall, Englewood Cliffs, New Jersey.

Rotter, J.B. (1966) Generalised expectancies for internal versus external control of reinforcement. *Psychological Monographs*, **80**, (1, whole no. 609).

Sampson, E.E. (1981) Cognitive psychology as ideology. *American Psychologist*, **36**, 730–43.

Schenkel, R.J., Rogers, J.P., Perfetto, M.A. and Levin, R.A. (1985–6) Importance of 'significant others' in predicting cooperation with diabetic regimen. *International Journal of Psychiatry in Medicine*, **15**, 149–55.

Schlenk, E.A. and Hart, L.K. (1984) Relationship between health locus of control, health value, and social support and compliance of persons with diabetes mellitus. *Diabetes Care*, **7**, 566–74.

Schwartzer, R. (1992) Self-efficacy in the adoption and maintenance of health behaviors: theoretical approaches and a new model, in *Self-Efficacy: Thought Control of Action*, (ed R. Schwartzer), Hemisphere Publishing Corporation, Washington, pp. 217–43.

Sherr, L. (1987) An evaluation of the UK government health education campaign on AIDS. *Psychology and Health*, **1**, 61–72.

Silver, R.L. and Wortman, C.B. (1980) Coping with undesirable life events, in *Human Helplessness*, (eds J. Garber and M.E.P. Seligman), Academic Press, New York, pp. 271–341.

Sonne, J.L. and Janoff, D.S. (1982) Attributions and the maintenance of behaviour change, in *Attributions and Psychological Change: Applications of Attributional Theories to Clinical and Educational Practice*, (eds C. Antaki and C.R. Brewin), Academic Press, London, pp. 83–96.

Stone, G.C. (1979) Psychology and the health system, in *Health Psychology* (eds G.C. Stone, F. Cohen and N.E. Adler), Jossey-Bass, San Francisco, pp. 47–75.

Strickland, B.R. (1978) Internal-external expectancies on health-related behaviors. *Journal of Consulting and Clinical Psychology*, **46**, 1192–211.

Taylor, C.B., Bandura, A., Ewart, C.K., Miller, N.H. and DeBusk, R.F. (1985) Exercise testing to enhance wives' confidence in their husbands' cardiac capability soon after clinically uncomplicated acute myocardial infarction. *American Journal of Cardiology*, **55**, 635–8.

Taylor, S.E., Lichtman, R.R. and Wood J.V. (1984) Attributions, beliefs about control and adjustment to breast cancer. *Journal of Personality and Social Psychology*, **46**, 489–502.

Tennen, H., Affleck, G. and Gershmann, K. (1986) Self-blame among parents of infants with perinatal complications: the role of self-protective motives. *Journal of Personality and Social Psychology*, **50**, 690–96.

Timko, C. and Janoff-Bulman, R. (1985) Attributions, vulnerability, and psychological adjustment: the case of breast cancer. *Health Psychology*, **4**, 521–44.

Turk, D.C., Rudy, T.E. and Salovey, P. (1986) Implicit models of illness. *Journal of Behavioural Medicine*, **9**, 453–74.

Wallston, K.A. and McLeod, E. (1979) Predictive factors in the adherence to an antihypertensive regimen among adult male outpatients. Unpublished manuscript, School of Nursing, Vanderbilt University.

Wallston, K.A. and Wallston, B.S. (1982) Who is responsible for your health? The construct of health locus of control, in *Social Psychology of Health and Illness*, (eds G.S. Sanders and J. Suls), Lawrence Erlbaum, Hillsdale, NJ, pp. 65–95.

Wallston, B.S. and Wallston, K.A. (1984) Social psychological models of health behavior: an examination and interaction, in *Handbook of Psychology and Health, vol. IV: Social Aspects of Health*, (eds. A. Baum, S. Taylor, and J.E. Singer), Lawrence Erlbaum, Hillsdale, NJ, pp. 23–53.

Wallston, K.A., Maides, S. and Wallston, B.S. (1976) Health-related information seeking as a function of health-related locus of control and health value. *Journal of Research into Personality*, **10**, 215–22.

Wallston, K.A., Wallston, B.S. and DeVellis, R. (1978) Development of the multidimensional health locus of control (MHLC) scales. *Health Education Monographs*, **6**, 160–70.

Wallston, K.A., Wallston, B.S., Smith, S. and Dobbins, C.J. (1987) Perceived control and health, in *Applications in Health Psychology*, (eds M. Johnston and T. Marteau) Transaction Books, New Brunswick, pp. 5–25.

Weinberger, M., Cohen, S. and Mazzuca, S.A. (1984) The role of physicians' knowledge and attitudes in effective diabetes management. *Social Science and Medicine*, **19**, 965–9.

Weiner, B. (1979) A theory of motivation for some classroom experiences. *Journal of Educational Psychology*, **71**, 3–25.

Weinstein (1988) The precaution adoption process. *Health Psychology*, **7**, 355–86.

Winett, R.A. (1985) Ecobehavioral assessment in lifestyles: concepts and methods, in *Measurement Strategies in Health Psychology*, (ed. P. Karoly), John Wiley and Sons, New York, pp. 147–81.

Wynne, G., Marteau, T.M., Johnston, M. *et al.* (1987) Inability of trained nurses to perform basic life support. *British Medical Journal*, **294**, 1189–9.

Chapter two

Stress, coping and physical health

Tom Cox

Introduction

Over the past two decades there has been an increasing belief that the experience of stress has undesirable consequences for health. It has become a common assumption, if not a 'cultural truism' (Leventhal and Tomarken, 1987), that it is associated with the impairment of health. Despite this, the evidence is otherwise: the experience of stress *per se* does not **necessarily** have pathological sequelae. Many of a person's responses both psychological and physiological, to such an experience, are comfortably within the body's normal homoeostatic limits and, although taxing the psychophysiological mechanisms involved, need not cause any lasting disturbance or damage. However, it is also obvious that the negative emotional experiences which are associated with the experience of stress detract both from the general quality of life and form the person's sense of wellbeing. Thus the experience of stress, while necessarily reducing that sense of wellbeing, does not inevitably contribute to the development of physical disorder for most people. For some, however, the experience does influence pathogenesis. That influence will not only be part of a wider aetiological process,

involving a variety of factors and processes, but will also be part of a two-way interaction between the experience of stress and the state of the person's health. Stress may affect health but, at the same time, a state of ill health can both act as a significant source of stress and also sensitize the person to other sources of stress by reducing their ability to cope.

Within these limits, the common assumption of a relationship between the experience of stress and poor physical health appears justified. However, for this hypothesis to have any social importance or practical usefulness it has to be examined in greater detail. Such an examination must address not only the fact of the relationship, but also the nature of the psychophysiological mechanisms that might underpin it. The definition of stress is central to this examination, and is the initial focus of this chapter.

Definition of stress

The definition of stress is not simply a question of semantics and it is important that there is agreement, at least in broad terms, on the nature of the concept. A lack of any such agreement would seriously hamper research into stress and the subsequent development of effective stress management strategies. Given this, it is an unfortunate but popular misconception that there is little consensus on the definition of stress as a scientific concept or, worse, that stress is in some way undefinable and unmeasurable. Such a belief belies a lack of knowledge of the relevant literature.

It has been concluded in several reviews of the literature that there are essentially three different, but overlapping, approaches to the definition and study of stress (see, for example, Lazarus, 1966; Appley and Trumbull, 1967; Cox, 1978, 1990; Cox and Mackay, 1981; Fletcher, 1988). The first approach conceptualizes stress as an aversive or noxious characteristic of the environment and, in related studies, treats it as an independent variable – the environmental cause of ill health. This approach has been termed the 'engineering model'. The second approach, on the other hand, defines stress in terms of the common physiological effects of a wide range of aversive or noxious stimuli. It treats stress as a dependent variable, as a particular physiological response to a threatening or damaging environment. This approach has been termed the 'medicophysiological model'. The third approach conceptualizes stress in terms of the dynamic interaction between the person and their environment. When studied, stress is either inferred from the existence of difficult person–environment interactions, or measured in terms of the cognitive and emotional processes that underpin those interactions. This final approach has been termed the 'psychological model'. The engineering and medicophysiological models are obvious among the earlier theories of stress, whereas the more psychological models characterize contemporary stress theory.

Engineering approach

The engineering approach has treated stress as a **stimulus characteristic** of the person's envir-

onment, usually conceived in terms of the load or level of demand placed on the individual, or as some aversive or noxious element of that environment (see Cox, 1978, 1990; Cox and Mackay, 1981; Fletcher, 1988). Occupational stress, for example, is treated as a property of the work environment, and usually as an objectively measurable aspect of that environment. In 1947, Symonds, in relation to psychological disorders in RAF flying personnel, wrote that '... stress is that which happens *to* the man, not that which happens *in* him; it is a set of *causes* not a set of *symptoms*.' According to this approach, stress was said to produce a strain reaction which, although often reversible, could on occasions prove to be irreversible and damaging (Cox and Mackay, 1981; Sutherland and Cooper, 1990). The concept of a stress threshold grew out of this way of thinking, and individual differences in this threshold have been used to account for differences in stress resistance and vulnerability.

Medicophysiological approach

The medicophysiological approach to the definition and study of stress received its initial impetus from the work of Selye (1950, 1956). He defined stress as 'a state manifested by a specific syndrome which consists of all the non-specific changes within the biologic system' that occur when challenged by aversive or noxious stimuli. Stress is treated as a generalized and non-specific physiological response syndrome. For many years, the stress response was largely conceived of in terms of the activation of two neuroendocrine systems, the anterior pituitary–adreno cortical system (PAC) and the sympathetic–adrenal medullary system (SAM) (see, for example, Cox, Cox and Thirlaway, 1983). Selye (1950, 1956) argued that this response was triphasic in nature, involving an initial alarm stage (sympathetic–adrenal medullary activation) followed by a stage of resistance (adrenocortical activation) giving way, under some circumstances, to a final stage of exhaustion (terminal reactivation of the sympathetic–adrenal medullary system).

Selye (1950) also argued that the wear and tear on the body caused by the stress response can significantly contribute to physical pathology. This was true where the response was frequent, of long duration or severe. The diseases that had such a stress-related aetiology, Selye termed 'diseases of adaptation'. This seemingly paradoxical situation arose because the stress response had evolved as adaptive in the short term, increasing the animal's (or person's) ability to respond actively to an aversive or noxious environment. However, in the long term it could contribute to the disease process.

Criticisms of the engineering and medicophysiological approaches

There have been two main criticisms of the engineering and medicophysiological approaches: first, do they account for the existing data, and second, are they conceptually adequate?

Do such theories account for the existing data?

It must be concluded that, in general, engineering and medicophysiological theories do not adequately account for the existing data. This is particularly so for the medicophysiological approach. Both the non-specificity and the time course of the physiological response to aversive and noxious stimuli have been shown to be different from those described by Selye (1950, 1956) and demanded by the model (see Mason, 1968, 1971). Mason (1971), for example, has shown that some noxious physical stimuli do not produce the stress response in its entirety. In particular, he has cited the effects of heat. Furthermore, Lacey (1967) has argued that the low correlations observed among different physiological components of the stress response are not consistent with the notion of an iden-

tifiable response syndrome. There is also a difficulty in distinguishing between those physiological changes that represent stress and those that do not, particularly as the former may be dissociated in time from the stressor (Fisher, 1986).

There is now much research which suggests that, if the stress response syndrome exists, it is not non-specific, and that there are subtle but important differences in the overall pattern of response to different stimuli. There is evidence, for example, of differentiation in the response of the catecholamines (reflecting sympathetic–adrenal medullary activation) to stressful situations (Cox and Cox, 1985). Several dimensions have been suggested as a basis of this differentiation: many relate to the expenditure of effort of different types, for example, physical versus psychological (Dimsdale and Moss, 1980a,b; Cox et al., 1982). Dimsdale and Moss (1980b) studied plasma catecholamine levels using a non-obtrusive blood withdraw pump and radio-enzymatic assay. They examined 10 young physicians engaged in public speaking and found that, although levels of both adrenaline and noradrenaline increased under this set of demands, the levels of adrenaline were far more sensitive. This sensitivity was associated with feelings of emotional arousal which accompanied the public speaking. Cox and her colleagues (1982) examined the physiological response to three different types of task associated with short-cycle repetitive work. Urinary catecholamine excretion rates were measured using an adaptation of Diament and Byers' (1975) assay technique. She found that both adrenaline and noradrenaline were sensitive to work characteristics, such as pay scheme and pacing, but differentially so. She suggested that noradrenaline activation was related to the physical activity inherent in the various tasks, and to the constraints and frustrations present, whereas adrenaline activation was more related to feelings of effort and stress.

Are such theories conceptually adequate?

The second criticism is that the engineering and medicophysiological models of stress are conceptually dated, in that they are set within a relatively simple stimulus–response paradigm and largely ignore individual differences of a psychological nature and the perceptual and cognitive processes which might underpin them (Cox, 1990; Sutherland and Cooper, 1990). Furthermore, these models treat the person as a passive vehicle for translating the stimulus characteristics of the environment into psychological and physiological response parameters. They largely ignore the interactions between the person and their various environments which are an essential part of systems-based approaches to biology, behaviour and psychology.

Psychological approach

The third approach to the definition and study of stress generally conceptualizes it in terms of the dynamic interaction between the person and their environment. When studied, stress is either inferred from the existence of difficult person–environment interactions or measured in terms of the cognitive and emotional processes that underpin those interactions. This approach has been termed the 'psychological model'. Variants of this psychological model dominate contemporary stress theory, and among them two distinct types can be identified: the interactional and the transactional. The former focuses on the structural features of the person's interaction with their environment, whereas the latter is more concerned with the psychological processes underpinning that interaction. Transactional models are primarily concerned with cognitive appraisal and coping. In a sense they represent a development of interactional models, and offer little which is not consistent with such models. Transactional theories owe much to the work of Lazarus (1966) and his notion of 'cognitive appraisal'.

Interactional theories of stress

Interactional theories of stress focus on the structural characteristics of a person's interaction with their environment. Two particular interactional theories stand out among the various which have been offered: those of French, Caplan and van Harrison (1982) and Karasek (1979). Both focus on the work environment, but could be extended to non-work situations, and have clear implications for health psychology.

Person–environment fit

Several researchers have shown that the goodness of fit between the person and their environment frequently offers a better explanation of behaviour than individual or situational differences (see, for example, Bowers, 1973; Ekehammer, 1974). Largely as a result of such observations, French and his colleagues formulated a theory of work stress based on the explicit concept of the person (P)–environment (E) fit (see, for example, French, Caplan and van Harrison, 1982). Two basic aspects of fit were identified: the degree to which a worker's attitudes and abilities meet the demands of the job, and the extent to which the job environment meets the worker's needs, and in particular the extent to which the individual is permitted and encouraged to use their knowledge and skills in the job setting. It has been argued that stress is likely to occur, and wellbeing is likely to be affected, when there is a lack of fit in either or both (French, Rogers and Cobb, 1974).

A clear distinction is made in person–environment fit theory between objective reality and subjective perceptions, and between environmental variabless (E) and person variables (P). Given this simple 2×2 configuration of $P \times E$ interaction, lack of fit could occur in four different ways and each might challenge health. There can be a lack of both subjective and objective P–E fit: these are the main foci of attention, with particular interest being expressed in the lack of subjective fit. This provides a strong link with other psychological theories of stress. However, there can also be a lack of fit between the objective environment (reality) and the subjective environment (hence lack of contact with reality), and also a lack of fit between the objective and subjective persons (hence poor self-assessment).

Job demands/decision latitude

Karasek (1979) defined 'decision latitude' as 'the working individual's potential control over his tasks and his conduct during the working day', and defined 'job demands' as 'the psychological stressors involved in accomplishing the workload'. He has also provided a structural model of work stress which draws attention to these two critical dimensions of the person–environment fit. He has suggested that such work characteristics may be non-linearly associated with health, and that they might combine interactively in relation to health. He demonstrated this theory through secondary analyses of data from the USA and Sweden, finding that workers in jobs perceived to have both low decision latitude and high job demands were particularly likely to report poor health and low satisfaction. Later studies appeared to confirm this theory. For example, a representative sample of the male Swedish workforce was examined for depression, excessive fatigue, cardiovascular disease and mortality. Those workers whose jobs were characterized by heavy workloads combined with little latitude for decision making were represented disproportionately on all these outcome variables. The lowest probabilities for illness and death were found among work groups with moderate workloads combined with high control over work conditions (Karasek, 1981; Ahlbom, Karasek and Theorell, 1990; Karasek and Theorell, 1990). The combined effect of

these two work characteristics is often described as a true interaction (synergy), but despite the popular appeal of this suggestion there is only weak evidence in its support. Karasek's (1979) own analyses suggest an additive rather than a synergistic effect, and he has admitted that 'there is only moderate evidence for an interaction effect, understood as a departure from a linear additive model'. Simple additive combinations have been reported by a number of researchers (see Warr, 1990).

Transactional definitions

Most transactional theories of stress focus on the cognitive processes underpinning the person's interaction with their environment, and nowhere is this more obvious than in relation to theories of appraisal and coping, such as those of Lazarus and Folkman in the USA (e.g. Lazarus and Folkman, 1984) and of Cox and Mackay in the UK (e.g. Cox, 1978; Cox and Mackay, 1981; Cox, 1990).

According to transactional models, stress is a **psychological state** involving aspects of both cognition and emotion. They treat stress as the internal representation of a particular and a problematic transaction between the person and their environment, but the term psychological stress is ambiguous. Although the experience of stress is psychological in nature, its antecedents and outcomes are not restricted to any particular domain, psychological or otherwise.

Appraisal is the evaluative process that gives these person–environment transactions their meaning (Holroyd and Lazarus, 1982). According to Lazarus and Folkman (Lazarus, 1966; Folkman and Lazarus, 1986). It is comprised of primary and secondary processes. With regard to the former, individuals ask themselves the question: 'is this particular encounter relevant to wellbeing and in what way?'. If the encounter is relevant and is defined as stressful rather than as benign or irrelevant, then more specific appraisals are made, such as those of loss or threat (of harm). Primary appraisal is associated with the emotional content of stressful transactions. Secondary appraisal is concerned with the question of coping.

Stress arises when the person perceives that he or she cannot adequately cope with the demands being made on them or with threats to their wellbeing (Lazarus, 1966, 1976; Cox 1990), when coping is of importance to them (Sells, 1970; Cox, 1978) and when they are anxious or depressed about it (Cox and Ferguson, 1991).

The experience of stress is therefore defined first by the person's realization that they are having difficulty coping with demands and threats to their wellbeing, and secondly, by the fact that coping is important and their difficulty in coping worries or depresses them. This approach allows a clear distinction between, say, the effects of lack of ability on performance and those of stress. If a person does not have the necessary knowledge or level of skill to complete a task, then their performance will be poor. They may not realize this, or if they do, it might not be felt to be of importance. This is not a 'stress' scenario. However, if the person does (a) realize that they are failing to cope with the demands of a task, and (b) experiences concern about that failure, then this is a 'stress' scenario. The effects of such stress might then cause a further impairment of performance over and above that caused by lack of ability.

It is useful to think of this stress state as embedded in an ongoing process which involves the person interacting with their environment, making appraisals of that interaction and attempting – and sometimes failing – to cope with the problems that arise.

Cox (1978) described the stress process in terms of a five-stage model. The first stage, it was argued, represents the sources of demand faced by the person and is part of their environment. The person's perception of these demands in relation to their ability to cope represents the second stage: effectively, primary appraisal. Stress was described as the psychological state that arose when there was a personally significant imbalance or mismatch between the person's perceptions of the demands on them and their ability to cope with those demands. The psychological and physiological changes which are associated with the recognition of such a stress state, and which include coping, represent the third stage of the model. Emotional changes are an important part of the psychological response to stress. These tend to be negative in nature and often define the experience of stress for the person. The fourth stage is concerned with the consequences of coping. The fifth stage is the general feedback (and feedforward) which occurs in relation to all other stages of the model.

This model has been further developed in several ways, and there has been some discussion of the problem of measuring stress based on this approach (Cox, 1985, 1990), with the development of possible subjective measures of the experiential (mood) correlates of the stress state (see Mackay *et al.*, 1978; Cox and Mackay, 1985).

Measurement of stress

The measurement of stress should be based primarily on self-report measures which focus on the emotional experience of stress (or related mood changes) and on the appraisal process (Cox, 1985). Measures relating to appraisal need to consider aspects of the person's perceptions of the demands on them, their ability to cope with those demands, the control they have over the demands and the support they receive in relation to those demands. However, Dewe (1991) has shown that it is necessary to go beyond simply asking people whether particular demands (etc.) are present or absent, and measure various dimensions of demand (etc.), such as their frequency, duration and level. Such measures need to be used in a way that allows for the possibility of interactions between perceptions, such as demand with control (Karasek, 1979; Warr, 1990) or demand and control with support (Payne and Fletcher, 1983; Cox, 1985; Karasek and Theorell, 1990). The importance of coping with particular combinations also needs to be taken into account (Sells, 1970; Cox, 1978).

Despite their obvious centrality and importance, self-report measures of appraisal and the experience of stress are, on their own, insufficient. Although their reliability can be established without reference to other data, their validity cannot. Therefore, data from other domains are required. Triangulation is a recommended process for validation in many different disciplines. Applying this principle would require data to be collected from at least three different domains (Cox, 1990). This can be achieved by considering evidence relating to the objective antecedents of the stress experience, the self-report of stress, and the various changes in behaviour, physiology and health status which may be correlated with the former. The influence of moderating factors, such as individual and group differences, may also be assessed.

What is being measured is a process: antecedents through perceptions and experience (and moderating factors) to immediate outcomes to health status. This approach underlines both the complexity of measurement, when approached scientifically, and the inadequacy of asking for or using single one-off measures of stress.

The experience of stress, however measured, is usually accompanied by attempts to deal with the underlying problem – coping – and by more general changes in cognition, behaviour and physiological function. Although probably adaptive in the short term, taken together in the long term they may threaten health.

Coping

Lazarus (1966) sees coping as having three main features. First, it is a process: it is what the person actually thinks and does in a stressful encounter. Secondly, it is context dependent: coping is influenced by the particular appraisal that initiates it, and by the resources available to manage that encounter. Finally, coping as a process should be defined 'independent of outcome', that is, independently of whether or not it was successful (see Folkman, 1984; Lazarus and Folkman, 1984; Folkman *et al.*, 1986). There have been two approaches to the study of coping: those attempting to classify the different types of coping process that exist and produce a comprehensive taxonomy of such strategies, and those that consider coping as a problem-solving process.

Coping taxonomies

Lazarus (1966) has argued that people usually combine task- and emotion-focused coping strategies. Task-focused strategies attempt some form of action directly targeted on dealing with the source of stress – adaptation *of* the environment – whereas emotion-focused strategies attempt to attenuate the emotional experience associated with that stress – adaptation *to* the environment.

The perceived success, or otherwise, of such strategies feeds back into the appraisal process to alter the person's perception of the situation. Lazarus and his colleagues also emphasize that the importance of the situation to the individual is critical in determining the intensity of their response.

Dewe (1987) examined sources of stress and strategies used to cope with them in New Zealand ministers of religion. Using factor-analytical techniques, he identified five clusters of coping strategies: seeking social support; postponing action by relaxation and distracting attention; developing a greater ability to deal with the problem; rationalizing the problem; and drawing on support through spiritual commitment. It was possible to classify 33% of the strategies which made up these clusters as task focused and 67% as emotion focused. The most frequent source of stress experienced by the ministers related to the emotional and time difficulties associated with crisis work, and the experience of such problems appeared to be associated with coping by seeking social support and rationalizing the problem.

Pearlin and associates (Pearlin and Schooler, 1978; Pearlin et al., 1981) have further developed this general approach and distinguished between responses concerned with changing the situation, those concerned with changing its meaning and those relating to the management of the symptoms of stress. In a different vein, Miller (Miller, 1979; Miller, Brody and Summerton, 1988) has distinguished between two informational styles which she terms 'blunters' and 'monitors'. The former tend to use denial strategies and the latter information-seeking strategies in relation to stressful situations. The various coping strategies described in the literature are not meant to be mutually exclusive, and most authors emphasize that no one type is necessarily better than any other in solving a problem. Most people use a mixture of strategies in most situations, although certain situations may tend to be associated with particular types of strategy.

Coping as problem solving

Coping is increasingly being viewed as a problem-solving strategy (Cox, 1987; Fisher, 1986). Cox (1987), for example, has described a cycle of activities, beginning with recognition and diagnosis (analysis) following through actions and evaluation to reanalysis, which possibly represents the ideal problem-solving process. However, all this implies only the positive side of a double-edged sword, and Schonpflug and Battmen (1988) have empha-

sized a more negative 'problem-generation' side. That is, by adopting the wrong actions or by failing in coping, a person may create further problems and stress. At the same time, Meichenbaum (1983) argues that 'catastrophizing' or overreacting to such failure serves a maladaptive purpose. It is often said that one of the few positive aspects to coping with stress is that the person learns from such experience. However, Einhorn and Hogarth (1981) suggest that there are at least three problems with this proposition: first, one does not necessarily know that there is something to be learned; secondly, what is to be learned is not clear; and thirdly, there is ambiguity in judging whether one has learned. Furthermore, the problem solver may be fully occupied and not have any spare cognitive capacity for learning, and the emotion associated with stress may interfere with the learning process (Mandler, 1982).

Coping may be seen as functional in its attempts to manage demands, by either changing them, redefining them or adapting to them. The styles and strategies used need to be relevant and applicable to the situation in hand. The choice and successful use of these responses will be determined by the nature of the situation, the personal and social resources available and also the type of causal reasoning adopted (appraisal).

Stress and health

The experience of stress can alter the person's emotional state, the way they think and behave, and can also produce changes in their physiological function (Stainbrook and Green, 1983; Cincirpini et al., 1984). Many of these changes simply represent a modest dysfunction and possibly some associated discomfort. Many are easily reversible, although still damaging to the quality of life at the time. However, for some, and under some circumstances, they might translate into poor physical health. Overall, however, the strength of the relationship between the experience of stress and its antecedents on one hand, and health status on the other, is consistent but only moderate (Kasl, 1980, 1984; Baker, 1985).

The psychological effects of stress may be expressed in a variety of different ways, and involve changes in cognitive–perceptual function, emotion and behaviour. Some of these changes may represent attempts to cope. Much of what the person thinks and does in a stressful situation can be accounted for by models of coping, including changes in health-related behaviours. There is evidence that some health-promoting behaviours, such as exercise and relaxation, sleep and good dietary habits, are impaired by the experience of stress, while other health-risk behaviours, such as smoking and drinking, are enhanced. Other behaviours, such as sexual behaviour, which may be health neutral, can also be impaired and that impairment can become a secondary cause of stress. Similarly, increases in health-risk behaviours can also become secondary causes of stress if sustained, for example alcohol or smoking. In addition to changes in health-related behaviour, the experience of stress is often related to changes in physiological function. Together, these changes describe two pathways by which the psychological experience of stress translates into physical ill health (Cox *et al.*, 1983).

Physiological change and physical health

Since the early work of Cannon (1929) and Selye (1950, 1956), much of the physiology of stress has focused on two neuroendocrine systems: the sympathetic–adrenal medullary system (SAM) and the hypothalamo–anterior pituitary–adrenal cortical system (HPAC). In a sense, both these systems focus on the function of the adrenal glands, and there have been several reviews of the role of the adrenals in stress physiology (for example, Selye, 1950; Levi, 1972; Cox and Cox, 1985). Recent studies in psychophysiology have extended beyond

consideration of these two systems to psycho-neuroimmunology.

There are now a number of studies, many of them Norwegian, which demonstrate a link between the experience of stress (at work) and changes in immune system activity, both cellular and humoral. Vaernes *et al.* (1991) have reported a study of Norwegian airforce personnel in which they showed significant correlations between perceived work stress and immunoglobulin levels, and also with health complaints related to immune system activity. Levels of complement component C3 (humoral immunity) appeared particularly sensitive to perceived work stress, and 31% of the variance in this measure could be accounted for by three work stress items relating to taking the job home, having to lead other people, and problems with subordinates. Interestingly, levels of IgM and IgG (cellular) did not correlate in any substantial way with the work stress measures. There was weak evidence of a linkage between IgA (cellular) and some aspects of perceived work stress. The immunological measures correlated with the measures of health complaints related to immune system activity.

Endresen *et al.* (1991) have reported a somewhat similar study of Norwegian bank workers. Their data suggested that T-cell number (not examined in the Vaernes *et al.* (1991) study), C3 (both cellular) and IgM (humoral) were sensitive to both perceived work stress and associated emotional distress. There are a number of other Norwegian studies which support the finding of a linkage between the experience of work stress and immune system activity. These include studies on offshore divers (Bergan *et al.*, 1987), submarine officers (Vaernes *et al.*, 1987), nursing staff (Arnestad and Aanestad, 1985; Endresen *et al.*, 1987), primary school teachers (Ursin *et al.*, 1984) and shift workers in the processing industry (Vaernes *et al.*, 1988). Although it may be safe to conclude that such a linkage exists, particularly in relation to cellular mechanisms, the direction of this relationship is not yet clear – the data are correlational – nor is its significance for health. Animal studies, not generally referred to in this chapter, do, however, suggest that environmental stimuli (stressors) can alter the effectiveness of the immune system and in some circumstances, reduce its ability to defend against both external infective agents and tumour growth. Much of this evidence has been usefully summarized in reviews of the role of psychosocial factors and psychophysiological processes in cancer(s) (Ader, 1981; Fox, 1981; Sklar and Anisman, 1981; Cox and Mackay, 1982; Irwin and Anisman, 1984; Cox, 1984).

Work by Riley (1981) provides one possible account of the way the experience of (work) stress may influence the development of cancers. Riley (1981) has argued that stress-associated pathologies will not be observed, despite the presence of stress, if there is no disease process already in existence. He argues here for a role for stress in the development of existing cancers, not in the aetiology of new cancers. Secondly, even if there is an existing latent pathology, the effects of stress will not be observed unless the disease is under the control of the immune system. This may account for stress effects on the development of some cancers and not others. Thirdly, the effects of stress will only be observed if there is some functional balance between the individual's defences and the developing cancer. Where one or other is obviously dominant, any additional effects of stress may be impossible to detect. This means that the effects of stress may not be detectable in the early and terminal stages of cancer development. This model was largely developed from Riley's studies on rodents to account for cancer development (see Riley and Spackman, 1977; Riley, 1979, 1981; Riley et al., 1979, 1981) but might be usefully applied to other diseases that involve the immune system activity (see, for example, Cox, 1988).

A considerable variety of different physical pathologies have been associated with the experience of stress through work (Holt, 1982). Those diseases usually cited as being stress related include bronchitis, coronary heart disease, thyroid disorders, skin diseases, certain types of arthritis, obesity, tuberculosis, peptic ulcers, ulcerative colitis and diabetes (Selye, 1956; Kroes, 1976; Cooper and Marshall, 1978; Cox, 1978). Furthermore, the general occurrence of physical ill health has also been related to the experience of stress. For example, Nowack (1991) has reported on the relationship between perceived stress and coping style on the one hand, and self-reported ill health on the other. The frequency and severity of physical ill health (Wyler, Masuda and Holmes, 1968, 1970) were measured. After controlling for demographic variables and for psychological wellbeing, perceived stress was shown to be a strong predictor of both the frequency and severity of physical ill health. About 30% of the variance in the latter was accounted for by perceived stress.

The exact nature of the role played by the experience of stress in these various pathologies and in physical ill health in general is not yet clear. Although it is likely that stress-related changes in psychophysiological function and health-related behaviour do underpin much of that role, the detail of those mechanisms is still being discovered, and there may be other mechanisms as yet undiscovered. As always, more research is indicated.

Conclusions

This chapter has reviewed three different approaches to the definition of stress, and described contemporary stress theory in terms of a psychological approach based on the interaction between the person and their environment. It has considered in some detail transactional models of the person–environment interaction and focused on the concepts of appraisal and coping. It has discussed theories of coping in terms of coping taxonomies and coping as problem solving. Finally, it has considered how the response to stress, including coping, may translate into physical pathology. It concludes by suggesting that, although much is known about stress and physical health, there is still a need for further research to refine our understanding of both the fact of that relationship and the complexity of the mechanisms that underpin it.

References

Ader, R.A. (1981) *Psychoneuroimmunology*, Academic Press, New York.

Ahlbom, A., Karasek, R.A. and Theorell, T. (1977) Psychosocial occupational demands and risk for cardio-vascular death. *Lakartidningen*, 77, 4243–5.

Appley, M.H. and Trumbull, R. (1967) *Psychological Stress*, Appleton-Century-Crofts, New York.

Arnestad, M. and Aanestad, B. (1985) Work environment at a psychiatric ward: stress, health and immunoglobulin levels. Unpublished PhD thesis, University of Bergen, Bergen.

Baker, D.B. (1985) The study of stress at work. *Annual Review of Public Health*, 6, 367–81.

Bergan, T., Vaernes, R.J., Ingebrigsten, P. *et al.*, (1987) Relationships between work environmental problems and health among Norwegian divers in the North Sea, in *Diving and Hyperbaric Medicine*, (eds. A. Marroni and G. Oriani), Academic Press, New York.

Bowers, K.S. (1973) Situationalism in psychology: an analysis and critique. *Psychological Review*, 80, 307–35.

Cannon, W.B. (1929) *Bodily Changes in Pain, Hunger, Fear and Rage: An Account of Recent Researches in the Function of Emotional Excitement*, Appleton, New York.

Cincirpini, P.M., Hook, J.D., Mendes de Leon, C.F. and Pritchard, W.S. (1984) *A Review of Cardiovascular, Electromyographic, Electrodermal and Respiratory Measures of Psychological Stress*, National Institute for Occupational Safety and Health, contract no: 84–257, Cincinnati, Ohio.

Cooper, C.L. and Marshall, J. (1978) Occupational sources of stress: a review of the literature relating to coronary heart disease and mental ill health. *Journal of Occupational Psychology*, 49, 11–28.

Cox, S., Cox, T., Thirlaway, M. and Mackay, C.J. (1982) Effects of simulated repetitive work on urinary catecholamine excretion. *Ergonomics*, 25, 1129–41.

Cox, T. (1978) *Stress*, Macmillan, London.

Cox, T. (1984) Stress: a psychophysiological approach to cancer, in *Psychosocial Stress and Cancer*, (ed. C.L. Cooper), Wiley, Chichester.

Cox, T. (1985) The nature and measurement of stress. *Ergonomics*, 28, 1155–63.

Cox, T. (1987) Stress, coping and problem solving. *Work and Stress*, 1, 5–14.

Cox, T. (1988) AIDS and stress. *Work and Stress*, 2, 109–12.

Cox, T. (1990) The recognition and measurement of stress: conceptual and methodological issues in *Methods in Ergonomics*, (eds J. Wilson and N. Corlett), Taylor & Francis, London.

Cox, T. and Cox, S. (1985) The role of the adrenals in the psychophysiology of stress, in *Current Issues in Clinical Psychology*, vol. 2, (ed. E. Karas), Plenum, New York.

Cox, T. and Ferguson, E. (1991) Individual differences, stress and coping, in *Personality and Stress: Individual Differences in the Stress Process*, (eds C.L. Cooper and R. Payne), Wiley, Chichester.

Cox. T. and Mackay, C.J. (1981) A transactional approach to occupational stress, in *Stress, Work Design and Productivity*, (eds N. Corlett and P. Richardson), Wiley, Chichester.

Cox, T. and Mackay, C.J. (1982) Psychosocial factors and psychophysiological mechanisms in the aetiology and development of cancers. *Social Science and Medicine*, 16, 381–96.

Cox, T. and Mackay, C.J. (1985) The measurement of self reported stress and arousal. *British Journal of Psychology*, 76, 183–6.

Cox, T., Cox, S and Thirlaway, M. (1983) The psychological and physiological response to stress, in *Physiological Correlates of Human Behaviour*, (eds A. Gale and J.A. Edwards), Academic Press, London.

Dewe, P. (1987) New Zealand ministers of religion: identifying sources of stress and coping strategies. *Work and Stress*, 1, 351–63.

Dewe, P. (1991) Measuring work stressors: the role of frequency, duration and demand. *Work and Stress*, 5, 77–91.

Diament, J. and Byers, S.O. (1975) A precise catecholamine assay for small samples. *Journal of Laboratory and Clinical Medicine*, 85, 679–93.

Dimsdale, J.E. and Moss, J. (1980a) Plasma catecholamines in stress and exercise. *Journal of the American Medical Association*, 243, 340–2.

Dimsdale, J.E. and Moss, J. (1980b) Short term catecholamine response to psychological stress. *Psychosomatic Medicine*, 42, 493–7.

Einhorn, H.J. and Hogarth, R.M. (1981) Behavioural decision theory: processes of judgement and choice. *Annual Review of Psychology*, **32**, 53–88.

Ekehammar, B. (1974) Interactionism in personality from a historical perspective. *Psychological Bulletin*, **81**, 1026.

Endresen, I.M., Ellertsen, B., Endresen, C. *et al.*, (1991) Stress at work and psychological and immunological parameters in a group of Norwegian female bank employees. *Work and Stress*, **5**, 217–27.

Endresen, I.M, Vaernes, R.J., Ursin, H. and Tonder, O. (1987) Psychological stress factors and concentration of immunoglobulins and complement components in Norwegian nurses. *Work and Stress*, **1**, 365–75.

Fisher, S. (1986). *Stress and Strategy*, Lawrence Erlbaum Associates, London.

Fletcher, B.C. (1988) The epidemiology of occupational stress, in *Causes, Coping and Consequences of Stress at Work*, (eds C.L. Cooper and R. Payne), Wiley, Chichester.

Folkman, S. (1984) Personal control and stress and coping processes: a theoretical analysis. *Journal of Personality and Social Psychology*, **46**, 839–52.

Folkman, S. and Lazarus, R. (1986) Stress process and depressive symptomatology. *Journal of Abnormal Psychology*, **95**, 107–13.

Folkman, S., Lazarus, R.S., Dunkel-Schetter, C. *et al.* (1986). Dynamics of a stressful encounter: cognitive appraisal, coping, and encounter outcomes. *Journal of Personality and Social Psychology*, **50**, 992–1003.

Fox, B.H. (1981) Psychosocial factors and the immune system in human cancer, in *Psychoneuro-immunology*, (ed R. Ader), Academic Press, New York.

French, J.R.P., Caplan, R.D. and van Harrison, R. (1982) *The Mechanisms of Job Stress and Strain*, Wiley, New York.

French, J.R.P., Rogers, W. and Cobb, S. (1974) A model of person–environment fit, in *Coping and Adaptation*, (eds Coehlo, G.W., Hamburg, D.A. and Adams, J.E.), Basic Books, New York.

Holroyd, K.A., and Lazarus R.S. (1982) Stress, coping and somatic adaptation, in *Handbook of Stress*, (eds L. Goldberger and S. Breznitz), Free Press, New York.

Holt, R.R. (1982) Occupational stress, in *Handbook of Stress: Theoretical and Clinical Aspects*, (eds L. Goldberger and S. Bremtz), Free Press, New York.

Irwin, J. and Anisman, H. (1984) Stress and pathology: immunological and central nervous system interactions, in *Psychosocial Stress and Cancer*, (ed C.L. Cooper) Wiley, Chichester.

Karasek, R. A. (1979) Job demands, job decision latitude and mental strain; implications for job redesign. *Administrative Science Quarterly*, **24**, 285–308.

Karasek, R.A. (1981) Job socialisation and job strain: the implications of two psychosocial mechanisms for job design, in *Working Life: A Social Science Contribution to Work Reform*, (eds B. Gardell and G. Johansson), Wiley, Chichester.

Karasek, R. and Theorell, T (1990) *Healthy Work: Stress, Productivity and the Reconstruction of Working Life*, Basic Books, New York.

Kasl, S.V. (1980) Epidemiological contributions to the study of work stress, in *Stress at Work*, (eds C.L. Cooper and R. Payne), Wiley, Chichester.

Kasl, S.V. (1984) Stress and health. *Annual Review of Public Health*, **5**, 319–41.

Kroes, W. H. (1976) *Society's Victim – The Policeman*, C.C. Thomas, New York.

Lacey, J.I. (1967) Somatic response patterning and stress: some revisions of activation theory, in *Psychological Stress*, (eds M.H. Appley and R. Trumbull), Appleton-Century-Crofts, New York.

Lazarus, R.S. (1966) *Psychological Stress and the Coping Process*, McGraw-Hill, New York.

Lazarus R,S, (1976) *Patterns of Adjustment*, McGraw-Hill, New York.

Lazarus, R.S. and Folkman, S. (1984). *Stress, Appraisal and Coping*, Springer Publications, New York.

Leventhal, H. and Tomarken, A. (1987) Stress and illness: perspectives from health psychology, in *Stress and Health: Issues in Research Methodology*, (eds S. Kasl and C. Cooper) Wiley, Chichester.

Levi, L. (1972) Stress and distress in response to psychosocial stimuli. *Acta Medica Scandinavica*, **191**, Supplement: 528.

Mackay, C.J., Cox, T., Burrows, G.C. and Lazzerini, A.J. (1978) An inventory for the measurement of self reported stress and arousal. *British Journal of Social and Clinical Psychology*, **17**, 283–4.

Mandler, G. (1982) Stress and thought processes, in *Handbook of Stress*, (eds L. Goldberg and S. Breznitz), Free Press, New York.

Mason, J.W. (1968) A review of psychoendocrine research on the pituitary–adrenal cortical system. *Psychosomatic Medicine*, **30**, 576–607.

Mason, J.W. (1971) A re-evaluation of the concept of non-specificity in stress theory. *Journal of Psychiatric Research*, **8**, 323–42.

Meichenbaum, D. (1983) *Coping with Stress*, Century Publishing, London.

Miller, S. (1979) Controllability and human stress: method, evidence and theory. *Behavioural Research and Therapy*, **17**, 287–304.

Miller, S., Brody, D. and Summerton, J. (1988). Styles of coping with threat: implications for health. *Journal of Personality and Social Psychology*, **54**, 142–8.

Nowack, K.M. (1991) Psychosocial predictors of health status. *Work and Stress*, **5**, 117–31.

Payne, R. and Fletcher, B. (1983) Job demands, supports and constraints as predictors of psychological strain among school teachers. *Journal of Vocational Behaviour*, **22**, 136–47.

Pearlin, L. and Schooler, C. (1978). The structure of coping. *Journal of Health and Social Behavior*, **19**, 2–21.

Pearlin, L., Menaghan, E., Lieberman, M. and Mullan, J. (1981). The stress process. *Journal of Health and Social Behavior*, **22**, 337–56.

Riley, V. (1979) Stress–cancer contradictions: a continuing puzzlement. *Cancer Detection and Prevention*, **2**, 159–62.

Riley, V. (1981) Psychoneuroendocrine influences on immunocompetence and neoplasia. *Science*, **212**, 1100–9.

Riley, V. and Spackman, D. (1977) Cage crowding stress: absence of effect on melanoma within protective facilities. *Proceedings of the American Association for Cancer Research*, **18**, 173.

Riley, V., Fitzmaurice, M.A. and Spackman, D.H. (1981) Psychoneuroimmunologic factors in neoplasia: studies in animals, in *Psychoneuroimmunology*, (ed R. Ader), Academic Press, New York.

Riley, V., Spackman, D., McClanahan, D. and Santisteban, G.A. (1979) The role of stress in malignancy. *Cancer Detection and Prevention*, **2**, 235–55.

Schonpflug, F. and Battmenn, A (1988) The costs and benefits of coping, in *Handbook of Life Stress, Cognition and Health*, (eds S. Fisher and J. Reason), Wiley, Chichester.

Sells, S.B. (1970) On the nature of stress, in *Social and Psychological Factors in Stress*, (ed J. McGrath), Holt, Rinehart and Winston, New York.

Selye, H. (1950) *Stress*, Acta Incorporated, Montreal.

Selye, H. (1956) *Stress of Life*, McGraw-Hill, New York.

Sklar, L.S. and Anisman, H. (1981) Stress and cancer. *Psychological Bulletin*, **89**, 369–406.

Stainbrook, G.L. and Green, L.W. (1983) Role of psychosocial stress in cardiovascular disease. *Houston Heart Bulletin*, **3**, 1–8.

Sutherland, V.J. and Cooper, C.L. (1990) *Understanding Stress: Psychological Perspective for Health Professionals. Psychology and Health 5*. Chapman and Hall, London.

Ursin, H., Mykletun, R., Tonder, O. *et al.* (1984) Psychological stress factors and concentrations of immunoglobulins and complement components in humans. *Scandinavian Journal of Psychology*, **23**, 193–9.

Vaernes, R.J., Knardahl, S., Romsing, J. *et al.* (1988) Relationships between environmental problems, defense strategies and health among shiftworkers in the process industry. *Work and Stress*, **1**, 7–15.

Vaernes, R.J., Myhre,G., Aas, H. *et al.* (1991) Relationships between stress, psychological factors, health and immune levels among military aviators. *Work and Stress*, **5**, 5–16.

Vaernes, R.J., Warncke, M., Eidsvik, S. *et al.* (1987) Relationships between perceived health and psychological factors among submarine personnel: endocrine and immunological effects, in *Diving and Hyperbaric Medicine*, (eds A. Marroni and G. Oriani), Academic Press, New York.

Warr, P.B. (1990) Decision latitude, job demands and employee wellbeing. *Work and Stress*, **4**, 285–94.

Wyler, A., Masuda, M. and Holmes, T. (1968) Seriousness of illness scale. *Journal of Psychosomatic Research*, **11**, 363–75.

Wyler, A., Masuda, M. and Holmes, T. (1970) Seriousness of illness scale: reproducibility. *Journal of Psychosomatic Research*, **14**, 54–64.

Chapter three

Placebos: their effectiveness and modes of action

Phil Richardson

Introduction

The suggestion that a pill made from powdered dolphin's penis might enhance a man's virility would presumably be greeted with derision by most western physicians and their patients. The fact that such a pill is still sold for this purpose at several retail outlets in London would, however, come as no surprise to anyone acquainted with traditional Chinese medicine. To the western medical practitioner a therapeutic result obtained from this pill would fall within the category of 'placebo effects' – effects which have long been viewed as a hindrance to the proper evaluation of active or 'specific' treatments. However, it is now widely recognized that the placebo effect is a phenomenon worthy of investigation in its own right.

A placebo has been defined as 'any therapy or component of therapy that is deliberately used for its non-specific, psychological or psychophysiological effect, or that is used for its presumed specific effect, but is without specific activity for the condition being treated (Shapiro and Morris, 1978). Although this is probably the best-known definition (Plotkin, 1985), several alternatives have been proposed (Brody,

1980; Grunbaum, 1981; Ross and Buckalew, 1985; Wickramasekera, 1985) and there has been considerable debate concerning the language which best describes placebo-related phenomena. For example, Wilkins (1979) has criticized the use of the terms 'specific' and 'non-specific', and Grunbaum has proposed an alternative terminology for placebo phenomena (Grunbaum, 1981, 1985, 1986). These issues will not be taken up here but for a further discussion of them the reader is referred to Borkovec (1985), Brody (1985), Critelli and Neumann (1984), Grunbaum (1985) and Peek (1977).

Although survey findings indicate that the administration of placebos is far from rare (Goldberg, Leigh and Quinlan, 1979; Goodwin, Goodwin and Vogel, 1979; Gray and Flynn, 1981) it seems unlikely that many doctors would openly endorse their routine use as part of daily clinical practice (Blaschke, Nies and Mamelok, 1985; Laurence and Bennett, 1980). Ethical considerations and the fear of generating widespread distrust in the patient population has led to the restriction of placebo use to a few 'special cases' and patients in double-blind trials (Brody, 1980). For this reason it might be thought that findings from research on placebos could have few implications for the practice of medicine. In subscribing to such a view, however, it would be necessary to maintain a clear dichotomy between 'real' (i.e. specific) treatments on the one hand and placebos on the other. This dichotomy fails to allow for the possibility that a real treatment could, in addition to its specific effects, have a non-specific (i.e. placebo-related) impact on the patient. If we abandon this simplistic dichotomy then it becomes clear that information concerning the effectiveness and mode of action of placebos is potentially relevant to all clinical practice.

This chapter summarizes the current state of knowledge concerning the range and extent of placebo effects. Following this, evidence from placebo studies exploring the importance of patient variables, therapist variables and the nature of the treatment itself will be examined. Finally, selected theories of placebo action will be briefly reviewed.

Range and extent of placebo effects

Historians of medicine are virtually unanimous in describing the majority of medicines and medical procedures in use prior to the 20th century as inert, or in some cases positively toxic (Shapiro, 1960). Therapeutic properties have been ascribed throughout history to an enormous array of bizarre substances, ranging from fly specks to crocodile dung. To the extent that they were therapeutic they presumably achieved much of their effectiveness through psychological processes. It could also be argued that, since many illnesses are self-limiting, patients recovered not as a result of the efforts of their physicians but rather despite them. Similar considerations apply when considering the frequently cited evidence for the effectiveness of healing rituals in primitive societies (Frank, 1973) and of alternative medicines such as acupuncture (Richardson and Vincent, 1986).

Scientific interest in the placebo effect arose largely through the introduction of the placebo-controlled trial in the 1950s as a means of assessing the efficacy of drug treatments (Demarr and Pelikan, 1955; Lasagna, 1955). An examination of this literature indicates that the disorders for which placebos have been reported to produce symptom relief are legion, and include allergies, angina pectoris, asthma, cancer, cerebral infarction, diabetes, enuresis, epilepsy, insomnia, migraine, multiple sclerosis, neurosis, depression, parkinsonism, psychosis, skin diseases, ulcers and warts (Hass, Fink and Hartfelder, 1959; Horningfeld, 1964; Souza and Goodwin, 1991; Totman 1987: White, Tursky and Schwartz, 1985). Indeed, there appears to be almost no limit to the disorders for which placebos have been reported to produce some degree of symptomatic relief (Ross and Olson, 1982). It should be noted, however, that much of the available evidence for the effectiveness of placebos comes from studies in which the administration of the placebo itself constituted the control condition for the evaluation of some other active treatment, and where improvement due to the placebo was inferred from differences between pre- and post-treatment scores. As most studies have failed to incorporate a no-treatment control condition, the inferences which may be drawn about the true size and extensiveness of the effects are limited. Effects attributed to the influence of the placebo may well be the result of spontaneous fluctuations in the symptoms of the disorder. Notwithstanding these problems of interpretation, it appears that in a large number of studies significant placebo responses are reported for at least a substantial minority of treated patients. The proportion of placebo responders in particular samples may vary from 0 to 100%, although the number commonly falls in the 30–50% range; where psychiatric disorders are concerned it is not infrequently as high as 75% (Jospe, 1978; Parkhouse, 1963; Shapiro and Morris, 1978).

The most extensively researched symptom is pain, where it is commonly claimed that 35% of patients with severe clinical pain will respond to a placebo with the degree of relief which might normally result from the administration of 10 mg of morphine (Beecher, 1955; Evans, 1974a). This figure is by no means fixed, however, and reports of substantially higher rates are common (e.g. Grevert, Albert and Goldstein, 1983; Langley *et al.*, 1984). Indeed, since placebo responses are assessed in a variety of different ways it would be surprising to find an invariant response rate across different studies. For example, different clinical measures of pain (e.g. subjective versus observer ratings) may be only moderately correlated with each other (Pearce and Richardson, 1987) and response rates to placebo analgesia may therefore depend, in part, on the particular measures used. Placebo effects do not appear to be confined to subjectively reported symptoms but can also occur on objectively recorded measures (e.g. lung function: Butler and Steptoe, 1984; postoperative swelling: Hashish, Feinman and Harvey, 1988) and on measures of bodily functions of which the patient would normally have no awareness, such as mild to moderate changes in blood pressure (Vogel, Goodwin and Goodwin, 1980) and pulse rate (Ross and Buckalew, 1983)). Moreover, in studies of healthy volunteers placebos have been found to influence performance on a wide range of laboratory tasks involving cognitive and psychomotor functions (Ross and Buckalew, 1983). In addition to their therapeutic impact, placebos may also provoke adverse reactions in the form of side-effects, symptom-worsening and dependence. Commonly reported side-effects include both subjective ones (e.g. drowsiness, nausea, lack of concentration) and more objective manifestations (e.g. sweating, vomiting, skin rashes) (Gowdey, 1983; Haegerstam *et al.*, 1982). A small number of patients will sometimes report a worsening of their symptoms following placebo administra-

tion, and this has been referred to as the nocebo effect (Kissel and Barrucand, 1974). Single case reports have also appeared documenting the occurrence of dependence on placebos (Vinar, 1969; Boleloucky, 1971). All in all, when we consider the published documentation of the range and extent of placebo effects it seems that Beecher (1955) was justified in referring to 'the powerful placebo'.

Variables which have been claimed to influence placebo responsiveness may be subdivided into three major categories: those concerned with the patient, the treatment itself and the therapist. These will be examined in turn.

Patient characteristics

The fact that only a proportion of patients in any treatment trial respond positively to a placebo has given rise to the suggestion that placebo responders may differ in some significant way from non-responders. This line of reasoning has given rise to a quest for the characteristics of the typical placebo responder – a quest which for the most part has proved fruitless. Although it has been reported that placebo reactors are more likely to be emotionally dependent (Lasagna, *et al.*, 1954), extrovert (Campbell and Rosenbaum, 1967), neurotic (Gartner, 1961), suggestible (McGlashan, Evans and Orne, 1969) and possess a fair number of other qualities (see Shapiro and Morris, 1978), the overall picture emerging from research in this area is one of conflicting, equivocal and often unreplicated findings (Buckalew, Ross and Starr, 1981). For example, although certain investigators have identified high scores on extraversion as being predictive of increased placebo responsivity (Knowles and Lucas, 1960; Gartner, 1961; Black, 1966; Campbell and Rosenbaum, 1967), others report the reverse effect, with introverts responding most (Morison, Woodmansey and Young, 1961; Thorn, 1962; Luoto, 1964). If placebo reactors differ in consistent ways from non-reactors, then their particular characteristics have yet to be reliably identified.

The complexities of investigating individual differences in placebo responsiveness are underlined by the findings of a placebo treatment study by Shapiro, who examined a number of different predictor variables (e.g. age, sex, personality measures) and took a range of different measures of the placebo response. The individual characteristics that best predicted the occurrence of a placebo response were found to vary according to which particular measure of the response was used (Shapiro, Wilensky and Struening, 1968). This underlines the fact that placebo responsivity is not a unidimensional phenomenon. Different studies may therefore be tapping different aspects of the placebo response, and hence obtaining inconsistent findings.

A more fundamental problem for research in this area is the fact that the concept of a 'typical placebo reactor' may itself be called into question. It is possible that placebo responsivity may not be enduring characteristic. Studies taking repeated measures of placebo responses across different contexts of administration have suggested that different individuals may respond on different occasions (Liberman, 1964; Frank, 1968). Liberman, for example, demonstrated this with the pain associated with childbirth. Positive responses to a placebo administered for labour pain were only weakly and insignificantly correlated with placebo responses during the postpartum period (Liberman, 1964).

The above findings suggest that a simple trait-based model of placebo responsivity has little predictive potential. This is consistent with findings on the prediction of behaviour in other areas (Mischel, 1976), where trait measures have likewise proved to be of only limited value. If enduring individual characteristics have any significance in determining placebo responsivity, then it is probably that they interact with a range of other situational variables (e.g. treatment type, therapist etc.) and/or with more variable aspects of the individual's state (e.g. fatigue, state anxiety, beliefs about particular treatments, etc.).

Treatment characteristics

Placebo have been administered in many forms. Although the sugar pill is the popular stereotype, an injection of 5% saline is probably the most common form of placebo administered (Gray and Flynn, 1981). In addition to bogus pills, capsules and injections, there have also been reports of placebo surgery (Cobb, Thomas and Dillard, 1959; Dimond, Kittle and Cockett, 1960) in which patients received an operation scar but nothing more. Placebo effects have also been reported in response to exposure to technically sophisticated equipment, such as X-rays (Schwitzgebel and Traugott, 1968). Forms of treatment which are reliant on such equipment (e.g. transcutaneous nerve stimulation, biofeedback, ultrasound etc.) have often been presented in a bogus (i.e. theoretically inactive) form as part of the evaluation of their effectiveness. (Wickramasekera, 1977; Thorsteinsson *et al.* 1978; Hashish, Feinman and Harvey, 1988). Finally, placebo treatment procedures with impressive sounding names have been devised expressly in order to capitalize upon the therapeutically persuasive potential of modern technology and sophisticated equipment, for example, subconscious reconditioning therapy (Lent, Crimmings and Russell, 1981), tachistoscope therapy (Tori and Worrell, 1983), subliminal pulse therapy (Langley, Sheppeard and Wigley, 1983).

Where placebo pills and capsules are concerned, variations in their effectiveness have frequently been attributed to differences in their physical characteristics, e.g. size, apparent dosage level and colour (Buckalew and Ross, 1981). For example, it has been reported that large pills work better than little ones, but also that little ones work better than large ones

(Berg, 1977); two pills may work better than one (Blackwell, Bloomfield and Buncher, 1972). That the colour of the pill may also be important, has been reported by several investigators Evans, for example, has recommended the use of a very large brown or purple pill, or a very small bright red or yellow one (Evans, 1974a). On the basis of a comparative study, Shapira recommends green for anxiety and yellow for depression (Shapira et al., 1970). Unfortunately, the data upon which his recommendations were made are far from clear-cut, the majority of green-yellow comparisons failing to reveal statistically significant differences. Blackwell, Bloomfield and Buncher (1972) have reported that red tends to stimulate, whereas blue is more likely to have sedative effects. This claim was based on the results of a pharmacology laboratory class in which (presumably healthy) medical student volunteers recorded what were essentially minor variations in their bodily state over the course of an hour following the ingestion of one or two red or blue capsules. Whether such an effect would generalize to an unhealthy patient population is far from clear.

More compelling findings emerge from an examination of the treatment modality itself (e.g. injection vs pill). It seems that treatments that are ostensibly more 'serious' or 'major' in some respect are associated with reports of greater placebo responsiveness. For example, in studies of the treatment of obesity and of hypertension, dummy injections had a greater therapeutic impact than placebo pills (Carne, 1961; Grenfell, Briggs and Holland, 1961). In addition, unusually high improvement rates have been reported following placebo surgery. As many as 85% of patients with angina pectoris achieved clinically significant reductions in their painful symptoms following simulated surgery in which they received nothing more than an operation scar (Cobb, Thomas and Dillard, 1959; Dimond, Kittle and Cockett, 1960). Placebos which make use of sophisticated scientific equipment may also have enhanced therapeutic potential (Wickramasekera, 1977; Langley and Sheppeard, 1987).

It is easy, when conducting comparative treatment research, to vary the vehicle or mode of treatment administration. To experiment with the colour of an empty capsule, for example, requires little effort and no psychological sophistication. A problem with this kind of research is that it all too easily leads to meaningless reification of the qualities under investigation. It is inherently nonsensical to suggest that an injection has any greater or lesser therapeutic force in general than a pill, a capsule or anything else. Similarly, there can be nothing about greenness per se, or largeness or smallness, which imbues a placebo with special curative powers. These qualities can have no influence independently of the recipient's perception of them. It is therefore unlikely that further investigations of the 'efficacy' of hitherto untested combinations of size, colour, shape etc. will contribute to our understanding of placebo effects in the absence of explicit hypotheses linking these qualities to the knowledge, perceptions or expectations of the patients to whom they are given.

Therapist variables

Therapist variables also appear to have an influence on placebo responsivity. For example, placebos administered by therapists of high status or prestige have been reported to work better than those given by lower-status individuals (Liberman, 1961; Lesse, 1962; Shapiro, 1964). Similar findings have also emerged from studies of faith healing and folk remedies (Jaspers, 1965; Frank, 1973). This phenomenon is reminiscent of social psychological research findings on the effects of persuasive communications upon attitude change (Hovland, Janis and Kelley, 1953). In these studies the credibility of a message has been shown to be influenced by the status of its source. The importance of treatment credibility has been established in recent years, both in psychotherapy (Kazdin and Wilcoxon, 1976) and in the treatment of pain (Petrie and Hazleman, 1985). Although certain treatments, notably those involving sophisticated equipment and elaborate scientific-sounding rationales, may have inherent credibility for the patient (Borkovec and Nau, 1972), it may be that the apparent value or credibility of more routine treatments (pills, injections) will depend more on the perceived qualities of the therapist than on the treatment itself.

There seems little doubt that the style of treatment administration can have an effect on outcome. For example, the confidence with which a placebo is administered appears to affect its strength of action (Uhlenhuth *et al.*, 1959). The apparent concern with which a treatment is administered may also be important. In a study exploring the role of the endogenous opioids in placebo analgesia, Grevert, Albert and Goldstein (1983) presented the 'pain-killing' placebo injection to patients with exaggerated concern, asking them to report any side-effects immediately and hovering in anxious anticipation of any complications that might arise. The positive placebo response rate following this style of presentation was 62%, far higher than the commonly reported rate of 35% for placebo-induced pain relief. Evidence such as this is at best indirect, since the level of the doctors' concern was not systematically varied. There is, however, a large body of evidence concerning the association between the interest level of therapists and the outcome of treatment. The research is well reviewed by Shapiro and Morris (1978), who state: 'an inescapable conclusion is that the therapist's interest in the patient, treatment and results is related to success in treatment and placebo effects' (p. 384).

The possibility that the pill may only be important in so far as it symbolizes the healing powers of the doctor is suggested by a pilot study conducted by Park and Covi (1965) at Johns Hopkins University Medical School. In their small, uncontrolled study, patients were given the following instructions: 'Many patients with your kind of condition have been helped by what are sometimes called sugar pills and we think that a sugar pill may help you too. Do you know what a sugar pill is? A sugar pill is a pill with no medicine in it at all. Are you willing to try it?' Fourteen out of the 15 patients agreed to take part and of these all but one derived clinically significant benefit. This study does not appear to have been replicated.

In the above study the effect of the doctors' (verbal) behaviour on the patients' response is self-evident. In contrast with this, it appears that doctors' beliefs, expectations or wishes may influence patients' responses in far less obvious ways – ways which may bypass the normal constraints of the double-blind trial. The study by Uhlenhuth *et al.* (1959) is a good example. Their double-blind drug trial involved two sedatives and a placebo in which all patients received each substance for 3 weeks. A balanced design was used and both patient and physician measures of improvement were taken. Of the two psychiatrists involved in the trial, one (Dr A) had an organic orientation and was optimistic about the therapeutic impact of the two active substances. The other (Dr B) was of a more psychotherapeutic persuasion and expected little in the way of additional specific benefits of the two drugs over and above their placebo effect. The adequacy of the double-blind procedure was assessed by asking each doctor to make repeated guesses concerning the identity of each of his patients' current medication. These guesses were not accurate above chance level, confirming their ignorance of the drug/placebo allocations. Despite this, each doctor obtained results from his patients directly in accord with his expectations: for Dr A the active drugs were significantly more effective than placebo; for Dr B there were no significant differences in effectiveness. The doctors' beliefs therefore appear to have had a direct influence on patients' responses.

A similar result was reported by Gracely *et al.* (1985). Patients undergoing wisdom tooth extractions were given either fentanyl (an analgesic), placebo or naloxone (an opiate antagonist), and were told that their pain might decrease, remain the same or increase. In reality there were two groups of patients: one which indeed might receive any of the three substances and one which, in fact, would receive only placebo or naloxone. The doctors were blind to the precise drug allocation but did know to which of the two broad groups each of the patients belonged. The patients' reported responses to the placebo in these two conditions were markedly different. Where the patient might have received fentanyl the placebo was clearly effective. The subjects in the other group showed no significant placebo response. Since the patients were unaware of the existence of the two conditions, this difference in response to the placebo must presumably be attributed to some aspect of the doctors' behaviour. Unfortunately, this finding was reported in letter form, with insufficient detail to allow more than a speculative interpretation of the results.

From these and a range of other findings it seems probable that the behaviour of the therapist may have subtle yet powerful influences on the patient's response to a placebo (Barbour, 1991). This conclusion is paralleled by findings from research on psychotherapy (Garfield and Bergin, 1986) and in the broader field of doctor–patient communication, where therapist behaviour has been shown to be an important influence on patient satisfaction, compliance with medical advice and a number of other outcome variables (see, Pendleton and Hasler, 1983 and Ley and Llewelyn, this volume). What has yet to be clearly established where placebos are concerned is which particular aspects of the therapist's behaviour influence which particular aspects of the patient's

response, and through which particular mechanisms of action. The following section examines selected theories of the mechanisms of placebo action.

Mechanisms of placebo action

Numerous theories of placebogenesis have been proposed. These include accounts couched in terms of operant conditioning, classical conditioning, guilt reduction, transference effects, suggestion, persuasion, role demands, hope, faith, labelling, misattribution, cognitive dissonance, anxiety reduction and expectancy effects. For comprehensive reviews of these the reader is referred elsewhere (see, for example, Jospe, 1978; Shapiro and Morris, 1978; Brody, 1980; White, Tursky and Schwartz 1985).

Expectancy

The concept of 'expectancy effects' is ubiquitously encountered in the placebo literature. At times the term appears to be used almost synonymously with 'placebo effects' (*cf.* Evans, 1974b). At other times its use appears to have explanatory intent, i.e. the placebo effect occurred because the patient expected it. There is certainly extensive evidence that patients' expectations may be predictive of the outcome of psychotherapy (Wilkins, 1973; Gomes-Schwartz, Hadley and Strupp, 1978) and may influence responses to chemotherapy (Lyerly *et al.*, 1964; Reed and Witt, 1965; Sotsky *et al.*, 1991). For example, Reed and Witt (1965) eliminated the hallucinogenic effect of LSD on habitual users by leading them to believe that they were taking a placebo. Parallels between placebo and drug effects, in which similar time–effect curves, similar dose–response relationships and similar side-effects are obtained, are also frequently taken as evidence for the importance of patient expectations in determining placebo effects (e.g. Ross and Olson, 1982; Wall, 1992). Despite the current popularity of cognitive conceptualizations of clinical problems, it is still difficult to ascribe much explanatory force to the concept of expectancy in the absence of some further specification of the mechanisms by which an expectation of therapeutic change is translated into a blood pressure reduction, say, or an improvement in a painful condition. Few expectancy accounts of placebo action go this far. An exception is to be found in the work of Ross and Olson (1981), who present a carefully formulated model of expectancy effects within the framework of attribution theory. In their article they provide a thorough review of early studies relevant to the expectancy–attribution perspective. Later work by Voudouris, Peck and Coleman (1990) on the relative importance of verbal expectancies in the placebo effect is referred to later in this chapter.

Reporting error

This account of placebo effects ascribes them largely to some form of error or misreporting, either on the part of the observer or on that of the patient. The implication is that the observed changes are either illusory or artefactual. Where the observer is the therapist, a wish or expectation to see therapeutic effects may bias his or her perception and/or recording of the symptoms. Where the patient is concerned, a wish to please the doctor (Tedeschi, Schlenker and Bonoma, 1971) may produce altered symptom reporting. This might involve conscious misrepresentation of symptoms or some form of error – perhaps in the attribution of perceived symptom change (see Ross and Olson, 1981).

Experimenter expectancy effects have been widely documented in laboratory-based psychological research (Rosenthal, 1966) and parallel therapist expectancy effects have been noted in clinical settings (Felman, 1956; Breuning, Ferguson and Cullari, 1980). Indeed, the use of the placebo in double-blind trials arose in part from the need to control for such effects (Wilkins, 1985). That patients might also misreport their symptoms does not seem unlikely, and may account for some instances of improvement following placebo administration. Accounts of placebo action based simply on the wish to please the doctor are not, however, consistent with the concurrence of positive therapeutic effects alongside negative ones (e.g. side-effects) in the same patient (see, for example, Shapiro et al., 1968). Moreover, the possibility that placebo effects could be accounted for entirely by misreporting on the part of the patient is eliminated by the observation of placebo-induced changes in bodily processes of which the patient would normally have no awareness (see above).

Cognitive dissonance

Totman (1979, 1987) proposed that dissonance reduction may account for some placebo effects. According to cognitive dissonance theory (Festinger, 1957), when an individual holds two or more beliefs which are psychologically inconsistent a state of tension arises (dissonance) which motivates the individual to reduce the inconsistency. Where placebos are concerned, the belief that no therapeutic change has occurred is potentially inconsistent with the knowledge of having received treatment, the fact that the doctor said the treatment would work, the possible belief that only very sick people don't get better, and so on. To reduce dissonance, one course open to patients may be to alter their perception of the occurrence of change.

Social psychological research has shown dissonance arousal to be a powerful motivating force, producing physiological as well as psychological change (Zimbardo, 1969). Moreover, the relevance of dissonance theory to clinical phenomena has been demonstrated in a number of investigations. For example, in an analogue study of relaxation training, Gordon

(1976) showed that a dissonance-enhancing procedure (manipulation of choice and personal commitment) could increase the perceived benefits of treatment.

More direct tests of the dissonance reduction hypothesis of placebo effects can be found in the work of Totman (1976, 1977, 1987). In an application of the well-known forced compliance paradigm, Totman (1977) offered placebo analgesia to subjects taking part in a study of the treatment of experimentally induced pain. The placebo – an injection of sterile water – was described as a new experimental drug and presented in such a way as to maximize the subjects' anxiety about it. One group of subjects was given justification for choosing to take the 'drug' by dint of the offer of payment; the potential benefits to science and to pain sufferers were also stressed. The second group was offered no such justification, and only minimal pressure was applied to ensure their participation. Totman reasoned that the low-justification group would experience the greatest dissonance if the drug failed to work. He predicted greater placebo analgesia in this group and this prediction was confirmed, whereby lending support to a dissonance reduction interpretation of the placebo effect.

Alternative interpretations are, however, possible. For example, far from reducing dissonance, the offer of payment in the high-justification group might have increased patients' anxiety about the drug. Since anxiety may influence pain perception (Sternbach, 1968), the manipulation could have reduced the analgesic effects of the placebo. Furthermore, the use of healthy volunteers as subjects in this study limits the clinical significance of its findings.

In a clinical study of the effectiveness of placebo hypnotic medication, Totman (1976) employed the technique of post-decisional dissonance induction in which the individual is forced to make a difficult (i.e. dissonance-arousing) choice between two barely distinguishable alternatives. Insomniac patients on a chest ward who were made to choose between two placebo sleeping pills subsequently slept an average of 2 hours longer per night (according to self- and nurse-observer ratings) than those to whom no such choice was offered. This study offers a more compelling demonstration of the clinical significance of putative dissonance manipulations where placebo effects are concerned. However, no direct check was made on the psychological effects of the manipulations (e.g. dissonance arousal, anxiety reduction etc.), so it cannot be firmly concluded that the differences in sleep times resulted from differences in dissonance arousal rather than differential effects of the manipulation on other psychological responses, such as anxiety levels and/or the patients' capacity for relaxation.

Conditioning processes

The principles of classical conditioning have been invoked to account for some placebo effects. On the grounds that many of the features of treatment settings (doctors, white coats, pills, syringes etc.) are potential conditioned stimuli, it is argued that placebo effects may be equivalent to conditioned therapeutic responses (Gleidman, Gantt and Teitelbaum, 1957; Wickramasekera, 1980, 1985). Conditioned stimuli associated with the onset of an unconditioned stimulus that provides symptom relief, or associated with the offset of the disease process, could therefore acquire placebo power. By this analysis, nocebos can be viewed as conditioned stimuli associated with disease onset. A detailed elaboration of this model has recently been put forward by Wickramasekera (1985).

Conditioned pharmacological effects have been demonstrated in both animals (see Siegel, 1985) and humans (Dafters and Anderson, 1982). For example, Herrnstein (1962) showed that the performance of rats on a learning task which had previously been disrupted by injections of scopolamine hydrobromide could subsequently be impaired by similarly administered injections of 5% saline (Herrnstein, 1962). There is also now a growing research literature on the environmental specificity of drug effects in humans (Annear and Vogel-Sprott, 1985; Shapiro and Nathan, 1986). Whether conditioning processes account for patients' responses to placebo treatments is less clear, and there is as yet only limited direct evidence.

There are certainly a number of placebo research findings which are amenable to a conditioning interpretation and which therefore provide indirect support for the model. For example, placebo-induced analgesic responses in laboratory studies of experimentally induced pain are generally far weaker and less consistent than those for clinical pain (Evans, 1974b). This could be due to the relative absence in laboratory settings of the usual clinical accompaniments of treatment administration (conditioned stimuli), which may normally promote placebo effects. Furthermore, therapeutic responses to many drugs often occur earlier in time than any pharmacological action could possibly have taken place. For example, a patient may obtain almost instant headache relief following the ingestion of a pill known to contain aspirin (Petrie, 1960). This kind of 'placebo' effect is consistent with the generally shorter latency of conditioned responses than of unconditioned ones. Although consistent with a conditioning account of placebo responses, both the above examples are amenable to alternative interpretations, for example in terms of anxiety reduction (see below). There appears to have been only a small number of direct tests of the classical conditioning model of placebo effects in humans. Voudouris, Peck and Coleman (1985) obtained either raised or lowered pain thresholds following the application of a placebo

cream that had preciously been paired with decreased or increased shock intensity. This finding was replicated in a later study, in which the authors also found evidence of generalization of the conditioned placebo response (Voudouris, Peck and Coleman, 1989). A further study in the same series (Voudouris, Peck and Coleman, 1990) examined the relative contribution of conditioning and verbal expectancy to the occurrence of placebo-induced pain relief. Conditioning produced more powerful placebo responses than the expectancy manipulation. As the authors themselves recognize, however, the two processes are not readily separable: conditioning procedures may themselves generate strong expectations.

Anxiety reduction

Several writers have suggested that the reduction of anxiety may be responsible for certain placebo effects (Thorn, 1962; Sternbach, 1968; Beecher, 1972; Evans, 1974b, 1985). The influence of anxiety on symptom levels could be direct. Sternbach (1968) has claimed, for instance, that placebo analgesia may be understood in terms of the influence of anxiety upon pain perception – the relief of a patient in pain after receiving analgesic medication leading to a direct reduction in experienced pain. Such effects might be expected to be mediated by changes in autonomic arousal, and might thus be most likely to occur in bodily systems which are at least partially under autonomic control (e.g. cardiovascular and respiratory systems). More recently it has been suggested that a reduction in hyperventilation (associated with a lowering of arousal) might be a causal mechanism in some placebo effects (Timmons, in press).

Alternatively, the cognitive aspects of anxiety might influence symptom perception. In this way, anxiety may have an indirect influence. For example, ceasing to worry about a symptom may reduce attention to it and hence its perceptual salience (*cf.* Pennebaker, 1982).

Several of the placebo findings reviewed in earlier sections of this chapter are amenable to an anxiety-reduction interpretation. Studies that purport to enhance or reduce placebo effects by manipulating cognitive dissonance (Totman, 1976, 1977; Totman, Reed and Craig, 1977) might equally well be having converse effects on anxiety levels. For example, in the study of post-decisional dissonance (Totman, 1976), the group of insomniacs who received a choice of treatments (and slept longer as a result) might consequently have felt less anxious than the group to whom no choice was offered. In the absence of concomitant measurement of dissonance and anxiety, the validity of these alternative interpretations of the results cannot be differentiated.

Differences in placebo response rates for experimental as opposed to clinical pain have been interpreted by Beecher (1972) as reflecting different levels of anxiety in the two situations; patients in pain, who may also be ill, are more likely to be anxious than healthy experimental volunteers. In the clinical group, therefore, the placebo has more scope to alleviate anxiety and thus reduce pain. Likewise, the accelerated analgesic response to the ingestion of a supposed painkiller may not be an example of a short-latency conditioned response, but simply a result of the relief engendered by the knowledge of having received treatment. It should be noted, however, that conditioning and anxiety reduction interpretations of placebo effects are not mutually exclusive. Anxiety itself may influence the conditioning process (Spence and Taylor, 1951; Wickramasekera, 1985).

Direct evidence of the relevance of anxiety to placebo effects is sparse. For trait anxiety the available evidence is mixed and inconsistent (Evans, 1974a). This is akin to the findings of research on other characteristics of placebo responders (see above). For state anxiety the situation is no clearer. Few studies have taken repeated measures of anxiety over the course of placebo therapy. A notable exception is the

work of Evans and colleagues (McGlashan, Evans and Orme, 1969; Evans, 1977), who took measures of both trait and state anxiety in an experimental study of placebo analgesia. Those patients who experienced anxiety reduction following placebo administration subsequently showed higher pain tolerance levels than the group for whom placebo administration led to increased anxiety. Interestingly, this placebo analgesic effect was significantly more pronounced in subjects with high trait anxiety, suggesting an interaction of trait anxiety and situationally determined responses.

Inconsistent with the above findings, however, are the results of an investigation of the effects of placebo on bronchoconstrictive responses in asthmatics. Butler and Steptoe (1984) obtained positive placebo effects on objective measures of lung function but found no association between these and ratings of tension, state anxiety or trait anxiety.

Psychiatric studies in which measures of psychopathology constitute the main dependent variable leave us in little doubt that placebo therapy can reduce anxiety (Solomon and Hart, 1978; Downing and Rickels, 1983), but the role of anxiety reduction in placebo effects on other response systems awaits further empirical clarification. Although the anxiety reduction hypothesis could, in principle, be applied to many different symptom domains, its most widespread application has been in the field of pain. With this in mind, it is interesting to note that the widely cited association between anxiety and pain is for from unequivocally established (Wardle, 1985). Moreover, Gross and Collins (1981) have pointed out that indices of the two are very often confounded. For example, measures of autonomic arousal which are used as physiological indices of pain are frequently identical with those which are used to monitor anxiety (pulse rate, galvanic skin response etc.). Similar considerations also apply to subjective and behavioural measures. To infer that one state is influencing another, however, we should at least be able to define ways of differentiating the two states.

Conclusions

Positive findings on the psychology of the placebo effect are few and far between. It seems that, through its analogy with physical medicines, the placebo concept is dangerously prone to reification. When a placebo is viewed as a treatment just like any other, then it is natural to ask which characteristics will maximize its therapeutic potential. In the absence of pharmacologically active ingredients to experiment with, this can all too readily lead to the absurdity of considering whether a large purple or brown placebo capsule is 'more effective' than a small green and yellow pill. As stated earlier, however, these qualities could have no therapeutic existence independently of the patient's psychological response to them. In an imaginary society in which all medicines were yellow, then a green placebo pill might be found to have less power than a yellow one; yet we would presumably search for an explanation for this effect, not via a better understanding of yellowness but through an investigation of the patient's perception of treatment in determining their response to it. As the above review indicates, process research of this kind has barely begun in the field of placebo effects.

More fundamentally, one might argue that the use of a single term to describe disparate phenomena is potentially misleading, and creates a spurious impression of homogeneity. In so far as placebos and placebo responses are highly varied and influenced in a variety of ways, then 'placebo' can be regarded as a portmanteau concept having limited explanatory power and serving largely to obfuscate the ways in which different psychological processes can influence different response systems. For example, many psychological processes are thought to influence pain perception (Melzack and Wall, 1982 and de Williams and Erskine,

this volume). Effective placebo analgesia could conceivably be achieved through the manipulation of any of these processes. Thus, one placebo may divert the patient's attention (e.g. placebo transcutaneous nerve stimulation, cf. Langley and Sheppeard, 1987), another may reduce anxiety and reassure the patient (e.g. a traditional placebo pill or injection: Evans, 1974b), and yet another may involve social influence processes (e.g. some form of group pseudotherapy: Craig, 1986). It is not at all clear that grouping these separate phenomena, involving separate processes, under the single term 'placebo', will in any way increase our understanding of their effects.

One reason for grouping phenomena together is to facilitate communication between scientists. Where pharmacologists are concerned, the term 'placebo response' may be a convenient way of describing any patient reaction not directly attributable to the pharmacological action of a drug. This could include numerous psychologically mediated forms of change. To the psychologist seeking to elucidate the psychological mechanisms of change, it is no longer clear that the term confers any particular advantage. Further difficulties of differentiation arise when the term 'placebo' is being used in relation to forms of treatment whose primary mechanisms of change are themselves thought to be psychological. Critelli and Neumann (1984) discuss the different ways in which 'specific' and 'non-specific' factors can be distinguished, and conclude that the only viable use of the term placebo in psychotherapy research is for it to refer to factors common to all therapies.

In view of the above considerations, it is unlikely that a single winner will ever be declared from among the rival theories of placebo action. Each is likely to have some part to play in accounting for changes occurring after placebo administration as a result of incidental features of a non-placebo treatment (Grunbaum, 1981). This is not to say that all theories will prove equally valuable. For example, placebo effects can occur in different response modalities: physiological, subjective (cognitive–affective) and behaviourial. A theory which can account for change in each of these may be more useful than one which is restricted to a particular level of response. Of the theories examined in this chapter, it may transpire that dissonance and classical conditioning accounts of placebo effects will have more limited spheres of applicability (cognitive and physiological, respectively) than those based on anxiety (reduction) for which a multiple-response system has already been postulated (Lang, 1968). On the other hand, the range of physiological responses that can be modified through classical conditioning may be broader than that for which a placebo-induced change in anxiety levels may be effective. Only further empirical research can settle these issues.

References

Annear, W.C. and Vogel-Sprott, M. (1985) Mental rehearsal and classical conditioning contribute to ethanol tolerance in humans. *Psychopharmacology*, 87, 90–3.

Barbour, A. (1991) Research report: intrapersonal communication and the placebo effect. *Journal of Group Psychotherapy, Psychodrama and Sociometry*, 44(1), 44–6.

Beecher, H.K. (1955) The powerful placebo. *Journal of the American Medical Association*, 159, 1602–6.

Beecher, H.K. (1972) The placebo effect as a non-specific force surrounding disease and the treatment of disease, in *Pain: Basic Principles, Pharmacology, Therapy*, (eds R. Janzen, W. Keidel, A. Herz, C. Steichele, J. Payne and R. Burt), Thieme, Stuttgart.

Berg, A.O. (1977) Placebos: a brief review for family physicians. *Journal of Family Practice*, 5, 97–100.

Black, A.A. (1966) Factors predisposing to placebo response in new outpatients with anxiety states. *British Journal of Psychiatry*, 112 (4870), 557–62.

Blackwell, B., Bloomfield, S.S. and Buncher, C.R. (1972) Demonstration to medical students of placebo responses and non-drug factors. *Lancet*, i, 1279–82.

Blaschke, T.F., Nies, A.S. and Mamelok, R.D. (1985) Principles of therapeutics, in *The Pharmacological Basis of Therapeutics*, 7th edn, (eds A. Goodman Gilman, L. S. Goodman, T.W. Rall and F. Murad), Macmillan, New York, pp. 49–65.

Boleloucky, Z. (1971) A contribution to the problems of placebo dependence: case report. *Activitas Nervosa Superior*, 13, 190–1.

Borkovec, T.D. (1985) Placebo: defining the unknown, in *Placebo, Theory, Research, and Mechanisms*, (eds L. White, B. Tursky and G.E. Schwartz), Guilford Press, New York, pp. 59–64.

Borkovec, T.D. and Nau, S.D. (1972) Credibility of analogue therapy rationales. *Journal of Behaviour Therapy and Experimental Psychiatry*, 3, 257–60.

Breuning, S.E., Ferguson, D.G. and Cullari, S. (1980) Analysis of single-double-blind procedures, maintenance of placebo effects, and drug-induced dyskinesia with mentally retarded persons. *Applied Research in Mental Retardation*, 1, 175–92.

Brody, H. (1980) *Placebos and the Philosophy of Medicine*, University of Chicago Press, Chicago.

Brody, H. (1985) Placebo effect: an examination of Grunbaum's definition, in *Placebo, Theory, Research, and Mechanisms*, (eds L. White, B. Tursky and G.E. Schwartz), Guilford Press, New York, pp. 37–58.

Buckalew, L.W. and Ross, S. (1981) Relationship of perceptual characteristics to efficacy of placebos. *Psychological Reports*, 49, 955–61.

Buckalew, L.W., Ross, S. and Starr, B.J. (1981) Nonspecific factors in drug effects: placebo personality. *Psychological Reports*, 48, 3–8.

Butler, C. and Steptoe, A. (1984) Placebo responses: and experimental study of psychophysiological processes in asthmatic volunteers. *British Journal of Clinical Psychology*, 25, 173–83.

Campbell, J. and Rosenbaum, P. (1967) Placebo effect and symptom relief in psychotherapy. *Achives of General Psychiatry*, 16, 364–8.

Carne, S. (1961) The action of chorionic gonadotrophin in the obese. *Lancet*, ii, 1282–4.

Cobb, L.A., Thomas, G.I., Dillard D.H. (1959) An evaluation of internal-mammary-artery ligation by a double blind technique. *New England Journal of Medicine*, 260, 1115–18.

Craig, K.D. (1986) Social modelling influences on pain, in *The Psychology of Pain* 2nd edn (ed R.A. Sternbach), Raven Press, New York, pp. 67–96.

Critelli, J.W. and Neumann, K.F. (1984) The placebo: conceptual analysis of a construct in transition. *American Psychologist*, 39, 32–9.

Dafters, R. and Anderson, G. (1982) Conditional tolerance to the tachycardia effect of ethanol in humans. *Psychopharmacology*, 78, 365–7.

Demarr, E.W. and Pelikan, E.W. (1955) Use of placebos in therapy and in clinical pharmacology. *Modern Hospital*, 84, 108–18.

Dimond, E.G., Kittle, C.F. and Cockett, J.E. (1960) Comparison of internal mammary-artery ligation and sham operation for angina pectoris. *American Journal of Cardiology*, 4, 483–6.

Downing, R.W. and Rickels, K. (1983) Physician prognosis in relationship to drug and placebo response in anxious and depressed psychiatric patients. *Journal of Nervous and Mental Disease*, 171, 182–5.

Evans, F.J. (1974a) The power of the sugar pill. *Psychology Today*, April, 55–9.

Evans, F.J. (1974b) The placebo response in pain reduction. *Advances in Neurology*, 4, 289–96.

Evans, F.J. (1977) The placebo control of pain: a paradigm for investigating non-specific effects in psychotherapy, in *Psychiatry: Areas of Promise and Advancement*, (eds J.P. Brady, J. Mednels, W.R. Reiger and M.T. Orne), Spectrum, New York.

Evans, F.J. (1985) Expectancy, therapeutic instructions and the placebo response, in *Placebo: Theory, Research, and Mechanisms*, (eds L. White, B. Tursky and G.E. Schwartz), Guilford Press, New York, pp. 215–28.

Feldman, P.E. (1956) The personal element in psychiatric research. *American Journal of Psychiatry*, 113, 52–4.

Festinger, L. (1957) *A Theory of Cognitive Dissonance*, Stanford University Press, Stanford, California.

Frank, J.D. (1968) The role of hope in psychotherapy. *International Journal of Psychiatry*, 5, 383–95.

Frank, J.D. (1973) *Persuasion and Healing*, Johns Hopkins University Press, Baltimore.

Garfield, S. and Bergin A.E. (1986) *Handbook of Psychotherapy and Behavior Change*, 3rd edn, John Wiley and Sons, New York.

Gartner, M.A. (1961) Selected personality differences between placebo reactors and non-reactors. *Journal of the American Osteopathic Association*, 60, 377–8.

Gleidman, L.H., Gantt, W.H. and Teitelbaum, H.A. (1957) Some implications of conditional reflex studies for placebo research. *American Journal of Psychiatry*, 113, 1103–7.

Goldberg, R.J., Leigh, H. and Quinlan, D. (1979) The current status of placebo in hospital practice. *General Hospital Psychiatry*, 1, 196–201.

Gomes-Schwartz, B., Hadley, S.E. and Strupp, H.H. (1978) Individual psychotherapy and behavior therapy. *Annual Review of Psychology*, 29, 435–71.

Goodwin, J.S., Goodwin, J.M. and Vogel, J.M. (1979) knowledge and use of placebo by house officers and nurses. *Annals of Internal Medicine*, 91, 106–10.

Gordon, R.M. (1976) Effects of volunteering and responsibility on the perceived value and effectiveness of a clinical treatment. *Journal of Consulting and Clinical Psychology*, 44, 799–801.

Gowdey, C.W. (1983) A guide to the pharmacology of placebos. *Canadian Medical Association Journal*, 128, 921–5.

Gracely, R.H., Dubner, R., Deeter, W.R. and Wolskee, P.J. (1985) Clinical expectations influence placebo analgesia. *Lancet*, i, 43.

Gray, G. and Flynn, P. (1981) A survey of placebo use in general hospital. *General Hospital Psychiatry*, 3, 199–203.

Grenfell, R., Briggs, A.H. and Holland, W.C. (1961) A double-blind study of the treatment of hypertension. *Journal of the American Medical Association*, 176, 124–67.

Grevert, P., Albert, L.H. and Goldstein, A. (1983) Partial antagonism of placebo analgesia by naloxone, *Pain*, 16, 129–43.

Gross, R.T. and Collins, F.L. (1981) On the relationship between anxiety and pain: a methodological confounding. *Clinical Psychology Review*, 1, 375–86.

Grunbaum, A. (1981) The placebo concept. *Behaviour Research and Therapy*, 19, 157–67.

Grunbaum, A. (1985) Explication and implications of the placebo concept, in *Placebo, Theory, Research, and Mechanisms*, (eds L. White, B. Tursky and G.E. Schwartz), Guilford Press, New York, pp. 9–36.

Grunbaum, A. (1986) The placebo concept in medicine and psychiatry. *Psychological Medicine*, 16, 19–38.

Haas, A., Fink, H. and Hartfelder, G. (1959) Das Placeboproblem. *Fortschritte der Arzneimittelforschung*, 1, 279–454.

Haegerstam, G., Huitfeldt, B., Nilsson, B.S. *et al.* (1982) Placebo in clinical drug trials – a multidisciplinary review. *Methods and Findings in Experimental and Clinical Pharmacology*, 4(4), 261–78.

Hashish, I., Feinman, C. and Harvey, W. (1988) Reduction of postoperative pain and swelling by ultrasound: a placebo effect. *Pain*, 83, 303–11.

Herrnstein, R. (1962) Placebo effect in the rat. *Science*, 138, 677–8.

Horningfeld, G. (1964) Nonspecific factors in treatment: Review of placebo reactions and placebo reactors. *Diseases of the Nervous System*, 25, 145–56; 225–39.

Hovland, C.I., Janis, I.L. and Kelley, H.H. (1953) *Communications and Persuasion: Psychological Studies of Opinion Change*, Yale University Press, New Haven, Connecticut.

Jaspers, K. (1965) *The Nature of Psychotherapy*, University of Chicago Press, Chicago, Illinois.

Jospe, M. (1978) *The Placebo Effect in Healing*, Heath, Lexington, Massachusetts.

Kazdin, A.E. and Wilcoxon, L.A. (1976) Systematic desensitization and non-specific treatment effects: a methodological evaluation. *Psychological Bulletin*, 83, 729–58.

Kissel, P. and Barucand, D. (1974) *Placebos et effet – placebo en médicine*, Masson, Paris.

Knowles, J.B. and Lucas, C.J. (1960) Experimental studies of the placebo response. *Journal of Medical Science*, 106, 231–40.

Lang, P. (1968) Fear reduction and fear behavior: problems in treating a construct, in *Research in Psychotherapy*, (ed J. Schlien), American Psychological Association, Washington DC, pp. 90–102.

Langley, G.B. and Sheppeard, H. (1987) Transcutaneous electrical nerve stimulation (TNS) and its relationship to placebo therapy: a review. *New Zealand Medical Journal*, 100, 215–17

Langley, G.B. Sheppeard, H. and Wigley, R.D. (1983) Placebo therapy in rheumatoid arthritis. *Clinical and Experimental Rheumatology*, 1, 17–21.

Langley, G.B., Sheppeard, H., Johnson, M. and Wigley, R.D. (1984) The analgesic effects of transcutaneous electrical nerve stimulation and placebo in chronic pain patients. *Rheumatology International*, 2, 1–5.

Lasagna, L. (1955) The controlled clinical trial: theory and practice. *Journal of Chronic Diseases*, 1, 343–67.

Lasagna, L., Mosteller, F., Von Felsinger, J. and Beecher, H. (1954) A study of the placebo response. *American Journal of Medicine*, 16, 770–9.

Laurence, D.R. and Bennett, P.N. (1980) *Clinical Pharmacology*, 5th edn, Churchill Livingstone, Edinburgh.

Lent, R.W., Crimmings, A.M. and Russell, R.K. (1981) Subconscious reconditioning: evaluation of a placebo strategy for outcome. *Behaviour Research and Therapy*, 12, 138–43.

Lesse, S. (1962) Placebo reactions in psychotherapy. *Diseases of the Nervous System*, 12, 313–19.

Liberman, R. (1961) Analysis of the placebo phenomenon. *Journal of Chronic Diseases*, 15, 761–83.

Liberman, R. (1964) An experimental study of the placebo response under three different situations of pain. *Journal of Psychiatric Research*, 2, 33–46.

Luoto, K. (1964) Personality and placebo effects upon timing behaviour. *Journal of Abnormal and Social Psychology*, 68, 54–61.

Lyerly, S., Ross, S., Krugman, A. and Clyde, D. (1964) Drugs and placebos: the effects of instructions upon performance and mood under amphetamine sulfate and chloral hydrate. *Journal of Abnormal and Social Psychology*, 68, 321–7.

McGlashan, T.H., Evans, F.J. and Orne, M.T. (1969) The nature of hypnotic analgesia and placebo response to experimental pain. *Psychosomatic Medicine*, 31, 227–46.

Melzack, R. and Wall, P. (1982) *The Challenge of Pain*, Penguin, Harmondsworth.

Mischel, W. (1976) *Introduction to Personality*, 2nd edn, Holt, Rinehart and Winston, New York.

Morison, R.A.H., Woodmansey, A, and Young, A.J. (1961) Placebo response in an arthritis trial. *Annals of Rheumatic Diseases*, 20, 179–85.

Park, L.C. and Covi, L. (1965) Nonblind placebo trial. *Achives of General Psychiatry*, 12, 336–45.

Parkhouse, J. (1963) Placebo research, *Nature*, 199, 308–10.

Pearce, S. and Richardson, P.H. (1987) Chronic pain: investigation, in *A Handbook of Clinical Adult Psychology*, (eds S. Lindsey and G. Powell), Gower, Aldershot, pp. 561–77.

Peek, C.J. (1977) A critical look at the theory of the placebo. *Biofeedback and Self-Regulation*, 2, 327–35.

Pendleton, D. and Hasler, J. (eds) (1983) *Doctor–Patient Communication*, Academic Press, London.

Pennebaker, J.W. (1982) *The Psychology of Physical Symptoms*, Springer-Verlag, New York.

Petrie, A. (1960) Some psychological aspects of pain relief and suffering. *Annals of the New York Academy of Science*, 86, 13–27.

Petrie, J. and Hazleman, B. (1985) Credibility of placebo transcutaneous nerve stimulation and acupuncture. *Clinical and Experimental Rheumatology*, 3, 151–3.

Plotkin, W.B. (1985) A psychological approach to placebo: the role of faith in therapy and treatment, in *Placebo: Theory, Research and Mechanisms* (eds L. White, B. Tursky and G.E. Schwartz), Guilford Press, New York, pp. 237–54.

Reed, C.F. and Witt, P.N. (1965) Factors contributing to unexpected reactions to human drug–placebo experiments. *Confina Psychiatrica*, 8, 57–68.

Richardson, P.H. and Vincent, C.A. (1986) Acupuncture for the treatment of pain: a review of evaluative research. *Pain*, 24, 15–40.

Rosenthal, R. (1966) *Experimenter Effects in Behaviourial Research*, Appleton-Century-Crofts, New York.

Ross, M. and Olson, J.M. (1981) An expectancy-attribution model of the effects of placebo. *Psychological Review*, 88, 408–37.

Ross, M. and Olson, J.M. (1982) Placebo effects in medical research and practice, In *Social Psychology and Behaviourial Medicine*, (ed J.R. Eiser), John Wiley and Sons, Chichester, pp. 441–58.

Ross, S. and Buckalew, L.W. (1983) The placebo as an agent in behavioural manipulations: a review of problems, issues, and affected measures. *Clinical Psychology Review*, 3, 457–71.

Ross, S. and Buckalew, L.W. (1985) Placebo agentry: assessment of drug and placebo effects, in *Placebo: Theory, Research and Mechanisms*, (eds L. White, B. Tursky and G.E. Schwartz), Guilford Press, New York, pp. 67–82.

Schwitzgebel, R. and Traugott, M. (1968) Initial note on the placebo effect of machines, *Behavioural Medicine*, 13, 267–73.

Shapira, A.K., McClelland, H.A., Griffiths, N.R. and Newell, D.J. (1970) Study on the effects of tablet colour in the treatment of anxiety states. *British Medical Journal*, 2, 446–9.

Shapiro, A.K. (1960) A contribution to a history of the placebo effect. *Behavioral Science*, 5, 398–430.

Shapiro, A.K. (1964) Etiological factors in placebo effect. *Journal of the American Medical Association*, 187, 712–14.

Shapiro, A.K. and Morris, L.A. (1978) The placebo effect in medical and psychological therapies, in *Handbook of Psychotherapy and Behavioral Change*, 2nd edn, (eds A.E. Bergin and S. Garfield), John Wiley and Sons, New York, pp. 369–410.

Shapiro, A.K., Wilensky, H. and Struening, E.L. (1968) Study of the placebo effect with placebo test. *Comprehensive Psychiatry*, 9, 118–37.

Shapiro, A.P. and Nathan P.E. (1986) Human tolerance to alcohol: the role of Pavlovian conditioning processes. *Psychopharmacology*, 88, 90–5.

Siegel, S. (1985) Drug-anticipatory responses in animals, in *Placebo: Theory, Research and Mechanisms*, (eds L. White, B. Tursky and G.E. Schwartz), Guilford Press, New York, pp. 288–305.

Solomon, K. and Hart, R. (1978) Pitfalls and prospects in clinical research on antianxiety drugs: benzodiazepines and placebo – a research review. *Journal of Clinical Psychiatry*, 39, 823–31.

Sotsky, S.M., Glass, D.R., Shea, M.T. *et al.* (1991) Patient predictors of response to psychotherapy and pharmacotherapy: findings in the NIMH Treatment of Depression Collaborative Research Program. *American Journal of Psychiatry*, 148(8), 997–1008.

Souza, F.G. and Goodwin, G.M. (1991) Lithium treatment and prophylaxis in unipolar depression: a meta-analysis. *British Journal of Psychiatry*, 158, 666–75.

Spence, K. and Taylor, J.A. (1951) Anxiety and the strength of the UCS as determiners of the amount of eyelid conditioning. *Journal of Experimental Psychology*, 42, 183–8.

Sternbach, R. (1968) *Pain: A Psychophysiological Analysis*, Academic Press, New York.

Tedeschi, J.T., Schlenker, B.R. and Bonoma, T.V. (1971) Cognitive dissonance: private ratiocination or public spectacle. *American Psychologist*, 26, 685–95.

Thorn, W.A. (1962) The placebo reactor. *Australian Journal of Pharmacy*, 43, 1035–7.

Thorsteinsson, G., Stonnington, H.H., Stillwell, G.K. and Elveback, L.R. (1978) The placebo effect in transcutaneous electrical stimulation. *Pain*, 5, 31–41.

Timmons, B.H. (in press) Breathing-related issues in therapy, in *Behavioural and Psychological Approaches to Breathing Disorders*, (eds B.H. Timmons and L. Ronald), Plenum Press, New York.

Tori, C. and Worrell, L. (1983) Reduction of human avoidant behaviour: a comparison of counter conditioning, expectancy and cognitive information approaches. *Journal of Consulting and Clinical Psychology*, 40, 69–77.

Totman, R. (1976) Cognitive dissonance in the placebo treatment of insomnia – a pilot experiment. *British Journal of Medical Psychology*, 49, 393–400.

Totman, R. (1977) Cognitive dissonance and the placebo response: the effect of differential justification for undergoing dummy injections. *European Journal of Social Psychology*, 5(4), 441–56.

Totman, R. (1979) *The Social Causes of Illness*, Souvenir Press, London.

Totman, R. (1987) *The Social Causes of Illness*, 2nd edn, Souvenir Press, London.

Totman, R., Reed, S.E. and Craig, J.W. (2977) Cognitive dissonance, stress and virus-induced common colds. *Journal of Psychosomatic Research*, 21, 55–63.

Uhlenhuth, E.H. Canter, A., Neustadt, J.O. and Payson, H.E. (1959) The symptomatic relief of anxiety with meprobamate, phenobarbital and placebo. *American Journal of Psychiatry*, 115, 905–10.

Vinar, O. (1969) Dependence on a placebo: a case report. *British Journal of Psychiatry*, 115, 1189–90.

Vogel, A.V., Goodwin, J.S. and Goodwin, J.M. (1980) The therapeutics of placebo. *American Family Physician*, 22, 106–9.

Voudouris, N.J., Peck, C. and Coleman, G. (1985) Conditioned placebo responses. *Journal of Personality and Social Psychology*, 48(1), 47–53.

Voudouris, N.J., Peck, C.L. and Coleman, G. (1989) Conditioned response of the placebo phenomenon: further support. *Pain*, 38, 109–16.

Voudouris, N.J., Peck, C.L. and Coleman, G. (1990) The role of conditioning and verbal expectancy in the placebo response. *Pain*, 43, 121–8.

Wall, P.D. (1992) The placebo effect: an unpopular topic. *Pain*, 51, 1–3.

Wardle, L. (1985) Pain, in *New Developments in Clinical Psychology*, (ed F.N. Watts), John Wiley and Sons, Chichester, pp. 16–32.

White, L., Tursky, B. and Schwartz, G.E. (1985) placebos in perspective, in *Placebo: Theory, Research, and Mechanisms*, (eds L. White, B. Tursky and G.E. Schwartz), Guildford Press, New York, pp. 3–8.

Wickramasekera, I. (1977) The placebo effect and medical instruments and biofeedback *Journal of Clinical Engineering*, 2, 227–30.

Wickramasekera, I. (1980) A conditioned response model of the placebo effect: predictions. *Biofeedback and Self-regulation*, 5, 5–18.

Wickramasekera, I. (1985) A conditioned response model of the placebo effect: predictions from the model, in *Placebo: Theory, Research and Mechanisms*, (eds L. White, B. Tursky and G.E. Schwartz), Guilford Press, new York, pp. 255–87.

Wilkins, W. (1973) Expectancy of therapeutic gain: an empirical and conceptual critique. *Journal of Consulting and Clinical Psychology*, 40, 69–77.

Wilkins, W. (1979) Getting specific about nonspecific. *Cognitive Therapy and Research*, 3, 319–29.

Wilkins, W. (1985) Placebo controls and concepts in chemotherapy and psychotherapy research, in *Placebo: Theory, Research, and Mechanisms*, (eds L. White, B. Tursky and G.E. Schwartz), Guilford Press, New York, pp. 83–109.

Zimbardo, P.G. (1969) *The Cognitive Control of Motivation*, Scott, Foresman, Illinois.

Chapter four

Psychology in health and social care settings: the new opportunities

Bernard J.B. Kat

Introduction

The first edition of this book was published in 1989. Since then there have been profound and far-reaching changes in the organization and management of health and social care in Great Britain. The government intends that as a result of these changes there will be specific, measurable improvements in the health and wellbeing of the population and a greater emphasis on the outcomes of health and social care than on the means of producing them. In order to achieve these policy objectives, the government and its agencies (including the National Health Service) are building on a broader conception of health and its determinants than hitherto. Among the origins of this broader understanding has been the application of social and behavioural sciences to health and social care. Psychologists now have many new and challenging opportunities to contribute to the improvement of public and individual health.

This chapter discusses the agencies now responsible for health and social care and the further changes in which they may be involved; next, one of their main responsibilities, the improvement of the health of the population, is discussed in the context of a three-dimensional model of health outcomes, or 'health gains'. The third section identifies a range of issues of interest to psychologists, and finally there is a very brief discussion of the next steps for psychology as a profession in the UK in relation to the new systems.

Organization of health and social care

In a chapter such as this it is possible to provide only a very brief overview. The reader who requires a more thorough account is advised to consult appropriate texts, such as those by Ham (1991) or Levitt and Wall (1991). The following account applies to

England and Wales; there are different arrangements in Scotland and Northern Ireland.

The Audit Commission, in a report which provides a very useful summary of community care policy and the problems of implementation, recently expressed the view that 'the organisational framework [for community care] inherited from the past has not kept pace with recent developments.... It evolved to provide a particular style of care that does not easily fit with current thinking. Many of the problems of community care can be attributed to trying to manage the new way of working within the old organisational framework.' (Audit Commission, 1992).

Some of the problems arise from the way in which money raised by central government through taxation and allocated to health and social care flows to other agencies. However, the existing organization of health and social care also incorporates certain distinctions which, if current reforms achieve their objectives, may soon be redefined or disappear altogether.

Distinctions 1: social care, health care, community care

Social care has deep roots in history. Local authorities with responsibility for the welfare of their populations can be traced back to the times of the first Queen Elizabeth and through the Poor Laws of the 19th century (Watkin, 1975). However, Departments of Social Services as we now understand them go back no further than the Seebohm Report (DHSS, 1968) and subsequent legislation. Local government is provided through authorities run by councillors who are elected by the population they serve. They have the power to raise revenue through local taxation, although a substantial proportion of the income to local authorities comes in the form of a support grant from central government. None the less, spending on 'social care' still has some ele-

ments of local decision-making. At the time of writing, outside the larger cities there are two quite separate and independent levels of local government. Some elements contributing to social care, particularly social services, are the responsibility of County Councils. Others, such as housing and environmental health, are the responsibility of District Councils. The local government scene is, of course, changing rapidly.

The history of health care is just as complex. The National Health Service Act 1946 brought the NHS into operation in 1948, following the recommendations of the Beveridge Report (1942). Unlike with social care, there is very little local control of health care. The management boards of Regional and District Health Authorities and NHS Trusts include a small number of non-executive members who are appointed, not elected. Spending on health care is determined directly by Parliament and the NHS is largely controlled from the centre by the Secretary of State for Health and a number of junior ministers. Current government policy on health care is outlined in a remarkable sequence of White Papers, the publication of which spanned three Parliaments and five Secretaries of State: *Promoting Better Health* (Department of Health, 1987); *Working for Patients* (Department of Health, 1989a); and *The Health of the Nation* (Department of Health, 1992a).

The concept of community care blurs the distinction between health care and social care. The aim of providing as much care as possible in the community for people who would otherwise have needed long-stay hospital care (the elderly, people with long-term mental health problems or severely disabled in some way) can be traced back to the Macmillan Report in 1926 (Watkin, 1975). Current policies on community care have been worked out in a sequence of government and other reports during the 1980s (DHSS, 1981; Social Services Committee, 1985; Audit Commission, 1986;

Griffiths, 1988). The White Paper *Caring for People* (Department of Health, 1989b) was a landmark; the principles are enacted in the National Health Service and Community Care Act 1990.

Community care has become the focus and vehicle of a new approach to public services. Valuing each person as an individual and aiming to promote as full and as socially normal a lifestyle as possible, implies services tailored to that person's needs. This reverses the previous emphasis on assessing people to see if they fitted criteria for service provision. A catchphrase of the new approach is 'seamless care': in other words, care that is so well coordinated and integrated that the recipient is unaware that it is being provided by several different agencies.

The new arrangements for community care have meant changes in the role of social services departments. They now have specific responsibilities for the assessment of individuals' needs for care and for enabling the required care to be provided by a range of agencies, including those in the private and voluntary sectors, as well as the NHS and their own organization. The implementation of community care policies in the future will undoubtedly lead to further governmental review of the organizational arrangements for health, social and community care.

Distinctions 2: primary, secondary and tertiary health care

Four levels can be recognized in all health care systems. They are characterized by the size of the population and the nature of the diseases and disorders with which each level is concerned:

> The first level of care is *self-care within a family*, of say 1–10 persons. The majority of symptomatic minor and chronic disorders are self cared for at this level. It is like-

ly that less than 1 in 4 of all symptoms is taken by the public to a professional medical worker.... *Primary medical care* provides the first level of professional care within a locality or neighbourhood. The first contact need not necessarily be with a physician; other trained paramedical workers can provide such care. The population cared for is around 2 500 per physician in developed countries, but is very much greater in an underdoctored developing country.... Primary care in a neighbourhood will deal with minor, major and chronic disorders.... When more specialised care is necessary, it is to the *general specialists working in a district* that may have 50 000 to 500 000 people that referral is made.... These will work from the base of a district hospital.... The base for *subspecialty units is the Region*. The modern subspecialties need a population base of 0.5 to 5 million to warrant the expensive facilities that are now necessary. The special clinical problems referred to these units will be the very rare conditions that may occur less than once a year in primary care, but will become everyday problems in a subspeciality unit (Fry, 1980)

During its first 25 years, the National Health Service was primarily concerned with making hospital services available to the population. The hospital and community health services were integrated into one organization through the 1974 reorganization of the NHS. That major change was intended, in part, to rectify the lack of development of domiciliary and community health services and to increase the emphasis on prevention through early detection and treatment.

The distinction between primary and secondary health care incorporates the distinction in medicine between general practitioners and hospital specialists. The latter evolved in the second half of the 19th century (Loudon,

1977), and was not based on specialization, as it is now. The hallmark of the consultant was that he or she depended for his or her living on being 'called in' and consulted by other medical practitioners. Pure consultants were rare. Their income came primarily from the rich people to whom they were general practitioners; their consultant functions arose from honorary appointments to provide hospital outpatient services. The hospital outpatient departments became serious competitors to urban general practitioners, who therefore insisted that no-one should be seen as an outpatient unless they had been referred with a letter of introduction – the principle of 'referral'.

The pattern of acute hospital services has been changing. By reducing lengths of stay and increasing day cases, acute hospitals are treating more people and discharging them more quickly. Some hospital consultants now undertake outpatient clinics at general practitioners' premises, and the effect of giving some GPs their own budgets (GP fundholders) has been to prompt some of those GPs to experiment with local substitutes for hospital referrals. Primary health care has become central to the policies of the government (Department of Health, 1987) and the World Health Organization (WHO, 1978) because of its importance in the promotion of health and the prevention of ill-health. More integration of primary and secondary health care has become a specific policy objective (Department of Health NHSME, 1991). Meanwhile, tertiary health care (consultant-to-consultant referrals, reflecting the high-tech nature of medicine) has come under the explicit financial control of Health Authorities.

The longer-term effects of these changes, and others which cannot be described within the space available, is expected to be a transfer of some areas of work from hospitals and secondary care to GPs and associated primary care staff, organized as 'primary care teams'.

Distinctions 3: primary, secondary and tertiary prevention

Intervening before ill-health has developed in order to prevent it has many attractions. Preventive interventions can be undertaken at a number of stages. The usual categorization comes from Caplan (1964):

> ... programs for reducing (1) the incidence of mental disorders of all types in a community (primary prevention) (2) the duration of a significant number of those disorders which do occur (secondary prevention) (3) the impairment which may result from disorders (tertiary prevention).

Successive governments have placed ever-greater emphasis on prevention. The programme initiated by the document *Prevention and Health: everybody's business* (DHSS, 1976) was a major initiative in the 1970s. *The Health of the Nation* (Department of Health, 1992a) is strongly influenced by the World Health Organization's programme 'Health for All by the Year 2000' (WHO, 1981). Although GPs are now paid to provide structured health promotion programmes on their practice premises, recent initiatives tend to reflect the insights of McKeown (1979), whose review concluded that the main influence on health – nutrition, environment and behaviour – lie outside the medical care system. The ultimate aim of the current reforms of health care is improvements in 'health':

> The Government's overall goal is to secure continuing improvement in the general health of the population of England by:
>
> *adding years to life*: an increase in life expectancy and reduction in premature death; and
>
> *adding life to years*: increasing years lived free from ill-health, reducing or minimising the adverse effects of illness and disability,

promoting healthy lifestyles, physical and social environments and, overall, improving quality of life. (Department of Health, 1992a)

Health is no longer seen as the business of the Health Service alone:

Success will come through, for example:

public policies: by policy-makers at all levels, not only across Government but also in other public bodies and industry, considering the health dimension when developing policies;

healthy surroundings: by the active promotion of physical environments conducive to health – in the home, in schools, at work, on the roads, at leisure, in public places;

healthy lifestyles: by increasing knowledge and understanding about how the way people live affects their health, and enabling families and individuals to act on this;

high quality health services: by identifying and meeting the health needs of local populations and securing the most appropriate balance between health promotion, disease prevention, treatment, care and rehabilitation. (Department of Health, 1992a)

The government acknowledged its debt to the World Health Organization in *The Health of the Nation*. In 1977 the 30th World Health Assembly passed a resolution that: the main social target of governments and the World Health Organization in the coming decades should be the attainment by all the citizens of the world by the year 2000 of a level of health (WHO, 1978). Note that the WHO suggests that a socially and economically productive life is the ultimate goal, rather than health as an end in itself. So, the prevention of ill health, by whatever means, is subsidiary to superordinate goals concerned with quality of life.

The range of purchasers of health and social care

Under the National Health Service and Community Care Act 1990, certain organizations have the responsibility to assess needs for services, specify what services are required and commission an appropriate organization to provide them. The collective noun for these organizations is 'purchasers'. In the field of health care this means Health Authorities (District HAs and Special HAs); Family Health Services Authorities (FHSAs); Joint Commissioning Consortia (several HAs formed into a single organization); and GP fundholders (GPFHs). In the field of social care this means social services care managers. Although there are important differences between purchasing health care and social care, and between different types of health care, the major components of the purchasing function are the same: definition and measurement of outcomes, needs assessment, service specification, monitoring of the impact of services, and rationing and prioritization.

There are two systems of purchasing in health care, Health Authorities and GP fundholders. District Health Authorities are allocated budgets by Regional Health Authorities to purchase services for their resident population, excluding certain services for people who are registered with a fundholding practice. Family Health Services Authorities (FHSAs) are responsible for purchasing and managing the services provided by GPs, general dental practitioners and retail pharmacists. These providers are 'independent contractors'; in other words, they are not employees of the NHS but self-employed individuals or independent companies and partnerships who contract with the NHS via FHSAs.

One of the most important functions of FHSAs is to work with Regional Health Authorities on the introduction of GP fundholding. The general practice funding scheme enables GPs in the scheme to choose the hospital to which they send their patients and pay those hospitals directly, thereby having a direct and personal influence on the way that hospital services are delivered.

The purchasing role of Health Authorities can be seen as a practical application of utilitarianism. They are concerned not with the needs of individuals but with the needs of their resident population; they have to achieve the greatest health for the greatest number with the money they have available to them. However, like social services care managers, GP fundholders are primarily concerned with the needs of individuals. So is the government's Patient's Charter (Department of Health, 1991b), which is intended to give entitlements to the citizens of the country through the creation of mandatory standards for public services.

'Healthy alliances' (Powell, 1993) are partnerships between all the organizations in an area which can bring about improvements in the health of the population – the health authorities, primary care teams, local authorities, voluntary bodies, businesses and the media, and the local community. They are being promoted by the NHS Management Executive as a mechanism for developing a shared agenda for promoting positive health within communities. Another development, 'locality purchasing' by 'joint consortia' formed by Health Authorities and FHSAs, is encouraging the formation of healthy alliances.

A report from the University of Manchester (1993) envisages the processes of joint commissioning and locality purchasing taken to their logical conclusion, and calls for a 'fundamental rethink' of purchasing arrangements to avoid major problems in implementing the community care reforms. Joint arrangements between health and local authorities are too fragmented, lack clear accountability and fail to use resources effectively. Changes would ensure that services are more responsive to patients' needs and uphold equal access, now

threatened by 'large authorities wielding substantial purchasing power'. The report suggests single agencies which would commission all services that have an impact on health outcomes. Called Social, Health and Welfare Commissioning Agencies (SHWCAs), they would each cater for a population of 250 000. The agencies would consist of executive officers and locally elected members, and could raise revenue by setting a rate. Services would be based in 'social, health and welfare centres' serving 10–20 000 people.

In Northern Ireland the same agency has been responsible for both social and health care for many years. In England, non-statutory coordinated purchasing of health, social and community care may prove to be a step towards statutory agencies which abolishes the distinctions between different types of care for good.

Providers: the blurring of boundaries between sectors

'Providers' is a convenient collective noun for individuals and organizations that provide services under contract to purchasers. In principle, purchasers can commission services from whomsoever and whichever organization they wish, whether the provider is based in the public, the voluntary or the private sector. NHS Trusts, quasi-autonomous providers of hospital and community health services, have attracted a great deal of public comment because they are public-sector organizations that are being encouraged by the government to behave like commercial businesses. Conversely, many voluntary organizations that enter into contracts to provide services find that they are now expected to accept procedures for accountability which used to be characteristic of the public sector. One effect of these changes is that 'working for the NHS' is no longer synonymous with employment in the NHS. In future, many self-employed people and people employed by private-sector agencies will be 'working for the NHS' through contracts to provide particular services.

Health outcomes and 'health gain'

A large body of literature has grown up around the question 'what is health?' Seedhouse (1986) believes that in modern western society many theories of health, with many purposes, are in use:

- The theory that health is an ideal state:
  - a 'Socratic' goal of perfect wellbeing in every respect;
  - an end in itself;
  - to count as health, disease, illness, handicap and social problems must be absent.
- The theory that health is the physical and mental fitness to do socialized daily tasks (i.e. to function normally in the person's own society):
  - a means towards the end of social functioning;
  - to count as health, all disabling disease, illness and handicap must be absent.
- The theory that health is a commodity which can be brought or given:
  - the rationale which lies behind medical theory and practice;
  - usually an end for the provider and a means for the receiver;
  - health is lost in the presence of disease, illness, pain, malady. It might be restored piecemeal.
- A group of theories which hold that health is a personal strength or ability, either physical, metaphysical or intellectual:
  - These strengths and abilities are not commodities which can be given or purchased. Nor are they ideal states. They are developed as personal tasks. They can be lost. They can be encouraged.

Seedhouse argues that these theories constitute clusters of ideas, but individuals have complex

and changing ideas about health and draw on different elements of the different theories at different times. Out of his review of theories of health and approaches to increasing health, he draws a number of conclusions:

1. Health is not a word that has a single uncontroversial meaning. This is demonstrated by the fact that the different theories of health are all legitimate and plausible but regard health in different and conflicting ways.
2. Health can be seen as a means or as an end: it depends on the point of view of the person giving the description. It can also be important to point out to a person that what they see as an end (perhaps their own physical wellbeing) is also a means by which they can grow and develop in their lives.
3. People cannot be fully understood in isolation from what they do in their lives. Also, people cannot be fully understood in purely biological terms (i.e. they must also be understood in relation to the social groups of which they are a member).
4. Although there are some conflicts between the various theories and approaches, there is a significant common factor: all theories of health and all theories designed to increase health are intended to advise against, to prevent the creation of, or to remove, obstacles to the achievement of human potential. These obstacles may be biological, environmental, societal, familial or personal. A person's health can be considered to be equivalent to the state of the set of conditions that fulfil or enable a person to work to fulfil his or her realistic chosen and biological potentials.

This is an analysis of personal health and clearly comes to a different focus from the World Health Organization resolution quoted earlier (i.e. 'which will permit them to lead a socially and economically productive life'). The phenomen with which Health Authorities and other purchasers are concerned is one which relates to populations and can be improved by intervention. For example, 'DHAs are charged with securing measurable improvements in the health of their resident population' (Department of Health, 1991a).

Working for Patients highlighted the importance of assessing outcomes, often referred to as 'health gains', since the term was introduced by the consultative document on targets for health (Department of Health, 1991a). The definitions currently under development by the Depart-

ment of Health for use in outcome evaluation are as follows:

Outcome – an end result which is attributable to intervention, or lack of intervention. The end result may manifest itself as a change in status, which may be absolute, or relative to expectation, e.g. deterioration in health when the expectation is no change.

Health outcome – an end result expressed in terms of health which is attributable to *any* intervention, i.e. not only a health services intervention. Health includes broader

---

Coronary heart disease (CHD) and stroke

To reduce death rates for both CHD and stroke in people under 65 by at least 40% by the year 2000 (Baseline 1990)

To reduce the death rate for CHD in people aged 65–74 by at least 30% by the year 2000 (Baseline 1990)

To reduce the death rate for stroke in people aged 65–74 by at least 40% by the year 2000 (Baseline 1990)

Cancers

To reduce the death rate for breast cancer in the population invited for screening by at least 25% by the year 2000 (Baseline 1990)

To reduce the incidence of invasive cervical cancer by at least 20% by the year 2000 (Baseline 1986)

To reduce the death rate for lung cancer under the age of 75 by at least 30% in men and by at least 15% in women by 2010 (Baseline 1990)

To halt the year-on-year increase in the incidence of skin cancer by 2005

Mental illness

To improve significantly the health and social functioning of mentally ill people

To reduce the overall suicide rate by at least 15% by the year 2000 (Baseline 1990)

To reduce the suicide rate of severely mentally ill people by at least 33% by the year 2000 (Baseline 1990)

HIV/AIDS and sexual health

To reduce the incidence of gonorrhoea by at least 20% by 1995 (Baseline 1990), as an indicator of HIV/AIDS trends

To reduce by at least 50% the rate of conception amongst the under 16s by the year 2000 (Baseline 1989)

Accidents

To reduce the death rate for accidents among children aged under 15 by at least 33% by 2005 (Baseline 1990)

To reduce the death rate for accidents among young people aged 15–24 by at least 25% by 2005 (Baseline 1990)

To reduce the death rate for accidents among people aged 65 and over by at least 33% by 2005 (Baseline 1990)

Note: The 1990 baseline for all mortality targets represents an average of the three years centred around 1990.

FIGURE 4.1 Health of the Nation targets for health gain (Department of Health, 1992).

aspects such as function, social handicap, well being and health-related quality of life, and relates to patients', public and professional values and expectations.

Outcome of health services – any end result (health or otherwise) which is attributable to a health services intervention.

The main development issue is how each of these can be measured. (Department of Health, 1992b)

The selection of outcome targets is a matter of policy, often political policy; *how* those targets are to be achieved is left to a much greater extent to providers, those given the responsibility of achieving them. This is true of the *Health of the Nation* initiative. Targets in key areas were selected by the government, using three criteria: the area must be a major cause of premature death or avoidable ill-health; there must be interventions which are known to be effective in reaching the target; and it must be possible to set and monitor targets and monitor progress towards them (Fig. 4.1).

The measurement of health

Needs assessment and the setting of measurable targets implies the existence of a technology of measurement. Indeed, when 'health gain' is defined in terms of target outcomes, measuring need and measuring outcomes become two sides of the same coin: the same measures can be used for both purposes. It is not the content of the measures but the use to which they are put which defines the difference between needs assessment and outcome measurement. There has been a flood of books listing and evaluating measures of health (for example, McDowell and Newell, 1987; Streiner and Norman, 1989; Fallowfield, 1990; Bowling, 1991; Larson, 1991; Wilkin, Hallam and Doggett, 1992). The Department of Health has also established a UK Clearing House on Outcomes based at the University of Leeds to collect, critically

appraise, collate and disseminate developments. Outcome research is a major focus in the NHS programme of research and development (Peckham, 1991), and the indicators by means of which progress towards *Health of the Nation* targets will be monitored have been published (Department of Health, 1992c). In the USA, action by federal agencies has led to the creation of PORTS – Patient Outcome Research Teams (Lancet, 1992).

Reviews of measures of health status can seem confusing; there are so many measures addressing so many different issues, categorized in apparently arbitrary ways. For example, Bowling (1991) categorizes the measures under five headings: the measurement of functional ability; broader measures of health status; measures of psychological wellbeing; measuring social networks and social support; measures of life satisfaction and morale. Wilkin, Hallam and Doggett (1992) use similar but not identical categories. Fallowfield (1990) adopts a different approach and focuses on quality of life in particular kinds of ill-health.

The three dimensions of 'health gain' (outcomes)

The three dimensions of the model used in this section derive from the WHO definitions, the Department of Health definition quoted above, and distinctions that we make in our everyday language. For the purposes of discussions it is helpful to visualize the dimensions as orthogonal, even though they coexist and interact in complex ways (Fig. 4.2). The basis of the model is the distinction between observable, experiential and social phenomena and the idea that a full description of outcomes needs to take account of all three dimensions. The next section shall turn to the processes that create outcomes, and note the ways in which events in one dimension have an impact on health outcome in another.

The three dimensions are explicit in the technical language of health care. Doctors have traditionally made a distinction between 'signs' – observable changes in bodily structure or function indicative of disease – and 'symptoms' – changes in the patient's experience of themselves or their world which are also indicative of disease. Susser (1990) provides a valuable personal account of the definitions of other key words used to talk about negative states of health: 'disease', 'illness', 'sickness', 'impairment', 'disability', 'handicap':

> 'Disease' is the word used to refer to objective physiological or mental disorder at the organic level and confined to the individual organism.

> 'Illness' is reserved for a subjective state, a psychological awareness of dysfunction at the personal level also confined to the individual.

> The word 'sickness' derives its technical meaning from Parson's concept of the 'sick role' and is used to refer to a state of social dysfunction, a social role assumed by the individual that is variously specified according to the expectations of a given society, and thereby extends beyond the individual to include relations with others. (Susser, 1990)

The definitions of impairment, disability and handicap adopted by the World Health Organization in the International Classification of Impairments, Disabilities and Handicaps (ICIDH) (WHO, 1980) were based on definitions developed by Susser and colleagues which were intended to parallel those of disease, illness and handicap:

> 'Impairment', analogous to disease, refers to a stable and persisting defect in the individual at the organic level which stems from known or unknown molecular, cellular, physiological or structural disorder.

> 'Disability', analogous with illness, refers to a stable and persisting physical or psychological dysfunction at the personal level, by necessity again confined to the individual; this dysfunction stems from the limitations imposed by the impairment and by the individual's psychological reaction to it.

> Like sickness, 'handicap' refers to persisting social dysfunction, a social role assumed by the impaired or disabled individual that is assigned by the expectations of society. Handicap stems not from the individual but from social expectations; it follows from the manner and degree in which expectations alter the performance of social roles by impaired or disabled persons. (Note: This definition was modified when adopted by the World Health Organization) (Susser, 1990).

Psychological and social problems lead to a significant proportion of primary health care contacts. The World Health Organization is therefore sponsoring research on a triaxial classification (physical, psychological, social) of health problems (Clare, Gulbinat and Sartorius, 1992) to complement traditional medical diagnoses.

What about positive states of health? In the English-speaking world we use a set of words – health, heal, hale, whole – all of which derive from the Germanic vocabulary of the Anglo-Saxons. Perhaps the demands of farming and warfare in the world of the Anglo-Saxons meant that health was synonymous with soundness and wholeness of the body. This meaning of health – the absence of disease and bodily damage is at the heart of what many authors call 'the medical model of health' (Larson, 1991).

Modern English also has a word for excellent physical health – 'fitness' – which carries some connotations of subjectivity but is measurable in terms of cardiovascular function, weight for height etc. Indeed, it could be said that one current preoccupation of many 'healthy' members of the UK population is to move along the dimension of physical health from absence of disease, but below optimum functioning, to a state of excellent health. However, our concept of health has evolved and broadened from that of the Anglo-Saxons. The World Health Organization's definition, used in its constitution in 1947, is well known: 'a state of complete physical, mental and social well-being'. This is a 'holistic' definition, that is, it refers to the health of a whole, socially active person.

Wellness or wellbeing are the words usually used to denote an excellent state of subjective health, the opposite of which is, by reference to the definitions quoted above, 'illness'. In clinical practice, psychologists tend to differentiate two aspects of sickness and handicap, the words used for the social-role dimension of ill-health. People may be either socially incompetent or socially unacceptable or both, as a result of behavioural deficits or excesses, problems of appearance, self-image and so on. However, these are usually judgements made by people about others; that is, they are socially determined judgements. There appear to be no conventional words for excellent health in terms of social competence and social acceptability, but the notion of a person who fulfils their roles to the full or who is a role model for others perhaps captures what is involved.

Kaplan (1990) asserts that it is behaviour that is the central outcome of health care: that biological, environmental and psychological outcomes are simply predictors or mediators of behavioural outcomes. Sullivan (1966) (quoted by Kaplan) had argued that behavioural indicators such as absenteeism, bed-disability days and institutional confinement are the most important consequences of disease and disability; death is also a behavioural outcome in the sense that it is the point at which there is no observable behaviour.

There are only two health outcomes that are of importance. First, there is life expectancy. Second, there is function or quality of life during the years that people are alive. Biological and physical events are mediators of these behavioural outcomes. Individuals are concerned about cancer, high blood pressure, high cholesterol, or other problems because they may shorten the life expectancy or make life less desirable prior to death. (Kaplan, 1990)

Emphasis on observable biological and behavioural outcomes is widespread: we shall find it again when we consider the definition of 'need' in the next section. But it results in insufficient attention being given to important experiential outcomes, such as pain, suffering and acceptance of current health status, and important social outcomes such as changes in carers' judgements of a person. It also leads to underestimates of the importance of experiential and social factors in the processes that produce the outcomes.

'Need', 'demand', 'dependence' and 'deviance'

Efforts to distinguish 'need' from 'demand' for health care are well known; the topic has become important in the context of debates about the legitimacy of service provision and has been given particular attention by health economists. 'Need' is a word with a long history in psychology (Brewin, 1992). Discussions about 'need' and 'demand' and the use of health services imply theories about why people behave in the way that they do, or become attempts to generate such a theory. Both words carry a lot of excess meaning. There is an unexplored psycholinguistic dimension in our everyday usage: I experience my need (a subjective state) but I observe your demand (a piece of behaviour). But the use of the two words in health care is almost exactly the reverse of everyday usage.

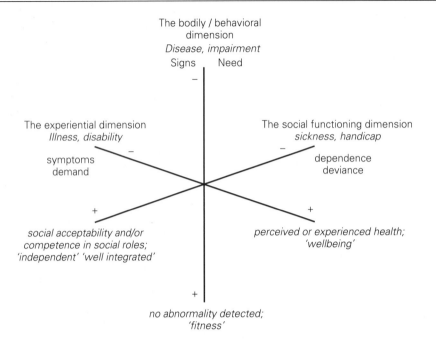

The bodily / behavioral
dimension
Disease, impairment
Signs   Need

−

The experiential dimension   The social functioning dimension
Illness, disability   *sickness, handicap*

−   −

symptoms   dependence
demand   deviance

+   +

social acceptability and/or   perceived or experienced health;
competence in social roles;   'wellbeing'
'independent' 'well integrated'

+

no abnormality detected;
'fitness'

FIGURE 4.2 Three dimensions of health gain (outcomes).

For example, Culyer (1976) took the view that: need for health care is defined by reference to some third party's view as to what a particular individual or class of individuals ought to receive. The demand for health care, however, is indicated by the individuals themselves in making claims upon health care resources'.

The ways in which 'need' and 'demand' are used in health care may reflect the different attitudes to medical care as a national welfare service (which offers free choice of a doctor and free access to consult him or her at will) which were identified by Wadsworth, Butterfield and Blaney (1971).

The first of these two attitudes includes a fear that free choice and free access will result in overwhelming demand from people with trivial complaints, and the second focuses on the benefits of early diagnosis and treatment in reducing need and improving health.

McKillip (1987) observed that: '... need involves the recognition of a problem by observers. A need has a more dispassionate quality than a demand and, because of this, is more popular with planners and academic researchers than with politicians. 'Objective' or rational indicators of need are frequently cited as alternatives to political assessments. However, the person that another person believes to be in need may neither recognise a problem nor use its solution. Many of the more familiar techniques of need identification share this drawback: they are aimed at helping observers identify problems that a target population has.'

'Need' is thought to imply more objectivity than 'demand', but someone still has to make a judgement about whether a need exists. 'Need' has not proved satisfactory because it is not a unitary concept: many different kinds of 'need' have been identified:

Normative need is that which the expert or professional, administrator or social scientist defines as need in any given situation. A 'desirable' standard is laid down.... [Felt need] is equated with want. When assessing the need for a service, the population is asked whether they feel they need it.... Expressed need or demand is felt need turned into action.... Comparative need is obtained by studying the characteristics of the population in receipt of a service. If there are people with similar characteristics not in receipt of a service, then they are in need. (Bradshaw, 1972)

When the Department of Health established a Needs Assessment project, the first problem facing the project team was terminology. The team chose to be definitive about the meaning of needs for the purposes of the role of a District Health Authority as a purchaser of health care and differentiated between need for care and neediness: '... there is only a need where there is a potential benefit, i.e. where the intervention and/or care setting is effective' (DHSS, 1991b).

In the three-dimensional model, 'demand' is identified with experiential outcomes on the illness/disability–wellbeing dimension. 'Need' is identified with outcomes on the disease/impairment–fitness dimension. This is consistent with the NHS usage in which 'need' relates to those phenomena which are more objectively measurable, whereas 'demand' reflects the wishes and behaviour of consumers or customers.

Outcomes on the social function dimension of sickness/handicap–role fulfilment are, in practice, very important. Service provision is elicited and legitimized in terms of two concepts about which there is a very large literature which it is not feasible to summarize here: 'dependence' and 'deviance'. Dependency, i.e. loss of independence, is an integral element of Talcot Parsons' notion of the 'sick role':

The occupant of the sick role, according to Parsons, is exempt from responsibility for his incapacity, as it is beyond his control, and he is also exempt from normal social role obligations. Definition of the incapacity in medical terms provides a legitimate basis for the sick individual's exemption (to varying degrees and for varying periods) from his normal role and task obligations. This partial and conditional legitimation also depends on the recognition by the sick person that to be ill is inherently undesirable and hence there is an obligation to try to get well. In addition, the sick person has an obligation to seek technically competent help (i.e. from a physician) and to co-operate in the process of getting well. (Based on Segall, 1976)

Some of the groups with whom health psychologists have been concerned for longest – people with chronic ill health and disability, brain damage, psychiatric disorders or learning disabilities – are often among the most rejected by the rest of the population. Some are caught in a vicious circle: as a result of behaving in a way that breaks social rules, they find themselves rejected and respond by exaggerating their behaviour. Deviance is social behaviour that is subject to social sanctions:

Deviant behaviour is thus defined in terms of social attitudes rather than intrinsic quality and may include deviance from group norms that are themselves deviant from more widely accepted norms.

Norms are established and expected forms of social behaviour. Norms are sets of implicit social rules, models of what should happen. Durkheim developed the notion of norms in his analysis of social fact, that is the conventions of behaviour and standards of value which exist independently of individuals and which exercise a coercive influence. Breaches of norms can result in the imposition of sanctions. (Bullock, Stallybrass and Trombley, 1988)

The 15 outcome targets specified in *The Health of the Nation* (see Fig. 4.1) consist of a mixture of 'bodily' and behavioural' outcomes. Ten refer to reductions in death rates, of which two refer specifically to suicidal behaviour; three refer to reductions in the rate of onset of disease (cancer, gonorrhoea); one refers to a direct consequence of behaviour (rate of conceptions); one refers broadly but non-specifically to the health and social functioning of a segment of the population.

Generally speaking, current measures of functional ability seek to quantify needs and outcomes on all three dimensions, but with a special emphasis on behavioural and dependency issues. Measures of psychological well-being, life satisfaction and morale tend to focus more specifically on experiential issues, whereas measures of social networks and social support encompass both the experiential and social functioning dimensions.

From health outcomes to health services

Implicit in these indicators for service provision ('need', 'demand', 'deviance', 'dependence') are the grounds for increasing or decreasing the provision of services.

In the case of needs, the grounds are provided by the perceived legitimacy of the need. By developing new methods of diagnosis and treatment, the medical profession tends to increase the areas of need regarded as legitimate, but so far as NHS provision is concerned, certain areas of potential need are not considered legitimate because of political and managerial decisions not to fund the services involved. Examples include complex dental work and, increasingly, long-term care of elderly and dependent people (who may, however, be eligible for social care).

Where patient demand is believed to under-represent need, there is usually a wish to increase demand; this is a common reason for screening programmes for non-symptomatic conditions. Where patient demand is considered to be in excess of need (and for the most part this arises in primary care settings because demand on hospitals is controlled directly by GPs), then patients' GPs will manage that demand by the way they respond to it. For example, GPs, by their behaviour, played a major part in increasing and then decreasing demand for minor tranquillizers and for antibiotics for viral upper-respiratory tract infections.

Dependency and deviance arise from the interaction between the individual and their social setting. Typically, the aim of care is to increase independence and/or decrease deviance; this may be done by encouraging the people with whom the patient interacts not to foster dependency and to be more accepting of the patient's behaviour. In the new health and social care systems, the case manager has the job of determining what level of services is required in the individual case and in relation to the needs of carers (Department of Health SSI, 1991a,b). Thus the responsibility of prioritizing some kinds of care over others, and rationing services so that they do not require more than the resources available, also falls to the case manager. Figure 4.3 summarizes the issues associated with the three dimensions of outcome.

Psychology's contribution to the new service systems

Thus far, this chapter has been 'setting the scene', describing and identifying aspects of the new health and social care systems which not only invite but, many psychologists would say, also require a substantial input from our discipline. Psychologists alone cannot unravel the mysteries of behavioural, experiential and

	'Observable' dimension	Experiential dimension	Social dimension
Acute state:	Disease	Illness	Sickness
Recognized by:	Signs	Symptoms	Dependence/deviance
Chronic state:	Impairment	Disability	Handicap
Excellent health:	Fitness	Wellbeing	Role fulfilment
Service indicator:	Need	Demand'	Complaints about excessive dependence/deviance
Rationing by:	Redefining Legitimacy	Management of demand	Care management

FIGURE 4.3 Summary of issues associated with the three dimensions of outcome.

social health outcomes, of demand, deviance and dependency; far from it. Substantial, measurable improvements in the health of the population rely on developments in many disciplines and subdisciplines, from anthropology to economics, from neuropsychoimmunology to cognitive social psychology. Indeed, psychology as a discipline may be making less of a contribution than it could, due to an excessive concern with intrapersonal processes. In the field of public health, social, economic and political changes are at least as important as individual behavioural and cognitive change, as the reviews by Ashton and Seymour (1988) and the Research Unit in Health and Behavioural Change (1989) illustrate. Orford (1992) analyses psychology's excessive bias towards the individual and makes a powerful case for correcting this by conceptualizing people within the social settings and systems of which they are part, or which influence them.

This book is about the applications of psychology to health care, but because the research and theory reported by authors preceded the current reforms, the relevance across the whole of health and social care is not always made explicit, and the focus is on service provision rather than the commissioning of services. It is important that these organiza-tional boundaries do not become boundaries in psychologists' thinking.

Definition and measurement of outcomes

At present, health care in the UK is a maelstrom of competing ideologies. The two systems of purchasing – Health Authorities and GP fundholders – illustrate the point:

> What is most significant about the new-style NHS – and the point most frequently neglected in discussions about it – is that it actually incorporates two different models. While the hospital model is management and provider-led, the primary health care model is much more consumer-led. Even if competition is going to be conspicuous by its absence in both models – except at the margins – the nature of the markets will be very different. In the hospital model, purchasers are proxy consumers, while in the primary care model, GPs are proxy consumers. (Day and Klein, 1991)

The NHS Management Executive now see 'healthy alliance' as the way of reconciling these two approaches (Powell, 1993). This author's own experience suggests that GPs have a more immediate awareness of the experiential and social dimensions of care than the officers of Health Authorities, whereas the latter attach greater importance to 'observable' need. But these can be seen as differences of priority and emphasis within an overall framework, and may become easier to debate and resolve as the technology for measuring social and experiential health outcomes improves. Epidemiologists who have sought to use existing psychometric instruments in public health research have found them to be poorly developed for the purpose (Gallacher and Davey Smith, 1989; Gallacher, 1992). A great deal of work based on generalizability theory (Cronbach *et al.*, 1972; Streiner and Norman, 1989) is required, and there is clearly a very important role for psychologists here. James (1978), an American reflecting on his introduction to community psychology, reported:

> ... I was somewhat surprised to learn that one major contribution I could make to ongoing departmental teaching and research activities was in guiding the selection or construction of psychometrically sound psychosocial scales for inclusion in population-based research. While this may not seem very exciting at first glance, the important thing is that this is the kind of technical assistance psychologists are more or less uniquely qualified to give in multi-disciplinary research settings, and meeting this need eventually widened my opportunities to draw upon relevant theory and research findings from clinical, personality and social psychology to influence the choice of variables to be studied in departmental research. (James, 1978)

Processes leading to outcomes

Many hospital doctors are primarily concerned with the biology of health care: anatomical, physiological and biochemical dysfunction. Illness, sick role and social behaviour which is apparently unrelated to biological dysfunction can appear bizarre, and give rise to great confusion and puzzlement, for example: alexithymia (Apfel and Sifneos, 1979; Lesser and Lesser, 1983); the 'Ganser syndrome' (Enoch, 1990); the 'Gaslight Phenomenon' (Smith and Sinanan, 1972); 'hypochondria' (Salkovskis and Warwick, 1986); 'hysteria'; mass psychogenic illness (Colligan, Pennebaker and Murphy, 1982); Munchausen syndrome (Asher, 1951; Wimberley, 1981); Munchausen-by-proxy syndrome (Meadow, 1977); 'non-compliance' with professional advice; 'psychosomatic' disorders; self-harm and suicidal behaviour; somatization (Katon, Ries and Kleinman, 1984; Kellner, 1986; Bridges and Goldberg, 1992); the 'worried well' (Miller, Acton and Hedge, 1988).

There is no place in psychology for a mind/body split or a distinction between physical and mental illness: often it is the same people who are suffering both. Kramer *et al.* (1992) report an analysis of data collected in Eastern Baltimore as part of the Epidemiologic Catchment Area program of the National Institute of Mental Health. Overall:

- 23.5% of people had at least one mental disorder.
- 41.7% of people had at least one physical disorder.
- 53.6% of people had *either* a physical or a mental disorder.
- 11.6% of people had *both* a physical *and* a mental disorder.
- 11.9% of people had a mental disorder *but* no physical disorder.
- 30.1% of people had a physical disorder *but* no mental disorder.
- 46.4% of people had *neither* a physical *nor* a mental disorder.
- 27.8% of people with a physical disorder *also* had a mental disorder.

Life events are social and experiential events that affect experiential and physical health status. Social deprivation and low social class affect health in many ways, although the multiple pathways from cause to effect are not yet clear; perceived lack of control over one's life may well be an important mediator. Neuropsychological phenomena affect experiential and social health outcomes. Modifiable beliefs have both direct and indirect effects on physical and experiential health status. Jones (1992), a physician, emphasized the importance of patients' perception of health as an outcome:

> Breathlessness is the most disabling symptom of patients with lung disease. Psychophysical studies have shown wide variability in the perception of breathlessness, even in normal individuals. In patients with pulmonary disease it is not possible to predict a given patient's breathlessness from measurements of lung function. It is not surprising, therefore, to find that there is a poor correlation between disturbed lung function and patients' resulting disability. It is also worth noting that while breathlessness is a troublesome and distressing symptom, it appears that the disturbances of daily life that result from it cause greater distress than the symptom itself .... If we are concerned with measurement and setting of standards for the alleviation of suffering caused by diseases, particularly those that are chronic, then measurements of patients' health and well-being must form major criteria of therapeutic efficiency. (Jones, 1992)

Psychology's particular contribution surely concerns the interactions between biology, behaviour, experience and social functioning.

Risk factors

An important concept in prevention is that of a 'risk factor'. Most forms of ill-health are multifactorial, that is, they have multiple interacting causes. In few, if any, forms of ill-health, is it certain that all the causes or how they interact with each other are known. A risk factor is an aspect of personal behaviour of lifestyle, an exposure to an environmental event or an inborn or inherited characteristic which epidemiological research has shown to be related to some form of ill-health. 'Having' a risk factor implies that the person has an increased risk or probability of that form of ill-health. But risk factors are correlates or predictors: a risk factor does not necessarily cause the form of ill-health in question.

In *The Health of the Nation*, the government has established targets for modification of certain risk factors, nearly all of which refer to forms of personal behaviour: smoking, drinking, diet, sharing of needles by injecting drug users (Fig. 4.4). Some psychologists believe that psychology should put particular effort into developing programmes to change these behaviours; others share the view expressed by the Research Unit in Health and Behavioural Change (1989) and shared by Gabbay (1992), that '... there remains a disconcerting belief that much of the improvement [in the health of the population] will come about by exhorting individual people to live more healthily. It is crucial that social and economic policies are changed to allow people to choose the healthy options'.

Psychology in health and social care in Britain: clinical, health, community and public health psychology?

In August 1982, *American Psychologist* published a special section with papers on public health and psychology (DeLeon and Pallak, 1982), and Winett, King and Altman published their volume attempting to integrate the theory and practice of health psychology and public health in 1989. In 1991, Ewart published a major paper attempting to provide an adequate theoretical basis for development.

Smoking

To reduce the prevalence of cigarette smoking to no more than 20% by the year 2000 in both men and women (a reduction of a third) (Baseline 1990)

To reduce consumption of cigarettes by at least 40% by the year 2000 (Baseline 1990)

In addition to the overall reduction in prevalence, at least 33% of women smokers to stop smoking at the start of their pregnancy by the year 2000

To reduce smoking prevalence of 11–15-year-olds by at least 33% by1994 (to less than 6%) (Baseline 1988)

Diet and Nutrition

To reduce the average percentage of food energy derived by the population from saturated fatty acids by at least 35% by 2005 (to no more than 11% of food energy) (Baseline 1990)

To reduce the average percentage of food energy derived from total fat by the population by at least 12% by 2005 (to no more than about 35% of total food energy) (Baseline 1990)

To reduce the proportion of men and women aged 16–64 who are obese by at least 25% and 33% respectively (to no more than 6% of men and 8% of women) (Baseline 1986/87)

To reduce the proportion of men drinking more than 21 units of alcohol per week and women drinking more than 14 units per week by 30% by 2005 (to 18% of men and 7% of women) (Baseline 1990)

Blood Pressure

To reduce mean systolic blood pressure in the adult population by at least 5 mmHg by 2005 (Baseline to be derived from new national survey)

HIV/AIDS

To reduce the percentage of injecting drug misusers who report sharing injecting equipment in the previous 4 weeks from 20% in 1990 to no more than 10% by 1997 and no more than 5% by the year 2000

FIGURE 4.4 Health of the Nation risk factor targets (Department of Health, 1992).

The UK is approximately 10 years behind the USA in relating the work of the discipline to the needs of populations. Ingham (1988), a clinical psychologist whose field of research has been epidemiology, reviewed the implications of the discipline for clinical psychologists. Cooke and Brewin, also clinical psychologists, have published epidemiological research (Cooke, 1982, 1987; Brewin *et al.*, 1987, 1988). Orford's recent plea for a more socially aware and community-oriented practice of psychology was preceded by a slim volume by Bender (1976). As Health Authorities started to undertake their new responsibilities for population needs assessment in 1991, Kat (1991a) noted that no more than two or three were known to be employing psychologists for their professional skills in this area.

In his account of community psychology, Orford (1992) observes that:

> Once psychology is practised outside the clinics, schools and penal establishments in which it has found its institutional homes in the past, and emerges into the community, then the familiar separations of clinical, educational, occupational, criminological and legal, and other branches of applied psychology make less and less sense. The central ideas of community psychology transcend these artificial boundaries as do many of the most exciting innovations in practice.

The same point must be made about psychology in relation to health and social care. As the responsibility for the care of people with long-term problems shifts from NHS institutions to social services-based care managers, as more services are shifted from general hospital outpatient departments to primary care settings, as artificial distinctions between people's social problems and their health problems cease to be made because all service provision is on the same site, so the current boundaries within professional applied psychology make less and less sense. The conclusion can be drawn that neither psychologists nor their employers, nor the recipients of their services, are likely to benefit if many small groups of psychologists seek to represent themselves separately from those with political and managerial control of health and social care. Whatever may be the apparent benefits of distinguishing different groups within professional applied psychology, such groups are too small to attract the financial resources the profession needs for development, and are vulnerable to ideologically based attempts to create commercial and political competition between them. In order to make best use of the new opportunities available, and counteract the undesirable effects of too many small groupings, all the psychologists interested in health and social care need to be represented to government and the agencies of the NHS through one structure. The British Psychological Society is the national organization within which all the current groupings are based. Efforts are now being made to bring about a review of the Society's structures, with the aim of achieving effective professional representation irrespective of specialist title (Mowbray, 1991; Kat, 1991b, 1993).

References

Apfel, R.J. and Sifneos, P.E. (1979) Alexithymia: concept and measurement. *Psychotherapy and Psychosomatics*, **32**, 180–90.

Asher, R. (1951) Munchausen's syndrome. *Lancet*, i, 339–41.

Ashton, J. and Seymour, H. (1988). *The New Public Health*, Open University Press, Milton Keynes.

Audit Commission for Local Authorities and the National Health Service in England and Wales (1986) *Making a Reality of Community Care*, HMSO, London.

Audit Commission for Local Authorities and the National Health Service in England and Wales (1992) *Community Care: Managing the Cascade of Change*, HMSO, London.

Bender, M. (1976) *Community Psychology*, Methuen, London.

Beveridge, W. (1942) *Report on Social Insurance and Allied Services*, HMSO, London.

Bowling, A. (1991) *Measuring Health. A Review of Quality of Life Measurement Scales*, Open University Press, Milton Keynes.

Bradshaw, J. (1972) A taxonomy of social need, in G. McLachlan, *Problems and Progress in Medical Care*, 7th series, Oxford University Press, London, pp. 70–82.

Brewin, C.R. (1992) Measuring individual needs for care and services, in *Measuring Mental Health Needs*, (eds) G. Thornicroft, C.R. Brewin and J.K. Wing, Gaskell, London, pp. 220–36.

Brewin, C.R., Wing, J.K., Mangen, S.P. *et al.* (1987) Principles and practice of measuring needs in the long-term mentally ill: the MRC Needs for Care Assessment. *Psychological Medicine*, **17**, 971–81.

Brewin, C.R., Wing, J.K., Mangen, S.P. *et al.* (1988) Needs for care among the long term mentally ill: a rapport from the Camberwell High Contact Survey. *Psychological Medicine*, **18**, 457–68.

Bridges, K.W. and Goldberg, D.P. (1992) Somatization in primary health care. Prevalence and determinants, in *Primary Health Care and Psychiatric Epidemiology*, eds B. Cooper and R. Eastwood, Tavistock/Routledge, London, pp. 341–50.

Bullock, A., Stallybrass, O. and Trombley, S. (eds) (1988) *The Fontana Dictionary of Modern Thought*. 2nd edn, Fontana Press, London.

Caplan, G. (1964) *Principles of Preventive Psychiatry*, Basic Books, New York.

Clare, A., Gulbinat, W. and Sartorius, N. (1992) A tri-axial classification of health problems presenting in primary health care. *Social Psychiatry and Psychiatric Epidemiology*, **27**, 108–16.

Colligan, M.J., Pennebaker, J.W. and Murphy, L.R. (eds) (1982) Mass psychogenic illness: a social psychological analysis. Lawrence Erlbaum Associates, Hillsdale, New Jersey.

Cooke, D.J. (1982) Depression: demographic factors in the distribution of different syndromes in the general population. *Social Psychiatry*, **17**(1), 29–36.

Cooke, D.J. (1987) The significance of life events as a cause of psychological and physical disorders, in (ed) B. Cooper *Psychiatric Epidemiology: Progress and Prospects*, Croom Helm, London, pp. 67–80.

Cronbach, L.J., Gleser, G.C., Nanda, H. and Rajaratnam, N. (1972) *The Dependability of Behavioural Measurements*, Wiley, New York.

Culyer, A.J. (1976) *Need and the National Health Service*, Martin Robinson, London.

Day, P. and Klein, R. (1991) Britain's health care experiment. *Health Affairs*, 10(3), 39–59.

DeLeon, P.H. and Pallak, M.S. (1982) Public health and psychology: an important, expanding interaction. *American Psychologist*, 37(8), 934–5.

Department of Health (1987) *Promoting Better Health: the Government's Programme for Improving Primary Health Care*, (Cm. 249), HMSO, London.

Department of Health (1989a) *Working for Patients*, (Cm. 555), HMSO, London.

Department of Health (1989b) *Caring for People. Community Care in the Next Decade and Beyond*, (Cmnd 849), HMSO, London.

Department of Health (1991a) *The Health of the Nation: a Consultative Document for Health in England*, (Cm. 1523), HMSO, London.

Department of Health (1991b) *The Patients' Charter*, HMSO, London.

Department of Health (1992a) *The Health of the Nation*, (Cm. 1986), HMSO, London.

Department of Health (1992b) *On the State of the Public Health: the Annual Report of the Chief Medical Officer of the Department of Health for the Year 1991*, HMSO, London.

Department of Health (1992c) *The Health of the Nation, Specification of National Indicators*, HMSO, London.

Department of Health and Social Security (1968) *Report of the Committee on Local Authority and Allied Personal Social Services* (The Seebohm Report), HMSO, London.

Department of Health and Social Security (1976) *Prevention and Health: Everybody's Business*, HMSO, London.

Department of Health and Social Security (1981) *Care in Community*. A consultative document on moving resources for care in England. DHSS, London.

Department of Health NHS Management Executive (1991) *Integrating Primary and Secondary Health Care*, NHSME, London.

Department of Health NHS Management Executive (1992) *The Extension of the Hospital and Community Health Services Elements of the GP Fundholding Scheme from 1 April 1993 – Supplementary Guidance*, HSG(92)53, NHSME, London.

Department of Health Social Services Inspectorate (1991a) *Care Management and Assessment. Manager's Guide*, London.

Department of Health Social Services Inspectorate (1991b) *Care Management and Assessment. Practitioner's Guide*, HMSO, London.

Enoch D. (1990) Ganser syndrome and Munchausen's syndrome, in (eds) R. Bluglass and P. Bowden, *Principles and Practice of Forensic Psychiatry*, Churchill Livingstone, London.

Ewart, C.K. (1991) Social action theory for a public health psychology. *American Psychologist*, 46, 931–46.

Fallowfield, L. (1990) *The Quality of Life. The Missing Measurement in Health Care*, Souvenir Press, London.

Fry, J. (1980) *Primary Care*, Heinemann Medical, London.

Gabbay, J. (1992) The Health of the Nation. Seize the opportunity. Editorial. *British Medical Journal*, 305, 129–30.

Gallacher, J.E.J. (1992) Methods of assessing personality for epidemiological study. *Journal of Epidemiology and Community Health*, 46, 465–9.

Gallacher, J.E.J. and Davey Smith, G. (1989) A framework for the adaption of psychological questionnaires for epidemiological use: an example of the Bortner Type A scale. *Psychological Medicine*, 19, 709–17.

Griffiths, R. (1988) *Community Care: Agenda for Action. A Report to the Secretary of State for Social Services*, HMSO, London.

Ham, C. (1991) *The New National Health Service: Organisation and Management*. Radcliffe Medical Press, Oxford, for NAHAT (the National Association of Health Authorities and Trusts).

Ingham, J.G. (1988) Implications of epidemiology for clinical psychologists. *British Journal of Clinical Psychology*, 27, 201–12.

James, S.A. (1978) The psychologist in a public health setting: implications for training. *Journal of Community Psychology*, 6(4), 324–7.

Jones, P.W. (1992) Patients' perception of health as a measure of outcome. *Medical Audit News*, 2(4), 57–8.

Kaplan, R.M. (1990) Behavior as the central outcome in health care. *American Psychologist*, 45, 1211–20.

Kat, B.J.B. (1991a) *Public Health Psychology: Review and Prospects*, Paper given at the Annual Conference of the British Psychological Society, Bournemouth.

Kat, B.J.B. (1991b) Response to Mowbray. *The Psychologist. Bulletin of the British Psychological Society*, 4(8), 362–3.

Kat, B.J.B. (1993) The death and rebirth of psychology in health care. *The Psychologist*. Bulletin of the British Psychological Society, 6(3), 123–5.

Katon, W., Ries, R.K. and Kleinman, A. (1984) The prevalence of somatization in primary care. *Comprehensive Psychiatry*, 25, 208–11.

Kellner, R. (1986) Somatization and hypochondriasis. Praeger, New York.

Kramer, M., Simonsick, E., Lima, B. and Levav, I. (1992) The epidemiological basis for mental health care in primary health care: a case for action, in

Primary Health Care and Psychiatric Epidemiology, (eds) B. Cooper and R. Eastwood, Tavistock/ Routledge, London, pp. 69–98.

Lancet (1992) Outcomes and PORTS. Editorial. *Lancet*, **340**, 1439.

Larson, J.S. (1991) *The Measurement of Health: Concepts and Indicators*, Greenwood Press, Westport, Connecticut.

Lesser, I.M. and Lesser, B.Z. (1983) Alexithymia: examining the development of a psychological concept. *American Journal of Psychiatry*, **140**, 1305–8.

Levitt, R. and Wall, A. (1991) *The Reorganised National Health Service*, 4th edn, Chapman and Hall, London.

Loudon, I.S.L. (1977) Historical background, in *Trends in General Practice*, (ed) J. Fry, British Medical Association for the Royal College of General Practitioners, London, p. 83.

McDowell, I. and Newell, C. (1987) *Measuring Health: A Guide to Rating Scales and Questionnaires*, Oxford University Press, Oxford.

McKeown T. (1979). *The Role of Medicine*, Basil Blackwell, Oxford.

McKillip, J. (1987) *Need Analysis. Tools for the Human Services and Education*. Sage Applied Social Research Methods Series Volume 10, Sage Publications, London.

Meadow, R. (1977) Munchausen by proxy: the hinterland of child abuse. *Lancet*, ii, 343–5.

Miller, D., Acton, T.M.G. and Hedge, B. (1988) The worried well: their identification and management. *Journal of the Royal College of Physicians*, **22**, 158–65.

Mowbray, D. (1991) Towards a College of Health Care Psychology? *The Psychologist. Bulletin of the British Psychological Society*, 4(8), 360–1.

Orford, J. (1992) *Community Psychology: Theory and Practice*, Wiley, Chichester.

Peckham, M. (1991) Research and development for the National Health Service. *Lancet*, **338**, 367–71.

Powell, M. (1993) *Healthy Alliances*, Department of Health, London.

Research Unit in Health and Behavioural Change (1989) *Changing the Public Health*, Wiley, Chichester.

Salkovskis, P.M. and Warwick, H.M.C. (1986) Morbid preoccupations, health anxiety and reassurance: a cognitive behavioural approach to hypochondriasis. *Behaviour Research and Therapy*, **24**, 597–602.

Seedhouse, D. (1986) *Health: the Foundations for Achievement*, Wiley, Chichester.

Segall, A. (1976) The sick role concept: understanding illness behaviour. *Journal of Health and Social Behaviour*, **17**, 163–70.

Smith, C.G. and Sinanan, K. (1972) The 'Gaslight Phenomenon' reappears. A modification of the Ganser syndrome. *British Journal of Psychiatry*, **120**, 685–6.

Social Services Committee of the House of Commons (1985) *Second Report, Session 1984–85. Community Care with Special Reference to Adult Mentally Ill and Mentally Handicapped People*, HMSO, London.

Streiner, D.L. and Norman, G.R. (1989) *Health Measurement Scales. A Practical Guide to their Development and Use*, Oxford University Press, Oxford.

Sullivan, D.F. (1966) *Conceptual Problems in Developing an Index of Health*, (Monograph series II, No. 17), Office of Health Statistics, National Center for Health Statistics, Washington DC.

Susser, M. (1990) Disease, illness, sickness, impairment, disability and handicap. *Psychological Medicine*, **20**, 471–3.

University of Manchester (1993) Discussion document on Social, Health and Welfare Commissioning Agencies. Cited in the *Health Services Journal*, 7th January, p. 6.

Wadsworth, M.E.J., Butterfield, W.J.H. and Blaney, R. (1971) *Health and Sickness: the Choice of Treatment*, Tavistock, London.

Watkin, B. (1975) *Documents on Health and Social Services: 1834 to the Present Day*, Methuen, London.

Wilkin, D., Hallam, L. and Doggett, M. (1992) *Measures of Need and Outcome for Primary Health Care*, Oxford University Press, Oxford.

Wimberley, T. (1981) The making of a Munchausen. *British Journal of Medical Psychology*, **54**, 121–9.

Winnett, R.A., King, A.C. and Altman, D.G. (1989) *Health Psychology and Public Health*, Pergamon Press, Oxford.

World Health Organization (1978) *Alma-Ata 1978. Primary Health Care*. 'Health for All' series number 1, World Health Organization, Geneva.

World Health Organization (1980) *International Classification of Impairments, Disabilities and Handicaps (ICIDH)*, World Health Organization, Geneva.

World Health Organization (1981) *Global Strategy for Health for All by the Year 2000*. 'Health for All' series number 3, World Health Organization, Geneva.

Chapter five

Improving patients' understanding, recall, satisfaction and compliance

Philip Ley and Sue Llewelyn

Introduction

This chapter will examine some of the problems involved in giving information to patients. It will be shown that in general patients want information about their condition and their treatment, but many feel that they are not told enough, many do not understand what they are told, and many do not remember what is said. If it is accepted that patients should be adequately informed, this is clearly a state of affairs which needs to be remedied. It is also likely that patients' compliance with advice and the speed and ease of recovery from illness are adversely affected by this lack of information. Although the main emphasis of this chapter will be on the improvement of information giving by health

care providers, this is only one aspect of communication in the clinical encounter. Roter, Hall and Katz (1988) reviewed content analyses of consultation communications between doctors and patients. Figure 5.1, based on tables in their review, shows the median percentage of the consultation spent in various forms of communication. The role of some of these other aspects of communication will be discussed later in the chapter. Also, although it does not appear in the chart, women seem to receive more information than men in clinical consultations (Hall, Roter and Katz, 1988; Weisman and Teitelbaum, 1989).

The emphasis here is on the ways in which the clinician's behaviour needs to change to improve communication. Specifically, patients'

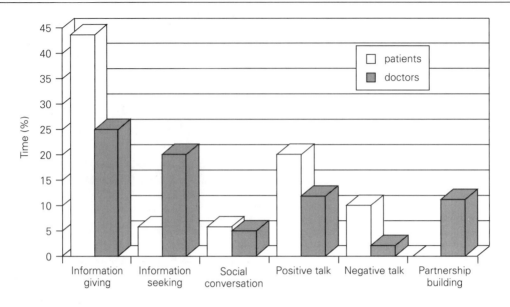

FIGURE 5.1 Median percentage of time spent by patients and doctors in various types of communication activity in consultations.

satisfaction with, understanding of and memory for the information given to them, their compliance with advice, and the interrelationships of these variables will be reviewed. Following this the effectiveness of some suggested methods for improving communication will be assessed.

Patient satisfaction

For a considerable period of time survey evidence has shown that most people seem to want to know as much as possible about their illnesses and their treatment (e.g. Cartwright, 1964; 1967; Ley and Spelman, 1967; Ley, 1982a; 1988; Morris, 1990). This is true even if the information concerned is 'bad news', such as a diagnosis of cancer, or information about the dangers and risks of investigative or treatment procedures (Kalish and Reynolds, 1976; Ley, 1982a; 1988; Levy, 1983). Survey evidence also shows that substantial proportions of patients do not feel that they have been adequately informed about their condition, and that there has been no drop in the percentage dissatisfied over the last 20 years or so. Ley (1988) reviewed 21 surveys of hospital patients and found that the mean percentage dissatisfied was 41, with a standard deviation of 20%. The correlation between date of survey and percentage dissatisfied was +0.16, which is not statistically significant. For 11 general practice studies also reviewed, mean dissatisfaction was 28%, with a standard deviation of 15%. The correlation between date of survey and percentage dissatisfied was −0.19: again, not statistically significant. These correlations suggest that the problem has not spontaneously remitted over the time period concerned (1961–1985). This interpretation has to be somewhat guarded, because the surveys involved have differed in sample and methodology. Also, even if the data are accepted at face value, other interpretations such as rising patient expectations of how much information they should be given, could account for the apparent lack of improvement.

Satisfaction with communications in more specific areas of communication also remains low; for example, Gibbs, Waters and George (1989a,b; 1990) reported on satisfaction with information about prescribed medication in eight samples of patients. The mean percentage feeling that they had been given enough information was only 29.5% (s.d. 8.04). Thus, an average of 70% or so wanted more information than they were given.

Satisfaction with communications is highly correlated with satisfaction with the other aspects of the consultation, such as general satisfaction, satisfaction with the affective aspects of the consultation and satisfaction with the behavioural aspect or the clinician's competence. In addition, patients' satisfaction is correlated with their compliance with advice (Ley, 1988; Hall and Dornan, 1988; 1990). The meta-analysis of 107 studies of satisfaction by Hall and Dornan (1988) suggested that satisfaction with the amount of attention paid to psychosocial problems was the lowest-ranked aspect of all indices of satisfaction. Interestingly, sociodemographic variables such as age, sex and race have very low correlations with satisfaction (Hall and Dornan, 1990).

It has also been found that even when clinicians feel that they have made special efforts to be lucid in their communication endeavour, the same proportion of patients remains dissatisfied (Ley, 1972a; 1988). This unexpected result is due, at least in part, to patients not understanding and/or forgetting what they are told, combined with their diffidence about asking questions. For whatever reasons, patients seem reluctant to ask questions in clinical settings (Fig. 5.1). For example, Carstairs (1970) reported that 53% of patients who wanted more information did not ask for it; Mayou, Williamson and Foster (1976) found that 70% of their patients did not intend to ask questions, even though many of them wanted more information; and Klein (1979) reported that half of those who wanted to make a request for

more information failed to do so. This reluctance to ask questions has two main undesirable effects. First, it deprives patients of information that they would like, and secondly, it prevents clinicians from obtaining the feedback they need if they are to improve as communicators.

Methods for providing clinicians with feedback have been reviewed by Sharf (1988). One method has involved trying to directly persuade patients to ask questions, and to instruct them in the questions they might wish to ask and how to ask them. These studies have included face to face and written instruction, accompanied by modelling and rehearsal. Other methods tried have included making patients co-authors of their case notes, and providing clinicians with the result of surveys of their patients. Results have been mixed in the small number of studies conducted to evaluate these techniques. Usually, patients in the experimental group have asked more questions than controls, and sometimes their compliance has been higher, but usually there has been either a negative or no effect on satisfaction (e.g. Roter, 1977; Greenfield, Kaplan and Ware, 1985; Tabak, 1988). Survey feedback to physicians does not necessarily improve their communicative behaviour (Adamson, Schann and Gullion, 1988).

Patients' understanding

Patients' understanding of what they are told has been assessed in a number of ways, including tests of understanding of medical vocabulary; tests of knowledge of illnesses; patients' own reports about their understanding; clinicians' interview judgements of patients' understanding; and quasi-behavioural tests. The results of all of these methods of assessment are likely to be time- and culture-bound. Lay levels of knowledge of medical matters are constantly changing. However, whenever such assessments have been made they have found that patients do not always understand what they are told, so it would be prudent to assume that this state of affairs will continue unless special steps are taken.

Several researchers have expressed surprise at some of the terms being used in an undefined fashion in communications to patients. For example, in an early study, Boyle (1970), using a multiple-choice test with a patient sample, found that the percentages correctly defining, for example, 'arthritis', 'jaundice', 'palpitation' and 'bronchitis' were 85%, 77%, 52% and 80%, respectively. Using the same test with samples of medical and dental undergraduates, and postgraduate students of education, Tring and Hayes-Allen (1973) found that the percentages correctly defining these words were 82%, 61%, 68% and 80%, respectively. These are just a few examples from these investigations. Boyle also investigated patients' knowledge of the location of major organs. Again, a multiple-choice format was used and it was found that, for example, 42% of patients knew the location of the heart, 20% the stomach, and 49% the liver. In a further investigation of understanding of medical terminology, Cole (1979) found that over half of samples of general practice patients and polytechnic students did not understand terms such as 'dilated', antiemetic' and 'haemorrhoids'. There is probably little point in multiplying these examples further. Similar findings are reported in more recent studies, for example Gibbs, Gibbs and Henrich (1987), Bourhis, Roth and MacQueen (1989). It is clear that some of the vocabulary used in communications to patients is unlikely to be familiar to them, and that some of the words which are unfamiliar to patients are assumed by professionals to be known by patients. This further reinforces the suggestion made earlier that feedback from patients is essential to the improvement of communicative performance.

Patients also have errors in their understanding of illness. Not unnaturally, they will interpret information given to them in terms of their 'model' of the illness in question. This can cause difficulties in communication. For example, Roth et al. (1962) reported that patients with peptic ulcer knew that acid caused ulcers, but they had unorthodox ideas about where the acid came from. Some thought it came from the teeth or the gums when food was chewed or swallowed, others that it was in the food which they ate, and only 10% had a reasonably clear idea that acid is secreted by the stomach. Another example comes from Leventhal, Meyer and Nerenz (1980), who found that nearly a third of hypertensive patients thought that their condition was likely to be cured by short-term treatment. The beliefs about how acid enters the stomach could militate against patients complying with advice about eating small frequent meals. The belief that hypertension can be cured by a short period of treatment might reduce the chances of long-term compliance with treatment regimens. Once more, the clinician needs feedback from the patient to be able to spot these different conceptions of illness, and provide corrective information.

In the light of the studies just reviewed, it is perhaps not surprising that patients frequently say that they have not understood what they have been told. Thus, in four samples of general practice patients, Kincey, Bradshaw and Ley (1975), Ley, Skilbeck and Tulips (1975) and Ley et al. (1976) found that the percentages claiming not to have understood what they had been told about various aspects of their condition ranged from 7% to 53%.

These high levels of not understanding are confirmed by studies in which patients have been interviewed by clinicians to assess their understanding. A good example of such a study is that of Parkin (1976) and Parkin et al. (1976), who followed up 130 patients after discharge from hospital medical wards, and found that 49% had poor or no knowledge of their illness, and that over a third had little or no comprehension of their drug regimen. Similar findings with regard to treatment emerged from a number of studies reviewed by Ley (1988), who reported that the percentages of patients judged by experts not to have adequate understanding of their treatment regimen ranged from 5 to 69%.

Investigations using quasi-behavioural methods also suggest frequent misunderstandings. In these investigations, patients have been asked to say, for example, exactly when they would take their prescribed drugs. Using this methodology, Herman (1973) found that the patients' stated interdose intervals were frequently far from optimal. Thus the interdose intervals for tablets to be taken twice a day ranged from 3 to 21 hours; three times a day, from 0 to 24 hours; and four times a day from 0 to 21 hours. Other investigators have reported similar confusion about interdose intervals, e.g. Norell *et al.* (1984), and Sanazaro (1985) found that 45% of a sample of diabetics could not correctly describe the procedure for good foot care. The conclusion must be that patients will often not understand important aspects of the information they receive.

Patients' recall

Studies of what patients remember of what they are told have been conducted in a variety of hospital and general practice settings. The material involved has consisted of the clinician's conclusions about the illness, its treatment, investigation and prognosis, and advice to the patient, or of some subset of this material, or of informed consent information. Analogue studies have also been conducted. In these, healthy volunteers have been presented with material which might have been given to a real patient, and asked to recall it. Patients frequently forget some of the information given to them. Table 5.1, based on the review by Ley (1988), summarizes these studies.

Investigations have differed considerably in methodology (Ley, 1988). In addition to the differences in content already alluded to, the patients involved in some studies have been making their first attendance with a particular illness, whereas other studies have taken all comers, including those making a repeat attendance with their illness. The first of these options allows better experimental control, in that if repeat attenders are studied there is no control over what they will have been told on previous visits. Against this is the argument that the use of samples that include repeat attenders has greater ecological validity, because those attending at clinics and other consultations always include a large proportion of repeat attenders (Bartlett *et al.*, 1984).

There are also differences in how memory is assessed. Some investigations have used free recall, i.e. patients are simply asked to state what they were told. Others have used cued recall, where patients are asked what they were told about the diagnosis, what they were told about the treatment, what they were told about investigations, etc. Yet other studies have used probed recall, in which the investigator continues to probe the patient's recall, usually with

TABLE 5.1 Summary of studies of memory for medical information

Type of subject	Number of samples	Mean percentage recalled	Range
Hospital patients	8	54	40–70
General practice patients	6	65	50–88
Patients given informed consent materials	9	47	29–72
Analogue subjects	10	47	28–64

prompting questions until sure that the patient can recall no more. Finally, some of the investigations of memory for informed consent materials have used a multiple-choice recognition task. It is not known which of these methodological variants yields the most valid predictor of patients' memory outside the experimental situation.

Another complication is that, at least for common illnesses, patients will have 'base rate' expectations of what is likely to be said. For example, Ley (1988) outlined the likely expectations of a mother taking a school-aged child with a sore throat to the general practitioner. The expectations will include that the child has tonsillitis, that an antibiotic will be prescribed, that it should be taken four times a day, that plenty of fluids should be provided, that the child should be kept off school for a few days, and possibly have to stay indoors for a day or two. In many cases, particularly in general practice consultations, some or all of these expectations will be met, thus making it easier to remember what has been said. Similarly, many general practitioners will give the same lifestyle advice about weight, smoking habits and exercise to particular patients on each encounter. This predictability would be expected to apply less to visits to a less familiar clinician in an outpatient clinic. These complications should be kept in mind when considering studies of forgetting (Ley, 1988).

Findings in relation to patient characteristics can be summarized as follows:

- No consistent relationship between age and recall has been found (Ley, 1988).
- Intellectual level has shown a low but consistent relationship to recall, the correlations ranging from 0.18 to 0.26 (Ley, 1988).
- Anxiety is related to recall, but not in the curvilinear fashion reported by Ley and Spelman (1967), the more common finding being that the more anxious the patient, the more is recalled (Kupst *et al.*, 1975;

Anderson *et al.*, 1979; Leeb, Bowers and Lynch, 1976).
- The higher the medical knowledge, the better the recall (Ley, 1988).

Characteristics of the material presented also affect recall. The main findings are as follows:

- There is a primacy effect in the recall of medical information: material presented first is better recalled (Ley and Spelman, 1967; Ley, 1972b; 1982b).
- Statements which are perceived as important are better recalled than those that are seen as less important (Ley and Spelman, 1967; Ley, 1972b).
- The greater the number of statements the smaller the mean percentage recalled (Ley, 1979; 1982b; 1988). The drop in percentage recalled is linear in studies of free recall by new outpatients, and in analogue studies. Note, however, that the absolute amount recalled rises with increased amount of information presented. Surprisingly, forgetting by outpatients and by analogue subjects is almost identical (Fig. 5.2). The fact that the information is true and personally relevant seems to make no difference.
- Also surprisingly, there seems to be no tendency for forgetting to increase with the passage of time. What patients can recall shortly after the consultation they tend to retain for a considerable time (Ley, 1982b; 1988).

Patients' non-compliance and compliance

Compliance is the patient following the advice given by the doctor. Failure to follow such advice is referred to as non-compliance (see also discussion of this issue in Chapter 12). Note that, as we shall see later, non-compliance is not confined to patients. Health care professionals also show high levels of non-compliance with rules for optimal patient care, (Ley, 1980; 1988; Meichenbaum and Turk, 1987). For research purposes, patients' non-compliance

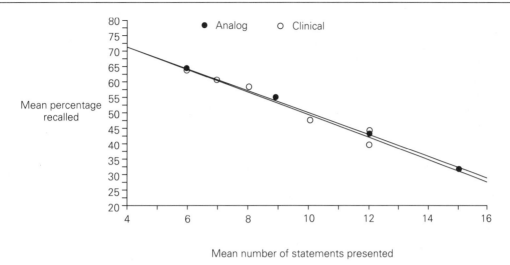

FIGURE 5.2 Relationship between mean number of statements presented and mean number recalled.

with advice has been defined in a variety of ways. In the case of medication, these include not taking enough medicine; taking too much medicine; not observing the correct interval between doses; not observing the correct duration of treatment; and taking additional non-prescribed medications. Advice about lifestyle changes such as dieting and giving up smoking has used analogous definitions of non-compliance. A decision also has to be made about the amount of deviation from the prescribed regimen which is permitted before the patient is judged to be non-compliant. Sometimes any deviation puts a patient in this category, sometimes complying on less than a given percentage of occasions, e.g. 75%, is used as the criterion.

The measurement of compliance also causes problems. Methods use have included patients' reports; pill and bottle counts; blood and urine tests; mechanical devices; direct observation; outcome, i.e. changes in the condition or behaviour; and clinicians' judgements. None of these methods is without its difficulties (Gordis, 1979; Caron, 1985; Roth, 1987; Ley, 1988). The one most commonly used in research is the patient's report. Caron (1985) reviewed a sam-

ple of investigations conducted between 1977 and 1983, and found that this was used as either the sole criterion, or one of the criteria, in 68% of cases. Outcome was used in 40%, direct observation in 14%, pill count in 12%, mechanical devices in 10% and blood or urine test in 6%. The use of outcome has been particularly common in studies of obesity and hypertension, while direct observation has been largely confirmed to appointment keeping/dropout. The mechanical devices used provide a record of the times at which, for example, the medicine container has been opened, or a relaxation tape has been played (e.g. Norell, 1981; Rudd and Marshall, 1987). Of the methods listed, clinicians' estimates are generally considered the least valid.

In clinical practice, as in the research studies, it is likely that the patient's report will be the commonest criterion for assessing compliance. Investigations reporting correlations between patient's report and other methods of assessing compliance have been summarized by Ley (1988). In these studies, the patient's report showed a mean correlation of +0.47 with pill counts, +0.80 with mechanical devices and +0.15 with physicians' estimates. As the number of studies reporting relevant information is small, these figures should be treated with some caution, but as they stand they suggest that the patient's report will give similar results to other methods on *relative* standing on the compliance dimension. However, there is ample evidence to show that patients' reports yield higher *absolute* estimates of compliance than more objective measures (Ley, 1988).

There is general agreement that questions concerning non-compliance should be prefaced by some introductory statement that makes the questions seem non-judgemental. For example, Haynes *et al.* (1980) introduced their compliance question by saying: 'People often have difficulty taking their pills for one reason or another and we are interested in finding out any problems that occur so that we can understand them better'. Having introduced the topic in some such way, it is worth noting the four questions asked by Morisky, Green and Levine (1986). A simple score based on these ques-

tions has shown validity as a predictor of blood pressure control over a 6-month period ($r = +0.43$) and a 42-month period ($r = +0.58$). The questions are as follows:

- Do you ever forget to take your medicine?
- Are you careless at times about taking your medicine?
- When you feel better do you sometimes stop taking your medicine?
- Sometimes when you feel worse do you stop taking your medicine?

The percentages of patients found to be non-compliant with health-related advice are summarized in Table 5.2 (Ley, 1976, 1978; Department of Health, Education and Welfare, 1979a; Sackett and Snow, 1979). It can be seen that the three reviews agree reasonably well with one another.

Patients' non-compliance is also expensive in material and human terms. The Department of Health and Human Services (1980) estimated

TABLE 5.2 Patients' non-compliance with advice

Area of advice	Mean percentage non-compliant in review by:		
	Ley (1976, 1978)	Department of Health, Education and Welfare (1979a)	Sackett and Snow (1979)
Medication			
Antitubercular	38.5	42.0	41.0
Antibiotic	49.0	47.7	–
Cardiovascular	–	39.3	38.7
Miscellaneous	48.0	52.0	42.5
Multiple drug regimen	–	60.0	–
Psychiatric	38.6	42.0	52.0
All medications	43.4	48.2	40.9
Attendance at clinics			
Obesity	47.7	–	–
Other	–	–	46.6
Diet			
Various	49.4	–	–
Other advice			
Miscellaneous	54.6	–	57.7

the annual costs (in 1979 US dollars) of non-compliance in the USA, in relation to ten major classes of commonly used drugs, to lie in the range 396–792 million dollars. In addition, non-compliance is a frequent cause of admission to medical wards. For example, Ausburn (1981) found that in 20% of cases admission was probably, and in a further 5% possibly, due to non-compliance with medication regimens. Thus success in reducing non-compliance could be expected to save significant amounts of money and reduce suffering by lessening the need for hospitalization, and by increasing the probabilities of cure or relief.

Determinants of, and relationships between, understanding, memory, satisfaction and compliance

Hall, Roter and Katz (1988) reviewed studies of the relationships between aspects of provider communication (shown in Fig. 5.1) and the outcome variables: patients' satisfaction, compliance and knowledge. A meta-analysis was conducted which yielded the average correlations shown in Table 5.3. Note that the provider communication variables have different patterns of effect on the outcome

variables. Only provider information-giving is related to all three outcome variables.

Ley (1982c) has suggested that, as well as having direct effects on the probability of compliance, understanding and memory will have indirect effects through their influence on satisfaction. To assess this possibility further, Ley (1986a, 1988) reviewed investigations from which correlations between understanding, memory, satisfaction and compliance could be derived. The mean correlations found are shown in Fig. 5.3, These findings will be discussed further below, in relation to the likely effectiveness of various intervention strategies to reduce non-compliance and increase satisfaction.

Remedies 1: Improving oral communications

Techniques used to increase understanding and memory of, and (sometimes) satisfaction with, orally presented communications are listed below. Also given are the absolute changes in recall found in key studies of the techniques.

- Use of primacy effects (increased recall by 36%; Ley, 1972b);
- Stressing importance (increased recall by 15%; Ley, 1972b);

TABLE 5.3 Correlations between provider communication variables and patients' satisfaction, compliance and recall/understanding

Provider communication variable	Correlations with outcome variables		
	Satisfaction	Compliance	Recall/understanding
Information giving	0.33	0.16	0.40
Question asking	−0.08 (ns)	−0.24	−0.18
Technical competence	0.22	–	–
Interpersonal competence	0.33	–	–
Partnership building	0.27	−0.06 (ns)	0.29
Positive talk	0.26	0.08 (ns)	0.05 (ns)
Negative talk	0.01 (ns)	−0.05	–
Total amount of communication (provider and patient)	0.35	0.17 (ns)	–

All correlation significant at P < 0.05, except those marked (ns), which are not significant.

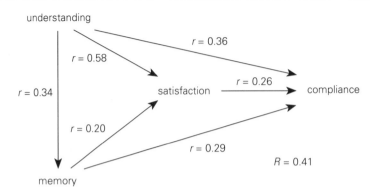

FIGURE 5.3 Relationships between understanding, memory, satisfaction and compliance.

- Simplification – use of shorter words and shorter sentences (increased recall by 13%; Bradshaw *et al.*, 1975);
- Explicit categorization – categorizing the material, listing the category names to the patient before presenting the information, and then repeating the appropriate category name before each category of information is presented (increased recall by 9–18%; Ley, 1979a; Ley *et al.*, 1973; Reynolds *et al.*, 1981) (This study did not actually use explicit categorization, but a half-distant relative thereof.)
- Repetition (recall increased by 14–19%; Kupst *et al.*, 1975; Bertakis, 1977; Ley, 1979a; satisfaction also increased; Bertakis, 1977);
- Use of specific rather than general statements (increased recall by 35%; Bradshaw *et al.*, 1975);
- Mixtures of the above techniques (increased recall by 9–21%; Ley *et al.*, 1976);
- Additional interviews to see that information has been understood (increased satisfaction by 3% to 33%; Ley *et al.*, 1976; Ley, 1983). (The intervention group has been compared with the combined placebo and no treatment group in Ley *et al.* (1976). This is probably the best comparison. Its result is a little worse than comparing experimental and placebo groups.)

In addition, phoned and mailed reminders have been used to increase compliance in appointment-keeping. In studies reviewed by Ley (1988), the mean absolute increase in the percentage of patients keeping their appointments was 17.1% (s.d. 7.2%).

It should be noted that although the use of reminders would be expected to increase recall, its effects on appointment-keeping might be due to other factors as well. Patients might perhaps see the clinic as a more caring place if it goes to the trouble of issuing reminders, or perhaps the reminder makes patients feel that they cannot use forgetting as an excuse for not keeping their appointment, and so on. (For a more detailed discussion of the use of reminders see Levy and Loftus, 1983 and Ley, 1988).

Remedies 2: use of written information

There are a number of reasons for considering the use of written information to augment or reinforce any oral communications. The first of these is that none of the oral techniques discussed above has been completely successful in eliminating problems of understanding, memory, satisfaction and compliance. Something more is needed. A second problem is that, even if such techniques were discovered, in the light of the evidence available on the frequency with which health care personnel fail to comply with recommended practices, it is unlikely that they would be universally adopted. Reviews by Ley (1981, 1988) of investigations of dentists, nurses, paramedical personnel, pharmacists, physicians, psychologists and surgeons found rates of non-compliance with recommended good health and medical care practices to range from 12% to 95%, with a mean of 60% and standard deviation of 27%.

In addition, there are a number of positive advantages in the use of written information. Its content can be more carefully thought out; it can be designed to maximize understanding and memory; it can be used for reference; and further, patients want it. Morris and Groft (1982) reviewed a number of USA surveys and reported that the median percentage wanting such information was 77%. Reviews by Ley and Morris (1984) and Ley (1988) confirm that the majority of people say that they would like written information about their medication and other aspects of their health care. A further example comes from a large-scale British investigation by Gibbs, Waters and George (1990), who reported that 97% of a nationwide sample of patients were in favour of receiving written information about their medication.

However, for the benefits of written information to be realized, the materials have to be noticed, read, understood, believed and remembered. There seems to be little direct evidence about how often written materials about prescribed medication are noticed, probably because it is assumed that they always are. However, the extent to which they are noticed can be inferred to some extent from the frequency with which patients claim to have read them: 49–97% of recipients claim to have read such information (Ley, 1988). Perhaps the best estimates are those derived by Ley (1988) from the 32 samples of patients in the Rand Corporation study for the US Food and Drug Administration (Kanouse *et al.*, 1981), and the data from a series of British studies (Ridout,

Waters and George 1986; Gibbs, Waters and George 1987; 1989a,b; 1990).

Across the US samples the mean percentage claiming to have read the information was approximately 72, with a standard deviation of approximately 9%. This investigation also provided data on the frequency with which patients kept and referred to their leaflets. Of those receiving the erythromycin, nitrazepam and oestrogen leaflets, the percentages claiming to have kept them for future reference were 54%, 57% and 45%, and claiming to have read them on more than one occasion were 32%, 22%, and 29%, respectively. In the British studies, Gibbs, Waters and George (1987) reported that 88% of 117 patients given a leaflet about their penicillin or non-steroidal anti-inflammatory drugs (NSAIDs) claimed to have read it. In a further investigation, Gibbs, Waters and George (1989a) found that 97% of 349 patients receiving a leaflet about NSAIDs, β-adrenoceptor antagonists or inhaled brochodilators claimed to have read it.

There has also been considerable research into the understandability of written information for patients, much of which has applied a standard readability formula to the information. These formulae enable one to predict how many years of schooling would need to have been successfully completed for easy understanding of the text in question. From this, and from knowledge of the percentage of the population who have completed that many years of schooling, it is possible to derive a rough estimate of the percentage of the population who would be able to understand the text. The formulae most often used in assessing medical information have been the Flesch Formula (Flesch, 1948), which yields a reading ease (RE) score, and the Dale–Chall Formula (Dale and Chall, 1948a,b). Others which have been used include the Readability Graph (Fry, 1968) and the SMOG Grading (McLaughlin, 1969). The cloze procedure (Taylor, 1953) has also been used. Further details of these formulae, the methods used in their derivation and their validity can be found in Klare (1963, 1974, 1976), while Ley and Morris (1984) and Ley (1988) provide reviews of problems connected with their use in medical contexts.

Investigations have included studies of information for diabetics (Thrush and Lanese, 1962); X-ray leaflets (Ley *et al.*, 1972); dental leaflets for children (Ley, 1973); patient package insets (Pyrzcak and Roth, 1976; Liquori, 1978; Holcomb, 1983); ophthalmic leaflets (French, Mellor and Parry, 1978); health education materials (Cole, 1979); informed consent forms (Grundner, 1980; Marrow, 1980); behaviour therapy self-help manuals (Andrasik and Murphy, 1977; O'Farrell and Keuther, 1983); welfare leaflets (Bendick and Cantu, 1978); written information about cancer (Department of Health, Education and Welfare, 1979b); a hundred leaflets and forms about a wide range of medical topics (Doak and Doak, 1980); and warning labels (Ley *et al.*, 1985). A summary based on the results of most of these investigations is shown in Table 5.4. For ease of comparison, results have been converted to the equivalent Flesch RE Score if another formula was used. Percentages likely to understand are based on USA 1979 Census data.

About a quarter of these materials would require college education for easy understanding, and thus would not be understood by approximately 70% of those aged 25 and over,

and by 83% of those aged over 65. Further, about a quarter of the over-25s and half of the over-65s would not be able to understand half of these written materials. The findings for the US welfare booklets are similar (Bendick and Cantu, 1978): 60% of these would be estimated to be too difficult for 70% of over-25s and 83% of over-65s. A quarter of the over-25s and half of the over-65s would find 87% of these leaflets too difficult.

More recent studies of written health materials in specific areas have reported continuing production of materials which are too difficult for their intended audiences, e.g. condom use (Richwald *et al.*, 1988); mental health leaflets (Le Bas, 1989); and cholesterol education materials (Glanz and Rudd, 1990).

It is clear that a considerable amount of written material for patients is at too high a difficulty level. The moral is obvious: anyone producing written information for patients should routinely apply a readability formula to it. If readability is low, then the material should be rewritten.

It will come as no surprise to hear that patients also forget written material. Ley and Morris (1984) reviewed studies of patients' recall of written information. In the small number of investigations which they were able to find, the mean percentage recalled ranged from 28% to 74%, with an overall mean of 60%. It would seem, then, that written information is

TABLE 5.4 Understandability of health-related written information for patients

Equivalent Flesch RE Score	Leaflets with this RE score (%) (n = 335)	Cumulative percentage of leaflets with this RE score or less	Percentage of population not expected to understand material with this RE score	
			All	Aged 65+
80 or more	1.5	100	5	12
60–79	31.7	98.6	10	23
50–59	40.3	66.9	23	50
30–49	23.9	26.6	69	83
Below 30	2.7	2.7	93	97

probably forgotten as frequently as orally presented information, but as we have seen, such written information can be, and often is, kept and referred to more than once.

Despite these problems, reviews by Morris and Halperin (1979), Morris and Groft (1982) and Ley and Morris (1984) found that the provision of written information about medication increased patients' knowledge in over 90% of investigations, increased compliance in about 60% and improved outcome in four out of seven. Similarly, Gibbs, Waters and George (1989a,b; 1990), in three large-scale studies, found that the provision of written information about their medication (β-adrenoceptor antagonists, benzodiazepines, diuretics, NSAIDs, penicillin) increased both patients' knowledge and their levels of satisfaction. For example, the mean percentage completely satisfied with the amount of information provided was 36.6% in the groups receiving leaflets, compared with a mean of 29.5% in the control groups ($t = 3.06$, d.f. 7, $P < .02$).

Written information can also be useful in other areas of health care. For example, Ellis *et al.* (1979) successfully increased patients' knowledge of their condition by providing them with a written copy of what they had been told; Young and Humphrey (1985) found that providing patients about to undergo a hysterectomy with a booklet about how to survive hospital and cope with anxiety, reduced distress and length of stay; Wallace (1986) found that one of the two booklets investigated reduced distress in gynaecological outpatients; and Ley (1986b) reported that obese subjects given written information alone showed weight losses ranging from 3.4 to 7.4 kg, which compares quite well with weight loss obtained by other methods. The chapter by Lewin in this volume also gives details of the benefits of written material for cardiac patients.

Written information can be improved. The simplest and most effective way of achieving this seems to be simplification, i.e. rewriting the material in shorter words and shorter sentences. Ley (1988) summarized the results of seven experiments involving 13 comparisons of the effects of simplification on recall of written information. In ten of these a significant increase in recall was found. The mean effect of simplification on understandability was equivalent to making the material understandable to people with 4 years' less schooling than would be required for understanding the control version. The mean increase in recall was approximately 55%. In addition, simplification was found to increase reading speed in an sample of elderly patients.

The effects of simplification on accuracy of medicine-taking were investigated by Ley, Jain and Skilbeck (1975), who compared three medication leaflets, differing in word and sentence length, with a control condition in which no leaflet was provided. The subjects were 160 psychiatric outpatients, and it was found that the easier the leaflet the lower the mean medication error. This result is shown in Fig. 5.4.

Surprisingly, more complicated attempts at improvement have not proved so successful. Thus, Ley (1978) reported that a package consisting of simplification, explicit categorization and repetition was only successful in increasing weight loss in obese women in one of three experiments. Kanouse *et al.* (1981), in the Rand Corporation study referred to earlier, devised a set of rules for improving written communications based on findings of laboratory studies of comprehension and memory. These included avoiding the use of negatives; using the active rather than the passive voice; using concrete nouns and sentences wherever possible; simplification; and filling subject, verb and object positions with important words rather than fillers. Incorporating these features into written information about medication had no effect on knowledge or compliance.

Other attempts to improve written information have involved the use of illustrations, cartoons, colour and highlighting of certain sorts

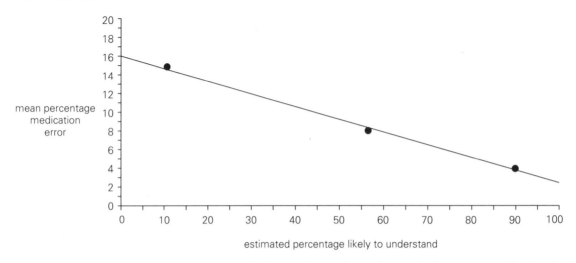

FIGURE 5.4 Relationship between percentage likely to understand a medication leaflet, as assessed by the Flesch Formula, and mean percentage medication errors in an outpatient sample.

of contact which it is desired to emphasize. No consistent findings seem to have emerged from this array of investigations. (For a more detailed review of these studies see Ley and Morris, 1984 and Ley, 1988).

Warnings: a subclass of written information

Increasingly, health care professionals are urging that patients, clients and the community in general should be warned about the possible hazards of medications, and other potentially dangerous products and behaviours. The minimal conditions for any health or warning message to be effective in achieving these aims require that it must be noticed; legible; read; understood; believed to be true; believed by its target audience to be relevant to them; and (sometimes) remembered. In addition, the label (or accompanying text) should ideally alert the user to the fact that there is a danger; specify what that danger is; and (preferably) specify what steps should be taken to avoid that danger. Finally, the message should lead to the desired behaviour change.

Research into factors influencing the effectiveness of warning messages in general has pro-duced the list of factors involved and possible methods for increasing effectiveness shown in Table 5.5 (Ley, 1991; Centre for Behavioural Research in Cancer, 1992).

In addition to the factors summarized in Table 5.5, it is known that the effectiveness of warnings is affected by familiarity with the product, amount of experience of engaging in the warned-against activity and frequency of exposure to the warning. All of these factors seem to reduce the effectiveness of warnings.

For example, in a series of papers, Goldhaber and de Turck (1988a,b,c) have shown that whether a warning sign about diving into the shallow end of a swimming pool was noticed by high-school students was related to swimming experience and history of diving into the shallow end of swimming pools or into above-ground pools. In a different topic area, Godfrey and Laughery (1984) found that women were less likely to notice a warning message about toxic shock syndrome on the brand of tampons they were using if they had previously been users of a different brand. There is also some evidence to suggest that the effects of warnings on perceptions of risk are reduced if people have had previous experience

TABLE 5.5 Desirable characteristics of a health message or warning and the psychological and physical packaging features which increase effectiveness

Desirable feature of message	Psychological packaging feature(s) likely to help	Physical packaging feature(s) likely to help
That it be noticed	Verbal symbol: e.g. 'Warning'; 'Danger' 'Hazard' Graphic symbol Novelty	Highlighting by use of: colour borders space different type face pointers Size Position
That it be legible		Contrast Where possible use matt, non-glossy, non-reflective surfaces Black letters on white backgrounds are easiest to read Size of type Print should be at least 8 point, and preferably 10 point Avoid text all in capitals Spacing leading of 1 or 2 points, depending on letter size and line length
That it be read	Ensure high 'readability' use short words use words familiar to the reader use short sentences avoid negatives Specify vulnerable groups Personalize message by use of 'you' Vary wording and content	High legibility
That it be understood	Ensure high 'readability' Explain technical terms Use active rather than passive sentences Be specific in any instructions Use headings where possible	High legibility
That it be believed to be true	Cite sources for the message who are likely to be seen as high in: credibility expertness attractiveness Use two-sided communications	

TABLE 5.5 *contd*

Desirable feature of message	Psychological packaging feature(s) likely to help	Physical packaging feature(s) likely to help
That it be believed by its target audience to be relevant to them	Explicitly mention target groups Deal with likely counter-propaganda	
That it be remembered if necessary	Ensure high 'readability' Use repetition Use specific/concrete statements Use explicit categorization Use primacy effect	Highlighting parts of message that need to be remembered

with potentially dangerous products. Thus, Karnes, Leonard and Rachwal (1986) reported that warnings had much less effect on perceptions of dangers and risks in the use of 'all-terrain vehicles' (cross-country mechanized vehicles with balloon-type tyres) among experienced than among naive users.

Further, Wright, Creighton and Threlfall (1982) investigated the factors determining whether people read product instructions or not. Among the determinants of whether people would read the instructions was their familiarity with the product. A related finding is that of the Centre for Behavioural Research in Cancer (1992), who reported that older (more experienced) smokers had a lower mean recall of four warning messages on cigarette packs than younger smokers, in each year following their introduction in 1986.

With regard to frequency of exposure to warnings, Skilbeck, Tulips and Ley (1977) compared the effect of a single presentation of a health warning with the effect of repeated daily presentations for a 16-week period on weight loss in obese women. All were exposed to a brief lecture on the health dangers of obesity and the benefits of weight reduction. All were given the same weight-reducing diet, and all asked to keep daily records of food intake on record sheets which were provided.

Half of the subjects (multiple-exposure group) had a reminder of the health risks of obesity printed at the top of their record sheets. The other half (single-exposure group) had no reminders or warnings, other than in an initial lecture presentation, which the multiple-warning group also received. The groups also varied in how frightening the initial lecture had been. Three levels of fear arousal were used. At all three levels, the women given repeated exposure to the message lost less weight than those who were only exposed to the message once: repeated exposure led to less weight loss. The most likely explanation for this finding is that the women receiving repetitions of the message had become accustomed to the idea of the dangers the message described. Results for the combined groups are shown in Fig. 5.5.

In addition, research into recall of cigarette pack warnings (mentioned above) showed that repeated exposure to the warnings does not lead to increases in recall after the first year. These effects on compliance and memory are likely to be due in part to habituation and extinction of the fear arousal elicited by warnings. This problem has been theoretically elaborated by Breznitz (1984), in a book on the psychology of false alarms. Breznitz argues that false alarms reduce both the credibility of warnings and people's willingness to take

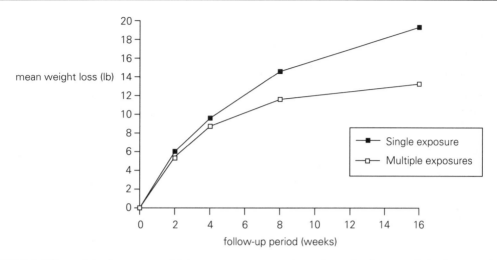

FIGURE 5.5 Effect of single versus multiple exposures to warnings about the dangers of obesity on weight loss.

health-protective measures. Taking smoking as an example, Breznitz states: 'Consider for instance the case of smoking. In spite of all the information to the contrary, one smokes a cigarette and nothing happens. One smokes another cigarette, and again nothing happens. Thus, in the absence of any clear signals that may indicate the dangers involved, these threats turn out subjectively to be false alarms'.

Some evidence that the credibility of warnings will be lower to those with greater familiarity with the product has been provided by Borland and Naccarella (1991) and the Centre for Behavioural Research in Cancer (1992). In these investigations it was found that the older the smoker, the lower was the belief in associations between smoking and various illnesses. It is also possible that the lower recall of warnings by older smokers is a further example of the effects of familiarity.

A further problem is that even 'true' alarms do not always induce people to change their behaviour. It has often been noted that, on average, those who have actually experienced a threatened accident or injury seem no more likely than those who have not had such an experience to take precautions in future. This has been found, for example, in relation to seatbelt usage after being injured in a car accident (Bragg, 1973), and safe storage of toxic products in households where a child has been poisoned (Baltimore and Meyer, 1969). Similarly, it is known that many smokers continue to smoke even after the 'alarm' has in fact eventuated and their emphysema or heart disease is well established and causing them problems.

Benefits of improved communication

The aims of improved communication include the following:

- Increased patient knowledge and recall;
- Increased patient satisfaction;
- Genuinely informed consent;
- Increased patient compliance;
- Quicker recovery from illness.

We have seen that patients' understanding and recall can be improved by a variety of techniques: primacy effects, stressed importance, simplification, explicit categorization, specific statements and repetition all increase patients' recall and understanding of their condition. The provision of written information also seems reliably to increase patients' knowledge and understanding. This is despite the fact that written information is frequently pitched at too high a level for its intended audience. The techniques of meta-analysis have also been applied to the assessment of the effectiveness of improved communication in increasing patients' knowledge and understanding. Mullen, Green and Persinger (1985) analysed a variety of methods likely to improve the communication of information, including the provision of additional face-to-face consultation, group education, written information and combinations of some of these. The mean effect size was +0.53. This can be interpreted as showing that the average patient who received these additional educational inputs had better knowledge and understanding than 70% of those who had not. Thus the provision of information increases knowledge and understanding. Also, understanding and recall can be further enhanced by the use of special techniques and by the provision of suitably prepared written materials.

Because most patients want to know as much as possible about their condition, it is hardly surprising that there is experimental and correlational evidence to show that informed patients are more satisfied. Using the Binomial Effect Size Display described by Rosenthal and Rubin (1982) in the manner suggested by Ley (1986a), it is possible to estimate that if all patients had adequate understanding, satisfaction rates would rise to somewhere in the region of 79%.

With regard to 'genuinely informed consent', there are major problems of definition (President's Commission, 1982; Faden, Beauchamp and King, 1986). It is easy enough to indicate situations where it does not exist, e.g. when patients are presented with a written consent form that they do not understand, a situation which, as we have seen, is probably all too common (Morrow, 1980). Clearly, a minimal requirement for informed consent is that the material presented to the patient should be understandable. It should also be constructed

and presented in such a way that patients can recall it, and thus reconsider it if they wish. Thus, techniques that increase understanding and recall can at least be said to contribute to the attainment of properly informed consent.

Evidence that techniques that increase understanding and memory can also affect compliance has already been presented. There have also been meta-analyses of this problem. In addition to summarizing the effects of techniques likely to increase understanding and recall on compliance, these analyses have also compared them with the effects of behavioural techniques (see DiMatteo and DiNicola, 1982; Epstein and Cluss, 1982; and Meichenbaum and Turk, 1987 for descriptions of these). Mazzuca (1982) reported a meta-analysis of what he classified as didactic and behavioural patient education. The didactic category included studies that used lectures, pamphlets, audiovisual media and prescription labels in an attempt to present standard information about the condition and its treatment to all patients with that condition. The behavioural category included studies that tried to individualize instruction for patients and fit regimens into their individual daily routines, and other behavioural techniques. The mean effect sizes were +0.26 for didactic techniques and +0.64 for behavioural techniques. Thus it would be expected that the average patient exposed to didactic techniques would be more compliant than 60% and the average patient receiving behavioural instruction more compliant than 73% of those given no such instruction.

Mullen, Green and Persinger, (1985) reported an effect size of +0.37 for the effects of instructional and educational methods on compliance with medication regimens. Behavioural methods yielded an effect size of +0.50. These figures suggest that the average patient exposed to such interventions is likely to be more compliant than 64% (overall result) and 69% (behaviour modification) of patients receiving no intervention.

A further way of interpreting the results of meta-analyses, if a baseline value is known, has been suggested by Ley (1987). If we take the weighted mean of the medication compliance studies reported by the Department of Health, Education and Welfare (1979a) as a base, this gives us an expected compliance rate of 52% without any intervention. Using Ley's method, it would be estimated that the use of Mazzuca's didactic interventions and the techniques summarized by Mullen *et al.* would increase the percentage compliant to 62% and 66% respectively. For behavioural techniques the corresponding figures would be 75% and 71%. These estimates are consistent with the average figure of a 23% increase in compliance in the review of behavioural methods by Haynes (1982) which, given a base of 52% compliant, would suggest that the use of behavioural techniques would lead to 75% or so being compliant.

Ley (1986a) also applied the Binomial Effect Size Display technique to this problem. Using the method in this way, it would be estimated that 68% of patients with adequate understanding, and 63% of patients with adequate levels of satisfaction would be compliant.

The conclusions from these studies are that both didactic and behavioural approaches can lead to improvement in compliance, but that the behavioural approach leads to greater gains. However, because of the expense of behavioural procedures, interventions such as the use of written information might be more cost-effective. For example, Ley (1986a) calculated that, if the use of written information increased compliance rates to 66%, then there would be a saving in the USA of 114–228 million 1979 dollars, just for the ten drugs reviewed by the Department of Health, Education and Welfare (1979a). Further complications in the interpretation of studies on the comparative effectiveness of informational and other intervention strategies are discussed in some detail by Ley (1988).

Finally, the effects of enhanced communication on the speed and quality of patients'

recovery, and on reactions to invasive investigative and dental procedures, have received attention. Narrative reviews have been provided by Ley (1977), Anderson and Masur (1983), and Mathews and Ridgeway (1984). All of these reviewers agree that psycho-educational interventions can reduce distress and speed recovery.

There have also been meta-analytic studies of this topic. Mazzuca (1982) reported that the mean effect sizes for didactic methods on progress and outcome were +0.18, and +0.19, respectively, suggesting that the average patient exposed to these interventions would be better off than about 57% of those not treated in this way. Behaviourally oriented methods were better, producing effect sizes of +0.74 for progress and +0.31 for outcome.

Mumford, Schlesinger, and Glass (1982) analysed the effects of interventions, including most of those already described, on recovery from surgery and heart attack. Educational approaches produced a mean effect size of +0.30. Thus the average patient receiving an educational intervention would be expected to progress better than 61% of those not receiving this intervention. These reviewers also reported that patients receiving interventions were discharged about 2 days earlier from hospital. However, the mean difference between those receiving an informational intervention and their controls was a little less, being only 1.21 days.

In another meta-analysis, Devine and Cook (1983) reported a mean effect size of +0.36, and confirmed that psycho-educational interventions reduced the length of stay in hospital, on average by 1.31 days, but more recent studies have yielded a lower reduction in length of stay. This might be because the value of psychoeducational intervention is now so well accepted that it has become part of the usual routine, or it might be due to the more analytical nature of the more recent studies, which have been trying to ease out the effects of different components in such interventions. This has inevitably led to the use of quite narrow and highly circumscribed interventions. Devine and Cook suggest that the best results are obtained with intervention packages with include more than one component. In conclusion, it is clear that providing information to patients leads to the fulfilment of the aims listed at the beginning of this section. Enhanced communication leads to better understanding and recall, greater satisfaction, better informed consent, greater compliance and better recovery from illness.

References

Adamson, T.E., Schann J.M. and Gullion, D.S. (1988) Patient feedback as a tool to influence physician counselling. *Patient Education and Counselling*, **11**, 109–17.

Anderson, J.L., Dodman, S., Kopelman, M. and Fleming, A. (1979) Patient information recall in a rheumatology clinic. *Rheumatology and Rehabilitation*, **18**, 18–22.

Anderson, K.O. and Masur, F. (1983) Psychological preparation for invasive medical and dental procedures. *Journal of Behavioural Medicine*, **6**, 1–40.

Andrasik, F. and Murphy, W.D. (1977) Assessing the readability of thirty-nine behavior-modification training manuals. *Journal of Applied Behavior Analysis*, **10**, 341–4.

Ausburn, L. (1981) Patient compliance with medication regimes, in *Advances in Behavioural Medicine, Vol. 1*, (ed) J.L. Sheppard, Cumberland College, Sydney.

Baltimore, C. and Meyer, R.J. (1969) A study of storage, child behavior, traits, and mothers' knowledge of toxicology in 52 poisoned families and 52 comparison families. *Pediatrics*, (Supplement) **44**, 816–20.

Barlett, E.E., Grayson, M., Barker, R. *et al.*, (1984) The effects of physician communications skills on patient satisfaction, recall, and adherence. *Journal of Chronic Diseases*, **37**, 755–64.

Bendick, M. and Cantu, M.C. (1978) The literacy of welfare clients. *Social Services Review*, March, 56–68.

Bertakis, K.D. (1977) The communication of information from physician to patient: a method for increasing retention and satisfaction. *Journal of Family Practice*, **5**, 217–22.

Borland, R. and Naccarella, L. (1991) Reactions to the 1989 Quit campaign: results from two telephone surveys. *Quit Evaluation Studies No. 5*. Victorian Smoking and Health Program, Melbourne.

Bourhis, R., Roth, S. and MacQueen, G. (1989) Communication in the hospital setting, a survey of medical and everyday language use amongst patients, nurses and doctors. *Social Science and Medicine*, **28**, 339–46.

Boyle, C.M. (1970) Differences between patients' and doctors' interpretations of common medical terms. *British Medical Journal*, **2**, 286–9.

Bradshaw, P.W., Ley, P., Kincey, J.A. and Bradshaw, J. (1975) Recall of medical advice: comprehensibility and specifity. *British Journal of Social and Clinical Psychology*, **14**, 55–62.

Bragg, B.W. (1973) *Seat Belts – Good Idea, but are They too Much Bother? An Analysis of the Relationship Between Attitudes Toward Seat Belts and Reported Seat Belt Use*, Department of Transport, Road and Motor Vehicle Traffic Safety, Ottawa.

Breznitz, S. (1984) *Cry Wolf: the Psychology of False Alarms*, Lawrence Erlbaum Associates, Hillsdale, NJ.

Caron, H.S. (1985) Compliance: the case for objective measurement. *Journal of Hypertension*, **3**, (Suppl.1), 11–17.

Carstairs, V. (1970) *Channels of Communication*, Scottish Home and Health Department, Edinburgh.

Cartwright, A. (1964) *Human Relations and Hospital Care*, Routledge and Kegan Paul, London.

Cartwright, A. (1967) *Patients and Their Doctors*, Routledge and Kegan Paul, London.

Centre for Behavioural Research in Cancer (1992) *Health Warnings and Contents Labelling on Tobacco Products*, Centre for Behavioural Research in Cancer, Melbourne.

Cole, R. (1979) The understanding of medical terminology used in printed health education materials. *Health Education Journal*, **38**, 111–21.

Dale, E. and Chall, J.S. (1948a) A formula for predicting readability. *Educational Research Bulletin*, **27**, 11–20.

Dale, E. and Chall, J.S. (1948b) A formula for predicting readability: instructions. *Educational Research Bulletin*, **27**, 27–54.

Department of Health and Human Services (1980) Prescription drug products: patient package insert requirements. *Federal Register*, **45**, 60754–817.

Department of Health, Education and Welfare (1979 a) Prescription drug products: patient labelling requirements. *Federal Register*, **44**, 40016–41.

Department of Health, Education and Welfare (1979b) *Readability Testing in Cancer Communications*, DHEW (NIH 79–1689), Washington DC.

Devine, E.C. and Cook, T.D. (1983) A meta-analysis of the effects of psycho-educational interventions on length of postsurgical hospital stay. *Nursing Research*, **32**, 267–74.

DiMatteo, M.R. and DiNicola, D.D. (1982) *Achieving Patient Compliance: The Psychology of the Medical Practitioner's Role*, Pergamon Press, New York.

Doak, L.G. and Doak, C.C. (1980) Patient comprehension profiles: recent findings and strategies. *Patient Counselling and Health Education*, 2, 101–6.

Ellis, D.A., Hopkin, J.M., Leitch, A.G. and Crofton, J.(1979) 'Doctors orders': controlled trial of supplementary, written information for patients. *British Medical Journal*, 1, 456.

Epstein, L.H. and Cluss, P.A. (1982) A behavioural medicine perspective on adherence vs long-term medical regimens. *Journal of Consulting and Clinical Psychology*, 50, 950–71.

Faden, R.R., Beauchamp, T,L. and King, N.M.P. (1986) *A History and Theory of Informed Consent*, Oxford University Press, Oxford.

Flesch, R. (1948) A new readability yardstick. *Journal of Applied Psychology*, 32, 221–33.

French, C., Mellor, M. and Parry, L. (1978) Patients' views of the ophthalmic optician. *Ophthalmic Optician*, 28, 784–6.

Fry, E.B. (1968) A readability formula that saves time. *Journal of Reading*, 11, 513–16; 575–8.

Gibbs, R.D., Gibbs. P.H. and Henrich, J. (1987) Patient understanding of commonly used medical vocabulary. *Journal of Family Practice*, 25, 176–8.

Gibbs, S., Waters, W.E. and George, C.F. (1987) The design of prescription information leaflets and the feasibility of their use in general practice. *Pharmaceutical Medicine*, 2, 23–33.

Gibbs, S., Waters, W.E. and George, C.F. (1989a) The benefits of prescription information leaflets (1). *British Journal of Clinical Pharmacology*, 27, 723–39.

Gibbs, S., Waters, W.E. and George, C.F. (1989b) The benefits of prescription information leaflets (2). *British Journal of Clinical Pharmacology*, 28, 345–51.

Gibbs, S., Waters, W.E. and George, C.F. (1990) Communicating information to patients about medicine. Prescription information leaflets: a national survey. *Journal of the Royal Society of Medicine*, 83, 292–7.

Glanz, K. and Rudd, J. (1990) Readability and content analysis of printed cholesterol education materials. *Patient Education and Counselling*, 16, 109–18.

Godfrey, S.S. and Laughery, K.R. (1984) The biasing effect of product familiarity on consumers' awareness of hazard. *Proceedings of the Human Factors Society, 28th Annual Meeting*.

Goldhaber, G.M. and de Turck, M.A. (1988a) Effects of consumers' familiarity with a product on attention to and compliance with warnings. *Journal of Product Liability*, 11, 29–37.

Goldhaber, G.M. and de Turck, M.A. (1988b) Effectiveness of warning signs: gender and familiarity effects. *Journal of Product Liability*, 11, 271–84.

Goldhaber, G.M. and de Turck, M.A. (1988c) Effectiveness of warning signs: "familiarity effects". *Forensic Reports*, 1, 281–301.

Gordis, L. (1979) Conceptual and methodological problems in measuring compliance, in *Compliance in Health Care*,(eds R.B. Haynes, D.W. Taylor, and D.L. Sackett), Johns Hopkins University Press, Baltimore.

Greenfield, S., Kaplan, S. and Ware, J.E. Jr. (1985) Expanding patient involvement in care: effects on patient outcomes. *Annals of Internal Medicine*, 102, 520–8.

Grundner, T.M. (1980) On the readability of surgical consent forms. *New England Journal of Medicine*, 302, 900–2.

Hall, J. and Dornan, M.C. (1988) What patients like about their medical care and how often they are asked: a meta-analysis of the satisfaction literature. *Social Sciences and Medicine*, 27, 935–9.

Hall, J. and Dornan, M.C. (1990) Patient sociodemographic characteristics as prediction of satisfaction with medical care: a meta-analysis. *Social Sciences and Medicine*, 30, 811–18.

Hall, J.A., Roter, D.L. and Katz, N.R. (1988) Meta-analysis of correlates of provider behavior in medical encounters. *Medical Care*, 26, 657–75.

Haynes, R.B. (1982) Improving patient compliance: an empirical view, in *Adherence, Compliance and Generalisation in Behavioural Medicine*, (ed R.B. Stuart), Brunner Mazd, New York.

Haynes, R.B., Taylor, D.W., Sackett, D.L. *et al.* (1980) Can simple clinical measurements detect non-compliance? *Hypertension*, 2, 757–64.

Hermann, F. (1973) The out-patient prescription label as a source of medication errors. *American Journal of Hospital Pharmacy*, 30, 155–9.

Holcomb, C.A. (1983) The cloze procedure and readability of patient-oriented drug information. *Journal of Drug Education*, 13, 347–57.

Kalish, R; and Reynolds, D. (1976) *Death and Ethnicity: a Psycho-Cultural Study*, University of Southern California Press, Los Angeles.

Kanouse, D.E., Berry, S.H., Hayes-Roth, B., *et al.* (1981) *Informing Patients About Drugs: Summary Report*, Rand Corporation. Santa Monica, CA.

Karnes, E.W., Leonard, S.D. and Rachwal, G. (1986) Effects of benign experiences on the perception of risk. *Proceedings of the Human Factors Society*, 30th Annual Meeting, 121–5.

Kincey, J.A., Bradshaw, P.W. and Ley, P. (1975) Patients' satisfaction and reported acceptance of advice in general practice. *Journal of the Royal College of General Practitioners*, 25, 558–66.

Klare, G.R. (1963) *The Measurement of Readability*, Iowa State University Press, Iowa.

Klare, G.R. (1974) Assessing readability. *Reading Research Quarterly*, **10**, 62–102.

Klare, G.R. (1976) A second look at the validity of readability formulas. *Journal of Reading Behavior*, **8**, 129–52.

Klein, R. (1979) Public opinion and the National Health Service. *British Medical Journal*, **1**, 1296–7.

Kupst, M.J., Dresser, K., Schulman, J.L. and Paul, M.H. (1975) Evaluation of methods to improve communication in the physician–patient relationship. *American Journal of Orthopsychiatry*, **45**, 420–9.

Le Bas, J. (1989) Comprehensibility of patient education literature. *Australian and New Zealand Journal of Psychiatry*, **23**, 542–6.

Leeb, D., Bowers, D.G. and Lynch, J.B. (1976) Observations in the myth of informed consent. *Plastic and Reconstructive Surgery*, **58**, 280–2.

Leventhal, H., Meyer, D. and Nerenz, D. (1980) The common sense representation of illness danger, in *Contributions to Medical Psychology* 2 (ed) S. Rachman, Pergamon Press, Oxford, pp. 7–30.

Levy, R.L. and Loftus, G.R. (1983) Compliance and memory, in *Everyday Memory*, (ed) P. Morris, Academic Press, London.

Levy, S. M. (1983) The process of death and dying: behavioral and social factors, in *Coping with Chronic Disease*, (eds) T.G. Burish and L.A. Bradley, Academic Press, New York.

Ley, P. (1972a) Complaints by hospital staff and patients: a review of the literature. *Bulletin of the British Psychological Society*, **25**, 115–20.

Ley, P. (1972b) Primacy, rated importance and the recall of medical information. *Journal of Health and Social Behavior*, **13**, 311–17.

Ley, P. (1973) Communication in the clinical setting. *British Journal of Orthodontics*, **1**, 173–7.

Ley, P. (1976) Towards better doctor–patient communications: contributions from social and experiment psychology, in *Communication between Doctors and Patients*, (ed) A.E. Bennett, Oxford, University Press, Oxford.

Ley, P. (1977) Psychological studies of doctor–patient communication, in *Contributions to Medical Psychology* 1, (ed) S. Rachman, Pergamon Press, Oxford. pp. 9–42.

Ley, P. (1978) Psychological and behavioural factors in weight loss, in *Recent Advances in Obesity Research* 2. (ed) G.A. Bray, Newman Publishing, London.

Ley, P. (1979) Memory for medical information. *British Journal of Social and Clinical Psychology*, **18**, 245–56.

Ley, P. (1980) Practical methods of improving compliance, in *Banbury Report 6: Product Labelling and Health Risks*, (eds L.A. Morris, M.B. Mazis and I. Barofsky) Cold Spring Harbor Laboratory, Cold Spring Harbor, Long Island.

Ley, P. (1981) Professional non-compliance: a neglected problem. *British Journal of Clinical Psychology*, **20**, 151–4.

Ley, P. (1982a). Giving information to patients, in *Social Psychology and Behavioural Medicine*, (ed) J.R. Eiser, Wiley, New York.

Ley, P. (1982b) Studies of recall in medical settings. *Human Learning*, **1**, 223–33.

Ley, P. (1982c) Understanding, memory, satisfaction and compliance. *British Journal of Clinical Psychology*, **21**, 241–54.

Ley, P. (1983) Patients' understanding and recall in clinical communication failure, in *Doctor–Patient Communication* (eds) D. Pendleton and J. Hasler, Academic Press, London.

Ley, P. (1986a) Cognitive variables and non-compliance. *Journal of Compliance in Health Care*, **1**, 171–88.

Ley, P. (1986b) Obesity in *Community Clinical Psychology*, (ed) H. Koch, Croom Helm, London.

Ley, P. (1987) A possible method for interpreting the results of meta-analyses of the comparative effectiveness of different treatments. *Behavior Research and Therapy*, **25**, 165–6.

Ley, P. (1988) *Communicating with Patients*. Croom Helm, London.

Ley, P. (1991) *Suggested Guidelines for Warning Labels: Report to the Preventive Strategies Panel of The National Health and Medical Research Council*. National and Medical Research Council, Canberra.

Ley, P. and Morris, L.A. (1984) Psychological aspects of written information for patients, in *Contributions to Medical Psychology* 3. (ed S. Rachman), Pergamon Press, Oxford.

Ley, P. and Spelman, M.S. (1967) *Communicating with the Patient*, Staples Press, London.

Ley, P., Bradshaw, P.W., Eaves, D. and Walker, C.M. (1973) A method for increasing patients' recall of information presented by doctors. *Psychological Medicine*, **3**, 217–20.

Ley, P., Bradshaw, P.W., Kincey, J.A. and Atherton, S.T. (1976) Increasing patients' satisfaction with communication. *British Journal of Social and Clinical Psychology*, **15**, 403–13.

Ley, P., Flaherty, B., Smith, F. *et al.* (1985) *A Comparative Study of the Effects of Two Warning Messages about Volatile Substances*, Drug and Alcohol Authority, Sydney.

Ley, P., Goldman, M., Bradshaw, P.W. *et al.* (1972) The comprehensibility of some X-ray leaflets. *Journal of the Institute of Health Education*, **10**, 47–53.

Ley, P., Jain, V.K. and Skilbeck, C.E. (1975) A method for decreasing patients' medication errors. *Psychological Medicine*, **6**, 599–601.

Ley, P., Skilbeck, C.E. and Tulips, J.C. (1975) Satisfaction, understanding and compliance in a general practice sample. Unpublished manuscript.

Ley, P., Whitworth, M.A., Skilbeck, C.E. *et al.* (1976) Improving doctor–patient communication in general practice. *Journal of the Royal College of General Practitioners*, **26**, 720–4.

Liguori, S. (1978) A quantitative assessment of the readability of P.P.I.s. *Drug Intelligence and Clinical Pharmacy*, **12**, 712–16.

McLaughlin, H. (1969) SMOG grading: and new readability formula. *Journal of Reading*, **22**, 639–46.

Mathews, A. and Ridgeway, V. (1984) Psychological preparation for surgery, in *Health Care and Human Behaviour*, (eds A. Mathews and A. Steptoe), Academic Press, London.

Mayou, R., Williamson, B. and Foster, A. (1976) Attitudes and advice after myocardial infarction, *British Medical Journal*, **1**, 1577–9.

Mazzuca, S.A. (1982) Does patient education in chronic disease have therapeutic value? *Journal of Chronic Diseases*, **35**, 521–9.

Meichenbaum, D. and Turk, D.C. (1987) *Facilitating Treatment Adherence: a Practitioner's Guidebook*, Plenum Press, New York.

Morisky, D.E., Green, L.W. and Levine, D.M. (1986) Concurrent and predictive validity of a self-reported measure of medication adherence. *Medical Care*, **24**, 67–74.

Morris, L.A. (1990) *Communicating Therapeutic Risks*, Springer Verlag, New York.

Morris, L.A. and Groft, S. (1982) Patient package inserts: a research perspective, in *Drug Therapeutic Concepts for Clinicians*. (ed) K. Melmon, Elsevier, New York.

Morris, L.A. and Halperin, J. (1979) Effects of written drug information on patient knowledge and compliance: a literature review. *American Journal of Public Health*, **69**, 47–52.

Morrow G. (1980) How readable are surgical consent forms? *Journal of the American Medical Association*, **244**, 56–8.

Mullen, P.D. Green, L.W. and Persinger, G.S. (1985) Clinical trials of patient education for chronic conditions: a comparative meta-analysis of intervention types. *Preventive Medicine*, **14**, 753–81.

Mumford, E., Schlesinger, H.J. and Glass, G.V. (1982) The effects of psychological intervention on recovery from survey and heart attacks: an analysis of the literature. *American Journal of Public Health*, **72**, 141–51.

Norell, S.E. (1981) Accuracy of patient interviews and estimates by clinic staff in determining medication compliance. *Social Science and Medicine*, **15E**, 57–61.

Norell, S.E., Alfredsson, L., Bergman, U. *et al.* (1984) Spacing of medications schedules t.i.d. American *Journal of Hospital Pharmacy*, **41**, 1183–5.

O'Farrell, T.J. and Keuther, N.J. (1983) Readability of behaviour therapy self-help manuals. *Behavior Therapy*, **14**, 449–54.

Parkin, D.M. (1976) Survey of the success of communications between hospital staff and patients. *Public Health, London*, **90**, 203–9.

Parkin, D.M., Henney, C.R., Quirk, J. and Crooks, J. (1976) Deviations from prescribed treatment after discharge from hospital. *British Medical Journal*, **2**, 686–8.

President's Commission for the Study of Ethical Problems in Medicine and Biomedical and Behavioral Research (1982) *Making Health Care Decisions*, US Government Printing Office, Washington DC.

Pyrczak, F. and Roth, D.H. (1976) Readability of directions on non-prescription drugs. *Journal of the American Pharmaceutical Association*, **16**, 242–3.

Reynolds, P.M. Sanson-Fisher, R.W., Poole, A.D. *et al.* (1981) Cancer and communication: information-giving in an oncology clinic. *British Medical Journal*, **282**, 1449–51.

Richwald, G.A., Wamsley, M.A., Coulson, A.H. and Moriskey, D.E. (1988) Are condom instructions readable? Results of a readability study. *Public Health Reports*, **103**, 355–9.

Ridout, S., Waters, W.E. and George, C.F. (1986) Knowledge of and attitudes to medicines in the Southampton community. *British Journal of Clinical Pharmacology*, **21**, 701–11.

Rosenthal, R. and Rubin, D.B. (1982) A simple general purpose display of magnitude of experimental effect. *Journal of Educational Psychology*, **74**, 166–9.

Roter, D. (1977) Patient participation in the patient–provider interaction: the effects of patient question. Asking on the quality of the interaction, satisfaction and compliance. *Health Education Monographs*, **5**, 281–315.

Roter, D.L., Hall, J.A., and Katz, N.R. (1988) Patient–physician communication: a descriptive summary of the literature. *Patient Education and Counselling*, **12**, 99–119.

Roth, H.P. (1987) Measurement of compliance. *Patient Education and Counselling*, **10**, 107–16.

Roth, H.P., Caron, H.S., Ort, R.S. *et al.* (1962) Patients' beliefs about peptic ulcer and its treatment. *Annals of Internal Medicine*, **56**, 72–80.

Rudd, P. and Marshall, G. (1987) Resolving problems of measuring compliance with medication monitors. *Journal of Compliance in Health Care*, **2**, 23–35.

Sackett, D.L. and Snow, J.C. (1979) Magnitude of compliance and non-compliance, in *Compliance in Health Care* (eds R.B. Haynes, D.W. Taylor and

D.L. Sackett), Johns Hopkins University Press, Baltimore.

Sanazaro, P.J. (1985) A survey of patient satisfaction, knowledge and compliance. *Western Journal of Medicine*, **142**, 703–5.

Sharf, B.F. (1988), Teaching patients to speak up: Past and future trends. *Patient Education and Counselling*, **11**, 95–108.

Skilbeck, C.E., Tulips, J.G. and Ley, P. (1977) Effects of fear arousal, fear position, fear exposure, and sidedness on compliance with dietary instructions. *European Journal of Social Psychology*, **7**, 221–39.

Tabak, E. (1988) Encouraging patient question asking: a clinical trial. *Patient Education and Counselling*, **12**, 37–49.

Taylor, W.L. (1953) Cloze procedure: a new tool for measuring readability. *Journalism Quarterly*, **30**, 415–33.

Thrush, R.S. and Lanese, R.R. (1962) The use of printed material in diabetes education. *Diabetes*, **11**, 132–7.

Tring, F.C. and Hayes-Allen, M.C. (1973) Understanding and misunderstanding of some medical terms. *British Journal of Medical Education*, **7**, 53–9.

Wallace, L.M. (1986) Communication variables in the design of pre-surgical preparatory information. *British Journal of Clinical Psychology*, **25**, 111–18.

Weisman, C.S. and Teitelbaum, M.A. (1989) Women and health care communication. *Patient Education and Counselling*, **11**, 109–17.

Wright, P., Creighton, P. and Threlfall, S.M. (1982) Some factors determining what instructions will be read, *Ergonomics*, **25**, 225–37.

Young, L. and Humphrey, M. (1985) Cognitive methods of preparing women for hysterectomy: does a booklet help? *British Journal of Clinical Psychology*, **24**, 303–4.

Chapter six

Institutional versus client-centred care in general hospitals

Keith A. Nichols

Introduction

Good teachers will monitor their pupils, assessing the need of each child and adjusting the teaching accordingly to suit those needs. Such a style is called pupil-centred teaching. In contrast, teacher-centred style follows objectives tied to issues *other* than how the pupil is doing, such as the teacher's own needs or a mechancial link with a syllabus and a narrow style of teaching. In general terms, good educational practice leans towards the pupil-centred approach, although never completely so.

General hospitals are institutions engaged with clients in a care-giving rather than an educational role. Nevertheless, there are sufficient similarities to justify asking if the hospital service should be seen as having a similar choice in approach. Ought the aim to be the creation of a system which is clearly client- or patient centred as opposed to institution-centred or, more specifically, administrator-, doctor- or nurse-centred? This chapter will serve as an argument for the client-centred approach to hospital care, and will try to convey some aspects of the character of such an approach.

Hospitals and institution-centred care

Where do things stand at the moment? This is not a new question: in 1980, Kennedy wrote:

> In the practice of medicine the consumer is the patient. His interests, which consumerism would seek to assert, are those of self-determination and the power to participate responsibly in decisions made about his life. The challenge to that power comes from the doctor who, in the exercise of his professional role, threatens to infantilise his patient, to undermine his power of self-determination, to act in a paternalistic manner.

Kennedy, like many others since, was both angered and depressed at the extent to which the institution-centred approach remains the dominant feature of contemporary hospital care in the UK. How has this come about?

It is a matter of history that the manner of creation of the National Health Service (NHS) in 1948 led to institutions which were almost wholly doctor-centred, primarily because the medical consultants were in a position to withdraw services if displeased (Gould, 1985). Added to this, the evolved emphasis in doctor training and initiation to the role similarly led to doctor-centredness (Hauser, 1981; Mizrahi, 1985). Other factors also played a part in maintaining this orientation; for example, the way in which the medical profession functioned in order to preserve its power position, in particular the maintenance of social distance and witholding information (Waitzkin and Stoeckle, 1972). Gould (1985), himself a doctor, views the situation in NHS hospitals as such an extreme case of doctor-centredness that he uses the phrase 'the medical mafia'.

Although the nursing profession has a wholly different role, training and background, equivalent problems are known to exist here too. Heyman and Shaw (1984) give a review of these, noting that nurse-centredness originates from the perpetuation of attitudes and practices which are basically defensive in nature, protecting the nurses from close emotional involvement with clients by the devices of fragmenting relationships, inhibiting initiative-taking and fostering subservience to medical authority. There is one encouraging difference, though: the problem is very much recognized and strenuous efforts towards change are being made through innovations such as primary nursing which emphasizes holistic care (McMahon and Pearson 1991). This trend is evident in the clear shift in emphasis in recent years seen in nursing periodicals such as *Nursing Times*.

Opposition to this institution-centredness is gaining strength in the UK, and more voices are heard in a plea to move towards a client-centred regime (Bennett, 1987; Coles, 1990; Nichols, 1993). However, in parallel to this, a new competitor has emerged in the form of hospital administration. Empowered by government legislation and armed with a brief to reduce spending, this expanding profession has, within a very short space of time, fostered a 'money-centred' regime in hospitals which can divert attention from individual client needs even further. It is a new and potentially very damaging form of institution-centredness. Planning decisions, resource allocation, staff management, staff welfare and the conduct of cases are now often influenced by criteria related to 'money-care' as distinct from health care and the need of the individual client.

Of what concern is this to health psychology? It has to be of *central* concern. Many health professions (e.g. nurses, speech therapists) concerned with the psychological well-being of people who are physically ill. They must deal with the fact that an institution-centred rather than a client-centred care regime bodes ill for hospital users. The issue is captured in the author's paradoxical personal experience: he finds that doctors and nurses, who are almost always of a caring nature, frequently foster a regime which is characterized by psychological neglect. This is rarely intentional, of course, but comes as a mechanical product of institution-centredness. The overall result, as described by Nichols (1987), is that *hospital-induced stresses* (as opposed to illness-induced stresses) figure to a large extent in the experience of the ill and injured. For example, because hospital staff are often out of touch with their clients' needs they attach little importance to the work of keeping clients reliably informed with usable information. There is normally no scheme to guarantee information provision, and thus the work is more often than not neglected. Similarly, because the personal needs of clients are not a key focus of attention, there has been sparse development in the emotional care of the seriously ill. In the earlier years at the renal unit from which these observations are drawn, the medical and nursing staff tended to treat normal, predictable emotional processes as if they were bacterial infections, that is, something to do battle with and 'put down', thus further stressing and isolating the clients with feelings of shame. The true needs of the clients lay in the opposite direction, that is, in the supportive companionship of a close, confiding relationship.

It would be inaccurate and quite unfair to suggest that there have been no improvements in recent years. There are some impressive examples of work that shifts care regimes towards a more 'whole-person' needs-related approach. This is especially so in the development of psychological care as part of the treatment for illness and disability. Davis and Fallowfield (1991) have collected a series of review articles covering fields such as cancer care, spinal cord injury, neurological disease, chronic pain and infertility, which demonstrate this. However, such improvements are almost always found to be the product of special projects or isolated to individual units and wards. The author knows of no instances in which whole hospitals have changed towards a more client-centred approach.

Information exchange and the institution-centred approach

A major need on the part of most seriously ill people and their partners is for good, clear, frequent and honest information. Waitzkin (1984) reports studies indicating that between 69% and 90% of doctors actively withheld information. In contrast, a similar percentage of people with advanced cancer wanted to have the information. Similarly, Reynolds (1978) confirmed that 97% of a group of cancer victims wanted full information. Speedling (1982) followed the fortunes of whole families dealing with the

aftermath of severe myocardial infarction. The lack of provision of information prior to discharge and subsequent abandonment of the family by the coronary care unit led to an enormous increase in stress, stress to which the unit staff remained oblivious. Ellian and Dean (1985) revealed the apparently grossly uncaring approach that consultant neurologists took in failing to inform 167 people of their diagnosis of multiple sclerosis, or caring for them in the ensuing reaction. Only 27% were spontaneously informed of the diagnosis by the diagnosing consultant, while 'a large group' found out by accident from casual remarks made by receptionists or domestics. Similarly, Newell, Gadd and Priestman (1987) discovered that 70% of a group of cancer victims relied on non-medical sources for information concerning their illness. Reynolds (1978) reported that 80% of patients in a general surgical ward had no advance warning, no explanation and no feedback on X-ray procedures. Ley (1988) and Stewart and Rotter (1989) present much more evidence on this general theme.

Coles (1990), in a most useful article, illustrates how people can emerge from even a well-intentioned interview with a doctor or nurse (that is, where there is a conscious effort to be client-centred by checking health beliefs, experiences and understanding etc.) still little the wiser, the problem being that the patient-centredness is superficial in that the person ends up being told what the professional assumes they need to know. In other words, actual needs are not really dealt with. The absence of a true client-centredness in hospital care can be very damaging. For example, the whole business of psychological care in terminal illness cannot even begin unless there has been full and honest information exchange. When this is absent, people suffer gross psychological neglect. Likewise, in general terms, it is known that most people need to be kept informed because, as Steptoe (1983) illustrates, stress and feelings of helplessness are generated in situations in which an individual has no control. No information inevitably means no control and, therefore, leads to needless stress.

Emotional care and the institution-centred approach

The doctor–nurse-centredness bias in care similarly leads to frequent failure to perceive the emotional needs of the seriously ill and, therefore, promotes a second area of neglect. Again, this is well documented but space allows only a brief example. Mayou and Howton (1986) review studies of the prevalence of psychological disorder in general hospital populations and also include comments on the performance of medical staff in detecting these disorders. Prevalence figures for medical cases under the age of 65 years ranged from 14.6% to 61%. Detection rates were acknowledged to be well below this but difficult to assess accurately, since both the screening devices and doctors' records which tend to be used as the index of detection have marked unreliability. However, in seven separate studies cited, the proportion of undetected cases of emotional disturbance ranged between 84% and 72%. Brody (1980) conducted a study in which the ability of 58 junior doctors to detect frank psychiatric disorder and recent stressful life events among 235 people in a general medical outpatient department was assessed. Despite knowing that the study was under way, the doctors failed to detect 34% of the psychiatric disorders and 76% of those people experiencing stressful life situations. Maguire (1985) reports much the same in his work with mastectomy cases, who were dealt with by both doctors and nurses: '... cancer causes substantial psychological morbidity. So it might be expected that most of it would be recognized and dealt with by the clinician or general practitioner. Unfortunately, this is not so'. The problem is so prevalent that worries are even voiced within the medical profession itself (Lancet, 1979).

This phenomenon is partly explained by the institution-centred mode of functioning in hospitals. In a previously mentioned study (Nichols, 1987), staff did not set aside time to discover how their clients were managing and what difficulties were being encountered. They were plainly out of touch, committing their time to issues other than assessing client needs. Of course, this was not the only reason. Inadequate training, poor role models, and the mobilization of individual psychodynamic defences to minimize personal trauma by maintaining a distant, blocking relationship with the seriously ill, are all factors known to influence the behaviour of doctors and nurses (Nichols, 1993).

Basis of client-centred psychological care

Pursuing the analogy with pupil-centred teaching, we might now reasonably ask how client-centred care in a general hospital would look – what would be different? This has, in fact, been the author's brief during the last 15 years: to explore the options within the general hospital system for improving psychological care by devising a means of shifting the bias away from institution-oriented care towards a system recognizing and dealing with the psychological needs of the clients. Much of this work has been conducted in a renal unit, but has included activity in coronary care, oncology, orthopaedics, etc. Early on, two things became clear. First, an approach urging medical, nursing or administrative staff simply to be a little more caring and offer a little counselling now and then is unlikely to change much. It is the neglectful elements of institutionalized attitudes and practice that need to be changed, rather than the behaviour of isolated individuals. Secondly, adding a sprinkling of clinical psychologists or more social workers to hospital personnel lists in order that they may attend to psychological casualties is also likely to prove ineffectual. Again, the real 'patient' needing treatment is the institutional orientation of the care system. To leave this system intact means that therapists will spend much of their time trying to undo the damage the system creates. Furthermore, their presence in such a role may possibly compound problems by letting in an atmosphere of 'leave well alone, the psychologist will deal with it'. Certainly, more psychologists and social workers are urgently needed in general hospitals, but their energy must go primarily towards creating a framework and motivation for change, together with a training/support structure to assist the implementation of any changes.

This chapter will not deal in any detailed way with the particular scheme of psychological care which has developed in the work at the renal unit. This has been described elsewhere (Nichols, 1989, 1993). However, it is relevant to outline the basic principles on which this scheme is based in order to highlight the features of client-centredness that are essential in this type of work.

Kornfield (1972) has described the impact that a modern technologically advanced hospital may have on people. Those unfamiliar with hospital life have much to learn and master. For example, apart from the shock and fright of illness and injury, engagement with the general hospital system can cause:

Geographic confusion — Where should one go? Where can one go? What is 'patient territory', etc?

Subcultural confusion — Who is who? Who does what? When are things done? What is good or bad conduct on the part of staff?

Role confusion — How is one to relate and behave? What is appropriate communication to staff? How are physical needs which do not fit work schedules to be met?

Close attention to the experience of the seriously ill and hospital users will reveal that such confusion adds to stress, and often means that people have to endure unnecessary discomforts. The client-centred approach would naturally bring an awareness of these demands on clients and seek to address them directly with an appropriate induction into the hospital environment. Ideally, this would be tailored to each individual's past experience and present knowledge. In straightforward terms this amounts to expanding the nursing role to include a basic teaching and guiding component. This has to be linked to an effort to enquire as to how people are coping and what aspects of hospital affairs, diagnosis and treatment they are confused, unsure or unhappy about. The key idea is that people using the hospital service need to understand it and be in harmony with it. For this to be so, the staff have to work at assisting them to gain understanding in a direct, practical way. As Coles (1990) illustrates, to be truly client-centred we have to help the client discover the questions they need to answer and, as Rutter (1989) shows, 'where they are coming from' in terms of health beliefs. Contrast this with the observations of Hawker (1983) that during visiting time on certain wards nurses *decreased* easy accessibility for questioning by anxious relatives through the device of apparent busyness and rush.

Perhaps the one feature of hospital life which endures to be the very flag of institution-centred care is the persistent use of the concept and role termed 'patient'. Effectively, the message associated with the patient role is one which ascribes powerlessness, helplessness and insignificance. A 'patient' sits or lies passively while all responsibility, decisions, procedures, basic care functions and planning are undertaken by the members of the institution, often without the person involved having access to knowledge about these other than fragments of information which may or may not be relayed. All this strips away personal status, dignity and control. Occasionally such dependence is necessary; usually it is not. Thus, in contrast to the phenomenon of learned helplessness, it has been argued elsewhere (Nichols, 1986) that entry into the typical general hospital involves the adoption of a role whose central feature is required helplessness. Schain (1980) writes forcefully on the disastrous effect that this 'paternalism in health care' can have on women treated for breast cancer or undergoing mastectomy: 'In any given anxiety-provoking situation, and especially in the face of major illness or radical surgery, people need to feel that they have some control over their lives and over the events about to occur ... the absence of power is strongly correlated with feelings of helplessness (or impotence) and is a precipitant to depression'.

Other than this general negative impact on the individual, the continuing use of the patient role has a paradoxical function in undermining medical endeavours. In many disabling or life-threatening conditions, survival, the degree of rehabilitation, the success of treatment and the risk of further physical complications have a close link with the motivation to comply with treatment and dietary regimen, together with a willingness to maintain good self-care skills. For example, the control of blood glucose levels in diabetics through rigorous dietary and insulin management may avert retinopathy, peripheral neuropathy and renal failure. The maintenance of good sterile techniques by people surviving with peritoneal dialysis may avert recurrent peritonitis and greatly extend the time available for the use of this technique (recurrent infections lead to a deterioration in the quality of dialysis). Similarly, the occurrence of a second myocardial infarction can be influenced by the degree of compliance with the regimen of diet, exercise, antihypertensives and change in life style. The author's experience reveals time and again that problems in compliance and self-care are often either created or compounded by the failure of hospital staff to introduce clients to a role which emphasizes personal responsibility and to then support them in this role by giving full involvement and information. A well disciplined and intimidated 'patient' is in no way prepared to take on the demands and rigours of self-care in the conditions mentioned above. Much the same will apply to any serious injury or illness in which an effort at personal mastery is needed for rehabilitation or survival.

Often, the immediate needs of the staff and institution are for a relatively passive, non-questioning, non-challenging person; hence the origin of the phrase 'the best patient is a comatosed patient'. It makes life easier to be sure: not having to make the effort to educate, inform and engage with the client on issues of personal feeling certainly has advantages for staff. The whole complex of roles, behaviour and attitudes centred around the notion of 'patient' is thus institution-centred. However, these same institutions find themselves having to deal with many more problems in the long term as a result, since poorly informed people who have known only the passive patient role are not well placed to become their own care agents, which is what has to happen in many instances.

Again, we should ask what might a client-centred alternative be like? The renal unit in Exeter has tried to work out a comprehensive scheme of care with a solid, psychological component, the so-called psychological care scheme (Nichols, 1993). Two aspects had to be taken into account. First, the successful operation of the psychological care scheme depended on people *using it*; secondly, surviving as a dialysand or dialysand's partner requires good physical and personal self-care. What the unit sought to establish was a role that emphasized client participation and mastery, but which at the same time felt comfortable to the staff. Thus the joint aims of the psychologist and nursing staff were formulated as follows:
We aim to create a situation in which:

1. We do not have passive patients but clients who are 'associates' to the health care team and are included wherever and whenever possible.

2. The clients are asked to honour the following *responsibilities* in terms of education and self-care:

   (a) to use the informational care facility in order to keep informed, thus reducing the stress of 'not knowing' and allowing participation in medical objectives and decisions;

   (b) to use the educational facility in order to achieve self sufficiency in dialysis, diet, exercise and physical self-care;

   (c) to use the emotional care and support facility in order to prevent isolation with stress and to promote a self-care awareness in stress and problem management.

One of the messages buried in this information is that an efficient and successful client-centred regime requires a reciprocal input from the client as well as from the staff. This is controversial, and arguments have often been put that people prefer not to have responsibilities or are unable to honour them when seriously ill. Certainly, to be truly client-centred this approach should be offered at the level of an invitation. A small proportion of people will have needs that take them, temporarily at least, into the conventional patient role of dependency and passivity, but the author's experience is that the majority of people gratefully take up the invitation and make the effort towards mastery. Kornfield (1972) cites an interesting study by Klagsbrun in which a programme of mutual care and self-care was set up on a residential cancer unit. The clients were progressively given more responsibility for looking after one another and themselves, even when very seriously ill. The study reports a very positive impact on morale, including that of the staff.

As another example of this type of approach the author has included some material developed at Exeter renal unit (with acknowledgements to Clinical Nurse Manager Polly Woodhams and Sister Julie Butler). This is used to make the run-up to a kidney transplant more client-centred. One of the problems in preparing people for transplantation is that there can be considerable individual variation, and standard information packages leave a lot to be desired. People must be adequately informed, though, so that they can maintain proper self-care. One way around this problem has been to assist clients in asking the correct questions, in order to obtain reliable and complete information. The following extracts illustrate the strategy.

The invitation:
'We have prepared and helped you to cope with life on dialysis and now we need to prepare you for living with your kidney transplant. By caring for yourself in a certain way, you may be able to extend the length of time that your kidney works for you.

Set out below are some very important questions. Your job during the next week or so is to arrange time with your primary nurse to obtain answers to these questions (your primary nurse is expecting you to do this), and any additional questions that you would like to ask.

It is also important for you to arrange to meet with the dietician and pharmacist to obtain information regarding diet and drugs; your primary nurse will help you to arrange this.'

The questions:
How long will I be in hospital?
Can I mix with other people when I leave hospital?
What if they have a cold?
Who should I contact if I feel unwell?
What form of exercise is suitable for me

and how much?

How should I treat my kidney – can I press it? What if it gets knocked?

Is there anything 'special' about my diet?

How much fluid should I drink? Do I need to measure and record it at home?

When may I return to school/work/household duties?

Would smoking be harmful to me?

Can I have normal sexual relations – are there positions to avoid?

Do I need to use contraception – what method is suitable?

What drugs must I take and how do I get supplies?

Are there any side-effects that I may experience from these drugs?

Does having a transplant control high blood pressure?

Does high blood pressure damage the transplant?

etc.

Finally, total repolarization to a mechanistically client-centred regime in hospitals should not be mistaken as the ideal. Staff also have needs and require consideration and care. A balanced negotiated compromise is most likely to succeed. We need staff who can explore clients' needs, articulate their own needs and construct an approach which mediates between the two. If psychological care is to become the practical consequence of health psychology, there is no other viable route.

References

Bennett, C. (1987) *The Wound and the Doctor*, Secker and Warburg, London.

Brody, D.S. (1980) Physician recognition of behavioural, psychological and social aspects of medical care. *Archives of Internal Medicine*, **140**, 1286–9.

Coles, C. (1990) Diabetes education: letting the patient into the picture. *Practical Diabetes,* **7** (3), 110–12.

Davis, H. and Fallowfield, L (eds) (1991) *Counselling and Communication in Health Care.* John Wiley and Sons, Chichester.

Ellian, M. and Dean, G. (1985) To tell or not to tell: the diagnosis of multiple sclerosis. *Lancet,* ii, 27–8.

Gould, D. (1985) *The Medical Mafia*, Hamish Hamilton, London.

Hauser, S.T. (1981) Doctor–patient relationships, in *Social Contexts of Health, Illness and Patient Care,* (eds E.G. Mishler *et al.*), Cambridge University Press, Cambridge, pp. 104–40.

Hawker, R. (1983) *Interaction Between Nurses and Patients' Relatives*, Unpublished PhD thesis, University of Exeter, Devon.

Heyman, B. and Shaw, M. (1984) Looking at relationships in nursing, in *Understanding Nurses*, (ed. S. Skevington), John Wiley and Sons, Chichester, pp. 29–47.

Kennedy, I. (1980) Unmasking medicine – consumerism in the doctor–patient relationship. *Listener*, 11 December.

Kornfield, D.S. (1972) The hospital environment: its impact on the patient. *Advances in Psychosomatic Medicine*, **8**, 252–70.

Lancet (1979) Psychiatric illness among medical patients. Editorial *Lancet*, i, 478–9.

Ley, P (1988) *Communicating With Patients*, Croom Helm, London.

Maguire, P. (1985) Improving the detection of psychiatric problems in cancer patients. *Social Science in Medicine*, **20**, 819–23.

McMahon, R. and Pearson, A. (1991) *Nursing as Therapy*, Chapman and Hall, London.

Mayou, R. and Hawton, K. (1986) Psychiatric disorder in the general hospital. *British Journal of Psychiatry*, **149**, 172–90.

Mizrahi, T. (1985) Getting rid of patients: contradictions in the socialisation of internists to the doctor–patient relationship. *Sociology of Health and Illness*, **7**, 214–33.

Newell, D.J., Gadd, E.M. and Priestman, T.J. (1987) Presentation of information to cancer patients: a comparison of two centres in the UK and USA. *British Journal of Medical Psychology*, **60**, 127–31.

Nichols, K.A. (1986) Self-care in medicine – overcoming obstructive health beliefs in staff and clients. *Proceedings of the London Conference of the British Psychological Society* (unpublished MS).

Nichols, K.A. (1987) Teaching nurses psychological care, in *Teaching Nurses Psychological Skills*, (ed. D. Miller), British Psychological Society, Leicester, pp. 5–14.

Nichols, K.A. (1989) Psychological care in renal failure, in *Psychological Management of Physical Illness*, (eds J.H. Lacey and T. Burns), Churchill Livingstone, London, pp. 261–282.

Nichols, K.A. (1993) *Psychological Care in Physical*

Illness, Chapman and Hall, London.

Reynolds, M. (1978) No news is bad news: patients' views about communication in hospital. *British Medical Journal*, 1, 1673–6.

Rutter, D. R. (1989) Models of belief–behaviour relationships in health. *Health Psychology Update*, 4, 3–10.

Schain, W. S. (1980) Patients' rights in decision-making. *Cancer*, 46, 1035–41.

Speedling, E.J. (1982) *Heart Attack – the Family response at Home and in the Hospital*, Tavistock Press, New York.

Steptoe, A. (1983) Stress, helplessness and control: implications of laboratory studies. *Journal of Psychosomatic Research*, 27, 361–7.

Stewart, M. and Rotter, D. (eds) (1989) *Communication with Medical Patients*, Brooks-Cole, California.

Waitzkin, H. (1984) Doctor–patient communication. *Journal of the American Medical Association*, 252, 2441–6

Waitzkin, H. and Stoeckle, J.D. (1972) The communication of information about illness. *Advances in Psychosomatic Medicine*, 8, 180–215.

Chapter seven

Caring: the costs to nurses and families

Sue Llewelyn and Sheila Payne

Introduction

There is increasing evidence that providing care for seriously and chronically ill patients is both stressful and damaging to the health of the carer, whether that carer is a professional or not. This chapter outlines why and how these stresses and risks to health occur, and what can be done to alleviate such problems. Since carers can be found both within and outside the health professions, caring by both families and nurses will be considered. After a discussion of the general conceptual issues involved, the focus will be first on caring families and their problems, and next on the difficulties faced by nurses who work with the chronically or seriously ill. It will be seen that although some of the problems faced by different types of carers differ, many of the issues are similar. Some of the coping strategies that have been developed to help these two groups of carers will then be outlined. A particularly important issue that will be highlighted here is the lamentable absence of conceptual clarity of many of these interventions in reducing the cost of caring. Finally, some suggestions will be made for alternative ways of dealing with what is likely to become an increasing problem in the future.

Nature of the problem

A number of different groups of people will be in need of a significant level of care from others for some part or even for all of their lives. These groups include the chronically sick or dementing elderly, the mentally handicapped, the physically handicapped, the brain-injured and the younger chronically sick, such as those suffering from multiple sclerosis, rheumatoid arthritis or strokes. The number of people requiring long-term care is increasing steadily, a trend which is unlikely to reverse in the foreseeable future. There are also major changes in the age structure of the population in Britain (Table 7.1).

TABLE 7.1 Comparison of the population structure 1900 and 1990 (from Midwinter, 1991)

Age group	1900	1990
% under16	31	20
% 16–60	64	64
% over 60	5	16

Since the beginning of this century there has been a marked increase in the number of people who live longer and a marked decline in the proportion of the population who are dependant children. It is estimated that by the end of this century there will be a million people over 85 years of age. The majority of elderly people are able to care for themselves, but about 10% of people aged 75 years or more are housebound or bedridden (Midwinter, 1991). The proportion of the population between 16 and 60 years who make up the labour force and provide the majority of care has remained unchanged. It is the relative proportion of informal care and services that need to be directed to younger and older people that has changed. A minority of elderly people do require services, such as supervised housing, meals on wheels and health care, rather more frequently than other groups in society.

Who are the carers?

Most of the bulk of caring for the old, the handicapped and the chronically sick undoubtedly falls into two groups: first families, and in particular women, and secondly nursing staff and social workers, in particular those working in non-teaching hospitals or in the community. These two groups of carers will be considered separately, although in the latter group most of the discussion will centre on nurses rather than social work staff. The issues for nurses are, however, remarkably similar to those for social work staff.

Carers within the home: families

Over the past few decades changes in philosophies concerning the nature of care, increasing medical sophistication and tighter financial stringencies have meant that the majority of people of all ages requiring constant care now live with their relatives, and are cared for by parents, a spouse or children. According to Rossiter and Wicks (1982) there are over 1¼ million people in Britain engaged in providing full-time care for a dependent. Much of this

caring work is essentially invisible, becoming visible only when there is a breakdown or crisis. Many caring families do not question their role in looking after their sick or handicapped relative, although considerable time away from other activities and disruption to family and social patterns may result.

The burden of care is not equally distributed among family members: caring is predominantly a female occupation. According to the UK Equal Opportunities Commission (1980), over 75% of carers for the elderly mentally infirm are women, and similar figures have been reported in families with handicapped children. The peak age of being a carer is between 45 and 64 years (Spackman, 1991). A study by Nissel and Bonnerjea (1982) showed that over 50% of wives caring for elderly relatives (who may well include the husband's parents) spent more than 3 hours per day caring, whereas their husbands did not contribute at all. These findings have been confirmed in studies by Levin, Sinclair and Gorbacj (1983) and Gilhooly (1984). Caring is also a very demanding occupation in financial terms: although 60% of carers also have paid employment, most work only part-time and suffer considerable financial hardship as a result (Equal Opportunities Commission, 1980). Nissel and Bonnerjea's study also showed that any financial assistance provided by the state did not effectively compensate for loss of earnings or increased financial demand.

Recent legislation (the NHS and Community Care Act, 1990) has recognized the needs and demands of the domestic carer's role. When this Act is implemented, dependent people and their carers will be assessed by a Care Manager who will provide a range of health and social services for the family. It is anticipated that people will have greater choice over the services they receive, and that they will be provided in their homes rather than in residential care facilities. Of course, what will be provided in practice will probably depend largely on

government funding policies and local implementation practice.

There is also growing evidence that providing care for a sick or handicapped relative has enormous implications in terms of demand on interpersonal relationships, and on the psychological and physical wellbeing of the carer. Using the example of caring for a handicapped child, Bicknell (1983) points out that 'a handicapped child is a handicapped family'. In other words, the fact of having to provide care is as disruptive to patterns of living as the handicap or illness itself. Nevertheless, it also has to be pointed out that caring for a loved one can bring many satisfactions, and while some may feel that caring is just a duty, others provide care because they dearly love the patient.

Carers from outside the home: nurses

Recent evidence suggests that the responsibility of providing care for the elderly or chronically sick is also very demanding on the services of professionals, and in particular on nurses and social work staff. The nursing profession (on which this chapter concentrates) is predominantly female, and recruits are found very largely from among school leavers aged around 18 (although the numbers of graduate nurses are slowly increasing). Staff turnover is high, and responsibility for wards sometimes falls on the shoulders of student nurses, simply because there are not enough staff nurses available to provide trained cover in all situations (West and Rushton, 1986). This situation is most likely to occur in areas which are relatively unpopular, such as geriatric or mental handicap nursing. Nurses are therefore often obliged to shoulder a considerable level of responsibility, sometimes at a very young age and without adequate backup. The growth of an ideology of community-based care has also led to an increase in the numbers of nursing staff working in relative isolation in community settings, again often without the immediate support of

their colleagues or supervisors. There is substantial evidence for high rates of mortality and morbidity among nurses, including deaths from suicide and stress-related disease (OPCS, 1978), burnout and absenteeism (Firth and Britton, 1989) and psychiatric and physical illness.

At the same time, the nursing profession is becoming increasingly confident. Many nurses are eager both to renounce the role of 'handmaiden' to the expert instruction of the doctor, and to assume yet more responsibility for patient care. In addition, changes in nurse education and the widespread adoption of the nursing process have led to the rejection of the detached professionalism of the past in favour of a more personally based service, in which the nurse has a real, human relationship with patients. All of these changes mean that nurses working with the elderly, the chronically sick or the handicapped are more likely than in the past to be working on their own, to be taking considerable initiatives and to be forming genuine personal relationships with their patients.

Stress in carers

Someone who is caring for chronically sick or disabled person faces a number of emotional, physical and, in the case of families, financial demands, and has a limited fund of resources with which to cope with them. This situation often leads to a complex of feelings and physical reactions known as stress. As already described in the chapter by Cox (this volume), there are a number of theories and models concerning the nature of stress. Many of these models are based on the rather simplistic assumption that stress is a fixed quality of any given situation or event, with the implication that what is stressful for one individual will be stressful for all, leaving little room for individual circumstances or variation. Many theories are also confused about whether stress is a physical or a psychological phenomenon, and about whether the appropriate way to deal with it is to alter the individual or to modify the situation. However, perhaps one of the more sophisticated of the models of stress is the transactional model described by Lazarus (1975) and Cox and Mackay (1981). This model, which will form the basis of the discussion of stress in this chapter, proposes that stress is a cognitive state with psychophysiological concomitants. According to Cox (1985), (see also Cox, this volume) stress is defined by a discrepancy between what individuals perceive to be their abilities and resources and what they believe is being demanded of them. In other words, stress results from an imbalance between existing resources and perceived demand. An important component of this model is the importance of individual perception: there is no 'objective' definition of either resources or demands. What is stressful for one individual may not be for another; furthermore, stress may result from either excessive demand or underutilization of resources.

An important component of this model is that it allows for the fact that stress can be alleviated, either by increasing individuals' perception of their resources or by altering their perception of the demands made upon them. Acceptance of this model would appear to have clear implications for those wishing to reduce the severity of stress in carers, both family and professional. Nevertheless, despite its apparent appeal and advance over previous models, a number of criticisms have been made of this model, notably by systems theories. These views are summarized by Handy (1986), who points out that the model's conceptual framework is inadequate in failing to note that, on the one hand, individuals may not be conscious of or able to label cognitively all the factors that are causing them to experience stress, for both organizational and intrapsychic reasons, and on the other, that attempts to solve the problem may fail to take note of hidden situational factors, such as the power structure

operating in the system. The implication of these criticisms is that the transactional model must be modified to incorporate the fact that a stressed individual exists within a particular context, and that the factors precipitating the experience of stress may actually be an important component of the stability of the system within which the individual exists. In other words, the system may well only be able to function at the cost of the stress of the individual; hence any attempt to uncover or reduce the individual's stress may well be resisted, not only by the system as a whole but also by the stressed individual, who may fear the collapse of the system or feel powerless or unwilling to change the situation. These points have considerable implications for attempts to reduce the stress experienced by carers, and will be returned to later in the chapter.

Stress in families

There is evidence that the process of caring for someone can lead to ill-health in the carer. The most reliable estimate of the prevalence of ill-health in carers is the 1985 General Household Survey (OPCS, 1988), the results of which are based on 18 500 interviews in a national sample. It demonstrates that about one-third of carers had an illness that limited their activities. In carers who spent 20 hours or more each week on caring tasks, and were over 45 years of age, about half reported a long-standing illness. Although it is difficult to prove a casual relationship between caring and illness, many factors in a carer's life may influence his or her health. The 1985 GHS found that 45% of carers spent 50 hours or more per week in caring. Many have regularly disturbed nights and they are expected to do heavy tasks such as lifting the dependent person.

The overwhelming picture of the experience of caring is that it is stressful. One of the best-known studies in this area was that carried out by Gilleard, Wall and Boyd (1981), who gave the General Health Questionnaire (GHQ) to relatives of elderly mentally infirm patients in order to measure the carer's level of psychological distress. Results showed that between 75% and 73% of relatives obtained GHQ scores above the threshold for psychiatric disturbance, with symptoms which were sufficient to warrant psychiatric diagnosis. Symptomatology was most marked in women, and was most clearly associated with demanding, disruptive behaviour of the dependant. Age or type of relationship with the patient made no difference.

This study was one of the first to suggest that a serious problem existed which was receiving very little attention from policy-makers. In another study, Thompson and Haran (1985) looked at carers for patients who had undergone leg amputations, and found that psychiatric symptomatology was present in 40% of carers. Levin, Sinclair and Gorbacj (1983), again using the GHQ, found that one-third of carers for elderly relatives were sufficiently psychiatrically disturbed to warrant psychiatric care for themselves. However, a study by Gilhooly (1984) found rather conflicting results: she reported that although morale among carers was low, mental health was either good or only mildly impaired. In agreement with the study by Gilleard, Wall and Boyd (1981), Gilhooly found that the mental health of the male carers was better than that of the female carers, but unlike Gilleard *et al.*, Gilhooly found that the longer the carer had been providing care the better their mental health was.

It may be helpful to consider one particular study in some detail. Hubert (1992), an anthropologist, worked closely with 20 families who had a young adult child with severe learning difficulties living at home. These young people were typically unable even to undertake basic self-care needs such as feeding and dressing themselves, some were incontinent and some were unable to use language. At times the par-

ents had to cope with disruptive and violent behaviour and epileptic fits. The constant caring demands of these adult children had had profound effects on the families, predominantly the mothers. Many mothers had established close relationships with their children but they had become isolated from their communities and, in some cases, other family members. The poor facilities available to learning-disabled people after they complete formal educational provision compounded the problems. Many parents were reluctant to use respite care because they found the custodial care offered, and the frequent use of antipsychotic drugs, were damaging to their child. This study highlights the ongoing nature of the stress that affects carers. The experience of people caring for Alzheimer's disease sufferers may be fairly similar.

These studies and others reviewed by Goodman (1986) suggest that the underlying source of distress for carers is, as implied by the transactional model of stress, an imbalance between the tasks of caring as perceived by the carer and the resources perceived to be available to the carer. The poverty of resources available stems in part from the financial drain of being a carer, due partly to the emotional demands associated with providing long-term care for a handicapped or sick relative who may not be able to provide much company or gratitude in return, partly to the physically tiring nature of the work, and in partly to the inability to replenish existing resources because of the isolated nature of the task. All these factors contribute to the experience of stress, especially when the tasks of caring are seen as never-ending.

In addition, there are more deep-seated causes of stress of which the carer may not be fully aware. These are feelings of anger, guilt and grief. Bicknell (1983) described the typical psychological response of parents when told of the handicap of their child as being essentially similar to that facing any bereaved parent, except that there are additional problems of adaptation and acceptance of their child in the long term. The parents may feel on some level that the handicap is a punishment for some past misdemeanour or immoral act, or may impute blame to their partner. Such feelings may never be voiced because on a conscious level they are acknowledged as illogical, and are also recognized to be socially unacceptable. The parents may also dread the future, or feel very angry with the child who has been born handicapped, but again will be unable to voice such feelings. Similarly, Cooper (1985) describes the immense distress of caring for the body of a beloved person whose personality and individuality have changed radically as a result of progressive disease, for example Alzheimer's disease. In these cases, unrecognized and unacceptable feelings will have to be suppressed and denied, which only adds to the sense of stress and resentment. These factors are not given adequate recognition even by the transactional model of stress.

Nurses and stress

Stress within nursing has been extensively described, although there has been an overemphasis on the learner nurse (Cundey, 1981), the specialist nurse, especially those working in intensive care units (Bailey, Steffen and Grant, 1980) and the nurse manager (Baglioni, Cooper and Hingley, 1990). Hipwell, Tyler and Wilson (1989) investigated the general ward nurse's stress and found that 'work overload' and 'death and dying' were the key factors. Foxall, Zimmerman and Bene (1990) compared the stresses of nurses working in intensive care, hospice and medical–surgical units. The overall levels of stress were similar, but differences were observed in the areas of stress causation. Intensive care nurses and hospice nurses were found to perceive more stress from 'death and dying' than the medical–surgical nurses, whose main stressor was 'work overload'.

Nursing is predominantly a female profession, with only about 10% male practitioners. The last 10 years have seen huge changes within the profession: the basic education has gone from an apprenticeship model, where students spent much of their time in the wards caring for patients, to a higher-education model. The new courses (called Project 2000) make much greater intellectual demands on the student and provide them with less time to develop practical skills. However, they have helped to reduce the high attrition rate from nursing courses, although this might also be due to the general economic conditions in the UK in the early 1990s, with high unemployment.

Nurses have also developed a systematic method of providing care, called the Nursing Process. This emphasizes the unique role of nursing care and challenges the nurses' function as subservient to medical care. However, the orientation to a more holistic model of care has placed demands on nurses who may not be skilled or even trained in more psychosocial aspects of care, such as counselling, (Fallowfield, 1991). Concurrent changes in the organizational structure of the NHS have altered the management role of senior nurses and introduced a business ethos of 'purchasers and providers' not previously present.

A recurrent finding in the nursing stress research is the perception of work overload or high demands. This is largely caused by inadequate staffing, and has been compounded recently by organizational change (Tyler and Cushway, 1992). It is certainly the case that hospitals are encouraged to achieve a greater throughput of patients, with a decrease in the average length of hospital stay and more day surgery. For example, a hernia repair operation, which formerly required 10 days in hospital, may now be treated as a day case. This means patients actually in hospital are likely to be more dependent and those discharged home may require community nursing services.

The second major area of stress in nursing has been related to specific aspects of patient care, especially to death and dying. The majority of hospitalized people die in general hospitals in ordinary wards, with only about 3% of deaths occurring in hospices. In the last decade there have been fundamental changes in the way dying people are cared for, probably as a result of the improvements pioneered by hospices. Palliative care is now a specialist branch of medicine and nursing. It is now common for cancer patients to be told their diagnosis. However, a number of studies (Field and Kitson, 1986) have found that a major source of stress is the perception of poor educational preparation of nurses to care for dying patients and their families. This may be increasingly important as patients no longer collude with staff in not discussing these issues. Likewise, the area of HIV/AIDS care may prove to be particularly stressful for nurses as they care for young dying people (Dworkin, Albrecht and Cooksey, 1991). Kelsey (1992) has argued that modern nurses are more aware of the problems faced by the families of the terminally ill, but they lack the confidence and competence to provide this total support. Nevertheless, it is also the case that communicating with sick and dying people and their relatives may be a source of satisfaction (Wilkinson, 1987).

Over the last few years, the way in which nursing work and nursing staff are organized in hospital wards has been regarded as affecting both the processes and the outcomes of care. The traditional pattern of nursing care was the allocation of tasks to individual nurses, who carried out each task on all patients (Merchant, 1985). For example, one nurse might take all the temperatures or give all the medicines. Tasks were divided into basic care or technical care. These had different status, and the nurse allocated to each task acquired that status. This care tended to produce impersonal, fragmented care for the patient. An alternative organizational approach, called primary nursing, has been demonstrated as having beneficial effects for patients and nurses. Qualified nurses using primary nursing care reported more supervisor support, more autonomy and less work pressure than those on traditionally organized wards. Nevertheless, this has problems too: nurses now feel more personally involved with patients and yet less supported emotionally.

These interprofessional issues, although superficially operating in different ways, actually combine both aspects of the transactional model of stress to predict high levels of stress among nurses. Some nurses may feel that their resources are not being used, whereas others may feel that they are taken for granted and not recompensed by recognition or gratitude. In other words, there is an imbalance between demands in terms of skills available and used, and resources in terms of recognition or support. In addition, as suggested earlier, the transactional model of stress is inadequate to explain the other issues which are also operating here. There has been little attempt by nurses to challenge the social system in which they work. Further, and as might be predicted, there are the ubiquitous communication difficulties that tend to occur in any large organization and which hamper the open discussion of such problems.

Similarities and differences between carers

As will have become clear, both families and nursing staff who work with dependent groups experience considerable stress. Nursing is a profession which is characterized by a number of features similar to those found within caring families: the need to be caring, considerate and respectful of the patient while performing intimate tasks which may be distasteful or distressing; the seemingly endless nature of the care, often without much prospect of recovery or cure; poor financial reward; the perpetual shortage of supervision or support from others, meaning that jobs are rarely done as well as they should or could be; and emotional demands inevitably involved in being in close contact with suffering or loss. Furthermore, as with domestic caring, nursing is female-dominated, with concomitant problems of status and recognition.

However, there are clearly a number of differences between caring for a patient at work and for a relative at home: although the emotional demand on nurses is considerable, they are obviously able to take breaks away from the job, but this is less possible for relatives. For example, Levin, Sinclair and Gorbacj (1983) found that 25% of carers studied never left their elderly relative or spouse alone, and 50% never left them alone for more than 3 hours. Nurses do have the opportunity to go off duty, an option not available to many carers. In addition, the family carer may not only have the practical burden of caring for the relative but, as noted, may also experience feelings of grief, anguish or guilt concerning the patient. It may in some ways be easier to care for a complete stranger than a loved one (Cooper, 1985). However, many nurses do form considerable attachments to their patients and may suffer feelings of anxiety or grief when they deteriorate or die. This is probably most acute when dealing with younger patients or children (Chiriboga, Jenkins and Bailey, 1983), but is also experienced by nurses working with the elderly and the handicapped, and AIDS sufferers of any age.

What can be done to reduce stress in carers?

This section will consider two examples of practical programmes that have been suggested as ways of reducing the incidence of stress in carers, both in families and in the nursing profession. A number of additional coping strategies will also be mentioned. It has to be pointed out that, although stress in carers is not new, it is only relatively recently that much attention

has been paid to the problem. Many writers have outlined the considerable cost to human service organizations of stress-related illnesses, and organizations representing the interests of patients have started to publicize the evidence that documents the demanding nature of the tasks carried out by carers (Ineichen, 1986). However, as has already been suggested, most attempts to deal with this problem have been based on inadequate models of stress, in that they tend to assume that the stress is caused by the quality of an event or situation, rather than the perception (conscious or unconscious) of an individual within that particular situation. Hence they ignore the fact that what is stressful for one individual may not be so for another, as well as assuming that what is helpful for one will be helpful for all. In addition, they frequently ignore the considerable systemic reasons for resisting attempts to reduce or remove stressful experiences.

Self-help and support groups

One of the most popular approaches to dealing with stress has been the establishment of self-help or mutual-aid groups and support groups (although the types of groups are technically distinguishable from each other, the terms will be used interchangeably in the following discussion). In all areas of health care, self-help groups have, over recent years, proliferated at a phenomenal rate: for example, Wright, Green and Hibson (1984) estimate that in the USA the number of self-help groups grew from 2000 in 1972 to over 500 000 in 1984, such that groups now exist which cover almost every type of illness, handicap, disorder or problem imaginable. Similar growth has been observed in the UK, where the provision of support groups for the relatives of the elderly, the handicapped or the chronically sick has also grown enormously. As an example, support groups for families with patients suffering from Alzheimer's disease are becoming more common (Ory *et al.*, 1985) and have been described as being 'an invaluable resource and source of social support' (p. 633).

Some writers, such as Pesznecker and Zahlis (1986), see the establishment of mutual-help groups for family care-givers as a major new role for community nurses, and provide suggestions as to how such groups can be set up and developed. They point out that, for the individual carer, sharing experiences with other care-givers can both reduce the problems of isolation and provide emotional and practical support. Some groups whose members care for patients who are incontinent, for example, supply members with information about the availability of aids or protective clothing, while others will simply create a forum in which a carer can unburden his or her feelings of isolation and grief. Yet other groups allow individuals to pool ideas and energies for fund-raising activities.

Although they seem to be a positive development, a number of researchers have recently expressed reservations about the helpfulness of some of these groups. Wambach (1985), for example, has described how a support group for widows imposed a view of the 'grief process' on members which did not allow for flexibility of individual experience. Further, in studies carried out by Llewelyn and Haslett (1986) and Block and Llewelyn (1987), some negative aspects of self-help or mutual-aid groups were noticed, such as the insistence by group leaders that members conform to the group's ideology, even when this appeared to conflict with the member's progress. Other problems included the domination by some individuals of the whole group, such that their views were imposed on other group members, since they felt that what worked for them must also work for others.

The difficulty in drawing any firm conclusions in this area is that many groups are not open to outsiders, and will only admit people who are both entitled and willing to become members. Objective research is therefore sadly lacking. It is only possible to conclude that self-help or support groups for carers may or may not be helpful, and that more information is needed about the ways in which they should function. Nevertheless, it does seem clear that an unexamined application of an oversimplified view of stress and its relief can lead to considerable problems for some members.

Support groups for carers in the nursing profession are also becoming more common. As with support groups for carers in the family, not much research has been carried out into the activities and outcomes of such groups. However, some studies do exist, and they indicate that such groups can be effective in combating the effects of stress in nurses. For example, Gray-Toft and Anderson (1983) describe a successful group in which nurses working in a hospice were given a 9-week counselling support programme in which discussion of recent stressful situations was encouraged, and techniques such as role-play and communication exercise were used to increase group support and individual skills. Results showed that measured stress diminished for these nurses, and satisfaction with co-workers increased. A reduction in staff turnover was also noted. Another set of studies by Weiner and Caldwell (1984) and Weiner, Caldwell and Tyson (1983) suggest that staff support groups can be helpful, but that they are likely to fail if seen by the nurses involved as having been imposed from above, or as being focused on the personal emotional problems of the members. They are likely to succeed if oriented around specific difficulties experienced in the workplace, such as the distress caused by the death of a particular patient. Lastly, a review of staff support groups by Kanas (1986) provides further evidence that, on the whole, staff support groups are an effective means of stress reduction in nursing staff, but such groups are most likely to be helpful when they have an active task-oriented leader, and least helpful when leaders or members attempt to use the group for personal therapy.

As predicted by the transactional model of stress, an important aspect in support groups is to allow individuals to decide for themselves what their stresses are and how best they can learn to cope. Nevertheless, it seems likely that the achievements of such groups will inevitably be limited, as they often fail to confront the organizational issues that lie at the root of many of the stresses experienced. It is interesting that they are most likely to be successful when they do look specifically at workplace issues.

Communication training for nurses

The second approach to be considered is applicable specifically to nurses, and concerns the provision of training in communication or interpersonal relationship skills. Such work has in part been based on the findings of researchers such as Cassee (1975) and others, which suggests that communication in health care systems is often lacking precisely where it is most needed, and where stress levels are highest. It is assumed to follow that better communication would limit uncertainty and anxiety, and thus reduce overall stress levels. Good communication between nurse and patient is also known to be helpful to the patient, and is associated with faster recovery and greater patient satisfaction (Ley, 1982; Hayward, 1975; Devine and Cook, 1983). It would therefore seem beneficial to all concerned to encourage better nurse–patient communication. This view underlies many recent developments in nurse education (for example Project 2000).

However, it has recently been suggested (for example, Fielding and Llewelyn, 1987) that such training, if carried out without attention to organizational issues, may actually exacerbate the problems it attempts to solve. As might be predicted from the criticisms of the transactional model of stress noted earlier, it

may be that poor communication actually serves several purposes, such as the protection of the emotional energies of individual nurses as well as the maintenance of organizational interests. The implications of this view are that communication training, if successful, would mean that nurses would be in even closer contact with patients' distress. Hence they might feel even less able to cope and might leave nursing in even greater numbers. Another more likely consequence is that such close communication would be resisted by the health care system, even while lip-service is paid to its piecemeal implementation. There are some suggestions that this is indeed the case.

Stress-management training for carers

Brief mention will now be made of some additional efforts which have been made to help carers to deal with the cost of caring. Some writers (for example, Ekberg, Griffith and Foxall, 1986) have suggested that relaxation techniques should be taught to the supporters of chronically ill patients in order to help them cope with the demands of caring, while for staff, von Baeyer and Krause (1983) outlined a stress-management course for nurses working in a burns treatment unit. In addition, Bailey (1984) and Murphy (1983) described a range of methods of providing autogenic regulation training for student nurses. Again, the key to success seems to be the opportunity for people to choose the means of stress reduction that suits them personally. Numerous studies have shown that relaxation procedures are an effective method for reducing general levels of anxiety, and are therefore likely to be effective for carers both within the family and in the profession, but again, they do not seem to be equally beneficial to all.

Other stress-management techniques which have been noted include the establishment of regular exercise patterns; the modification of diet; reorganization of personal routines; and the establishment of better social support networks (see, for example, Green, 1985; Constable and Russell, 1986; Evison, 1986; Llewelyn and Trent, 1987). All these approaches probably do have positive effects in reducing stress, especially if they are chosen and controlled by the individual who is experiencing stress. However, they may be at best irrelevant, and at worst actually counterproductive, if they are imposed on people without regard for individual circumstances.

Alternative suggestions

So far in this chapter it has been suggested that carers, both within the family and within the nursing profession, face considerable stress and that many of the attempts that have been made to deal with it are based on an inadequate understanding of the nature of stress. In this last section, some suggestions will be made for more appropriate and effective means of reducing the cost to the carers which involve more than a piecemeal attempt to bolster their individual attempts, and which do take account of the context within which the stresses occur. These suggestions are based on an acknowledgement of the importance of the points made by Handy (1986) and others, that people do not exist in isolation from their social contexts, nor are they always aware of all the personal and organizational conflicts underlying the stress they experience. Social systems may resist awareness of the costs and causes of stress, because awareness could lead to a challenge to the system itself, whereas individuals may resist awareness because the price of challenging the situation can appear greater in the short term than putting up with it.

Modification of the structure of nurse training and the nursing profession

If stress develops as a result of an imbalance between perceived demands and perceived resources, further complicated by the fact that perceptions may be distorted for both organizational and psychological reasons, then the nursing profession as a whole needs to devote considerable time and attention to understanding stress and translating that understanding into action (see also Chapter 4). To take an example, one repeated cry of distress from nurses is that they have less influence over the treatment of patients than doctors, even when they know individual patients much better than doctors do. Yet it is apparent that this occurs for political and economic reasons, not necessarily logical or medical ones. For an individual to point out that it should not be this way will not change the interests maintaining the situation as it is, and is not likely to be successful. It is also likely to be stressful for the individual concerned. Challenges are best made at an organizational and political level and, at the same time, support has to be provided for those who are challenging, since challenging often proves very expensive for individuals. Hence, nurses need to be taught about how organizations function, and why change is difficult and threatening to those who work in them. Only then will nurses be able to reduce their feelings of powerlessness and hence their experience of stress.

To take another example: nurses often complain that they feel stressed because they have too much to do and inadequate numbers of staff to do it with. Yet so long as nurses continue to accept the high turnover of their profession, workloads will remain too high, which will in turn lead to high stress levels: a never-ending cycle. The answer has to lie in collective change aimed to bring about alterations to the structure of nurse education and professional work in terms of pay, professional recognition, the provision of supervision and support, and so on. Nurses should not be asked to shoulder impossible burdens without emotional and practical backup, but so long as they do not protest effectively, they will probably be asked to do just that.

Family education and structure

Just as in nursing, stress experienced by carers in the family is caused by an imbalance between perceived demands and resources. It is also caused by feelings of anger and grief, which may not be recognized, yet most carers are not able to express these frustrations in any public forum, nor are they often encouraged to do so in the family itself. Until very recently, no financial assistance was given to female carers since it was assumed that caring was part of a woman's job and the cost to the economy as a whole of providing care allowances was assumed to be excessive.

Several changes to the structure of caring are therefore essential, both economic and personal and familial. First, it is essential that the financial cost of caring for relatives is recognized, together with an acceptance that care in the community should not be care on the cheap. Although money cannot possibly compensate for the distress of caring for a loved one who is dementing or who has been born handicapped, it can make life easier and less isolated. Carers should become more vociferous and public in their demands. Secondly, individual family members, and in particular boys and men, need to be educated to regard care for the sick, the elderly and the handicapped as an essential part of their responsibility in life. Only then will the burdens of care become more truly shared and some aspects of caring become less stressful.

It has been pointed out that all these issues are closely linked to the need for an increase in the status of women (Gunning, 1983). Consideration of the relative and roles of the two sexes is never very far from any discussion of caring, in nursing and in the family. It has to be anticipated that in a society which sees caring as predominantly women's work, and as something which should be provided without consideration for financial return or compensation, any attempt to change the balance will lead to an enormous degree of resistance from both institutions and individuals. More discussion of these issues, in the professions and as a part of general education, is clearly paramount if these problems are not to multiply in the future, with enormous consequences for the carer and the cared-for alike.

References

Baglioni, A.J., Cooper, C.L. and Hingley, P. (1990) Job stress, mental health and job satisfaction among UK senior nurses. *Stress Medicine*, 6, 9–20.

Bailey, J.T., Steffen, S.M. and Grant J.W. (1980) The stress audit: identifying the stressors of ICU nursing. *Journal of Nursing Education*, 19(6), 15–25.

Bailey, R. (1984) Autogenic regulation training and sickness absence amongst student nurses in general training. *Journal of Advanced Nursing*, 9, 581–7.

Bicknell, J. (1983) The psychopathology of handicap. *British Journal of Medical Psychology*, 56, 167–78.

Block, E. and Llewelyn, S. (1987) Leadership skills and helpful factors in self-help groups. *British Journal of Guidance and Counselling*, 15, 257–70.

Cassee, E. (1975) Therapeutic behaviour, hospital culture and communication, in *A Sociology of Medical Practice*, (eds C. Cox and A. Mead), Collier Macmillan, London, pp. 224–32.

Chiriboga, D.A., Jenkins, G. and Bailey, J. (1983) Stress and coping among hospice nurses: test of an analytic model. *Nursing Research*, 32, 294–9.

Constable, J.F. and Russell, D.W. (1986) The effect of social support and the work environment upon burnout among nurses. *Journal of Human Stress*, 12, 20–6.

Cooper, K. (1985) The person you loved has gone. *New Society*, 18 October, 106–7.

Cox, T. (1985) *Stress*, Macmillan, London

Cox, T. and Mackay, C.J. (1981) A transactional approach to occupational stress, in *Stress, Work Design and Productivity*, (eds N. Corlett and P. Richardson), John Wiley and Sons, Chichester, pp. 91–113.

Cundey, B. (1981) Coping with death – a time stress. *Nursing Mirror*, 3 June, 23–4.

Devine, E.C. and Cook, T.D. (1983) A meta-analytic analysis of the effects of psycho-educational interventions on length of post-surgical hospital stay. *Nursing Research*, 32, 267–74.

Dworkin, J., Albrecht, G. and Cooksey, J. (1991) Concern about AIDS among hospital physicians, nurses and social workers. *Social Science and Medicine*, 33(3), 239–48.

Ekberg, J., Griffith, N. and Foxall, M.J. (1986) Spouse burnout syndrome. *Journal of Advanced Nursing*, 11, 161–5.

Equal Opportunities Commission (1980) *The Experience of Caring for Elderly and Handicapped Dependents*, Equal Opportunities Commission, London.

Evison, R. (1986) Self-help in preventing stress build-up. *Professional Nurse*, March, 157–9.

Fallowfield, L. (1991) *Breast Cancer*, Routledge, London.

Field, D. and Kitson, C. (1986) Formal teaching about death and dying in UK nursing schools. *Nursing Education Today*, 6, 270–6.

Fielding, R.G. and Llewelyn, S.P. (1987) Communication training in nursing may damage your health and enthusiasm: some warnings. *Journal of Advanced Nursing*, 12, 281–290.

Firth, H. and Britton, P. (1989) Burnout, absence and turnover among British nursing staff. *Journal of Occupational Psychology*, 62, 55–9.

Foxall, M.J., Zimmerman, S.R. and Bene, B. (1990) Comparison of frequency and sources of nursing job stress perceived by intensive care, hospice and medical–surgical nurses. *Journal of Advanced Nursing*, 15, 577–84.

Gilhooly, M. (1984) The impact of care giving on care givers. *British Journal of Medical Psychology*, 57, 35–44.

Gilleard, C.J., Wall, G. and Boyd, W. (1981) Problems of caring for the elderly mentally ill at home. *Archives of Gerontological Geriatrics*, 1, 151–8.

Goodman, C. (1986) Research on the informal carer: a selected literature review. *Journal of Advanced Nursing*, 11, 705–12.

Gray-Toft, P. and Anderson, J. (1983) A hospital staff support program: design and evaluation. *International Journal of Nursing Studies*, 20, 137–7.

Green, K. (1985) Consumer views of self-care: promise of panacea. *Journal of RSH*, 2, 65–7.

Gunning, C.S. (1983) The profession itself as a source of stress, in *Nurses Under Stress*, (eds S.F. Jacobson and H.M. McGrath), John Wiley and Sons, Chichester, pp. 113–26.

Handy, J.A. (1986) Considering organizations in organizational stress research: a rejoinder to Glowinkowski and Cooper and to Duckworth. *Bulletin of the British Psychological Society*, 39, 205–10.

Hayward, J. (1975) *Information, a Prescription Against Pain*, Royal College of Nursing, London.

Hipwell, E.A., Tyler, P.A. and Wilson, C.M. (1989) Sources of stress and dissatisfaction among nurses in four hospital environments. *British Journal of Medical Psychology*, 62, 71–9.

Hubert, J. (1992) *Too Many Drugs, Too Little Care*, Values into Action, London.

Ineichen, B. (1986) The people who have half a mind to help themselves. *Guardian*, 3 March.

Kanas, N. (1986) Support groups for mental health staff and trainees. *International Journal of Group Psychotherapy*, 36, 279–96.

Kelsey, S. (1992) Can we care to the end? Do nurses have the skills for terminal care? *Professional Nurse*, January, 216–19.

Lazarus, R.S. (1975) *Patterns of Adjustment*, McGraw Hill, New York.

Levin, E., Sinclair, I. and Gorbacj, P. (1983) *The Supporter of Confused Elderly Persons at Home, Final Report to DHSS, Vol.1*, National Insititute of Social Work Research Unit, London.

Ley, P. (1982) Satisfaction, compliance and communication. *British Journal of Clinical Psychology*, 31, 241–5.

Llewelyn, S.P. and Haslett, A. (1986) Factors perceived as helpful by members of self-help groups: an exploratory study. *British Journal of Guidance and Counselling*, 14, 252–62.

Llewelyn, S.P. and Trent, D.R. (1987) *Nursing in the Community*, The British Psychological Society/Methuen, London.

Merchant, J. (1985) Why task allocation? A review. *Nursing Times*, Occupational Paper, 71 (28), 65–8.

Midwinter, E. (1991) *Oldness Equals Illness: the Association of Ill-Health and Old Age*. Institute of Health Policy Studies, Southampton.

Murphy, L. (1983) A comparison of relaxation methods for reducing stress in nursing personnel. *Human Factors*, 25, 431.

Nissel, M. and Bonnerjea, L. (1982) *Family Care of the Handicapped Elderly, Who Pays?* Policy Studies Institute, London.

OPCS (1978) *Occupational Mortality: the Registrar General's Decennial Supplement for England and Wales 1970–72*, HMSO, London.

OPCS (1988) *General Household Survey 1985: Informal Carers*, HMSO, London.

Ory, M.G., Williams, T.F., Emr, M. *et al.* (1985) Families, informal supports, and Alzheimer's Disease. *Research on Ageing*, 7, 623–43.

Pesznecker, B.L. and Zahlis, E. (1986) Establishing mutual-help groups for family-member care givers: a new role for community health nurses. *Public Health Nursing*, 3, 29–37.

Rossiter, C. and Wicks, M. (1982) The future of family care. *Community Care*, 22 September, 19.

Spackman, A (1991) *The Health of Informal Carers*, Institute of Health Policy Studies, Southampton.

Thompson, D. and Haran, D. (1985) Living with an amputation: the helper. *Social Science and Medicine*, 20, 319–23.

Tyler, P. and Cushway, D. (1992) Stress, coping and mental well-being in hospital nurses. *Stress Medicine*, 8, 91–8.

von Baeyer, C. and Krause, L. (1983) Effectiveness of stress management training for nurses working in a burn treatment unit. *International Journal of Psychiatry in Medicine*, 13, 13–125.

Wambach, J.A. (1985) The grief process as a social construct. *Omega*, 16, 201–11.

Weiner, M.F. and Caldwell, T. (1984) The process and impact of an ICU nurse support group. *International Journal of Psychiatry in Medicine*, 13, 47–55.

Weiner, M.F., Caldwell, T. and Tyson, T. (1983) Stresses and coping in ICU nursing: why support groups fail. *General Hospital Psychiatry*, 5, 179–83.

West, M. and Rushton, R. (1986) The drop-out factor. *Nursing Times*, 31 December, 29–31.

Wilkinson, S.M. (1987) The reality of nursing cancer patients. *Lampada*, 12, 12–19.

Wright, H.H., Green, R.L. and Hibson, M. (1984) The role of the self-help group in the delivery of health services to underserved populations in the 1980s. *Psychiatric Forum*, 12, 42–7.

Chapter eight

Patients' contributions to the consultation

Elizabeth J. Robinson

Introduction

This chapter identifies some of the ways in which patients can contribute to their consultations with general practitioners, not simply by giving an account of the symptoms they wish the doctor to consider, but by presenting their ideas about the diagnosis, cause or treatment of their problem, and by commenting on or seeking clarification of information, instructions and advice offered by the doctor. The author considers what might be the causes and consequences of patients' making or failing to make these kinds of contributions, and suggests possible ways of encouraging patients to make contributions which might help achieve the aims of the consultation.

Throughout the chapter examples will be provided of patients' contributions to general practice consultations which were tape recorded in Bristol and Birmingham as part of research projects funded by the Economic and Social Research Council, by the South West Regional Health Authority and by the West Midlands Regional Health Authority. Twenty-two doctors and their patients kindly allowed the author to tape record several of their surgery sessions, and the patients also agreed to being interviewed.

Incidence of patients' contributions

It is common for general practice consultations to open with the doctor inviting the patient to say why he or she has come. The patient may offer the doctor in return a fairly minimal clue:

D: What can I do for you today?
P: (Has recently had a baby) I'm a bit worried about inside.
D: Worried about what?
P: Well I don't know really.
D: What were you worried about might be happening?
P: Well the prolapse or something like that.
D: You want me to have a look do you?
P: Yes please.

On the other hand, the patient may offer, without prompting, an account of symptoms, a hypothesized diagnosis, a cause, an account of treatment which has been tried and a request for an alternative treatment:

D: What can I do for you?
P: It's my elbow again. It's extremely painful. I've been decorating you see. During the winter I get no trouble at all because I think it's covered up, but it's very painful. I wondered if you could give me some antibiotics. It's begin-

ning to weep now so it's getting a bit easier – it's like a boil you know. (further exchange)

P: Sunday night I didn't know what to do with myself. It's a bit easier now but as I say, once it starts. I keep putting it in warm water.

D: Yes, yes that's fine.

P: And once it starts to weep – but I think in future I will just have to keep it covered, do you?

When the consultation has moved on to discussion about management of the problem presented, some patients receive the doctors' suggestions only with thanks, while others seek to clarify those suggestions, and may make comments expressing disagreement with those suggestions: 'Are they likely to upset my stomach at all?'; 'What about lozenges?'. 'And that will stop the itching will it?'. 'We've tried this before, come to the conclusion it's a waste of time'.

Most patients behave in a way somewhere between the two quoted examples, but the evidence suggests that many patients lie towards the 'passive' end of the continuum, and relatively few towards the 'active' end Ley, 1976; Boreham and Gibson, 1978; Tuckett *et al.*, 1982, 1985. In the study by Tuckett *et al.* (1982), patients' behaviour during their consultation was rated and people were scored as having minimum participation, covert active participation (making indirect requests) or overt active participation. The patient's part in the consultation was divided into six tasks, such as presenting symptoms, requesting clarification, expressing doubts. For each of these six tasks, at least half of the patients fell into the minimum participation category.

The following sections will discuss possible reasons why patients tend to play such a passive role, whether it would be better if they were more active, and what are the possible ways of achieving a higher incidence of contributions. It will be useful first, however, to make a distinction between two types of patient contributions to the consultation:

1. Type 1: comments and queries, not directly invited by the doctor, which could in principle have been formulated *prior to* the consultation in that they arise from the patient's own knowledge and experience (although it will be suggested that sometimes contributions of this type are actually not clearly formulated before the consultation, but may become so during it or afterwards). The following are examples of this type, all of which were presented by patients in the absence of direct invitation by the doctor to present their views: 'I thought query mastitis'. 'Whether I'm getting used to the tablets or what'. 'My friend said you would probably squeeze them out'. 'Sometimes my hands go numb and that so maybe it's affecting my eye in that way'. 'Do you think it's connected with the throat?'. 'I'm not wildly keen on taking antibiotics and things, but I just feel it's going on a bit'.

2. Type 2: comments and queries, not directly invited by the doctor, which could only have been formulated *during or after* the consultation, in that they arise from information, instructions or advice offered by the doctor during the consultation (although it will be argued that some of this second type are not formulated until after the consultation). Examples of this type are: 'Take two in the morning. Both at the same time?'. 'Is that all right with the stuff I'm already taking?'; 'Eczema's not catching is it?' (patient's parent having suggested a diagnosis of measles, but been given a diagnosis of eczema); 'It would go on this long would it?' (doctor having diagnosed a strained ligament).

In studies of the extent of patients' participation in consultations, the incidence of contributions has generally been assumed implicitly to be determined by the same factors throughout the consultation. However, as will be shown later, different factors may be responsible for the incidence of each of these two types of contribution, and the presence or absence of each may have different consequences. Because of this the two kinds will be considered separately.

Contributions arising from patients' preconsultation knowledge and experience: type 1 contributions

Reasons why patients fail to make type 1 contributions

It is possible that some of the 'passive' patients really have no more to contribute: that they cannot verbalize anything more about why they have come or what they hope to receive from the doctor. Two days after the consultation by the woman quoted who had recently had a baby, the author interviewed her at home. There was no sign that she could elaborate very much on what she had been worried about: 'I wasn't feeling happy about inside, just having the baby, everything seemed a bit droopy. He's put my mind at rest, he said there's nothing to worry about, he'd keep an eye on me'.

A second possibility, however, is that some of the 'passive' patients could give a more complete account of why they have come to see the doctor, but some reason fail to produce it spontaneously during their consultation. It is understandable that patients who are worried that they have cancer or AIDS might be loath to verbalize their fears, but there are cases that appear to be much more straightforward. One example is of a woman who consulted her doctor about a mole on her ear:

P: It's that that's bothering me, I don't know what it is but it's grown since it came there – it's been there some time but just lately it's been itching and I've got the devil's own job to keep my fingers off and it's bothering me.

(further discussion and examination)
D: Yes well I think they're just moles both of them. I think the only thing to do if this is uncomfortable is to have it removed. (The woman was referred to a consultant.)

When this woman was interviewed at home 2 days later, she reported surprise at having been referred to a consultant: 'I thought there might be something I could dab on myself to get rid of it. (Did you ask Dr ... about that?) I didn't ask, you don't like to waste anybody's time on trivialities. I don't consider it's anything serious or radical. I don't like the look of it. It's the itching that pushed me up there'. She still wondered whether there was not some cream she could have used herself to get rid of the mole and hoped that I might be able to give her the answer. She did not ask her doctor the quick and straightforward question: 'Is there any cream I could use to get rid of it?', although her account of her problem was quite lengthy and contained considerable redundancy; in that respect she appeared not to be greatly concerned to take the minimum amount of time for her consultation.

A second example is of a woman who consulted her doctor about a discharging ear, from which she suffered every 2 years or so and which always cleared up when she used some drops. The doctor gave her a prescription for the drops, and when I interviewed her at home she said: 'I said to my husband this morning "My ear's better". (So have you stopped the drops?) I haven't stopped actually. You have a little bottle and they would last quite a long time but I've never been quite sure how long I should use it. Antibiotics you go on with them, don't you? I've never asked, it gets better so I stop usually. I don't remember anyone ever saying use the whole bottle like they would with antibiotics'. Again, for some reason this woman did not ask her doctor: 'How long should I go on with the drops?' This was a question which she could have prepared prior to her consultation, since she was expecting to be prescribed the usual drops, and it was a question which she could have been reminded to ask by the doctor's giving of instructions for using the drops. Yet she did not ask it.

These examples appear to be consistent with the idea that people may have ideas and questions formulated prior to their consultation which for some reason they do not produce during it. The way in which the doctor interacts with the patient, both non-verbally and verbally, is likely to be an important determinant of whether or not patients actually produce questions during the consultation. Clearly, doctors might, either deliberately or unintentionally, behave in ways that inhibit patients from saying or asking what they intended. It is also likely to be the case that, irrespective of what cues they are being given by this particular doctor in this particular consultation, some patients choose not to behave in ways which they judge to be inappropriate to the 'patient' role. Presenting one's own ideas about diagnosis, cause and suitable treatment may be considered to be inappropriate behaviour.

These are straightforward reasons why patients may fail to present views or ask questions which they report in post-consultation interviews. However, the fact that these views and questions are reported *after* the consultation may be relevant. Could it be that the consultation itself serves to clarify people's ideas, and that they can formulate views and queries afterwards which existed only in embryonic form beforehand? If this is the case, then it would not be accurate to describe these patients as having being 'inhibited' in the presentation of their views. A further reason why we might suspect that patients' preconsultation views may not be clearly formulated is that people who think it inappropriate to play an active part in their consultation may have no reason to plan beforehand precisely what they wish to say to or obtain from the doctor. Why would we expect to find clearly formulated ideas among people who have no intention of presenting them?

That people do have ideas about health and illness, and about when and why to consult a doctor, has been demonstrated by research connected with the Health Belief Model. These ideas may arise directly or indirectly from a variety of sources, both medical and non-medical (e.g. Stimson and Webb, 1975; DiMatteo and DiNicola, 1982; Pill and Stott, 1982; Baxter, 1983). The results of studies such as these suggest that consultation with the doctor is usefully seen as but one event in a chain, albeit a significant event, possibly having been preceded by considerable thought and planning, and possibly being followed by discussion with non-medical friends and relatives and pharmacists. However, we cannot tell from this research, nor from the research in which patients have been interviewed after their consultation, what form patients' ideas took immediately prior to their consultation.

Studies in which patients have been interviewed immediately prior to their consultation have asked them to indicate which of a list of possible 'services' they wish to obtain from their doctor (e.g. Lazare, Eisenthal and Wasserman, 1975) or which of a set of categories of information (about diagnosis, prognosis, treatment etc.) they hope to be given (Kindelan and Kent, 1986, 1988). This technique provides useful data about the relative incidence of different types of request, but we cannot tell from ticks on a questionnaire how clearly or vaguely formulated are people's wishes.

An implication of the suggestion made above is that one function of the consultation may be to clarify patients' thinking about the problem presented and its management. This may be particularly true of patients who have not had any interpersonal discussion about the problem prior to their consultation. This view is similar to one put forward by Bensing and Verhaak (1982) and Verhaak (1986). Verhaak has examined ways in which doctors help patients to reflect on their problem during the consultation. He argues that for many general practice patients all that is needed is that the doctor helps the patient to put his or her symptoms in perspective.

Consequences of failure to make type 1 contributions

It has been argued (Eisenthal and Lazare, 1979; DiMatteo and DiNicola, 1982; Pendleton *et al.*, 1984; Tuckett *et al.*, 1985; Weston and Brown, 1989) that the aim of the consultation should be for doctor and patient to reach mutual understanding and agreement about the problem presented and its management, and that this is more likely to be achieved if both make their ideas explicit. Value judgements about patients' autonomy and responsibility might underlie this view, but this aspect will not be discussed here.

Evidence consistent with this view is that significant failures of communication arise when doctors do not know what ideas and expectations patients bring to their consultation. Tuckett *et al.* (1982, 1985) tape recorded consultations and also interviewed people at length shortly afterwards and tried to ascertain which aspects of the doctor's information, instructions and advice they had understood and accepted, and what their understanding was of the problem presented. In a statistical analysis of 328 consultations with associated interviews, Tuckett *et al.*, identified several variables which were associated with whether or not patients gave an accurate account of, and understood, what had been said in their consultation. They found that consultations in which doctors 'inhibited' or 'evaded' patients' expression of ideas were more likely to result in failures of recall or understanding than those in which they did not. However, it appears that in nearly all consultations in which there was considered to be no inhibition or evasion, the patients had made no attempt to express their ideas. We cannot be

sure, therefore, whether it was the inhibition/ evasion which was relevant to the subsequent errors in recall, or whether it was the patients' attempts to present their ideas *per se*. This second possibility, along with evidence consistent with it, is presented by Robinson and Whitfield (1988).

Tuckett *et al.* (1985) examined a subsample of 60 the 328 cases in more detail, without statistical analyses, in order to try to pinpoint more precisely what factors were associated with misremembering and misunderstanding in patients' post-consultation accounts. They report that in this subsample, patients who gave accurate accounts were more likely than those who made errors to have received the diagnoses or treatment they said they expected. Tuckett *et al.*, conclude that: 'The explanatory framework with which patients entered the consultation was the crucial factor in determining what patients remembered and understood (p. 144). When there was a mismatch between doctor's and patient's views, the patient's views were not explored in the consultation and the consultation was 'unsuccessful' (unsuccessful here means that the patient misinterpreted or did not accept what the doctor had said about the problem presented or its treatment).

As suggested above, the assumption that post-consultation interviews provide an accurate account of the ideas patients held prior to their consultation, may not be valid. Nevertheless, whether patients were, in the post-consultation interviews, expressing ideas they had elaborated prior to, during or following the consultation, the evidence remains that there was apparently a link between the match or mismatch of doctor's and patient's ideas on the one hand, and the extent to which patients understood and accepted the doctor's ideas on the other. It seems that when a patient revealed, through the post-consultation interview, a personal view which differed from that of the doctor, that patient was likely not to understand what the doctor had said.

One possible implication of results such as these is that patients' post-consultation understanding would be more accurate if their ideas, however vaguely formulated, were made explicit during the consultation. That is, this kind of communication failure might be avoided if the doctor knew more about the patient's thinking, so that information, instructions or advice could be presented in a way that fitted more comfortably into the patient's frame of reference. This possibility is discussed further below.

It should, however, be mentioned that there may be negative aspects associated with active participation by patients. Tuckett *et al.*, report that more tension was apparent in consultations in which patients attempted to present their views than in consultations in which they did not.

Increasing the incidence of Type 1 contributions

The possibilities presented above lead to suggestions as to how patients might be encouraged to contribute more to their consultation. One obvious way of enabling patients to produce ideas and questions which they have formulated prior to the consultation is for doctors to make it clear by their verbal and non-verbal behaviour that contributions from patients are welcome. One possible risk here is that patients might feel so relaxed that they talk at length about their holidays and their grandchildren. We need to ensure that the doctor feels in control, and that talk remains mainly problem-oriented.

A second possible though perhaps not practicable way of encouraging patients to present preformulated ideas might be to help patients to plan precisely what they want to say before they enter the consultation. This same intervention might enable patients to clarify and/or formulate ideas. Roter (1977) carried out an

intervention of this kind with low-income black women patients. Women in the experimental group had an interview with a health-educator immediately before they saw their doctor. The health-educator went through a list of areas: aetiology, duration, severity and prevention of illness, medication, smoking etc. For each area, the patient was asked whether she had any questions. For example, the educator might say: 'Sometimes patients forget to take their medicine. Do you have any questions about what you should do if you missed taking your medicine?' When women said they did, and agreed that they would like to ask the doctor, the educator wrote the question down. The women entered their consultation with a list of questions which they had been encouraged to ask. Control patients went into their consultation with a similar-looking piece of paper which had telephone numbers of clinics, in order to disguise from the doctor which patients were in the experimental group.

Women in the experimental group did, as predicted, ask more direct questions, although their consultations were no longer than those of the women in the control group. Women in the experimental group were more likely to keep subsequent appointments. However, there were undesirable outcomes of the intervention: in the consultations of the experimental group, both doctors and patients expressed more negative affect, anger and anxiety.

Perhaps problems of this kind would be less likely to arise if the patient's comments and questions were produced at the doctor's invitation: instead of leaving patients to take the initiative in presenting their ideas or questions, the doctor could ask patients why they have come and what they think about the problem presented. The doctor's questions could not only elicit ideas which have already been formulated, but could also act as a way of clarifying and structuring the patient's thoughts. However, the recommendation that doctors should try to elicit patients' views in this way has been put forward by researchers who assume that patients have preformulated ideas about what is wrong with them and/or what 'service' they wish to receive from their doctor. If these ideas were made explicit, it is argued, the result would be more effective doctor–patient communication (Lazare *et al.*, Eisenthal and Wasserman, 1975; Kleinman, Eisenberg and Good, 1978; DiMatteo and DiNicola, 1982 Pendleton *et al.*, 1984; Tuckett *et al.*, 1985). For further discussion of this topic, see Hinckley, Craig and Anderson (1988) and Stewart and Roter (1989).

Lazare and colleagues have carried out a number of studies of what they call the 'negotiated approach' in psychiatric clinics. Here, the clinician aims to understand the patient's perspective about the problem and its management, recognizes the legitimacy of disagreements between patient and clinician, and tries to negotiate their resolution. In these studies, patients were asked to rate how satisfied they were with their consultation, and in one of them (Eisenthal and Lazare, 1979) the researchers recorded whether or not patients kept a subsequent appointment (a measure of adherence to the agreed plan of action). Sometimes the consultations themselves were coded in terms of the extent to which the clinician used the negotiated approach (Eisenthal, Koopman and Lazare, 1983). Sometimes there was no such coding and patients' ratings of, for example, the extent to which the clinician understood their requests were used to assess use of the negotiated approach. The results are consistent with the view that patients are more satisfied, and are more likely to keep future appointments, when the doctor either uses or is seen by the patient as having used the negotiated approach. However, in these studies we are given no information about what contributions the patients actually made, since there were no separate analyses of the doctor's

and the patient's role in the negotiation process. Furthermore, by far the most powerful predictor of keeping the subsequent appointment was whether or not the patient's request was met, and it is not clear to what extent the other measures were independent of this.

The apparent positive consequence of there being a match, as opposed to mismatch, between patients' and doctors' views, is consistent with the results of Tuckett *et al.*'s (1985) study, in that, as mentioned above, patients who understood and accepted what the doctor said had apparently often been offered what they expected. In Tuckett's data there were few if any examples of what Lazare and colleagues would consider to be the 'negotiated approach' by doctors, and Tuckett *et al.*'s interpretation was that if only the mismatch had been made explicit during the consultation, it could have been dealt with effectively so that doctor and patient could have reached agreement. From Lazare and colleagues' studies, however, we do not yet have a powerful demonstration that this is what happens when doctors invite patients to say why they have come and what they hope to receive.

The evidence available, then, while being consistent with the view that doctor–patient communication can be more successful when patients' ideas are made explicit during the consultation, is also consistent with the idea that whether or not that happens, the most important predictor of a positive outcome is that the doctor offers information and advice which fits easily into the patient's preconsultation framework. Clearly, one would not draw the conclusion that doctors should invite patients to present their ideas and then accept them whether or not they agree with them. However, perhaps in future research we need to look more closely at what happens when there is a mismatch, either implicit or explicit, between the ideas of the patient and those of the doctor.

Contributions concerning information, instructions and advice given during the consultation: type 2 contributions

Reasons why patients fail to make type 2 contributions

Some patients presumably do fully understand and accept the instructions and advice offered by their doctor, and have no need to ask any clarifying questions.

A second reason why patients fail to ask clarifying questions is that when the doctor presents information, instructions or advice, patients may think they understand and accept them only to realize later that they have doubts or queries. Robinson and Whitfield (1985) suggested that for various reasons, such as anxiety about the problem presented, concern about time or about appropriate patient behaviour, patients are likely to be inefficient at processing new information given during a consultation. A consequence is that they may think they have understood what has been said, only to discover later that they have not. This problem was not seen as particular to doctor–patient consultations, but as a more general difficulty with processing new information given orally in fairly stressful circumstances.

Robinson and Whitfield (1985) predicted that if patients were helped to be more efficient at checking their understanding of what was said during the consultation, they would become aware of uncertainties and would be able to raise these with the doctor. They should then emerge from their consultation with a more complete understanding of what their doctor wanted them to do. A study was carried out to test this prediction. Patients were given one of three forms of written information before they went in to consult their doctor. One form simply told patients that research was being done into how well doctors and patients understand each other, and asked for their permission to tape record their consultation. The

second form told patients in addition that people often think of questions once they get home after seeing their doctor, that it would be better if these questions were dealt with during the consultation, and that their doctor was very willing to answer any questions they might have about their problem. Patients given this second form, then, were given explicit permission to ask questions. The third form included the contents of the other two, but also advised patients to check their understanding of any instructions and advice they were offered: patients were asked to imagine carrying out such instructions or advice to see if any problems occurred to them, and were also asked to notice whether the instructions they were offered differed from those they expected. That is, these latter patients were given two strategies to help them process information more effectively. All the patients were then tape recorded in consultation with their doctor, and were interviewed immediately afterwards. In the interview they were asked to give a complete account of any instructions and advice they had been offered, with prompts from the interviewer until they said there was nothing more.

The people who had been given the advice to check their understanding differed from the others in two ways: during their consultations they produced a higher incidence of comments and questions which arose from instructions or advice given by the doctor, and in their post-consultation interviews they gave more complete and accurate accounts of the instructions and advice they had been offered. The people who were given permission to ask questions, but who were not given any strategy to use to check their understanding, behaved no differently from those who were told only the purpose of the research. However, the doctors who took part in this research were volunteers who were sympathetic to the aim of finding ways of increasing patient participation, and it may be that their patients were already aware that it was acceptable for them to ask questions.

These results were consistent with our idea that patients may fail to ask clarifying questions about what the doctor says because they are not aware of those questions during the consultation. It appeared to be the case that helping patients to process new information more effectively and to check their understanding made them aware of questions, and also allowed them to achieve a better understanding of what had been suggested.

Consequences of failure to make type 2 contributions

If patients do indeed have questions and doubts about what the doctor said during their consultation, it is presumably better to raise them during the consultation rather than make a guess about what was meant or have to seek clarification from friends, relatives or the pharmacist. There may also be misunderstandings and misrememberings which remain undetected by patients, who then unintentionally fail to carry out the instructions.

Without feedback from patients, doctors have little evidence on which to judge whether they have presented instructions and advice in a way which will keep the patient to understand and remember them. Patients' diffidence during the consultation has been seen as a major cause of failures to remember and/or understand instructions and advice. This in turn is likely to be an important cause of unintentional non-compliance. This argument and the evidence for it are presented by Ley (1976); see also Ley and Llewelyn, this volume.

As would be predicted on the basis of this argument, Heszen-Klemens and Lapinska (1984) found more accurate recall among patients who asked more questions. However, results which at first sight are inconsistent with the view presented above are reported by Anderson (1979), who found no association

between patients' level of participation in the consultation and their recall of information given. Alternatively, it may be that if patients' initiatives had been subdivided, for example into those that expressed ideas which could have been formulated prior to the consultation (which may be unrelated to recall) and those that sought to clarify information given during the consultation (which seem likely to be related to recall), clearer relationships would have emerged. However, in a study of customers' recall of information given by community pharmacists (rather than by doctors), Wilson et al. (1992) found that customers who asked more questions received more information and remembered more, but also forgot more, than did customers who played a more passive role.

Further results which appear to cast doubt on Ley's case concern the extent to which patients forget (rather than misunderstand) what the doctor says to them. Until recently, the evidence consistently demonstrated a high incidence of forgetting and/or misunderstanding by patients (e.g. Ley and Spelman, 1965; Ley, 1976, 1982; Anderson, 1979; Anderson. et al., 1979). This evidence, along with suggestions for reducing levels of forgetting, has been widely disseminated to practitioners. However, Tuckett, Boulton and Olson (1985) report that in their large study, recall of the main points made in the consultation was high. A similar finding is reported by Pendleton in work which is unpublished. Tuckett's et al. (1985) more detailed analysis of which patients fail to remember and/or understand what the doctor said has already been summarized. In this section the focus is on the overall incidence of forgetting and/or misunderstanding.) Tuckett et al., draw a firm distinction between accuracy of recall and accuracy of understanding, a distinction which it has been found difficult to maintain (Robinson and Whitfield, 1985, 1987a,b). For example, one woman was asked to note when pains in her arm occurred, and was told that if the pain came when she was at rest it was not significant, but if it came after excessive use it was more worrying. In her post-consultation interview, the woman reported these two possibilities the wrong way round. Was this because she was trying to remember by rote without understanding the underlying reasoning? If so, had she failed to remember or failed to understand? What follows will treat failures to remember and to understand as a single problem.

Tuckett *et al.* (1985) suggest that Ley's technique of questioning patients may not have made the task demands clear to them. They also suggest that giving equal weighting to all the points made by the doctor is inappropriate, on the grounds that patients detect and remember the more important aspects. These criticisms seem valid (although the former does not apply to Anderson's work), but there is also a problem with the Tuckett study in that patients were helped to reconstruct the whole consultation in a way which presumably would not happen if they were not taking part in a research project. The fact that patients can remember most of what was said when helped to do so may not be relevant to their recall in everyday life.

However, there is another difference between the studies: in those in which a high incidence of forgetting was found, patients were interviewed immediately after leaving their consultation, but in Tuckett *et al.*'s (1985) study, interviews took place a few days after the consultation. Whereas a simple learning theory account would lead to the expectation that recall would be highest immediately after input, a cognitive account would predict that recall might be better after patients have had time to reflect upon what has been said, and to begin to carry out instructions. Patients may also have experienced events relevant to the instructions and advice offered, which could have reminded them of the doctor's suggestions. For example, one mother in the

author's sample was advised that her daughter, suffering from measles, might develop discomfort in her eyes, and that if this happened the mother could phone in for some drops. In an immediate post-consultation interview the mother failed to report this suggestion, but in a later home interview it appeared that problems with the child's eyes had arisen and the mother had remembered to ask for drops. It may be that home interviews are more likely than immediate post-consultation ones to provide evidence which is relevant to non-compliance.

In one study (Robinson and Whitfield, 1988) the authors interviewed 81 patients both immediately after their consultation and again at home 2 days later. In the immediate post-consultation interview, 28 patients made at least one error or omission in their account of the instructions and advice they had been offered, but in the home interview, eight of them gave fully complete and accurate accounts. Nevertheless, 20 patients made the same error or omission in both interviews, and we can assume that those people really did forget, misunderstand or fail to take in what the doctor had suggested.

Quite apart from misremembering what the doctor said, a substantial proportion of patients report 'residual queries', that is questions they wish they had asked the doctor at the time. In a study by Robinson and Ross (1990), the authors initially construed these as a sign of communication failure, along with misremembering and misunderstanding what had been said. Patients were interviewed immediately before they consulted their doctor, and again 2 days later. The expectation was that people who arrived well prepared for their consultation, having thought about possible diagnoses, causes and treatments of their problem, would take a more active part in their consultation and be less likely to report residual queries afterwards. However, results suggested that these preconceptions were too simplistic, and there were a number of variables associated with the incidence if residual queries. It appeared that patients who think in depth about their problem may continue to think about it after the consultation, and hence to become aware of further queries. Residual queries may not always be a sign of communication failure, but rather one sign of a thoughtful patient.

Increasing the incidence of type 2 contributions

What follows assumes that there is indeed a significant incidence of forgetting and/or misunderstanding by patients of doctors' instructions and advice. One approach to solving these problems has been to presume that patients will be reticent, and to identify ways in which doctors can present instructions and advice in such a way as to maximize the chances that patients will remember them (Ley, 1983). For example, there is evidence that people remember advice better when it is presented in specific rather than general form: 'Aim to lose three pounds in the next fortnight', rather than 'Try to lose weight' (Bradshaw *et al.*, (1975), and when it is structured for the patient rather than unstructured: 'I'll tell you what's wrong with you, what the treatment will be, and what you must do to help yourself. Now, what's wrong with you ...' (Ley *et al.*, 1973). Clearly, it is valuable to know how to present information in the way which is most easily remembered, but this approach has limitations in that the doctor remains unaware of the individual needs and concerns of the patient, and idiosyncratic queries may not be dealt with.

An alternative approach, which arises from the suggestion that patients fail to check their understanding of what the doctor says, is to identify ways in which doctors might help patients to process new information more effectively, and thereby formulate comments and queries about what has been said. That is,

we might try to find out how doctors themselves can achieve the same outcome as the written advice to check understanding which was used by Robinson and Whitfield (1985).

In a series of informal studies carried out in collaboration with trainee GPs, the author tried out ways of encouraging patients to check their understanding of the instructions and advice they had been offered. When the doctor said something like 'Any questions about that?' or' Do you understand all that?', there were very few clarifying questions: these were apparently not effective ways of encouraging patients to process new information more effectively. However, when the doctors said something like 'Can you imagine any problems with doing that?', a substantial proportion of patients did raise questions. Not surprisingly, though, the doctors were uneasy about using a stock phrase again and again.

There was, however, a strategy the trainee GPs used spontaneously which seemed to be effective in encouraging patients to produce questions and comments: while making suggestions for treatment, some doctors, particularly trainees, asked questions such as 'Have you tried anything in the past that you found good?' 'Have you tried lots of hot drinks?'. As well as answering the questions, these patients were likely subsequently to produce further contributions which sought to clarify something already said by the doctor, such as: 'So I needn't finish the course then?'; 'Which is the one for the headache?'.

In contrast, when doctors allowed patients to be passive, there were few contributions of this kind. Robinson and Whitfield (1985, 1987b) found a significant correlation between the incidence of doctors' questions to patients about the proposed treatment and the incidence of patients' questions and comments which were likely to have been formulated during, rather than prior to, the consultation (Type 2). However, the incidence of Type 1 contributions was not associated with any coded feature of the doctors' verbal behaviour. The finding that the two kinds of patient contributions were related in different ways to the doctors' behaviours, suggests that the doctors' questioning did not simply indicate to patients that they were permitted to take a generally more active part in the consultation. Instead, it may be that the doctors' questions prevented patients from being passive recipients of information and encouraged them to think in depth about the proposed treatment. As a consequence, they became aware of queries they might otherwise not have thought of until after the consultation. We do not yet know whether the use of this strategy by doctors leads to more accurate post-consultation accounts by patients, and further research is being carried out to test this.

Summary and conclusions

It was suggested that a number of different factors could be responsible for patients' tendency to behave in a passive way during their consultation:

- They have not formulated any clear idea about why they are there or what they hope to obtain.
- They have formulated ideas but think it inappropriate to produce them.
- They fully understand and accept the information, instructions and advice offered by the doctor, and so have no clarifying questions or comments.
- They have processed the information, instructions and advice too superficially to be aware of problems.

Presumably it is better if patients do not leave their consultations with unanswered questions, and with comments which they had planned to produce but for some reason did not. Other reasons why it might be better if patients did take a more active part in their consultation are that when patients present their ideas and

expectations, agreement is more likely to be reached on the problem and its management; when this happens, patients are perhaps more likely to understand, accept and adhere to the agreed plan; and it may be that when patients produce questions and comments about what the doctor says during the consultation, they remember and understand better what the treatment regimen is to be, and have fewer residual questions.

Two kinds of evidence have been used to support the view that it would be better if patients' ideas, wishes and questions were made explicit during the consultation: evidence which identifies problems of remembering and understanding in consultations in which those contributions were not made, and evidence which demonstrates positive outcomes of consultations in which those contributions were made. However, the evidence so far available is consistent with the idea that a major factor causing problems in doctor–patient communication is mismatch between doctor's and patient's views, rather than failure to make that mismatch explicit. It is not yet clear whether, when a mismatch is made explicit, doctor and patient can reach agreement within the consultation and whether the consultation then has a positive outcome.

Possible ways of achieving a higher incidence of patients' contributions are by altering the nature of the doctor–patient interaction, so that patients feel free to present ideas and expectations which they have formulated prior to the consultation; and by presenting information, instructions and advice in a way that prevents patients from being passive recipients and encourages them to become aware of misunderstandings and problems.

Alternatively, or in addition, we can accept that patients may not spontaneously make the contributions which are desirable, and the doctor may invite them to present their ideas and expectations, or present information, instructions and advice in ways which are best

References

understood and remembered by patients generally.

There could be important differences between consultations in which patients spontaneously contribute their ideas and expectations, and those in which doctors invite patients to present them. The doctor's invitation may act not only as a way of eliciting preformulated views, but also as a way of allowing the patient to formulate and/or clarify views which were present only in embryonic form beforehand. If so, this possible clarification function may turn out to be desirable.

Even if the patient's views are only elicited, rather than clarified, by the doctor's invitations, it is not necessarily the case that the consultation would be equivalent to one in which the patient spontaneously contributed the same views. There is some evidence that tension, anxiety or anger are more likely to occur when patients contribute spontaneously than when they do not, and this is perhaps less likely to happen if the patient's views are invited. Furthermore, the order in which doctor's and patient's views occur in the consultation is likely to differ according to whether the patient's views are presented spontaneously or in response to an invitation. Levels of remembering and understanding may be influenced by the order of presentation of information. This may apply not only to the patient's level of remembering and understanding of what the doctor's says, but also to the doctor's remembering and understanding of what the patient says, a factor which in turn may influence the clarity with which the doctor presents instructions and advice.

Even more complexity can be introduced into this analysis by considering what might happen over time if doctors began to invite patients to present their ideas and expectations. Eventually patients' conceptions of the 'patient' role might change, and they might begin spontaneously to present the kinds of views which in earlier consultations the doctor had invited.

Would patients then leave their consultations with a more complete understanding of their problem and its management, more likely to adhere to the suggested plan of action? The evidence so far available does not allow us to predict with any certainty.

What has emerged from this discussion of patients' contributions to the consultation is that the general observation that patients are often 'passive' rather than 'active' can usefully be developed to give a much more detailed analysis of the kinds of contributions patients might make, and of what determines whether or not they are made. What use can be made of this kind of account depends in large part on what the aims of the consultation are considered to be, and what judgements are made about the responsibilities and rights of patients and doctors. If, for example, one judges patients to be autonomous individuals responsible for their own health and well-being, who should use doctors as expert sources of information and as ways of obtaining access to particular services, then one might aim to put into practice any of the ways of increasing the incidence of patients' participation in their consultations. If, on the other hand, one considers that there are circumstances when it is appropriate for doctors to take a paternalistic role and make decisions on behalf of patients, rather than to aim for a shared understanding of the problem, then one might be much more cautious about aiming to increase patients' participation. However, the relationships between value judgements and interpretations or use of research findings are not so straightforward as these examples imply, and readers might usefully reflect on their value judgements before seeing implications for action in the research literature.

References

Anderson, J.L. (1979) Patients' recall of information and its relation to the nature of the consultation, in

135

Research in Psychology and Medicine, vol. 2, (eds D.J. Oborne, M.M. Gruneberg and J.R. Eiser), Academic Press, London pp. 238–246

Anderson, J.L., Dodman, S., Kopelman, M. and Fleming, A. (1979) Patient information recall in a rheumatology clinic. *Rheumatology and Rehabilitation*, **18**, 18–22.

Baxter, M. (1983) The causes of disease. *Social Science and Medicine*, **17**, 59–69

Bensing, J. and Verhaak, P. (1982) Room for the patient. *Nederlands Tijdschrift voor de Psychologie*, **37**, (English version available), 19–31.

Boreham, P. and Gibson, D. (1978) The informative process in private medical consultations. *Social Science and Medicine*, **12**, 409–16.

Bradshaw, P.W., Ley, P. and Kincey, J.A. (1975) Recall of medical advice: comprehensibility and specificity. *British Journal of Social and Clinical Psychology*, **14**, 55–62.

DiMatteo, M.R. and DiNicola, D.D. (1982) *Achieving Patient Compliance*, Pergamon, New York.

Eisenthal, S. and Lazare, A. (1979) Adherence and the negotiated approach to patienthood. *Archives of General Psychiatry*, **36**, 393–8.

Eisenthal, S., Koopman, C. and Lazare, A. (1983) Process analysis of two dimensions of the negotiated approach in relation to satisfaction in the initial interview. *Journal of Nervous and Mental Disease*, **171**, 49–54.

Heszen-Klemens, I. and Lapinska, E. (1984) Doctor–patient interaction, patients' health behaviour and effects of treatment. *Social Science and Medicine*, **19**, 9–18.

Hinckley, J.J., Craig, H.K. and Anderson, L.A. (1989) Communication characteristics of provider–patient information exchanges, in *Handbook of Language and Social Psychology*, (eds) H. Giles and W.P. Robinson, Wiley, Chichester. pp. 519–536.

Kindelan, K. and Kent, G. (1986) Patients' preferences for information. *Journal of the Royal College of General Practitioners*, **36**, 461–3.

Kindelan, K. and Kent, G. (1988) Concordance between patients' information preferences and general practitioners' perceptions. *Psychology and Health*, **1**, 399–410.

Kleinman, A., Eisenberg, L. and Good, B. (1978) Clinical lessons from anthropologic and cross-cultural research. *Annals of Internal Medicine*, **88**, 251–8.

Lazare, A., Eisenthal, S. and Wasserman, L. (1975) The customer approach to patienthood. *Archives of General Psychiatry*, **32**, 553–8.

Ley, P. (1976) Towards better doctor–patient communication, in *Communication between Doctors and Patients*, (ed) Bennett, A.E., Oxford University Press, Oxford. pp. 75–98.

Ley, P. (1982) Satisfaction, compliance and communication. *British Journal of Clinical Psychology*, **21**, 241–54.

Ley, P. (1983) Patients' understanding and recall in clinical communication, in *Doctor–Patient Communication*, (eds) Pendleton, D. and Hasler, J., Academic Press, London, pp. 89–108.

Ley, P. and Spelman, M.S. (1965) Communications in an outpatient setting. *British Journal of Social and Clinical Psychology*, **4**, 114–16.

Ley, P. Bradshaw, P., Eaves, D. and Walker, C.M. (1973) A method for increasing patients' recall of information presented by doctors. *Psychological Medicine*, **3**, 217–20.

Pendleton, D., Schofield, T., Tate, P. and Havelock, P. (1984) *The Consultation: An Approach to Learning and Teaching*, Oxford University Press, Oxford.

Pill, R. and Stott, N. (1982) Concepts of illness causation and responsibility: some preliminary data from a sample of working class mothers. *Social Science and Medicine*, **16**, 43–52.

Robinson, E.J. and Ross E. (1990) *Match or Mismatch Between Patient's and Doctor's Ideas in Relation to Patient's Recall and Understanding of the Doctor's Suggestions*, Unpublished manuscript, University of Birmingham.

Robinson, E.J. and Whitfield, M.J. (1985) Improving the efficiency of patients' comprehension monitoring. *Social Science and Medicine*, **21**, 915–19.

Robinson, E.J. and Whitfield, M.J. (1987a) Participation of patients during general practice consultations: consultations of trainees compared with those of experienced doctors. *Family Practice*, **4**, 5–10.

Robinson, E.J. and Whitfield, M.J. (1987b). Participation of patients during general practice consultations. *Psychology and Health*, **1**, 123–32.

Robinson, E.J. and Whitefield, M.J. (1988) Contributions of patients to GP consultations in relation to their understanding of doctors' instructions and advice. *Social Science and Medicine*, **27**, 895–900.

Roter, D.L. (1977) Patient participation in patient–provider interaction: the effect of patient question asking on the quality of interaction, satisfaction and compliance. *Health Education Monographs*, **5**, 281–315.

Stewart, M. and Roter D. (eds) (1989) *Communicating with Medical Patients*, Sage, London.

Stimson, G. and Webb, B. (1975) *Going to See the Doctor*, Routledge and Kegan Paul, London.

Tuckett, D., Boulton, M. and Olson, C. (1985) A new approach to the measurement of patients' understanding of what they are told in medical consultations. *Journal of Health and Social Behaviour*, **26**, 27–38.

Tuckett, D., Boulton, M., Olson, C. and Williams, A. (1982) *Final Report on the Patient Project,* Health Education Council, London.

Tuckett,, D., Boulton, M., Olson, C. and Williams, A. (1985) *Meetings between Experts*, Tavistock, London.

Verhaak, P. (1986) *Detection of Psychological Complaints by General Practitioners.* Paper given at conference on The Doctor, the Patient, the Illness, Durham, July, 1986.

Weston, W.W. and Brown, J.B. (1989) The importance of Patients' beliefs, in *Communicating with Medical Patients*, (eds) M. Stewart and D. Roter, Sage, London. pp. 77–85.

Wilson, M., Robinson, E.J., Blenkinsopp, A. and Panton R. (1992) Customers' recall of information given in community pharmacies. *International Journal of Pharmacy Practice*, **1**, 152–9.

Part Two

Applications

Chapter nine

Cardiac disorders

Bob Lewin

Introduction

Since the 1900s the incidence of heart disease in the western world has grown to epidemic proportions, and it is now the major cause of premature death. In the UK, about a third of the middle-aged population are believed to have coronary artery disease (CAD), and approximately 180 000 people survive the physical and psychological trauma of a heart attack every year. If the present situation continues, 50% of us will die prematurely from a cardiac disorder (Julian, 1992). As might be expected, such an extensive health crisis has produced an enormous research effort. No single review is likely adequately to summarize its many topics. Excellent reviews of most areas already exist and are referenced below.

Psychology has made almost no impact on the practice of cardiology. Psychologists who work in the area are mainly found in cardiac rehabilitation settings and even there are a scarce resource (Maes, 1992). One of the most popular cardiology texts (Julian, 1992) devotes only three out of 320 pages to psychological factors in heart disease. However, there are signs that things may be changing. As therapeutic interventions and imaging techniques become more effective, it is becoming increasingly clear that renovating the mechanical parts of the cardiovascular system is often not enough to restore the patient's quality of life. Recently the interaction between stress, the autonomic nervous system and the cardiovascular system has been attracting increasing interest from medical researchers.

This chapter will give a brief overview of the current medical model of heart disease and an equally brief introduction to some attempts at developing a more satisfying psychobiosocial model. The second half of the chapter will discuss psychological adjustment to heart attack and psychological issues in cardiac rehabilitation. The chapter concentrates on the theoretical and research background to applications in the area, although there is also some discussion of applications, as appropriate to Part 2 of this volume.

Aetiology of CAD: the medical model

The current medical model holds that the disease is largely the consequence of a maladaptive lifestyle, the result of behaviours such as smoking, poor dietary habits and lack of exercise. These 'risk factors' combine in a multiplicative and largely unknown way to injure the coronary arteries. The body responds by forming atheromatous plaques, thereby narrowing the coronary blood vessels and restricting the blood flow to the heart muscle (myocardium).

Symptoms: the biomechanical model

The early stages of the disease are silent and acute presentation generally takes one of three forms. In 42% of new cases the first indication that a problem exists is a heart attack. This is usually caused when a thrombus or a detached plaque permanently blocks a cardiac blood vessel. This causes the death of that part of the heart muscle and creates a myocardial infarction (MI). In 30–50% of cases death will occur, usually because the strong electrical signal produced by the dying tissue upsets the orderly contractions of the four chambers of the heart, thereby leading to cardiac arrest. More rarely, death is the direct result of the extent of myocardial damage (heart failure). Thirty eight percent of new cases will present with chest pain (angina), which is due to transient myocardial ischaemia brought about by increased demand (exercise or emotional arousal) or reduced supply (coronary artery spasm or reduced cardiac output). In 13% of cases the first symptom of coronary disease will be sudden death, usually as the result of cardiac arrest.

Primary prevention: the medical model

It is generally agreed that the disease is largely preventable (O'Brien, 1991). This fact immediately suggests a challenging task for a psychological intervention, to change the health behaviours of the western world. Over the last 20 years a number of large-scale community-based educational programmes have been evaluated. Despite some reports of success in bringing about lifestyle changes (e.g. Farquhar, Macoby and Solomon, 1984) the results were generally disappointing. Elder (1985) has reviewed the use of behavioural strategies in primary prevention programmes. One reason for the poor results may be that most studies have been conducted in the USA against a background of a 50% decline in mortality from

CAD. Part of this reduction is the result of new medical treatments, but there is no doubt that large numbers of Americans have altered their lifestyle without being part of such an intervention or having had any assistance from a psychologist. With the exception of Finland, no similar reductions in mortality have occurred in Europe. Indeed, in a number of eastern European countries there have been marked increases.

'High-risk group' interventions

Targeting whole communities is expensive. A cheaper strategy is to target only those who show evidence of one or more of the major modifiable risk factors (e.g. smoking, hypertension, raised cholesterol levels). A study that incorporated a number of psychological techniques for behaviour change and involved over 12 000 high-risk men was the Multiple Risk Factor Reduction Intervention Trial (MRFIT). Subjects were randomized to receive either routine medical care or, where necessary, to interventions designed to change their diet (Gorder *et al.*, 1986), help them stop smoking (Hughes *et al.*, 1981) or treat hypertension. Although the intervention produced significant behavioural and risk factor changes total mortality was only reduced by 7% compared to the control group. The difference was not statistically significant. The clinical efficacy and cost-effectiveness of such interventions have been seriously challenged (e.g. McCormick and Skrabanek, 1988).

The most interesting study to date, perhaps because of its unequivocal grounding in behavioural psychology, compared three increasingly intensive programmes designed to reduce weight, encourage regular exercise and reduce smoking and hypertension. The best of these treatments, the most intensive, produced a very worthwhile (41%) reduction in the current overall risk of CHD (coronary heart disease) at 1 year follow-up (Lovibond, Birrell and

Langeluddecke, 1986). An interesting strategy employed by the study was to give participants regular feedback on the risk of having a heart attack. The authors conjecture that programmes that address multiple risk behaviours simultaneously are more likely to succeed, because the benefits of a generally improved lifestyle interact to increase feelings of well-being and aid compliance. For example, weight loss and smoking cessation make exercise easier and more rewarding, and exercise compliance can help to bring about weight loss.

Secondary prevention: the medical model

The most striking evidence that secondary prevention might be worthwhile is the culmination of 10 years of work by Ornish, a cardiologist. His 'lifestyle' programme included dietary change, exercise and stress management (yoga and meditation). At 1 year follow-up angiograms revealed that 85% of patients had experienced a regression in the underlying disease state (Ornish *et al.*, 1990). Symptomatically patients reported a 90% reduction in the frequency of angina. This study can be criticized on practical grounds for the high refusal rate of potential subjects (50%), because of the degree of lifestyle change required (e.g. a strict vegetarian diet) and because of its intensive nature. Patients attended a special centre for 8 hours per week indefinitely. The regression of disease may have been the result of the large changes made in the conventional risk factors. However, Ornish maintains that the psychological aspects, stress management, the provision of social support and the opportunity to share emotions in a non-judgemental group setting were the most therapeutically active part of the treatment.

Psychosocial risk factors

The simple biomechanical model outlined above has a number of problems. Most strikingly, all of the known risk factors do not account for 50% of the actual cases of CAD, and they are poor predictors of the distribution, severity and rate of disease progression. A major risk factor in one culture may not correlate with CAD incidence in another country. For example, the Japanese have nearly doubled their intake of saturated fat over the last 10 years, as a nation they are enthusiastic smokers, and yet their CHD mortality rate, already one of the lowest in the world, has declined by 23% over the same period (Office of Health Economics, 1990). Even ignoring intercultural differences, which may simply reflect differences in the co-occurrence of particular risk factors, major differences in incidence may also occur within the same 'conventional' risk factors (Jenkins, 1983).

It may well be that further epidemiological work will fill the gaps in the present theory. At present there is an interesting aetiological niche to be filled and a number of psychobiological theories have laid claim to the territory. No convincing theory has emerged, and several related species of explanation are currently competing for dominance. All propose a roughly similar biological pathway. High levels of 'arousal' produce a strong neuroendocrine response through the sympathetic-adrenal medullary system or the pituitary–adrenal cortical system. Excess levels of the associated neurohormones foster the formation of atheroma, and may also be cardiotoxic or arrhythmogenic. In brief, many years of chronic over-arousal contributes to the development of CAD, and further acute over arousal in an already compromised individual may produce sudden cardiac death (Eliot and Buell, 1985). Some support for this is available from animal studies. For example, stress or the administration of exogenous catecholamines can produce sudden cardiac death in animals with CAD analogues (Lown *et al.*, 1980), and monkeys kept in high stress environments and fed a 'western' diet develop CAD (Manuck *et al.*, 1988a,b).

Among the many psychological factors that have been suggested as producing this over-arousal are maladaptive behavioural repertoires, such as the Type A Behaviour Pattern (TABP, Rosenman *et al.*, 1975) or 'anger-in' (Dembroski *et al.*, 1985). It is increasingly being suggested that these intrapersonal characteristics may only become risk factors in certain environments (Byrne and Reinhart, 1989). A number of other researchers have chosen to emphasize environment rather than intrapersonal factors, highlighting problems such as high-stress/low-control work situations (Marmot, 1983; Marmot, Shipley and Rose, 1984), poor social support or high work strain (for a review see Krantz and Raisen, 1988).

Personality theories

Space does not permit a review of all the intrapersonal risk factor theories that have been proposed; however, the best-known is the TABP. Type A persons are highly competitive, crave recognition, are hostile and impatient with others and are constantly impelled by a sense of urgency and a need to win. Type B people are low in these behavioural attributes (Friedman and Rosenman, 1959). Several thousand papers have been published in this area, the early studies seeming to show that it was indeed a risk factor of equal strength with the 'classic' risk factors. Since then many contradictory results have been reported. Most seriously, a number of large-scale trials of high-risk subjects have failed to find an increased risk for Type A subjects, and one study found increased mortality among Type B survivors of MI (Ragland and Brand, 1988). Sub-elements of the TABP, in particular hostility (Williams, Hanley and Lee, 1980; Barefoot, Dahlstrom and Williams, 1983; Barefoot *et al.*, 1987; but see McCranie *et al.*, 1986), have been proposed as the true pathogenic element. An introduction to this debate, as well as to reactivity studies and hypertension is provided by Carroll

(1992). For a hostile review of Type A research see Freeman and King (1986). A comprehensive meta-analysis of this area concluded that: 'The picture of coronary proneness revealed by this review is not one of a hurried, impatient workaholic but instead of a person with one or more negative emotions' (Booth-Kewley and Friedman, 1987).

Finally, there is now some doubt as to how specific TABP is to heart disease. A recent study of 1949 male and female adults in Belgium showed that Type A subjects reported a higher incidence of CHD, peptic ulcers, thyroid problems, asthma and rheumatoid arthritis. The authors concur with Booth-Kewley in seeing TABP as only one part of a '...generic disease-prone personality that involves depression, anger/hostility, anxiety and possibly other aspects of personality' (Rime *et al.*, 1989).

Cardiac reactivity

A further contribution of stress to cardiac morbidity may be through a biological predisposition to an excessive 'cardiac reactivity' to psychological challenge. This is also believed to be implicated in the development of hypertension. Hypertension studies form an important subtopic in cardiovascular psychology, and there is evidence that behavioural techniques can be an effective method of treatment for some patients (Steptoe, 1988). For an introduction to some of the current research issue in this area see Elbert *et al.* (1988).

Life events as risk factors

A number of efforts have been made to link aversive life events to the development of CAD: these have also provided contradictory results (Wells, 1985). Byrne and Byrne (1990) have recently reviewed this literature and, despite highlighting some individually interesting results, came to the conclusion that: 'The field will, for some time, remain enigmatic; apparent enough to tantalize but lacking sufficiently in concept and substance to preclude definitive statements.... It is certain that whatever future evidence is presented, the links between stress, anxiety, and CHD will not be simple, straightforward or uniform across individuals or settings' (Byrne and Byrne, 1990).

Social risk factors

Once more common in the middle and upper classes, CAD is now inversely related to socioeconomic status. Strong social class differences in incidence exist within communities and in shared working environments (Marmot, Shipley and Rose, 1984). This is still the case when all the other major risk factors are statistically controlled for (Krantz and Raisen, 1988). Even within manual occupations, social class appears to be 'dose dependent', and the effects of variables such as home ownership vs renting can be discriminated, ownership being associated with a lower incidence of CAD (Woodward et al., 1992). Unemployment has also been studied, and when associated variables such as financial difficulties and family disruption were also measured a significant increase in the incidence of cardiovascular disease was found within 2–3 years of job loss (Brenner, 1979). Of course, social deprivation is a powerful predictor of both morbidity and mortality in all disease states (Davey Smith, Bartley and Blane, 1990). Failure to consider these issues can greatly reduce the efficacy and applicability of interventions. For example, many adults in poverty deny themselves food for the sake of their children, and smoke to control their hunger. For many, cigarettes may represent their only item of 'personal ownership'. Behavioural strategies are unlikely to benefit many of those most in need, if such factors are ignored.

The production of symptoms

The biomedical model of symptom production has been outlined above. Evidence is rapidly accumulating to suggest that this too may be overly simplistic. Psychological factors may be involved in the production of symptoms in several ways. First, through psychophysiological pathways, it may contribute to producing myocardial ischaemia or even sudden death. Secondly, it is now well accepted that pain, like any perception, is actively constructed by the brain and its intensity is influenced by a number of psychological variables. Thirdly, the patient's response to the illness may exacerbate the symptoms; for example, if they drastically reduce their activity level the subsequent loss of fitness is likely to lower the ischaemic threshold. Finally, patients vary widely in their symptom reporting and seeking of medical aid.

Psychological factors in the production of myocardial ischaemia and acute events

The association of strong emotion, especially anger, with angina and sudden death was noted as early as the 18th century (Heberden, 1772). As the details of the circulation became better understood and the biomechanical model became dominant, these observations were increasingly ignored. Following the discovery that ischaemia and even MI may be produced by coronary artery spasm (Maseri et al., 1978), there has been a renewal of interest in the role of autonomic activity in the regulation of the cardiovascular system. The role of various stressors in the production of ischaemia or arrhythmias has been confirmed by a number of authors (Schwartz, Weinberger and Singer, 1981; Reich et al., 1981; Krantz, 1991). It appears that in individual with CAD, arteries constrict rather than dilate (the normal response) when the individual is under stress (Yeung, Vekshtein and Krantz, 1991). High-reactivity patients are more likely to show stress-induced ischaemia than low-reactivity subjects; they may also show lower levels of trait anxiety, neuroticism and depression (Zotti *et al.*, 1991). Rozanski, Bairey and Krantz (1988) demonstrated that a personally relevant speaking task produced as much 'cardiac dysfunction' as exercise. Verrier, Hagestad and Lown (1987), using dogs in which the coronary circulation could be reversibly compromised, concluded that delayed myocardial ischaemia could be produced as a response to anger, and that this was the result of arousal of the sympathetic nervous system. Depression may be linked to acute events in a number of ways. A study of Channer *et al.* (1988) showed that depressed patients not only walked less far on an exercise stress test but also developed earlier ST depression (an electrophysiological marker for ischaemia), despite having levels of CAD similar to non-depressed patients. Carney *et al.* (1988) followed up 52 patients who had had angiography for suspected CAD. At 12-month follow-up 77.8% of the depressed patients had sustained at least one major cardiac event, compared with 34.9% of the non-depressed. Multiple regression analysis showed that depression was an independent predictor of events when all other demographic and physiological variables were entered. A significant weakness of this study is that one of the cardiac events was coronary artery bypass surgery: nearly twice the number of depressed patients had received surgery. This may have been because the more depressed and lethargic patients reported more pain, or because they were viewed as more functionally disabled than the non-depressed.

A number of studies have hinted that psychosocial variables are related to survival independently of the severity of CAD. Anxiety and depression have been associated with early death in a number of studies (e.g. Stern, Pascal and Ackerman, 1977; Kennedy, Hofer and Cohen, 1987). A prospective study of 2300 male survivors of MI (Ruberman *et al.*, 1984) found that, with other risk markers held constant, patients initially classified as being social-ly isolated and having a high degree of life stress had four times the risk of death over the following 3 years.

Psychological variables and symptom report

It is true that in patients with very advanced disease states certain combinations of physical findings (e.g. low exercise tolerance plus left ventricular failure) give an approximate guide to survival time. However, for the great majority of patients it is impossible to use disease measures to predict the degree of disability reported by the patient. Several studies have shown that the self-report of pain and disability (Jenkins *et al.*, 1983; Smith, Follick and Korr, 1984) and the success of medical treatment (Williams, Haney and McKinnis, 1986; Channer *et al.*, 1988) is related to scores on questionnaires measuring features such as anxiety, depression, hypochondriasis, anger, TABP and sleep disturbance, but not to disease measures.

The perception of pain

A small but significant number of people are unaware of having had a myocardial infarction. Some of these patients may have congenitally high pain thresholds (Sheps, Hinderlier and Bragdon, 1988; Falcone *et al.*, 1988). However, it is not uncommon to find that 50% of the ischaemic episodes recorded by a 24-hour continuous ambulatory ECG recording are not perceived by the patient, whereas the other 50% are accompanied by self-report of pain. Nor is it uncommon for the patient to report pain when no evidence of ischaemia is present on the tape. Although the spontaneous regression of CAD has occasionally been reported, it is thought to be extremely rare, yet angina often remits after causing years of pain and disability.

It is now well established that the meaning of an illness in terms of patient's life, their beliefs about the illness or the pain, their level of autonomic arousal, their mood state, the amount of attention directed to the pain, various 'personality' variables, their coping style and their previous experience of pain, greatly influences the amount of pain and disability reported and the demand for medical intervention (Elton and Stanley, 1983). There is no reason to believe that patients with CAD are any different in this respect. However, once lesions are found, unless the amount of pain and disability are grossly disproportionate, they are taken to account for all of the pain reported and treatment will proceed on this basis. Unless there are clear survival advantages for the patient in having coronary artery bypass surgery, the initial therapeutic intervention will be drug treatment. For many patients this will prove sufficient; others will continue to complain of pain, and many of these (especially in America) will progress to surgery, either bypass graft or angioplasty. The success of bypass grafts in improving exercise tolerance and reducing symptoms is substantial: 70–90% of patients report acceptable to excellent levels of improvement. Functional improvements may not be accompanied by similar psychosocial gains: two studies showed that about 30% of patients do not benefit in terms of quality of life (Mayou and Bryant, 1987; Channer *et al.*, 1988). The risk are not inconsiderable either: in one study 37% showed measurable cognitive deficits 8 weeks after surgery (Newman, Smith and Treasure, 1987) and about 3% of patients do not survive the operation (Mock, Ringqvist and Fisher, 1982). In their study of quality of life following bypass graft surgery, Mayou and Bryant found that the best predictors of outcome 'were *not* medical factors but mental state and a group of variables suggesting a cautious, passive approach to illness.' (Mayou and Bryant, 1987).

Symptoms without CAD

Over 20 % of those patients referred to cardiology whose symptoms are 'typical' enough for them to advance to angiography (an invasive and expensive investigation) are found to have little or no CAD. At 1 year post-catheterization, Bass and Wade (1984) found that 63% continued to take (cardiac) medication for their symptoms, 60% were still regularly consulting their GP or hospital doctor, 23% had visited an A&E department and 'extreme fatigue' prevented 30% performing simple household chores. There is little spontaneous remission. At 10-year follow-up few patients have improved (Proudfit, Bruschke and Sones, 1980). These patients do not seem to suffer from higher rates of acute cardiac events than people without CAD. Numerous suggestions have been made about underlying medical conditions that may account for the symptoms, including a possible hotly debated cardiological problem labelled syndrome X (Favaro *et al.*, 1989). No medical treatment has been found that reliably reduces the pain. As a group they have a psychological profile similar to patients suffering from other illnesses with a large psychological overlay, such as chronic back pain, non-organic pelvic pain, irritable bowel syndrome and other 'psychophysiologic disorders' (Ockene, Shay and Alpert, 1980). They also exhibit high rate of neuroticism, anxiety, depression and somatic concerns (Bass and Wade, 1984; Costa *et al.*, 1985; Cormier *et al.*, 1988), as well as unexplained breathing problems (Bass and Wade, 1984; Freeman and Nixon, 1985) and panic symptoms (Lantinga *et al.*, 1988; Beitman *et al.*, 1988; Cormier *et al.*, 1988). Obviously, such findings have to be treated with caution, and do not indicate that an individual patient's pain is largely psychosomatic, because it is not known to what degree the psychological distress is a consequence of failing to receive a satisfying medical explanation or treatment. A psychological treatment has reported useful improvements in both pain report and activity levels in these patients (Klimes, Mayou and Pearce, 1990).

Psychological interventions to reduce symptoms and disability

The facts reviewed above suggest that attending to psychological wellbeing may have a favourable impact on symptoms and disability. In an early study by Ornish (which did not include exercise), a 1-month intensive residential stress-management programme (yoga, meditation and group discussion of coping methods) was found to reduce self-report of angina by over 90% (Ornish et al., 1983). A programme of stress management for patients with angina, carried out by Wallace and Bundy in Birmingham, also produced symptomatic improvement, including improvement in asymptomatic myocardial ischaemia (Bundy, 1992). This finding is particularly important because it precludes the possibility that the intervention introduced a reporting bias or had converted previously symptomatic ischaemia into silent ischaemia.

In a study conducted by the author and others, groups of 6–10 patients with established CAD and angina took part in an 8-week 'angina management programme'. This included techniques drawn from pain management, attention to misperceptions about heart disease, yoga, breathing retraining, stress management, biofeedback and moderate exercise. In all, 62 patients received treatment and large improvements were recorded in both symptomatic and functional measures. Following an independent review by the patients' cardiologists, who were not involved in the research, 60% of the patients were withdrawn from surgery as it was felt that it was unlikely to add to the gains made. It is not clear which parts of the treatment were responsible for the changes, and it is possible that the exercise component alone might have produced similar results.

Further evidence that teaching cardiac patients ways of reducing arousal might reduce levels of angina is available from an intervention aimed (successfully) at treating primary hypertension. The treatment involved patients attending group sessions for relaxation, biofeedback and yoga. Useful reductions in blood pressure were maintained to 4-year follow-up, and mortality was reduced in the intervention group, as was the incidence of angina (Patel et al., 1985).

Psychological interventions and sudden death

A reanalysis of data from the Recurrent Coronary Prevention Project, the intention of which was to alter Type A behaviour, found that sudden cardiac death had predominantly psychosocial predictors, whereas non-sudden cardiac death and non-fatal recurrences were predominantly predicted by biological factors. Type A behaviour was an independent predictor of sudden, but not non-sudden, cardiac death in this population. The authors claim that: 'These results are first demonstration of a direct relation between stress and sudden cardiac death in a large prospective clinical study, and provide insight into the future of past prospective studies to find an association between type A behaviour and cardiac mortality' (Brackett and Powell, 1988).

It should be noted that, although TABP and cardiac mortality were reduced in the treatment group, the study is unable to tell us whether these facts were causally related. This is because other psychological predictors of mortality (depression, anxiety and social support) were not reported. Indeed, the intervention group received twice the amount of 'attention', delivered though regular group meetings, one of the stated aims of which was to act as a source of social support (Thoresen et al., 1982).

A particularly interesting study in this area is one by Frasure-Smith and Prince (1989). The 'stress' level of post-MI patients was monitored by monthly telephone administration of the General Health Questionnaire. Patients reaching the 'caseness' criteria were visited by a nurse, who attempted to determine the cause of the distress and then intervened or brought in others to attempt to solve the problem Mortality in the experimental group was significantly reduced compared to an untreated control group. When those patients in the intervention group who exhibited caseness prior to discharge were compared with similar patients in the control group, the long-term reduction in mortality was 50%. The success of this programme has led to the NIH (National Institutes of Health) sponsoring a multicentre trial that is currently under way.

Synthesis

The findings presented above suggest that psychological interventions may bring about a number of worthwhile clinical gains, which may include a reduction in early mortality. It is not clear how such results are produced: it may be that the psychobiological theories are correct, or it may be that they succeed by altering symptom perception or reporting behaviour, health behaviours (e.g. smoking and exercise), beliefs about the illness, anxiety, depression, social support, medical contact or illness behaviour. We need to know a great deal more about these variables in patients with CAD. Most of what is known is as a result of work with the survivors of acute events, almost exclusively MI.

Psychological reaction to acute myocardial infarction

During an acute MI, people are often shocked, still in acute pain, possibly lapsing in and out of consciousness and the subject of active medical attention. The predominant emotion during the acute event is anxiety (Cay et al., 1972). This may be seen as a 'normal' reaction and not unique to MI. Vetter et al. (1977) found anxiety levels to be no different from those of patients admitted to hospital for other medical

emergencies. There has been considerable debate about the contribution that the 'high-tech' nature of the cardiac care unit (CCU) may make to the patient's distress, but reviewers have come to contradictory conclusions (see Byrne and Byrne, 1990). Once the patient's medical condition is stabilized, usually within 12–48 hours, they are transferred to a 'step-down' or general ward.

Course of the psychological reaction in hospital

It is generally agreed that there is a recognizable pattern to psychological adjustment to such an acute episode (Cay et al., 1972; Dellipiani et al., 1976; Billing et al., 1980). Severe anxiety during the height of the acute episode is sometimes followed by a brief, almost euphoric, period once the condition is stabilized and the patient realizes he or she is going to live. This quickly dissipates as the reality of the situation sinks in and the patient begins to realize that they have a life-threatening illness and to consider the effect it will have on their future life (Dellipiani et al., 1976).

Denial

There is, however, a group of patients who appear to cope with MI by denying its significance. Studies have reported 12–20 % of patients as being sceptical about having had a heart attack, and some flatly contradicted the physician's diagnosis (Almeida and Wenger, 1982; Baile et al., 1982). An extreme form of denial has also occasionally been described in which the recently discharged patient deliberately tests himself against fate by indulging in strenuous activity or 'saturnalian excess' (Soloff, 1978). It is not recorded whether this has ever proved fatal. Denial has been viewed as a healthy coping strategy and has been claimed to reduce mortality, speed recovery (Tesar and Hackett, 1985) and to be a predictor of better long-term psychosocial adjustment (Croog, Shapiro and Levine, 1971; Stern, Pascal and Ackerman, 1977). However, these findings are contentious. Critics have suggested that empirical evidence is conflicting or missing (Doehrman, 1977; Croog, 1983) and that a number of covariate predictors of adjustment and survival have not been controlled for (Croog, 1983).

Psychiatric morbidity

It is common to find raised levels of anxiety and depression in the first weeks following discharge (Wishnie, Hackett and Cassem, 1971; McGrath and Robinson, 1973; Thompson, Cordle and Sutton, 1982), but for the majority of patients these problems remit within 6–12 weeks (Mayou, 1984). Stern, Pascal and McLoone (1976) found that 70% of patients reporting depression at 6 weeks and 67% of the patients who were anxious at 3 months were still depressed or anxious at 1 year follow-up. There is general agreement that 25–35% of patients will record clinical levels of anxiety and depression at 1 year, and that there will be little further spontaneous remission. It is equally well established that there is no significant association between the psychological reaction to MI and the severity of the infarct (Cay et al., 1972; Lloyd and Cawley, 1982, 1983; Wiklund et al., 1984a,b; Schleifer et al., 1989; Laerum et al., 1988). The degree to which poor preinfarct psychiatric status accounts for variance in the eventual adjustment is not clear. One week after the acute MI, Lloyd and Cawley (1983) found three groups of patients, those with psychiatric morbidity predating the infarct (17%), those whose psychiatric distress was reactive to the MI (20%), and a third group (63%) who showed no psychiatric symptomatology. Some caution must obviously be exercised in *post hoc* diagnosis of this kind. At 12-month follow-up 75% of the first group were still disturbed, as were 25% of

the second group. Partners and other family members are often more psychologically disturbed than the patient, and this may have an important influence on the patient's anxiety and long-term outcome (Doerr and Jones, 1979; Cay, 1982). Ideally they should be equally involved in any therapeutic process, although they may have diferent educational and psychological needs (Taylor, Bandura and Ewart, 1985). Patient and spouse should be forewarned of the transitory emotional upset – 'homecoming depression' – that commonly follows discharge (Wiklund et al., 1985a). A small proportion of patients will succumb to a restricted and fearful lifestyle that has been labelled in many different ways over the last 100 years, as 'cardiac neurosis', 'neurocirculatory asthenia', 'effort syndrome' or 'soldier's heart'. Such patients are typified by high levels of anxiety, increasing physical deconditioning due to avoidance of any exercise, a hopeless and dependent attitude and an almost obsessional preoccupation with physical symptoms and details of their medical history (Julian, 1991). They are well known to their general practitioners and cardiologists, and are frequently hospitalized for further, usually fruitless, investigations (Stern, 1977).

Poor adjustment following MI

Surveys that only use psychiatric criteria such as anxiety and depression often miss the profound influence MI may have on one or more aspects of the patient's life. In an excellent review of psychological interventions in rehabilitation, Wiklund commented:

> despite medical evidence that healing of the MI is usually complete within 2 months and the fact that a majority of patients have a preserved physical capacity, the high incidence of emotional disturbance, pessimism, self-reported symptoms, avoidance behaviour, and sexual decline indicate that a

majority of the patients unjustifiably consider themselves severely impaired both during convalescence and one year after the MI. (Wiklund *et al.*, 1985a).

Return to work

Reports of the overall rate of return to work following survived MI vary between 62% and 92% (Wiklund *et al.*, 1985b). Failure to re-enter employment has been associated with increased anxiety and depression in a number of studies (Cay *et al.*, 1973; Stern, Pascal and McLoone, 1976; Stern, Pascal and Ackerman, 1977; Mayou, 1979) but the direction of causality is difficult to establish. Certainly many patients give a fear of unemployment as their greatest worry only days after the MI (Cay *et al.*, 1972). Many who return to work will reduce the quality or quantity of their output (Mayou, 1979; Wiklund *et al.*, 1985b; Maeland and Havick, 1986), earn less (Doehrman, 1977; Hinohara, 1970) and experience greater work-related stress (Stern, Pascal and Ackerman, 1977). Croog (1983) found that 30% believed reduced health status had harmed their work.

Return to work is, however, a somewhat naive endpoint to choose when assessing the efficacy of psychological interventions, because it is often influenced by environmental factors not amenable to rehabilitation (Walter, 1985) and also because, for many people, reducing their work effort or choosing to retire to sickness benefits may be an adaptive strategy and one to be actively encouraged in rehabilitation (Wenger and Alpert, 1989).

Sexual adjustment

It is commonly believed that great excitement can lead to a heart attack and it is therefore not surprising that: 'There are many myths about sudden death from heart attack during sexual intercourse' (Freeman, 1986). In fact, a survey by Ueno (1963) of 5559 sudden cardiac deaths found that only 18 (0.03%) were related to coitus and that in 14 of these the deceased had been drinking heavily and was with an extra-marital partner who was on average 12 years younger. Of course, these figures may simply indicate that a doctor called to a death in a family home is more discreet then when called to a hotel room! In another widely quoted study, middle-aged married men who were wearing ambulatory monitoring devices during coitus showed a mean maximum heart rate at orgasm of 117 beats per minute; a similar pulse rate was elicited by driving in traffic, climbing two flights of stairs or discussing business on the phone (Hellerstein and Friedman, 1970). Again, caution must be exercised in extrapolating from these results: the study population was 101 men, of whom only 50% had sustained an MI; the others were at high risk of CAD. The patients were not specifically asked to indulge in, or to report, intercourse and only 14 did report conjugal sexual activity during the monitoring period. It must be asked how typical these patients were. Many patients find wearing the monitor awkward and constraining enough without attempting intercourse as well. Despite these reservations, it is important to assure patients that intercourse is not only safe but may be beneficial. The work levels involved in sexual activity have been estimated as 3.5 mets (metabolic equivalents) for foreplay, rising to 4.7–5.5 mets for orgasm: well within the safe limits for most post-MI patients, who can achieve 8–9 mets without harm (Douglas and Wilkes, 1975).

MI has consistently been reported to have a deleterious effect on sexual activity and investigators have reported that 10–58% admit to sexual difficulties or a reduction in frequency or satisfaction following MI (Horgan and Craig, 1978; Masur, 1979; Mehta and Krop, 1979; Sjorgen and Fugl-Meyer, 1983). Once again, such figures must also be interpreted with caution: a survey of 131 post infarct men reported extensive sexual problems prior to

MI, 64% had been impotent, 28% had experienced a 'substantial decrease of sexual interest and activity', and 8% premature ejaculation (Wabrek and Burchell, 1980). Sexual problems in cardiac patients may also be iatrogenic, as many cardiac drugs have potential side-effects that increase sexual dysfunction. Hypertensive agents and diuretics may cause impotence and problems with ejaculation in as many as 30% of patients (Reichgott, 1979) and β-blockers have been shown to produce impotence in 15%, decrease potency (the ability to maintain erection to ejaculation) in 28% and decrease libido in 4% (Burnet and Chahine, 1979).

A study by Sjorgen recruited 49 males who had been sexually active prior to MI, and found that overall there was a reduction in satisfaction of 45%. Of these patients, 45% mentioned fatigue, 39% fear, 8% reduced libido and 39% pain on intercourse among the reasons for reduced satisfaction. Only 22% reported erectile or orgasmic incompetence. It has been asserted that, although sexual adjustment may be affected in many ways, '...the fear response usually dominates and may become a phobia' (Dangrove, 1968). Hellerstein and Friedman (1970) found that there was little relationship between the severity of the MI and the level of post-MI sexual activity.

Most studies have been restricted to men, although it may be that women are particularly badly affected. A study by Papadopolous *et al.* (1983) found that 50% of women admitted being afraid of resuming intercourse. Abramov (1976) interviewed 100 women aged 40–60 and found sexual dissatisfaction present in 65% of post-MI patients compared to 24% of age-matched controls hospitalized for other reasons. For both groups the problem was mainly secondary to sexual dysfunction in the partner. An MI does not inevitably result in poorer sexual functioning: some authors have reported that a number of patients had improved sexual function, and suggest that this is generally as the result of an improvement in

the marital relationship (Hellerstein and Friedman, 1970; Laerum *et al.*, 1988). Stern, Pascal and Ackerman (1977) found that 10% of patients reported increased frequency and quality in their sexual activity.

Medical staff commonly neglect to give sexual advice following MI. A 'simple survey' conducted by Freeman and King (1986) at the Charing Cross Hospital, London, found that 65% of the physicians said that they did not discuss return to sexual activity. Of the 35% who did discuss it, 70% spent less than 5 minutes on the subject and only 30% discussed it with the spouse. The majority of junior hospital doctors said that they would advise against the resumption of coitus if the patient had had a severe MI or had 'many risk factors'. How much of the abandonment of intercourse is as the result of poor communication or inaccurate medical advice is known.

The partner and family

The quality of the marital and familial relationships may be an important determinant of psychological recovery (Lloyd and Cawley, 1982; Adsett and Bruhn, 1968). Marriages high in intimacy appear to have a 'buffering effect' protecting the patient from anxiety and depression (Waltz *et al.*, 1988). Of course, it may be that patients capable of forming particularly good marital relationships have innate qualities that also aid their psychological recovery.

The effect of MI on those close to the patient has been poorly researched. In a long-term qualitative follow-up of 72 patients, Finlayson and McEwen (1977) found a number of marriages in which long-lasting changes in the role relationships, decision-making patterns and the balance of power had occured. These changes, which were often initiated when the patient was convalescing, were still evident 4 years later. Some patients accepted these changes all too willingly, and secondary gains may play a causal role in the development of 'cardiac neurosis'. By way of contrast, many patients felt over protected, and this often resulted in tension or increased family rows.

Stern, in a study of 52 spouses, reported that among the anxious or depressed spouses, 26% felt guilty, believing that their own actions might have caused the problem. In several cases this belief had been directly fostered by the patient. There appeared to be three major causes of distress: first, a fear of provoking another infarct by doing or saying something that might cause the patient worry or annoyance; secondly, as noted by Finlayson and McEwen (1977), the balance of power had altered. The spouse was attempting to handle all the family problems without asking for support from the 'invalid'. This often caused the healthy spouse to feel stressed and/or resentful. A third factor emerged in a small number of spouses which appeared to reflect a long-standing reaction, that of becoming depressed or anxious in the face of any problem. The wives of high deniers may be at particular risk of psychological disturbance (Stern and Pascal, 1979). Similar findings have been reported by Skelton and Dominian (1973), who also reported that many wives felt in a double-bind: if they showed any concern or anxiety they were accused of being overprotective, but if they were less involved, they were accused of being uncaring.

The patient's increased irritability has been widely reported as a source of friction in relationships. The family often report feeling that dealing with the patient is like 'walking on eggshells' or 'living with a volcano' or 'sitting on a keg of dynamite' (Skelton and Dominian, 1973; Stern and Pascal, 1979; Bedsworth and Molen, 1982).

Illness behaviour following MI

The most common reaction of patients after an MI is to fear and deliberately avoid activity (Croog and Levine, 1977; Mallaghan and

Pemberton, 1977; Wiklund *et al.*, 1984a). Normal or explicable feelings of fatigue or minor symptoms tend to be interpreted as relating to the heart, which often leads to a reduction in social and physical activity and further preoccupation with symptoms (Wiklund *et al.*, 1984b). As reduced activity automatically leads to physical deconditioning, producing more fatigue and further anxiety, patients often become trapped in a downward spiral of increasing disability. Finlayson and McEwen (1977) found that at 1 year 30% and at 4 years 50% of their sample of post-MI patients reported a reduction in social and leisure activities. Croog found that 70% of an American group reported being less active 12 months later (Croog and Levine, 1977).

Byrne and White (1978) gave the Illness Behaviour Questionnaire to 120 post-MI patients 10–14 days after admission. In a principal components analysis, eight factors were identified. The largest factor, accounting for 19.9% of the variance, was one previously isolated by Pilowsky and labelled by him as 'hypochondriasis'. These six items and their loadings were: jealousy of other people's good health; disease attention through radio, TV etc.; thinks something wrong with the mind; upset by appearance of face or body; thinks more liable to illness than others; more sensitive to pain than others. Several of these items will be familiar to anyone who has treated cardiac patients. The first item is often expressed as 'why me?'. If prompted, some patients may complain that child molesters or others perceived as wicked or useless are allowed to enjoy good health, whereas they, who have always worked hard and stuck to the rules, have been punished. Item two is also commonly observed: patients often become hyperaware of references to heart disease in the media, and these may trigger intrusive and distressing thoughts about their illness. Patients are often hardly aware of these thoughts, and only notice the sudden emotional lability they produce. This in turn is often a cause of great distress, especially in previously phlegmatic patients who may wonder of their 'mind has been damaged' or if they are 'going mad' (Wishnie, Hackett and Cassem, 1971).

Wynn (1967) examined 400 male CAD patients attending a work assessment centre specifically designed to 'help in the prevention and treatment of unnecessary invalidism in patients with heart disease'. Using a standardized (but unvalidated) interview, he reported that unwarranted emotional distress and invalidism was present in 50% of the patients referred to the centre. Overall, he found that psychological distress contributed more to the level of disability than did physical impairment.

A study of 383 post-MI patients in Norway (Maeland and Havick, 1989) showed increased hospitalizations were independently related to a higher number of pre-MI hospitalizations for heart disease, less cardiac lifestyle knowledge and higher levels of anxiety and depression 1–2 weeks after the MI. Twenty percent were readmitted for chest pain without a new infarction, and discriminant analysis identified female sex and patients' initial expectation of reduced emotional control following MI as the best predictor. The severity of the MI (estimated from peak enzyme levels) had no effect on the use of hospital or physician services. The authors concluded that: '...psychological factors influence health service utilisation to a comparable extent as medical factors' (Maeland and Havick, 1989).

Why do some patients fail to adjust?

The outlook for most patients is relatively optimistic: the majority will not experience another heart attack and will make a rapid functional recovery. Treadmill testing has shown that within 4 weeks 50% of patients have age-adjusted normal work rates (DeBusk, 1982). Although there is no doubt that a substantial minority of patients fail to make a successful adjustment, it is also true that the majority do not show gross levels of disturbance, and as many as 20% of patients regard the MI as having had a beneficial effect on their life (Laerum et al., 1988) What differentiates those who successfully incorporate the event, and even draw strength from it, from those who are psychologically damaged? Very little psychological research has been done to answer this question, and that which has suggests that the patient's thoughts and beliefs play a central role in determining the psychological outcome.

The 'health perception' model

Undue illness behaviour can be viewed as a rational response to mistaken beliefs about the seriousness of an illness and its long-term prognosis (Garrity et al., 1976). In a series of papers, Garrity (1973a,b) attempted to show that differences in adjustment to MI can often be explained in terms of perceived health. He showed that, in male MI patients, psychological morale covaried with perceived health status. It also predicted return to work and community involvement. There was only a weak connection between clinical measures of health and patients' subjective health perceptions.

Using retrospective reports of pre-MI self-perceived health, and then following patients for 3–5 years, Maeland and Havick demonstrated the profound effect that an MI has on a patient's beliefs about their health: 67% retrospectively rated their premorbid perceived health as high. This reduced to 21% at discharge, 31% at 6 weeks and 42% at 3–5 years. Patients also rated their maximal physical ability at these times, and their estimates appeared fairly accurate. Despite being aware of the improvement in their physical ability, and despite the fact that 75% of them had returned to work within 6 months, their perceived health scores generally did not shift to any extent after the first 6 weeks of convalescence

(Maeland and Havick, 1988). Once again, there was no meaningful correlation between perceived health and the severity of the MI. Perceived health was associated at all measurement points with levels of emotional distress, including sensitization (involvement with symptoms), expectation of reduced emotional control, anxiety and depression. Winefield and Martin (1981) have also reported that anxiety prior to discharge was strongly related to self-reported health 30 weeks later. It seems, therefore, that anxious patients view themselves as more ill than less anxious patients, despite having similar views about their preserved functional capacity. Patients appear to see health and exercise capacity as independent of each other. Perhaps this is not surprising when one considers the lesson they have just received: they thought they were healthy but without warning they nearly died! It may help to explain a common finding in rehabilitation: that increasing patients' functional capacity (through exercise classes) does not alter their anxiety or make return to work more likely.

Cardiac misconceptions

There is increasing evidence to suggest that, at least in some patients, poor adjustment may be related to misperceptions about heart disease. Maeland and Havick, in the study of the use of health services following MI reported above, found that 'false alarm' admissions were related to a number of unrealistic fears, for example: 'believing that the infarction had left a weak area in the heart wall that easily could rupture; or that the risk for recurrence would remain high indefinitely seemed to be of special importance' (Maeland and Havick, 1989).

Wynn (1967) analysed the most reasons for unwarranted distress of illness behaviour. He judged that 38% of patients were primarily upset due to an inadequate understanding of what had happened: 'Patients not infrequently made comments like "the main artery to my

heart is blocking up" or "half my heart is dead and the other half is dying".' Patients with residual angina were unduly afraid that each episode of angina was similar to another but smaller heart attack. Twenty-two percent of patients were considered to have had the majority of their anxiety caused by medical staff:

> Often it is the symbolic significance of the doctors' remarks, rather than his words, which did so much harm.... In the convalescent phase, comments such as 'you will be alright if you are careful' were interpreted by some patients as 'If I am not careful I will die'.... Other commonly used and frightening phrases were 'you were lucky this time' (patient's interpretation – 'I won't be lucky next time'); 'It is only a warning' (interpretation – 'something terrible is yet to come').

A further 11% '....were suffering the dire psychological distress of anticipating early death' (Wynn, 1967). This was usually the result of an overly cautious or guarded prognosis given by their doctor, or because pessimistic opinions that had been given confidentially to wives or other relatives had been conveyed to the patient.

Patient attributions for MI

Fielding (1987) interviewed 102 post-MI patients. Patients listed the factors that they '...felt caused their heart attack' in order of perceived pathogenicity and then rated them for controllability. All patients had been strongly advised to stop smoking, and had received health education relating to their MI. The causes most frequently given by these patients were 'overwork' (62 times), smoking (60 times) and 'worry' (59 times). The medical risk factors (smoking, lack of exercise, lifestyle, overweight and diet) were rated as significantly more controllable than the psychological ones (overwork, worry, stress). Patients also saw the psychosocial causes as more dangerous than the biological causes, with the single exception of smoking. Murray (1989), in a small-scale ($n = 25$) replication of Fielding's study, broadly confirmed his results.

In work carried out at the author's centre, involving more than 180 patients, the same factors emerged. Many patients appeared to view the heart as a kind of battery or fuel tank that is depleted by work, worry or stress, but also by too much pleasurable excitement. They perceived the heart attack as 'a warning' that very little charge is left in the battery. Given these two beliefs, the most logical thing to do is to conserve the remaining energy by avoiding work, worry and excitement. As rest, or 'taking things easy' is often seen as recuperative, it is easy to imagine how such beliefs may lead to the 'fearful and restricted lifestyle' reported by Mayou and Bryant (1987).

Cardiac misconceptions and the patient's attributions for MI are probably socially normative, and in many cases they are reinforced by the patient's family and friends. The fact that medical staff sometimes unintentionally reinforce these misconceptions and unhelpful causal attributions has been noted above. It seems likely that a naive understanding of psychological theories such as TABP or the 'dangers' of stress may also contaminate the interactions of therapists with patients. The actions of therapists, just as much as what is actually said, may reinforce these mistaken beliefs. For example, some patients remarked that the purpose of the relaxation training that they always received after their exercise classes was to rest the heart to allow it to 'recover'. In fact, there is no evidence that normal levels of enjoyable arousal or exertion contribute to an acute MI. The truth – perhaps even more alarming – is that the formation of a new thrombus or the rupture or detachment of an atherosclerotic plaque is to a large extent a random event.

Fielding (1987) regards current rehabilitation programmes as failing the patient because 'the focus on biological factors in rehabilitation...fails to address those specific areas of concern held by MI patients'.

A rehabilitation intervention carried out by the author and others (Lewin, Robertson and Cay, 1991) attempted to address cardiac misconceptions and patient attributions. The intervention took the form of a 6-week self-help home-based rehabilitation programme in the form of a workbook and two audio tapes. It was administered by a specially trained nurse who explained the programme and provided brief contacts to encourage compliance and solve problems with its execution. The programmes included information deliberately designed to undermine the most common unhelpful attributions and misconceptions. It also included a relaxation and stress-management programme, the intention of which was to increase the patient's subjective belief in the controllability of stress and worry and therefore the likelihood of further MIs. The package produced marked improvements in anxiety, depression and caseness in patients who were distressed prior to discharge. It also significantly reduced both the number of contacts with the GP and readmissions to hospital over the following 12 months. Some caution must be applied in interpreting these psychological improvements as being as the result of changing the patient's beliefs. First, data on changes in these factors was not collected; secondly the numbers available to the 12-month follow-up were low; thirdly, patients were encouraged to self-diagnose unusual levels of anxiety and depression and were advised how to make appropriate self-referral if the self-help advice and time had not significantly reduced the problem; and finally, patients also carried out a home exercise programme, and it is possible that this also contributed to the results.

Cardiac rehabilitation

Despite the endorsement of many authoritative bodies (Parmley, 1986; International Society and Federation of Cardiology, 1981; Health and Public Policy Committee, American College of Physicians, 1988), a recent survey found that considerably less than half the health districts in the UK had any form of cardiac rehabilitation programme (Horgen, Bethell and Carson, 1992). Most were run by a physician with a physiotherapist. The relative importance of psychosocial interventions compared to physical training is still a contentious issue. The statement of the American College of Physicians that 'Medically supervised physical exercise is the core element of cardiac rehabilitation' (Health and Public Policy Committee, 1988) probably represents the current view in all countries.

Components of comprehensive rehabilitation programmes

Exercise training

It is established that appropriate levels of exercise may produce a 20% increase in maximal work capacity, with a beneficial effect on metabolic and circulatory demands. Some patients may be capable of further gains, producing useful changes in cardiac function such as a higher ischaemic threshold and greater myocardial contractility (DATTA, 1987; Greenland and Chu, 1988; Oberman, 1988). Not all exercise trials have reported an improvement in exercise tolerance or other cardiological variables. Indeed, some have reported negative outcomes (Wenger, 1979; Froelicher, Jensen and Genter, 1984; Grodzinski et al., 1987). Up to 50% of patients may gain no physiological benefit from a training programme (van Dixhoorn et al., 1989). It is not established that these physiological effects have any impact on the disease or affect survival, and this is probably why car-

diac rehabilitation services have been so slow to develop. Recently, two meta-analyses (Oldridge, 1988; O'Connor et al., 1989) have reported a 20–25% reduction in total mortality and a 20% reduction in cardiovascular mortality. Such studies are problematic because of the high dropout and differential refusal rates among those offered exercised-based rehabilitation: as many as 50% of patients drop out of treatment before the end of the programme (Oldridge, 1988). Strategies to improve long-term compliance with exercise prescription and the factors that contribute to dropout have been studied (Oldridge et al., 1988). In view of the evidence reviewed above, it is equally reasonable to hypothesize that any reduction in mortality following rehabilitation is as the result of treatments such as relaxation and stress management that are increasingly being included in such programmes.

It has often been asserted that exercise has a beneficial effect on the psychological adjustment of post-MI patients (e.g. Barr Taylor et al., 1986). Many health professionals believe that exercise can operate as an anxiolytic or antidepressant (Byrd, 1963). However, the majority of investigators looking for this effect in post-MI patients have found no such improvement (Plavsic et al., 1976; Mayou et al., 1981; Stern and Cleary, 1982). The study by Stern is noteworthy for the fact that it was controlled, had large number (651), used spouse rating as well as self-report and took measures to eliminate non-compilers. A study by O'Rourke and the present author (O'Rourke et al., 1990) of post coronary bypass patients who were anxious or depressed on entry to an exercise programme found an improvement that remitted following discharge from the programme. At 12-month follow-up, levels were the same as on entry to the programme. Exercise therapy does not seem to influence return to work (Danchin and Goepfert, 1988), but may help patients to feel that they are fighting back, and thus improve their self image and their belief in the controllability of the illness. This is likely to improve their quality of life, but the opposite effects may result if, once discharged, they fail to comply. There may also be reassurance and important social support in attending regular exercise classes. One solution may be to set up community-based classes that patients and their families can attend indefinitely.

Post-MI cardiac education and secondary prevention

A major element of most comprehensive rehabilitation programmes is education about the causes of heart disease and relevant health behaviours. The effectiveness of post-MI education has been poorly evaluated. It has been claimed that it can help to reduce negative psychosocial consequences at 1 year (Theorell, 1983). However, the majority of evidence suggest that education alone does not lead to worthwhile additional long-term changes in smoking behaviour (Sivarajan, Newton and Almes, 1983), diet (Barbarowicz et al., 1980) or exercise (Oldridge et al., 1988). Of course, many patients make such changes spontaneously and it seems that, for those who do not, something more than education is required.

Relaxation training

A study by Hase and Douglas (1987) showed a significant reduction in state but not trait anxiety in cardiac patients who were given a relaxation tape. At 4-month follow-up the experimental group reported walking more (6.66 km per week compared to 2.73 km per week) significantly fewer episodes of chest pain (0.4 vs 2.13) and less than half the number of self-reported 'psychological problems' (10 vs 25). The study was limited by small number ($n = 30$), pseudo randomization (on a monthly basis) and the failure to control for severity of infarct.

Guzzetta (1989) compared the 'stress'-reducing properties of two different relaxation procedures. One group of 27 patients were instructed in Benson's 'respiratory one-method'; the second group of 26 received relaxation plus 'music therapy', which involved choosing one of three categories of music cassette to listen to for 20 minutes twice a day. Both experimental groups had significantly lower heart rates and higher peripheral temperature than the normal-care control group. Asked 'How helpful were the sessions in helping you to relax?', 92% endorsed 'extremely helpful' and 77% said that they intended to continue to practise the method.

Van Dixhoorn et al. (1989) randomly allocated 156 post-MI patients to 5 weeks exercise only (group B) or exercise plus relaxation and breathing retraining (group A). Group A patients showed a more pronounced training bradycardia, greater improvement in S-T abnormalities and less angina. The authors used a composite measure of outcome to form a tripartite disposition of cases: successful, no change and worse. The chances of achieving 'success' were doubled when relaxation was added to the exercise programme. At 2–3-year follow-up, group A had suffered significantly fewer cardiac events (17%) than the exercise-only group (37%). The effects on psychological adjustment included an increase in feelings of wellbeing and a reduction in anxiety and invalidism in group A, but not in group B (Van Dixhoorn et al., 1989).

A similar study of 105 male patients attending a 4–6-week rehabilitation programme in Germany also found a disproportionate improvement in those patients who received relaxation training as well as exercise (Krampen and Ohm, 1984). In particular, they found an improved performance on exercise stress testing, lower levels of hopelessness (using the Beck Hopelessness Scale) and higher subjective ratings of their general state of health and wellbeing at the end of the rehabilitation programme.

Bohachick (1984) has reported a significant reduction in psychological distress in patients taught relaxation. Using the Speilberger State Anxiety Scale and the Symptoms Check-list 90R, she reported lower anxiety, depression, interpersonal sensitivity and somatization.

Stress-management training (SMT)

The beneficial effects of several SMT interventions have been reported above.

Langosch conducted a controlled comparison between SMT and relaxation alone (R). Patients were attending a 3-week post-MI inpatient rehabilitation programme; a control group received standard rehabilitation treatment alone. The study is marred by a high refusal and dropout rate, by pseudo-randomization (patients were free to select which group to attend and by a large variation in educational level: 29% of the SMT group had high-school education, compared with 4% of the R group. At 6 months the SMT patients had fewer cardiac complications (10% vs 31%) than the relaxation-only group (Langosch et al., 1982). They also reported themselves as better able to handle stress, whereas the R group's confidence had significantly declined.

There have been many studies aimed at reducing TABP, and the largest and most successful has been mentioned above. SMT alone has been shown to successfully reduce TABP (Roskies et al., 1986). The contentious nature of the TABP calls into question the value of such programmes. Johnston (1986) has addressed this question in a paper entitled 'Can and should type A behaviour be changed?' In brief, his answers were yes and yes. In reviewing this area, Evans (1991) advised caution, pointing out that in post-MI patients TABP may improve prognosis.

Counselling and psychotherapy

Research in this area is sparse, poorly conducted and inconclusive. Studies by Ibrahim et al. (1974), Rahe, Ward and Hayes (1979) and Gruen (1975) have reported some gains but were fundamentally flawed by poor control procedures and non-standard assessments. One of the few studies to meet modern standards of design compared cardiac education plus relaxation training (both delivered on audio tapes) with the same package plus six sessions of individual counselling. The addition of counselling did not improve outcome; both groups made highly significant and nearly identical psychological and lifestyle gains, compared to a normal care control group (Oldenberg and Perkins, 1985).

Summary

As yet there are no definitive conclusions regarding psychological risk factors. The cardiology text alluded to in the introduction (Julian, 1992) remains neutral on topics such as TABP and hostility. Given the current plethora of theories and conflicting evidence such a judgement seems both wise and fair. A weakness of such theories is that they have been developed in a top-down fashion. There is probably a limitless number of permutations of innate physiological vulnerability, personality or coping styles and environmental contingencies that could combine to produce 'chronic overarousal'. Psychological risk factors are likely to be particularly fluid elements in this equation, their pathogenicity varying over the individual's lifespan, according to the degree of person–environment match–mismatch, and possibly even with changing cultural mores and values.

In the same text, the role of stress in producing episodes of angina is acknowledged, as is the fact that 'circumstantial evidence' is sometimes available to suggest its role in MI or cardiac arrest. These topics are beginning to interest medical researchers, which hopefully will lead to a better understanding of the mechanisms by which chronic overarousal could produce vascular damage. Psychological treatment trials that have employed a wide variety of strategies to target stress or emotional distress have produced encouraging results. A pressing problem is to develop reliable stress measures, both subjective and psychophysiological. At present there is no evidence that psychological treatments have achieved their results by altering stress. There is no mention in the text of the role of psychological factors as codeterminants of symptom burden or the success of medical treatment. It seems likely that, as health psychology advances and such factors become more widely appreciated in medicine in general, this topic will attract more attention.

As regards cardiac rehabilitation, the need for psychological input to such programmes is increasingly being acknowledged in clinical practice. A start has been made toward answering a fundamental question: why do physically restored patients often fail to return to active life? Hopefully the thrust of research will now move away from quantifying levels of psychiatric disturbance to examining the self-concept and belief systems of patients with CAD, including those who have not yet sustained an acute event. What are the psychological effects on patients of receiving such a diagnosis? What is different about the 20% who claim that their quality of life has been improved by experiencing an MI? In other illnesses the patient's feelings of having control over the disease process have been shown to be important. For this reason, as well as for secondary prevention, it is important to help patients change their health behaviours. Better ways of doing this have to be developed.

At present there is no clear evidence that the majority of patients either want, or benefit from, psychodynamic psychotherapy or unstructured counselling. This is not to deny that a significant number of patients require psychological treatment for anxiety, depression, hypochondriasis, obsessional thoughts, undue illness behaviour or sexual or marital problems. Too few patients currently receive such help. Given that around one million people have symptomatic CAD, services must be easily administered, economical with the use of expensive specialists and equipment and, in today's economic climate, be shown to be cost-effective. It seems that there will be plenty for health psychologists to do in the years to come.

References

Abramov, L.A. (1976) Sexual life and sexual frigidity among women developing acute myocardial infarction. *Psychosomatic Medicine*, **38**, 418–23.

Adsett, C.A. and Bruhn, J.G. (1968) Short-term psychotherapy for post-myocardial infarction patients and their wives. *Canadian Medical Association Journal*, **99**, 577–84.

Almeida, D. and Wenger, N.K. (1982) Emotional responses of patients with acute myocardial infarction to their disease. *Cardiology*, **69**, 303–9.

Baile, W.F., Bigelow, G.E., Gottlieb, S.H. *et al.* (1982) Rapid resumption of cigarette smoking following myocardial infarction. *Addictive Behaviour*, **7**, 373–80.

Barbarowicz, P., Nelson, M., DeBusk, R.F. and Haskell, W.L. (1980) A comparison of in-hospital education approaches for coronary bypass patients. *Heart Lung*, **9**, 127–33.

Barefoot, J.C., Dahlstrom, J.W. and Williams, R.B. (1983) Hostility, CHD incidence, and total mortality: a 25 year follow-up study of 255 physicians. *Psychosomatic Medicine*, **45**, 59–63.

Barefoot, J.C., Williams, R.B., Dahlstrom, W.G. *et al.* (1987) Predicting mortality from scores of the Cook–Medley Scale: a follow-up of 118 lawyers. *Psychosomatic Medicine*, **49**, 210–20.

Barr Taylor, C., Houston-Miller, N., Ahn, D.K. *et al.* (1986) The effects of exercise training programs on psychosocial improvement in uncomplicated post-myocardial infarction patients. *Journal of Psychosomatic Research*, **30**, 581–7.

Bass, C. and Wade, C. (1984) Chest pain with normal coronary arteries: a comparative study of psychiatric and social morbidity. *Psychological Medicine*, **14**, 51–61.

Bedsworth, J.A. and Molen, M.T. (1982) Psychological stress in spouses of patients with myocardial infarction. *Heart Lung*, **11**, 82–92.

Beitman, B.D., Mukerji, V., Flaker, G. and Basha, I.M.

(1988) Panic disorder, cardiology patients, and atypical chest pain. *Psychiatric Clinics of North America*, 11, 387–97.

Billing, E., Lindell, B., Sederholm, M. and Theorell, T. (1980) Denial, anxiety and depression following myocardial infarction. *Psychosomatics*, 21, 639–45.

Bohachick, P. (1984) Progressive relaxation training in cardiac rehabilitation: effects on psychological variables. *Nursing Research*, 33, 283–7.

Booth-Kewley, S. and Friedman, H.S. (1987) Psychological predictors of heart disease: a quantitative review. *Psychological Bulletin*, 101, 343–62.

Brackett, C.D. and Powell, L.H. (1988) Psychosocial and physiological predictors of sudden cardiac death after healing of acute myocardial infarction. *American Journal of Cardiology*, 61, 979–83.

Brenner, M.H. (1979) Mortality and the national economy: a review, and the experience of England and Wales. *Lancet*, 2, 568–73.

Bundy, E.C. (1992) *Stress Management Training in Chronic Stable Angina*, PhD Thesis, Birmingham University.

Burnet, W.C. and Chahine, R.A. (1979) Sexual dysfunction as a complication of propranolol therapy in men. *Cardiovascular Medicine*, 4, 811–13.

Byrd, O.E. (1963) A survey of beliefs and practices on relief of tension by moderate exercise. *Journal of School Health*, 33, 426–7.

Byrne, D.G. and Byrne, A.E. (1990) Anxiety and coronary heart disease, in *Anxiety and the Heart*, (eds D.G. Byrne and R.H. Rosenman), Hemisphere, New York.

Byrne, D.G. and Reinhart, M.I. (1989) Occupation, Type A behaviour and self-reported angina pectoris. *Journal of Psychosomatic Research*, 33, 609–19.

Byrne, D.G. and Whyte, H.M. (1978) Severity of illness behaviour in survivors of myocardial infraction. *Journal of Psychosomatic Research*, 22, 485–91.

Carney, R.M., Rich, M.W., Freedland, K.E. *et al.* (1988) Major depressive disorder predicts cardiac events in patients with coronary artery disease. *Psychosomatic Medicine*, 50, 627–33.

Carroll, D. (1992) *Health Psychology: Stress, Behaviour and Disease*, Falmer Press, London.

Cay, E.L. (1982) Psychological problems in patients after a myocardial infarction. *Advances in Cardiology*, 22, 108–12.

Cay, E.L., Vetter, N., Philip, A. and Dugard, P. (1972) Psychological status during recovery from an acute heart attack. *Journal of Psychosomatic Research*, 16, 425–35.

Cay, E.L., Vetter, N., Philip, A. and Dugard, P. (1973) Return to work after a heart attack. *Journal of Psychosomatic Research*, 17, 231–43.

Channer, K.S., O'Connor, S., Britton, S., *et al.* (1988)

Psychological factors influence in success of coronary artery surgery. *Journal of the Royal Society of Medicine*, 11, 629–32.

Cormier, L.E., Katon, W., Russo, J. *et al.* (1988) Chest pain with negative cardiac diagnostic studies: relationship to psychiatric illness. *Journal of Nervous and Mental Disease*, 176, 351–8.

Costa, P.T., Zonderman, A.B., Engel, B.T. *et al.* (1985) The relation of chest pain symptoms to angiographic findings of coronary artery stenosis and neuroticism. *Psychosomatic Medicine*, 47, 285–93.

Croog, S.H. (1983) Recovery and rehabilitation of heart patients: psychosocial aspects, in *Handbook of Psychology and Health, Vol. 3, Cardiovascular Disorders and Behaviour,* (eds D.S. Krantz, A. Baum and J.S. Singer), Lawrence Erlbaum Associates, Hillsdale NJ.

Croog, S.H. and Levine (1977) *The Heart Patient Recovers*, Human Science Press, New York.

Croog, S.H., Shapiro, D.S. and Levine, S. (1971) Denial among heart patients. *Psychosomatic Medicine*, 33, 382–97.

Danchin, N. and Goepfert, P.C. (1988) Exercise training, cardiac rehabilitation and return to work in patients with coronary artery disease. *European Heart Journal*, 9, 43–6.

Dangrove, E. (1968) Sexual responses to disease processes. *Journal of Sexual Research*, 4, 257.

Davey Smith, G., Bartley, M. and Blane, D. (1990) The Black report on socio-economic inequalities in health 10 years on. *British Medical Journal*, 301, 373–7.

DeBusk, R.F. (1982) Physical condition following myocardial infarction. *Advances in Cardiology*, 31, 156–61.

Dellipiani, A.W., Cay, E.L., Philip, A.E. *et al.* (1976) Anxiety after a heart attack. *British Heart Journal*, 38, 752–7.

Dembroski, T.M., MacDougall, J.M., Williams, R.B. *et al.* (1985) Components of Type A, hostility and anger-in: relationship to angiographic findings. *Psychosomatic Medicine*, 47, 219–33.

Diagnostic and Therapeutic Technology Assessment (DATTA) (1987) Coronary rehabilitation services. *Journal of the American Medical Association*, 258, 1959–62.

Doehrman, S.R. (1977) Psychosocial aspects of recovery from coronary heart disease: a review. *Social Science and Medicine*, 11, 199–218.

Doerr, B.C. and Jones, J.W. (1979) Effects of family preparation on state anxiety level of CCU patients. *Nursing Research*, 28, 315–16.

Douglas, J.E. and Wilkes, T.D. (1975) Reconditioning cardiac patients. *American Family Physician*, 11, 123.

Elbert, T., Langosh, W., Steptoe, A. and Vaitl, D. (eds) (1988) *Behavioural Medicine in Cardiovascular Disorders*, John Wiley & Sons, Chichester.

Elder, J.P. (1985) Applications of behaviour modification to community health education: the case of heart disease prevention. *Health Education Quarterly*, **12**, 151–68.

Eliot, R.S. and Buell, J.C. (1985) Role of emotions and stress in the genesis of sudden death. *Journal of the American College of Cardiology*, **5**, 195–8.

Elton, D. and Stanley, G. (1983) *Psychological Control of Pain*, Grune and Stratton, Sydney.

Evans, P. (1991) Coronary heart disease, in *The Psychology of Health, an Introduction*, (eds M. Pitts and K. Phillips), Routledge, London.

Falcone, C., Sconocchia, R., Guasti, L. *et al.* (1988) Dental pain threshold and angina pectoris in patients with coronary artery disease. *Journal of the American College of Cardiology*, **12**, 348–52.

Farquhar, J.W., Macoby, N. and Solomon, D.S. (1984) Community applications of behavioural medicine, in *Handbook of Behavioral Medicine*, (ed W.D. Gentry), Guilford Press, New York.

Favaro, L., Masini, F., Maffei, M.L. and Botti, G. (1989) Syndrome X. *Recenti Progressi in Medicina*, **80**, 281–5.

Fielding, R. (1987) Patients' beliefs regarding the causes of myocardial infarction: implications for information-giving and compliance. *Patient Education and Counselling*, **9**, 121–34.

Finlayson, A. and McEwen, J. (1977) *Coronary Heart Disease and Pattern of Living*, Croom Helm, London.

Frasure-Smith, N. and Prince, R. (1989) Long-term follow-up of the ischaemic heart disease life stress monitoring program. *Psychosomatic Medicine*, **51**, 485–513.

Freeman, L.J. and King, J.C. (1986) Sex and the post-infarction patient. *Cardiology in Practice*, November, 6–8.

Freeman, L.J. and Nixon, P.G.F. (1985) Chest pain and the hyperventilation syndrome – some aetiological considerations. *Postgraduate Medical Journal*, **61**, 957–61.

Freeman, Z. (1986) Is Type A behaviour a cause of coronary heart disease? *Medical Journal of Australia*, **45**, 262–70.

Friedman, M. and Rosenman, R.H. (1959) Association of specific overt behaviour pattern with blood and cardiovascular findings. *Journal of the American Medical Association*, **169**, 1289–96.

Froelicher, V., Jensen, D. and Genter, F. (1984) A randomized trial of exercise training in patients with coronary heart disease. *Journal of the American Medical Association*, **64**, 1116–24.

Garrity, T.F. (1973a) Social involvement and activeness as predictors of morale six months after myocardial infarction. *Social Science and Medicine*, **7**, 199–207.

Garrity, T.F. (1973b) Vocational adjustment after first myocardial infarction: comparative assessment of several variables suggested in the literature. *Social Science and Medicine*, **7**, 705–17.

Garrity, T.F., McGill, A., Becker, M. *et al.* (1976) Report of the task group of cardiac rehabilitation, in *Proceedings of the National Heart and Lung Institute Working Conference on Health Behaviour*, (ed S.M. Weiss), (DHEW Publication No. 76–868), US Government Printing Office, Washington DC.

Gorder, D.D., Dolecek, T.A., Coleman, G.C. *et al.* (1986) Dietary intake in the Multiple Risk Factor Intervention Trial (MRFIT): nutrient and food group changes over 6 years. *Journal of the American Dietetic Association*, **86**, 744–51.

Greenland, P. and Chu, J.S. (1988) Efficacy of cardiac services with emphasis on patients after myocardial infarction. *Annals of Internal Medicine*, **109**, 650–63.

Grodzinski, E., Jette, M., Blumchen, G. and Borer, J. (1987) Effects of a four week training program on left ventricular function as assessed by radionuclide ventriculography. *Journal of Cardiopulmonary Rehabilitation*, **7**, 517–24.

Gruen, W. (1975) Effects of brief psychotherapy during the hospitalization period on the recovery process in heart attacks. *Journal of Consulting and Clinical Psychology*, **43**, 223–32.

Guzzetta, C.E. (1989) Effects of relaxation and music therapy on patients in coronary care unit with presumptive acute myocardial infarction. *Heart and Lung*, **18**, 609–16.

Hase, S. and Douglas, A. (1987) Effects of relaxation training on recovery from myocardial infarction. *Australian Journal of Advanced Nursing*, **5**, 18–26.

Health and Public Policy Committee (1988) Position paper, American College of Physicians, Cardiac Rehabilitation Services. *Annals of Internal Medicine*, **109**, 671–3.

Heberden, W. (1772) Some account of a disorder of the breast. Read at the college, July 21, 1768. *Medical Transactions of the College of Physicians of London*, **2**, 59.

Hellerstein, H.K. and Friedman, E.H. (1970) Sexual activity and the postcoronary patient. *Archives of Internal Medicine*, **125**, 987–97.

Hinohara, S. (1970) Psychological aspects in rehabilitation of coronary heart disease. *Scandinavian Journal of Rehabilitation Medicine*, **2**, 53–9.

Horgan, J.H. and Craig, A.J. (1978) Resumption of sexual activity after myocardial infarction. *Journal of the Irish Medical Association*, **71**, 540–2.

Horgan, J.H., Bethell, H. and Carson, P. (1992) British Cardiac Society: Working Party report on cardiac rehabilitation. *British Heart Journal*, **67**, 412–18.

Hughes, G.H., Hymowitz, N., Ockene, J.K. *et al.* (1981) The Multiple Risk Factor Intervention Trial (MRFIT). V. Intervention on smoking. *Preventive Medicine*, **10**, 476–500.

Ibrahim, M.A., Feldman, J.G., Sultz, M.A. *et al.* (1974) Management after myocardial infarction: a controlled trial of effect of group psychotherapy. *International Journal of Psychiatric Medicine*, **5**, 253–68.

International Society and Federation of Cardiology Scientific Councils (1981) Secondary prevention in survivors of myocardial infarction. *British Medical Journal*, **282**, 894–6.

Jenkins, C.D. (1983) Psychosocial and behavioral factors, in *Prevention of Coronary Heart Disease*, (eds N. Kaplan and J. Stamler), Saunders, Philadelphia, pp. 98–112.

Jenkins, D.C., Stanton, B., Klien, M.D. *et al.* (1983) Correlates of angina pectoris amongst men awaiting coronary artery by-pass surgery. *Psychosomatic Medicine*, **45**, 141–53.

Johnston, D.W. (1986) Can and should type A behaviour be changed? *Postgraduate Medical Journal*, **62**, 785–8.

Julian, D.G. (1992) *Cardiology*, 6th edn, Baillière Tindall, London.

Kennedy, G.J., Hofer, M.A. and Cohen, D. (1987) Significance of depression and cognitive impairment in patients undergoing programmed stimulation of cardiac arrhythmias. *Psychosomatic Medicine*, **49**, 410–14.

Klimes, I., Mayou, R.A. and Pearce, M.J. (1990) Psychological treatment for atypical non-cardiac chest pain: a controlled evaluation. *Psychological Medicine*, **20**, 605–11.

Krampen, G. and Ohm, D. (1984) Effects of relaxation training during rehabilitation of myocardial infarction patients. *International Journal of Rehabilitation Research*, **7**, 68–9.

Krantz, D.S. and Raisen, S.E. (1988) Environmental stress, reactivity and ischaemic heart disease. *British Journal of Medical Psychology*, **61**, 3–16.

Krantz, D.S., Helmers, K.F., Bairey, C.N. *et al.* (1991) Cardiovascular reactivity and mental stress–induced myocardial ischaemia in patients with coronary artery disease. *Journal of Psychosomatic Medicine*, **53**, 1–12.

Laerum, E., Johnsen, N., Smith, P. and Larsen, S. (1988) Myocardial infarction may induce positive changes in life style and in the quality of life. *Scandinavian Journal of Primary Health Care*, **6**, 67–71.

Langosch, W., Seer, P., Brodner, G. *et al.* (1982) Behaviour therapy with coronary heart disease patients: results of a comparative study. *Journal of Psychosomatic Research*, **26**, 475–84.

Lantinga, L.J., Sprafkin, R.P., McCroskery, J.H. *et al.* (1988) One-year psychosocial follow-up of patients with chest pain and angiographically normal coronary arteries. *American Journal of Cardiology*, **62**, 209–13.

Lewin, B., Robertson, I.H. and Cay, E.I., (1992) Effects of self-help post-myocardial infarction rehabilitation on psychological adjustment and use of health services. *Lancet*, **339**, 1036–40.

Lloyd, G.G. and Cawley, R.H. (1982) Psychiatric morbidity after myocardial infarction. *Quarterly Journal of Medicine*, **51**, 33–42.

Lloyd G.G. and Cawley, R.H. (1983) Distress or illness? A study of psychological symptoms after myocardial infarction. *British Journal of Psychiatry*, **142**, 120–5.

Lovibond, S.H., Birrell, P. and Langeluddecke, P. (1986) Changing coronary heart disease risk-factor status: the effects of three behavioural programs. *Journal of Behavioral Medicine*, **9**, 415–37.

Lown, B., DeSilva, R.A., Reich, P. and Murawaski, B.J. (1980) Psychophysiological factors in sudden cardiac death. *American Journal of Psychiatry*, **137**, 1325–35.

McCormick, J. and Skrabanek, P., (1988) Coronary heart disease is not preventable by population intervention. *Lancet*, **2**, 839–41.

McCranie, E.W., Watkins, L.O., Brandsma, J.M. and Sisson, B.D. (1986) Hostility, coronary heart disease (CHD) incidence, and total mortality: lack of association in 25 year follow-up study of 478 physicians. *Journal of Behavioural Medicine*, **9**, 119–25.

McGrath, F.J. and Robinson, J.S. (1973) The medical social worker in the coronary unit. *Medical Journal of Australia*, **2**, 1113–16.

Mæland, J.G., and Havik, O.E. (1986) Return to work after a myocardial infarction: the influence of background factors, work characteristics and illness severity. *Scandinavian Journal of Social Medicine*, **14**, 183–95.

Mæland, J.G. and Havik, O.E. (1988) Self-assessment of health before and after a myocardial infarction. *Social Science and Medicine*, **27**, 597–605.

Mæland, J.G. and Havik, O.E. (1989) Use of health services after a myocardial infarction; *Scandinavian Journal of Social Medicine*, **17**, 93–102.

Maes, S. (1992) Psychosocial aspects of cardiac rehabilitation in Europe. *British Journal of Clinical Psychology*, **31**, 473–83.

Mallaghan, M. and Pemberton, J. (1977) Some behavioural changes in 493 patients after an acute myocardial infarction. *British Journal of Preventative Medicine*, **31**, 86–90.

Manuck, S.B., Kaplan, J.R., Adams, M.R. and Clarkson, T.B. (1988a) Stress, behaviour, and cardiovascular disease: a basic science perspective using animal models. *Health Psychology*, **7**, 113–24.

Manuck, S.B., Kaplan, J.R., Adams, M.R. and Clarkson, T.B. (1988b) Effects of stress and the sympathetic nervous system on coronary artery atherosclerosis in the cynomolgus macaque. *American Heart Journal*, **116**, 328–33.

Marmot, M.G. (1983) Stress, social and cultural variation in heart disease. *Journal of Psychosomatic Research*, **27**, 377.

Marmot, M.E., Shipley, M.J. and Rose, G. (1984) Inequalities in death-specific explanations of a general pattern. *Lancet*, **1**, 1003–6.

Maseri, A., L'Abbate, Baroldi, G. *et al.* (1978) Coronary vasospasm as a possible cause of myocardial infarction. *New England Journal of Medicine*, **299**, 1271–7.

Masur, F.T. (1979) Resumption of sexual activity following myocardial infarction. *Sexual Disability*, **2**, 98–114.

Mayou, R. (1979) The course and determinants of reactions to myocardial infarction. *British Journal of Psychiatry*, **134**, 588–94.

Mayou, R. (1984) Prediction of emotional and social outcome after a heart attack. *Journal of Psychosomatic Research*, **28**, 17–25.

Mayou, R. and Bryant, B. (1987) Quality of life after coronary artery surgery. *Quarterly Journal of Medicine*, New series, **62**, 239–48.

Mayou, R. MacMahon, D., Sleight, P. and Florencio, M.J. (1981) Early rehabilitation after myocardial infarction. *Lancet*, **2**, 1399–1401.

Mehta J. and Krop, H. (1979) The effect of myocardial infarction on sexual functioning. *Sexual Disability*, **2**, 115–21.

Mock, M.B., Ringqvist, I. and Fisher, L.D. (1982) Survival of medically treated patients in the coronary artery surgery study (CASS) registry. *Circulation*, **66**, 562–8.

Murray, P.J. (1989) Rehabilitation information and health beliefs in the post-coronary patient: do we meet their information needs? *Journal of Advanced Nursing*, **14**, 689–93.

Newman, S., Smith, P., Treasure, T. (1987) Acute neuropsychological consequences of coronary artery bypass surgery. *Current Psychological Research Reviews*, **6**, 115–124.

Oberman, A. (1988) Rehabilitation of patients with coronary artery disease, in *Heart Disease: a Textbook of Cardiovascular Medicine*, (ed E. Braunwald), W.B. Saunders Co., Philadelphia.

O'Brien, B.J. (1991) Introduction, in *Cholesterol and Coronary Heart Disease: Consensus or Controversy?* Office of Health Economics, London.

Ockene, I.S., Shay, M.J. and Alpert, J.S. (1980) Unexplained chest pain in patients with normal coronary arteriograms. A follow-up study of functional status. *New England Journal of Medicine*, **303**, 1249–52.

O'Connor, G.T., Collins, R., Buring, J.E. *et al.* (1989) Rehabilitation with exercise after myocardial infarction. *Circulation*, **82**, 324–44.

Office of Health Economics (1990) *Coronary Heart Disease: the Need for Action*, Office of Health Economics, London.

Oldenberg, B. and Perkins, R.J. (1985) Controlled trial of psychological intervention in myocardial infarction. *Journal of Consulting and Clinical Psychology*, **53**, 852–9.

Oldridge, N.B. (1988) Cardiac rehabilitation exercise programme compliance and compliance enhancing strategies. *Sports Medicine*, **6**, 42–55.

Oldridge, N.B., Guyatt, G.H., Fischer, M.E. and Rimm, A.A. (1988) Cardiac rehabilitation after myocardial infarction, combined experience of randomized clinical trials. *Journal of the American Medical Association*, **260**, 945–50.

Ornish, D., Brown, S.E., Scherwitz, L.W. *et al.* (1990) Can lifestyle changes reverse coronary heart disease? *Lancet*, **336**, 129–33.

Ornish, D., Scherwitz, L.W., Doody, R.S. *et al.* (1983) Effects of stress management training and dietary changes in treating ischemic heart disease. *Journal of the American Medical Association*, **249**, 54–9.

O'Rourke, A., Lewin, B., Whitecross, S. and Pacy, W. (1990) The effects of physical exercise training and cardiac education on levels of anxiety and depression in the rehabilitation of coronary artery bypass graft patients. *International Disability Studies*, **12**, 104–6.

Papadopoulos, C., Beaumont, C., Shelley, S.I. *et al.* (1983) Myocardial infarction and sexual activity of the female patient. *Archives of Internal Medicine*, **143**, 1528.

Parmley, W.W. (1986) President's Page: Position Report on Cardiac Rehabilitation, Recommendations of the American College of Cardiology on cardiovascular rehabilitation. *Journal of the American College of Cardiology*, **7**, 451–3.

Patel, C., Marmot, M.G., Terry, D.J. *et al.* (1985) Trial of relaxation in reducing coronary risk: four year follow up. *British Medical Journal*, **290**, 1103–6.

Plavsic, C., Turkulin, K., Perman, Z. *et al.* (1976) The results of exercise therapy in coronary prone individuals and coronary patients. *Italian Journal of Cardiology*, **6**, 422–32.

Proudfit, W.L., Bruschke, A.V.G. and Sones, F.M. (1980) Clinical course of patients with normal of slightly or moderately abnormal coronary arteriograms: 10 year follow-up 521 patients. *Circulation*, **62**, 712–17.

Ragland, D.R, and Brand, R.J. (1988) Type A behaviour and mortality from coronary heart disease. *New England Journal of Medicine*, **318**, 65–9.

Rahe, R.M., Ward, H.W. and Hayes, V. (1979) Brief group therapy in myocardial infarction rehabilitation three to four year follow-up of a controlled trial. *Psychosomatic Medicine*, **41**, 229–42.

Reich, P., DeSilva, R.A., Lown, B. and Murawaski, B.J. (1981) Acute psychological disturbances preceding life-threatening ventricular arrhythmias. *Journal of the American Medical Association*, **246**, 233.

Reichgott, M.J. (1979) Problems of sexual function in patients with hypertension. *Cardiovascular Medicine*, **4**, 149.

Rime, B., Ucros, C.G., Bestgen, Y. and Jeanjean, M. (1989) Type A behaviour pattern: specific coronary risk factor or general disease-prone condition? *British Journal of Medical Psychology*, **62**, 229–40.

Rosenman, R.H., Brand, R.J., Jenkins, C.D. *et al.* (1975) Coronary heart disease in the Western Collaborative Group Study: final follow-up experience of eight and a half years. *Journal of the American Medical Association*, **233**, 872–7.

Roskies, E., Seragabianz, P., Oseasons, S.R. *et al.* (1986) The Montreal type A intervention project: major findings. *Health Psychology*, **5**, 1.

Rozanski, A., Bairey, C.N. and Krantz, D.S. (1988) Mental stress and the induction of silent myocardial ischemia in patients with coronary artery disease. *New England Journal of Medicine*, **318**, 1005–12.

Ruberman, W., Weinblatt, E., Goldberg, J.D. and Chaudhary, B.S. (1984) Psychosocial influences on mortality after myocardial infraction. *New England Journal of Medicine*, **311**, 552–9.

Schleifer, S.J., Macari-Hinson, M.M., Coyle, D.A. *et al.* (1989) The nature of depression following myocardial infarction. *Archives of Internal Medicine*, **149**, 1785–9.

Schwartz, G.E., Weinberger, D.A. and Singer, J.A. (1981) Cardiovascular differentiation of happiness, sadness, anger, and fear following imagery and exercise. *Psychosomatic Medicine*, **43**, 343.

Sheps, D.S., Hinderliter, A. and Bragdon, E.E. (1988) Endorphins and pain perception in silent myocardial ischemia. *American Journal of Cardiology*, **61**, 3–8.

Sivarajan, E.S., Newton K.M. and Almes M.J. (1983) Limited effects of outpatients teaching and counselling after myocardial infarction: a controlled study. *Heart and Lung*, **12**, 65–73.

Sjorgen, K. and Fugl-Meyer, A. (1983) Some factors influencing quality of sexual life after myocardial infarction. *International Rehabilitation Medicine*, **5**, 197–201.

Skelton, M. and Dominian, J. (1973) Psychological stress in wives of patients with myocardial infarction. *British Medical Journal*, **2**, 101–3.

Smith, T.W., Follick, M.J. and Korr, K.S. (1984) Anger, neuroticism, type A behaviour and the experience of angina. *British Journal of Medical Psychology*, **57**, 249–52.

Soloff, P.H. (1978) Denial and rehabilitation of the postinfarction patient. *International Journal of Psychiatric Medicine*, **8**, 125–32.

Steptoe, A. (1988) The processes underlying long-term blood pressure reductions in essential hypertensives following behaviour therapy, in *Behavioural Medicine in Cardiovascular Disorders*, (eds T. Elbert, W. Langosh, A. Steptoe and D. Vaitl), John Wiley & Sons, Chichester, pp. 139–48.

Stern, M.J. and Cleary, P. (1982) The National Exercise and Heart Disease Project: long term psychosocial outcome. *Archives of Internal Medicine*, **142**, 1093–7.

Stern, M.J. and Pascal, L. (1979) Psychosocial adaptation post-myocardial infarction: the spouse's dilemma. *Journal of Psychosomatic Research*, **23**, 83–7.

Stern, M.J., Pascal, L. and Ackerman, A. (1977) Life adjustment post myocardial infarction. Determining predictive variable. *Archives of Internal Medicine*, **137**, 1680–5.

Stern, M.J., Pascal, L. and McLoone, J.B. (1976) Psychosocial adaption following an acute myocardial infarction. *Journal of Chronic Disease*, **29**, 513–6.

Taylor, C.B., Bandura, A. and Ewart, C.K. (1985) Exercise testing to enhance wives' confidence in their husband's cardiac capability soon after clinically uncomplicated acute myocardial infarction. *American Journal Cardiology*, **55**, 635–8.

Tesar, G.T. and Hackett, T.P. (1985) Psychiatric management of the hospitalised cardiac patient. *Journal of Cardiopulmonary Rehabilitation*, **5**, 219–25.

Theorell, T. (1983) Psychosocial intervention as part of the rehabilitation after a myocardial infarction. *International Rehabilitation Medicine*, **5**, 185–8.

Thompson, D., Cordle, C. and Sutton, T. (1982) Anxiety in coronary patients. *International Rehabilitation Medicine*, **4**, 161–3.

Thoresen, C.E., Friedman, M., Gill, J.K. and Ulmer, D.K. (1982) The current coronary prevention project: some preliminary findings. *Acta Medica Scandinavica*, Suppl **600**, 172–92.

Ueno, M. (1963) The so-called coital death. *Japan Journal of Legal Medicine*, **17**, 535.

van Dixhoorn, J., De Loos, J. and Duivenvoorden, H.J. (1983) Contribution of relaxation technique training to the rehabilitation of myocardial infarction patients. *Psychotherapy and Psychosomatics*, **40**, 137–47.

van Dixhoorn, J., Duivenvoorden, H.J., Staal, H.A. and Pool, J. (1989) Physical training and relaxation therapy in cardiac rehabilitation assessed through a composite criterion for training outcome. *American Heart Journal*, **118**, 545–52.

Verrier, R.L., Hagestad, E.L. and Lown, B. (1987) Delayed myocardial ischaemia induced by anger. *Circulation*, **75**, 249–54.

Vetter, N.J., Cay, E.L., Philip, A.E. and Strange, R.C. (1977) Anxiety on admission to a coronary care unit. *Journal of Psychosomatic Research*, **21**, 73–8.

Wabreck, A.J. and Burchell, R.C. (1980) Male sexual dysfunction associated with coronary heart disease. *Archives of Sexual Behaviour*, **9**, 69–75.

Walter, P.J. (1985) *Return to Work after Coronary Artery Bypass Surgery: Psychosocial and Economic Aspects*, Springer Verlag, New York.

Waltz, M., Badura, B., Pfaff, H. and Schott, T. (1988) Marriage and the psychosocial consequences of a heart attack: a longitudinal study of adaption to chronic illness after 3 years. *Social Science and Medicine*, **27**, 149–58.

Wells, J.A. (1985) Chronic life situations and life change events, in *Measuring Psychosocial Variables in Epidemiologic Studies of Cardiovascular Disease*, (NIH publication no. 80 85-2270, 105-129) NIH, Betheseda, MD.

Wenger, N. (1979) Research related to rehabilitation. *Circulation*, **60**, 1636–9.

Wenger, N.K. and Alpert J.S. (1989) Rehabilitation of the coronary patient. *Archives of Internal Medicine*, **149**, 1505–6.

Wiklund, I., Sann, H., Vedin, A. and Wilhelmsson, C. (1984a) Psychosocial outcome one year after a first myocardial infarction. *Journal of Psychosomatic Research*, **28**, 309–21.

Wiklund, I., Sanne, H., Elmfeldt, D. *et al.* (1984b) Emotional reaction, health preoccupation and sexual activity two months after a myocardial infarction, health preoccupation and sexual activity two months after a myocardial infarction. *Scandinavian Journal of Rehabilitation Medicine*, **16**, 47–56.

Wiklund, I., Sanne, H., Vedin, A. and Wilhelmsson, C. (1985a) Copping with myocardial infarction: a model with clinical applications, a literature review. *International Rehabilitation Medicine*, **7**, 167–75.

Wiklund, I., Sanne, H., Vedin, A. and Wilhelmsson (1985b) Determinants of return to work one year after a first myocardial infarction. *Journal of Cardiopulmonary Rehabilitation*, **5**, 62–72.

Williams, R.B., Hanley, T.H. and Lee, K.L. (1980) Type A behaviour, hostility, and coronary atherosclerosis. *Psychosomatic Medicine*, **42**, 539–49.

Williams, R.B., Haney, T.H. and McKinnis, R.A. (1986) Psychosocial and physical predictors of anginal pain relief with medical management. *Psychosomatic Medicine*, **48**, 200–10.

Winefield, H. and Martin, C.J. (1981) Measurement and prediction recovery after myocardial infarction. *International Journal of Psychiatric Medicine*, **11**, 145–54.

Wishnie, H.A., Hackett, T.P. and Cassem, N.H. (1971) Psychological hazards of convalescence following myocardial infarction. *Journal of American Medicine*, **215**, 1296–9.

Woodward, M., Shewry, M.C., Cairns, W. *et al.* (1992) Social status and coronary heart disease: results from the Scottish Heart health study. *Preventive Medicine*, **21**, 136–48.

Wynn, A. (1967) Unwarranted emotional distress in men with ischaemic heart disease. *Medical Journal of Australia*, **2**, 847–51.

Yeung, A.C., Vekshtein, V.I. and Krantz, D.S. (1991) The effects of atherosclerosis on the vasomotor response of coronary arteries to normal stress. *New England Journal of Medicine*, **325**, 1551–6.

Zotti, A.M., Bettinardi, O., Soffiantino, F. *et al.* (1991) Psychophysiological stress testing in post infarction patients. Psychological correlates of cardiovascular arousal and abnormal cardiac responses. *Circulation*, **83**, 1125–35.

Chapter ten

Dermatology

Peter James

Introduction

This chapter summarizes the psychological mechanisms that can contribute to the formation and expression of dermatological symptoms. It will also review the psychosocial impact of skin diseases generally and raise many research questions which need urgent attention. A number of specific conditions will be presented, with a view to drawing implications for current health care practice.

Background

Over 20 years ago, considerable interest in a range of skin disorders was evident in the psychosomatic literature, and was reviewed comprehensively by Whitlock (1976). However, the concern was often with personality traits which were thought to predispose individuals to skin complaints. Psychodynamic formulations were also presented quite extensively to explain how certain inner psychic conflicts could be manifested symbolically as skin dysfunction (e.g. Alexander, 1950). Indeed, the literature could be criticized for making a fundamental error by assuming that, in the absence of organic explanations for observed pathophysiology, there must be a 'functional', 'psychological' or 'neurotic' explanation. With the development of medical science, it soon became evident that these psychological formulations were in error as organic explanations were found.

Although the psychosomatic and health psychology literatures have sharpened and developed their scientific tools, dermatologists' attitudes remain shaped by their past exposure. Consider the way psychodermatology is generally introduced in dermatology textbooks: they often suggest that the role of psychological factors in causing or aggravating skin disease is controversial. Much nonsense has been written on the subject, uncritical and uncontrolled work has produced a reaction among some dermatologists. There is no sign of a significant revival in psychodermatology, as reflected by the few recent research papers quoted here. Perhaps dermatologists' attitudes towards health psychology need to be developed. Attempts to create formal psychodermatological training for dermatologists are a welcome innovation (Van Moffaert, 1986).

The skin is a large visible organ prone to a wide range of painful, itchy and disfiguring conditions which are all too often chronic in nature. That psychological factors are associated with changes in the skin is obvious: emotional expression involves both sensory and visible changes in the skin. Further, body image is largely affected by the skin.

The liaison psychiatry (Cotterill, 1989) and health psychology (Koo, 1989) literatures, although using different underlying explanatory models, suggest that emotional distress, behavioural disorders, excessive disability and characteristic cognitive patterns are both prevalent and require explanation. In a typical dermatology clinic there is a high incidence of psychiatric problems, ranging from depression to delusional symptoms (Cotterill, 1983), especially with dermatology inpatients (Hughes *et al.*, 1983a). Despite the comments noted above, many authors have urged dermatology services to broaden their approach from the dominant medical model to incorporate these psychiatric or psychological dimensions (Medansky, 1980; Engles, 1982). Some have gone so far as to say that the incorporation of psychological models to dermatology is of greater relevance than to other specialties such as cardiology, renal dialysis and cosmetic surgery, which have all received considerably more attention (Van Moffaert, 1982). Others have promoted the role of clinical psychology in the management of skin problems in primary care (Mackie, 1991). The first step towards incorporating health psychology must be to introduce some conceptual clarity as to how psychological processes can influence the skin.

First, we have to identify problems where individuals express their distress in a way that leads to dermatological attention, without skin pathology or disorder. This has been referred to as 'dermatological non-disease' (Cotterill, 1981), and would include such problems as dysmorphobia (perceived physical defect without objective evidence) and delusions of parasitosis (perceived skin infestation without adequate objective evidence). These are problems beyond the scope of this chapter, but we will make a distinction between psychological processes that influence the course of a skin condition and psychological consequences which directly result from that condition. Both are important in clinical practice, and are considered separately below.

Psychological consequences of skin disorders

The exact impact of a skin condition on an individual will depend upon the way it interferes with their ability to meet their needs, and the extent to which it proves stressful for them and their family. People may react differently to the same skin condition, and yet certain skin complaints may tend to result in people experiencing a common cluster of problems. Given this complexity of individual-vs-condition interaction, typical of approaches to chronic illness (Turk, Meichenbaum and Genest, 1983), we should not expect to find a neat list of psychological problems encountered by all patients for each skin condition. What follows is a checklist of likely consequences which apply to all skin conditions, the disabling consequences sometimes ranking with heart failure or renal failure in magnitude (Ryan, 1991). Skin lesions or disturbances can lead to reduced mobility and dexterity; certain provoking environmental factors may have to be avoided; treatments with bandages and ointments can be restricting. These and other factors lead to levels of actual and perceived physical disability, the latter being more important from a psychological perspective. Individuals further impose limits on their behaviour because of the perceived consequences, e.g. negative social reactions to unsightly and 'contagious' lesions. Therefore, a discrepancy will exist between the wishes or expectations of individuals and what they perceive they are able to do. They may inappropriately attribute disappointments or failures in life to their skin condition. These combined effects can construed by the sufferer as a loss of function. If temporary, it may lead to a depressed mood if the sufferer judges life to have little to offer, either now or in the future (Beck, 1976). If relatively permanent, this loss can lead to a form of bereavement process, with the usual emotional sequelae (Worden, 1991). In dermatology, this loss may not be accepted because of the promise of medical treatment or the hope of remission. The bereavement process may thus be prolonged and, as with other physical illnesses, it may not be recognized by patients and clinicians.

It can be seen that in every step of the argument outlined above there is scope for understanding how the impact of a condition can vary in magnitude according to the way an individual is thinking. Using health psychology, these cognitions become amenable to comprehension and intervention (Merluzzi, Glass and Genest, 1981). For instance, cognitive models can help to explain how some individuals can be severely socially disabled by mild acne, whereas others can be cheerful despite physically incapacitating chronic psoriasis. Psychology would expect to find a wide range of such cognitions or attitudes, and hypothesize that these will show a degree of independence from the severity and nature of the skin condition.

Adjustment could be construed as individuals minimizing the discrepancy between their expectations and what they actually achieve. As chronic skin conditions often affect people in adolescence and early life, where ambitions and expectations are at a formative stage, these health-related cognitions may be of particular clinical interest. Research into these skin-related attitudes, adjustment and the associated mood has recently begun for acne.

Popular models of stress (Meichenbaum and Jaremko, 1982) predict increased vulnerability where individuals perceive themselves to be in a demanding situation, or in situations where they perceive threat to their physical wellbeing, personal control or self-esteem, including body image and socially valid role. Chronic skin conditions are typically unpredictable, uncontrollable, provoke negative reactions from onlookers, affect body image perceptions (Shuster et al., 1978; Leichtman, Burnett and Robinson, 1981), interfere with sexual activity (Buckwalter, 1982) and lead to some physical and social disability. It is clear that, for some individuals, the skin condition may serve as a major stressor as outlined above, because of the perceived threat or demand. This is particularly pertinent to children, where disturbances in body image and psychosocial development are less reversible (e.g. Pines, 1980). There may be additional stressors in the form of pain and itchiness, which are integral elements of many skin disorders. Accumulating stress may be given the emotional labels of anxiety, frustration or anger, and it is interesting that these are so often observed in dermatology patients.

Stress involves an increase in peripheral bodily activation, and these psychophysiological changes may exacerbate the skin condition directly. It is worth noting a clinical observation: when stressed, individuals may perceive their skin condition to be worse than it actually is, although empirical evidence is not available to support this contention. Using the stress model, one would predict that anxiety or stress experiences could be best predicted by looking at the way individuals assess the impact of the condition on them, rather than looking at the objective nature of the skin condition itself. As in the section above, the emphasis is on identifying patients' attitudes towards their condition. It is likely that the assessment and clinical tools developed could be equally applied to a number of skin conditions, such as eczema, psoriasis and acne.

Although extreme examples of poor adjustment can be cited, the vast majority of dermatology patients seem to adapt to their condition reasonably well. However, we still need to know if there is scope for improving moderate or poor levels of coping in the individual, or in the family in the case of children, perhaps with the use of self-help literature (e.g. Orton, 1981). With both children and adults the clinician may need to check that the skin condition does not have rewards or secondary gains for the patient or the family (Minnuchin, 1974). Some of the adverse consequences outlined above may, in turn, further exacerbate the skin complaint, thus tending to a 'vicious

169

cycle.' The next section includes a discussion about the possible mechanisms involved in this process.

Pathological routes to skin disorders

There have been a number of attempts to classify psychosomatic skin conditions (e.g. Walton, 1985). These often discriminate between groups of disorders on the basis of hypothesized aetiology. An alternative approach is to identify a number of distinct psychological processes involved in any skin condition, and three are identified below. However, it is worth emphasizing that to acknowledge the full picture, psychological processes have to be considered in combination with a range of constitutional and environmental factors. This results in the application of multicausal models (Rees, 1976). It is no longer tenable to ask whether a condition is psychological or not, a practice which led to the unfortunate use of the diagnostic label 'neurodermatitis' (Brocq and Jacquet, 1891). There is a psychological component to all skin conditions, even if this is just manifested as a degree to which an individual can comply with medical treatment, but it is the magnitude which will justify clinical intervention. The following three processes are not mutually exclusive, and one may well expect all three to be interacting.

Primary psychophysiological process

Psychological states such as stress, emotional distress and styles of thinking are accompanied by physiological changes in the skin and to the immune system. Furthermore, the hypnotic induction of skin changes also demonstrates the potential role of psychophysiological processes (Barber, 1984). These psychologically induced bodily changes may be necessary – but not necessarily sufficient – to lead, over time, to the initial generation of a skin disorder. Specificity theories have tried to explain how these psychophysiological mechanisms result in an individual being susceptible to one condition and not another, for example perhaps eczema but not hives.

One approach is to hypothesize that certain individuals have a tendency to show persistently more reactivity in some physiological systems as opposed to others, and that this individual response-specificity results in physiological dysfunction or damage, culminating in skin pathology (Sternbach, 1966). Differences in reactivity or recovery in skin functioning, e.g. blood flow, skin temperature and skin conductance, have rarely been researched across skin conditions, despite the obvious theoretical attractions. In one study, stress-induced psychophysiological activation in psoriasis and atopic dermatitis showed few group differences (Arnetz et al. 1991).

Another approach is the 'organ weakness' model, which states that under conditions of equal psychophysiological reactivity, the prone individual has an organic predisposition to exhibit pathophysiology, whereas a non-prone individual does not. Given the genetic and clearly identified environmental factors in many skin conditions, this organic weakness model does seem quite plausible. However, it can be hypothesized that despite this weakness some individuals would not have developed skin disorders had it not been for a sufficiently extreme or prolonged psychophysiological excitation. There are suggestions that some cases of alopecia (Medansky and Handler, 1981), psoriasis (Fava et al. 1980) and urticaria (Meynadier et al., 1985) may fall into this category. Logically, it is possible that further episodes of skin disease may be avoidable: if the skin changes are reversible, if psychological mechanisms are reduced and if the other organ weakness/environmental factors in the multicausal model remain insufficient to precipitate disease.

Secondary psychophysiological process

When the skin has a preexisting pathology, its new properties may mean that the psychophysiological processes identified above exacerbate the disease process. These psychophysiological processes are secondary. The distinction is important clinically because it helps achieve face validity with dermatologists and encourages realistic expectations for therapeutic outcome. Psychophysiological manipulations such as relaxation, biofeedback and stress management might reduce the intensity and frequency of the skin disorder, but the underlying disease process would remain unaffected. To investigate this process, specific disease groups would need to be studied psychophysiologically, as generalization from normal subjects would be inappropriate. This secondary process is likely to account for the evidence, reviewed later, that many skin conditions are made worse by variants of stress.

Itching, known as pruritus, is a common symptom in dermatology, and results from various physiological and pathophysiological processes stimulating nerve endings in the skin. Mild stimulation of the neuronal pathways involved in slow mediated pain seems to produce itch (Tonnesen, 1979). In fact, chronic pruritus can be seen as producing a range of problems typical of chronic pain (Gilchrist, 1982). It has often been asserted that psychophysiological process in the skin can further influence the level of itchiness (Whitlock, 1976). Despite these obvious suggestions that health psychology has much to offer our understanding of itch, progress is very slow. There are no widely used and acceptable measures of pruritus, and there are no recent psychophysical studies. Initial attempts at producing experimentally induced itch by cowhage (Shelley and Arthur, 1959) and by electrical stimulation (Edwards et al., 1976) have not been reliably replicated. The effect of emotional arousal, depression and fatigue on

pruritus levels has not been properly investigated. With a few exceptions (e.g. Bjornberg, Lowhagen and Tergberg, 1979) individual differences in itch threshold and itch tolerance have not been scientifically examined. Given the prevalence and impact of pruritus and the damaging nature of scratching, it would seem that the condition is in urgent need of attention. There is every reason to believe that the models and experimental tools so prolific in pain research could be applied in pruritus. As an example, Hajek, Jakoubek and Hadil, (1990) successfully manipulated cutaneous pain thresholds in controls and atopic eczema sufferers using repeated hypnotic suggestions.

Behavioural processes

Unlike most organs, the skin is amenable to direct conscious or unconscious manipulation. Hair-pulling (trichotillomania), self-harm (dermatitis artefacta), rubbing, scratching and intense scratching (excoriations) are all behaviours directly involved in dermatology. The extensive behavioural and self-control literature in health psychology (e.g. Russell, 1986) could thus be applied. For example, dermatological problems can become the focus of obsessive–compulsive problems (Stein and Hollander, 1992), especially in troubled adolescents (Koo and Smith, 1991a). Psychological therapies might therefore be very important.

Of particular interest is scratching behaviour and the relationship to the noxious sensation of itchiness (urge to scratch). Scratching without itchiness may occur in displacement activities (Musaph, 1968), through classical conditioning (Jordan and Whitlock, 1974) or through operant conditioning (Allen and Harris, 1966). Most scratching will be positively correlated with itchiness, although the types of dyssynchrony are of major clinical interest; 'itch without scratch' would be an important therapeutic goal. Scratching during the day can be recorded using forearm EMG (Savin et al., 1975) and at night by monitoring bed movements (Felix and Shuster, 1975). Given that most of the damaging scratching occurs at night, it might be possible to use these measures as a form of biofeedback to wake the patient and deter such nocturnal behaviour, although, to the author's knowledge, this has not been tried. Later in the chapter there are many examples of these behavioural processes in action. Meanwhile, let us conclude this section by referring to the less tangible illness behaviours of an individual that will influence the course of the skin disease indirectly:

- At what point does the skin rash merit health-seeking behaviour?
- Is an individual complying with medical advice?
- Does an individual show initiative or take an active role in the management of their condition?

With chronic skin conditions it is not unusual for patients to spend several months as inpatients and be very frequent outpatient attenders. This may shape up certain sorts of illness behaviour and dependency, especially in children. Here, then, are further avenues for research.

Skin disorders

Acne

Acne is one of the commonest of complaints, and varies greatly in severity. Excessive sebum is produced by glands in the skin and outflow is obstructed. It is related to hormonal activity, hence its peak instance during adolescence, and so the relevant psychophysiology would include the neuroendocrine system. A review by Kenyon (1966) of studies relating acne to personality concluded that this condition was not primarily influenced by psychological dimensions. However, individual characteris-

tics, e.g. tough mindedness, do influence the individual's perception of acne-related disability (Lim and Tan, 1991). More pervasively, dissatisfaction with acne-affected skin can have a wider influence on general body image (Gupta et al., 1990). Although acne does cause a drop in self-esteem and an increase in social isolation, these effects do not seem to be extreme in adolescents, and improve with an improvement in the skin (Koo and Smith, 1991b). One useful tool has been developed to assess acne-related disability (Motley and Finley, 1989), and this could be used to assess therapy that addresses these psychosocial issues in addition to standard medical treatment.

It has been noted that some individuals do seem to show a worsening of acne during emotional distress (Kenyon, 1966; Kraus, 1970), and patients with more severe acne as rated by a dermatologist do seem to have higher levels of anxiety and anger (Wu et al., 1988). Whitlock (1976) suggests that, in more sensitive adolescents, emotional reaction given a biological predisposition to acne leads to secondary exacerbation. More research is needed to elucidate the percentage of people for whom stress can exacerbate their acne. A more serious version of this scenario occurs in acne excorie, where the sufferer goes to excessive lengths of self-surgery, with resultant scarring. Not surprisingly, such presentations are noted to occur in individuals with underlying emotional problems, even though their emotional status may not be immediately apparent in the clinic (Sneddon and Sneddon, 1981).

In a controlled clinical trail with 30 acne patients treated with biofeedback (frontalis EMG), assisted relaxation training and cognitive imagery, Hughes et al. (1983b) showed a statistically clinically significant improvement in acne in the psychological treatment group, compared to an attention comparison and medical treatment group. The rationale for therapy was to reduce emotional distress, thereby reducing the hormonal activity involved in acne pathophysiology. Follow-up showed that many of the gains were lost, and that this could be largely accounted for by some subjects discontinuing the relaxing cognitive imagery. Since frontalis EMG is an unreliable indicator of general relaxation, other standard methods could more usefully be employed instead of biofeedback. Whether such results could be observed and maintained in a wider sample of severe acne patients remains an empirical question, although the 12 therapy sessions over 6 weeks could well have been extended with booster sessions.

Eczema

Eczema is a variety of conditions in which the skin swells, weeps and itches significantly. Given its greater prevalence and chronicity, we shall consider atopic eczema in this section. This affects mostly children, but in approximately 10% of cases it continues into adult life. It can involve large areas of the skin, and the dermis can also become thickened and tough in appearance. The course is unpredictable. That eczema can be a social stigma and that it has an adverse effect upon body image seems obvious, but this has not been systematically researched. The sufferer struggles to resist the urge to scratch, as this produces further lesions and itchiness. Frustration seems inevitable, either because the sufferer gives in and scratches, or because there is a failure to satisfy the biological call to scratch. Itch can be seen as the core symptom in eczema (Rajka, 1975). Many of the lesions are caused by scratching, both during the day and especially the night (Savin, 1980). There is therefore, no doubting the importance of behavioural process in this condition, but specific psychophysiological processes are difficult to discern other than by their influence on itch.

Some of the evidence that indicates the relevance of psychological factors in atopic eczema will now be reviewed. In a detailed summary of the long-term characteristics of eczema patients, Graham (1972) was convinced that there were high levels of suppressed hostility, and that this was a consequence of unsatisfied dependency needs. This led to clinical attempts to influence maternal bonding, which it was believed could be severely disrupted by eczema-induced parental rejection and disappointment, and by child irritability and anxiety (Williams, 1951). There are no recent methodologically acceptable empirical studies to shed light on these possibilities, although some clinicians still seem to find the constructs useful (Fritz, 1979). The most significant difference between eczema patients and controls seems to be an elevated anxiety in the former (Jordan and Whitlock, 1974; Garrie, Garrie and Mole, 1974). Following a 9-year longitudinal study of eczema patients by Rechardt (1970), we can be fairly confident that most of these characteristics result from the skin condition, rather than from predisposing personality characteristics of aetiological significance. He showed that where skin had improved for some time, there was no longer any evidence of emotional lability or extreme personality characteristics. Tentatively, it might be said that eczema does lead to significant levels of emotional distress in some children and adults, but research is needed to develop appropriate clinical assessment tools to examine levels of adjustment.

In a psychophysiological analysis of ten atopic eczema patients who were compared with ten matched controls, Faulstisch et al. (1985) provided some evidence to suggest that patients become more anxious than controls to laboratory-produced stress, as measured by a subjective anxiety scale, forearm EMG and heart rate. They concluded that atopic eczema patients show a greater autonomic arousal which, according to the authors, suggests a psychophysiological component to the condition. Interesting though this finding is, we still do not know whether patients are just generally more prone to anxiety because of their skin condition, whether the psycho-physiological processes are acting according to the organ weakness model, or whether, as the authors suggest, the autonomic arousal is itself increasing the itchiness. This latter belief gains support and further clarification from research with 18 atopic eczema patients which found that autonomic reactivity to stressors was higher than in controls, and patients particularly prone to marked itching uniquely showed an increase in stress-induced skin temperature (Munzel and Schandry, 1990). Another approach used hypnotic suggestions of pain in eczema patients, and produced a skin temperature increase (Hajek *et al.*, 1992). These psychophysiological studies hold promise and deserve more attention.

Given the age of onset and the genetic dimension of eczema, most authors assume that psychological factors are acting by the secondary, rather than the primary, psychophysiological route. In a 20-year follow-up of patients with atopic eczema, Roth, Kierland and Rochester (1964) documented, on the basis of patients' self-report, that 66% of mild and 80% of severe atopic eczema patients say that emotional distress or fatigue exacerbates their condition. Using more independent measures of stress, and recording actual rather than perceived measures of eczema, Brown (1972) surveyed 82 successive referrals and compared them with controls on interview-derived life-event measures. Although a statistically significant difference was found, suggesting a relationship between life events and eczema, this difference was accounted for by a relatively small number of patients showing the effect strongly. The implications for the practitioner are that patients with eczema should be screened for levels of life events or emotional distress, and these related to the severity of their eczema. This author would predict that, for a small proportion of patients, therapy to reduce stress effects could actually decrease the severity of the eczema. In a large proportion of

patients, eczema-induced stress may be worth addressing to improve quality of life. Therefore, for many, the realistic goal would be for an improvement in emotional adjustment rather than a change in their eczema severity.

There are few large-scale controlled intervention studies incorporating psychological factors into the treatment of atopic eczema. Brown and Bettley (1971) randomly assigned 72 patients diagnosed as having eczema to medical treatment with or without psychotherapy. Psychotherapy involved identifying stressors and expressing concerns and, where appropriate, using relaxation and hypnosis. Although some patients did benefit from the additional psychotherapy, at 14-month follow-up those in receipt of psychotherapy who were unmotivated or could identify no problem area did not benefit. This accords well with the earlier observation that psychological factors are relevant to the disease in only a proportion of patients. It also suggests that the random or routine allocation of patients to a psychological regimen is inappropriate, and that the relevance of psychological factors should first be established if possible.

In a study of eight atopic eczema patients, Haynes *et al.* (1979) used frontalis EMG feedback and taped relaxation after a baseline and a non-specific stage. Their hypothesis was that itching may be reduced in a relaxed state. They took itching ratings and photography-derived measures of the percentage of skin affected. The study took place over 11 weekly sessions, eight involving a 20-minute intervention phase. There was a significant decrease in itching ratings during each treatment session, but there was no change across sessions. This supports the hypothesis that itch can be reduced with relaxation. Given the poor relation to the frontalis EMG and other measures of relaxation, it is not surprising that there was no correlation between frontalis EMG and itching. Affected skin areas were reduced across sessions by 15%, although this may be the result of spontaneous remission. No substantial follow-up was carried out. One can probably best assume from this study that the systematic use of relaxation, in total amounting to less than 4 hours in this study, could be beneficial in eczema, and its effect may largely be by reducing the levels of itch. A similar study on five adult eczema patients showed that EMG biofeedback and muscle relaxation improved skin and self-reported symptom irritation levels in all five patients, and at a 2-year follow-up three were asymptomatic (McMenamy, Katz and Gipson, 1988). Another small study on three eczema patients used a cognitive behavioural approach, essentially noting potential triggers to a flare and using relaxation and habit reversal, and showed a good outcome for symptom severity and reductions in the use of medication (Horne *et al.*, 1989).

There is a series of single case reports showing how different behavioural approaches have been used successfully to reduce scratching, an important behavioural process in eczema. Avoiding reinforcements such as social attention to scratching (Walton, 1960), reinforcing non-scratching behaviour (Bar and Kuypers, 1973), self-aversive conditioning with electric shock (Ratcliff and Stein, 1968), self-monitoring (Cataldo *et al.*, 1980), and self-control using stroking and self-reinforcement (Watson, Thorp and Krisber, 1972), have all been used as part of a programme to successfully reduce scratching behaviour. In a convincing study of 17 unselected atopic eczema patients, Melin *et al.* (1986) demonstrated that an intervention called 'behavioural habit breaking' significantly decreased scratching and improved skin status, but had no effect on levels of itchiness. They found that the skin status largely reflected the amount of scratching, demonstrating the need to influence scratching behaviour while the itch levels probably remain unchanged. Although long-term results are not available, this provides a good model of a flexible psychological

approach and so will be described in a little more detail. It seems particularly useful as it will have high face validity to eczema patients who do not see themselves as anxious or under stress. Subjects were asked to self-monitor their scratching using a golf counter, and transfer this daily to a diary. They were asked to identify early warning signs when their hands moved towards scratchable skin, and to develop situation awareness about where their scratching was at its most frequent. They were thus being encouraged to take more conscious control of what would otherwise have been automatic scratching behaviour. In the treatment programme they discussed the unpleasant aspects of scratching in order to decrease the likelihood of scratching when experiencing strong urges. Finally, behaviour incompatible to scratching was introduced in two phases: First, hands were put firmly on the itchy skin for 1 minute and were then moved to the side of the thigh, or were required to grasp objects. The second phase had the subjects occupy their hands without touching the affected skin. This behavioural repertoire was practised while imagining themselves to be in an itch-provoking situation, to increase generalization. The therapist provided feedback on all stages of their skills acquisition.

Eczema provides a good example of how patient-specific assessments could identify where the problem lies, following which a range of psychological approaches can be offered to improve the quality of life. Itch levels may be manipulated by lowering sympathetic activity; scratching behaviour may be manipulated by behavioural methods, even though itchiness remains the same; stress management could reduce exacerbation and counselling could help families and individuals cope. There does seem to be good evidence that health psychology can have a clinical role for some eczema patients, but the task of selecting suitable individuals would be made easier with the development of screening tools which are applicable to a typical clinic population.

Dermatitis artefacta

This term refers to skin lesions which are self-inflicted in the absence of an underlying cause, such as itching. Some patients may admit to their actions, but often the dermatologist is faced with a diagnostic challenge, given that patients can show incredible ingenuity in producing skin damage. The dermatologist looks for unusual lesions in accessible places, which appear suddenly and which fail to respond to therapy other than by the use of permanent masking bandages. The diagnosis should be used carefully by all concerned to ensure that there is no unnecessary stigmatizing, which can accompany this diagnosis (Lyell, 1979), and also to ensure there is no underlying organic cause (Cox and Wilkinson, 1992). In a large survey of 130 patients, it was noted that 90% were female, 66% were under 30 and 74% were unmarried (Hollender and Abram, 1973). Fabisch (1980) conceptualized the problem as having an underlying dimension of self-harm, one end involving habitual scratching or rubbing, the other end more serious harm typical of dermatitis artefacta. We are then in need of explanations as to what reinforces or motivates the behaviour, which probably starts at the mild end of this dimension but then progresses to the other. The most predetermined examples are those where there are obvious gains, such as financial compensation and avoiding unpleasant or dangerous tasks. Possibly less conscious would be the achievement of a 'sick role' (Parsons, 1951), wherein the individual is excused responsibilities and stressors in a socially legitimized way. Cotterill (1983) concluded that episodes often follow precipitatory events, such as sexual or matrimonial problems, bereavement and school or work problems. He concludes that the lesions may be used as an alternative method of communication. The literature on psychological processes in somatization (e.g. Ford, 1984) provides ways of understanding individual differences.

A fascinating clinical aspect of this condition is in the therapist–patient relationship, where the patient denies apparently self-injurious behaviour. The therapist will have difficulty in accurately empathizing with the patient in a genuine way and explaining the rationale for therapy, although all are agreed that in most cases the therapist should not be confronting (Lyell, 1979; Cotterill, 1983). It is reminiscent of hysterical-conversion patients, where it would seem that initial rapport has to be established on the patient's terms and emphasis given to the hypothesized motives for the individual behaving the way they do (Jones, 1980). The dermatology service is probably prone to seeing the patient as a malingerer rather than as a person in distress. Psychiatric reviews suggest that psychological distress is particularly prevalent in this population (Fabisch, 1980), and that they are unwilling to receive psychological or psychiatric care (Sheppard, O'Loughlin and Malone, 1986). Therefore, the health psychologist's goal could be to develop guidance on how the dermatologist can best manage such presentations psychologically.

Hyperhidrosis

In this condition, patients chronically suffer excessive sweating in the palms and axillae, and sometimes in the face, feet, chest and anogenital area. There is a range of neuronal and hormonal mechanisms that influence apocrine and eccrine sweating, and therefore organic pathology can lead to hyperhidrosis. It has been demonstrated that heat, emotional arousal and mental concentration are accompanied by significant sweating (Kuno, 1956). It is quite clear that in anxiety, and in the flight/flight stress reaction, significant sweating levels may result. It is possible that such 'normal' sweating reaches a level which is defined by the individual as excessive, i.e. a primary psychophysiological role, as there are no other organic or pathophysiological cause. More usually, psychophysiological sweating will be acting upon an already abnormal sweating response, that is, excessive sweating would still be evident in the absence of sweat-producing psychological stimuli. Daily record keeping would be needed to identify whether sweating was responsive to psychological stimuli. Regardless of the initial cause, one consequence of hyperhidrosis is a fear of sweating caused by an embarrassment at having wet hands (sudophobia).

In a single case report, Bar and Kuypers (1973) used assertiveness training and systematic desensitization to social anxiety, apparently in this case a major psychological triggering stimulus of the sweating response. After treatment, and after a 12-month follow-up, there was still a positive outcome, although sweat gland activity was not completely normal.

A clinical trial of 14 patients with chronic hyperhidrosis was conducted by Duller and Gentry (1980) using a Meeco water vapour analyser to measure and provide feedback about the sweat response. The triggering stimuli to create the response were both emotionally arousing topics and stress from being asked to complete arithmetic tasks. With at least ten sessions of 30 minutes duration, patients were given biofeedback until no further improvement was discerned. Six months following the final therapeutic session, 11 of the 14 patients demonstrated clinical improvement, based on either self-report or therapist's ratings. Although their outcome measures are weak, and we have no evidence as to whether general relaxation or specific sweat gland control was achieved, the results do suggest that this approach should be repeated.

From our contemporary understanding of biofeedback effects and the complexity of neuronal and hormonal sweating control, it does seem that relaxation methods are likely to be as effective as biofeedback in the long term. However, biofeedback is likely to have high face validity to patients, and may therefore help motivate individuals while they achieve active control by other methods. Active control, or increased self-efficacy, in the self management of hyperhidrosis may help to reduce the associated sudophobia. However, as there are relatively few reports of effective psychological or medical treatments (Manusov and Nadeau, 1989), perhaps another role might be to help people adjust to this condition with the minimum psychosocial impact.

Psoriasis

This is a common and chronic non-infective inflammatory skin disorder involving red plaques with a scaly surface. The psoriatic skin produces new cells some 20–50 times faster than the normal skin. Vulnerability seems to depend upon the action of a number of genes which, in accumulation, reach a threshold, whereupon environmental factors can precipitate disease. Commonly recognized factors are trauma, infection and hormonal changes. It has also been suggested that psychological factors can precipitate psoriasis, hence it is a good example of the need for a multicausal aetiology model.

The impact of psoriasis on individuals is varied (Gupta, Gupta and Hakerman, 1987). Perception of body image can be adversely affected, and the greater the severity of psoriasis the greater the disturbance (Leichtman, Burnett and Robinson, 1981). Sexual function is disrupted to some extent in the majority of patients (Weinstein, 1984), especially when the genital area is affected (Buckwalter, 1982). Psoriasis patients may be more vulnerable to having high measures of outward aggression (Matussek, Agerer and Seibt, 1985), anxiety and depression (Fava *et al.*, 1980) and alcoholism (Morse, Perry and Hurt, 1985). Although there does seem to be a wide range of sequelae to having psoriasis, there will be many who are well adjusted and minimally affected.

To be more specific about the prevalence of distress, more refined adjustment measures must be developed. A useful approach to measuring disability in psoriasis has been developed by Finlay and Kelly (1987), who identified ten independent and relevant items about daily activity, work, leisure and treatment. An example question is: 'Is your psoriasis making it difficult for you to do any sport?', this being rated from one to seven. This Psoriasis Disability Index (PDI) can then be used as a therapy outcome measure, or as an adjunct to clinical assessment. The Sickness Impact Profile (SIP) has also been validated in this population (Finlay et al., 1990), but does not measure attitudes or feelings towards psoriasis.

In reviewing the psychological processes involved in the development or exacerbation of psoriasis, one difficulty is the lack of readily accessible psychophysiological measures directly reflecting the psoriatic process. However, the greater turnover of cells is accompanied by greater heat production, and so skin temperature may be important. Non-specific psychoendocrine and metabolic variables in psychophysiological research on psoriasis, including serum growth hormone levels, are of general interest (Arnetz et al., 1985). This Swedish group exposed ten psoriasis patients and ten matched controls to stressors. During resting levels there was no difference between groups, but after exposure to stressors the psoriasis patients showed more mental stress, higher levels of urinary adrenaline and lower level of plasma cortisol. They concluded that psoriasis patients were more likely to perceive stress, and under stress reacted differentially from the control group. Research of this sort is notoriously difficult to interpret, however, and at best can only be seen as an interesting pilot study into the psychophysiological processes in psoriasis.

Much more convincing evidence that psychological factors influence the course of psoriasis comes from a range of reports suggesting that there is a temporal connection, and therefore possibly a causal role, between stress and psoriasis exacerbation. Largely on the basis of interview or questionnaire data, it has been reported that 40% of 2144 psoriasis patients said that worry brings on their psoriasis, and 37% said that it makes existing psoriasis worse (Farber, Bright and Nall, 1968). Similarly, Farber and Nall (1974) reported that, in 5600 patients, one-third thought worry made the psoriasis worse, one-third thought it did not and one-third were unsure. Critics of the hypothesis that stress has a causative role in psoriasis could claim that anecdotal evidence inflates this correlation (Baughman and Sobel, 1976), and that much of the emotional stress is a reaction to, and not a cause of, psoriasis (Shuster, 1979).

Three more recent studies have used life-events questionnaires to look objectively for stress before psoriasis flares. The first study used a checklist of undesirable events that occurred in the last month, and found that in 33% of cases, stress was an important precipitating factor (Seville, 1977). In a study of 60 patients; a comparison of equal numbers of psoriasis, chronic urticaria and fungal infection patients, a Paykel-derived life-events scale showed a greater instance of life-events up to 6 months prior to the disease onset in psoriasis and urticaria (Fava et al., 1980). In contrast to these two studies, the third failed to show a difference in life-event scores between 16 psoriasis patients and 16 well matched patients with cutaneous neoplasms, viral warts and fungal infections (Payne, Payne and Marks, 1985). However, this postal survey reported life events over the last year, and hence may have missed the most critical time.

From all evidence available, it is most likely that for some individuals their psoriasis is made worse during stress. However, the proportion of psoriasis sufferers thus affected, and by what mechanism, remains unanswered. Longitudinal studies with more sensitive measures of everyday stress would be particularly interesting.

Despite the available rationale to justify the inclusion of psychological counselling in the management of some patients with psoriasis, there has been little documented clinical activity. Benoit and Harrell (1980) offered biofeedback of skin temperature in three patients with psoriasis. They monitored cellular proliferation rate, and tentatively suggested that a reduction in temperature would reduce the psoriasis severity by decreased cellular proliferation. Across a biofeedback training session, small but significant reductions in temperature of the affected skin were noted. Cell proliferation reduced from pre- to post training. In one patient the plaque to which biofeedback was given had fewer scales and changed from red to pink. Other psoriasis plaques on this patient did not change. However, in the other two patients the plaques subjected to therapy improved significantly, as did plaques on a contralateral limb. In this sort of research there is a need for control subjects, as spontaneous remission is likely.

In one controlled study four treatment groups were used: meditation alone, meditation and imagery, waiting list controls and no treatment (Gaston et al., 1991). Group size was small, four or five patients, and so time-series multivariate statistical methods were used. Experimental groups showed a significant reduction in symptoms as rated by dermatologists, but no additional benefit accrued from imagery. Price, Motta Redin and Mayo (1991) compared a control group with a problem discussion/relaxation group. The treatment group were significantly less anxious, but only a trend was noticed in symptom improvement, and we must await more outcome trials of this kind.

Raynaud's disease

This is an episodic vasospasmic attack characterized by the affected area – hands and some-

times feet – going through a three-stage colour change: first blanching, then cyanotic blue and finally becoming bright red. The condition can be painful. The vasoconstriction is precipitated by cold and, in some cases apparently by emotional factors (Jobe et al., 1986). As psychophysiological studies show that finger blood flow can be reduced in certain anxiety-provoking situations (Sampson, 1977), psychological factors may well contribute to the severity of the attack. However, there is no good evidence that Raynaud's patients are particularly prone to emotional stress (Connors, 1980). Intervention studies have typically addressed either the reduction of emotional arousal and sympathetic activity by relaxation methods, or the voluntary control of peripheral blood flow by temperature biofeedback of affected digits.

Following a number of promising case reports in the literature, Keefe, Surwit and Pilon (1979) compared relaxation by autogenic training with and without finger temperature biofeedback in 30 patients with Raynaud's disease. Using the response to a cold stress test as one outcome measure, they found an improvement initially. After 1-year follow-up, the response to the stress test had returned to baseline levels even though patients still reported a significant symptomatic improvement. There was no extra beneficial effect by adding biofeedback. The research group then repeated the design with 21 patients, but this time added a progressive muscle relaxation group, used more sensitive temperature recordings and used repeated exposure to the cold stressor task (Keefe, Surwit and Pilon, 1980). Biofeedback, autogenic training and relaxation were equally effective in significantly reducing symptoms; biofeedback added no specific therapeutic value. Other studies suggest finger temperature feedback to be more effective than autogenic training in causing actual increases in blood flow (Freedman, 1989) and in causing temperature increases (Freedman et al., 1991).

Clinical research has recently shifted its

approach to facilitate relaxation and digital temperature increase when the individual is actually exposed to a cold stressor. Freedman, Ianni and Wenig (1983) showed that this specific 'cold stress' training improved outcome at 1 year follow-up from a 66% to a 92% reduction in attacks. Freedman's group also found that temperature feedback was superior to both the frontalis EMG feedback and autogenic training in decreasing subject vulnerability to attack under decreasing temperature. The symptom reduction for 20 training sessions over 10 weeks does seem to justify the expense and specialized equipment associated with biofeedback. A similar finding in 14 patients showed training to vasodilate in a 'cooling environment' produced a 31% decrease in vasospasmic attacks (Stambrook, Hamel and Carter, 1988).

A series of studies by Jobe and colleagues has used a classical conditioning approach, with promising results. The whole body is exposed to a 0°C environment (conditioned stimulus) while the hands are immersed in hot water (unconditioned stimulus). This alternative model does not suppose that emotional arousal is a meditator. The initial clinical improvement with 27 treatment sessions for patients (Jobe *et al.*, 1982) was replicated with eight subjects who had 54 10-minute conditioning sessions over 6 weeks (Jobe *et al.*, 1986). The latter study compared classical conditioning with temperature biofeedback. Initially, there was no difference immediately but after a 1-year follow-up the classical conditioning was more effective.

To conclude, there is good evidence that psychological approaches have something to offer Raynaud's disease sufferers, although there is much to be done in the search for the most effective combination of operant, classical-conditioning and stress-management approaches. From among these different options it is likely that patients will be able to choose an approach which has face validity for them.

Future research is likely to discern the actual mechanisms involved (e.g. Freedman *et al.*, 1991).

Trichotillomania

This is a rare form of dermatitis artefacta where the patient has strong urges to pull their own hair or eyebrows, resulting in alopecia. Hair pulling and twisting are common habits in childhood which, even if taken to maladaptive extremes, need not indicate psychiatric disorder (Chang *et al.*, 1991). However, reports of hair pulling are observed in learning disabled children, emotionally maladjusted children and adolescents, and in adults who have needed psychiatric care (Dean, Nelson and Moss, 1992). It is most common in females.

Analytic models briefly reviewed by Risch and Ferguson (1981) formulated trichotillomania as arising from such dynamics as domineering mothers and unsatisfied dependency needs, sensual pleasure from infantile nursing and as a masturbatory substitute. The reported results of analytic psychotherapy have been very mixed, and are generally unconvincing (Mannino and Delgardo, 1969).

Although possibly related to an obsessive–compulsive disorder (hair pulling is conceptualized as tension-reducing by DSM III Psychiatric Classification), clinical studies of children (Reeve, Bernstein and Christenson, 1992) and adults (Stanley *et al.*, 1992) fail to support this view. It is likely that this population is a heterogenous one, and several models will be needed to explain the phenomenon.

An alternative approach is to apply behavioural models (Vitulano *et al.*, 1992). A behavioural analysis would look for antecedents of the unwanted behaviour to assess the strength of the urge and look to see what triggering stimuli there were. It would also identify the consequences of the hair-pulling behaviour to see if there is anxiety reduction or inappropriate environmental re-inforcement. On the basis of self-report at interview, diary keeping and other observational methods, a programme can be constructed and tailored to the particular presentation. Where anxiety is particularly in evidence a form of relaxation may be used, and this has been applied with good effect (Fabbri and Dy, 1974). Other methods to reduce conditioned anxiety, such as cognitive desensitization, have also been reported (Bornstein and Rychtarik, 1978).

Using self-control methods, success has been reported with self-monitoring (Bayer, 1972) and stimulus control with self-reinforcement (Cordle and Long, 1980). Reinforcing behaviour incompatible with hair pulling and habit reversal (Rosenbaum and Ayllon, 1981) has also been applied, with good effect. Finally, hair-pulling behaviour has been subjected to punishment by using electric aversion therapy (Horne, 1977; Crawford, 1988). Other social 'punishments' used have been the response cost of collecting and sending pulled hairs to the therapist (McLaughlin and Nay, 1975), and public exposure of the affected scalp (Cordle and Long, 1980). Most of the programmes have used a combination of the components outlined above.

It would appear that a variety of behavioural methods can be employed successfully. In many cases long-term follow-up exceeds a year without evidence of spontaneous remission. Operant principles employed within a self-control framework seem to be the most widely used approaches. However, there are indications that for some individuals anxiety may need to be addressed more directly.

Urticaria

Urticaria, alternatively known as hives is an episodic flare in the skin that produces nettle-like wheals and itching and can last from 1 to 25 hours. Patients may identify precipitants such as food substances, temperature changes or physical pressure in the skin. However, often these unsightly lesions will appear and disappear without the individual having any control or understanding of the causes. There is no contention that stress and heat are the major precipitants in cholinergic urticaria (Pegum and Baker, 1979), a variant with pinhead wheals on larger flares, where sympathetic nerve-end activity in sweat glands is involved. In chronic urticaria more generally, the physiological routes by which emotional factors may influence the skin are varied and complex. For example, acetylcholine, immune reactions and vasodilation are all cited in the pathophysiology of this condition, and are associated with stress reactions. An interesting observation is the tendency of the skin to produce a hive-like lesion in response to pressure. The parameters of this reaction could be usefully explored in the psychophysiology laboratory to see how responsive it is to psychological stimuli. Cutaneous vascular reactions in urticaria patients have been monitored psychophysiologically (Graham, 1950), but generally the evidence from laboratory studies about the role of psychophysiological processes in hives is not yet available. In chronic urticaria the estimated importance of psychological factors in aetiology seems to have diminished over time. Rees (1957) studied 76 individuals and compared them with patients from a medical ward. The onset of hives was reported to coincide with the stress situation in 51% of the hives sample, significantly higher than in the medical patients. More recent studies suggest an association between life events prior to onset and chronic urticaria. In a systematic study of 225 new cases, only 12 were attributed to psychological factors, whereas in a further 48 cases psychological factors were seen to be contributing within a multifactorial context (Meynadier *et al.*, 1985). Further attacks in prone individuals have been correlated with emotional arousal in 64% of a sample of 76 patients (Rees, 1957) and 7% of 300 patients (Juhlin, 1981). One explanation to account for this large difference is that Juhlin asked patients their opinions, whereas Rees' data are based on the clinician's judgement.

Another approach is to look at so-called specific personality profiles which were thought to have aetiological significance. Although there are increased levels of frustration and anxiety in hives patients (Whitlock, 1976), and psychiatric vulnerability (Juhlin, 1981), these are probably best interpreted as a reaction to the condition and not the initial cause. The incidence of psychological distress following this condition is less than that seen in eczema and psoriasis, probably because of its intermittent nature. In chronic idiopathic urticaria there is a higher prevalence of anxiety and depression than in a normal population (Sheehan-Dare, Henderson and Cotterill, 1990). Furthermore, in this same population a psychological assessment (Symptom Checklist 90) of 19 patients showed significantly higher problems than in controls of anxiety and interpersonal relationships (Sperber, Shaw and Bruce, 1989). The latter authors conclude that stress management and group therapy for interpersonal issues would be a useful addition to therapeutic efforts.

Many dermatology reviews refer to the importance of addressing the psychological factors cited above, although they are probably less relevant than in eczema and psoriasis. There are few clinical outcome trials or single case reports.

Daniels (1973) reports the successful application of relaxation therapy and desensitization for a 23-year-old woman with urticaria who had evident emotional problems with her family. The hives episodes reduced in frequency and then stopped completely after 12 weeks of intervention, and had not returned at a 23-month follow-up. Although spontaneous remission may be an explanation, there was a reduction in family conflict, as one would

expect from a psychological explanation citing anxiety as a precipitant. The intermittent nature of this condition produces a problem in discerning whether intervention is effective or not. Clinical data would need to be kept over several months to see if the frequency and duration of the attacks changed with psychological intervention. This means that in the short term there may be difficulty in motivating both the client and the therapist, because changes are not obvious.

The next step in exploring the psychology of hives might be to identify the relatively small percentage of individuals who, according to self-report, experience attacks in relation to psychological precipitants.

Conclusions

There is overwhelming evidence that the psychological consequences of skin disorders give rise to a level of distress which must be investigated. The development of simple screening devices to assess emotional and behavioural adjustment is needed to pick out those individuals who become excessively distressed. If left unattended, these individuals may well developed more severe problems that may eventually necessitate psychiatric referral. As many skin conditions are directly influenced by behavioural processes such as scratching, health psychology's sophisticated tools for behavioural change (e.g. Russell, 1986) are particularly relevant.

The exact role of psychophysiological processes in the onset and exacerbation of skin disorders is far from clear, yet the available evidence is sufficiently suggestive to merit further investigations. A range of therapeutic options would follow if positive results were found (Steptoe, 1989). Most surprising is the lack of information we have about the psychological parameters of itch, when given the available analogue in pain. However, psychodermatology is in its infancy, and it has not been helped in its development by the understandably cautious attitudes in dermatology towards psychological models. Nevertheless, the psychological approach deserves more attention. For instance, if health psychology approaches can make inroads into unravelling the itch–scratch cycle to enable therapeutic intervention, this would have a major impact on dermatology services. Perhaps even more of a challenge would be to introduce models and constructs into everyday dermatology practice which recognize the complex interplay between psychology and the skin.

References

Alexander, F. (1950) *Psychosomatic Medicine: Its Principles and Applications*, Norton, New York.

Allen, K. and Harris, F. (1966) Elimination of a child's excessive scratching by reinforcement procedures. *Behaviour Research Therapy*, 4, 79.

Arnetz, B., Fjellner, B., Eneroth, P. and Kallner, A. (1985) Stress and psoriasis: psychoendocrine and metabolic reactions. *Psychosomatic Medicine*, 47, 528–41.

Arnetz, B., Fjellner, B., Eneroth, P., and Kallner, A. (1991) Endocrine and dermatological concomitants of mental stress. Acta *Dermato Venereologica*, (Stockholm), Suppl. 156, 9–12.

Bar, L. and Kuypers, B. (1973) Behaviour therapy in dermatological practice. *British Journal of Dermatology*, 88, 591–8.

Baughman, R. and Sobel, R. (1976) Emotional factors in psoriasis, in *Psoriasis*, (eds E. Farber and E. Cox), Yorke Medical Books, New York.

Bayer, C.A. (1972) Self monitoring and mild aversion treatment of trichotillomania. *Journal of Behaviour Therapy and Experimental Psychiatry*, 3, 13–20.

Beck, A.T. (1976) *Cognitive Therapy and the Emotional Disorders*, International University Press, New York.

Benoit, L.J. and Harrell, E.H. (1980) Biofeedback and control of skin cell proliferation in psoriasis. *Psychological Reports*, 46, 831–9.

Bjornberg, A., Lowhagen, B. and Tergberg, J. (1979) Skin reactivity in workers with and without itching. *Acta Dermatovenereologica*, 59, 49–53.

Bornstein, P.H. and Rychtarik, R.G. (1978) Multicomponent behavioural treatment of trichotillomania; *Behavioural Research and Therapy*, 16, 217–20.

Brocq, L. and Jacquet, L. (1891) Notes pour servir à l'histoire des névrodermites. *Annales de Dermatologie et de Syphilographie (Paris)*, 97, 193.

Brown, D. (1972) Stress as a precipitant of eczema. *Journal of Psychosomatic Research*, 16, 34.

Brown, D. and Bettley, F.(1971) Psychiatric treatment of eczema; a controlled trial. *British Medical Journal*, 2, 729–34.

Buckwalter, K. (1982) The influence of skin disorders on sexual expression. *Sex Disability*, 5, 98–106.

Cataldo, M., Varnia, J., Ruso, D. and Estes, S. (1980) Behaviour therapy techniques in the treatment of exfoliative dermatitis. *Archives of Dermatology*, 116, 919.

Chang, C., Lee, M., Chiang, Y. and Ly, Y. (1991) Trichotillomania: a clinical study of 36 patients. *Taiwan I Msaiah-Tasa-Chih*, 90 (2), 176–80.

Connors, C.K. (1980) Behavioural and psychophysiological aspects of Raynaud's disease, in *Comprehensive Handbook of Behavioural Medicine, Vol. 1*, (eds. R.J. Ferguson and H.L. Taylor), Springer, New York, pp. 29–40.

Cordle, C.J. and Long, C.G. (1980) Trichotillomania. *Journal of Behaviour Therapy and Experimental Psychiatry*, 11, 127–30.

Cotterill, J. (1981) Dermatological non-disease. *British Journal of Dermatology*, 104, 611–19.

Cotterill, J. (1983) Psychiatry and skin disease, in *Recent Advances in Dermatology*, (eds A. Rook and H. Maibach), Churchill Livingstone, Edinburgh, pp. 189–212.

Cotterill, J.A. (1989) Psychiatry and the skin. *British Journal of Hospital Medicine*, 42, 401–4.

Cox, N.H. and Wilkinson, D. (1992) Dermatitis artefacta as the presenting syndrome in autoerythrocyte sensitization syndrome, *British Journal of Dermatology*, 126 (1), 86–9.

Crawford, D. (1988) Aversion therapy in the treatment of trichotillomania. *Behavioural Psychotherapy*, 16, 57–63.

Daniels, I.K. (1973) Treatment of urticaria and severe headache by behaviour therapy. *Psychosomatics*, 14, 347–51.

Dean, J., Nelson, E. and Moss, L. (1992) Pathological hair-pulling: a review of the literature and case reports. *Comprehensive Psychiatry*, 33 (2), 84–91.

Duller, P. and Gentry, W. (1980) Use of biofeedback in treating chronic hyperidrosis: a preliminary report. *British Journal of Dermatology*, 103, 143.

Edwards, A., Shallow, W., Wright, T. and Dignam, E. (1976) Pruritic skin disease, psychological stress, and the itch sensation. *Archives of Dermatology*, 112, 339–43.

Engles, W.D. (1982) *Dermatologic disorders. Psychosomatics*, 23 (12), 1209–19.

Fabbri, R. and Dy, A.J. (1974) Hypnotic treatment of

trichotillomania: two cases. *International Journal of Clinical and Experimental Hypnosis*, **22**, 210–15.

Fabisch, W. (1980) Psychiatric aspects of dermatitis artefacte. *British Journal of Dermatology*, **102**, 29–34.

Farber, E., and Nall, N. (1974) The natural history of psoriasis in 5,600 patients. *Dermatologica*, **148**, 1.

Farber, E., Bright, R. and Nall, M. (1968) Psoriasis, a questionnaire survey of 2144 patients. *Archives of Dermatology*, **98**, 248–59.

Faulstitch, M., Williamson, D., Duchman, E. *et al.* (1985) Psychophysiological analysis of atopic dermatitis. *Journal of Psychosomatic Research*, **29** (4), 415–17.

Fava, G., Perini, G., Santonastaso, P. and Fornash, C. (1980) Life events and psychological distress in dermatologic disorders. *British Journal of Medical Psychology*, **53**, 277–82.

Felix, R. and Shuster, S. (1975) A new method for the measurement of itch. *British Journal of Dermatology*, **93**, 303.

Finlay, A. and Kelly, S. (1987) Psoriasis – an index of disability. *Clinical and Experimental Dermatology*, **12**, 8–11.

Finlay A.Y., Khan, G.K., Luscombe, D.K. and Salek M.S. (1990) Validation of sickness impact profile and psoriasis disability index. *British Journal of Dermatology*, **123** (6), 751–6.

Ford, C.V. (1984) *The Somatization Disorders*, Elsevier Biomedical, New York.

Freedman, R. (1989) Quantitative measurement of finger blood flow during behavioural treatments for Raynaud's disease. *Psychophysiology*, **26** (4), 437–41.

Freedman, R., Ianni, P. and Wenig, P. (1983) Behavioural treatment of Raynaud's disease. *Journal of Consulting and Clinical Psychology*, **51**, 539–49.

Freedman, R., Keegan, D., Migaly, P. *et al.* (1991) Plasma catecholamines during behavioural treatments for Raynaud's disease. *Psychosomatic Medicine*, **53** (4), 433–9.

Fritz, G. (1979) Psychological aspects of atopic dermatitis. *Clinical Pediatrics*, **18**, 360–4.

Garrie, E., Garrie, S. and Mole, T. (1974) Anxiety and atopic dermatitis. *Journal of Consulting and Clinical Psychology*, **42**, 742.

Gaston, L., Crombez, J., Lassonde, M. *et al.* (1991) Psychological stress and psoriasis. *Acta Dermato Venereologica*, (*Stockh*), Suppl. **156**, 37–43.

Gilchrist, B. (1982) Pruritis. *Archives of Internal Medicine*, **142**, 101–4.

Graham, D. (1950) The pathogenesis of hives. *Proceedings of the Association for Research in Nervous and Mental Disease*, **29**, 987–1009.

Graham, D. (1972) Psychosomatic medicine, in *Handbook of Psychophysiology* (eds N. Greenfield and R. Sternbach), Hutt, New York, pp. 839–924.

Gupta, M., Gupta, A. and Hakerman, H. (1987) Psoriasis and psychiatry. *General Hospital Psychiatry*, **9**, 157–66.

Gupta, M., Gupta, A., Schork, N. *et al.* (1990) Psychiatric aspects of the treatment of mild to moderate facial acne. *International Journal of Dermatology*, **29** (10), 719–21.

Hajek, P., Jakoubek, B., and Radil, T. (1990) Gradual increases in cutaneous threshold induced by repeated hypnosis of healthy individuals and patients with atopic eczema. *Perceptual and Motor Skills*, **70** (2), 549–50.

Hajek, P., Jakoubek, B., Kyhus, K. and Radi, T. (1992) Increase in cutaneous temperature by hypnotic suggestion of pain. *Perceptual and Motor Skills*, **74**, 737–8.

Haynes, S., Wilson, C., Jaffee, P. and Britton, B. (1979) Biofeedback treatment of atopic dermatitis. *Biofeedback and Self Regulation*, **4**, 195–209.

Hollender, H. and Abram, H. (1973) Dermatitis factitia, *Southern Medical Journal*, **6**, 1279–85.

Horne, D.J. (1977) Behaviour therapy of trichotillomania. *Behavioural Research and Therapy*, **15**, 192–6.

Horne, D.J., White, A. and Varigas, G.A. (1989) A preliminary study of psychological therapy in the management of atopic eczema. *British Journal of Medical Psychology*, **62** (3), 241–8.

Hughes, J., Barraclough, B., Hamblin, L. and White, J. (1983a) Psychiatric symptoms in dermatology patients. *British Journal of Psychiatry*, **143**, 51–4.

Hughes, H., Brown, B., Lawlis, G. and Fulton, J. (1983b) Treatment of acne vulgaris by biofeedback, relaxation and cognitive imagery. *Journal of Psychosomatic Research*, **27**, 185–91.

Jobe, J., Sampson, J., Roberts, D. and Beetham, W. (1982) Induced vasodilation as treatment for Raynaud's disease. *Annals of Internal Medicine*, **97**, 706–9.

Jobe, J., Sampson, J., Roberts, D. and Kelly, J. (1986) Comparisons of behavioural treatments for Raynaud's disease. *Journal of Behavioural Medicine*, **9**, 89–96.

Jones, M. (1980) Conversion reaction. *Psychological Bulletin*, **87**, 127–41.

Jordan, J. and Whitlock, F. (1974) Atopic dermatitis, anxiety and conditioned scratch response. *Journal of Psychosomatic Research*, **18**, 297.

Juhlin, L. (1981) Recurrent urticaria. *British Journal of Dermatology*, **104**, 369–81.

Keefe, F., Surwit, R. and Pilon, N. (1979) A 1 year follow up of Raynaud's patients treated with behavioural therapy techniques. *Journal of Behavioural Medicine*, **2**, 385–91.

Keefe, F., Surwit, R. and Pilon, N. (1980) Biofeedback, autogenic training and progressive muscle relaxation in the treatment of Raynaud's disease. *Journal of Applied Behaviour Analysis*, **13**, 3–11.

Kenyon, F. (1966) Psychosomatic aspects of acne. *British Journal of Dermatology*, **78**, 344.

Koo, J.Y.M. (1979) *Psychodermatology: Current Concepts*, Crawley, Upjohn.

Koo, J. and Smith, L. (1991a) Obsessive–compulsive disorders in pediatric dermatology practice. *Paediatric Dermatology*, **8** (2), 107–13.

Koo, J.Y. and Smith, L.L. (1991b) Psychological aspects of acne. *Paediatric Dermatology*, **8** (3), 185–8.

Kraus, S.J. (1970) Stress, acne and free fatty acids. *Psychosomatic Medicine*, **32**, 503.

Kuno, Y. (1956) *Human Perspiration*, C. Thomas, Illinois.

Leichtman, S., Burnett, J. and Robinson, H. (1981) Body image concerns of psoriasis patients. *Journal of Personality Assessment*, **45** (5), 478–84

Lim, C. and Tan, T.C. (1991) Personality, disability and acne in college students. *Clinical and Experimental Dermatology*, **16** (5), 371–3.

Lyell, A. (1979) Cutaneous artefactual disease. *Journal of American the Academy of Dermatology*, **1**, 391–407.

Mackie, D. (1991) The psychology of skin disorders. *The Practitioner*, **235**, 356–60.

McLaughlin, J.G. and Nay, R.W. (1975) Treatment of trichotillomania using positive coverants and response cost. A case report. *Behaviour Therapy*, **6**, 87–91.

McMenamy, C.J., Katz, R.G. and Gipson, M. (1988) Treatment of eczema by CMG biofeedback and relaxation training. *Journal of Behavioural Therapy and Experimental Psychiatry*, **19** (3), 221–7.

Mannino, F.V. and Delgardo, R.A. (1969) Trichotillomania in children. *American Journal of Psychology*, **126**, 505–11.

Manusov, E.G. and Nadeau, M.T. (1989) Hyperidrosis: a management dilemma. *Journal of Family Practice*, **28** (4), 412–15.

Matussek, P., Agerer, D. and Seibt, G. (1985) Aggression in depressives and psoriatics. *Psychotherapy and Psychosomatics*, **43**, 120–5.

Medansky, R. (1980) Dermatopsychosomatics: an overview. *Psychosomatics*, **21**, 195–200.

Medansky, R.S. and Handler, R.M. (1981) Dematopsychosomatics. *Journal of the American Academy of Dermatology*, **5** (2), 125–36.

Meichenbaum, D.H. and Jaremko, M. (1982) *Stress Prevention and Management*, Plenum Press, New York.

Melin, L., Frederiksen, T., Noren, P. and Swebilius, B. (1986) Behavioural treatment of scratching in patients with atopic dermatitis. *British Journal of Dermatology*, **115**, 467–74.

Merluzzi, T.V., Glass, C.R. and Genest, M. (1981) *Cognitive Assessment*, Guilford Press, New York.

Meynadier, J., Guillot, B., Boulanger, A. *et al.* (1985) Aetiology of chronic urticaria, in *The Urticarias*, (ed. R. Champion), Churchill Livingstone, Edinburgh.

Minnuchin, S. (1974) *Families and Family Therapy*, Harvard University Press, Cambridge, Mass.

Morse, R.M., Perry, H.O. and Hurt, R.D. (1985) Alcoholism and psoriasis. *Archives of Dermatology*, **9**, 396–9.

Motley, R.J. and Finlay, A.Y. (1989) How much disability is caused by acne? *Clinical and Experimental Dermatology*, **14** (3), 194–8.

Munzel, K. and Schandry R. (1990) Atopic eczema: psychophysiological reactivity with standardized stressors. *Hautarzt*, **41** (11), 606–11.

Musaph, H. (1968) Psychodynamics in itching states. *International Journal of Psychoanalysis*, **49**, 336–40.

Orton, C. (1981) *Learning to Live with Skin Disorders*, Souvenir Press, London.

Parsons, T. (1951) *The Social System Process*, Free Press, New York.

Payne, R., Payne, C. and Marks, R. (1985) Stress does not worsen psoriasis. *Clinical and Experimental Dermatology*, **10**, 239–45.

Pegum, J.S. and Baker, H. (1979) *Dermatology*, Baillière Tindall, London.

Pines, D. (1980) Skin communication. *International Journal of Psychoanalysis*, 61, 315.

Price, M.L., Mottahedin, I. and Mayo, P.R. (1991) Can psychotherapy help patients with psoriasis? *Clinical and Experimental Dermatology*, **16** (2), 114–7.

Rajka, G. (1975) *Atopic Dermatitis*, W.B. Saunders and Co, Eastbourne.

Ratcliff, R. and Stein, N. (1968) Treatment of neurodermatitis by behaviour therapy – a case study. *Behavioural Research and Therapy*, **6**, 397.

Rechardt, E. (1970) *An Investigation into the Psychosomatic Aspects of Prurigo Besnier*, Psychiatric Clinic of Helsinki University Central Hospital.

Rees, L. (1957) An aetiological study of urticaria and angioneurotic oedema. *Journal of Psychosomatic Research*, **2**, 172.

Rees, L. (1976) Stress, distress and disease. *British Journal of Psychiatry*, **128**, 3–18.

Reeve, E., Bernstein, G. and Christenson, G. (1992) Clinical characteristics and psychiatric comorbidity in children with trichotillomania. *Journal of the American Academy of Childhood and Adolescence Psychiatry*, **31** (1), 132–8.

Risch, C. and Ferguson, J. (1981) Behavioural treatment of skin disorders, in *The Comprehensive*

Handbook of Behavioural Medicine, Vol. 2, (eds R.J. Ferguson and H.L. Taylor), Spectrum Inc., New York, pp. 29–40.

Roth, H., Kierland, R. and Rochester, M. (1964) The natural history of atopic dermatitis. *Archives of Dermatology*, **89**, 209–14.

Russell, M.L. (1986) *Behavioural Counselling in Medicine*, Oxford University Press, New York.

Ryan, T. (1991) Disability in dermatology. *British Journal of Hospital Medicine*, **46** (1), 33–6.

Sampson, J.B. (1977) Effects on anxiety of temperature response to cold water immersion. *Annual Meeting of the Society for Psychophysiological Research.* Abstract.

Savin, J. (1980) Itching, in *Recent Advances in Dermatology, 5*, (eds A. Rook and J. Savin), Churchill Livingstone, New York, pp. 221–335.

Savin, J., Paterson, W., Oswand, I. and Adam, K. (1975) Further studies of scratching during sleep. *British Journal of Dermatology*, **93**,. 297–302.

Seville, R. (1977) Psoriasis and stress. *British Journal of Dermatology*, **97**, 297–302.

Sheehan-Dare, R., Henderson, M. and Cotterill, J. (1990) Anxiety and depression in patients with chronic urticaria and generalized pruritus. *British Journal of Dermatology*, **123** (6), 769–74.

Shelley, W. and Arthur, R. (1959) Studies on cowhage. *Archives of Dermatology*, **72**, 399–406.

Sheppard, N.P., O'Loughlin, S.O. and Malone, J.P. (1986) Psychogenic skin disease. *British Journal of Psychiatry*, **149**, 636–43.

Shuster, S. (1979) Stress and psoriasis. *British Journal of Dermatology*, **97**, 297–302.

Shuster, S. Fisher, G.I.K., Harris, E. and Binnell, D. (1978) The effect of skin disease on self image. *British Journal of Dermatology*, **99** (Suppl. 16), 18–19.

Sneddon, I. and Sneddon, J. (1981) Acne excorie – a protective device. *British Journal of Dermatology*, **91** (Suppl. 19), 29.

Sperber, J., Shaw, J. and Bruce, S. (1989) Psychological components and the role of adjunct interventions in chronic idiopathic urticaria. *Psychotherapy and Psychosomatics*, **51** (3), 135–41.

Stambrook, M., Hamel, E., and Carter, S. (1988) Training to vasodilate in a cooling environment. *Biofeedback-Self-Regulations*, **13** (1), 9–23.

Stanley, M., Swann, A., Bowers, T. *et al.* (1992) A comparison of clinical features of trichotillomania and obsessive–compulsive disorder. *Behaviour Research Therapy*, **30** (1), 39–44.

Stein, D.J and Hollander, E. (1992) Dermatology and conditions related to obsessive–compulsive disorder.

Journal of the American Academy of Dermatology, **26** (2), 237–42.

Steptoe, A. (1989) Psychophysiological interventions in behavioural medicine, in *Handbook of Clinical Psychophysiology*, (ed. G. Turpin), Wiley, Chichester.

Sternbach, R.A. (1966) *Principles of Psychophysiology*, Academic Press, Orlando.

Tonnesen, M. (1979) Pruritis, in *Dermatology in General Medicine*, (eds T. Fitzpatrick, K. Arndt, W. Clark *et al.*), McGraw-Hill, New York.

Turk, D., Meichenbaum, D. and Genest, M. (1983) *Pain and Behavioural Medicine*, Guilford Press, New York.

Van Moffaert, M. (1982) Psychosomatics for the practising dermatologist. *Dermatologica*, **165**, 73–87.

Van Moffaert, M. (1986) Training future derma-tologists in psychodermatology. *General Hospital Psychiatry*, **8** (2), 115–18.

Vitulano, L.A., King, R.A., Scahill, L. and Cohen, D. (1992) Behavioural treatment of children and adoles-cents with trichotillomania. *Journal of the American Academy of Childhood and Adolescence Psychiatry*, **31** (1), 139–46.

Walton, R. (1960) The application of learning theory to the treatment of a case of neurodermatitis, in *Therapy and Neuroses*, (ed. H. Eysenck), Pergamon Press, New York, pp. 272–4.

Walton, R. (1985) Stress factors in dermatology. *Stress Medicine*, **1**, 55–60.

Watson, D., Thorp, R. and Krisber, J. (1972) Case study in self-modification: suppression of infantile scratching. *Journal of Behaviour Therapy and Experimental Psychiatry*, **3**, 213.

Weinstein, M. (1984) Psychosocial perspective on psoriasis. *Dermatology Clinic*, **2**, 507–15.

Whitlock, F.A. (1976) *Psychophysiological Aspects of Skin Disease*, W.B. Saunders & Co, Eastbourne.

Williams, D. (1951) Management of atopic dermatitis in children *Archives of Dermatology and Syphilology*, **63**, 545.

Worden, J.W. (1991) *Grief Counselling and Grief Therapy*, Tavistock Publications, London.

Wu, S.F., Kinder, B., Trunnel, T. and Fulton, J. (1988) Role of anxiety and anger in acne patients. *Journal of the American Academy of Dermatology*, **18**, 325–33.

Chapter eleven

Diabetes mellitus

Richard Shillitoe

Introduction

Diabetes mellitus is a disease that has a bearing upon almost all areas of psychological functioning, from cognitive development, schooling and family life when young, to mood and interpersonal relationships when adult. The management regimen requires lifelong self-regulation of behaviour, and the degree of control a patient achieves over the disease is affected by stress, attitudes, social support, the manner in which health care is delivered, and the expertise and beliefs of care professionals. Some patients will develop serious degenerative complications and will benefit from counselling. In short, the problems posed by the disease and its management encompass almost every area of health psychology.

The disease

For practical purposes there are two main types of diabetes, although research workers recognize several more. Type I diabetes corresponds to what used to be called 'juvenile onset' or 'insulin-dependent' diabetes. The neutral label type I is to be preferred because some patients who fall into this category do not develop diabetes until adulthood, and because others who are not 'insulin-dependent' actually require insulin for adequate disease control. Type II diabetes used to be known as 'maturity onset' and 'non-insulin-dependent'; these labels have been largely replaced because they, too, are

confusing. Both types of diabetes are disorders of the metabolic systems responsible for the storage and utilization of glucose, the principal energy source released from food. The regulation of the blood level of glucose is carried out principally by the hormone insulin. The relative or absolute absence of insulin, or the body's inability to use it, leads to widespread metabolic abnormalities. Although patients with type II diabetes retain some insulin action, this is not to say that this type of diabetes is relatively innocuous: the disease may be present undetected for several years, during which time the degenerative changes associated with diabetes may proceed silently.

The underlying lesion is quite different in type I and type II diabetes. Type I diabetes is probably due to an autoimmune disease of the insulin-producing cells of the pancreas. There is a genetic predisposition, although less than 50% of identical twins are concordant for the disease. Onset is usually during childhood or early adulthood, with a peak age of incidence between 12 and 14 years of age.

The type II disorder has a stronger genetic component, with a concordance rate for identical twins approaching 100%. There is both a reduction of insulin receptors in peripheral tissue and a deficiency in insulin secretion. It is predominantly a disease of ageing, with more than 70% of patients being older than 55 years. The great majority of these are obese.

Degenerative complications, such as

neuropathy, peripheral vascular disease, renal failure and visual impairment are, to some degree, observable in a majority of patients after many years. The development of long-term complications is largely a consequence of poor disease management (Diabetes Control and Complications Trial, 1993), although genetic susceptibility also plays a part (Strowig and Raskin, 1992).

Prevalence and incidence

Diabetes is a common disease of affluent societies, present in about 1–2% of the population and rising to 5–10% of the population over 40 years of age. Of the total number with diabetes, approximately 75% will have the type II disorder (Jarrett, 1986). The prevalence of diabetes has probably doubled in recent decades, and is still rising. Studies worldwide show that the adoption of a westernized lifestyle, with a sedentary existence and the eating of energy-dense foods, is an important contributory factor for the rise in prevalence of type II diabetes (Taylor and Zimmet, 1983). Minority groups, such as Asian communities in Britain, among whom type II diabetes is common, present significant difficulties for health professionals, who tend to be unfamiliar with their cultural values, views of disease and treatment, lifestyle and language.

Higher rates of the type II disease have been reported in the UK and the USA in localities with poor social and economic conditions and low family income (see Jarrett, 1986). Part of this may be accounted for by the link between obesity and family income. Adults in low-income groups consume twice as much sugar as adults in high-income groups, and diets for people with diabetes are significantly more expensive than the everyday diets of most healthy individuals (Hanes and De Looy, 1987). Persons in lower-income groups are less likely to engage in self-care behaviours or to have a 'future-oriented' view of health (DiMatteo and DiNicola, 1982). These factors all constitute barriers to dietary adherence, both as a preventive measure and as a means of controlling the disease once diagnosed.

Management of diabetes mellitus

Management consists of balancing events that raise blood glucose (e.g. eating foodstuffs which contain carbohydrate) with events that lower blood glucose (e.g. activity, injections of insulin, taking oral hypoglycaemic medication). The aims are to keep the blood glucose within the normal range as far as possible and, in the long term, to avoid degenerative complications.

Although management is usually thought of in terms of metabolic control, it is primarily a problem of behavioural self-management: the regulation of blood glucose by deliberate actions in the absence of the body's natural control mechanisms (Wing *et al.*, 1986) The main self-management tasks are as follows:

- Eating specific amounts of food at specific times to attain and maintain normal growth and optimal body weight.
- Taking medication in the correct dosage at the correct time, to keep blood glucose levels as near normal as possible.
- Monitoring blood glucose accurately at specific times to obtain feedback about the success of self-management behaviours and to direct future efforts.
- Taking exercise and other preventative measures appropriately, to improve and maintain good physical condition.

Management by diet

Diets are necessary for the regulation of energy intake in all patients with diabetes. Obese patients will require reducing diets. Diets are unpopular and poorly adhered to; this is less a reflection upon diets specifically for diabetes than it is upon the general difficulty that people experience in any long-term dietary adherence. Modern dietary recommendations for people with diabetes emphasize fibre, complex carbo-hydrates and low fat intake and, as such, they are very similar to healthy eating patterns appropriate for the general population. This could have the desirable effect of bringing a patient's diet and the eating habits of other family members into line, and thus reducing one important barrier to dietary adherence. However, high-fibre complex carbohydrate low-fat diets are still not normally followed in western society, and cultural changes will need to occur if they are to achieve widespread acceptance.

The general body of psychological research concerning the modification of eating behaviour is relevant, especially for obese patients who are prescribed a reducing diet. Most behaviourally orientated clinicians favour a multifaceted approach requiring intensive long-term contact, a combination of behavioural strategies and formal exercise targets (see Wing, 1989). The use of behavioural management techniques gen-erally results in some weight loss, but gradual reversion to the starting weight in subsequent months. On the other hand, alternative approaches such as medical advice or dietary education and counselling generally fare considerably worse (Wilson, 1980).

Diabetes and eating disorders

The coexistence of an eating disorder with dia-betes could cause problems with metabolic control through, for example, repetitive binge eating or self-induced vomiting. Given that dia-betes management focuses attention on food, and that insulin causes weight gain, it is not surprising that some authors have found an increased prevalence of eating disorders in ado-lescents and young adults with diabetes (Rodin et al., 1985; Steel et al., 1987). Clinicians report that management is difficult; cognitive behaviour therapy may be helpful (Peveler and Fairburn, 1989).

The prevalence of eating disorders among people with diabetes is not known with any

accuracy. In young diabetic women, it has been reported to be as high as 20% (Rodin et al., 1985). However, the use of assessment scales standardized on the physically healthy, such as the Eating Attitudes Test (EAT), as used by many researchers, is inappropri-ate. People with diabetes are expected to avoid foodstuffs containing sugar and to have an extensive knowledge of the carbo-hydrate content of foods; such knowledge and behaviour in healthy individuals is taken to indicate eating pathology. Rosmark et al. (1986) excluded such items from the EAT and showed that the preva-lence of eating problems in female clinic attenders (9%) was significantly higher than for males and normative samples, but considerably lower than earlier estimates. Using a semistructured clinical interview – the Eating Disorder Examination – Fairburn et al. (1991) did not show a higher prevalence of eating disorders in young diabetic women than in matched non-diabetic controls. Whatever the final figure, one conclusion that can be safely made is that researchers who abandon the basic psychometric principles of test construc-tion and usage do so at their peril. Tests should be designed for, and standardized on, the populations for whom they are intended.

Management by medication: tablets

The frequency with which patients with chronic disease fail to take prescribed oral medication has been extensively documented (DiMatteo and DiNicola, 1982). There is no reason to sup-pose that patients with diabetes fare any better than other patient groups, but there is little direct evidence. Measurement of serum concen-trations of oral hypoglycaemics by Wiholm (1980) indicated not only irregular drug intake but also a discrepancy between biochemical evi-dence and patients' self-reports. The importance of this is that clinical decisions made on the basis of self-reports may be inappropriate.

Management by medication: insulin

The body's natural pattern of insulin release is low basal output supplemented by 'spurts' at mealtimes. To mimic this, a regimen of up to four injections per day is often recommended for the insulin-requiring patient, that is, a night-time injection of slow-acting insulin to provide the basal level, and an injection of rapid-acting insulin before each meal. The patient also has to adjust the amount of insulin injected and the timing of injections in the light of current blood glucose, predicted activity level and food intake.

A number of devices have been developed to make insulin delivery less onerous. The insulin injector 'pen', a fully self-contained syringe containing a vial of insulin and about the size of a fountain pen, is one. It makes self-injection significantly easier and more convenient. Pens have a high patient acceptability (Jefferson et al., 1985) but there is no clear evidence that they result in improved blood glucose control.

Another device is the infusion pump, a small battery-powered pump worn on the belt, with an indwelling needle delivering insulin continuously. Pumps can allow very precise control to be obtained. The use of continuous subcutaneous insulin infusion (CSII) may appear to be a great management advance, yet many patients find it unacceptable. In one study, given the choice of CSII, a multiple injection regimen or the continuation of less intensive insulin regimen, many patients initially chose CSII but dropped out after a few weeks (Ward, 1984). The use of diabetes-specific attributional scales showed that the patients who had selected CSII scored significantly higher on external medical control scales and lower on internal personal control scales than did the patients who selected the other treatment options (Bradley et al., 1987). As CSII actually requires continual vigilance from its users, those who selected it may have been hoping for less personal involvement and may not have been those best suited to meeting its demands. The area of individual differences and treatment preference has been little explored so far, although it is of fundamental importance in the management of a chronic disease such as diabetes, which requires the continual active involvement of sufferers.

Hypoglycaemia

A common complication of treatment by insulin is hypoglycaemia. The more determined attempts are made to keep blood glucose within the normal range, throughout the day, the greater the chances of it falling too low, causing a hypoglycaemic reaction. As the body and brain become deprived of glucose, cognitive, behavioural, mood and other disturbances become progressively more evident. These may be embarrassing, inconvenient or life-threatening. Judgement is generally impaired when blood glucose is low, and signs, clearly noticeable to observers, may not be appreciated by patients themselves, who may not recognize the need to take corrective action until they are unable to do so. Hopes that patients could be taught to recognize early warning symptoms of hypoglycaemia have met with mixed results. Many patients cannot do so with sufficient accuracy to derive significant clinical benefit, although many believe that they can: a potentially dangerous situation. Children and adolescents in particular find it difficult to estimate their blood glucose level accurately (see Gonder-Frederick, Snyder and Clarke, 1991).

Repeated hypoglycaemia may cause mild, but measurable, brain damage. Young children who have repeated hypoglycaemic episodes have slightly but significantly lowered scores on tests of intelligence, school achievement, visuospatial ability, memory functions, motor speed and hand-eye coordination when assessed in later years (Ryan, Vega and Drash, 1985; Rovet, Ehrlich and Hoppe, 1987). Several retrospective studies on the effects of repeated hypoglycaemia in adulthood have reached similar conclusions (e.g. Pramming *et al.*, 1986; Langan *et al.*, 1991), but the only prospective study so far to appear (Reichard, Britz and Rosenqvist, 1991) was unable to show any signs of cognitive deterioration in patients on intensified insulin regimens, despite an increased frequency of severe hypoglycaemia.

Clinicians who advocate very tight blood glucose control should be aware that they are exposing patients to an increased risk of hypo-glycaemic episodes. The consequences of this will vary from transient behavioural disturbances to permanent cognitive impairment.

Management by monitoring

It is essential to monitor the effectiveness of the regimen. Patients require accurate feedback of their current blood glucose level so that they can make immediate decisions concerning adjustments to the management regimen. Most patients with type I diabetes, for whom wide and rapid variability of blood glucose can be a great problem, monitor their own blood glucose using a pocket-sized battery-powered meter and glucose-sensitive reagent strips. The patient obtains a blood sample by finger pricking, and applies it to the glucose-sensitive strip. This is then 'read' by the meter, which give a rapid reading of the current blood glucose. The strips can also be used on their own and read visually. The procedure is known as self-monitoring of blood glucose (SMBG), and is often associated with multiple injection regimens, of up to four injections per day.

Long-term studies of the efficacy of such intensive regimens are lacking. In the short-term they can improve control, although staff attention and prompting may be prime components in causing improvements (Worth *et al.*, 1982). It is known that the procedure is often carried out inaccurately by adults with type I diabetes (Fairclough *et al.*, 1983), adults with type II diabetes (Campbell *et al.*, 1992), children (Wing *et al.*, 1986) and health professionals (Ting and Nanji, 1988). Few patients understand how to adjust their insulin in the light of SMBG results (Gill and Redmond, 1991), and it is not known with what frequency patients need to self-monitor in order to improve their disease control.

Some researchers have used meters with hidden 'memory chips' to record secretly the time when each assessment is made and the reading obtained, in order to examine the accuracy of patients' own records of meter usage. These studies show that adults (Mazze *et al.*, 1984), adolescents (Wilson and Endres, 1986) and apparently well-motivated groups of patients such as pregnant women (Langer and Mazze, 1986) frequently omit to record abnormal results, change abnormal results to more normal values and record totally fictitious readings. Once again, clinical decisions made on the basis of patient-kept records are likely to be inappropriate.

These sorts of findings are generally greeted with dismay, but they should come as no surprise to those who have studied communication in health care (see the chapter by Ley and Llewelyn, this volume). The challenge for health psychology is to develop effective ways to help patients incorporate the procedure into routine life, to ensure its long-term performance and to use the findings as a basis for the modification of other aspects of the regimen, in particular insulin dosage. The most effective ways of achieving this have yet to be determined. Self-learning via written instructions is insufficient for many (Ward, Haas and Beard, 1985); for children, peer modelling may be of value (Warzak, Ayllon and Delcher, 1982); with adolescents, success has been reported using problem-solving groups (Anderson *et al.*, 1989); and for staff, annual assessments of competence can be valuable (Lawrence *et al.*, 1989).

Management by prevention

Exercise, no smoking and a moderate alcohol intake are desirable for people with diabetes who are at greater risk from the deleterious effects of an unhealthy lifestyle then their non-diabetic counterparts. Aerobic exercise is valuable for weight loss, reduces insulin resistance in patients with type II diabetes and diminishes the risk of hypertension and cardiovascular disease (Stein *et al.*, 1984). Incorporating the necessary amount of exercise into a regular routine for the sake of a long-term risk reduction, however, may be perceived as a chore not worth undertaking. Ways of overcoming this difficulty have been discussed by Dubbert, Martin and Epstein (1986). Whether preventative measures on a large scale are feasible is difficult to say, but an interesting attempt to improve the physical activity of a whole population at risk for the development of diabetes, the Zuni Indians of New Mexico, has been described by Leonard, Leonard and Wilson (1986).

Both diabetes and smoking are risk factors for the development of cardiovascular disease. The prevalence of smoking among people with diabetes is not markedly different from that of the general population (Jones and Hedley, 1987). Alcohol has effects upon carbohydrate metabolism, may increase the likelihood of hypoglycaemia in type I patients and leads to weight gain (Connor and Marks, 1985). The introduction of audit into diabetes care means that many services now routinely monitor the number of patients who drink immoderately or smoke, and may make reduction a specific target. Quite how this may be achieved is not clear, but management strategies derived from the field of addictive behaviours are of obvious potential benefit here. Controlled evaluations have yet to be reported with diabetic samples.

From compliance to empowerment

From the preceding sections (see also Chapter 5) it may have been concluded that compliance with management advice is often poor. In a general sense this is undoubtedly correct. Compliance, however, is a construct of dubious value.

There are three main problems. First, the word implies that the patient has been given a specific set of treatment guidelines to follow. For many aspects of the regimen (e.g. exercise) this may not be the case. Secondly, authors such as Webb *et al.* (1984) have shown that adequate performance of one aspect of the regimen (e.g. the timing of a meal in relation to insulin administration) does not predict adequate performance of any of the others to which it might be expected to relate (e.g. the carbohydrate or fat content of the meal itself). Thirdly, one of the hallmarks of the regimen is that it is almost infinitely variable: the patient is expected to modify diet, insulin etc. in accordance with blood test results, activity levels, infections and other factors that affect blood glucose. Under these circumstances, defining and measuring compliance with some loosely prescribed, independent and constantly changing criteria is a practical and theoretical nightmare.

In recognition of this, Glasgow, Wilson and McCaul (1985) proposed that instead of 'compliance' one should think in terms of 'levels of self-care behaviour'; that is, the setting of explicit and specific behavioural goals in the light of assessed need, and the measurement of the extent to which the targeted behaviours are actually carried out. The application of behaviourally based methods of management to diabetes has been reviewed by Wing *et al.* (1986) and, for children, by Stark, Dahlquist and Collins (1987). The abandonment of a term such as 'compliance', which also carries overtones of 'doctor's orders' and which sees 'non-compliance' in terms of some deficit in the patient, is long overdue. It is the antithesis of the concept of self-regulation, which lies at the heart of diabetes management.

It is just a short step from this to the open acknowledgement that not only do patients make and carry out many of the day-to-day decisions regarding the management of their diabetes independently of medical advice, but that they also have the right to be the active decision makers regarding their own care: professionals may know what is best for an individual's diabetes, but this is not the same as knowing what is best for the individual who has the diabetes (Anderson *et al.*, 1991). There are similarities here with the deliberations of health economists, health care planners and others concerning the identification of health wants and health needs (e.g. Brewin, Bradley and Home, 1991).

In terms of empowerment, however, there is a long way to go, as the experience of many patients during the changeover to 'human' insulin makes clear. A wholesale changeover of insulin prescription took place throughout the 1980s, in which patients were switched to newer genetically engineered forms of insulin (so-called 'human' insulin) with the minimum of information and discussion. The reasons for this were commercial rather than clinical. A proportional of patients subsequently reported that their subjective sensations of hypoglycaemia had changed, but received short shrift from their medical advisors and were frequently (and falsely) told that changing back to their old insulin preparation was impossible, as it was no longer available (Tattersall, 1992). It is only recently that scientific evidence is beginning to emerge that such complaints could be valid (e.g. Egger, Davey Smith and Teuscher, 1992), although the arguments still rage. In the meantime, much trust and goodwill has been lost. The only winners may be the lawyers, who are actively encouraging disaffected patients to sue their clinicians and/or the pharmaceutical companies.

Education and diabetes management

Patients of all ages (and the parents of children with diabetes) display considerable ignorance of the disease and its management (see the review by Shillitoe, 1988). A wide variety of educational programmes have been devised in response to this unsatisfactory state of affairs, ranging from fairly informal methods, which can be offered at routine clinic attendance, to interactive computer programs and formal residential courses for patients and their families. Although some of these methods might be relatively efficient at imparting information, there is no evidence of a straightforward relationship between knowledge and metabolic control, or between what a patient knows and what a patient does (Shillitoe, 1988), and little evidence that traditional educational programmes have any lasting or beneficial effect. This is in line with evidence from other disease populations that standardized informational packages are of limited value in influencing behaviour and clinical outcomes (Mazzuca, 1982).

In the last decade there has been a move away from the passive, theoretical type of educational programme to more experimental, practical approaches, which rely heavily (but not always explicitly) upon social learning theory for their design and implementation. This has often involved group methods, where opportunities for modelling and imitation can be maximized. Peer modelling and guided practice have been used to teach injection skills to youngsters (Gilbert *et al.*, 1982) and self-monitoring of blood glucose (Warzak, Ayllon and Delcher, 1982). Other researchers have used role-play to teach aspects of the regimen (Lucey and Wing, 1985) or social skills training to modify dietary behaviour (Kaplan, Chadwick and Schimmell, 1985). The techniques have been used most often with children and adolescents, but are applicable to adults as well.

The use of techniques that focus upon behavioural change in real life (e.g. McCulloch *et al.*, 1983); which require the active participation of family members (e.g. Delamater *et al.*, 1990);

which are derived from cognitive behaviour therapy (Campbell *et al.*, 1990); and modules which are introduced according to identified needs (Mazzuca *et al.*, 1986) have all been claimed to be superior to traditional educational procedures.

In the past, many researchers and clinicians have simply embarked upon an educational programme without being explicit about its purpose, whether it is knowledge acquisition, skills development, behavioural change or some other objective. The tendency has also been to develop complicated packages, the individual components of which have not been assessed, and to operate outside a theoretical framework of education. Until these points are addressed, much time spent in educating patients will continue to be wasted.

Knowledge and education among health professionals

The education of health professionals presents as great a challenge as does the education of patients. One problem is that staff may perceive their knowledge or skills to be better than they actually are (Drass *et al.*, 1989). Another is that staff and patients' views of what is important to know may differ markedly (Genev *et al.*, 1992), and staff may have optimistic views of what patients know or what tasks they are capable of performing correctly (Wysocki *et al.*, 1992). Education for staff might target the correct use of reflectance meters (Lawrence *et al.*, 1989), dietary management (Scheiderich, Freibaum and Peterson, 1983), the modification of inappropriate beliefs about acceptable glycaemic ranges (Mellor *et al.*, 1985) or the likelihood of developing degenerative complications (Marteau and Baum, 1984). As with patients, educational objectives for staff should be explicit and determined by an assessment of education needs.

Stress management

Stress can exert an effect upon diabetes control in two ways: directly, through metabolic pathways concerned with the stress response, and indirectly, through effects upon behaviour. There is evidence that self-care behaviours are often performed less strictly during periods of stress. For example, Cox *et al.* (1984) and Hanson and Pichert (1986) showed that harassment and worry are associated with changes in eating patterns and, according to Fisher *et al.* (1982): 'emotional conflict or negative emotions' directly preceded one-quarter of all dietary violations. The counter-regulatory or 'stress' hormones reduce insulin sensitivity, so it might be expected that stress in an individual with diabetes will result in an elevation of blood glucose. In fact, the situation is quite complicated. In response to laboratory stressors, blood glucose levels have been reported to increase, decrease and remain unchanged. These findings can, in part, be attributed to methodological flaws (see Goetsch, 1989 for a review) but it is also clear that many variables are at work. These include the nature, context and degree of stress, the prevailing level of glycaemic control and the amount of free insulin in circulation (Bradley and Cox, 1978); cognitive appraisal of the stressor (Cox *et al.*, 1985); individual difference (Stabler *et al.*, 1987); recency of eating (Wing *et al.*, 1985; Kemmer *et al.*, 1986); and changes in blood flow affecting the absorption of insulin (Greenhalgh *et al.*, 1992). Much more investigation of the relationships between these variables is required.

Perhaps because of these complexities, the results of experiments designed to teach stress-management skills by such means as relaxation training and biofeedback techniques, have generally been disappointing. It is difficult to predict which patients are likely to respond to stress-management training. Although some authors have reported improvements in glycaemic control (e.g. Fowler, Budzynski and VandenBergh, 1976; Seeburg and DeBoer, 1981; Landis *et al.*, 1985), others have not done so (e.g. Feinglos, Hastedt and Surwit, 1987). When authors have reported improvements, the levels of improvement reported have generally been low, blood glucose remaining above the normal range in nearly all cases. The role of individual differences in determining responses to stress and to stress-management procedures requires further exploration before their clinical utility can be evaluated.

Blood glucose discrimination training

One form of biofeedback which has received a good deal of attention is blood glucose discrimination training, which was referred to earlier. In this procedure patients are asked to make a prediction of their current blood glucose level using mood state, bodily sensations etc. as cues. SMBG provides immediate feedback of the accuracy of the prediction and allows the possibility of improving predictive accuracy. This would be of clinical value especially, for example, for adolescents and children whose awareness of blood glucose levels has been reported as inferior to that of other age groups (Nurick and Johnson, 1991; Gonder-Frederick *et al.*, 1991). Some patients are able to improve their predictive accuracy, and do so by learning to attend to external cues (such as time since last eating) as well as internal states (Cox *et al.*, 1985, 1989). However, for many people the relationship between subjective experiences and blood glucose level is variable over time (Cox *et al.*, 1983): it is certainly subject to great individual variation, and may also be subject to the overall degree of metabolic control and the structural integrity of the nervous system. These factors are likely to limit the clinical utility of the procedure and make its use by some patients potentially dangerous.

Stressful life events

Major life events or minor events (daily hassles) have not been shown conclusively to cause glycaemic changes or to precipitate the onset of diabetes, although there is some evidence that suggests such associations. Investigators have focused upon children and adolescents (Brand, Johnson and Johnson, 1986); young adults (Robinson and Fuller, 1985); the middle aged (Lloyd *et al.*, 1991); and older patients showing retinopathy (Jacobson, Rand and Hauser, 1985). Insensitive or inappropriate measures of stressors, the stress response or metabolic control may be responsible for this state of uncertainty. The validation of a diabetes-specific Barriers to Adherence Scale (Glasgow, McCaul and Schafer, 1986) measuring the occurrence of daily hassles which might influence self-care behaviours points the way to more standardized assessment procedures.

Brittle diabetes

A small group of type 1 patients, commonly females in their teens or early 20s and overweight, present particular management problems. They show large-scale variability in blood glucose and have a history of multiple hospital admissions. Generally, substantial emotional and family problems feature in their personal lives. Some may be 'superlabile' in their physiological response to stress (Baker and Barcai, 1970), but the evidence for this is minimal and it has been proposed that control in the majority is brittle because of 'wilful metabolic sabotage' (Keen, 1985). In other words, control is deliberately manipulated by the patient to secure hospital admission in order to avoid some intolerable domestic or personal crisis (Tattersall and Walford, 1985). Readers may feel uncomfortable with this apparent blaming of the patient and the use of emotive language, but repeated admissions obviously try the patience and tolerance of care staff, who feel frustrated and misused. This is a situation in which it is only too easy for staff to blame and reject the patient. Team work probably provides the most appropriate method of management, with easy access to a psychologist who can take an advisory, supportive or consultatory role to the first-line diabetes team (Shillitoe, 1991).

Attitudes and beliefs

A patient's personal beliefs about the disease and about the regimen should be reflected in which self-care behaviours are actually performed. The main lines of research into the role of attitudes and beliefs have concerned locus of control and the Health Belief Model.

Locus of control (LOC)

A person's control orientation could have an indirect effect on metabolic outcome via its effects upon the frequency of self-management behaviours (Schlenk and Hart, 1984) or directly upon physiology (see Wallston et al., 1987). The experimental findings as far as diabetes is concerned are inconsistent and contradictory, and this is true for all age groups (see Shillitoe, 1988, for a fuller discussion). It has been argued (Bradley et al., 1984) that published LOC scales are too general for use with specific disease. Bradley and colleagues have therefore developed diabetes-specific causal attributional scales, versions of which are available for patients treated with insulin (Bradley et al., 1984) and for those treated with oral hypoglycaemics (Bradley et al., 1990). In a similar vein, Grossman, Brink and Hauser (1987) have published a Self-Efficacy for Diabetes Scale specifically constructed for use with adolescents. Agreement is clearly necessary concerning measuring instruments before apparently similar studies can be compared and some of the confusions, hopefully, resolved.

The Health Belief Model (HBM)

The situation is even worse as far as the HBM is concerned. Authors have tended to construct their own scales and have seldom reported adequately upon their psychometric properties. Researchers have used different versions of the model, have often failed to define the nature of their patient samples and have used invalid measures of outcome (see Shillitoe and Christie, 1989). The model has not been well served by many investigations performed in its name.

Some authors, such as Given et al. (1983), Jenny (1984) and Bradley et al. (1984) have reported on the development of diabetes-specific health belief scales, but even so there are conceptual problems with the HBM when it is applied to a chronic disease such as diabetes. Not least of these concerns is the relationship between beliefs, behaviours and outcomes (King, 1983). Behaviours and outcomes must modify beliefs and expectations, so that the beliefs measured after some outcome has been achieved (such as a particular body weight or a particular level of metabolic control) may not be the same as those that predated and perhaps initiated the behaviours. The predictive power of health beliefs in chronic disease may be intrinsically limited by the existence of such a feedback loop.

Finally, what about the attitudes and beliefs of care professionals? General practitioners have been shown to have a bleaker outlook on diabetes than hospital doctors, perceiving the disease to carry more risks and having less confidence that achieving treatment goals will reduce those risks (Marteau and Kinmonth, 1988). In keeping with their beliefs, GPs tolerated a wider range of blood glucose levels in their patients. Physicians with an internal LOC have been shown to be more likely to foster self-care in their patients than those with an external control expectancy (Linn and Lewis, 1979), and Gamsu and Bradley (1987) noted a number of mismatches between staff attributions and patient attributions for various diabetes-related outcomes. Negative outcomes (such as having a hypoglycaemic attack) were rated as being more foreseeable by staff than they were by patients, whereas the reverse was the case for positive outcomes. Patients rated themselves as having more control over these than did staff. The existence of such differences is likely to have an effect upon the quality of patient–carer communication, and hence patient behaviour and outcome.

Personal and social functioning in diabetes

Children and adolescents with diabetes

Two-thirds of newly diagnosed children and adolescents show symptoms, lasting a few months, of depressed mood, irritability, feelings of friendlessness, social withdrawal and anxiety (Kovacs *et al.*, 1985a). A minority display greater affective disturbance. A poor marital relationship between the parents may be a risk factor for adaptational difficulties.

There is no good evidence that children and adolescents with diabetes have self-esteem or adjustment problems, nor that the incidence of emotional or behavioural problems is higher than it is in healthy youngsters. These statements are at variance with the view of many earlier writers, who claimed that poor self-esteem and relationship problems are the norm. Such views, based on inadequate assessment methods and vague criteria of disturbance, were convincingly challenged in a review by Johnson (1980), and subsequently in well-controlled investigations (e.g. Jacobson *et al.*, 1986). The implications of this are that children and adolescents with lasting or significant behavioural or emotional problems are not following the normal path to adaptation, and may require special intervention.

Some children or groups of children may, however, be at greater risk for difficulties in coping. The age at which the child develops diabetes may be an important variable here, and there may be a sex difference in the effects of age of onset upon adaptation. Female adolescents who had developed diabetes before the age of 5 years were identified by Ryan and Morrow (1986) as having a higher incident of anxiety and concern about personal appearance than other groups of diabetic teenagers. Male adolescents between 9 and 12 years of age at diagnosis were found by Ahlfield, Soler and Marcus (1983) to display adjustment problems relatively more frequently.

Who is responsible for management?

The transfer of responsibility for management from parents to youngster starts in childhood and continues throughout adolescence. Children are capable of performing management tasks mechanically before they are capable of understanding the underlying rationale and responding flexibly to changing circumstances. There is often a stage when the views of parents, patients and health workers concerning a youngster's understanding and competence fail to match with each other or with reality. The timing of the transfer of management responsibility should take into account the stage of cognitive development of the child (Harkavy *et al.*, 1983). Peer support groups for adolescents (and parents) may facilitate adaptation (Marrero *et al.*, 1982; Brink, 1982; Marteau, Gillespie and Swift, 1987).

Family relationships and diabetes

Short-term affective disturbances are a natural response of parents to the diagnosis of diabetes in a child. These seldom reach clinical significance, and have generally resolved by 1 year after diagnosis (Kovacs *et al.*, 1985a) Although parents, especially mothers, con to worry about management and their child's future (Banion, Miles and Carter, 1983), there is no reliable evidence that parents show mal-adaptive nurturing behaviour (Johnson, 1984) or that the parents' relationship or family cohesion suffers (Kovacs et al., 1985b), despite the daily difficulties that must exist.

On the other hand, there is evidence that certain family characteristics are associated with the quality of metabolic control. In adolescent females, the presence of the emotionally charged relationship between patient and mother has been found to be associated with poor regimen adherence (Bobrow, AvRuskin and Siller, 1985), although causality is difficult to establish. Use of the Moos Family Environment Scale by a number of researchers (e.g. Anderson et al., 1981; Hauser et al., 1985; Wertlieb, Hauser and Jacobson, 1986) has shown an association between a relaxed, uncompetitive family atmosphere with an organized routine, and better outcome and adjustment. Marital conflict, the presence of a step-parent or adoptive parents and a lack of emotional expressiveness have also been associated with poorer control (Marteau, Bloch and Baum, 1987). Some families may be particularly poor at dealing with conflicts among members. They have been described as 'psychosomatic families' (Minuchin, Rosman and Baker, 1978). Minuchin and colleagues reported elevation of free fatty acids in the diabetic family member following stressful family interviews. Family therapy is said to be helpful. Despite the high regard in which Minuchin's views are generally held, they have not been subjected to controlled evaluation. They have, however, been critically discussed by Coyne and Anderson (1988). Sargent and Baker (1983) have produced guidelines for the clinical assessment of families, and Schafer, McCaul and Glasgow (1986) have published a Diabetes Family Behaviour Checklist for the paper-and-pencil assessment of family interactions.

Adults with diabetes

Few studies have been performed into the ways in which adults cope with the disease. There is general agreement, especially from spouses, that when one partner in a marriage has diabetes the disease places extra burdens on marital relationships (Surridge et al., 1984). Lassitude and irritability are often mentioned. Negative interpersonal relations correlate with poor regimen adherence (Schafer et al., 1986) although, once again, which comes first remains to be established. Where family support is high, adherence to the regimen is also likely to be high (Glasgow and Toobert, 1988). Jenny (1984) has reported that the worries and concerns of adults are age-related. In her sample, older patients (over 66 years) were most concerned with the cost of the regimen, whereas younger patients (16–24 years) were less convinced of the value of self-monitoring and believed diabetes to be less serious than did their older counterparts. Irrespective of age, dietary adherence was reported to be the major problem facing patients.

Age-related changes or degenerative changes due to complications can lead to the impairment of aspects of daily living, and can affect self-care in older people with diabetes. Such individuals have particular educational needs, may lack social support and may be looked after by relatively unskilled carers. The application of health psychology to older people with diabetes has hardly begun, Anderson (1990) and Funnell (1990) have provided overviews of some of the possibilities, but there is very little in the way of research findings.

Complications

Degenerative complications affect the quality of life and have effects on mood, self-care and adaptation (Lloyd et al., 1992). Clinically, patients often express fears of complications, particularly of blindness. Apart from Jacobson,

Rand and Hauser (1985), who reported higher levels of psychiatric symptomatology in patients with retinopathy, and Oehler-Giarratana and Fitzgerald (1980), who used group therapy with patients with serious visual impairment, little work has been published on the topic. A useful paper by Holmes (1986) provides an introduction to the effects of deteriorating functioning on patients, and presents guidelines for helping patients and their families.

There is a small literature on sexual problems (e.g. Anderson and Wolf, 1986; Newman and Bertelson, 1986). Psychosocial factors as well as organic ones need to be taken into account during the assessment process (Meisler *et al.*, 1989).

Mood disorders

A number of studies have shown greater lifetime prevalence and point prevalence rates for both depression and anxiety in people with diabetes compared with controls. This holds good both for young adults and older people, and for those with either the type I or the type II disorders (e.g. Lustman, Griffith and Clouse, 1988; Palinkas, Barrett-Connor and Wingard, 1991). Higher scores on depression inventories are associated with poorer metabolic control, although whether the relationship is a causal one and, if so, which comes first, is not known. There are several possible modes of action. Biochemical changes in the hypothalamic–pituitary axis which occur during depression could affect carbohydrate metabolism and thus increase glucose levels, or people who are depressed may be less likely to adhere to self-care regimens. Alternatively (perhaps additionally), the difficulties associated with a chronic disease and an awareness of the ever-present possibility of degenerative changes might render a person more vulnerable to major depression.

Delivery of health care

Since publication of the first edition of this book, the debate on the best form of service delivery has continued. It has been frustrated by the lack of good-quality data and complicated by political imperatives. The traditional pattern of care, of centralized hospital-based clinics to which patients are referred for stabilization and follow-up, is being superseded by alternative approaches which embrace the ethos that health care should be community-based, easily available, flexible and responsive to local need. The organization of care around GPs or community resource centres forms the mainstay of these approaches, with hospital-based services responding to acute medical crises and providing specialist assessment and treatment where necessary, In the UK there are now financial rewards for GPs who run their own specialist clinics. Different views have been expressed concerning the relative merits of such approaches (e.g. Singh, Holland and Thorn, 1984; Hayes and Harries, 1984; Bradshaw *et al.*, 1992), but there are few good-quality data to enable comparisons to be made. Politics and fashions in care seem to determine the content and delivery of services more than does scientific evidence.

The recent introduction of clinical audit to diabetes services (and to health services as a whole), with its emphasis upon specific and measurable outcomes and targeted changes, has been greeted enthusiastically by care providers (e.g. North Tyneside Diabetes Team, 1992). If experiences in the USA are anything to go by, the UK can expect purchasers of health services to require explicit standards of care to be laid down in key aspects of service delivery (Wheeler and Warren-Boulton, 1992), and attempts are being made to agree upon a core data set for service characteristics and clinical outcomes (Williams *et al.*, 1992). Behaviourally orientated health psychologists will be familiar with these concepts, and should be able to help care teams define, evaluate and refine their services. Teams also need education in the psychosocial aspects of living with a chronic disease. Attention should also be given to care-givers' attitudes and behaviours and training in the methods of behavioural self-management. Unless this is done, the opportunities that currently exist for altering not just the place of care but also the focus and philosophy of care, will have been missed.

Summary

The importance of the collaboration between psychological and biomedical science lies in three main areas. The first is the direct application of psychological methods of treatment to problems of management. This can be seen in the application of stress-control procedures, behaviour modification methods and so on. The second area is the use of psychological methods to enhance existing medical treatments and to facilitate their uptake. The design of educational programmes and the study of the variables that influence self-care behaviours are examples of this. The third role is in clarifying the processes of adaptation to chronic disease. All of these require an understanding of normal psychosocial development and performance. In their absence, technical medicine can be of limited benefit only.

References

Ahlfield, J.E., Soler, N.G. and Marcus, S.D. (1983) Adolescent diabetes mellitus: parent/child perspectives on the effect of the disease on family and social interactions. *Diabetes Care*, 6, 393–8.

Anderson, L.A. (1990) Health-care communication and selected psychosocial correlates of adherence in diabetes management. *Diabetes Care*, 13, (Suppl. 2), 66–76.

Anderson, B.J. and Wolf, F.M. (1986) Chronic physical illness and sexual behavior: psychological issues. *Journal of Consulting and Clinical Psychology*, 54, 168–75.

Anderson, B.J., Miller, J.P., Auslander, W.F. and Santiago, J.V. (1981) Family characteristics of diabetic adolescents: relationship to metabolic control.

Diabetes Care, 4, 586–94.

Anderson, B.J., Wolf, F.M. Burkhart, M.I. *et al.* (1989) Effects of peer-group intervention on metabolic control of adolescents with IDDM. *Diabetes Care*, 12, 179–83.

Anderson, R.M., Funnell, M.M., Barr, P.A. *et al.* (1991) Learning to empower patients. *Diabetes Care*, 14, 584–90.

Baker, L. and Barcai, A. (1970) Psychosomatic aspects of diabetes mellitus, in *Modern Trends in Psychosomatic Medicine*, vol. 2, (ed O.W. Hill), Butterworths, London, pp. 105–23.

Banion, C.R., Miles, M.S. and Carter, M.C. (1983) Problems of mothers in management of children with diabetes. *Diabetes Care*, 6, 548–51.

Bobrow, E.S., AvRuskin, T.W. and Siller, J. (1985) Mother–daughter interaction and adherence to diabetes regimens. *Diabetes Care*, 8, 146–51.

Bradley, C. and Cox, T. (1978) Stress and health, in *Stress* (ed T. Cox), MacMillan, London, pp. 91–111.

Bradley, C., Brewin, C.R., Gamsu, D.S. and Moses, J.L. (1984) Development of scales to measure perceived control of diabetes mellitus and diabetes-related health beliefs. *Diabetic Medicine*, 1, 213–8.

Bradley, C., Gamsu, D.S., Moses, J.L. *et al.* (1987) The use of diabetes-specific perceived control and health belief measures to predict treatment choice and efficacy in a feasibility study of continuous subcutaneous insulin infusion pumps. *Psychology and Health*, 1, 133–46.

Bradley, C., Lewis, K.S., Jennings, A.M. and Ward, J.D. (1990) Scales to measure perceived control developed specifically for people with tablet-treated diabetes. *Diabetic Medicine*, 7, 685–94.

Bradshaw, C., Eccles, M.P., Steen, I.N. and Choi, H.Y. (1992) Work-load and outcomes of diabetes care in general practice. *Diabetic Medicine*, 9, 275–8.

Brand, A.H., Johnson, J.H. and Johnson, S.B. (1986) Life stress and diabetic control in children and adolescents with insulin-dependent diabetes. *Journal of Pediatric Psychology*, 11, 481–95.

Brewin, C.R., Bradley, C. and Home, P. (1991) Measuring needs in patients with diabetes, in *The Technology of Diabetes Care: Converging Medical and Psychosocial Perspectives*, (eds C. Bradley, P. Home and M.J. Christie), Harwood Academic Publishers, Reading, pp. 142–55.

Brink, S. (1982) Youth and parents groups for patients with juvenile onset type I diabetes mellitus. *Pediatric and Adolescent Endocrinology*, 10, 234–40.

Campbell, L.V., Barth, R., Gosper, J.K. *et al.* (1990) Impact of intensive educational approach to dietary change in NIDDM. *Diabetes Care*, 13, 841–7.

Campbell, L.V., Ashwell, S.M., Borkman, M. and Chisholm, D.J. (1992) White coat hyperglycaemia: disparity between diabetes clinic and home blood glucose concentrations. *British Medical Journal*, **305**, 1194–6.

Connor, H. and Marks, V. (1985) Alcohol and diabetes. *Human Nutrition: Applied Nutrition*, **39A**, 393–9.

Cox, D.J., Gonder-Frederick, L., Pohl, S. and Pennebaker, J.W. (1983) Reliability of symptom – blood glucose relationships among insulin-dependent adult diabetics. *Psychosomatic Medicine*, **45**, 357–60.

Cox, D.J., Taylor, A.G., Nowacek, G. *et al.* (1984) The relationship between psychological stress and insulin-dependent diabetic blood glucose control: preliminary investigations. *Health Psychology*, **3**, 63–75.

Cox, D.J., Clarke, W.L., Gonder-Frederick, L. *et al.* (1985) Accuracy of perceived blood glucose in IDDM. *Diabetes Care*, **8**, 529–36.

Cox, D.J., Gonder-Frederick, L.A., Lee, J.H. *et al.* (1989) Effects and correlates of blood glucose awareness training among patients with IDDM. *Diabetes Care*, **12**, 313–8.

Coyne, J.C. and Anderson, B.J. (1988) The 'psychosomatic family' reconsidered: diabetes in context. *Journal of Marital and Family Therapy*, **14**, 113–23.

Delamater, A.M., Bubb, J., Davis, S.G. *et al.* (1990) Randomized prospective study of self-management training with newly diagnosed diabetic children. *Diabetes Care*, **13**, 492–8.

Diabetes Control and Complications Trial Research Group (1993) The effects of intensive treatment of diabetes. *New England Journal of Medicine*, **329**, 977–86.

DiMatteo, M.R. and DiNicola, D.D. (1982) *Achieving Patient Compliance: the Psychology of the Medical Practitioner's Role*, Pergamon Press, New York.

Drass, J.A., Muir-Nash, J., Boykin, P.C. *et al.* (1989) Perceived and actual level of knowledge of diabetes mellitus among nurses. *Diabetes Care*, **12**, 351–6.

Dubbert, P.M., Martin, J.E. and Epstein, L.H. (1986) Exercise, in *Self-Management of Chronic Disease*, (eds K.A. Holroyd and T.L. Creer), Academic Press, London, pp. 127–61.

Egger, M., Davey Smith, G. and Teuscher, A. (1992) Human insulin and unawareness of hypoglycaemia: need for a large randomised trial. *British Medical Journal*, **305**, 351–5.

Fairburn, C.G., Peveler, R.C., Davies, B. *et al.* (1991) Eating disorders in young adults with insulin dependent diabetes mellitus: a controlled study. *British Medical Journal*, **303**, 17–20.

Fairclough, P.K., Clements, R.S., Filer, D.V. and Bell, D.S.H. (1983) An evaluation of patient performance of and their satisfaction with various rapid blood glucose measurement systems. *Diabetes Care*, **6**, 45–9.

Feinglos, M.N., Hastedt, P. and Surwit, R.S. (1987) Effects of relaxation therapy on patients with type I diabetes mellitus. *Diabetes Care*, **10**, 72–5.

Fisher, E.B., Delamater, A.M., Bertelson, A.D. and Kirkley, B.G. (1982) Psychological factors in diabetes and its treatment. *Journal of Consulting and Clinical Psychology*, **50**, 993–1003.

Fowler, J.E., Budzynski, T.H. and VandenBergh, R.L. (1976) Effects of an EMG biofeedback relaxation program on the control of diabetes. *Biofeedback and Self-Regulation*, **1**, 105–12.

Funnell, M.M. (1990) Role of the diabetes educator for older adults. *Diabetes Care*, **13** (Suppl. 2), 60–5.

Gamsu, D.S. and Bradley, C. (1987) Clinical staffs' attributions about diabetes: scale development and staff vs. patient comparisons. *Current Psychological Research and Reviews*, **6**, 69–78.

Genev, N.M., Flack, J.R., Hoskins, P.L. *et al.* (1992) Diabetes education: whose priorities are met? *Diabetic Medicine*, **9**, 475–9.

Gilbert, B.O., Johnson, S.B., Spillar, R. *et al.* (1982) The effects of a peer-modeling film on children learning to self-inject insulin. *Behavior Therapy*, **13**, 186–93.

Gill, G.V. and Redmond, S. (1991) Self-adjustment of insulin: an educational failure? *Practical Diabetes*, **8**, 142–3.

Given, C.W., Given, B.A., Gallin, R.S. and Condon, J.W. (1983) Development of scales to measure beliefs of diabetic patients. *Research in Nursing and Health*, **6**, 127–41.

Glasgow, R.E. and Toobert, D.J. (1988) Social environment and regimen adherence among type II diabetic patients. *Diabetes Care*, **11**, 377–86.

Glasgow, R.E., McCaul, K.D. and Schafer, L.C. (1986) Barriers to regimen adherence among persons with insulin-dependent diabetes. *Journal of Behavioral Medicine*, **9**, 65–77.

Glasgow, R.E., Wilson, W. and McCaul, K.D. (1985) Regimen adherence: a problematic construct in diabetes research (Editorial) *Diabetes Care*, **8**, 300–1.

Goetsch, V.L. (1989) Stress and blood glucose in diabetes: a review and methodological commentary. *Annals of Behavioural Medicine*, **11**, 102–7.

Gonder-Frederick, L.A., Snyder, A.L. and Clarke, W.L. (1991) Accuracy of blood glucose estimation by children with IDDM and their parents. *Diabetes Care*, **14**, 565–70.

Greenhalgh, P.M., Jones, J.R., Jackson, C.A. *et al.* (1992) Changes in injection-site blood flow and plasma free insulin concentrations in response to stress in type I diabetic patients. *Diabetic Medicine*, **9**, 20–9.

Grossman, H.Y., Brink, S. and Hauser, S.T. (1987) Self-efficacy in adolescent girls and boys with insulin-dependent diabetes mellitus. *Diabetes Care*, **10**, 324–9.

Hanes, F.A. and De Looy, A.E. (1987) Can I afford the diet? *Human Nutrition: Applied Nutrition*, **41A**, 1–12.

Hanson, S.L. and Pichert, J.W. (1986) Perceived stress and diabetes control in adolescents. *Health Psychology*, **5**, 439–52.

Harkavy, J., Johnson, S.B., Silverstein, J. *et al.* (1983) Who learns what at a diabetes summer camp. *Journal of Pediatric Psychology*, **8**, 143–52.

Hauser, S.T., Jacobson, A.M., Wertlieb, D. *et al.* (1985) The contribution of family environment to perceived competence and illness adjustment in diabetic and acutely ill adolescents. *Family Relations*, **34**, 99–108.

Hayes, T.M. and Harries, J. (1984) Randomised controlled trial of routine hospital clinic care versus routine general practice care for type II diabetics. *British Medical Journal*, **289**, 728–30.

Holmes, D.M. (1986) The person and diabetes in psychosocial context. *Diabetes Care*, **9**, 194–206.

Jacobson, A.M., Rand, L.I. and Hauser, S.T. (1985) Psychologic stress and glycemic control: a comparison of patients with and without proliferative diabetic retinopathy. *Psychosomatic Medicine*, **47**, 372–81.

Jacobson, A.M., Hauser, S.T., Wertlieb, D. *et al.* (1986) Psychological adjustment of children with recently diagnosed diabetes mellitus. *Diabetes Care*, **9**, 323–9.

Jarrett, R.J. (1986) *Diabetes Mellitus*, Croom Helm, London.

Jefferson, I.G., Marteau, T.M., Smith, M.A. and Baum, J.D. (1985) A multiple injection regimen using an insulin injection pen and pre-filled cartridged soluble human insulin in adolescents with diabetes. *Diabetic Medicine*, **2**, 493–5.

Jenny, J.L. (1984) A comparison of four age groups' adaptation to diabetes. *Canadian Journal of Public Health*, **75**, 237–44.

Johnson, S.B. (1980) Psychosocial factors in juvenile diabetes. *Journal of Behavioral Medicine*, **3**, 95–116.

Johnson, S.B. (1984) Knowledge, attitudes and behavior: correlates of health in childhood diabetes. *Clinical Psychology Review*, **4**, 503–24.

Jones, R.B. and Hedley, A.J. (1987) Prevalence of smoking in a diabetic population: the need for action. *Diabetic Medicine*, **4**, 233–6.

Kaplan, R.M., Chadwick, M.W. and Schimmel, L.E. (1985) Social learning intervention to promote metabolic control in type I diabetes mellitus: pilot experiment results. *Diabetes Care*, **8**, 152–5.

Keen, H. (1985) Of mind and metabolism: an overview of brittle diabetes, in *Brittle Diabetes*, (ed J.C. Pickup), Blackwell Scientific Publications, Oxford, pp. 1–6.

Kemmer, F.W., Bisping, R., Steingrüber, H.J. *et al.* (1986) Psychological stress and metabolic control in patients with type I diabetes mellitus. *New England Journal of Medicine*, **314**, 1078–84.

King, J. (1983) Health beliefs in the consultation, in *Doctor–Patients Communication*, (eds D Pendleton and J. Hasler), Academic Press, London, pp. 109–25.

Kovacs, M., Feinberg, T.L., Paulauskas, S. *et al.* (1985a) Initial coping responses and psychosocial characteristics of children with insulin-dependent diabetes mellitus. *Journal of Pediatrics*, **106**, 827–34.

Kovacs, M., Finkelstein, R., Feinberg, T.L. *et al.* (1985b) Initial psychologic responses of parents to the diagnosis of insulin-dependent diabetes mellitus in their children. *Diabetes Care*, **8**, 568–75.

Landis, B., Jovanovic, L., Landis, E. *et al.* (1985) Effect of stress reduction on daily glucose range in previously stabilized insulin-dependent diabetic patients. *Diabetes Care*, **8**, 624–6.

Langan, S.J., Deary, I.J., Hepburn, D.A. and Frier, B.M. (1991) Cumulative cognitive impairment following recurrent severe hypoglycaemia in adult patients with insulin treated diabetes mellitus. *Diabetologia*, **34**, 337–44.

Langer, O., and Mazze, R.S. (1986) Diabetes in pregnancy: evaluating self-monitoring performance and glycemic control with memory-based reflectance meters. *American Journal of Obstetrics and Gynecology*, **155**, 635–7.

Lawrence, P.A., Dowe, M.C., Perry, E.K. *et al.* (1989) Accuracy of nurses in performing capillary blood glucose monitoring. *Diabetes Care*, **12**, 298–301.

Leonard, B., Leonard, C., and Wilson, R. (1986) Zuni diabetes project. *Public Health Reports*, **101**, 282–8.

Linn, L.S. and Lewis, C.E. (1979) Attitudes towards self-care among practising physicians. *Medical Care*, **17**, 187–90.

Lloyd, C.E., Robinson, N., Stevens, L.K. and Fuller, J.H. (1991) The relationship between stress and the development of diabetic complications. *Diabetic Medicine*, **8**, 146–50.

Lloyd, C.E., Matthews, K.A., Wing, R.R. and Orchard, T.J. (1992) Psychosocial factors and complications of IDDM. *Diabetes Care*, **15**, 166–72.

Lucey, D. and Wing, L. (1985) A clinic-based education programme for children with diabetes. *Diabetic Medicine*, **2**, 292–5.

Lustman, P.J., Griffith, L.S. and Clouse, R.E. (1988) Depression in adults with diabetes. *Diabetes Care*, **11**, 605–12.

McCulloch, D.K., Mitchell, R.D., Ambler, J. and Tattersall, R.B. (1983) Influence of imaginative teaching of diet on compliance and metabolic control in insulin dependent diabetes. *British Medical Journal*, **287**, 1858–61.

Marrero, D.G., Myers, G.L., Golden, M.P. *et al.* (1982) Adjustment to misfortune: the use of a social support group for adolescent diabetics. *Pediatric and Adolescent Endocrinology*, **10**, 213–8.

Marteau, T.M. and Baum, J.D. (1984) Doctors' views on diabetes. *Archives of Disease in Childhood*, **59**, 566–70.

Marteau, T.M. and Kinmonth, A.L. (1988) Doctors' beliefs about diabetes: a comparison of hospital and community doctors. *British Journal of Clinical Psychology*, **27**, 381–3.

Marteau, T.M. Bloch, S. and Baum, J.D. (1987) Family life and diabetic control. *Journal of Child Psychology and Psychiatry*, **28**, 823–33.

Marteau, T.M., Gillespie, C. and Swift, P.G.F. (1987) Evaluation of a weekend group for parents of children with diabetes. *Diabetic Medicine*, **4**, 488–90.

Mazze, R.S., Shamoon, H., Pasmantier, R. *et al.* (1984) Reliability of blood glucose monitoring by patients with diabetes mellitus. *American Journal of Medicine*, **77**, 211–7.

Mazzuca, S.A. (1982) Does patient education in chronic disease have therapeutic value? *Journal of Chronic Diseases*, **35**, 521–9.

Mazzuca, S.A., Moorman, N.H., Wheeler, M.L. *et al.* (1986) The diabetes education study: a controlled trial of the effects of diabetes patient education. *Diabetes Care*, **9**, 1–10.

Meisler, A.W., Carey, M.P., Lantigna, L.J. and Krauss, D.J. (1989) Erectile dysfunction in diabetes mellitus: a biopsychosocial approach to etiology and assessment. *Annals of Behavioral Medicine*, **11**, 18–27.

Mellor, J.G., Samanta, A., Blandford, R.L. and Burden, A.C. (1985) Questionnaire survey of diabetic care in general practice in Leicestershire. *Health Trends*, **17**, 61–3.

Minuchin, S., Rosman, B.L. and Baker, L. (1978) *Psychosomatic Families: Anorexia Nervosa in Context*, Harvard University Press, Cambridge, Massachusetts.

Newman, A.S. and Bertelson, A.D. (1986) Sexual dysfunction in diabetic women, *Journal of Behavioral Medicine*, **9**, 261–70.

North Tyneside Diabetes Team (1992) The diabetes annual review as an educational tool: assessment and learning integrated with care, screening, and audit. *Diabetic Medicine*, **9**, 389–94.

Nurick, M.A. and Johnson, S.B. (1991) Enhancing blood glucose awareness in adolescents and young adults with IDDM. *Diabetes Care*, **14**, 1–7.

Oehler-Giarratana, J. and Fitzgerald, R.G. (1980) Group therapy with blind diabetics. *Archives of General Psychiatry*, **37**, 463–7.

Palinkas, L.A., Barrett-Connor, E. and Wingard, D.L. (1991) Type 2 diabetes and depressive symptoms in older adults: a population-based study. *Diabetic Medicine*, **8**, 532–9.

Peveler, R.C. and Fairburn, C.G. (1989) Anorexia nervosa in association with diabetes mellitus – a cognitive–behavioural approach to treatment. *Behaviour Research and Therapy*, **27**, 95–9.

Pramming, S., Thorsteinsson, B., Theilgaard, A. *et al.* (1986) Cognitive function during hypoglycaemia in type I diabetes mellitus. *British Medicine Journal*, **292**, 647–50.

Reichard, P., Britz, A. and Rosenqvist, U. (1991) Intensified conventional insulin treatment and neuropsychological impairment. *British Medical Journal*, **303**, 1439–42.

Robinson, N. and Fuller, J.H. (1985) Role of life events and difficulties in the onset of diabetes mellitus. *Journal of Psychosomatic Research*, **29**, 583–91.

Rodin, G.M., Daneman, D., Johnson, L.E. *et al.* (1985) Anorexia nervosa and bulimia in female adolescents with insulin dependent diabetes mellitus: a systematic study. *Journal of Psychiatric Research*, **19**, 381–4.

Rosmark, B., Berne, C., Holmgren, S. *et al.* (1986) Eating disorders in patients with insulin-dependent diabetes mellitus. *Journal of Clinical Psychiatry*, **47**, 547–50.

Rovet, J.F., Ehrlich, R.M. and Hoppe, M. (1987) Intellectual deficits associated with early onset insulin-dependent diabetes mellitus in children. *Diabetes Care*, **10**, 510–5.

Ryan, C.M. and Morrow, L.A. (1986) Self-esteem in diabetic adolescents: relationship between age at onset and gender. *Journal of Consulting and Clinical Psychiatry*, **54**, 730–1.

Ryan, C., Vega, A. and Drash, A. (1985) Cognitive deficits in adolescents who developed diabetes early in life. *Pediatrics*, **75**, 921–7.

Sargent, J. and Baker, L. (1983) Behavior and diabetes care. *Primary Care*, **10**, 583–94.

Schafer, L.C., McCaul, K.D. and Glasgow, R.E. (1986) Supportive and nonsupportive family behaviors: relationships to adherence and metabolic control in persons with type I diabetes. *Diabetes Care*, **9**, 179–85.

Scheiderich, S.D., Freibaum, C.N. and Peterson, L.M. (1983) Registered nurses' knowledge about diabetes mellitus. *Diabetes Care*, **6**, 57–61.

Schlenk, E.A. and Hart, L.K. (1984) Relationship between health locus of control, health value, and social support and compliance of persons with diabetes mellitus. *Diabetes Care*, **7**, 566–74.

Seeburg, K.N. and DeBoer, K.F. (1981) Effects of EMG biofeedback on diabetes. *Biofeedback and Self Regulation*, **5**, 289–93.

Shillitoe, R.W. (1988) *Psychology and Diabetes: Psychosocial Factors in Management and Control*, Chapman and Hall, London.

Shillitoe, R.W. (1991) Counselling in health care: diabetes mellitus, in *Counselling and Communication in*

Health Care, (eds H. Davis and L. Fallowfield), Wiley, Chichester, pp. 71–83.

Shillitoe, R.W. and Christie, M.J. (1989) Determinants of health care: the health belief model. *Holistic Medicine*, 4, 3–17.

Singh, B.M., Holland, M.R. and Thorn, P.A, (1984) Metabolic control of diabetes in general practice clinics; comparison with a hospital clinic. *British Medical Journal*, 289, 726–8.

Stabler, B., Surwit, R.S., Lane, J.D. *et al.* (1987) Type A behavior pattern and blood glucose control in diabetic children. *Psychosomatic Medicine*, 49, 313–6.

Stark, L.J., Dahlquist, L.M. and Collins, F.L. (1987) Improving children's compliance with diabetes management. *Clinical Psychology Review*, 7, 223–42.

Steel, J., Young, R.J., Lloyd, G.G. and Clarke B.F. (1987) Clinically apparent eating disorders in young diabetic women: associations with painful neuropathy and other complications. *British Medical Journal*, 294, 859–62.

Stein, S.P., Goldberg, N., Kalman, F. and Chesler, R. (1984) Exercise and the patient with type I diabetes mellitus. *Pediatric Clinics of North America*. 31, 665-73.

Strowig, S. and Raskin, P. (1992) Glycemic control and diabetic complications. *Diabetes Care*, 15, 1126–40

Surridge D.H.C., William-Erdahl, D.L., Lawson, J.S. *et al.* (1984) Psychiatric aspects of diabetes mellitus. *British Journal of Psychiatry*, 145, 269–76.

Tattersall, R.B. (1992) Human insulin gone wrong. *Diabetes Medicine*, 9, 397.

Tattersall, R.B. and Walford, S. (1985) Brittle diabetes in response to life stress: cheating and manipulation, in *Brittle Diabetes*, (ed J.C. Pickup), Blackwell Scientific Publications, Oxford, pp. 76–102.

Taylor, R. and Zimmet, P. (1983) Migrant studies in diabetes epidemiology, in *Diabetes in Epidemiological Perspective*, (eds J.I. Mann, K. Pyörälä, and A. Teuscher), Churchill Livingstone, Edinburgh, pp. 58–77.

Ting, C. and Nanjii, A.A. (1988) Evaluation of the quality of bedside monitoring of the blood glucose level in a teaching hospital. *Canadian Medical Association Journal*, 138, 23–6.

Wallston, K.A., Wallston, B.S., Smith, S. and Dobbins, C.J. (1987) Perceived control and health. *Current Psychological Research and Reviews*, 6, 5–25.

Ward, D.J. (1984) Continuous subcutaneous insulin infusion (CSII): therapeutic options. *Diabetic Medicine*, 1, 47–51.

Ward, W.K., Haas, L.B. and Beard, J.C. (1985) A randomized, controlled comparison of instruction by a diabetes educator versus self-instruction in self-monitoring of blood glucose. *Diabetes Care*, 8, 284–6.

Warzak, W.J., Ayllon, T. and Delcher, H.K. (1982) Peer instruction of home glucose monitoring. *Diabetes Care*, 5, 44–6.

Webb, K.L., Dobson, A.J., O'Connell, D.L. *et al.* (1984) Dietary compliance among insulin dependent diabetics. *Journal of Chronic Diseases*, 37, 633–43.

Wertlieb, D., Hauser, S.T. and Jacobson, A.M. (1986) Adaptation to diabetes: behavior symptoms and family context. *Journal of Pediatric Psychology*, 11, 463–79.

Wheeler, M.L. and Warren-Boulton, E. (1992) Diabetes patient education programs. *Diabetes Care*, 15, (Suppl. 1), 336–40.

Wiholm, B.E. (1980) Irregular drug intake and serum chlorpropamide concentrations. *European Journal of Clinical Pharmacology*, 18, 159–63.

Williams, D.R.R., Home, P. and Members of a Working Group of the Research Unit of the Royal College of Physicians and British Diabetic Association (1992) A proposal for continuing audit of diabetes services. *Diabetic Medicine*, 9, 759–64.

Wilson, D.P. and Endres, R.K. (1986) Compliance with blood glucose monitoring in children with type I diabetes mellitus. *Journal of Pediatrics*, 108, 1022–4.

Wilson, G.T. (1980) Behavior modification and the treatment of obesity, in *Obesity* (ed A.J. Stunkard), W.B. Saunders and Co., Philadelphia, pp. 325–44.

Wing, R.R. (1989) Behavioral strategies for weight reduction in obese type II diabetic patients. *Diabetes Care*, 12, 139–44.

Wing, R.R., Epstein, L.H., Blair, E. and Nowalk, M.P. (1985) Psychologic stress and blood glucose levels in nondiabetic subjects. *Psychosomatic Medicine*, 47, 558–64.

Wing, R.R., Epstein, L.H., Nowalk, M.P. and Lamparski, D.M. (1986) Behavioral self-regulation in the treatment of patients with diabetes mellitus. *Psychological Bulletin*, 99, 78–89.

Worth, R., Home, P.D., Johnston, D.G. *et al.* (1982) Intensive attention improves glycaemic control in insulin dependent diabetes without further advantage from home blood glucose monitoring: results of a controlled trial. *British Medical Journal*, 285, 1233–40.

Wysocki, T., Meinhold, P.A., Abrams, K.C. *et al.* (1992) Parental and professional estimates of self-care independence of children and adolescents with IDDM. *Diabetes Care*, 15, 43–52.

Chapter twelve

Psychological aspects of physical disability

Stephen Wilkinson

Introduction

Approximately 8% of the population have a physical disability, with four per 1000 being severely disabled (needing special care) and one of these four being under the age of 65 years (Harris 1971; Martin, Meltzer and Eliot, 1988). An average Health District (250 000 people) may thus expect 250 people under the age of 65 years to need special care. This chapter will focus on disabled adults (16–65 years of age), the majority of whom live in the community and a minority, usually suffering from damage to the central nervous system, in institutional care.

There are many different types of condition leading to physical disability, most commonly arthritis, diseases of the respiration or circulation, and diseases of the central nervous system, such as cerebral palsy, stroke, multiple sclerosis and head injury. The World Health Organization's (1980) classification of diseases distinguishes between impairment, i.e. basic physical damage to the body or brain, disability (loss of function) resulting from impair-

ment, and handicap which is a perceived social or occupational disadvantage resulting from disability. Obviously such impairments, disabilities and handicaps may have profound effects on the individuals concerned and their families, affecting material and psychological wellbeing.

In considering psychological aspects of disability it is necessary to be cautious in making such general statements due to factors which may have a specific impact on adjustment:

- *Age of acquisition.* Conditions such as spina bifida, which affect people from birth, may have different implications for a family than diseases of later life, such as stroke or Parkinson's disease.
- *Insidious versus traumatic.* Diseases such as rheumatoid arthritis, which develop gradually in previously healthy people, may have a different psychological impact from traumatic injuries such as spinal cord lesions.
- *Stability of condition and prognosis.* Whether diseases remain relatively stable, e.g. cerebral palsy, or progressive, e.g. mus-

cular dystrophy, influences the person's perception of future disabilities or life expectancy.

- *Severity of disability and degree of dependency.* These will place different demands on carers and influence the degree of restriction placed on the individual. Sex differences will affect such basic features of care as the strength needed to assist the disabled person, which may have implications for home management.
- *Intellectual functioning and personality change.* Both these may be affected by brain damage and, as in the case of head injury may lead to multiple disabilities affecting mobility, memory, reasoning and social judgement. In some cases these behavioural problems require intensive supervision (see below for further discussion).
- *The presence or absence of pain and the frequency of periods of associated illness.*

Quality of research

The standard of research into psychological aspects of physical disability has been generally poor, with many ideas expressed and assumptions made without experimental verification or regard to the factors mentioned above. One reason for this is that many of the writers have not had a psychological or scientific background, and until recently psychologists have shown little interest in physical disability. In the field of rehabilitation, therapists and other workers using training procedures may have no theoretical bases for their practice. Furthermore, research into rehabilitation and therapeutic techniques is difficult, with the ethical problems of creating 'no-treatment' control groups (see Baddeley, Meade and Newcombe, 1980 for a discussion of research design problems). There have also been few standardized measures used in therapy. Critics of therapists' treatments (e.g. Miller, 1984) have highlighted the lack of evidence of the

effects of therapy compared to the progress made owing to natural recovery. Much of this criticism is justified and tempers the sometimes exaggerated claims for the effects of therapy. However, judging therapists' effectiveness by their ability to enhance natural recovery may devalue their essential role in the practical management of patients, e.g. ensuring a smooth transition between hospital and home.

In the UK higher standards of training for nurses and therapists have increased the perception of need for scientific rigour and objectivity when considering the efficacy of therapeutic efforts. Single-case methodology has enabled more sensitive study to be made of detailed aspects of rehabilitation. Better quality journals (*Clinical Rehabilitation, International Disability Studies, Neuropsychological Rehabilitation*) have provided a forum for multidisciplinary research presentations, and organizations such as the Society for Research in Rehabilitation have helped to improve understanding and the quality of research.

Theoretical considerations

In the 1950s it was realized that psychological reactions to disability did not run parallel to the course of the illness, stabilizing as the physical condition stabilized. Since then (see Shontz, 1978 and Russell, 1981 for reviews) there have been two main trends in ideas about psychological adjustment. For convenience, these may be termed 'personality-based' and 'social context'.

Personality-based

Psychoanalytical views of adjustment (e.g. Krueger, 1984) liken disability to loss, suggesting that the individual will undergo a sequence of stages in coming to terms with or accepting disability, before moving on to discovering new means of living a fulfilling life. These stages are seen as:

- shock;
- retreat, denial or disbelief;
- grief/mourning and depression;
- hostility and anger;
- adjustment.

Stage theorists have proposed that disabled people need to experience these stages, suggesting that psychotherapy or counselling should focus on enabling the individual to experience each stage in order to achieve adjustment. The onset of physical disability has also been compared by Krupnick (1984) to 'post-traumatic stress disorder', which has received wider attention in the psychiatric literature and is usually associated with the after-effects on victims of war or disaster. Given these assumptions, considerable psychological distress would be expected in physically disabled people. However, research in this area reveals conflicting opinions.

Rutter (1976) found a greater degree of depression and psychiatric disturbance in chronic bronchitics, and greater psychological disturbance than normal was found by Gardiner (1980) in a group of rheumatoid arthritis sufferers. However, the last two studies pointed to the absence of a relationship between severity of disease and psychological disturbance. Similarly Motet-Grigoras and Schuckit (1986) found higher levels of depression, alcohol and substance abuse in a group of congenitally disabled young men than in a group of non-disabled controls. In contrast, Richards (1986) found a moderate increase in depression and hostility immediately post discharge in a group of spinal cord-injured men. This depression had mostly resolved by the end of the first year following injury, with the absence of marked depression being predictive of good rather than poor outcome.

Further recent studies (Buckelew *et al.*, 1991; Fuhrer *et al.*, 1992) have examined life satisfaction and adjustment in spinal cord-injured men and women. Buckelew *et al.* found no cor-

relation between age or time since injury and health beliefs or psychological distress. Fuhrer *et al.* (1992) also found no correlation with chronological variables, but did find positive relationships between life satisfaction and self-assessed health, perceived control and social support. Both studies infer the influence of social policy and support available as major determinants of quality of life. Similarly, Kostin (1973) found disabled people rating their overall adjustment and life satisfaction as not significantly different from non-disabled people, and although significant depression may be found in 25–30% of stroke victims (Robinson and Price, 1982), there are clearly many who do not experience grief.

These and other studies (e.g. Treischman, 1980) have been critical of stage theory, which would expect depression to be a necessary phase in adjustment. As pointed out by Cook (1976), grief, although common, is by no means a universal reaction to disability and should not be assumed to be present by professionals.

There have also been attempts to identify particular personality types associated with different disabilities. Richman and Harper (1980) found personality differences between orthopaedically disabled adolescents and those with a cleft lip/palate, the former being more isolated and aloof towards interpersonal relationships, the latter being more preoccupied with relationships. Both groups were generally more inhibited than non-disabled controls. However, Harper (1983) also examined aspects of personality to see if there were differences between congenital and acquired disabilities. Although a greater sense of isolation, pessimism, alienation and self-centredness was found in a disabled group than in a non-disabled control group, no differences were found between types of disability. Moreover, no differences were discovered between progressive and non-progressive disorders, although speed of decline or setbacks was associated with social withdrawal. Thus there is no clear evidence of personality 'types' associated with particular congenital disabilities.

For individuals who were otherwise normal until physically disabled by disease or trauma, adjustment may be influenced by pre morbid coping skills.

Social context

From a sociological perspective (see Ben Sira, 1983 and Thoits, 1982, for reviews) adjustment has been seen as being related to the strength of social networks and control over resources. These authors have claimed that economic considerations are paramount, and may be of greater importance than professional help in determining an individual's reactions to disability. Ben Sira (1986) has also been critical of the power that welfare agencies have in making decisions which may radically affect the disabled person's housing, social and occupational opportunities, cautioning professionals not to allow their own interests to supercede those of their clients. In a comprehensive review, Wright (1983) considered many aspects of the potentially hostile and restrictive environment that disabled people encounter. Some of these are described below.

Shears and Jensema (1969) found acceptance of disabled people by the general population in many walks of life, but found less acceptance the more intimate the relationship. For example, marriage for disabled people was often considered inappropriate by non-disabled people. English (1971) found disabled people to be perceived similarly to other minority groups by non-disabled people, and the institutionalization of many disabled people has been viewed as a system of 'apartheid', denying disabled people the same rights as those enjoyed by the rest of the population. Wright (1983) viewed the search for personality characteristics of disabled people as part of the stereotyping associated with the stigma of disability in society.

Any difference from 'normal' would then be seen as a justification for treating disabled people differently, rather than focusing on the creation of opportunities for social and occupational integration and the removal of architectural barriers.

The assumption that disabled people must be suffering emotionally has also been vehemently challenged. Wright (1983) suggested that the general population (caring professionals included) assumes that disabled people must be emotionally disturbed, and adopts patronizing and pitying attitudes towards them. The term 'requirement of mourning' has been used to describe this phenomenon, and implies that disabled people should be looked after, not expected to have normal thoughts and feelings, nor to be able to manage their own affairs and have normal relationships. The roots of this prejudice are manifold, linked to the general public having little contact with disabled people, fear of the unknown and related to idealized images of normality, success and self-esteem being related to body image. Portrayal in the media of 'beautiful people' who acquire material wellbeing and status to which the general population aspires, identifies the disabled individual as different. Furthermore, Elliott and Byrd (1982) have discussed the image of disabled people in the media, pointing to their frequent portrayal as monsters or villains (e.g. Long John Silver, Frankenstein, Captain Hook) or saintly heroes, with no middle ground of being seen as simply ordinary people. Such attitudes are, of course, not the prerogative of non-disabled people and may lead to many disabled people wishing to have nothing to do with other disabled people. However, it is worth noting the view of Weinberg and Williams (1978) that disability may bring positive effects, such as increased sensitivity to others and the provision of a challenge.

Whether such attitudes in society are highly prevalent is unclear, but certainly reactions can be detected which are similar to those regarding learning disabled and mentally ill people. The Independent Living Movement reflects the wish of many disabled people to control their own lives and have access to the same opportunities as everyone else, guided by the principles inherent in 'normalization' as expounded by Wolfensburger (1976). This movement is far more advanced in the USA, but has gained ground in the UK and has considerable implications for the provision of services for disabled people. BBC Radio programmes such as 'Does he take Sugar?' have done much to foster rights for disabled people by encouraging the public to relate normally to disabled people, rather than regard them with fear or as children, only to be spoken to via their carers.

Behavioral learning view of disability

A behavioral learning view of disability would seem to offer some integration of both personality and socially based aspects of disability. Fordyce (1971) has described adaptation to disability as a learning process, based on principles of classical and operant conditioning. Hence the onset of disability is seen as changing the availability of reward or reinforcement for the individual. Loss, in behavioral terms, may be seen as the loss of previously satisfying conditions of life or the means of achieving them. These might be physical activities such as walking or cycling, or more mental pursuits such as problem-solving or communicating with others. It is probably true that individuals who, prior to the onset of their disability, derived great satisfaction from, for instance, athletic pursuits, will be more devastated by the loss of limb function than those to whom this was less important. Similarly, those who derived satisfaction and self-esteem from mental pursuits may be more affected by a stroke that limits their memory. To replace such loss depends both on the individual's abilities and the availability within the environment of alternative means of satisfaction.

In summary, both Shontz (1978) and Russell (1981) suggested some integration of personality and socially based theories whereby individuals are considered within their social context. They suggest that it is inappropriate to make general assumptions about psychological reactions to disability. Whereas phenomena such as depression, denial and resentment are commonly seen in the clinical context, they should not be viewed as necessary stages on the road to adjustment, nor should emotional suffering be expected in all disabled people. Analysis of individual behaviour and the environment within which the behaviour occurs suggests that a behavioural learning model is appropriate for understanding psychological reactions to disability.

Adjustment and coping with disability

Words like 'adjustment', 'coping' and 'acceptance' are frequently used but ill-defined terms to describe successful psychological reactions to disability. According to Wright (1983), adjustment entails:

- Enlarging the scope of one's values;
- Containing the effects of disability;
- Subordinating physical concerns;
- Transforming values based on comparison with others into values placed on one's own assets and strengths.

Similarly, a study by Moos and Tsu (1977) found six factors associated with adjustment:

- Cognitive restructuring, i.e. changing one's beliefs and goals;
- Emotional expression – negative expressions such as 'taking it out on other people' were associated with poor adjustment;
- Wish-fulfilment – the presence of time-consuming fantasies of getting better were related to poor adjustment;
- Acceptance of responsibility for one's disability was related to good adjustment, rather than seeing oneself as a burden on

others;

- Information-seeking – this was positively associated with adjustment;
- Threat minimization – tending to keep feelings to oneself was associated with good adjustment.

These findings were echoed by Felton, Revenson and Hinrichsen (1984), who found avoidance of information, ignoring advice and angrily blaming others all associated with poor self-esteem and poor adjustment. Similarly, Nerenz and Leventhal (1983) describe self-regulation theory, which views the structure of coping as being:

1. The representation of the illness, involving the reception and interpretation of information in order to define the health threat; this leads to
2. Action planning, involving the choice and trial of different coping strategies; this is followed by
3. Monitoring and appraisal of their effectiveness.

Coping is thus seen as a dynamic process, where clearly the nature and means of presentation of information by professionals may be critical.

There may be potential for teaching coping skills, but this remains to be tested for improving adjustment and outcomes in disability. Furthermore, there is a tendency for health professionals to see themselves as counsellors and to assume that disabled people need counselling. Counselling is a highly complex activity, with many schools of thought and little good research regarding the effectiveness either of the general process or of specific features of counselling efforts. There is also a tendency for counselling to be emotion-focused and to facilitate the expression of clients' distress and negative feelings. Research on coping suggests that this may be counterproductive, and more effective counselling may be achieved by well-defined problem-orientated active goal-setting and paying attention to positive rather than negative affect.

Another interesting concept related to adjustment is health locus of control (HLC), more fully described in Chapter 2 of this book. Briefly, people who perceive control over their lives as being determined by outside forces (an external locus of control) e.g. the state, are assumed to be prone to feelings of helplessness and depression, due to not taking responsibility for their own lives. Barton, Bates and Orzech (1980) examined this notion with respect to disability; contrary to expectations, better adjustment was found in a group of residents in an institution who had an external 'locus'. This was attributed to the constraints of the institutional policies which discouraged self-determined activities. In view of this, Reid (1984) has proposed a system of participatory control to balance the wishes of the individual with the needs of institutions.

Perceived control has been related to life satisfaction in people with spinal injury, and a study by Wassem (1991) found people with multiple sclerosis who had a high internal locus to have more knowledge of their disease, to practise more self-care and to have a more benign course of the disease. Harkapaa *et al.* (1991) found HLC related to treatment gains for patients with low back pain: those with stronger internal beliefs improved, learnt their exercises better and practised them more frequently than those with weaker internal beliefs.

More recently, locus of control has been examined in the context of stroke rehabilitation. Partridge and Johnston (1989) developed a Recovery Locus of Control scale for use with recently disabled adults. Patients with a greater internal locus showed a speedier recovery. In a further study (Johnston, *et al.*,1992) a simple letter designed to enhance internal locus was sent to patients about to receive physiotherapy. This was achieved in the experimental group, as was greater satisfaction about information provided, compared with a control group, although no significant differences were found with regard to expectations of therapy.

There appear to be many implications from the above work on coping skills and HLC and their relationship with psychological distress, rehabilitation recovery and the course of some physical disease. The suggestion is that coping skills could be taught, and that inculcating an internal HLC could enhance life satisfaction and psychological wellbeing. It could also influence treatment and rehabilitation efforts, the course of the disease and the level of disability. More research to test these ideas is obviously required.

Finally, the role of assertiveness has been examined in relation to adjustment (Elliott *et al.*, 1991) in spinal cord injury. Assertiveness may be beneficial in terms of controlling social support and making an independent life but, in accordance with Reid's findings above, may be detrimental if the opportunities for social control are limited. These authors found less depression in people who had a high level of support, facilitating social interaction and re-assuring personal worth. However, they were more prone to depression if they perceived themselves as a burden to others and if they felt a keen sense of responsibility for others' welfare.

Family reactions

Cleveland (1979) used illustrative case reports to describe family reactions to someone experiencing a spinal cord injury. All experienced grief, with behavioural concomitants such as weight loss, loss of sleep and appetite. The patients, mostly young men, tended to be cared for by their mothers, with younger siblings taking over the responsibility for household chores. Conflict within the family was described, with feelings of over-protectiveness on the one hand and feelings of anger and resentment at the disruption of their lives on

the other. Consequent feelings of guilt were then engendered by the feelings of resentment. Families were frequently isolated, but often not wishing to seek outside help. Relatives tended to overestimate the amount of distress the person was suffering. Cleveland also described the feelings of power the disabled people acquired through their moods dictating the mood of the household. It is unclear whether these observations hold for all acquired disability, or whether there are parallels with congenital disorders such as spina bifida, or disorders such as stroke acquired later in life.

Regarding the possibility of establishing intimate and family relationships, the 1988 OPCS survey showed that 66% of all disabled adults under 60 years of age are married. This figure, which is very similar to non-disabled adults, perhaps goes some way towards demystifying the nature of intimate relationships between disabled people, which tend to be regarded as taboo. As stated previously, there is probably still a prevailing attitude in society that disabled people cannot, or indeed should not, become involved in normal marital and sexual relationships. Paradowski (1977) studied 155 disabled people in institutional care and found many with difficulties in conducting a relationship (despite 35% having a partner), due to lack of opportunity and the conflict over the role of carers in helping to provide the opportunity. This tended to lead to relationships being conducted covertly. That disabled people maintain sexual interest was demonstrated by Fitting and Salisbury (1978), who found the majority of spinal cord-injured females retaining sexual interest, with 85% having had some form of sexual relationship since injury, despite some fear that sexual activity might lead to further physical damage, and also the inconvenience caused by bladder and bowel dysfunction. Elderly people suffering from Parkinson's disease maintain sexual interest and activity despite physical limitations; Ward and Wilkinson (1988) found that a group of

Parkinson's disease sufferers not only maintained their interest but welcomed the opportunity for discussion of these matters, expressing surprise at the reticence of the medical profession in broaching the subject.

Caring

Many disabled people are reliant on care-givers, either their family, friends or professionals. There is no adequate theory of caring that defines why people are willing to give care, or what attitudes, behaviour and emotional expression constitute 'caring'. Attempts have been made, especially in the nursing field, to refine definitions of caring, although it has tended to be a concept surrounded in mystique. A prevailing myth appears to be that the capacity for caring is inbuilt, a natural human trait, but this has not been tested.

A special issue of the *Journal of Advances in Nursing Science* (1990) examined various theories, three main ones being those expressed by Orem (1985), Watson (1988) and Leininger (1984). Orem's model views caring as making up 'self-care deficits', providing a helping system for self-maintenance and regulation. Watson's theory of caring emphasizes the importance of the relationships and transactions necessary between care-giver and receiver to promote and protect a patient's humanity. This system is very much seen as attending to the psychological, emotional and spiritual needs of patients. Leininger viewed caring from a transcultural perspective, citing the universality of knowing a person, being with them, enabling and doing things for them. Bottorff (1991), however, sees nursing as a practical science of caring. Broadly, the orientation of these theories varies between the extreme of carer as emotional provider, giving warmth and feeling, to the other extreme of the nurse as technician. One study by Cronin and Harrison (1988), mentioned in the above review, examined what patients felt had benefited them from nurses.

Of importance was feeling that they were treated as an individual, help with dealing with illness experiences (physical), having needs anticipated by nurses who were available (not having to wait and wait), and nurses who appeared relaxed and confident. This contrasts with nurses' own opinions of their efficacy, which focused on 'involvement' and the affective or emotionally expressive aspects of their caring actions. This questions the relevance of assumptions of intimacy and involvement which may motivate some professional care staff.

In an excellent review of this field (Hall, 1990) a four-component model of care is proposed in order to assist a more refined analysis of 'caring':

1. Identification of sets of beliefs or philosophies which guide care;
2. Identification of the goals and objectives of care;
3. Description of direct caring practices and acts;
4. Emotions and feelings accompanying care.

With regard to (1) above, Hall notes various philosophies which may underpin caring practice, such as the provision of minimal restriction, choice and normalization, in contrast to more parental models of care. Of concern is the observation that some carers may come from a background where physical punishment or scolding is a normal method of controlling behaviour, and may be resorted to when the cared-for are difficult to manage. Certainly some physically disabled people are physically and verbally abused, and an assessment of potential carers' attitudes would seem essential for entry into the caring professions.

Hall further notes the emergence of practical handbooks and training materials directed at the day-to-day practice and experience of informal carers (Association of Carers, 1985; Kolmer, 1988). Common characteristics to emerge from such literature include the simple presence of the carer, alertness and vigilance, assistance and aid for activities of daily living based on a clear assessment of the activities that need help. Methods of physical contact, style and content of verbal and non-verbal interaction, including the giving of information or instruction, facial expression and gesture, are also important caring skills.

The feelings of wellbeing, compassion and love involved in caring acts may give way over long periods of time to anger, resentment, guilt and depression, if carers receive no assistance for their fatigue and isolation. Carers' needs should be identified alongside the disabled person's to help maintain their quality of life. Similarly, attention needs to be paid to the environment in which care takes place (see also Llewelyn and Payne, this volume).

Work such as Hall's will assist in developing a better understanding of caring and the principles of carer training; this is essential in the light of the suggestion that five million people in the UK are in caring households, and that one in four of all adults will be a carer at some time in their lives (Randall, 1988).

Assessment of adjustment

It is worth mentioning some of the assessment techniques used in the foregoing research. Although much of the work in this field is flawed and open to criticism of observer bias, and of disabled people giving socially desirable responses, most of the papers quoted have used some form of standardized assessment, usually questionnaires or rating scales based on some underlying clinical assumptions, and with some confidence in their reliability.

There are numerous scales designed to measure *response to illness*. Examples of these are the Derogatis (1975) Psychosocial Adjustment to Illness Scale and Pritchard's (1981) Response to Illness Questionnaire. There has been much interest in measuring quality of life (see Katz, 1987 for a review), and its use in reaching decisions about resource allocation. There is

insufficient space here to discuss these scales, although general findings are that 'poor quality of life' is associated with high dependency, based on the value judgements of professionals or the general public, which equate mobility with life satisfaction. It is erroneous to assume that a quadriplegic who is totally dependent for physical care has the lowest quality of life next to death, just as it is false to believe that some highly dependent disabled people would be better off dead. Yet these seem to be assumptions made by some of the rating scales, which therefore need to be treated with caution.

General measures of psychological distress focusing on depression, anxiety or other psychiatric concepts, include the Beck Inventory for Depression (Beck *et al.*, 1961), the Hamilton (1960) Rating Scale for Depression and the Zung (1965) Self-Rating for Depression Scale. Anxiety has been measured by Taylor's (1953) Manifest Anxiety Scale or Spielberger, Gorsuch and Lushene's State Trait Anxiety Scale (1970). Apart from the usual question marks raised by the use of rating scales in representing a true picture of behavior, particular caution needs to be exercised in interpreting their use with disabled people. Many of the scales include items regarding preoccupation with physical health; this is quite understandable in the case of disabled people, but is often interpreted as a psychiatric sign. However, the Hospital Anxiety and Depression Scale (Zigmond and Snaith, 1983) has attempted to overcome this. A scale found to be useful for measuring psychiatric distress in carers is the General Health Questionnaire (Goldberg, 1978).

Other, more specific, scales of interest are Yuker and Block's (1979) Attitudes towards Disabled Persons Scale, which has been used to measure change in education programmes (see the discussion on implications for professionals, below). Linkowski (1971) developed a rating scale designed to measure acceptance of disability, based on Wright's (1983) assumptions (described above) regarding adjustment.

Rosenberg (1965) developed the well known Self Esteem questionnaire, and Toseland and Sykes (1977) designed a Life Satisfaction Index. Health locus of control has been measured by means of a rating scale (Wallston and Wallston, 1976), and there have been attempts to measure coping skills (e.g. Folkman and Lazarus 1980). Developments have also taken place on the measurement of 'coping with caring' (Matson and Moffat, 1988, personal communication).

Despite the proliferation of rating scales, results have seldom been validated by cross-checking with other indices. Lawson, Robinson and Bakes (1985) have developed a standard day interview which examines in more detail how disabled people occupy their time (e.g. sitting doing nothing, engaged in conversation, time spent in constructive activity). Such instruments, together with direct observation of individual behaviour and behavioural analysis should help to validate the use of the rating scales and provide more precise information about disabled persons' needs. Moreover, Treischman (1974) has outlined the importance of disabled people having clear goals, which may be provided by such assessments as Kiresuk and Lund's (1978) Goal Attainment Scaling.

Another practical application has come from work on driving assessment (Nouri, Tinson and Lincoln, 1987), which combines psychological test performance (e.g. reaction time, tracking tasks) with a practical driving assessment.

Intellectual impairment and multiple disability

Intellectual impairment is commonly associated with some congenital conditions involving physical disability and many acquired diseases such as stroke, head injury and multiple sclerosis. Owing to the complexities of damage to memory, perception, reasoning and aspects of personality, people with multiple disabilities of intellectual and physical functioning require separate consideration. The preceding sections have been mainly concerned with people with physical disability who have normal intellectual functions; those who may not be intellectually able to manage their own affairs have often been overlooked or misunderstood, and unwarranted conclusions may have been drawn from studies of their views.

Examples in the literature are easy to find. Matson and Brooks (1977) considered the relationship of self-concept to severity of physical disability, and found self-concept among a group of multiple sclerosis sufferers to have improved with severity of disability. Although this finding was not repeated by Zeldow and Pavlous (1984), who found the opposite, neither study controlled for the presence of dementia in their groups, which may have led to euphoric and otherwise unrealistic responses to questions. Head injury (Brooks, 1984) is a condition which also exemplifies some of these problems: people may be intellectually impaired, physically disabled and have disturbed behaviour, which may make them unrealistic and very difficult to live with. Despite being able to hold a conversation which they appear to understand, they may have forgotten that conversation within a few minutes. The person may feel well and deny any problems, but if left alone may be able to do virtually nothing unprompted. Without direct observation and rating by the family, reliance on the patient's judgement about their situation is hazardous. It is not uncommon for such individuals to be regarded by unknowing relatives and professionals as depressed or poorly motivated, as they may assign personality characteristics to what is in fact a consequence of a damaged brain, and an inability to make rational decisions.

Generally, accurate psychological assessment may well not have been undertaken, or if it has, such assessments often have no direct relevance to patient management. There have been important developments in this field, with the emergence of such assessments as the Rivermead Behavioural Memory Test (Wilson, Cockburn and Baddeley, 1985) and The Rivermead Perceptual Assessment Battery (Whiting *et al.*, 1988), and the increasing involvement of psychologists in patient management. An example of the latter has been the use of behavioural checklists to define steps in the teaching of skills to severely brain-damaged physically disabled people (Wilson, 1981; Wilson, Corkburn and Baddeley, 1985), along similar lines to those in work with people with learning difficulties.

Cognitive retraining

There has also been considerable interest in the possibilities of cognitive retraining, which has been critically reviewed by Miller (1984). It is beyond the scope of this chapter to review the evidence thoroughly, but until recently the findings have been somewhat pessimistic. Unlike damaged muscle, which may need considerable work to regain its function, the damaged brain does not appear to respond to intensive stimulation. Although training procedures aimed at exercising memory have been ineffective, especially in terms of being useful in everyday life, there have been more encouraging result when training in everyday tasks has been used. Patients may, for example, be taught to use a diary or checklists of tasks, in order not to lose track. The clinical management of memory problems has been described in more detail by Wilson and Moffat (1992), although psychological expertise in this area is in short supply.

Therapeutic approaches

In addition to the above-mentioned cognitive retraining, Lincoln (1983) classified the application of psychological principles in the management of disabled patients as follows:

- Behaviour modification
- Skills training
- Biofeedback

Each of these is considered below.

Behaviour modification

The use of behaviour modification principles has been implemented mainly with people in institutional settings who are not capable of managing their own affairs. Token economy systems are one example, systematically giving or withholding rewards to individuals depending on their behaviour. The aim of such methods is to reduce disruptive behaviour such as verbal or physical aggression, to shape behaviour and skills which are socially acceptable and to increase the individual's independence. Despite the common criticism that such methods deprive patients of their rights, or that they are manipulative, they may be seen as making the environment predictable. Such systems have also been effective with disturbed behaviour which has proved intractable by other methods. Readers are referred to Wood (1984) for further information and to Horton and Miller (1985) for a review of behavioural treatments in neuropsychology.

Ince (1980) also describes a wide range of behavioural applications in rehabilitation, ranging from behavioural analysis and goal setting to desensitization for the fear of falling in stroke victims.

Skills training

Psychological principles of learning, memory and skill acquisition should be fundamental to the practice of occupational, speech and physiotherapists, and in rehabilitation medicine and nursing. The importance of accurate and immediate feedback, the length and frequency of training sessions and the understanding of why disabled people may not be making progress or adjustment are all issues which need to be conceptualized and framed according to sound psychological theory; this is often not the case. Following survival from traumas such as strokes, head or spinal injuries, a process of recovery (ranging from 6 months to 2 years) takes place which can be expected to level off, leaving relatively stable levels of disability. Rehabilitation efforts are aimed at maximizing this recovery process and, where physical functions do not recover, teaching methods of adjustment and coping techniques. Much work needs to be done to understand the process of rehabilitation, including the optimal duration and frequency of therapists' training sessions and how they can best teach the techniques of mobilization and activities of daily living, which should be based on sound measurement and psychological understanding of learning processes. Some developments have taken place (Heller *et al.*, 1987; Sunderland, 1988, personal communication) in the construction of reliable assessments of motor function in order to examine the differences between various therapeutic strategies, e.g. the merits of intensive versus intermittent treatment sessions. Implications for health professionals include the questioning of trial-and-error learning and the need to provide clear instructions that keep failure to a minimum in rehabilitation tasks, otherwise the individual may learn these failures and incorporate them in their activities of daily living. Equally, errors may reinforce feelings of failure, depression and the tendency to give up rehabilitation efforts.

Biofeedback

Although there is a considerable literature on the use of biofeedback techniques in rehabilitation (e.g. Basmajian, 1981) for such conditions as footdrop, chronic pain and spasticity there is little evidence that effects demonstrated in the laboratory generalize to everyday settings. However, the use of EMG (electromyography) feedback and other psychophysiological methods remains to be tested thoroughly in

realistic settings. For a fuller review of this area see Young and Blanchard (1980).

Other therapeutic approaches

Cognitive behaviour therapy

The application of behavioural learning principles to help people identify and modify their negative views of their world has been effective in the treatment of depression (Beck *et al.*, 1979). In one of the few well-controlled studies of its application in physical disability, Larcombe and Wilson (1984) demonstrated its use in combating depression in multiple sclerosis (MS). They taught a group of MS sufferers to identify negative ways of thinking which were leading to resignation and depression; they then established aims and encouraged goal-directed activity for the group, who improved more than a control group that received general support. Another imaginative use of cognitive therapy (Evans, Halar and Smith, 1986) was the use of a telephone conference for disabled adults, based on goal-directed cognitive therapy which demonstrated greater benefits for the therapy group than a group which used the link purely as a means of social contact. Their greater goal attainment and decreased loneliness were confirmed by family members.

Computer technology

This has opened up new channels of communication and control for some disabled people. Computers linked to environmental control systems, the use of sophisticated switching devices, word processing and speech synthesis all offer greater freedom to disabled people. There is controversy over their use in cognitive retraining (see Robertson, 1990 for a review), but their full potential for disabled people, as a means of control and for constructive activity, has yet to be realized (see Cromwell, 1986 for a guide to their applications in occupational therapy).

Provision of information

Disabled people have to deal with numerous professions and agencies. It is often commented that the complexities of the system are designed to defeat sufferers, hence the establishment of organizations specifically to help them through the maze. Although doctor–patient communication has been studied extensively (Ley, 1977; Ley and Llewelyn, this volume), highlighting the importance of clear, concise information presented in manageable packages, there has been little work on the most efficient means of communicating with disabled people, which is often left to professional prerogative.

Sexual counselling

Some research has shown benefits for spinal cord-injured patients who attended a group providing information on physical and sexual functioning. Cole and Stevens (1970) found that almost 50% took up the offer of sexual counselling, and despite difficulties in genital sensation or ability to achieve orgasm, 32% described their sexual adjustment as good. Despite such evidence, the provision of sexual counselling is limited and has been highlighted as an area of neglect (Royal College of Physicians, 1986). There are too few specialists in this field, and health professionals receive too little training to know how to advise people. Often the assumption would appear to be that disabled people should be asexual, despite evidence to the contrary. The organization Sexual Problems of Disabled People (SPOD), which is an association to help with these difficulties, stands out as an example of good practice.

Implications for health professionals

Various authors have considered the attitudes of health and social service professionals towards disabled people, sometimes with alarming conclusions. Chubon (1982) showed negative attitudes towards disabled people among health professionals and, in the case of nurses (Mikulic, 1971), the reinforcement of dependency rather than independent behaviour. Miller and Keith (1973) also found passive isolation of patients being reinforced by understimulating hospital environments, with 60% of patients unoccupied in wards during the daytime and 90% unoccupied in the evenings and at weekends. It is worth mentioning that hospitals are generally designed for sick people, not for learning the new skills needed to cope with a disability, or for social placement, when a disabled person cannot return home. Many disabled people find themselves recurrently in hospital and not immediately able to return home following recovery from the acute stages of disease. Hospitals are not suitable environments at this stage of recovery, and there are too few transitional living arrangements or rehabilitation areas, which more closely approximate living conditions in the community. Rehabilitation performance in hospital may not be carried into the community, one reason for this being the artificiality of hospital settings and therapists' workshops or gymnasia. Rehabilitation and disability management is a process of learning or relearning to manage physical and mental limitations, but unfortunately, basic learning principles and their importance for medical, nursing and therapist practice, have often been overlooked. They should be a fundamental part of training, so long as they are taught in such a way that staff can see their clinical relevance.

Regarding the attitudes of health professionals, some studies of training programmes for attitude change show potential applications. There is some suggestion that disability simulation and role reversal (e.g. putting health professionals literally in a disabled person's chair or bed) may be useful. Pastalan (1974) demonstrated the benefits of such methods for architectural students by simulating sensory deficits in different settings. However, Wright

(1983) has cautioned against the indiscriminate use of such methods by pointing out research which shows that care staff can be left with more negative and overprotective attitudes towards patients after such training. To prevent this from occurring, they suggested that the tasks set, e.g. negotiating a ward with a wheelchair, were seen as being achievable rather than hopeless. Furthermore, Donaldson and Martinson (1977) reviewed studies which attempted to modify attitudes and found that live presentations on disabled living by disabled people were more effective than video or audio presentations. They also point out more favourable responses when studies have used disabled people presenting a coping model, rather than one of weakness or suffering. There is a suggestion from the foregoing research that disabled counsellors or teachers might be employed to educate the general public and health professionals, and that disabled counsellors might act as effective coping models in the rehabilitation process.

There is much to be learnt from work on coping skills and the importance of control which should be incorporated in professional training. Professionals should encourage the idea of carers being in partnership with disabled people and listening to their needs rather than providing services according to professionals' perceptions (see Chapter 4). Rarely does it seem that disabled people actually run services for themselves.

Service evaluation and planning implications

The plight of disabled people in institutional care was demonstrated by Miller and Gwynne in 1971, and there have been developments since then to try and improve services for disabled people. 'Living Options' (Prince of Wales Advisory Group, 1985) provided guidelines for those planning services. This recognized the disabled as people first and disabled second,

and warned against the overall 'classification' of 'the disabled'. The principles of planning outlined include:

- Choice
- Consultation
- Information
- Participation
- Recognition
- Autonomy.

The suggested ways forward are by:

- Involvement in committees.
- Establishment of Joint Care Planning Teams (because of the complexities of liaison between health, social services and other local government departments).
- Identification of the severely disabled and assessment of their needs.
- Acknowledgement of disabled people with behavioural problems, notably head injury.
- Creative funding.
- Improvement of domiciliary services.
- The provision of units for the young disabled, giving assessment, rehabilitation and respite care, with imaginative alternatives to permanent institutional care.
- Centres for independent living, special aids and equipment centres and peer counselling.
- Special equipment, housing schemes, carers' networks and improved transportation.

Despite such publications, it has been questioned whether statutory services are meeting needs (Thomas, 1985; Beardshaw, 1986; Fiedler, 1988). Concern was also expressed in the UK by the Royal College of Physicians (1986) regarding service organization and provision, calling for health authorities to spell out policies for 15 areas concerning disability, where there are usually no coherent planning and operational policies (e.g. head injury services, continence management, the young disabled school leaver). Developments of these services are slowly occurring. In a review of units for the young disabled in the UK (Royal

College of Physicians, 1986) wide variations in service provision were noted. Often, services were poorly funded, ill-organized and lacking in well defined policies.

Some projects have systematically examined need in health populations, but these are notable exceptions. Examples in the UK are the Southampton survey, resulting in the establishment of a register of disability enabling the monitoring of changes in dependency level and the amount of care required by disabled people (Dawson, 1984). Another survey (Holland, Crawford and Peberdy, 1986) also resulted in the provision of a service based on the expressed wishes of disabled people and their families. A similar survey has been conducted (Paediatric Research Unit, 1985) for disabled adolescents. Another imaginative initiative was a project entitled 'A Chance to Choose', (Neville, 1987) where Plymouth Health Authority actively involved disabled people and their representatives in policy-making. The King's Fund has also sponsored a series of projects involving disabled people in developing imaginative services (Fiedler, 1991). No follow-up studies have yet been undertaken to compare institutional-based care versus community-based care, and these are much needed. Readers are also referred to Warren (1987) for a review of some of the difficulties in assessing the needs of disabled people and translating these needs into appropriate services.

There is considerable concern in the UK at present regarding the implementation of the Community Care Act, which will place greater responsibility on local authorities to purchase care for disabled people. There is a move away from local authorities providing care themselves, as the present government considers it is more appropriate to provide them through the voluntary or private business sector. Although the legislation is claimed to offer greater choice of care for people, it is quite clear that 'social' care will be expected to be paid for (as is residential care) by individuals if they have the means, rather than be free (paid for by the state) like health care. There is considerable conflict between and social care agencies, as the definition of 'health' or 'social' care is debated. None of this is helpful for disabled people or their carers and whether this legislation will improve the quality of care in the community, allowing disabled people to remain living at home, remains to be seen.

A controversial scheme introduced in the UK a few years ago, whereby money was given directly to disabled people to purchase their own care (the Independent Living Fund) is to be wound up, seeming to disempower those who might have benefited. Although there were fears that disabled people might have been exploited and received little advice about becoming employers, the fund greatly enhanced quality of life for them and their carers (Kestenbaum, 1992; Wilkinson and Hughes, 1992).

Community-based solutions may be preferable to institutional ones only if adequate resources are provided and standards are monitored. If disabled people (not all independent and articulate) simply disappear into impoverished surroundings, this will place intolerable burdens on their carers. There may also be a minority, such as behaviourally disturbed brain-damaged adults and other physically disabled people with severe intellectual impairment, who require special residential facilities.

References

Association of Carers (1985) *Help at Hand: the Who, How, Where of Caring*, Association of Carers, Rochester.

Baddeley, A., Meade, T. and Newcombe, F. (1980) Design problems in research on rehabilitation after brain damage. *International Rehabilitation Medicine*, **2**, 138–42.

Barton, E.M., Bates, M.M. and Orzech, M.J. (1980) Aetiology of dependence in older nursing home residents during morning care. The role of staff behaviour. *Journal of Personal and Social Psychiatry*, **35**, 351–63.

Basmajian, J.V. (1981) Biofeedback in rehabilitation. A review of principles and practices. *Archives of Physical Medicine and Rehabilitation*, 62, 469–75.

Beardshaw, V. (1986) *Last on the List*, King's Fund, London.

Beck, A.T., Rush, A.J., Emery, G. and Shaw, B.F. (1979) *Cognitive Therapy of Depression: a Treatment Manual*, Guilford Press, New York.

Beck, A.T., Ward, C.H. and Mendelson, M. (1961) Inventory for measuring depression. *Archives of General Psychiatry*, 4, 561–71.

Ben Sira, Z. (1983) Loss, stress and readjustment. The structure of coping with bereavement and disability. *Social Science and Medicine*, 17(21), 1619–32.

Ben Sira, Z. (1986) Disability stress and readjustment: the function of the professionals' latent goals and affective behaviour in rehabilitation. *Social Science and Medicine*, 23(21), 43–55.

Bottorff, J.L. (1991) Nursing: a practical science of caring. *Journal of Advances in Nursing Science*, 14(1), 26–39.

Brooks, N. (1984) *Closed Head Injury: Psychological, Social and Family Problems*. Oxford University Press, Oxford.

Buckelew, S.P., Frank, R.G., Elliott, T.R. et al. (1991) Adjustment to spinal cord injury: stage theory revisited. *Paraplegia*, 29(2), 125–30.

Chubon, R.A. (1982) An analysis of research dealing with the attitudes of professionals towards disability. *Journal of Rehabilitation*, Jan/Feb/March, 25–30.

Cleveland, M. (1979) Family adaptation to the traumatic spinal cord injury of a son or daughter. *Social Work in Health Care*, 4(4), 459–71.

Cole, T.M. and Stevens, M.R. (1970) Rehabilitation professionals and sexual counselling for spinal cord injured adults. *Archives of Sexual Behaviour*, 4, 631–8.

Cook, D.W. (1976) Psychological aspects of spinal cord injury *Rehabilitation Counselling Bulletin*, 19, 535–43.

Cromwell, F.S. (1986) *Computer Applications in Occupational Therapy*, Haworth, London.

Cronin, S.N. and Harrison, B. (1988) Importance of nurse caring behaviours as perceived by patients after myocardial infarction. *Heart and Lung*, 17(4), 374–80.

Dawson, J. (1984) *Southampton and South West Hampshire Health District Care Attendant Scheme: report on fifth year of operation*, Rehabilitation Unit, University of Southampton.

Derogatis, L.R. (1975) *Psychosocial Adjustment to Illness Scale*, Clinical Psychosomatic Research, Baltimore.

Donaldson, J. and Martinson, M. (1977) Modifying attitudes towards physically disabled persons. *Exceptional Children*, 43, 337–41.

Elliott, T.R. and Byrd, E.K. (1982) Media and disability. *Rehabilitation Literature*, 43(11–12), 348–55.

Elliott, T.R., Herrick, S.M., Patti, A.M. et al. (1991) Assertiveness, social support and psychological adjustment following spinal cord injury. *Behavioural Research and Therapy*, 29(5), 485–93.

English, W.R. (1971) Correlates of stigma towards physically disabled persons. *Rehabilitation Research Practice Review*, 2(4), 1–51.

Evans, R., Halar, E. and Smith, M.A. (1985) Cognitive therapy to achieve personal goals: results of telephone group counselling with disabled adults. *Archives of Physical Medicine and Rehabilitation*, 66, 693–6.

Felton, B.J., Revenson, T.A. and Hinrichsen G.A. (1984) Stress and coping in the explanation of psychological adjustment among chronically ill adults. *Social Science and Medicine*, 18(10), 889–98.

Fiedler, B. (1988) *Living Options Lottery*, King's Fund, London.

Fiedler, B. (1991) *Living Options in Practice*, King's Fund, London.

Fitting, M. and Salisbury, S. (1978) Self-concept and sexuality of spinal cord injured females. *Archives of Sexual Behaviour*, 7(2), 143–56.

Folkman, S. and Lazarus, R.S. (1980) An analysis of coping in a middle aged community sample. *Journal of Health and Social Behaviour*, 21, 219.

Fordyce, W.E. (1971) in *Rehabilitation Psychology*, (ed W.R. Neff), American Psychological Association, New York.

Fuhrer, M.J. Rintala, D.H., Hart, K.A. et al. (1992) Relationship of life satisfaction to impairment, disability and handicap among persons with spinal cord injury living in the community. *Archives of Physical Medicine and Rehabilitation*, 73(6), 552–7.

Gardiner, B.M. (1980) Psychological aspects of rheumatoid arthritis. *Psychological Medicine*, 10, 159–65.

Goldberg, D. (1978) *Manual of the General Health Questionnaires*, NFER-Nelson, London.

Hall, J. (1990) Towards a psychology of caring. *British Journal of Clinical Psychology*, 29, 129–44.

Hamilton, M. (1960) A rating scale for depression. *Journal of Neurology Neurosurgery and Psychiatry*, 23, 56–62.

Harkapaa, J., Jarvikorski, A., Meuin, G. et al. (1991) Health locus of control beliefs and psychological distress as predictors for treatment outcome in lowback pain patients. *Pain*, 46(1), 35–41.

Harper, D.C. (1983) Personality concepts and degree of impairment in male adolescents with progressive and non-progressive physical disorders. *Journal of Clinical Psychology*, 39(6), 859–67.

Harris, A.I. (1971) *Handicapped and Impaired in Great Britain*, HMSO, London.

Heller, A., Wade, D., Wood, V.A. *et al.* (1987) Arm function after stroke: measurement and recovery over the first three months. *Journal of Neurology Neurosurgery and Psychiatry*, 50, 714–19.

Holland, R., Crawford, J. and Peberdy, C. (1986) *Towards a Better Service for People with a Severe Physical Disability in the Basingstoke and NE Hampshire Health Authority*, Basingstoke District Health Authority, Basingstoke.

Horton, A.M. and Miller, W.G. (1985) Neuropsychology and behaviour therapy, in *Progress in Behaviour Modification*, Vol. 19, Academic Press, London, pp. 1–65.

Ince, L.P. (1980) *Behavioural Psychology in Rehabilitation Medicine*, Williams and Wilkins, Baltimore.

Johnston, M. and Gilbert, P. (1992) Changing perceived control in patients with physical disabilities: an intervention study with patients receiving rehabilitation. *British Journal of Clinical Psychology*, 31(1), 89–94.

Journal of Advances in Nursing Science (1990) Special issue on 'Caring', 13(1).

Katz, S. (ed.) (1987) The Portugal Conference: Measuring quality of life and functional status in clinical and epidemiological research. *Journal of Chronic Diseases*, 40, Special issue No.6.

Kestenbaum, A. (1992) *Cash for Care. A Report on the Experience of Independent Living Fund Clients*, Independent Living Fund, Nottingham.

Kiresuk, T.J. and Lund, S.H. (1978) Goal attainment scaling, in *Evaluation of Human Service Programs*, (ed C. Atkinson), Academic Press, New York.

Kolmer, N. (1988) *Caring at Home*, National Extension College, Cambridge.

Kostin, M. (1973) The life satisfaction of non-normal persons. *Journal of Consulting and Clinical Psychology*, 41, 207–14.

Krueger, D.W. (1984) *Rehabilitation Psychology*, Aspen Publishers, Rockville, Maryland.

Krupnick, J. (1984) The diagnosis and treatment of post-traumatic stress disorders, in (ed D.W. Krueger), *Rehabilitation Psychology*, Aspen Publishers, Rockville, pp. 15–25.

Larcombe, N.A. and Wilson, P.H. (1984) An evaluation of cognitive behaviour therapy for depression in patients with multiple sclerosis. *British Journal of Psychiatry*, 145, 366–71.

Lawson, A., Robinson, I. and Bakes, C. (1985) Problems in evaluating the consequences of disabled illness: the case of multiple sclerosis. *Psychological Medicine*, 15, 555–79.

Leininger, M.M. (1984) (ed) *Care. The Essence of Nursing and Health*, Sluck, Thorofare, N.J.

Ley, P. (1977) Psychological studies of doctor–patient communication, *Contributions to Medical Psychology*, Vol. 11, (ed. S. Richman), Pergamon Press, Oxford.

Lincoln, N. (1983) Physical handicap, in *The Practice of Clinical Psychology in Great Britian*, (ed. A. Lidell), John Wiley & Sons, Chichester, pp. 187–202.

Linkowski, D.C. (1971) A scale to measure acceptance of disability. *Rehabilitation Counselling Bulletin*, June, 236–44.

Martin, J., Meltzer, H. and Eliot, D. (1988) *The Prevalence of Disability Among Adults*, HMSO, London.

Matson, R. and Brooks, N. (1977) Adjusting to multiple sclerosis. An exploratory study. *Social Science and Medicine*, 11, 245–50.

Mikulic, M. (1971) Reinforcement of independent and dependent patient behaviours by nursing personnel: an exploratory study. *Nursing Research*, 20, 148–55.

Miller, E. (1984) *The Recovery and Management of Neuropsychological Impairment*, Wiley, Chichester.

Miller, E.J. and Gwynne, G.V. (1971) *A Life Apart: a Pilot Study of Residential Institutions for the Physically Handicapped and the Young Chronic Sick*, Tavistock Publications, London.

Miller, R. and Keith, R.A. (1973) Behavioural mapping in a rehabilitation hospital. *Rehabilitation Psychology*, 20, 148–55.

Moos, R.H. and Tsu, V.D. (1977) The crisis of physical illness: an overview, in *Coping With Physical Illness* (ed R. Moss), Plenum, New York.

Motet-Grigoras, C.N. and Schuckit, M.A. (1986) Depression and substance abuse in handicapped young men. *Journal of Clinical Psychiatry*, 47, 234–7.

Nerenz, D.R. and Leventhal, H. (1983) Self-regulation therapy in chronic illness, in *Coping With Chronic Diseases*, (eds. T.G. Burrish and L.A. Bradley), Academic Press, London, pp. 13–37.

Neville, J. (1987) *A Chance to Choose*, Plymouth Health Authority, Plymouth.

Nouri, F.M., Tinson, D.J. and Lincoln N.B. (1987) Cognitive ability and driving after stroke. *International Disability Studies*, 9, 110–15.

Orem, D.E. (1985) *Nursing: Concepts of Practice*, 3rd edn, McGraw Hill, London.

Paediatric Research Unit (1985) *Needs of Handicapped Young Adults*, Royal Devon and Exeter Hospital, Exeter.

Paradowski, W. (1977) Socialisation patterns and sexual problems of the institutionalised chronically ill and physical disabled. *Archives of Physical Medicine and Rehabilitation*, 58, 53–9.

Partrige, C. and Johnston, M. (1989) Perceived control of recovery from physical disability: measurement and prediction. *British Journal of Clinical*

Psychology, **28**(1), 53–9.

Pastalan, L.A. (1974) The simulation of age-related sensory losses. A new approach to the study of environmental barriers. *New Outlook for the Blind*, **68**, 356–62.

Prince of Wales Advisory Group on Disability (1985) *Living Options: Guidelines for Those Planning Services for People with Severe Physical Disabilities*, Kings Fund, London.

Pritchard, M. (1981) Temporal reliability of a questionnaire measuring psychological response to illness. *Journal of Psychosomatic Research*, **25**, 63–6.

Randall, R. (1988) *Action for Carers*, Kings Fund Informal Caring Programme, London.

Reid, D. (1984) Participatory control and the chronic illness, adjustment process, in *Research with the Locus of Control/Construct*, Vol. 3, Academic Press, London, pp. 361–89.

Richards, J.S. (1986) Psychologic adjustment to spinal cord injury during the first post-discharge year. *Archives of Physical Medicine and Rehabilitation*, **67**, 362–5.

Richman, L.C. and Harper, D.C. (1980) Personality profiles of physically impaired young adults. *Journal of Clinical Psychology*, **36**(3), 668–71.

Robertson, I. (1990) Does computerised cognitive rehabilitation work? A review. *Aphasiology*, **4**, 381–405.

Robinson, R.G. and Price, T.R. (1982) Post stroke depressive disorders: a follow-up study of 103 patients. *Stroke*, **13**, 635–41.

Rosenberg, M.I. (1965) *Society and the Adolescent Self-Image*. Princeton University Press, Princeton NJ.

Royal College of Physicians of London (1986) Physical disability in 1986 and beyond. *Journal of the Royal College of Physicians of London*, **20**(3), 1–37.

Royal College of Physicians of London (1986) *The Young Disabled Adult. A Report of the Royal College of Physicians on the Use of Residential Homes and Hospital Units for the Age Group 16–64*. Royal College of Physicians, London.

Russell, R. (1981) Concepts of adjustment to disability: an overview. *Rehabilitation Literature*, **42**(11–12), 330–8.

Rutter, B.M. (1976) Measurement of psychological factors in chronic illness. *Rheumatology and Rehabilitation*, **15**, 174–8.

Shears, L.M. and Jensema, C.J. (1969) Social acceptability of anomalous persons. *Exceptional Child*, **36**, 91–6.

Shontz, F.C. (1978) Psychological adjustment to physical disability: trends and theories. *Archives of Physical Medicine and Rehabilitation*, **59**, 251–4.

Speilberger, C.D., Gorsuch, R.L. and Lushene, R.E. (1970) *Manual for the State Trait Anxiety Inventory*,

Counselling Psychology Press, Palo Alto, CA.

Taylor, J.A. (1953) Taylor manifest anxiety scale. A personality scale of manifest anxiety. *Journal of Abnormal and Social Psychiatry*, **948**, 285–90.

Thoits, P.A. (1982) Conceptual, methodological and theoretical problems in studying social support as a buffer against life stress. *Journal of Health and Social Behaviour*, **23**, 145–6.

Thomas, A. (1985) The health and social needs of physically handicapped young adults: are they being met by the statutory services? *Developmental Medicine and Child Neurology*, Suppl No. 50, August.

Toseland, R. And Sykes, J. (1977) Senior citizens centre participation and other correlates of life satisfaction. *Gerontologist*, **17**, 235–41.

Treischman, R.B. (1974) Coping with disability: a sliding scale of goals. *Archives of Physical Medicine and Rehabilitation*, **55**(12), 556–60.

Treischman, R.B. (1980) *Spinal Cord Injuries: Psychological, Social and Vocational Adjustment*, Pergamon Press, New York.

Wallston, B.S. and Wallston, K.A. (1976) Development and validation of the health locus of control (HLC) scale. *Journal of Consulting and Clinical Psychology*, **44**(4), 580–5.

Ward, C.D. and Wilkinson, S.M. (1988) *Sexual Functioning in Parkinson's Disease*, Unpublished, MS.

Warren, M. (1987) The prevalence of disability: measuring and estimating the number and needs of disabled people in the community. *Public Health*, **101**, 333–41.

Wassem, R. (1991) A test of the relationship between health locus of control and the course of multiple sclerosis. *Rehabilitation Nursing*, **16**(4), 189–93.

Watson, J. (1988) *Nursing: Human Science and Human Care. A Theory of Nursing*, NLN, New York.

Weinberg, N. and Williams, J. (1978) How the physically disabled perceive their disabilities. *Journal of Rehabilitation*, **44**(3), 31–3.

Whiting, S., Lincoln, N., Bhavnani, G. and Cockburn, J. (1988) *Rivermead Perceptual Assessment Battery*, NFER-Nelson, Windsor.

Wilkinson, S. and Hughes, D. (1992) *Care Free? An Evaluation of the Independent Living Fund*, United Bristol Health Care Trust, Bristol.

Wilson, B. (1981) A survey of behavioural treatments carried out a rehabilitation centre for stroke and head injuries, in *Brain Function Therapy*, (ed. G. Powell), Gower Press, Aldershot.

Wilson, B.A. and Moffar, N. (1992) *Clinical Management of Memory Problems*, Chapman and Hall, London.

Wilson, B., Cockburn, J. and Baddaley, A. (1985) *The Rivermead Behavioural Memory Test*, Thames Valley Test Co., Cambridge.

Wolfensburger, W. (1976) *The Principle of Normalisation in Human Services*, National Institute of Mental Retardation, Toronto.

World Health Organization (1980) *International Classification of Impairments, Disabilities and Handicaps*, World Health Organization, Geneva.

Wood, R.L. (1984) Behaviour disorders following severe brain injury: their presentation and psychological management, in *Closed Head Injury: Psychological, Social and Family Problems*, (ed N. Brooks), Oxford University Press, Oxford.

Wright, B. (1983) *Psychosocial Aspects of Physical Disability*, Harper and Row, London.

Young, L.D. and Blanchard, E.G. (1980) Medical applications of biofeedback training. A selected review, in *Contributions to Medical Psychology*, vol 2, (ed S. Rachman), Pergamon Press, New York, pp. 215–54.

Yuker, H. and Block, J. (1979) *Challenging Barriers to Change: Attitudes Towards the Disabled*. Albertson, New York National Centre on Employment of the Handicapped at the Human Resource Centre.

Zeldow, P.N. and Pavlous, M. (1984) Physical disability, life stress and psychosocial adjustment in multiple sclerosis. *Journal of Nervous and Mental Diseases*, **172**(2), 80–4.

Zigmond, A.S. and Snaith, R.P. (1983) The hospital anxiety and depression scale. *Acta Psychiatrica Scandinavica*, **67**, 361–70.

Zung, W. (1965) A self-rating depression scale (SDS). *Archives of General Psychiatry*, **12**, 63–70.

Chapter thirteen

Disorders of the gut

Paul Bennett

Introduction

Until recently, physicians and psychologists have legitimized psychology's interest in disorders of the gut by arguing that many were direct sequelae to psychological stress (see Whitehead and Schuster, 1985). While the evidence to support such an argument has become less sustainable over recent years, the importance of other psychological factors, such as sensitivity to pain in many bowel disorders, still provides fertile ground for psychological study. In addition, changes in aetiological models have not prevented a number of intervention studies evaluating the effectiveness of psychological methods in controlling the symptoms of many gastrointestinal disorders.

Rather than attempting a broad overview of all the psychological literature relating to disorders of the gut, this chapter examines the role of psychological factors in the aetiology and treatment of three of the most common disorders: the irritable bowel syndrome, peptic ulcer disease and inflammatory bowel disease. Readers seeking a review of psychological factors in other gastrointestinal disorders are recommended reviews by Whitehead (1992) and Whitehead and Schuster (1985).

Irritable bowel syndrome

The irritable bowel syndrome (IBS) is a disorder of the large bowel characterized by abdominal pain and changes in bowel habit in the absence of organic disease. To be diagnosed as IBS, the symptoms need to have been continuous or recurrent for a period of at least 3 months. Symptoms include both abdominal pain or discomfort, which is relieved by defecation or associated with a change of stool, and an irregular pattern of defecation that includes two or more of the following: altered stool form (hard or loose), altered stool passage (including straining or urgency), the passage of mucus and feelings of distension (Drossman et al., 1990). The symptoms of IBS may be severe, sufficiently to markedly restrict the individual's activity, which may be further restricted by fear of pain or diarrhoea (Bennett, 1987a).

Epidemiological data based on these diagnostic criteria have yet to be published. However, prevalence rates using less stringent diagnostic criteria suggest that the prevalence of IBS within the general population lies between 8% and 17% (Drossman et al., 1982; Whitehead et al., 1982; Talley et al., 1991).

Older studies (e.g. Fielding, 1977) suggest that IBS patients account for between 50% and 70% of referrals to gastroenterology clinics, although more recent evidence suggests that more IBS patients are being treated in primary care settings, with referral rates to specialists being as low as 10% (Everhart and Renault, 1991).

Aetiology of IBS

The cause of IBS remains unclear. Most commentators have argued that IBS results, at least in part, from psychological stress; that is, stress precedes the symptoms, and they form part of the stress response. This model assumes that IBS symptoms result from a hyperreactivity of the colon to stressful events or emotional stimuli. Some (e.g. Dinan et al., 1990) have argued that such reactivity may be mediated centrally, via the sympathetic nervous system, while others (e.g. Snape et al., 1977) have identified abnormal smooth muscle activity in the gut in response to stress or other insults such as food intolerances, as the probable cause of symptoms.

The strongest 'stress hypothesis' was proposed by Latimer (1981), who argued that the symptoms of IBS and anxiety stem from a common underlying autonomic reactivity, with symptom choice (IBS or anxiety) determined by vicarious learning and maintained by environmental contingencies. To argue his case, Latimer drew on a variety of sources of evidence, all based on studies of inpatient samples.

The first line of evidence Latimer invoked are findings that psychological stress is frequently reported as a major contributory factor to the onset or exacerbation of symptoms, both in case histories (e.g. Garrick, 1981; Youell and McCollough, 1975) and in studies of clinical populations (Hislop, 1971). Stressors reported in these studies are often minor concerns about family, finances and career. These may not be not objectively stressful, but are nevertheless associated with subjective anxiety for the individual (Whitehead and Schuster, 1985). Such evidence, although it may be of value as a hypothesis, must be treated with caution. Case histories are a particularly unreliable source from which to generalize, as they carry a number of biases which, however careful the investigator, are difficult to avoid. In addition, it has been suggested that many IBS patients may over report stressors in their lives as some form of justification for their seeking treatment.

A second potential source of evidence taken to suggest that IBS symptoms are caused by stress are findings that many patients have been assigned psychiatric diagnoses. Early studies suggested that between 72% and 100% (Liss, Alpers and Woodruff, 1973; Young et al., 1976; Latimer et al., 1981) of IBS patients could be assigned such a diagnosis. However, more recent British data suggests that the incidence of psychiatric diagnoses may be lower than in other populations. MacDonald and Bouchier (1980) found the incidence of psychiatric disorder amongst IBS patients to be 53%, while Whorwell et al. (1986) found the concurrence rates to be only 24%. The nature of any diagnoses varies considerably. Pooling data from a number of studies, Whitehead and Schuster (1985) estimated the most common diagnoses to be hysteria (20%), depression (20%) and anxiety neurosis (14%). Of course, such a relationship between psychiatric diagnoses and the diagnosis of IBS does not necessarily suggest that psychiatric morbidity *causes* IBS. Indeed, the opposite relationship could be proposed: IBS symptoms may cause depression, anxiety and other negative mood states.

A third source of support for the link between stress and IBS stems from a number of studies in which psychometric assessments of anxiety or other mood disturbances have been found to be associated with IBS (e.g. Whitehead, Engel and Schuster, 1980; Bergeron and Monto, 1985; Richter et al., 1986). Latimer and colleagues, in particular, have found high levels of depression and anxiety among IBS patients, equivalent to those of a matched group of psychiatric patients and greater than normal controls and those of patients with other gastrointestinal disorders (Latimer *et al.*, 1981). However, such a degree of psychopathology has not always been found. Two studies (Welch, Stace and Pomare, 1984; Cook, van Eeden and Collins, 1987) found no difference between IBS sufferers and patients with other gastrointestinal diseases on measures of depression, and Cook *et al.* found levels of anxiety to be no different from matched 'normal' controls.

A final source of evidence of the link between stress and IBS symptoms stems from life events research, where a number of studies have found patients with IBS to report a higher number of stressful events in the months preceding exacerbation, compared with patients having inflammatory bowel disease or appendectomy, or the general population (e.g. Fava and Pavan, 1976/7; Mendeloff *et al.*, 1970). Again, some caution must be exercised in interpreting these findings of retrospective studies, as the high levels of psychopathology found in clinic populations suggests that this population may selectively recall more subjectively stressful life events than controls.

Strong evidence to support Latimer's contention that IBS is, in *all* cases, a result of (or synonymous with) the stress process has proved difficult to find. At best, it can only reasonably be contended that in some cases IBS symptoms result directly from stress. Evidence from studies conducted in the general population suggests that the degree to which such symptoms are triggered or exacerbated by stress may indeed be quite modest.

General population-based research

Up to 80% of people with IBS do not consult a physician (Drossman *et al.*, 1988: Whitehead *et al.*, 1988). In addition, non-clinic attenders who have IBS visit their doctor less for other minor or vague symptoms than those who consult as a result of their IBS symptoms (Sandler *et al.*, 1984). Thus, the IBS patients seen in hospitals are probably a self-selected medical help-seeking group with relatively high levels of learned illness behaviour and anxiety or depression. It is possible that the majority of people with IBS have no degree of psychopathology or stress-related symptoms. Three more recent studies (Greenbaum *et al.*, 1983: Drossman *et al.*, 1988: Whitehead *et al.*, 1988) lend support to this suggestion. In all three studies, physician non-consulters were found to evidence no psychopathology or psychological distress. Accordingly, it can be argued that psychological symptoms do not cause IBS, but do influence the decision to consult a physician.

Although IBS would appear not to be linked directly to high levels of psychological distress, it is possible that more everyday stress may exacerbate or cause symptoms in those prone to IBS. Early evidence suggested that this may the case. Drossman *et al.* (1982) identified a group of non-clinic-attending people with IBS from a large random sample of hospital workers, 84% of whom reported that stressors caused them constipation and diarrhoea, while 69% said that stressors led to abdominal pain or discomfort.

A more recent prospective study (Whitehead *et al.*, 1992, reported in Whitehead, 1992) suggests that the role of stress in exacerbating symptoms may not be as strong as appears to be suggested by these results. They followed 39 women with clearly defined IBS, assessing them at 3-monthly intervals on measures of both bowel symptoms and stressful life events. Although the IBS group reported more life events than the control group, the correlations between symptoms and stressful events only accounted for about 10% of the variance in symptoms. However, the focus of this study on relative major life events may have missed the impact of more minor everyday stresses on IBS, which may be more strongly related to symptoms. In addition, they do not report how well the women coped with the stressors, which may be more important in exacerbating symptoms than the absolute number of life events (Corney *et al.*, 1991). The role of stress IBS still requires further explication.

Conclusion

The strong case proposed by Latimer, that IBS is synonymous with anxiety, cannot be supported. Nevertheless, there is evidence that stress has some mediating role in IBS, although the importance of that role is far from clear and may differ between individuals. Thus, a model of IBS proposed by Whitehead and Schuster (1985), which includes stress as one of potentially *several* triggers, including dietary intolerance as well as emotional states, to increased gut motility is most likely.

An additional mechanism by which IBS symptoms may arise is through individual differences in sensitivity to abdominal pain. Patients with IBS report pain at lower volumes when a balloon is inflated in the colon and rectum (Kullman and Fielding, 1981 Whitehead, Engel and Schuster, 1980) and also the small intestine (Kellow *et al.*, 1988) and oesophagus (Richter *et al.*, 1986). This may be a specific sensitivity, as it is not associated with reduced tolerance to aversive stimuli applied to the skin or correlated with measures of neuroticism.

Interventions in IBS

The findings that IBS may involve increased sensitivity to pain suggest that attention need be paid to interventions targeted at pain control (Whitehead, 1992). Whether traditional pain control methods are applicable to intervening in gut pain is an empirical question. It is certainly one for the future, as most of the published interventions in IBS have concentrated on attempting to lower bowel motility through some method of stress reduction. As IBS cannot now be considered to be strongly associated with stress, such interventions may, with hindsight, appear somewhat inappropriate. However, it must be noted that most *patients* with IBS *do* report symptoms of anxiety. Accordingly, therapeutic approaches that attempt to reduce stress may still be an appropriate and potentially effective way of helping such people.

Stress management training

Early studies into the effectiveness of stress management training were primarily single case histories (e.g. Cohen and Reed, 1968; Wise, Cooper and Ahmed, 1982). Their results suggested that relaxation techniques, either alone or in combination with other stress management strategies, could powerfully affect IBS symptomatology. Although such results are encouraging, they must be viewed in the light of the natural history of IBS and its placebo response to therapy. After 1 year without therapy, Waller and Misiewicz (1969) reported that 12% of previously symptomatic patients were symptom free and 36% reported themselves as improved. Similarly, Whitehead and Schuster (1985) note that the median response rate to placebo is 70%. Controlled trials are necessary to evaluate the effectiveness of stress management procedures in treating IBS.

One of the first of such trials to assess the impact of stress management procedures on a defined IBS population was conducted by Bennett and Wilkinson (1985). They compared the effectiveness of a stress management intervention, involving relaxation and cognitive restructuring techniques, with a standard medical treatment. By the end of the 8-week intervention, bowel symptoms (including pain and diarrhoea) had improved in both groups to a similar extent, but anxiety scores had reduced significantly in the psychological condition only. At 6-month follow-up (Bennett, 1987b), most participants in the stress management group had maintained the improvements made at the end of therapy. A second study to compare relaxation with medical treatment (Voirol and Hipolito, 1987) reported significantly greater reductions in episodes of pain and medical consultations among those in the relaxation condition over a 40-month follow-up period. Corney et al. (1991) found similar results up to 9 months follow-up.

In a series of studies, Blanchard and colleagues (Blanchard et al., 1992; Blanchard and Schwartz, 1987; Neff and Blanchard, 1987) evaluated a multicomponent intervention involving education about IBS and its causes, deep muscle relaxation, thermal biofeedback and cognitive therapy. In a pilot study conducted with four subjects, Neff and Blanchard (1987) found that two of them reported bowel activity within the normal range by the end of the intervention, while the others reported that their symptoms had improved by 45–50%. In their main study, they followed matched groups receiving the intervention (10 subjects) and in a symptom monitoring condition (nine subjects). Two weeks after treatment, six subjects in the treatment group and one in the control group reported a 50% reduction in symptoms. In addition, subjects in the treatment group reported significantly greater reductions in the reporting of abdominal pain and constipation, but only marginal differences on measures of diarrhoea and flatulence, compared to those in the control group. Four years later, Schwartz et al. (1990) followed up the patients in the active intervention group and those from a similar study conducted by Gerardi (1987). By this time, 90% of the participants rated themselves as improved by 50% or more, while half had maintained clinically significant improvements. In addition, all measures had improved over baseline measures. Unfortunately, in the absence of data concerning the control group, the significance of these findings is difficult to interpret.

A weakness of the Blanchard group studies described is that they compare an active treatment, where patient expectancies are of positive improvement, with a condition where the expectancies of outcome are at best neutral. Given the marked placebo response exhibited by patients with IBS, such a design does not permit us to state unequivocally that any changes in symptoms are associated with any particular intervention: they may represent a more generalized response to the expectancies of participants. In order to determine treatment effects it is necessary to compare the active intervention with a condition where participants are given some form of intervention which has face validity and leads to positive expectations of change, yet has no actual direct physiological effect.

Blanchard et al. (1992) addressed this issue by comparing their multicomponent intervention with a pseudomediation and EEG α suppression feedback and a symptom monitoring condition. At 6-month follow-up, no condition was found to be more effective than others in controlling a variety of IBS symptoms. Although this was a somewhat disappointing result, it may not necessarily suggest that stress management procedures work simply as a result of patients' positive expectation of treatment, as may be implied by the results. If this were the case, the symptom monitoring group would have been less successful than either of the other groups. In addition, subjects in the supposed control group actually appeared to be using relaxation methods and mental imagery to help them control stress more than those in the active intervention group. Thus, the placebo intervention may have helped people to cope with stress, making this study effectively a comparison between two active treatments.

Psychotherapy

A second method used to help IBS patients control stress has been through the use of psychotherapy. In one of the largest controlled trials of any intervention in IBS, Svedlund et al. (1983)

randomly allocated 101 patients to medication alone or in combination with psychotherapy. Psychotherapy comprised up to 10 hours of sessions aimed at helping participants modify maladaptive behaviour, find new solutions to problems and to cope more effectively with stress and emotional problems. Unfortunately, assessments carried out at baseline and immediately following the intervention were not blind to the treatment received by the patient, and were based on semistructured interview data assessing the severity of symptoms over the previous month. To offset some of the bias which may have resulted from this, postal questionnaires were used to gather 1-year follow-up data. The psychotherapy group evidenced significantly greater improvements than the medical treatment only group on measures of abdominal pain immediately following treatment and at 1-year follow-up, and on measures of bowel dysfunction at 1-year follow-up. Differences favouring the combined intervention were more pronounced at follow-up, as the subjects in the psychotherapy group continued to improve during the year following intervention, in contrast to those in the medical treatment group, where a slight increase in symptoms was evident.

Guthrie *et al.* (1991) reported a similar trial of psychotherapy, in which over 100 patients were randomly allocated to a standard medical regimen or a combination of medical therapy plus daily relaxation exercises and psychotherapy. After 3 months' intervention the combined treatment group had improved relative to the medical treatment group on measures of abdominal pain and diarrhoea, but not on constipation or bloating. Unfortunately, no follow-up data were reported, so the persistence of this advantage cannot be gauged.

Hypnotherapy

A British group, led by Whorwell, has led the research into the effectiveness of hypnosis in the treatment of IBS. In their first study, Whorwell, Prior and Colgan, (1987) randomly allocated 30 patients with refractory IBS into hypnotherapy alone or supportive psychotherapy combined with placebo medication. Hypnotherapy was directed at general relaxation and control of intestinal motility. Both conditions consisted of seven half-hour sessions over a period of 3 months. In addition, patients used audio tapes to practise self-hypnosis at home on a daily basis. Participants were independently assessed, and recorded their symptoms using diaries. By the 5th week of therapy, subjects in the hypnosis group evidenced significantly greater improvement on all measures. This improvement was maintained or increased by the end of therapy and at follow-up assessment, made around 18 months after the completion of therapy (Whorwell, Prior and Colgan, 1987). Whorwell (1989) suggests that 85% of patients will evidence significant reduction in symptoms, although older patients and those with significant levels of psychopathology are least likely to benefit from hypnosis.

Biofeedback

In contrast to the previous studies, which have attempted to moderate symptoms primarily through the use of relaxation techniques and the management of stress, bowel biofeedback interventions have attempted to teach patients to control bowel motility directly. In the first of such studies, Furman (1973) reported dramatic, albeit anecdotal, success after teaching five IBS patients to increase or decrease bowel sounds heard via an electronic microphage placed on the abdomen. All subjects, despite initially high levels of symptomatology, achieved normal bowel activity. Unfortunately, this initial success has not been replicated (Weinstock, 1976) and this technique is no longer used. Another form of colonic biofeedback also achieved encouraging initial results. Bueno-Miranda, Cerulli and Schuster (1976) taught 21 patients to control bowel motility following rectal distension by a balloon in a single 2-hour session.

Fourteen successfully learned the skill and were able to control motility equally well 2 months later. Whether this learning had an effect on day-to-day bowel activity was not reported. Whitehead (1985) further explored the clinical uses of this technique, comparing it to a programme of systematic desensitization. Subject numbers were small (four per condition), so statistical significance was not achieved; however, reductions in motility but not pain were reported in the biofeedback condition, and reductions in pain but not motility in the desensitization group. Not surprisingly, perhaps, desensitization was better tolerated by subjects than motility training. This remains the only comparison of biofeedback and stress management techniques.

Peptic ulcer disease

Peptic ulcer disease (PUD) is ulcerating lesions in the stomach or duodenum. Peptic ulcers are associated with epigastric pain, usually occurring several hours after eating, and relieved by food. Less frequently, intestinal bleeding and vomiting due to obstruction of the small bowel close to the stomach may be the presenting symptoms (Deckelbaum *et al.*, 1974). Approximately 10% of the population will develop PUD during their lifetime (Whitehead and Schuster, 1985).

Aetiology

Just as in IBS, early researchers (e.g. Draper and Touraine, 1932) argued that PUD resulted from psychological stress, with the archetypal stressed and hard-driving executive thought to be the typical PUD patient. Evidence to support this hypothesis arose from a variety of sources.

Epidemiological studies

Epidemiological evidence has shown there to be a higher incidence of duodenal ulcers during wartime than in times of peace; in urban rather than rural populations; and in a number of occupations thought to be particularly stressful, including surgeons, air-traffic controllers and business executives (Pflanz, 1971; Cobb and Rose, 1973). Unfortunately, such findings provide only modest support for the stress hypothesis, because large-scale epidemiological studies rely on diagnoses taken from medical notes, which may not be confirmed by radiological or endoscopic evidence: peptic ulcer disease is confirmed in only 30–90% of those presenting with ulcer-like symptoms (Pflanz, 1971; Myren, 1983); conversely, a small number of individuals develop PUD yet remain symptom free (Dunn and Etter, 1962). In addition, it is not clear whether those found to have ulcers were actually under stress. For example, surgeons and business executives frequently have a high degree of job latitude and control – factors associated with low levels of occupational stress (Karasek, 1989). These and other methodological difficulties have led researchers to concentrate their efforts on other methodologies, using patients with confirmed diagnoses. As with IBS, such a development may have led to differing biases.

Research with patient populations

In comparison with healthy or hospitalized controls, PUD patients have been found to be anxious, emotionally unstable, lack assertiveness, hypochondriacal and low achievers (Lyketsos *et al.*, 1982; Christodoulou, Alevizos and Konstantakakis, 1983; Feldman *et al.*, 1986; McIntosh *et al.*, 1983), quite the opposite of the stereotype. However, in the attempt to limit research to hospitalized patients with a confirmed diagnosis of PUD, the research has become biased to finding such traits. As with IBS, it is possible that individuals are more anxious or depressed and more likely to be seeking medical help. Support for this notion comes from studies conducted on a representative population (Pfeiffer, Fodor and Geizerova,

1973) and on individuals not attending hospital clinics (Sandberg and Bilding, 1976), where no association was found between ulceration and psychopathology. In addition, Sandberg and Bilding reported that clinic attenders were more anxious and depressed than non-attenders.

The life-events literature has also provided rather mixed evidence of how psychological stress may contribute to the development of PUD. A number of studies report comparatively high levels of acute stressors in PUD patients prior to the development of symptoms, compared with patients with other abdominal disorders or during periods free of ulceration (Davies and Wilson, 1937; Sapira and Cross, 1982). Gilligan et al. (1987), for example, found higher levels of chronic stress in duodenal ulcer patients than in the general population. Similarly, although Feldman et al. (1986) failed to find higher numbers of stressful events in the previous year reported by PUD patients, compared to patient or healthy controls, they perceived such events significantly more negatively and had less social support in coping with them. Only two studies have found increased numbers of stressful life events to be reported by gastric ulcer patients (Alp, Court and Kerr Grant, 1970; Sapira and Cross, 1982). Unfortunately, retrospective recall to up to 10 years, and a reliance on medical notes, renders the strength of the former result particularly questionable. Several studies have failed to find any association between stressful life events and the development of PUD (Feldman and Walker, 1984) and gastric ulcer (Piper et al., 1978; Thomas, Greig and Piper, 1980). Unfortunately these share with some of the other papers methodological problems that make it difficult to assess the true impact of life stresses on ulceration, including the use of insensitive simple life-event inventories, long-term retrospective recall in a subpopulation prone to recall bias (Minter and Kimball, 1978), and poor control of investigator bias. Well controlled prospective studies, although

difficult to set up, may provide more substantive evidence.

Although few in number, physiological studies have shown chronic psychological stress to result in hypersecretion of acid in the stomach (Peters and Richardson, 1983), and that relaxation can reduce gastric acid secretion (Stacher et al., 1975), suggesting that hypersecretion may be associated with the increased arousal found at times of stress. Peters and Richardson examined hydrochloric acid output in two men during and following periods of intense life stress. In both cases, both peak and basal acid output was high at the time of stress, reducing gradually over a period of months following relief from the stressor. In an experimental test of the relationship between stress and factors influencing the development of PUD, Statcher et al. (1975) examined the effects of hypnotic suggestions of relaxation to four normal volunteer subjects on basal and betazole-stimulated gastric acid secretion. Acid secretion was significantly reduced during hypnosis compared to identical conditions when no relaxation instructions were given. Finally, studies of patients with fistulas (e.g. Beaumont, 1833; Wolf and Wolff, 1943), allowing monitoring of gastric changes and secretions, provide many reports of increased acid secretion to high arousal, though the emotional states causing such fluctuations appear highly idiosyncratic.

The evidence for stress having an aetiological role in the development of PUD is, perhaps surprisingly, rather patchy, but enough to justify some form of psychological intervention, particularly with individuals experiencing stress concurrently with ulceration. However, few studies have examined the efficacy of such an intervention, probably due to the success of such medical treatments as cimetidine (Winship, 1978) and an expected unacceptability of psychological treatment to potential client groups (Whitehead and Schuster, 1985).

Interventions in PUD

Stress management interventions

As PUD has traditionally been associated with stress, it is not surprising that the majority of intervention studies have focused on the efficacy of stress management techniques in controlling PUD symptoms. Two early uncontrolled studies suggested that stress management training may produce symptomatic relief in PUD patients. Beaty (1976) taught three patients with frequent ulcer pain to relax using forehead EMG biofeedback combined with home relaxation practice. All three reported no pain or medication use at therapy completion or 6-month follow-up, although ulcer healing was not verified by X-ray or endoscopy. Using a similar combination, Aleo and Nicassio (1978) reported that by the end of the 12-week intervention, three of four subjects were free of pain, with radiographically confirmed ulcer healing. The fourth subject reported less ulcer pain than previously, and the ulcer was reduced in size.

Although these results suggest that such interventions are useful, they are compromised by small numbers and the lack of control groups. Under placebo treatment, both duodenal and gastric ulcers heal rapidly (Scheurer et al., 1977) and controlled trials, preferably with a placebo treatment group, are necessary to evaluate the effectiveness of any intervention.

The earliest report of a controlled evaluation of stress management in the treatment of PUD was reported by Chappell and colleagues (Chappell et al., 1936; Chappell and Stevenson, 1936). Volunteers were allocated to combined medical and psychological treatment or medical treatment alone. The psychological intervention consisted of small group meetings, 7 days a week for 6 weeks, and included an education phase, instruction in distraction techniques and the use of positive self-statements, and extinction of social reinforcement of illness-related behaviours. It was an extremely sophisticated package for its time, if rather intensive! By the end of the treatment phase, 30 of the 32 combined treatment subjects remaining in the study were asymptomatic. Not surprisingly, perhaps, 15 subjects had dropped out and were not included in the analysis. By 3-year follow-up most of the therapeutic gains had been maintained. Twenty-six of the 28 patients for whom data was available considered themselves healthy, although five had infrequent mild symptoms, and nine had frequent mild symptoms. The medically treated group was only followed up at 8 months, and by this time the two successfully treated subjects had suffered severe recurrences. The methodology of the study had a number of flaws, including non-random allocation of treatment groups, failure to distinguish between duodenal ulcer and gastric ulcer patients, no X-ray verification of healing, and non-blind assessment of symptomatology. Nevertheless, the study provided early evidence of the potential of a cognitive–behavioural approach to the treatment of PUD.

Rather more modern evidence is provided by Brooks and Richardson (1980). They randomly allocated 22 subjects with radiologically confirmed duodenal ulcers to either an intensive psychological intervention consisting of an educative phase, relaxation training, cognitive restructuring, the use of positive-self-talk and coping imagery, and assertion training, or placebo treatment consisting of three supportive meetings with a therapist. All subjects received antacid medication. Subjects completed a battery of psychological tests immediately before and after intervention, and at 60-day follow-up. Ulcer symptoms and the amount of medication used was monitored by weekly diaries. The psychological intervention proved successful. Patients high in anxiety or low on assertiveness showed substantial improvements in the active therapy but not in the placebo group. Similarly, subjects in active therapy experienced significantly fewer days of symptomatic pain and consumed less medication. X-ray revealed similar levels of ulcer healing in both groups. It is perhaps in the long-term follow-up (42 months) that the strength of the active intervention was most convincing. Fewer subjects (one in nine) had recurrences than in the placebo group (five in eight), they attended hospital less frequently, and none had surgery compared with two in the placebo group.

Biofeedback

Some studies have attempted to teach subjects to reduce acid secretion and gastric motility. Welgan (1974) taught 10 subjects with duodenal ulcers to control acid secretion by providing visual and auditory feedback of stomach pH levels. Compared to baseline, subjects were successful in reducing acid concentration and the volume of secretions. Using a similar technique, Whitehead, Renault and Goldiamond (1975) were also successful in teaching three out of four healthy subjects to increase acid secretion up to three times the baseline rate, or decrease it to baseline levels in each condition. Unfortunately, the strength of these results is weakened by Welgan's (1977) later finding that similar changes occurred when subjects were given false feedback. In an attempt to modify gastric motility (thought to mediate peptic ulcer pain), Whitehead and Drescher (1980) provided motility feedback to subjects from a pressure transducer placed in the stomach. During feedback subjects learned to successfully alter motility, but were unable to successfully modify motility without feedback, even after many learning trials. Biofeedback techniques are technically complex, uncomfortable and expensive to perform, and appear to produce few generalized skills. Further, their clinical utility has yet to be established. A more clinically useful approach may be found in stress management procedures.

Inflammatory bowel disease

The term inflammatory bowel disease (IBD) refers to two related diseases: Crohn's disease and ulcerative colitis. Both are remitting diseases, with alternating periods of exacerbation and remission. Ulcerative colitis results from inflammation and ulceration of the mucosa, or inner lining, of the colon. Initially, it usually affects the rectum and sigmoid colon, but it may extend to the entire colon. The principal symptoms are diarrhoea, rectal bleeding, abdominal pain and anorexia. Removal of the large bowel (colectomy) is required in many patients with severe or long-standing symptoms, usually to prevent malignancy. This results in an ileostomy. Crohn's disease affects the outer layers of the intestinal wall and may occur anywhere in the gastrointestinal tract. Inflammation leads to scarring and constriction of the bowel, which may lead to bowel obstruction and the need for bowel resection or partial or complete colectomy, resulting in a colostomy or ileostomy. The symptoms of Crohn's disease include diarrhoea, abdominal pain, anorexia and fever. The estimated prevalence of ulcerative colitis is 36–70 per 100 000, and of Crohn's 20–40 per 100 000 population (Mendeloff, 1975). The two disorders are usually considered as different manifestations of the same disease process, and for this reason are discussed together.

Aetiology of IBD

Evidence that psychological factors have an aetiological role in IBD symptomatology is less strong than for some other gastrointestinal disorders, and the early analytic theorists (e.g. Engel, 1955) have dropped from favour. However, some of the physiological systems thought to be involved in the aetiology of IBD, particularly the immune systems, are known to be affected by psychological factors (Ader, 1981). It is possible, therefore, that psychological factors may also affect IBD symptomatology.

Several uncontrolled studies and case reports (Daniels, 1942; Bonfils and Uzan, 1974; Schoenberg, 1983) have found relatively high levels of stressors reported by IBD patients prior to symptom exacerbation. For example, McKegney, Gordon and Levine, (1970) reported that a serious life crisis occurred within 6 months of illness in 86% of ulcerative colitis and 68% of Crohn's disease patients. Studies with comparison groups have also reported higher levels of stressors in IBD patients than controls. Hislop (1974) interviewed 50 consecutive IBD patients nd matched controls of hospital visitors, and found that the incidence of bereavement, marriage, divorce, pregnancy and childbirth and migration during the previous 12 months were all greater in the IBD group. Similarly, Fava and Pavan (1976/7) found more reports of recent life events in ulcerative colitis patients than in appendectomy patients, but less than IBS controls. Two substantial studies, however, failed to find any differences in life events preceding exacerbation. Mendeloff et al. (1970b) devised a stress scale examining social and cultural discontinuities, mobility, job changes and other adverse life changes in the previous 6 months. They interviewed 158 patients with ulcerative colitis, 102 with irritable bowel syndrome and 735 local residents. They found no differences between the ulcerative colitis and local residents groups, remarking that the ulcerative colitis group appeared to lead a more stable life than controls. Helzer et al. (1982), using the Holmes and Rahe life-events scale (Holmes and Rahe, 1967), also found no differences between ulcerative colitis patients and a control group with other chronic diseases. Unfortunately, all the studies were retrospective, often with the interviewer not blind to either the hypothesis or the illness of the patient. A well controlled prospective study is still awaited.

Psychometric studies have also failed to identify consistently any psychological characteristics in IBD patients that could contribute to their symptoms. Sheffield and Carney (1976) administered the Taylor Manifest Anxiety Scale (Taylor, 1953) to 28 outpatients with Crohn's disease, 17 with a chronic illness and 43 with psychosomatic illnesses (including ulcerative colitis). Scores for the Crohn's disease group were higher than the test norms and the scores of chronic medical patients, and the same as the psychosomatic patients. Crohn's patients were also found to be more neurotic than chronic medical patients. Some doubt as to the generalizability of their findings results from the disproportionately high number (eight) of Crohn's patients having a psychiatric illness (Helzer et al., 1982), the non-random acquisition of subjects and the comparison of Crohn's patients with a control group including patients with ulcerative colitis. In a more controlled study of consecutive admissions, Esler and Goulston (1973) found no difference on the Institute of Personality and Ability Testing anxiety scale (Cattell and Scheier, 1963) between normal controls and ulcerative colitis patients. Similarly, two other studies failed to find higher levels of neuroticism in ulcerative colitis patients than in normal controls (Esler and Goulston, 1973) or chronically ill patients (Helzer et al., 1982).

Apart from early impressionistic reports (e.g. Whybrow, Kane and Lipton, 1968), no study using appropriate diagnostic criteria (e.g. Goldberg, 1970), and even some using rather odd ones (Feldman et al., 1967) has shown a relationship between psychiatric disorder and IBD. Heltzer et al. (1982) gave a structured psychiatric interview to 57 ulcerative colitis patients and a control group of chronic medical patients, allowing diagnosis of lifetime psychiatric disorders. If anything, less psychiatric disturbance was found in the ulcerative colitis group (26% versus 30%). Thus, there is little evidence of any degree of psychopathology in this population, perhaps surprisingly in view of the unpleasant symptomatology of IBD. Evidence of the adverse impact of IBD on lifestyles is shown in a study of 84 outpatients by Mallett *et al.* (1982) who reported that two-thirds had changed their work routines, 85% had problems with their social life when their symptoms were severe and over half reported general irritability to be a problem during exacerbation. Similarly, Joachim and Milne (1985) report that 42% of IBD sufferers felt that their illness significantly reduced their life satisfaction, and IBD was seen as contributing to feelings of low energy (56%), depression (39%), nervousness (36%) and insomnia (32%). Perhaps surprisingly, only 25% were worried about their illness, despite its chronic recurring nature and ultimately poor prognosis.

Intervention in IBD

Despite there being little substantive evidence to suggest that stress may trigger or exacerbate the symptoms of IBD, a number of studies have been conducted attempting to moderate symptoms. In addition, acknowledging that distress may result from, rather than cause, IBD, a number of studies have attempted to alleviate some of this distress.

Symptom reduction

The early analytical models led to a number of reports of successful treatment of IBD using psychoanalytical techniques (e.g. Daniels, 1940), generating an interest in its psychological treatment that may not have been sustained in the absence of strong aetiological evidence. Successes reported in these analytical single case reports were supported by results from a number of uncontrolled group studies. For example, Weinstock (1962) reported on 28 patients receiving long-term analytical therapy

for between 18 months and 5 years. Although severely ill at the beginning of therapy, 21 of these had long periods of remission, with a mean duration of 9 years. Although interest in the analytical treatment of IBD remains (e.g. Schoenberg, 1983), successful reports of the use of relatively brief supportive psychotherapy (Groen and Bastiaans, 1951) has led researchers and clinicians to concentrate their efforts on this less intense approach. In an uncontrolled study, Groen and Birnbaum (1968) combined this approach with minimal medication to treat 27 ulcerative colitis patients. At 2-year follow-up, 20 were either cured or considerably better, four had improved but were still on steroids, one died and two were lost to follow-up.

In a poorly controlled series of studies Karush *et al.* (1977) evaluated this approach further, assigning patients to either medical treatment alone or in combination with supportive psychotherapy. Unfortunately, subjects were not randomly assigned to each condition and the subjects in the two conditions were far from alike, as patients receiving the combined therapy had a psychiatric diagnosis (including schizophrenia), while the others showed no psychopathology. The authors report that although gains made in the psychotherapy group were not immediately apparent, over the 8-year period of the study patients receiving the combined treatment experienced shorter and less severe exacerbations and longer periods of remission. Unfortunately, the degree of somatic change was not related to psychological improvement (Karush *et al.*, 1969). The only controlled study of the use of supportive psychotherapy in the treatment of ulcerative colitis was reported by Grace, Pinsky and Wolff, (1954). Thirty-four patients were treated with supportive psychotherapy, and their outcome was compared with a matched control group treated with a combination of diet, steroids and antibiotics. After a minimum follow-up of 2 years, patients in the psychotherapy group had fewer ileostomies or colostomies (three versus ten) and had spent less time in hospital; 26% were symptom free and 39% had improved, compared to 15% and 18% respectively. No placebo treatment group was included and ratings of symptomatology were not blind. Nevertheless, outcomes in the psychotherapy group were substantially better than in the medical group, even on the hard outcome measures.

A number of uncontrolled reports suggest that autogenic relaxation training may also have a beneficial effect upon the outcome of ulcerative colitis. For example, Schaeffer (1966) reports on 32 patients treated with autogenic training, combined in some cases with minimal drug therapy and hypnosis. Over follow-up periods of between 1 and 12 years, he reports that 23 patients were cured and six were significantly improved. Similarly successful reports, usually of autogenic training in combination with other techniques, including psychoanalytical therapy and hypnosis, have also been reported (see Luthe and Schultz, 1969). The uncontrolled nature of these reports and the tendency to combine treatments makes the exact role of autogenic training in the treatment of IBD unclear, but potentially useful.

A final strand of therapy aimed at reducing IBD symptomatology is the use of hypnosis. Unfortunately, the results of one study by Taub and colleagues attempting to evaluate the value of hypnosis in a controlled manner were never published due to criminal investigations at Taub's laboratory. The study is, however, described by Whitehead and Schuster (1985). Following a 3-month baseline period, 16 patients with poorly controlled ulcerative colitis were assigned to either between four and 12 psychodynamically oriented hypnotherapy sessions over a 3-month period, or to a symptom monitoring group. Of the treated subjects, seven reported significant symptomatic improvements, and this was confirmed by physical examination in five. No control patients improved. Unfortunately, following adverse publicity concerning the criminal proceedings, their success rate was drastically cut and the implications of their findings remain unclear. A well controlled trial of hypnotherapy versus placebo therapy is needed to resolve the question of their mixed findings.

Reduction of distress

Despite some success in attempts to control the symptoms of IBD through the use of psychological therapy, more recent aetiological models have led to an increased emphasis on the importance of minimizing adverse psychological sequelae to the disease process, instead of, or as well as, controlling symptoms. One of the first of such studies was conducted by Joachim (1983), who reported an uncontrolled pilot study in which 14 outpatients were taught deep breathing exercises and relaxation techniques over a period of four weekly meetings. Two weeks after the final session, nine patients reported an increased ability to sleep and to control their IBD pain, and 13 reported that they were more able to calm themselves. In a later controlled study Milne, Joachim and Niedhart (1986) randomly allocated 80 patients with IBD to either an intervention group in which they received six classes on stress management, or a control group which received no intervention. Assessments were made of psychological wellbeing, physical symptomatology and the amount of distress caused by their symptoms. Unfortunately, the randomization process was not successful, as the intervention group reported greater distress and symptomatology at baseline. Although the disease symptoms and wellbeing scores improved most in the intervention group over the course of the intervention and at 4-year follow-up, these results may represent a regression to the mean in their scores, rather than a direct effect of the intervention. A third controlled study was reported by Freyberger *et al.*

(1985), who randomly allocated 38 patients with ulcerative colitis to a brief psychotherapy group or no treatment control condition. Significant improvements on measures of state anxiety, depression and mood were reported in the treatment group but not the control group. Unfortunately, no follow-up assessments were made to assess the durability of these results.

Schwarz and Blanchard (1991) maintained the interest in the impact of psychological intervention, not only on physical symptoms but also in helping people cope with the sequelae to disease. In a study involving 21 patients, they compared a multicomponent behavioural intervention comprising an educational phase, progressive muscle relaxation, thermal biofeedback and training in cognitive stress management techniques with a symptom monitoring condition. Their results were somewhat mixed. The symptom monitoring group reported a reduction in all eight symptoms monitored during the course of the trial, whereas the intervention condition reported improvements in only five. More positively, intervention subjects saw themselves as coping better with IBD, feeling less stress as a result of their disease, and experiencing less depression and anxiety, despite their relatively small changes in symptoms. Retrospective analyses suggested that patients with ulcerative colitis benefited less in terms of reductions in physical symptoms than those with Crohn's disease. Clearly, larger studies are necessary to determine whether this is the case. Nevertheless, the findings that stress management had a positive impact on patients' ability to cope with the disease and reduced their levels of distress is an important finding, and is suggestive of a role for future psychological work.

Finally, Shaw and Ehrlich (1987) examined the impact of relaxation training on the pain associated with ulcerative colitis. A total of 40 patients were allocated to either a relaxation training or attention control conditions. Although there were no between-group differ-ences before treatment, immediately following the intervention and at 6-week follow-up patients in the relaxation condition reported significantly less frequent and intense pain, and that they were better able to control any pain and were less distressed by it. In addition, significantly fewer patients were taking anti-inflammatory drugs.

Summary and conclusions

Evidence linking psychological variables, particularly stress, to disorders of the guts is surprisingly sparse, and frequently confusing and contradictory, reflecting the many methodological weaknesses common to research in the disorders discussed. Most studies which have suggested a link between psychological factors and gut disorders have been conducted using hospitalized patients or those attending outpatient clinics. However, there is strong evidence to suggest that this methodology biases the results of such studies towards finding some degree of psychopathology among patients with disorders of the bowel, as those with some degree of distress are most likely to consult physicians.

Those studies conducted with more representative samples suggest that the role of stress in the aetiology of gut disorders may have previously been overemphasized. Nevertheless, there remains evidence to suggest that such a link does exist, albeit a less important one than has been previously thought. Three studies (Corney et al., 1991; Drossman et al., 1982; Whitehead et al, 1992; reported in Whitehead, 1992) have shown IBS symptoms to covary with levels of stress. Much of the literature relating to PUD is difficult to interpret, yet the physiological studies that have been conducted suggest at least the possibility that ulceration may be mediated via stress-related excess gastric acid secretion and motility. In the case of IBD, however, there is little evidence to suggest that stress either triggers or exacerbates symptoms. However, here the converse is true: the severity and chronicity of symptoms may lead to substantial distress and reduced quality of life.

Almost in the face of this mixed evidence, evaluation of the impact of psychological interventions on both symptoms and mood has been pursued. As these disorders cannot now be considered to be strongly associated with stress, such interventions may, with hindsight, appear somewhat inappropriate. However, as previously noted, most patients with IBS do report symptoms of anxiety or other negative mood states. Accordingly, therapeutic approaches which attempt to reduce stress may still be an appropriate and potentially effective way of helping such people. Indeed, in many cases this has proved to be the case.

There is reasonable evidence that interventions targeted at the alleviation of stress can positively influence the symptoms of IBS, and do so as much as medical intervention and better than no treatment. It is somewhat disappointing that the most rigorous evaluation of psychological intervention in IBS (Blanchard *et al.*, 1992), which compared stress management with a placebo intervention, found no advantage accruing to patients in the active intervention condition. However, the study involved only a small number of patients and reported other counterintuitive results. Accordingly, more studies should be conducted before it can be asserted that stress management procedures confer no more advantage than placebo treatment. Those studies that have been conducted also suggest that patients with PUD would benefit from learning stress management procedures, although the potential benefits are likely to be in terms of reduced recurrence rather than the immediate alleviation of symptoms. Finally, although stress management procedures have proved to be of mixed benefit in terms of symptom reduction in people with IBD, it does appear that they may help people both to manage any resultant pain and to man-

age the disease more effectively. In a chronic and debilitating condition these findings are not trivial, and suggest that psychosocial interventions may confer considerable benefits to this population. It is necessary to conduct well controlled trials which carefully assess the psychosocial as well as the medical benefits that may accrue from psychological interventions, as well as interventions reflecting the changing aetiological models for these disorders. In particular, the benefits of pain management strategies with IBS patients offer an exciting avenue for future research.

References

Ader, R. (1981) *Psychoneuroimmunology*, Academic Press, New York.

Aleo, S. and Nicassio, P. (1978) Autoregulation of duodenal ulcer disease: a preliminary report of four cases. *Proceedings of the Biofeedback Society of America* (Ninth Annual Meeting), Biofeedback Society of America. Denver, Colorado.

Alp, M.H., Court, J.H. and Kerr Grant A. (1970) Personality pattern and emotional stress in the genesis of gastric ulcer. *Gut*, **11**, 773–7.

Beaty, E.T. (1976) Feedback assisted relaxation training as a treatment for peptic ulcers. *Biofeedback and Self-Regulation*, **1**, 323–4.

Beaumont, W. (1833) *Experiments and Observations on the Gastric Juice and the Physiology of Digestion*, FP Allen, Plattsburgh, New York.

Bennett, P. (1987a) Psychological aspects of physical illness: irritable bowel syndrome. *Nursing Times*, **83**(46), 51–3.

Bennett, P. (1987b) Individual responses to medical and behavioural treatment of the irritable bowel syndrome. Paper presented at the Annual Conference of the British Association of Behavioural Psychotherapy, Exeter.

Bennett, P. and Wilkinson, S. (1985) A comparison of psychological and medical treatment of the irritable bowel syndrome. *British Journal of Clinical Psychology*, **24**, 215–16.

Bergeron, C.M. and Monto, G.L. (1985) Personality patterns seen in irritable bowel syndrome patients. *American Journal of Gastroenterology*, **80**, 448–51.

Blanchard, E.B., Schwarz, S.P., Suls, J. M. *et al.* (1992) Two controlled evaluations of a multicomponent psychological treatment of irritable bowel syndrome. *Behaviour Research and Therapy*, **30**, 175–89.

Bonfils, S. and de M. Uzan, M. (1974) Irritable bowel syndrome versus ulcerative colitis: psychofunctional disturbance versus psychosomatic disease? *Journal of Psychosomatic Research*, **18**, 291–6.

Brooks, G.R. and Richardson, F.C. (1980) Emotional skills training: a treatment program for duodenal ulcer. *Behaviour Therapy*, **11**, 198–207.

Bueno-Miranda, F., Cerulli, M. and Schuster, M.M. (1976) Operant conditioning of colonic motility in irritable bowel syndrome (IBS). *Gastroenterology*, **70**, 867.

Cattell, R.B. and Scheier, I.H. (1963) *Handbook for the IPAT Anxiety Scale Questionnaire*, Institute for Personality and Ability Testing, Champaign, Illinois.

Chappell, M.N. and Stevenson, T.I. (1936) Group psychological training in some organic conditions. *Mental Hugiene*, **20**, 588–97.

Chappel, M.N., Stefano, J.J., Rogerson, J.S. and Pike, F. H. (1936) The value of group psychological procedures in the treatment of peptic ulcer. *American Journal of Digestive Disease and Nutrition*, **3**, 813–17.

Christodoulou, G.N., Alevizos, B.H. and Konstantakakis, E. (1983) Peptic ulcer in adults. Psychopathological, environmental, characterological and hereditary factors. *Psychotherapy and Psychosomatics*, **39**, 55–62.

Cobb, S. and Rose, R.M. (1973) Hypertension, peptic ulcer and diabetes in air traffic controllers. *Journal of the American Medical Association*, **224**, 489–92.

Cohen, S.I. and Reed, J.L. (1968) The treatment of 'nervous diarrhoea' and other conditioned autonomic disorders by desensitization. *British Journal of Psychiatry*, **114**, 1275–80.

Cook, I.J., van Eeden, A. and Collins, SM. (1987) Patients with irritable bowel syndrome have greater pain tolerance than normal subjects. *Gastroenterology*, **93**, 727–33.

Corney, R.H., Stanton, R., Newell, R. *et al.* (1991) Behavioural psychotherapy in the treatment of irritable bowel syndrome. *Journal of Psychosomatic Research*, **35**, 461–9.

Daniels, G.E. (1940) Treatment of a case of ulcerative colitis associated with hysterical depressions. *Psychosomatic Medicine*, **24**, 276–85.

Daniels, G.E. (1942) Psychiatric aspects of ulcerative colitis. *New England Journal of Medicine*, **226**, 178–84.

Davies, D.T. and Wilson, A.T. (1937) Observation on the life history of chronic peptic ulcer. *Lancet*, ii, 1355–60.

Deckelbaum, R.J., Roy, C.C., Lussier-Lararoff, J. and Morin, C.L. (1974) Peptic ulcer disease: a clinical study of 73 children. *Canadian Medical Association Journal*, **111**, 225–8.

Dinan, T.G., Barry, S., Ahkion, S. *et al.* (1990) Assessment of central noradrenergic functioning in irritable bowel syndrome using a neuroendocrine challenge test. *Journal of Psychosomatic Research*, **34**, 575–80.

Draper, G. and Touraine, G.A. (1932) The man–environment unit and peptic ulcers. *Archives of Internal Medicine*, **49**, 615.

Drossman, D.A., Sandler, R.S., McKee, D.C. and Lovitz, A.J. (1982) Bowel patterns among subjects not seeking health care: use of a questionnaire to identify a population with bowel dysfunction. *Gastroenterology*, **83**, 529–34.

Drossman, D.A., Leserman, J., Nachman, G. *et al.* (1988) Psychosocial factors in the irritable bowel syndrome. A multivariate study of patients and non-patients with irritable bowel syndrome. *Gastroenterology*, **95**, 701–8.

Drossman, D.A., Thompson, W.G., Talley, N. J. *et al.* (1990) Identification of sub-groups of functional gastrointestinal disorders. *Gastroenterology International*, **3**, 159–72.

Dunn, J.P. and Etter, L.E. (1962) Inadequacy of the medical history in the diagnosis of duodenal ulcer. *New England Journal of Medicine*, **266**, 68–72.

Engel, G.L. (1955) Studies of ulcerative colitis. III. The nature of the psychologic processes. *American Journal of Medicine*, **17**, 231–56.

Esler, M.D. and Goulston, K.J. (1973) Levels of anxiety in colonic disorders. *New England Journal of Medicine*, **288**, 16–20.

Everhart, J.E. and Renault, P.F. (1991) Irritable bowel syndrome in office-based practice in the United States. *Gastroenterology*, **100**, 998–1005.

Fava, G.A. and Pavan, L. (1976/7) Large bowel disorders. I. Illness configuration and life events. *Psychotherapy and Psychosomatics*, **27**, 93–9.

Feldman, M. and Walker, P. (1984) A controlled study of psychosocial factors in peptic ulcer disease. *Gastroenterology*, **86**, 1075.

Feldman, F., Cantor, D., Soll, S. and Bachrach, W. (1967) Psychiatric study of a consecutive series of 34 patients with ulcerative colitis. *British Medical Journal*, **3**, 14–17.

Feldman, M., Walker, P., Green, J.L. and Weingarder, K. (1986) Life events stress and psychosocial factors in men with peptic ulcer disease. A multidimensional case-controlled study. *Gastroenterology*, **91**, 1370–9.

Fielding, J.F. (1977) A year in out-patients with the irritable bowel syndrome. *Irish Journal of Medical Science*, **146**, 162–6.

Freyberger, H., Kunsebeck, H-W., Lempa, W. *et al.* (1985) Psychotherapeutic interventions in alexithymic patients with special regard to ulcerative colitis and Crohn patients. *Psychotherapy and Psychosomatics*, **44**, 72–81.

Furman, S. (1973) Intestinal biofeedback in functional diarrhoea: a preliminary report. *Journal of*

Behaviour Therapy and Experimental Psychiatry, **4**, 317–21.

Garrick, T.R. (1981) Behaviour therapy for irritable bowel syndrome: A case report. *General Hospital Psychiatry*, **3**, 48–51.

Gilligan, I., Fung, L., Piper, D.W. and Tennant. C. (1987) Life event stress and chronic difficulties in duodenal ulcer: a case control study. *Journal of Psychosomatic Research*, **31**, 117–23.

Goldberg, D. (1970) A psychiatric study of patients with diseases of the small intestine. *Gut*, **11**, 459–65.

Grace, W.J., Pinsky, R.H. and Wolff, H.G. (1954) The treatment of ulcerative colitis, II. *Gastroenterology*, **26**, 462–8.

Greenbaum, D., Abitz, L., Van Egeren, L. *et al.* (1983) Irritable bowel symptom prevalence, rectosigmoid motility and psychometrics in symptomatic subjectts not seeing physicians. *Gastroenterology*, **84**, 1174.

Groen, J. and Bastiaans, J. (1951) Psychotherapy of ulcerative colitis. *Gastroenterology*, **17**, 344–52.

Groen, J. and Birnbaum, D. (1968) Conservative (supportive) treatment of severe ulcerative colitis. Methods and results. *Israeli Journal of Medical Science*, **4**, 130–9.

Guthrie, E., Creed, F., Dawson, D. and Tomenson, B. (1991) A controlled trial of psychological treatment for the irritable bowel syndrome. *Gastroenterology*, **100**, 450–7.

Helzer, J.E., Stillings, W.A., Chammas, S. *et al.* (1982) A controlled study of the association between ulcerative colitis and psychiatric diagnoses. *Digestive Diseases and Sciences*, **27**, 513–18.

Hislop, I. (1971) Psychological significance of the irritable colon syndrome. *Gut*, **12**, 452–7.

Hislop, I. (1974) Onset setting in inflammatory bowel disease. *Medical Journal of Australia*, **1**, 981–4.

Holmes, T.H. and Rahe, R.H. (1967) The social readjustment rating scale. *Journal of Psychosomatic Research*, **11**, 213–18.

Joachim, G. (1983) The effects of two stress management on feelings of well-being in patients with inflammatory bowel disease. *Nursing Papers*, **15**, 5–18.

Joachim, G. and Milne, B. (1985) The effects of inflammatory bowel disease on lifestyle. *Canadian Nurse*, **81**, 38–40.

Karasek, R.A. (1989) Control in the workplace and its health-related impacts, in *Job Control and Worker Health*, (eds. S.L. Sauter, J.J. Hurrell and C.L. Cooper), Wiley, New York.

Karush, A., Daniels, G.E., Flood, C. and O'Connor, J. F. (1977) *Psychotherapy in Chronic Ulcerative Colitis*, WB Saunders and Co., Philadelphia.

Karush, A., Daniels, G.E., O'Connor, J.F. and Stern, L.O. (1969) The response to psychotherapy in chronic ulcerative colitis. II. Factors arising from the therapeutic situation. *Psychosomatic Medicine*, **31**, 201–26.

Kellow, J.E., Phillips, S.F., Miller, L.J. and Zinsmeister, A.R. (1988) Dysmotility of the small intestine in irritable bowel syndrome. *Gut*, **29**, 1236–43.

Kullman, G. and Fielding, J.F. (1981) Rectal distensibility in the irritable bowel syndrome. *Irish Medical Journal*, **74**, 140–2.

Latimer, P.R. (1981) Irritable bowel syndrome: a behavioural model. *Behaviour Research and Therapy*, **19**, 475–83.

Latimer, P.R., Sarna, S, Campbell, D. *et al.* (1981) Colonic motor and myoelectrical activity: a comparative study of normal patients, psychoneurotic patients and patients with irritable bowel syndrome. *Gastroenterology*, **80**, 893–901.

Liss, J.L., Alpers, D. and Woodruff, R.A. Jr (1973) The irritable colon syndrome and psychiatric illness. *Diseases of the Nervous System*, **34**, 151–7.

Luthe, W. and Schultz, J.H. (1969) *Autogenic Therapy Volume II: Medical Applications*, Grune and Stratton, New York.

Lyketsos, G., Arapakis, G., Psaras, M. *et al.* (1982) Psychological characteristics of hypertensive and ulcer patients. *Journal of Psychosomatic Research*, **26**, 255–62.

MacDonald, A.J. and Bouchier, I.A.D. (1980) Nonorganic gastrointestinal illness: a medical and psychiatric study. *British Journal of Psychiatry*, **136**, 151–7.

McIntosh, J.H., Nasiry, R.W., Frydman, M. *et al.* (1983) The personality pattern of patients with chronic peptic ulcer. A case-control study. *Scandinavian Journal of Gastroenterology*, **18**, 945–50.

McKegney, F.P., Gordon, R.O. and Levine, S.M. (1970) A psychosomatic comparison of patients with ulcerative colitis and Crohn's disease. *Psychosomatic Medicine*, **32**, 153–66.

MacLeod, J.H. (1983) Biofeedback in the management of partial anal incontinence. *Diseases of the Colon and Rectum*, **26**, 244–6.

Mallet, S., Lennard-Jones, J., Bingley, J. and Gilon, E. (1982) Colitis. *Lancet*, **ii**, 619–21.

Mendeloff, A.I. (1975) The epidemiology of idiopathic inflammatory bowel disease, in *Inflammatory Bowel Disease* (eds J.B. Kirsner and R.G. Shorter), Lea and Febiger, Philadelphia, pp. 3–19.

Mendeloff, A.I., Monk, M., Sigel, C.I. and Lilienfeld, A. (1970) Illness experience and life stresses in patients with irritable colon and with ulcerative colitis. An epidemiologic study of ulcerative colitis and regional enteritis in Baltimore. 1960–1964. *New England Journal of Medicine*, **282**, 14–17.

Milne B., Joachim, G. and Niedhart, J. (1986) A stress management program for inflammatory bowel disease patients. *Journal of Advanced Nursing*, **11**, 561–7.

Minter, R.E. and Kimball, C.P. (1978) Life events and illness onset: a review *Psychosomtics*, **19**, 334–9.

Myren J. (1983) The natural history of peptic ulcer. Views in the 1980s. *Scandinavian Journal of Gastroenterology*, **18**, 993–7.

Neff, D.F. and Blanchard, E.B. (1987) A multicomponent and treatment for irritable bowel syndrome. *Behaviour Therapy*, **18**, 70– 83.

Peters, M.N. and Richardson, C.T. (1983) Stressful life events disease. *Gastroenterology*, **84**, 114–19.

Pfeiffer, C.J., Fodor, J. and Geizerova, H. (1973) An epidemiologic study of the relationships of peptic ulcer disease in 50–54 year old, urban males with physical, health and smoking factors. *Journal of Chronic Diseases*, **26**, 291–302.

Pflanz, M. (1971) Epidemiological and sociocultural factors in the aetiology of duodenal ulcer. *Advances in Psychosomatic Medicine*, **6**, 121–51.

Piper, D.W., Greig, M., Shinners, J. *et al.* (1978) Chronic gastric ulcer and stress. *Digestion*, **18**, 303–9.

Richter, J.E., Obrecht, W.F., Bradley, L.A. *et al.* (1986) Psychological comparison of patients with nutcracker oesophagus and irritable bowel syndrome. *Digestive Disease Scienc*e, **31**, 131–8.

Sandberg, B. and Bilding, A. (1976) Duodenal ulcer in army trainees during basic military training. *Journal of Psychosomatic Research*, **20**, 61–74.

Sandler, R.S., Drossman, D.A., Nathan, H.P. and McKee, D.C. (1984) Symptom complaints and health care seeking behaviour in subjects with bowel dysfunction. *Gastroenterology*, **87**, 314–18.

Sapira, J.D. and Cross, M.R. (1982) Pre-hospitalization life change in gastric ulcer (GU) versus duodenal ulcer (DU). *Psychosomatic Medicine*, **44**, 121.

Schaeffer, G. (1966) Ergebnisse des autogenen Trainings bei der Colitis ulcerosa, in *IV World Congress of Psychiatry, 5–11, IX* (ed. J.J. Lopez Ibor), Excerpta Medica Foundation, International Congress Series No. 117, 48, Amsterdam.

Scheurer, U., Witzel, L., Halter, F. *et al.* (1977) Gastric and duodenal ulcer healing under placebo treatment. *Gastroenterology*, **72**, 838–41.

Schoenberg, P. (1983) An experience of ulcerative colitis. *British Journal of Psychiatry*, **143**, 517–48.

Schwartz, S.P. and Blanchard, E.B. (1991) Evaluation of a psychological treatment for inflammatory bowel disease. *Behaviour Research and Therapy*, **29**, 167–77.

Schwartz, S.P., Taylor, A.E., Scharff, L. and Blanchard, E.B. (1990) Behaviourally treated irritable bowel syndrome patients: a four-year follow-up. *Behaviour Research and Therapy*, **28**, 331–5.

Shaw, L. and Ehrlich, A. (1987) Relaxation training as a treatment for chronic pain caused by ulcerative colitis. *Pain*, **29**, 287–93.

Sheffield, B.F. and Carney, M.W.P. (1976) Crohn's disease: a psychosomatic illness? *British Journal of Psychiatry*, **128**, 446–50.

Snape, W.J., Carlson, G.M., Matarrazo, S.A. and Cohen, S. (1977) Evidence that abnormal myoelectrical activity produces colonic motor dysfunction in the irritable bowel syndrome. *Gastroenterology*, **72**, 383–7.

Stacher, G., Berner, P., Naske, R. *et al.* (1975) Effect of hyponotic suggestion of relaxation on basal and betazole-stimulated gastric acid secretion. *Gastroenterology*, **68**, 656–61..

Svedlund, J., Sjodin, I., Ottosson, J.O. and Dotevall, G. (1983) Controlled study of psychotherapy in irritable bowel syndrome. *Lancet*, **ii**, 589–92.

Switz, D.M. (1976) What the gastroenterologist does all day. *Gastroenterology*, **70**, 1048–50.

Talley, N.J., Zinsmeister, A.R., van Dyke, C. and Melton, L.J. (1991) Epidemiology of colonic symptoms and the irritable bowel syndrome. *Gastroenterology*, **101**, 927–34.

Taylor, J.A. (1953) A personality state of manifest anxiety. *Journal of Abnormal Psychology*, **48**, 285–90.

Thomas, J., Greig, M. and Piper, D.W. (1980) Chronic gastric ulcer and life events. *Gastroenterology*, **78**, 905–11.

Voirol, M.W. and Hipolito, J. (1987) Relaxation anthropoanalytique dans les syndromes de l'intestin irritable: resultats a 40 mois. *Schweizerische Medizinische Wochenschrift*, **117**, 1117–19.

Waller, S.L. and Misiewicz, J.J. (1969) Prognosis in the irritable bowel syndrome. *Lancet*, **ii**, 753–6.

Weinstock, H.I. (1962) Successful treatment of ulcerative colitis by psychoanalysts: a survey of 28 cases with follow-up. *Journal of Psychomatic Research*, **6**, 243.

Weinstock, S.A. (1976) The re-establishment of intestinal control in functional colitis. *Biofeedback and Self-Regulation*, **1**, 324.

Welch, G.W., Stace, N.H. and Pomare, E.W. (1984) Specificity of psychological profiles of irritable bowel syndrome patients. *Australian and New Zealand Journal of Medicine*, **14**, 101–4.

Welgan, P.R. (1974) Learned control of gastric acid secretions in peptic ulcer patients. *Psychosomatic Medicine*, **36**, 411–19.

Welgan, P.R. (1977) Biofeedback control of stomach acid secretions and gastrointestinal reactions, in *Biofeedback and Behaviour*, (eds J. Beatty and H. Legewie), Plenum, New York, pp. 385–94.

Whitehead, W.E. (1985) Psychotherapy and biofeedback in the treatment of irritable bowel syndrome, in *Irritable Bowel Syndrome*, (ed. N.W. Read), Grune and Stratton, London, pp. 245–63.

Whitehead, W.E. (1992) Behavioural medicine approaches to gastrointestinal disorders. *Journal of Consulting and Clinical Psychology*, **60**, 605–12.

Whitehead, W.E. and Drescher, V.M. (1980) Perception of gastric contractions and self-control of gastric motility. *Psychophysiology*, **17**, 552–8.

Whitehead, W.E. and Schuster, M.M. (1985) *Gastrointestinal Disorders. Behavioural and Physiological Basis for Treatment*, Academic Press, London.

Whitehead, W.E., Winget, C., Fedoravicius, A.S. *et al.* (1982) Learned illness behaviour in patients with irritable bowel syndrome and peptic ulcer. *Digestive Diseases Science*, **27**, 202–8.

Whitehead, W.E., Bosmajian, L., Zonderman, A.B. *et al.* (1988) Symptoms of psychologic distress associated with irritable bowel syndrome. Comparison of community and medical clinic samples. *Gastroenterology*, **95**, 709–14.

Whitehead, W.E., Engel, B.T. and Schuster, M.M. (1980) Irritable bowel syndrome: physiological and psychological differences between diarrhoea-predominant and constipation-predominant patients. *Digestive Diseases and Sciences*, **25**, 404–13.

Whitehead, W.E., Renault, P.F. and Goldiamond, I. (1975) Modification of human gastric acid secretion with operant-conditioning procedures. *Journal of Applied Behaviour Analysis*, **8**, 147–56.

Whorwell, P.J. (1989) Hypnotherapy in irritable bowel syndrome. *Lancet*, **1**, 622.

Whorwell, P.J., McCallum, M., Creed, F.H. and Roberts C.T. (1986) Non-colonic features of irritable bowel syndrome. *Gut*, **27**, 37–40.

Whorwell, P.J., Prior, A. and Colgan, S.M. (1987) Hypnotherapy in severe irritable bowel syndrome: further experience. *Gut*, **28**, 423–5.

Whybrow, P.C., Kane, F.J. Jr and Lipton, M.A. (1968) Regional ileitis and psychiatric disorder. *Psychosomatic Medicine*, **30**, 209–21.

Winship, D.H. (1978) Cimetidine in the treatment of duodenal ulcer: review and commentary. *Gastroenterology*, **74**, 402–6.

Wise, T.N., Cooper, J.N. and Ahmed, S. (1982) The efficacy of group therapy for patients with irritable bowel syndrome. *Psychosomatics*, **23**, 465–9.

Wolf, S. and Wolff, H.G. (1943) *Human Gastric Function: An Experimental Study of a Man and his Stomach*, Oxford University Press, Oxford and New York.

Youell, K.J. and McCollough, J.P. (1975) Behavioural treatment of mucous colitis. *Journal of Consulting and Clinical Psychology*, **43**, 740–5.

Young, S.J., Alpers, D.H., Norland, C.C. and Woodruff, R.A. Jr (1976) Psychiatric illness and the irritable bowel syndrome: practical implications for the primary physician. *Gastroenterology*, **70**, 162–6.

Chapter fourteen

Elderly care medicine

Nicola Bradbury

Introduction

The impact of the rapid increase in the numbers of elderly people in most developed countries can be regarded as a major challenge of the late 20th century. There has been a dramatic rise in the numbers of those surviving to over 75 years of age. Current projections envisage some 20% of the population by the end of the century being over 65, with an increasing build-up of the over 80s. As elderly people are, proportionally, heavy users of both health and social services, the financial consequences for the NHS are likely to be considerable. The lower age limit which defines 'old age' – conventionally retirement age – is becoming increasingly vague. Pressure of numbers, as well as the anticipation that many people experience relatively good health for the first decade or more following retirement, means that some services for elderly people deal only with those over 75 years. With increasing longevity, two generations of a family (elderly children and their even older parents) can fall into this category. Elderly patients will provide a continuing challenge in the field of elderly care medicine as the emphasis changes from keeping people alive to ensuring that a good quality of life is maintained into advanced old age.

In spite of the increasing numbers of elderly people within our society, old age appears to be surrounded by more misconceptions than any other phase of the lifecycle. This final stage tends to be perceived, by both young and old, as a time of negatively valued change. The fundamental element of ageism is the view that elderly people are in some way different from our present and future selves, and therefore do not have the same desires, concerns or fears. Even our attempts at humour show the existence of largely negative attitudes about elderly people, highlighting the 'double standard' of ageing. With the cultural emphasis on female physical attractiveness, society is much more permissive about ageing in men (Palmore, 1971; Sontag, 1978).

Perhaps some of the greatest misconceptions concerning the ageing process are associated with age-related changes in intellectual functioning. Up to the mid-1960s, a view of intellectual development was prevalent which placed a strong emphasis on the apparent decline in abilities from a peak in the 20–30 age range. This view saw overall intellectual decline in parallel with physical decline, and was in line with the expectations of the man-in-the-street who is likely to have an expectancy of reduced mental ability combined with strong negative views of elderly people. The past 20 years have seen a re-examination of these hypotheses and an increasing awareness that most of the traditional conclusions were derived from cross-sectional studies which confound the age variable with other factors, such as education, social and cultural influences, health care etc. More recent longitudinal studies suggest that the expectation of general decline in elderly people is not justified (Britton, 1983).

Similar misconceptions have surrounded personality change with age. In the 1960s two main themes emerged. One emphasized withdrawal from the environment – 'disengagement' – as a primary need in successful adjustment; the other emphasized the need for continued activity. Both theories have been subject to much analysis and criticism. The majority of studies contradict the disengagement theory, stressing that active elderly people have been consistently found to be happier than younger people (Woods and Britton, 1985). Investigations over the past 20 years or so have shown that the majority of elderly people (60–70%) are satisfactorily adjusted in old age, with a small but significant number who are extremely well adjusted. It also appears that great personality change is not a reasonable expectation in most elderly people.

The majority of professional carers of elderly people will have been socialized into a society where the myths and stereotypes surrounding old age go relatively unchallenged. Many studies point to antipathy towards elderly people on the part of professionals as well as the general public. In an American study, medical students were found to show more prejudice towards elderly people than towards minority racial groups, a prejudice which did not improve during medical school years (Spence, Feigenbaum and Fitzgerald, 1968). Similar antipathy has been found among students in social work, law and medicine (Geiger, 1978). In a study of applicants for training in clinical

psychology, Liddell and Boyle (1980) found that the prospect of work with elderly people did not seem at all appealing, and was among the lowest-rated areas. Studies have demonstrated that young adults expect the problems associated with old age to be far more serious than they are for the elderly people who actually experience them (Hendricks and Hendricks, 1981). It is essential that people providing services to elderly individuals are encouraged to look at their own attitudes to elderly people and are provided with accurate information about cognitive and personality changes associated with the ageing process.

The aim of this chapter is to look at the psychological and emotional needs of elderly people in receipt of medical care, whether as part of an elderly care service, in other hospital departments, nursing homes or primary care settings. The application of psychological research and techniques can help to maintain the elderly individual at his or her optimum level of functioning, both mentally and physically, and slow down or prevent further deterioration. The potential contribution of applied psychology in two main areas will be outlined:

1. Establishing a psychotherapeutic environment, both physical and social;
2. Working with individuals to help them cope better within their existing environment, by considering:
   - the interaction of physical and mental health problems with psychological functioning;
   - psychological therapy with older people;
   - help with bereavement;
   - encouraging good practices in systems of care provision.

Establishing a psychotherapeutic environment

The importance of environmental influences, both physical and social, on behaviour has been well established through psychological research. In designing environments for elderly people which will promote the optimum functioning and wellbeing of both patients and staff, a variety of psychological factors should be borne in mind.

Physical environment

Environmental organization

A number of studies have demonstrated how minor environmental changes in institutions, such as altering seating arrangements, providing recreational materials and reorganizing ward routines, can have quite profound psychological effects, such as increasing the levels of communication and purposeful activity of elderly people (Jenkins *et al.*, 1977; Melin and Gotestam, 1981).

The physical environment affects behaviour in complex and sometimes unpredictable ways. The common effect of ageing is to reduce the body's spare capacity for dealing with change. This increases the elderly person's dependence on the environment in its broader sense (Church, 1986). Sick elderly people are more affected by their environment than any other population. The feedback they receive from their surroundings becomes less reliable due to the reduced effectiveness of sensory organs. Their resources may be depleted because of failing health, death of friends and relatives, less social and emotional support, financial difficulties etc. They therefore have proportionally less energy available for personal change, and their impaired physical abilities make it extremely difficult for them to impose change on their environment.

Because the absolute level of resources of an elderly person is usually low, their environment should be planned to minimize the amount of energy and effort required to make sense of and negotiate it. This implies a minimum of constraints and barriers which inhibit action and reduce choice. The environmental needs of elderly people will vary between individuals, so there is a need for a variety of environments, for example within a ward. For instance, an elderly man who is seriously ill will only be marginally aware of his surroundings. His basic psychological need will be to feel safe and secure. Therefore, his bed should be positioned so that he can be regularly and easily observed by staff, and know that this is the case. With reduced dependency comes an increased need for stimulation and a growing need to control privacy.

The following are examples of age-related changes, relevant to the design of environments such as hospital wards for elderly people:

- Uncontrolled natural light and light from unbalanced artificial sources produces uncomfortable glare. Light can be arranged to avoid this by using several independent light sources, and/or avoiding large expanses of unshaded windows on sunny sides of buildings.
- Depth perception is affected. It can be difficult to judge treads going down a flight of stairs which is carpeted with a floral print or painted the same colour overall. Conversely, the boundary between a pale-coloured floor surface and a dark one is often misperceived as a step. It is important to avoid visual cues which may be misinterpreted.
- Auditory losses can mean the inability to hear conversation clearly if there is background noise, while parts of words in conversations are frequently unintelligible. Audition can be assisted by minimizing intrusive noise and avoiding soaking up too much of the available sound with thick curtains, carpets and acoustic tiles.
- Old people rely proportionately more on secondary cues such as smell, temperature change, noise and particularly touch for information about their environment. These cues could be utilized in ward design.

- Cognitive changes suggest that equipment should be as conventional as possible, and particular care should be taken to avoid materials and items which communicate conflicting sensory information. For instance, a plastic tumbler communicates 'glass' visually but something quite different through temperature, touch and sound. Non-slip floors should not look slippery, although they frequently do.
- The common fear frail elderly people have of walking means that distance deters, so facilities that patients use should be as close together as possible. Apparent distance can be reduced by avoiding long open vistas and providing potential props along the circulation ways. It is the perception of environmental features as hazardous that operates as a barriers to mobility. (For a more detailed account see Henneman, 1982.)

Reality orientation

Without orientation for time, place and person, organized behaviour is impossible. The environment, as well as the behaviour of other people, plays a crucial role in making this information available. Reality orientation (RO) is an approach to the management of confused elderly people which originated in the USA in the 1960s. An essential part of the therapy is the design of the environment so as to constantly remind elderly people of the information they need in order to remain orientated. In unfamiliar places we all use signs to guide us, watches or clocks to tell us the time, and a diary, calendar or newspaper for the date and current events. RO incorporates these and other common memory aids into the elderly person's environment. A display of personal belongings and mementos on a bedside locker will help an elderly person remember where they sleep. Large, clearly visible name badges on members of staff will help patients remember who other people are. There should be a large calendar board showing place, day,

month and year (changed daily) in day areas, which the patients should be encouraged to refer to. Different colour schemes in the bays will help with orientation to place, and doors should be clearly marked with, for example, all toilet doors being painted the same colour. Colour-coded lines on floors or walls leading to particular areas can be useful as long as there are not too many of them. These simple and inexpensive modifications can help to minimize the amount of effort required by an elderly person, confused or not, to make sense of and negotiate their hospital environment.

Principle of normalization

Although the internal design of accommodation is crucial in order to promote maximum functioning, elderly people's physical environment also includes the neighbourhood in which they live, the size and appearance of the buildings, access to shops, public transport and leisure facilities. A concept originally applied to other client groups but equally relevant to older people is the principle of normalization. This involves making available to service users patterns and conditions of life as close as possible to those normally valued by society. It is likely that this will be a lifestyle similar to the one the elderly person would have chosen had not illness or disability brought him or her into contact with service providers.

Normalization represents a rejection of the patterns of care that segregate disabled and handicapped people from the rest of the community (Woods and Britton, 1985). This principle is a foundation for planning and running services as well as a vantage point for judging service quality. Elderly people are at risk in our society of being thought 'less valuable' than others (CMH, 1981). Current thinking is that the application of the normalization principle to services for elderly people (particularly those services where acute medical treatments are not a major concern) is likely to provide the best quality of life available within the limitations of their disability.

Social environment

Staff–patient communication

It is not only the content of a health care service that affects elderly people and their carers. The process by which the service is delivered can be as important, if not more so, than the service outcome (Calnan and Williams, 1991). Every contact between a service provider and a service user contains a psychological component, and the interaction between them is the central factor in a quality service.

Nursing staff, as well as other professional and care staff, are a major part of the social environment for elderly people during a spell in hospital; for people whose stay is an extended one, and particularly for those who live permanently in hospital, the social relationships established with ward staff are particularly important. When elderly patients on long-stay wards were asked to identify the essential requirements of a good service, the personal attributes of nurses, e.g. attentiveness, cheerfulness and willingness to listen, were valued most highly (Fitzpatrick, 1992).

In addition to making a significant contribution to patient satisfaction, the behaviour of care staff can have a considerable influence on the behaviour and wellbeing of elderly patients. Their responsibilities involve not only meeting the physical needs of the elderly people in their care, but also being aware of and promoting their emotional and social needs. The relationship between staff and patients is crucial in helping to maintain a sense of identity, promoting self-esteem and ensuring the recognition of spiritual needs. Staff have an important role in facilitating the maintenance of social and family relationships, encouraging the continuation of leisure interests and ensuring access to privacy when appropriate. Elderly people need encouragement to gain confidence in their own abilities and to regain maximum independence (Royal College of Nursing, 1975). Unfortunately, a number of studies of staff–patient interactions have suggested that staff behaviour actively reinforces dependent rather than independent behaviour. A consequence of this is the tendency for elderly patients to become increasingly inactive. Engagement studies seem invariably to find high levels of inactivity on geriatric wards (Jeffrey, 1986).

Staff–patient patterns of verbal communication have been found to be potentially 'infantilizing', and there is evidence that, particularly in their care of dying patient, doctors and nurses use distancing tactics, such as false reassurances or showing a preference for dealing with physical rather than emotional problems (Maguire, 1985). Although these tactics may be obvious to an observer, medical and nursing staff are usually unaware that they are using them. These strategies to avoid getting too close and unleashing strong emotions like despair and anger are also likely to be evident on geriatric wards where, although perhaps not terminally ill, many patients will be experiencing strong negative feelings about themselves and the future.

A number of studies have suggested that medical and nursing staff working with elderly people need more emphasis in their training on psychological issues and the importance of the nature and style of their interactions with patients. If staff are to feel confident in opening up and maintaining an effective dialogue with patients, they must be trained in the relevant interviewing and counselling skills, as well as being provided with personal emotional support.

Reality orientation therapy

On any elderly care ward a significant number of patients are likely to be suffering from a degree of cognitive impairment. However, nursing staff have been found to interact significantly less with confused than with lucid patients (Armstrong-Esther and Browne, 1986). Training in reality orientation therapy, a basic, informal communication approach developed from reality orientation and used by many staff unknowingly, can provide staff will useful skills in caring for confused people (Holden and Woods, 1982).

Certain basic attitudes underlie the approach (individuality, dignity, self-respect, choice and independence), and the content and form of the communications are specifically adapted for confused elderly people. The aim is to use each interaction with elderly patients to give them basic information about who they are, who other people are, where they are, the time, day and date, and what is going on in their lives. The elderly person is encouraged to interact with his or her environment and, whenever possible, all senses are involved. Staff need to take into account the short attention span by frequently changing the content of the interaction but repeatedly returning to the presentation of basic information. Helping the person succeed is a major aim, and prompts or cues are given so that the patient is able to find the answer for him or herself. Part of the popularity of the approach is likely to be that it provides a positive and structured technique for relating to this group of patients, who can present such a challenge to nursing and medical staff.

Reminiscence

Reminiscing is certainly not an activity restricted to old age, but elderly people have accumulated many years of memories and have more of their lives behind them than there is to look forward to. At one time thinking about the past was regarded as positively unhealthy for elderly people, but over the past 20 years this view has changed. It is now recognized that the process of life review can help elderly people evaluate, understand and accept their lives.

There are, however considerable individual differences in the attitudes held by older people themselves towards reminiscence and its value in their lives. Some regard their memories as their most treasured possession, while for others the past is unimportant. Carers of elderly people need to understand from the elderly individual's perspective his or her life history and circumstances (Coleman, 1986).

Reminiscing is a rich experience distinguished from the memory of less personal information by the fact that it involves the process of reliving the past rather than the factual recall of historical events (Norris, 1986). It is suggested that reminiscing helps elderly people accept the passing of time and assists them to come to terms with their approaching death. In facilitating reminiscence, staff are encouraging the elderly person to concentrate on a period of their lives that is best remembered, a time when they were most likely to have been active, healthy and productive. Because of this, people who have memory problems, and those who are withdrawn or depressed, are more likely to enjoy participating in this activity than many others.

Reminiscing can help to enhance the elderly person's feeling of self worth by focusing on past achievements as well as providing the opportunity to share their experiences and wisdom. Staff members have the opportunity to learn more about their patients' past lives and the events which have shaped them as individuals, while sharing in a mutually enjoyable experience.

Helping individuals to cope better within their existing environment

Interaction of physical and mental health problems with psychological functioning

The challenge of coping with acute and chronic physical health problems is more likely to face those in later life. A number of physical disease processes have an impact on psychological functioning, therefore most health staff working with elderly people will have contact with individuals suffering from some kind of psychological disturbance.

Depression

The majority of elderly people adjust satisfactorily to old age (Woods and Britton, 1985). Changes in the locomotor, cardiovascular and respiratory systems may impose restrictions on activity but, unless these occur simultaneously, a reasonable level of functioning can be maintained. However, poor physical health has often been linked to the onset of depression in older adults. For some, health problems are compounded by economic and social difficulties, leading to a relatively passive and sterile existence.

Depression in elderly people is one of the health problems most frequently missed by general practitioners, perhaps because the typical depressive symptomatology overlaps with changes associated with the normal ageing process, e.g. alterations in sleep, appetite and physical health (Kline, 1976).

Stroke

Stroke affects nearly 100 000 new patients per year in England and Wales, with approximately two-thirds of sufferers surviving the acute episode (House, 1987). Emotional distress and instability, anxiety, frustration and depression are common problems after stroke and other chronic disabling illnesses (Binder, 1984). In addition to physical disability, stroke patients are likely to experience a variety of psychological problems arising from concerns about their present plight. These include feelings of loss of control, fears about death and disfigurement, social isolation, helplessness and worry about the loss of social roles.

Acute confusional state

Medical services will deal with many elderly people in whom physical illness causes or contributes to a change (usually temporary) in mental functioning. Acute confusional states are the most likely cause of cognitive changes in elderly people and, because they are generally reversible, should always be thoroughly investigated. They can, of course, occur superimposed on a pre-existing mental illness.

Frequently, an acute confusional state is an early symptom of an undetected physical disorder, e.g. severe constipation, malnutrition, urinary tract or chest infection. An acute confusional state can also be a side-effect of prescribed medication. Because the elderly body is much slower at breaking down many drugs, there is always a risk of them accumulating in the system to reach toxic levels. In addition, a sudden change in social situation or environment can put a vulnerable elderly person at risk of developing an acute confusional state. A move into a residential or nursing home, a bereavement or an admission to hospital are all potential triggers.

Management of the acute confusional state depends on identifying and, where possible, treating the underlying organic cause.

Dementia

In the past, all kinds of brain disorders in old people were given the blanket name 'senility'. However, it is now recognized that dementia is not one but a number of different diseases, in which the cells of the brain die more quickly than in normal ageing. The effects of dementia are predominantly psychological in nature, affecting the sufferer's emotional state, capacity to think, personality attributes and interpersonal relationships.

Dementia can attack people in middle age but, as with many diseases, it becomes progressively more common as age increases. It has been estimated that around 20% of the over-

80s suffer from dementia. These individuals may, of course, also be subject to the whole range of physical health problems which would bring them into contact with general medical and elderly care services.

Interventions

Assessment

Comprehensive assessment consists of accurate diagnosis and the identification of strengths and needs across the whole range of biological, social and psychological functioning. Elderly people often have complex needs requiring a simultaneous response from a number of services. Care should provide a regular pattern of support based on retained strengths. The pattern has to be meaningful within the old person's daily routine.

One of the most useful sources of information about elderly people and the ways in which they relate to their surroundings is their past. An elderly individual's ability to adjust to physical illness or disability, as well as the psychological responses that accompany it, will depend not only on the nature of the disability but also on his or her success at coping with major crises in earlier life.

With elderly people there is literally almost a lifetime of evidence potentially available as to their style of personality and the coping strategies, both cognitive and behavioural, that they employed in the past to help them get through times of change and stress. If these strategies can be identified, they can be used in helping the elderly person adjust to present circumstances (Woods and Britton, 1985). This evidence is best gathered through a continuous and gradual process by a single identified and trusted assessor, using the basic principles of 'getting to know you', i.e. frequent contacts of short duration employing a conversational rather than interrogative style. The result will be a biographical account or life story.

There are three main approaches to help in the identification of strengths and needs in the areas of personal care, activities of daily living and behavioural difficulties. Whenever possible, behavioural assessments should take place in the person's own home.

- Rating scales
- Direct observation in a structured setting
- Observation of the elderly's person behaviour in their usual environment. (For more detail, see Woods and Britton, 1985.)

An important factor in any behavioural assessment of elderly people is the interaction between biological and environmental variables. Hodge (1984) draws attention to the fact that it cannot be assumed that the patient has the neuropsychological capabilities necessary to be able to perform all the steps to achieve a behavioural target. It is pointless designing behavioural programmes for cognitively impaired elderly people without first undertaking an assessment of any neuropsychological function needed to achieve the final behavioural goal. A neurophysiological impairment may be the unidentified cause of an inexplicably slow response to rehabilitation. Often, information from a thorough neuropsychological assessment can be incorporated into a management or training programme for the patient, and it will always help staff, relatives and the elderly patients themselves to gain a better understanding of their behaviour and responses.

Psychometric assessment can help in gathering information about the strengths and needs of elderly people showing signs of cognitive impairment. The past few years have seen increasing interest in the construction of psychological tests appropriate for older people which draw on vastly increased knowledge in such areas as information processing and neuropsychology (Britton, 1983). The Kendrick Battery for the Detection of Dementia (Gibson and Kendrick, 1979) and the Clifton Assessment Procedure for the Elderly (Pattie and

Gilleard, 1979) are psychological tests designed specifically for older people in the UK. They both attempt to assist in the identification and monitoring of change, and have been found to have extensive applications.

Two more recently published assessment tools have been designed to offer a more detailed examination of the range of cognitive functions in older people. The Cambridge Mental Disorders of the Elderly Examination (CAMDEX) is an interview schedule for the diagnosis and measurement of dementia in elderly people and includes a mini neuro-psychological battery (Roth *et al.*, 1986). The Middlesex Elderly Assessment of Mental State (MEAMS) has been designed to differentiate between functional illnesses and organically based cognitive impairments (Golding, 1989). The MEAMS systematically assesses the major areas of cognitive performance using a range of subtests.

The assessment of depression in elderly people has also received considerable attention. A number of scales measuring morale, life satisfaction and wellbeing have been developed. Woods and Britton (1985) recommend Bigot's Life Satisfaction Scale (Bigot, 1974) and a depression scale (Schwab, Holzer and Warheit, 1973) as being particularly useful. The 30-item Geriatric Depression Scale (Brink *et al.*, 1982) requires a simple Yes/No response and has been found to distinguish between depressed and control groups.

In addition to assessing the elderly person themselves it is equally important to carry out an assessment of his or her support network, including the needs of any unpaid carers. An elderly person's ability to live in the community is more dependent on the sources of support available than on their degree of disability.

Psychological therapy with older people

Within elderly care medicine, psychological therapy is likely to be appropriate for individ-uals whose reaction to, or recovery from, a physical illness is impeded by emotional, cognitive or relationship difficulties. The triggers for referral for assessment for a variety of types of psychological intervention might include:

- Is the person more disabled by their medical condition than would normally be expected?
- Is the person's recovery particularly slow for no clearly identifiable reason?
- Is the individual excessively tearful, worried or anxious?
- Is the person withdrawn and uncommunicative?
- Does the individual complain of a lot of minor symptoms for which there is no apparent medical cause?
- Is the person behaving in ways which might suggest that his or her needs are not being met by the ward regime?
- Is the person consistently disorientated as to time, place or person?
- Does the individual have particular difficulty in remembering things?

Elderly people are subject to all the psychological problems experienced by adults of any age. These may be of recent origin or have developed prior to or during early adulthood. They may have problems such as eating disorders, drug dependence, family, marital or sexual difficulties. There is also evidence that some problems occur more often in later life. Loss and bereavement, although not unique to older people, happen more frequently to this age group. Although generally borne without professional help, problems can include abnormal grief, role-performance dysfunction and depression. In fact, it has been suggested that up to 50% of elderly people in the community have some degree of depression. Survey data indicate that symptoms of anxiety occur at more than twice the rate in elderly people than in young adults (Sallis and Lichstein, 1982).

As well as increasing in frequency with age, these problems seem to manifest themselves rather differently in older people. Sallis and Lichstein suggest that elderly people engage in more body monitoring than those in younger age groups. This 'heightened vigilance' leads to psychological distress over physical symptoms and a reaction which can be seen as a symptom phobia. In addition, there is evidence that depressed elderly people experience more somatic physiological symptoms than emotional 'psychological' ones (Hanley and Baikie, 1984).

At one time it was commonly thought that, although their behaviour could be modified through the use of appropriate reinforcement, elderly people were unable to respond to other forms of psychotherapy. However, many of the psychological approaches found to be effective with younger people have now been used with older adults, and there are many studies demonstrating the success of cognitive and psychodynamic therapies. In spite of this, it cannot be assumed that therapy can be carried out in exactly the same manner as with younger adults.

A number of factors have been identified which seem to increase the effectiveness of therapeutic work with elderly patients, (Church, 1983; 1986).

- Because of changes in both language ability and abstract thinking, a less interpretive approach is more appropriate for older people, with the therapist taking an active rather than a passive role.
- The therapist should be free of any prejudice against older people, and able to appreciate what goals might be important for someone who has 5 or 10 years of life left to them.
- It is suggested that therapy with elderly people should be time-limited, with flexibility in both the location and the length of sessions.
- The therapist needs to be aware of possible drug effects in elderly people, and physical factors which may exacerbate 'psychological' problems.

Provided these factors are taken into account, there would seem to be no justification for not offering older people access to the range of therapeutic facilities available to younger adults.

Loss and bereavement

Loss is very much a part of the life of elderly people. Older patients in hospital may have had to give up their home, have lost their independence or a part of their body, and will almost certainly have experienced a number of losses through death. An understanding of the process of grief, as well as personal comfort with the concept of death, would seem to be vital prerequisites for working with elderly people.

Examination of research evidence indicates that the grief of elderly people often differs from the pattern of grieving typical in younger persons. Extreme outbursts of despair and rage seem to be less common in old age, and it has been suggested that even sudden bereavement seems less devastating for elderly women than for younger widows. In one study, elderly widows consulted their GPs less than younger widows for psychological symptoms but were more likely to have reported complaints of aching back and joints, as well as a variety of somatic problems (Parkes, 1985).

Working through the tasks of grieving can present particular problems for elderly people (Worden, 1982). The tendency to maintain a 'stiff upper lip' and the view that any expression of strong emotion is a weakness may make it difficult for some elderly people to experience and heal the pain of loss. Older people whose cognition may be only mildly impaired may fail to remember that their partner is dead. Confrontation with the facts may produce extreme distress or outright denial. An individual who has limited mobility, restricted social contacts and few financial resources may find it almost impossible to adjust to an environment in which the deceased is missing (particularly following the death of a spouse), let alone re-invest emotional energy in another relationship.

It has been suggested that there are circumstances under which it is inappropriate to encourage an elderly person to face the tasks of grieving. The most important deciding factor is likely to be the quality of life that will result from the grieving process. The 'young old' will have time to come to terms with their loss and have a life to look forward to. Some forgetful old people can live in blissful ignorance of the fact that their partner has died, while others succeed in avoiding reminders of their lost spouse. Parkes (1985) puts forward the view that carers have no right to interfere with ways of coping that are helping the individual get through a very difficult chapter in their lives. However, if an elderly person's way of coping with bereavement is prolonging their misery, and the misery of those around them, then it is necessary to help them undertake those tasks of grieving which have previously been avoided.

Constructional approach

There has recently been a gradual but significant change in the role and practice of many of the caring professions, clinical psychology included, working with elderly people. This change has involved a move away from custodial care towards a more interventionist approach. Many forms of delivering care are based on a pathological approach, tending to concentrate on the difficulties or problems that a patient has (e.g. the nursing process). An alternative to this is the constructional approach, introduced by American psychologist Israel Goldiamond in the 1970s. Since then it has been further developed and now provides a sophisticated means of analysing and changing behaviour (Flemming, Barrow-clough and Whitmore, 1983).

This approach places great emphasis on increasing the client's behaviour or range of possible behaviours. The constructional approach does not ignore difficulties, but aims to help these by concentrating on developing new ways for the elderly person to behave. This approach assumes that the behaviours thought to be problem can be developed and used to help the person reach a specified objective. In other words, rather than extinguishing behaviours, more satisfying behaviours are developed.

Using this approach, the goal of treatment for a patient described by staff as being 'attention seeking' would not be to reduce the amount of contact between staff and the patient: in a poorly staffed institutional setting a desire for personal contact seems hardly unreasonable. The constructional approach might ensure that the patient receives the attention that he or she needs, but at times which are more convenient for staff members, and as a result of more appropriate behaviour.

Similarly, in the case of an elderly person who is described as a 'wanderer', the goal of treatment using the constructional approach would not be to ensure that the individual spent more time in one place. His or her mobility and energy could be directed towards more purposeful activity, such as helping staff with domestic tasks or being taken out for a walk.

Goal planning

The introduction of individual programme planning (IPP) to a number of handicapped groups has highlighted the value of identifying needs, not only in terms of skills deficits but also in terms of opportunities or provisions required. At the same time, clients' strengths are highlighted and can then be used as the basis from which to develop new skills or, in the case of elderly people, compensate for losses. Building on and emphasizing retained abilities can help the elderly individual experience success and the feeling of mastery over his or her world.

Goal planning with elderly people (Barrowclough and Flemming, 1985) involves an assessment of the individual's strengths and needs, designing and carrying out programmes which will enable those needs to be met and evaluating the effectiveness of the programmes. This is likely to involve helping elderly patients relearn lost skills, and also to increase opportunities to make use of their remaining skills.

Some characteristics of goal planning are:

- The client is involved as fully as possible;
- The plan is formulated in clear behavioural language, thus maximizing clarity and consistency of approach;
- It is broken down into a series of steps, each of which can be accomplished in a short period of time;
- Training for staff emphasizes a constructional approach to client need (Barrowclough and Flemming, 1985).

Systems approaches

Since the arguments against individual psychotherapy with elderly people were refuted (Church, 1983), a healthy interest has been taken in psychological therapy with older adults. However, the criticism that individual therapy is not cost-effective is as relevant to this client group as any other. Psychological approaches to individual patient care can be unsuccessful because staff are unable to use their psychological skills, or management programmes are not adhered to consistently. Intervention can be focused not only on the individual, but also on the setting in which the elderly person is receiving care. Increasingly, psychological techniques have been used to change systems of care provision which were not allowing or encouraging good care practices.

Georgiades and Phillmore (1975) have shown that staff training is a poor solution to the problem of changing care systems. 'Giving away' therapy skills is not enough: it is necessary to deal with the managerial and organizational factors which will help or inhibit care staff's use of these skills. To do this the change agent must become a facilitator or manager of organizational change, recognizing that problems are located not within an individual but within the pattern of relationships of which the individual is a part. Any action on one part of this human system will impinge on other parts of the system.

There are a number of factors thought to be essential to guide successful systems approaches to changing care practices:

- Large-scale permanent organizational change requires a timescale of years to achieve.
- Change agents must maintain their power within the system and ensure that those in positions of power are recruited to support and facilitate the change initiative.
- The change agent must maintain manoeuvrability, avoiding covert alliances or making powerful enemies.
- It is necessary to understand the rules of the 'game', i.e. acquire a knowledge of the political processes and map out the hierarchies and boundaries within the organization.
- Change agents need to learn how organizations change spontaneously and how to capitalize on this in planned change endeavours.
- A strategy and tactics for the implementation of change, based upon the systems analysis of the organization, must be planned and followed in a flexible fashion.
- There are particular skills of observation, analysis, interaction and persistence involved in being a successful change agent (Jeffrey, 1986).

Family therapy is another application of human systems theory found to be applicable to elderly people. The presenting problem, rather than being sited in the individual, is seen as being due to or maintained by interactions and relationships within the social network of which the person is a part. Family therapy techniques have been carried out with family members and with the network of care staff within institutional settings (Herr and Weakland, 1979).

Problems of compliance

Problems of compliance are certainly not unique to older people, but can be a cause of particular difficulty with this patient group. For many older adults, compliance with prescribed health care depends on how well the regimen fits in with their usual lifestyle and goals. Where there is a marked difference, a high risk of non-compliance can be predicted. More than any other single factor over which the clinician has control, the quality of the relationship with the patient affects compliance. Adherence is consistently higher if patients believe they have some say in treatment (Schaffer, 1981).

The use of medication by elderly people has received considerable attention. In the UK it is estimated that the over-65s are responsible for approximately 30% of NHS expenditure on prescriptions. The use of both prescribed and non-prescribed medicines increases with age, women taking more medicines than men (Adamson and Smith, 1978). Increasing forget-fulness, confusion, failing eyesight, multiple disabilities, poor manual dexterity, lack of understanding of treatment, suspicion and mis-trust of drugs or of those administering them, can all contribute towards a failure to maintain drug regimens as prescribed (Wade and Bowling, 1986).

Medication regimens for elderly people should always be as simple as possible, using the fewest possible drugs. Directions for use should also be simple but specific, using words patients understand and preferably relating to signposts in the patient's daily routine (e.g. mealtimes, getting up or going to bed).

Medication aids have been developed to help those patients who take several different types of drug every day. For example, the Dosett dispensing box displays up to a week's supply in a closed plastic container. Many carers make use of egg cups or envelopes.

One successful way of increasing patient compliance on discharge is the practice of encouraging patients to take responsibility for their own self-administration of medicines while still in hospital. This provides an opportunity to educate patients in drug use, to tailor regimens to suit individual requirements, and to identify those patients who are likely to fail to take their medication at home because of physical or mental impairment. Relatives and community services can then be alerted to the possibility of non-compliance.

Studies of non-compliance have led to the recommendation that medicines should be shown to the patient with an explanation of their purpose and any possible side-effects (Barrowclough and Pegg, 1982). Although there is little evidence that the use of written material makes a significant difference to compliance in this patient group, it is generally accepted that oral instructions should be backed up with written instructions (Parish, Doggett and Colleypriest, 1983) (see also Ley and Llewelyn, this volume).

Summary

Over recent years, psychological studies of ageing individuals have provided us with a more positive and accurate picture of the ageing process. Health psychology is taking an increasing interest in applying its theories and skills to older people. Many of these applications are relevant to the provision of elderly care services.

It has been found that many of the psychological approaches developed for use with younger people are equally relevant to elderly patients, bearing in mind the special needs of this age group. Taking into account psychological factors in the design of living environments will promote optimum functioning in disabled elderly people. An awareness of the psychological needs of elderly patients and their carers and some expertise in the use of basic psychotherapeutic skills will enable health service staff to provide an improved level of care. Psychological intervention with the system of care provision will help to ensure that good care practices are permitted and encouraged.

The application of psychological knowledge and techniques can make a major contribution to the maintanance of a good quality of life in old age, in spite of illness or disability.

References

Adamson, K.A. and Smith, D.L. (1978) Non-prescription drugs and the elderly patient. *Canadian Pharmaceutical Journal*, **111**, (3), 80–5.

Armstrong-Esther, C.A. and Browne, K.D. (1986) The influence of elderly patients' mental impairment on nurse–patient interaction. *Journal of Advanced Nursing*, **11**, 379–87.

Barrowclough, C. and Flemming, I. (1985) *Goal Planning with Elderly People*, Manchester University Press, Manchester.

Barrowclough, F. and Pegg, M. (1982) Why don't they comply? *Nursing Mirror*, **155**, 32–3.

Bigot, A. (1974) The relevance of American life satisfaction indices for research on British subjects before and after retirement. *Age and Ageing*, **3**, 113–21.

Binder, L.M. (1984) Emotional problems after stroke. *Stroke*, **15**(1), 174–7.

Brink, T.L., Yesavage, J.A., Lum, O. *et al.* (1982) Screening tests for geriatric depression. *Clinical Gerontologist*, **1**, 37–43.

Britton, P.G. (1983) Psychology services for the elderly, in *The Practice of Clinical Psychology in Great Britain*, (ed. A. Liddell), John Wiley and Sons, Chichester, pp. 171–85.

Calnan, M. and Williams, S. (1991) Please treat me nicely. *Health Service Journal*, 17 January.

Campaign for People with Mental Handicap (1981) *The Principle of Normalisation: A Foundation for Effective Services*, CMH, London.

Church, M. (1983) Psychological therapy with elderly people. *Bulletin of the British Psychological Society*, **36**, 110–12.

Church, M. (1986) Issues in psychological therapy with elderly people, in *Psychological Therapies for the Elderly*, (eds I. Hanley and M. Gilhooly), Croom Helm, London, pp. 1–21.

Coleman, P. (1986) Issues in the therapeutic use of reminiscence with elderly people, in *Psychological Therapies for the Elderly*, (eds I. Hanley and M. Gilhooly), Croom Helm, London, pp. 41–64.

Fitzpatrick, B. (1992) Exploring patient advocacy. *Times Health Supplement*, November, 7–8.

Flemming, I., Barrowclough, C. and Whitmore, B. (1983) The constructional approach. *Nursing Mirror*, **156**(23), 21–3.

Geiger, D.L. (1978) How future professionals view the elderly: a comparative analysis of social work, law and medical students' perceptions. *Gerontologist*, **18**, 591.

Georgiades, N. and Phillmore, L. (1975) The myth of the hero innovator and alternative strategies for organizational change, in *Behaviour Modification with the Severely Retarded*, (eds C. Kiernon and P. Woodford), Associated Scientific Publishers, New York, pp. 313–19.

Gibson, J.A. and Kendrick, D.C. (1979) *The Kendrick Battery for the Detection of Dementia in the Elderly*, NFER Publishing Company, Windsor.

Golding, E. (1989) *The Middlesex Elderly Assessment of Mental State*, Thames Valley Test Company, Fareham.

Hanley, I. and Baikie, E. (1984) Understanding and treating depression in the elderly in *Psychological Approaches to the Care of the Elderly*, (eds I. Hanley and J. Hodge), Croom Helm, London, pp. 213–36.

Hendricks, J. and Hendricks, C.D. (1981) *Ageing in Mass Society: Myths and Realities*, 2nd edn, Winthrop Publishers, Cambridge, Mass.

Henneman, L. (1982) *Short Manual Discussing Psychological Factors in the Design of Environments for the Elderly Sick*, Evaluation and Services Development Team, Southernhay East, Exeter.

Herr, J. and Weakland, J. (1979) *Counselling Elders and Their Families*, Springer, New York.

Hodge, J. (1984) Towards a behavioural analysis of dementia, in *Psychological Approaches to the Care of the Elderly*, (eds I. Hanley and J. Hodge), Croom Helm, London, pp. 61–87.

Holden, U.P. and Woods, R.T. (1982) *Reality Orientation*, Churchill Livingstone, Edinburgh.

House, A. (1987) Mood disorders after stroke: a review of the evidence. International Journal of Geriatric Psychiatry, **2**, 211–21.

Jeffrey, D.P. (1986) The systems approach to changing practice in residential care, in *Psychological Therapies for the Elderly*, (eds I. Hanley and M. Gilhooly), Croom Helm, London, pp. 124–50.

Jenkins, J., Felce, D., Barry, L. and Powell, L. (1977) Increasing engagement in activity in old people's homes by providing recreational material. *Behaviour, Research and Therapy*, **15**, 429–34.

Kline, N. (1976) Incidence, prevalence and recognition of depressive illness, in *Disease of the Nervous System*, 37(3), 10–14.

Liddell, A. and Boyle, M. (1980) Characteristics of applicants to the MSc in Clinical Psychology at NELP. *DCP Newsletter No. 30*, 20–5.

Maguire, P. (1985) Barriers to psychological care of the dying. *British Medical Journal*, **291**, 1711–13.

Melin, L. and Gotestam, K.G. (1981) The effects of rearranging ward routines on communication and eating behaviours of psychogeriatric patients. *Journal of Applied Behaviour Analysis*, **14**, 47–51.

Norris, A. (1986) *Reminiscence with Elderly People*, Winslow Press, London.

Palmore, E. (1971) Attitudes to ageing as shown by humour. *Gerontologist*, **11**(3), 181–6.

Parish, P., Doggett, M. and Colleypriest, M. (1983) *The Elderly and their Use of Medicines*, King's Fund, London.

Parkes, C. Murray (1985) Bereavement in the elderly. *Geriatric Medicine Today*, **4**, 5.

Pattie, A.H. and Gilleard, C.T. (1979) *The Clifton Assessment Procedures for the Elderly*, Hodder and Stoughton, Sevenoaks.

Roth, M., Tym, E., Moutjoy, C.Q. *et al.* (1986) CAMDEX. *British Journal of Psychiatry*, **149**, 698–709.

Royal College of Nursing (1975) *Improving Geriatric Care in Hospital*, RCN, London.

Sallis, J.F. and Lichstein, K.L. (1982) Analysis and management of geriatric anxiety. International *Journal of Ageing and Human Development*, **15**(3), 197–211.

Schaffer, J.B. (1981) Getting elderly patients to eat properly. *Geriatrics*, **36**(10), 76–82.

Schwab, J.J., Holzer, C.E. and Warheit, G.J. (1973) Depressive symptomatology and age. *Psychosomatics*, **14**, 135–41.

Sontag, S. (1978) The double standard of ageing, in *An Ageing Population*, (eds V. Carver and P. Liddiard), Hodder and Stoughton, London, pp. 72–80.

Spence, D., Feigenbaum, E. and Fitzgerald, F. (1968) Medical students' attitudes towards the geriatric patient. *Journal of the American Geriatric Society*, **16**, 976.

Wade, B. and Bowling, A. (1986) Appropriate use of drugs by elderly people. *Journal of Advanced Nursing*, **11**(9), 47–55.

Worden, W. (1982) *Grief Counselling and Grief Therapy*, Tavistock Publications, London.

Woods, R.T. and Britton, P.G. (1985) *Clinical Psychology with the Elderly*, Croom Helm, London.

Chapter fifteen

Gynaecology

Myra Hunter

Introduction

Women attending gynaecological clinics experience particularly high rates of psychological distress and psychiatric morbidity (Ballinger, 1977; Worsley, Walters and Wood, 1977; Byrne, 1984). Such high levels of psychological distress may be understood in terms of the generally higher prevalence rates of distress in women (Briscoe, 1982), together with the finding that people seeking medical help have been shown to suffer from a considerable degree of emotional distress (Moffic and Paykel, 1975).

People seek medical help for complex reasons. There is a growing body of evidence to suggest that psychosocial stress and the perception of one's own general health are factors which discriminate more strongly between clinic attenders and non-attenders than illness *per se* (Tessler, Mechanic and Dimond, 1976; Mechanic, 1980).

Psychological explanations of sex differences in psychological distress also emphasize increased psychosocial stress associated with female roles as well as differences in socialization and possible differences in expression of distress. It seems plausible that some women who attend gynaecological clinics may be expressing a latent need, using a particular channel of complaint, about their lives and psychosocial position. In contrast, biological explanations tend to link high rates of distress

with hormonal changes, for example during menstruation, postpartum and during the menopause (see Dalton, 1977).

Gynaecology emerged as a separate specialty of medicine during the early part of this century. Prior to then general surgeons were responsible for major gynaecological problems. This may explain why gynaecology was and still is considered to be primarily a surgical specialty. Psychoanalytic and feminist writers suggest that it may be no accident that surgery has been used so extensively by physicians to remove female organs (Horny, 1932; Weideger, 1978).

Clearly, there appears to be a mismatch between the types of problems brought to gynaecologists and the general approaches used in gynaecological treatment. Beard, a leading gynaecologist, acknowledges that: 'gynaecologists see a large number of women with complaints that do not have their origin in recognized forms of pathology' (Beard, 1984). For example, two of the most commonly reported presenting symptoms, menorrhagia and pelvic pain, are frequently associated with distress but are without known organic pathology. These conditions may result in surgical intervention when a psychological approach may be a viable alternative (Pearce, Knight and Beard, 1982; Greenberg, 1983).

This chapter argues that a shift towards the psychological understanding of gynaecological problems is needed. Gynaecology is now recognized as an area in which psychology or behavioural medicine may have a useful contribution (Broome, 1980; Broome and Wallace, 1984; Ussher, 1992; Hunter, 1993).

In the following sections gynaecological problems are discussed in three major subgroups, based on the relevant psychological issues common among the various types of presenting problems and interventions. First, a considerable proportion of consultations are brief contacts or 'acute interventions' in that they involve consultation and possible physical examination, decision-making and perhaps surgical intervention. Under the heading of acute interventions, contraception, sterilization, termination of pregnancy and hysterectomy will be included as examples. The second group, 'chronic problems', usually involves continuing consultation, chronic distress and sometimes a series of interventions. Under this heading the psychological contribution to our understanding of pelvic pain, cancer, infertility, sexual problems and menorrhagia will be discussed. Finally, menstruation and the menopause will be discussed in the context of normal development, with reference to problems which may occur during the lifecycle. There will obviously be some overlap between these three sections, but the selective review will provide examples of major contributions made so far.

Psychological contributions to gynaecological problems

Acute interventions

Communication between doctors and patients is often hampered by use of jargon, complexity, inappropriate amounts of information, anxiety, forgetting and incompatible explanations of the presenting problem (Ley, 1977, 1982; see also Ley and Llewelyn, this volume).

Gynaecological consultations may be particularly prone to communication problems, for several reasons. First, all the patients are women and the majority of gynaecologists are men. The presenting problem is often considered private or embarrassing or a taboo subject, e.g. sexual life or menstruation. Second, vaginal examination is frequently a routine part of an initial visit. Many women experience embarrassment, considerable anxiety and feelings of degradation on undergoing vaginal examination (Osokosky, 1967; Magee, 1975; Areskog-Wijma, 1987), leading in a proportion of women to phobic avoidance of subsequent consultations (Reading, 1982). If embarrassment and anxiety are associated with the presenting problem, and with vaginal examination, then information may not be retained and decisions may be made without adequate consideration. Quite simple procedural changes have been shown to alleviate some of these problems, for example structuring and simplifying written and verbal information (Ley, 1977). In more complex cases, when anxiety is more intense, relaxation and desensitization could be used. Reading (1982) described the successful treatment of a woman suffering from fear of vaginal examination using these methods together with cognitive restructuring. In another study, Fuller, Endress and Johnson (1978) showed that relaxation in combination with sensory information resulted in less distress for women undergoing vaginal examination than did information alone.

Two additional problems met during consultations are more difficult to address. First, gynaecologists of both sexes may find certain problems and/or vaginal examinations quite stressful themselves, and may not have the opportunity to learn how to cope with their own feelings. Coping strategies may help the doctor, for example by distancing him or herself from the patient, but make it more difficult for the patient to feel at ease. In a recent survey, Areskog-Wijma (1987) found that only 4% of women awaiting a gynaecological examination preferred a male doctor; 42% preferred a female doctor and 54% did not mind either sex. If given no choice, then they preferred an older man. Women wished to be met on an equal footing with warmth and respect. Clearly, these women found young male doctors most threatening, but did want to be treated less formally.

The second problem, which is not specific to gynaecology, is that of discordant expectations about the consultation, the nature of the problem and its outcome. As discussed earlier there are various hypotheses available to both doctor and patient about the causes of symptoms, ranging from biological, hormonal, 'time of life', age and psychological stress to social problems. The impact of the patient's own explanations of their illness, and the implications of discordant doctor–patient explanations upon subsequent treatment decisions are important areas for future research.

The psychologist's major contribution to the area of acute intervention has been to provide information and coping strategies to deal with the actual procedure of surgery. Before describing this work it seems appropriate to describe some recent work investigating the decision-making processes leading up to the intervention. Also, attempts to identify and help women who may be at risk of longer-term emotional sequelae will be discussed.

Decision-making, risk factors and counselling

Beliefs that gynaecological interventions lead to considerable emotional reactions were prevalent in the early literature, assuming loss of femininity and emotional and sexual problems. However, better controlled studies carried out in the past 20 years have found that for most women suffering may at its most be short-lived, with a good long-term prognosis. For example, few serious psychological problems have been found following termination of pregnancy (Greer et al., 1976; Adler et al., 1990; Donnai, Charles and Harris, 1981) and many women

actually feel relief (Shusterman, 1979). A small proportion, estimated at 0–10%, do have some longer-term emotional disturbance. Several factors have been identified as predictors of subsequent emotional problems (Dunlop, 1978; Shusterman, 1979). (Table 15.1)

Clearly, social support and previous emotional problems are important. However, psychological processes involved in the decision to terminate are increasingly being emphasized. Women who are very ambivalent or feel pressure from others, e.g. coercion either for or against the decision, or lack of control over the decision because of medical reasons, may require further counselling. Women appear to seek support for their decisions from others, particularly other females (Allen, 1982).

Counselling may therefore actually provide an opportunity for a woman to weigh up the costs and benefits of the decision and to gain support for her own decision, involving her partner if possible. There is some evidence that counselling can improve satisfaction and support for the decision to terminate the pregnancy (Marcus, 1979). However, in this study future contraception or termination behaviour was not improved. Identification of those at risk and who need follow-up counselling would appear to be a sensible approach, but requires further study.

Tubal sterilization is one of the most popular forms of contraception for women who have completed their families. The majority of women suffer no ill effects in terms of psychiatric problems (Smith, 1979; Cooper et al., 1982). Improvements in sexual functioning have generally been reported (Alder et al., 1981; Cooper et al., 1982). Couples' satisfaction with previous contraception as well as selection procedures and counselling will obviously influence rates of emotional sequelae. Around 5% are estimated to regret the sterilization operation (Schwyhart and Kutner, 1973). Factors associated with dissatisfaction and emotional problems are shown in Table

15.1. Regret was particularly linked to decision-making factors. For example, sterilization for medical reasons and perceived coercion from doctors, spouse and family. The success rates of reversal following sterilization vary depending on the original surgery performed, with estimates ranging between 35% and 77% for tubal ligation, and more optimistic figures, 78–100%, for Falope ring or clip method. Women requesting reversal of sterilization were examined in a controlled study by Leader et al. (1981). These women tended to be younger than the women who were satisfied with their sterilization, and they tended to have been sterilized at the time of a termination of pregnancy or caesarean section. Reviewing the reasons for reversal, Lambers, Trimbos-Kemper and Van Hall, (1984) found that regret frequently followed a life change, e.g. change in relationship, death of a child, or attribution of other problems to the sterilization. Here again, counselling is recommended before the event in order to clarify decision-making, provide information and to examine possible external pressure. Women or couples who appear to be at risk, but who appear clear in their decision, could still be offered follow-up counselling. Factors influencing reproductive decision-making are discussed further by Christopher (1991) and Porter (1991).

Hysterectomy is one of the most commonly performed operations in gynaecology. Van Keep, Wildermeersch and Lehert, (1983) carried out a survey of 2066 women aged between 40 and 70 years in six European countries. On average, 11.4% had had a hysterectomy (the figures were 13.2% for the UK, 15.5% in Italy and 8.5% in France). The likelihood of women now aged 30 years having a hysterectomy by the age of 65 years was estimated at 21%. These figures have increased over time, but are estimated to be appreciably lower than those for USA and Australia, where twice as many hysterectomies are performed (Dennerstein and Ryan, 1982). The major reasons for hysterectomy are usually dysfunctional uterine bleeding, followed by fibroids and then malignant disease (Kincey and McFarlane, 1984).

Hysterectomy has long been associated with undesirable consequences, such as sexual, emotional and physical problems, including premature ageing and reduced femininity (see the

TABLE 15.1 Predicting emotional reactions following acute interventions

Intervention	Risk factors
Termination of pregnancy	Pressure/coercion in decision-making Previous psychiatric conditions Medical reasons for termination (Dunlop, 1978) Anger on discovering pregnancy Low intimacy with partner Dissatisfaction with termination decision (Shusterman, 1979)
Tubal sterilization	Previous psychiatric history (Cooper et al., 1982) Medical indications (Benjamin, Rubinstein and Kleinkopf, 1980) Multiparity and youth (Lambers, Trimbos-Kemper and van Hall, 1982) Perceived coercion from others (Leader et al., 1981)
Hysterectomy	Previous psychiatric history (Gath, Cooper and Day, 1982) Parity, age Expectations, beliefs, decision-making (Dennerstein, Wood and Burrows, 1977; Tsoi, Poon and Ho, 1983) Lack of social support (Webb and Wilson-Barnett, 1983)

review by Dennerstein and Ryan, 1982). Methodological problems abound in this area of research, possibly leading to an over-estimation of expected psychological problems in earlier retrospective studies.

In a recent prospective study Gath and co-workers (Gath and Cooper, 1981; Gath, Cooper and Day, 1982) found a decrease in psychiatric disorders, mainly neurotic depression, following hysterectomy performed for menorrhagia. The women in this study were suffering from severe menorraghia and had waited some time for operation. Symptomatic relief may have inflated the difference between pre- and postoperative assessments, and perhaps masked any smaller negative effects. A strikingly high rate of psychiatric disorder (58%) was identified preoperatively, which reduced to 29% 18 months postoperatively. Martin *et al.* (1980), in a prospective study, found no change in scores before and after hysterectomy. Both studies demonstrated that emotional state preoperatively was the best predictor of emotional problems after the operation (i.e. predictors of longer-term psychological problems, rather than short-term reactions to the operation, which are discussed in the next section). Other predictors have also been suggested, as shown in Table 15.1, including age, parity and absence of a perceived supportive social network.

Psychologists have begun to focus upon the effects of knowledge, expectations and beliefs about hysterectomy. Whether it is perceived as a loss, a relief, or whether fertility is an issue at that life stage may modify an individual's interpretation of the event. Dennerstein and Ryan (1982) and Tsoi, Poon and Ho (1983) both describe misconceptions and fears about what the operation will involve and its impact on self-concept and sexual life. Negative expectations of the operation predicted poor outcome in relation to sexual problems (Dennerstein, Wood and Burrows, 1977), and thus beliefs may be fulfilled. Further study of cognitive fac-

tors and differences in the personal impact of hysterectomy is needed. As well as providing adequate information about the operative procedures (see next section), it seems vital to provide the opportunity for information and discussion earlier in the decision-making process, in order to give time for consideration of expectations, beliefs about hysterectomy and, more importantly, the decision as to whether to have the operation. The symptom of menorrhagia, which commonly results in hysterectomy, will be discussed under the heading of chronic conditions.

Preparation studies apart, there is a lack of research on the effects of interventions for women who appear to be at risk. It would seem reasonable to recommend both gynaecological and psychological involvement for these women, and there is some evidence that a preoperative counselling session is valued by patients (Wilson-Barnett, Webb and Gould, 1982). An operation involving hospitalization may provide an opportunity to re-evaluate existing problems, and in some cases the surgery may become a focus for existing problems. Postoperative counselling may help women for whom hysterectomy has a particular impact, with implications for self-concept and future plans. Marteau and Johnston (1987) make an obvious but relevant statement when they emphasize the importance of the general context of the patient's life when considering the impact of surgical interventions.

Preparation for surgical interventions

Surgical interventions are commonly associated with anxiety and uncertainty prior to, during and for variable intervals after the operation. There is consistent evidence that preoperative anxiety is associated with postoperative anxiety, as well as postoperative pain and recovery (Johnston and Carpenter, 1980; Wallace, 1984). By providing information preoperatively, psychologists and others have attempted to decrease pre- and postoperative anxiety and facilitate recovery (Wilson-Barnett, 1991; and see Kincey, this volume).

In general, the results of preoperation studies seem favourable (see reviews by Ley, 1977; Matthews and Ridgeway, 1981). Certain methodological problems are common in this area of research, such as different types of operation and hospitals used, failure to control for placebo effects, focus on brief timescale before and after operation and lack of acknowledgement of individual fears and misconceptions (Wallace, 1984). Undergoing an operation is a process which may last several months or more, with possible long-term effects on health and lifestyle. Preparation studies frequently fail to emphasize the importance of the meaning of the outcome of the operation. Not surprisingly, Wallace (1983) found that fears about laparoscopy differed for those women seeking sterilization and those seeking fertility information.

Providing procedural information to women undergoing minor gynaecological surgery, for example laparoscopy, has produced mixed results (Reading, 1979; Hewson, 1979; Wallace, 1984). Reading (1979) found only a non-significant improvement in postoperative measures using verbal procedural information, compared to an attention control. Written information was found to be superior to verbal information in reducing preoperative anxiety (Hewson, 1979). In Wallace's well designed study (1983), patients given a detailed information booklet preoperatively reported significantly less anxiety and pain and recovered more rapidly on behavioural measures than women receiving routine care or routine care plus reassuring information. The experimental group of women were also more satisfied and reported more accurate expectations and fewer worries than the controls. No beneficial effects were demonstrated on medication usage or length of hospital stay. These variables appeared to be determined more by

hospital policy than patient variables. Detailed information therefore seems to produce more significant results. In an earlier study, Johnson and Leventhal (1974) found that adding information about sensory changes enhanced the effect of procedural information.

Procedural information alone may be less effective in alleviating postoperative distress in major gynaecological surgery, for example hysterectomy.

Ridgeway and Matthews (1982) compared procedural information with a booklet concentrating on cognitive coping given to women undergoing elective hysterectomy. They found that these preparations produced differential effects: information about surgery increased knowledge and satisfaction ratings, whereas cognitive coping had the most effect on indices of recovery, i.e. fewer analgesics and less pain. Patients in the latter group also reported fewer worrying thoughts. Again, neither intervention influenced length of hospital stay. As discussed in the previous section, there are psychosocial variables which may contribute to the level of distress experienced following major surgery. Cognitive coping strategies may be particularly useful in alleviating distress associated with misconceptions and worries about hysterectomy. An approach which is sensitive to the particular fears associated with each operation is advocated (Johnston, 1982; Wallace, 1984).

In addition, there is evidence suggesting that preparation may be most effective if tailored to the patient's preferred coping style. Miller and Mangan (1983) found an interaction between coping style (blunters vs monitors) and response to information in a group of women undergoing colposcopy. This finding was supported by Steptoe and O'Sullivan (1986) in a mixed gynaecological sample.

In conclusion, preparation, particularly that providing realistic expectations, does appear to have an impact on postoperative measures of distress and recovery. The benefits of these effects could be more pervasive if hospital regimes could be helped to increased sensitivity to patient's subjective states, for example pre-operative fear and postoperative pain levels. In view of the increased sensitivity of women in recognizing other patients' concerns (Johnston, 1982), the use of support groups could enhance the effects of psychological preparation both pre- and postoperatively.

Chronic problems

Under this heading are problems presenting particular difficulties, for example in diagnosis and/or treatment. Psychological contributions to problems of chronic pelvic pain, gynaecological cancer, psychosexual difficulties, infertility and menorrhagia are discussed

Chronic pelvic pain

This is a very commonly presented gynaecological problem, often leading to surgical treatment. Beard, Belsey and Lieberman (1977) suggest that, because of the difficulty in detecting organic conditions, it is generally appropriate to consider psychological factors in treatment. In a series of studies, Pearce has investigated psychological interventions aimed at alleviating chronic pelvic pain. In the study reported by Pearce, Knight and Beard (1982), relaxation training was compared with behavioural counselling and non-directive counselling: 32 patients with chronic pelvic pain (without obvious organic pathology, of at least 6 months' duration) were assigned to three treatment groups and a no-treatment control. All three treatment groups achieved significant increases in pain-free days at 3 months post-treatment. However, this was most marked for the non-directive counselling group. At 12-month follow-up, the relaxation group and the non-directive counselling group continued to improve. No significant changes in pain ratings were observed in the control condition. Although small numbers of patients were used

and the effective components in treatment are difficult to discern, this study offers a useful starting point for further application of psychological treatments. In a subsequent study two cognitive – behavioural treatments were compared, one offering stress management and relaxation, the other aimed at modifying the specific antecedents and consequences of pain. Improvements were evident for both treatment groups in terms of mood, pain intensity and behavioural disruption to daily life, when compared with a minimal intervention control condition (Pearce, 1989). Presenting such treatments to patients requires careful preparation and close collaboration between psychologist and gynaecologist, in order to encourage a multimodal model of pain. Patients with a determined physiological attribution of pain may be more difficult to engage in such treatment.

Gynaecological cancers

The endometrium is the most common site for gynaecological cancer, occurring mainly in peri- and postmenopausal women, followed by cancer of the cervix, the ovary and the vulva (Andersen and Andersen, 1986). Cervical cancer occurs throughout a wide age range, but the incidence worldwide had declined in response to early detection of the preinvasive phase of the disease.

Although ovarian cancer is relatively rare, detection is difficult because women are frequently asymptomatic. With early diagnosis and aggressive therapy, two-thirds of these women will survive for at least 5 years. However, the distress experience during the process of diagnosis and treatment is considerable. Marteau (1989, 1990) has drawn attention to the potential psychological costs of screening and suggests ways of reducing these, emphasizing the provision of information, choice and research to monitor the procedures involved in screening. In a detailed study of women's experiences of cervical screening and follow-up investigations,

Posner and Vessey (1988) revealed a range of reactions, including considerable distress, anxiety and embarrassment. Once again, consideration of psychological and social factors was recommended, such as the need for privacy, clear explanation and support.

Given the importance of early detection of cancer, women's initial appraisal of symptoms has been examined. A common misinterpretation of irregular bleeding, one of the commonest early signs, was that it was a sign of the menopause and delay in seeking medical help was associated with this attribution (Cochran, Hacker and Berek, 1986). Once cancer is diagnosed, intense depression and emotional confusion are generally experienced. Given the uncontrollability of the event, the frequent difficulty in locating a cause, the associated pain and long-term implications, it is not surprising that depression is the major emotional reaction. The effect of cancer and its treatment on sexual functioning has perhaps received most attention. Andersen and Andersen (1986) found that even in the early stages, 75% of women with cervical or endometrial cancer reported sexual dysfunction. These authors also compared women during treatment for cancer with women with benign gynaecological disease in a prospective study. They found a significant difference between groups in sexual behaviour but not in sexual desire (Andersen and Andersen, 1986). Not surprisingly, major sexual difficulties are common in women undergoing radical pelvic surgery particularly vulvectomy, with estimates ranging between 70 and 90% (Andersen and Hacker, 1983; Tamburini et al., 1986). Preliminary results suggest that information and psychosexual counselling made available both before and after radical surgery may reduce the frequency of these sexual problems (Lamont, Depetrillo and Sargeant, 1978; Capone et al., 1980).

A final area of research has focused on women's reactions to specific treatments, mainly chemotherapy and radiotherapy. Side-effects,

notably nausea and vomiting, hair loss, lowered energy and appetite, are reported following chemotherapy. Experience of side-effects can lead in some cases to anticipatory conditioned reactions, for example nausea and vomiting, to the hospital or time of appointment, and to non-compliance with treatment. Psychological interventions based on relaxation and imagery (Lyles et al., 1982), hypnosis and relaxation (Redd, Andresen and Minagawa, 1982), and systematic desensitization (Morrow and Morrell, 1982) have been found to reduce anxiety and, in some cases, the severity of nausea (Lyles et al., 1982).

Patients undergoing radiation therapy frequently report fears of damage, pain, burning and sterility; as well as distress and physical side-effects (King et al., 1985). Interventions aimed at alleviating distress and reducing fears have included the provision of detailed procedural information (Israel and Mood, 1982; Rainey, 1985) and psychosexual advice (Karlsson and Andersen, 1986). Since radiation leads to ovarian dysfunction, women often become postmenopausal experiencing hot flushes and vaginal dryness and, obviously, infertility. Preparation for and advice about these effects may be overlooked.

Although research has generally focused on specific treatments and specific reactions, the need for general counselling of women who face such personal loss is acknowledged (see Fallowfield 1991; Watson 1993). Hospital staff may also require regular discussions of their clinical work if they are to provide the necessary information and support to patients and maintain their own morale. National support groups may provide alternative and complementary methods of treatment, emphasizing a sense of personal control and offering individual and group support to patients and relatives.

Psychosexual functioning

This can be affected greatly by gynaecological interventions and may be a major aspect of the presenting complaint in others. However, because of embarrassment and taboos about sexuality, the problem may be ignored or treated as a biological symptom unrelated to interpersonal or environmental factors. Dodd and Parsons (1984) outline factors including information and training necessary to facilitate sensitive assessment and discussion of sexuality in gynaecological settings. Space does not permit a full discussion of psychosexual problems and their treatments; for general descriptions of assessment and psychological treatments see Bancroft (1983), LoPiccolo and LoPiccolo (1978) and Kaplan (1979).

It may be unrealistic to expect gynaecologists to provide psychosexual counselling, since understanding the problem inevitably involves detailed consideration of the couple's whole psychosocial situation (Bancroft, 1983). Equally, psychologists working with gynaecologists would be advised to understand and liaise closely concerning the physical effects of interventions such as vaginal surgery and oophorectomy. For example, postmenopausal women may experience reduced vaginal lubrication and dyspareunia as a result of hormonal changes.

The majority of sexual problems, however, do not have a physical or hormonal cause. In a medical setting it is important to emphasize the role of ignorance, negative attitudes, early relationship problems, current psychosocial problems, life changes and, obviously, current relationship difficulties in the genesis of sexual problems. Our knowledge of what is normal in sexual behaviour is limited (Bancroft, 1983), and there is discordance between the various reports of specific sexual problems, for example anorgasmia, and overall sexual satisfaction (Fisher, 1973; Frank, Andersen and Rubenstein, 1978).

When sexual problems are the main complaint there is evidence, from studies of couples attending psychosexual clinics (Bancroft and Coles, 1976; Mears, 1978), that for women the major problems are associated with reduced sexual desire or general unresponsiveness, followed by orgasmic dysfunction, with vaginismus affecting approximately 20% of cases. Since one-third of male partners also have a sexual problem, and in view of the difficulty in separating sexual and marital problems, both partners should be considered. Psychological interventions have been well documented, including relaxation, systematic desensitization, the use of vaginal dilatation and a general approach including sensate focus exercises and marital therapy. Attempts to evaluate specific treatment effects have been inconclusive, partly because of the complexity of the process under study and also because of methodological problems. An eclectic approach such as that advocated by Kaplan (1979) would seem to have the flexibility to deal with the variety of problems presented. For a fuller discussion of psychosexual problems associated with gynaecological problems see Dodd and Parsons (1984).

Infertility

Infertility is defined as the involuntary inability to conceive. It affects approximately 10% of couples of childbearing age (Pfeffer and Woollett, 1983), and it is now recognized that infertility and its treatment is often associated with considerable emotional distress (Edelmann and Connolly, 1987; Slade *et al.*, 1992).

The majority of early psychological studies were generally concerned with examining psychological factors as causes for unexplained infertility, rather than as reactions to infertility and its treatment (for review see Humphrey, 1984). Attempts to identify specific psychological characteristics of infertile women, particularly those for whom no organic cause could be identified, have been largely unsuccessful. Bell (1981) argues that the emphasis on unexplained infertility is somewhat misplaced, and that the needs of the majority of patients have been neglected. There is certainly evidence of a high rate of psychological distress in patients attending infertility clinic (Edelmann and Connolly, 1987) and an apparent lack of provision for emotional and psychological needs (Owens and Read, 1984).

Recent studies have focused on the secondary effects of psychological expectations and reactions and subsequent adjustment. For example, in Bell's (1981) study of couples at an infertility clinic, five individuals reported sexual dysfunction secondary to their infertility. Such reactions, whether due to mood changes or to performance anxiety during investigations, such as postcoital test, may obviously impede the process of treatment. There is some evidence that ovulation can be delayed by stress of various kinds (Peyser *et al.*, 1973), and that this may respond to psychological intervention. For a review of the possible impact of stress upon fertility problems see Edelmann and Golombok (1989).

Vere and Joyce (1979) report changes in the timing of ovulation in women after beginning artificial insemination by donor (AID) treatment. This ovulatory change from preclinic to treatment is attributed to the emotional stress of treatment. Harper, Lenton and Cooke (1985) illustrate the effect of psychological stress upon the physiological measures which are needed to investigate infertility. Prolactin levels were taken before the gynaecological interview and were found to coincide with subjective reports of state, but not trait, anxiety. Thus, measures to reduce stress in patients attending clinics are likely to be important to the subjective state of couples, and may also facilitate the process of investigation and treatment. A sympathetic atmosphere, adequate information and preparation prior to and during treatment would seem essential. In a consumer survey of 387 members of the National Association of the Childless who had attended infertility clinics, Owens and Read (1984) reported that about half the couples were

satisfied with investigations and treatment. However, there was considerably more criticism of the service by both partners when male infertility was the focus of investigation. Waiting times were generally regarded as too long, and couples felt that there was inadequate provision for the emotional aspects of infertility during investigation and treatment. In particular, too little time for discussion and lack of detailed information were areas pinpointed for improvement. These findings are supported by Connolly and Cooke (1987), who carried out a postal survey of 843 couples who had attended an infertility clinic. Emotional distress was associated with prolonged periods of investigation, and greater emotional and marital problems were encountered by both men and women when the cause for infertility lay in the male. Both these studies point to a need for increased understanding of the emotional needs of men who have fertility problems.

With the rapid development of new and controversial treatments such as *in vitro* fertilization (IVF) and ovum or semen donation, attention to psychological needs during treatment and the longer-term implications of treatment has lagged behind. IVF is regarded as the only hope of treatment for many couples, particularly for women with fallopian tubal damage or with ovarian failure due to premature menopause, or interventions such as radiotherapy or oophorectomy. This treatment is not widely available and couples experience long periods of investigation and delays before and during treatment. It is costly in time, emotional investment, disruption to lifestyle and, in many cases, financially. In addition, estimates of success in established centres are generally disappointing, with an average pregnancy rate of 11.6% per treatment cycle, increasing to 37% after three IVF cycles (Guzick, Wilkes and Jones, 1986).

The few psychological studies of couples entering IVF programmes have reported high levels of anxiety and distress (Haseltine, 1984; Keye, 1984; Morse and Dennerstein, 1985). Morse and Dennerstein (1985), in a pilot study of 30 couples in Australia, also noted a difference between women with organic causes and women with unexplained infertility the latter group being more distressed. Haseltine (1984) found that, whereas anxiety characterized women's reactions to treatment, male partners tended to react with depressed mood. When contacts were made post-treatment, couples stressed the immense impact that had resulted from the demands of the treatment and the failure of outcome (Morse and Dennerstein, 1985). Johnston, Shaw and Bird (1987) examined patients' estimates of outcome at stages during IVF treatment. In general, couples overestimated the likelihood of success.

Clearly, the cognitive task of being both adequately prepared for possible failure and positive enough to maintain motivation during treatment is considerable. Given the real possibility of failure, counselling prior to treatment could usefully explore the couple's future long-term options to help them to weigh up alternative lifestyles, both with and without children. Adoption is an alternative option, although there is now an acute shortage of adoptable infants (see Humphrey, 1984).

During treatment itself, preparation involving procedural and sensory information, using booklets as well as discussions, may reduce anxiety. Particularly anxious patients may benefit from stress inoculation and specific treatments aimed at anxiety reduction. The egg collection phase is regarded as particularly anxiety-provoking. As with other infertility treatments, involvement and support of the male partner is also important.

Ethical issues remain for the future, for example whether to tell the child about his or her origin. Perhaps because of the social stigma attached to infertility and the general wish for secrecy, many couples seeking artificial insemination by donor (AID) express the wish to bring up the child in ignorance, although ambivalent feelings exist (Humphrey, 1984). The Human Fertilization and Embryology Act (1990) recommends that counselling should be made available for all people seeking licensed treatment (i.e. IVF or treatment involving donated gametes). Specifically, this covers discussion of the medical procedures so that couples can make informed choices and discussion of the short and long-term emotional and social implications of the treatments. Counselling for those who donate eggs, embryos or sperm is also strongly advised.

Menorrhagia

This excessive menstrual bleeding is a common problem in women, particularly in their 30s and 40s, and one for which hysterectomy is often regarded as the only effective remedy. The specific causes of menorrhagia are still unknown, and a range of medications – for example progestogens, synthetic androgens and the contraceptive pill – are used, with varied effects and possible side-effects. Diagnosis is usually based on subjective reports which have been found to be only partially associated with blood loss as assessed by objective methods (Fraser, McCarron and Markham, 1984). In addition, the number of sanitary pads or tampons used bear little or no relationship to the amount of blood lost. Greenberg (1983) carried out one of the few psychological studies of menorrhagia. He found that 62% of women attending a gynaecology clinic complaining of menorrhagia were also suffering from mild to moderate neurotic depression, as assessed by the General Health Questionnaire (Goldberg, 1972) and clinical assessment. This group of depressed women had significantly higher haemoglobin levels, less specific and less severe gynaecological symptoms and a higher degree of social vulnerability. They had also experience more recent life stresses than non-depressed patients complaining of menorrhagia.

Several interpretation of these findings are possible. Severe menorrhagia could lead to considerable psychological distress. As discussed in the previous section, Gath's patients (Gath and Cooper, 1981; Gath, Cooper and Day, 1982) had waited approximately 1 year for their operation, and anticipation of the operation itself may also produce anxiety. Alternatively, some women with emotional problems may attend gynaecological clinics for help because of negative attitudes to mental illness. Attention to physical rather than emotional problems is reinforced by the medical system: when people feel depressed they are more likely to focus on bodily symptoms or perceive these more negatively.

Given that the menstrual cycle is controlled centrally by hormones which can be influenced by emotional states, it is certainly possible that significant emotional problems may disrupt the menstrual cycle. There is clearly a need for further research to attempt to clarify the relationship between these complex factors. For example, if we assume an illness behaviour explanation, then why is menstruation the focus of complaint and what factors serve to produce and maintain this pattern of illness behaviours? However, the first step is to confirm the above findings using objective assessments of blood loss. Such research could have important clinical implications since, as Gath's study illustrates, a considerable proportion of these women will undergo surgery rather than be offered psychological help.

The implications for the decision-making process prior to surgery have been stressed earlier. Assessment of women at this stage should include exploration of emotional and psychosocial problems. Pilot studies offering psychological treatments while assessing subjective complaints as well as blood loss would provide valuable information and possible clinical benefits.

The menstrual cycle

On average, women menstruate for 35–40 years. The menarche occurs between 12.8 and 13.2 years (range 9–16 years) and the mean age of menopause (last menstrual period) is 50.5 years. Medical interest and research has focused on specific phases of the menstrual cycle, such as the premenstruum and because studies have been based on clinic samples, they have emphasized negative aspects of the menstrual cycle (Asso, 1992).

Progress in menstrual cycle research has been hampered by conceptual assumptions and considerable methodological problems. Conceptually, there has been emphasis upon internal states and traits as causative factors and normative assumptions about expected female health and behaviour (Koeske, 1983). Methodological problems include variations in menstrual cycle length, the need to examine several cycles and the definition and measurement of vague concepts such as premenstrual syndrome (Walker, 1992).

Before discussing particular menstrual problems, the findings relating to the normal cycle will be summarized, based on the better-designed studies. Although it is generally assumed that hormonal fluctuations underlie cyclic mood changes in women, conclusive evidence of a specific physiological basis is lacking (see Ussher, 1992). There is some evidence of small changes in sensory acuity and sensitivity, and possibly small effects on motor activity.

However, when higher cognitive processes, moods and complex behaviours have been investigated, the evidence generally argues against a menstrual effect (Sommer, 1973; Parlee, 1983). Environmental factors have generally been found to account for more of the variation in measures than cycle phase (Wilcoxon, Schrader and Sherif, 1976; Strauss and Appelt, 1983).

Research interest in menstrual problems has been focused upon dysmenorrhoea and premenstrual tension. The psychological contributions to these areas, as well as to the menopause, will be described. Other aspects of the menstrual cycle, such as intermenstrual bleeding, amenorrhoea and menorrhagia, have been neglected, despite their frequency of presentation at gynaecology clinics. The particular problems of menorrhagia have been discussed earlier.

Dysmenorrhoea

This term refers to pain and discomfort during menstruation. Primary dysmenorrhoea occurs with no pelvic pathology, whereas secondary dysmenorrhoea is secondary to congenital problems or pathology such as endometriosis. There is now strong evidence that the former type of pain is associated with ovulatory cycles, and is caused by contractions of the uterus and increased blood flow, resulting in ischaemia stimulated by prostaglandin activity. Primary dysmenorrhoea commonly occurs in younger women, but prevalence rates are difficult to estimate. Approximately 10–14% of young women do not attend school because of dysmenorrhoea. Gynaecological treatments include suppression of ovulation and prostaglandin synthetase-inhibiting drugs, which are generally regarded as being successful (for reviews see Friederich, 1983; Calhoun and Burnette, 1984).

Dalton (1969) proposed a dichotomy of menstrual problems, with spasmodic dysmenorrhoea occurring menstrually and congestive dysmenorrhoea occurring premenstrually. Oestrogen deficiency was assumed to cause spasmodic dysmenorrhoea. However, there has been little support for her theory of menstrual types (Clare, 1983). Psychological treatments include relaxation, desensitization and counselling. Chesney and Tasto (1975), Duson (1976) and Cox and Meyer (1978) used relaxation and imaginary desensitization to cues of menstrual distress. Self-control procedures were added by Cox and Meyer (1978) and

Duson (1976) asking patients to monitor symptoms and reinforce treatment goals and increase positive cognitions. Such treatments have been found to be more effective than a no-treatment control. Chesney and Tasto (1975) found that desensitization was more effective than a placebo discussion group. Further research is necessary with plausible control conditions, longer follow-up intervals and different samples.

Given the considerable research on psychological treatments of pain problems, it is surprising that relatively little attention has been paid to dysmenorrhoea. The effects of negative beliefs, maternal modelling and behavioural reactions to the pain also deserve further study, and have treatment implications. Finally, the finding of a link between dysmenorrhoea, prostaglandin synthesis and stress (Stephenson, Denney and Aberger, 1983) may stimulate further psychological research.

Premenstrual tension or syndrome (PMS)

This is a term used to refer to a wide range of symptoms, including tension, depression, irritability, abdominal bloating, breast tenderness and headache occurring some 7–10 days before menstruation. There is no one set of symptoms and the duration of the premenstruum is ill-defined. Because of problems of definition and methodology described above, prevalence rates ranging between 25 and 90% have been reported (Coppen and Kessel, 1963; Reid and Yen, 1981). When larger unselected samples are studied, the existence of severe debilitating PMS is apparently relatively rare (Halbreich and Endicott, 1982; Steiner, Haskett and Carroll, 1980). There is also the suggestion from factor analytic studies that several separate clusters of symptoms may exist (Warner and Bancroft, 1986). Some women may experience premenstrual exacerbation of ongoing emotional problems. Only those without psychiatric disorder and with clear relief of severe symptoms on menstruation are now generally considered to be true sufferers (Steiner, Haskett and Carroll, 1980).

Hormonal theories implicating the role of oestrogen, progesterone or prolactin have failed to be substantiated as yet (Walker, 1992). Gynaecological treatments are used ranging from the contraceptive pill, oestrogen and progesterone therapy to synthetic progestogens. However, these only serve to disrupt the cycle and have no specific treatment effect. Further, in controlled trials they have been found to be no more effective than placebo treatment (Smith and Schiff, 1989).

To date, psychologists' contributions have been largely focused on improvements in methodology and emphasis on the psychosocial context of symptomatology. In these better-designed studies the only symptoms to be repeatedly shown to be linked to the premenstrual phase have been pain and water retention (Wilcoxon, Schrader and Sherif, 1976; Abplanalp et al., 1979). Stressful life events and environmental factors generally account for more of the variation in psychological symptoms than does cycle stage (Wilcoxon, Schrader and Sherif, 1976; Stephenson, Denney and Aberger, 1983; Strauss and Appelt, 1983). One of the main findings in Wilcoxon's study was an increase in mood differences between women at premenstruum and during menstruation.

In another branch of research the influence of cognitive factors has been emphasized: for example, knowledge of cycle phase has a considerable influence on symptom report (Ruble, 1977). Slade (1984) provides evidence to suggest that the discrepancy between beliefs about symptom occurrence and daily ratings of symptoms may be explained by the experience of random emotional fluctuations and differential patterns of attribution.

There is laboratory evidence to suggest that autonomic nervous system arousal may increase premenstrually (see Asso, 1992). The results of Wilcoxon, Schrader and Sherif's

(1976) study of increased variation in mood premenstrually may be explained by the interaction of internal changes in arousal with perceptual, attribution factors and environmental effects.

Very little research has focused on psychological treatment of PMS. Strong treatment effects with placebo in women presenting with PMS have been found, suggesting that psychological treatments may be usefully employed. Combined relaxation and systematic desensitization was found to be an effective treatment in a single group design (Cox and Meyer, 1978). Chesney and Tasto (1975), however, found a similar treatment to be no more effective than an attention placebo discussion group. It is too early to pinpoint specific treatment effects. Slade (1989) describes the treatment of four women using a cognitive – behavioural approach, which combined problem-solving, autogenic training and anxiety and anger-control strategies.

In the author's experience, the use of daily monitoring of mood and life events can lead to a useful problem-solving approach to clarify the appropriateness or usefulness of certain attributions of symptoms, e.g. to hormones, marital problems and life stresses. Specific therapeutic approaches, for example cognitive therapy, marital therapy, individual or group therapy, may then follow. The use of self-help guides (Birke and Gardner, 1981), counselling and self-help groups also has considerable potential for alleviating premenstrual distress (Fielding and Bosanko, 1984).

The menopause

The menopause is primarily a physiological event, marked by cessation of the menstrual cycle and experienced by all women who have not experienced an earlier surgical menopause. Defining stages during the process of the menopause is problematic and normally retrospective, relying on reports of menstrual changes. The term 'climacteric' refers to the period of gradual reduction in ovulation and decreased output of ovarian hormones. The generally accepted classification defines women as postmenopausal if no menstruation has occurred during the previous 12 months, and as perimenopausal if menstruation has become irregular but has occurred during the past 12 months (Jaszmann, 1973). Hormonal assessments of ovarian functioning can be made using hormone assays (Moore, Gustafson and Studa, 1975).

The menopausal transition has inevitably acquired considerable psychosocial and cultural meaning, being a definitive landmark of ageing in women and coinciding with middle age. Concepts such as 'empty nest', physical decline, loss of femininity, loss of sexuality, and even psychosis – i.e. involutional melancholia – have been used, resulting in varied stereotypes, usually with negative connotations in western cultures. With the development of oestrogen therapy as a treatment for hot flushes and vaginal dryness and, more recently, osteoporosis, the postmenopause has been viewed as a period of deficiency (Wilson, 1966).

Understanding of the normal experience of the menopause has been hampered by polarized theoretical views – medical versus sociocultural – as well as considerable methodological problems. In addition to the problems outlined above, which are common to menstrual cycle research, age effects and cohort differences need to be carefully considered when comparing groups of menopausal women (see Kaufert and Syrotuik, 1981). Hormone and menstrual changes occur over a much longer timescale.

It is generally agreed that hot flushes, night sweats and vaginal changes are definitely associated with menopausal status (McKinlay and McKinlay, 1973; Studd, Chakravarti and Oram, 1977). It is estimated that approximately 70% of women report hot flushes, with 15–20% of these experiencing moderate to severe symptoms. However, there is no conclusive evidence that psychiatric disorder increases in pre- or postmenopausal women (Ballinger, 1990), and little evidence that emotional problems are more prevalent during the menopause transition (Hunter, 1990).

Research drawn from anthropology, sociology and psychology has illustrated the effect of psychosocial context of symptom reports. Cross-cultural differences in experience of the menopause have been described, suggesting that symptoms are more prevalent when the menopause is associated with negative social change (Flint, 1975; Lock, 1986; Beyenne, 1986). The effects of diet and menstrual history are also emphasized in explaining cultural differences (Beyenne, 1986). The effects of life stresses have been examined (Greene and Cooke, 1980). Greene (1983) found that losses and bereavements occuring during the climacteric were the most potent predictors of somatic symptoms, particularly if they occurred in the context of other additional stresses. The effect of life stress on oestrogen levels has also been proposed (Ballinger *et al.*, 1979), implying an interaction of stresses and physiological aspects of menopause. There is little evidence, however, that the menopause itself is more stressful than other life stages, such as early motherhood. Regarding the 'empty nest syndrome', Krystal and Chiriboga (1979), in a comprehensive review of the literature, concluded that children leaving home is not necessarily stressful and is met with relief by many couples. In general, the results of recent longitudinal studies carried out in the 1980s using large general population samples, are showing that the main predictors of depressed mood and other psychological symptoms at peri- or postmenopause are previous emotional problems (Hunter, 1992; Holte, 1992; Kaufert, Gilbert and Tate, 1992; McKinlay, Brambilla and Posner, 1992). Bereavement may coincide with the menopause but not necessarily. Although it is generally acknowledged that negative attitudes, expectations and stereotypes exacerbate symptoms, these have rarely been systematically studied.

A number of cognitive factors were examined in the author's own research. In a 3-year follow-up study of 47 premenopausal women, drawn from a non-clinic sample, negative stereotyped beliefs about the menopause were found to predict depressed mood when these women later became peri- or postmenopausal. These beliefs were not, however, associated with concurrent levels of depression.

In Table 15.2, the results of a multiple stepwise regression analysis are shown, indicating the relative contributions of predictive variables. Negative stereotype provided additional predictive power and was relatively independent of previous levels of depression (Hunter, 1992). These findings suggest a general need for information and education and perhaps specific strategies to counteract certain beliefs. A study is currently in progress which aims to evaluate the effects of preparation groups for 45-year old women, involving provision of information, discussion of beliefs and health education (Liao and Hunter, 1994). Further investigation of the development of such stereotypes would be of interest, and may have implications for future intervention.

The implications of psychological and sociological research have been to attempt to increase awareness of the normality of the menopause and the need to consider psychosocial factors when treating menopausal women in a clinical setting. It is acknowledged that symptoms are inappropriately attributed to the menopause (Osborne, 1984; Endacott and Whitehead, 1983) and women may therefore receive oestrogen therapy rather than psychological treatment. Vasomotor symptoms (hot flushes, night sweats, and vaginal dryness) are certainly improved with oestrogen therapy (Studd, Chakravarti and Oram, 1977), but their precise causes are as yet unknown. In a detailed psychological investigation, Voda (1981) reported vast individual differences in the experience of hot flushes and their precipitants. Severe hot flushes can lead to embarrassment and social anxiety, and night sweats may cause sleeplessness, factors which may, in turn, exacerbate symptoms. If such internal changes are not understood, they may be interpreted as signs of sexual inadequacy or physical or mental illness. An exciting development has been the recent application of relaxation therapy and counselling to alleviate hot flushes (Stevenson and Delprato, 1983; Germaine and Freedman, 1985). Reductions in symptom frequency were found, and more objective and reliable psychophysiological methods of assessing hot flushes are being developed. A cognitive–relaxation treatment study for women with hot flushes is currently being carried out in a primary care setting (Liao and Hunter 1994).

There were 21 menopause clinics in the UK in 1982 catering for 3–4% of menopausal women (Whitehead, 1982). Clinical psychologists have recently described collaborative

TABLE 15.2 Predicting depressed mood at peri-post-menopause multiple stepwise regression analysis

Predictive factor Pre-menopause	Beta	Correlation	% Variance
Depressed mood	0.42	0.58	34
Negative stereotype	0.21	0.36	6
Employment	−0.27	−0.32	5
Socioeconomic status	−0.24	−0.18	6
			S1

work with gynaecologists in such clinics (Greene and Hart, 1987; Hunter, 1988) using exploration of attributions of symptoms, psychosexual and marital relationships, coping with life stresses, physiological changes, possible role changes and ageing. The menopause can provide a useful focus for evaluating the past and making adjustments for the future.

Conclusions

There are clearly many levels at which psychological approaches can be applied in gynaecological practice. First, and perhaps of most importance, is the provision of psychosocial models and interactive models of gynaecological complaints. The impact of environmental factors such as stressful life events and perceived social support has been underestimated. Similarly, information about normal developmental processes and the considerable range of normal experience has generally not been available. Appreciation of these factors may help to counter stereotypes about women, which are generally based on clinic samples. The development of interactive models could have several benefits, for example the pursuit of integrated psychological and physiological research, the avoidance of polarized views and dualistic thinking, such as organic versus functional, and the possibility of offering clients a broader range of treatments.

Psychological approaches have emphasized the clients' own perceptions and explanations of their problems. Negotiating the discussion of such explanations during gynaecological consultations, particularly when they are not concordant, could well be a useful topic in the education of medical students and gynaecologists. When clients see that gynaecologists and psychologists work together and share an integrative model, referral is less distressing for clients, who then are likely to be less resistant to psychological treatments (Pearce, Knight and Beard, 1982). Fears of 'psychological'

being equated with malingering, imaginary problems or being insane often require acknowledgement and discussion.

Space does not permit discussion of the full range of possible psychological interventions, but it may be useful to conclude with a few examples of the types of services that psychologists could usefully offer. One important aim is to provide information and training in communication skills to nurses, health visitors, medical students and junior gynaecologists. Seminars might focus on particular problem areas, such as doctor – patient communication dealing with PMT and sexual problems presenting as pelvic pain. Clinical input can be provided to outpatients referred from general gynaecological clinics, for example with menstrual problems or post-termination distress or hysterectomy, as well as to patients from specialist clinics offering help with menopausal, psychosexual or fertility problems. The psychologist's role can include education, staff training and support, helping people to make informed choices and setting up support groups for particular problems, as well as providing individual or group therapy. Research or project work might focus upon a particular problem, for instance to establish a new intervention method. Examples of project work include preparation for major gynaecological surgery, or problems of communication among staff involved with termination of pregnancy.

Action research and collaborative projects provide an interdisciplinary forum for discussion and can demonstrate the importance of psychological factors in gynaecological problems and service provision.

References

Abplanalp, J.M., Rose, R.M., Donnely, A.F. and Livingstone-Vaughn, C. (1979) Psychoendocrinology of the menstrual cycle: II. The relationship between enjoyment of activities, moods and reproductive hormones. *Psychosomatic Medicine*, 14(8), 605–15.

Alder, E., Cook, A., Gray, J. *et al.* (1981) The effects of sterilization: a comparison of sterilized women with the wives of vasectomized men. *Contraception*, **23**, 45–54.

Adler, N.E., David, H.P., Major, B.N. *et al.* (1990) Psychological responses after abortion. *Science*, **248**, 41–4.

Allen, C. (1982) A study of factors affecting decision making in women seeking TOP. Unpublished-dissertation for BPS Diploma.

Andersen, B.L. and Andersen, B. (1986) Psychosomatic aspects of gynecologic oncology: present status and future directions. *Journal of Psychosomatic Obstetrics and Gynecology*, **5**(4), 233–44.

Andersen, B.L. and Hacker, N.F. (1983) Psychosexual adjustment after vulva surgery. *Obstetrics and Gynecology*, **62**, 457–62.

Areskog-Wijma, B. (1987) The gynecological examination – women's experiences and preferences and the role of the gynecologist. *Journal of Psychosomatic Obstetrics and Gynecology*, **6**, 59–69.

Asso, D. (1992) A reappraisal of the normal menstrual cycle. *Journal of Reproductive and Infant Psychology*, **10**, 103–10.

Ballinger, C.B. (1977) Psychiatric morbidity and the menopause: survey of a gynaecological outpatient clinic. *British Journal of Psychiatry*, **131**, 83–9.

Ballinger, C.B. (1990) Psychiatric aspects of the menopause. *British Journal of Psychiatry*, **156**, 773–81.

Ballinger, S., Cobbin, D., Krivanek, J. and Saunders, D. (1979) Life stress and depression in the menopause. *Maturitas*, **1**, 191–9.

Bancroft, J. (1983) *Human Sexuality and its Problems*. Churchill Livingstone, Edinburgh and New York.

Bancroft, J. and Coles, L. (1976) Three years' experience in a sexual problems clinic. *British Medical Journal*, **1**, 1577.

Beard, R.W. (1984) Preface, in *Psychology and Gynaecological Problems*, (eds A. Broome and L. Wallace), Tavistock Publications, London.

Beard, R.W., Belsey, E.M. and Lieberman, J.C.M. (1977) Pelvic pain in women: gynaecologic psychiatric considerations. *American Journal of Obstetrics and Gynecology*, **77**, 806–23.

Bell, J.S. (1981) Psychological problems among patients attending an infertility clinic. *Journal of Psychosomatic Research*, **25**, 1–3.

Benjamin, L., Rubinstein, L.M. and Kleinkopf, V. (1980) Elective sterilization in childless women. *Fertility and Sterility*, **34**, 116–20.

Beyenne, Y. (1986) Cultural significance and physiological manifestations of menopause, a biocultural analysis. *Culture, Medicine and Psychiatry*, **10**, 47–71.

Birke, L. And Gardner, K, (1981) *Why Suffer? Periods and their Problems*. Virago Press, London.

Briscoe, M. (1982) Sex differences in psychological well-being. *Psychological Medicine Monographs Suppl.*, **1**, 1–46.

Broome, A. (1980) Clinical psychology with obstetrics and gynaecology. *Bulletin of the British Psychological Society*, **33**, 357–9.

Broome, A. and Wallace, L. (1984) *Psychology and Gynaecological Problems*, Tavistock Publications, London.

Byrne, P. (1984) Psychiatric morbidity in a gynecological clinic: an epidemiological study. *British Journal of Psychiatry*, **144**, 28–34.

Calhoun, K.S. and Burnette, M.M. (1984) Etiology and treatment of menstrual disorders. *Behavioral Medicine Update*, **5**(4), 21–6.

Capone, M.A., Good, R.S., Westie, K.S. and Jacobsen, A.F. (1980) Psychosocial rehabilitation of gynecologic oncology patients. *Archives of Physical Medicine and Rehabilitation*, **61**, 128–32.

Chesney, M.A. and Tasto, D.L. (1975) The effectiveness of behaviour modification with spasmodic and congestive dysmenorrhoea. *Behavioural Research Therapy*, **13**, 245–53.

Christopher, E. (1991) Family planning and reproductive decisions. *Journal of Reproductive and Infant Psychology*, **9**, 217–26.

Clare, A.W. (1983) Psychiatric and social aspects of premenstrual complaint. *Psychological Bulletin Monographs Suppl.*, **4**, 1–58.

Cochran, S.D., Hacker, N.F. and Berek, J. (1986) Correlates of delay in seeking treatment for endometrial cancer. *Journal of Psychosomatic Obstetrics and Gynecology*, **5**(4), 245–52.

Connolly, K.J. and Cooke, I. (1987) Distress and marital problems associated with infertility. *Journal of Reproductive and Infant Psychology*, **5**, 49–57.

Cooper, P., Gath, D., Rose, N. and Fieldsend, R. (1982) Psychological sequelae to elective sterilization in women: a prospective study. *British Medical Journal*, **284**, 461–4.

Coppen, A. and Kessel, N. (1963) Menstruation and personality. *British Journal of Psychiatry*, **109**, 711–21.

Cox, D.J. and Meyer, R.G. (1978) Behavioural treatment parameters with primary dysmenorrhoea. *Journal of Behavioural Medicine*, **1**, 297–310.

Dalton, K. (1969) *The Menstrual Cycle*, Panthean, New York.

Dalton, K. (1977) *The Premenstrual Syndrome and Progesterone Therapy*, Heinemann Medical Books, London.

Dennerstein, L. and Ryan, M. (1982) Psychosocial and emotional sequelae of hysterectomy. *Journal of*

Psychosomatic Obstetrics and Gynecology, **1–2**, 81–6.

Dennerstein, L., Wood, C. and Burrows, G.D. (1977) Sexual response following hysterectomy and oophorectomy, *Obstetrics and Gynecology*, **49**, 92–6.

Dodd, B.G. and Parsons, A.D. (1984) Psychological problems, in *Psychology and Gynaecological Problems*, (eds A. Broome and L. Wallace), Tavistock Publications, London, pp. 189–210.

Donnai, P., Charles, N. and Harris, R. (1981) Attitudes of patients after genetic termination of pregnancy. *British Medical Journal*, **282**, 621–2.

Dunlop, J.Z. (1978) Counselling patients requesting an abortion. *Practitioner*, **220**, 847–52.

Duson, B.M (1976) Effectiveness of relaxation desensitization and cognitive restructuring in teaching the self-management of menstrual symptoms of college women. Unpublished doctoral dissertation, University of Texas, Austin, Texas.

Edelmann, R.J. and Connolly, K.J. (1987) The counselling needs of infertile couples. *Journal of Reproductive and Infant Psychology*, **5**, 63–70.

Edelmann, R.J. and Golombok, S. (1989) Stress and reproductive failure. *Journal of Reproductive and Infant Psychology*, **7**, 79–86.

Endacott, J. and Whitehead, M.I. (1983) Female and male climacteric. *Nursing*, **2**(14), 399–403.

Fallowfield, L. (1991) Counselling patients with cancer, in *Counselling and Communication in Health Care*, (eds H. Davis and L. Fallowfield), Wiley, Chichester, pp. 253–70.

Fielding, D. and Bosanko, C. (1984) Psychological aspects of the menstruum and premenstruum, in *Psychology and Gynaecological Problems*, (eds A. Broome and L. Wallace), Tavistock Publications, London, pp. 211–42.

Fisher, S. (1973) *The Female Orgasm*, Basic Books, New York.

Flint, M. (1975) The menopause: reward or punishment. *Psychosomatics*, **16**, 161–3.

Frank, E., Andersen, C. and Rubenstein, D. (1978) Frequency of sexual dysfunction in 'normal couples'. *New England Journal of Medicine*, **299**, 111–15.

Fraser, I.S., McCarron, G. and Markham, R. (1984) A preliminary study of factors influencing perception of menstrual blood loss volume. *American Journal of Obstetrics and Gynecology*, **149**(7), 788–93.

Friederich, M.A. (1983) Dysmenorrhoea. *Women and Health*, Special issue, 91–106.

Fuller, S.S., Endress, M.P. and Johnson, J.E. (1978) The effects of cognitive and behavioural control in coping with an aversive health examination. *Journal of Human Stress*, **4**, 18–25.

Gath, D. and Cooper, P.J. (1981) Psychiatric disorder after hysterectomy. *Journal of Psychiatric Research*, **25**(5), 347–55.

Gath, D., Cooper, P. and Day, A. (1982) Hysterectomy and psychiatric disorder. 1. Levels of psychiatric morbidity before and after hysterectomy. *British Journal of Psychiatry*, **140**, 335–42.

Germaine, L.M. and Freedman, R.R. (1985) Behavioural treatment of menopausal hot flushes: evaluation by objective methods. *Journal of Consulting and Clinical Psychology*, **52**(6), 1072–9.

Goldberg, D.P. (1972) *The Detection of Psychiatric Illness by Questionnaire*, Oxford University Press, Oxford.

Greenberg, M. (1983) The meaning of menorrhagia: an investigation into the association between the complaint of menorrhagia and depression. *Journal of Psychosomatic Research*, **27**(3), 209–14.

Greene, J.G. (1983) Bereavement and social support at the climacteric. *Maturitas*, **5**(2), 115–25.

Greene, J.G. and Cooke, D.J. (1980) Life stress and symptoms at the climacterium. *British Journal of Psychiatry*, **136**, 486–91.

Greene, J.G. and Hart, P.M. (1987) The evaluation of a psychological treatment programme for menopausal women. *Maturitas*, **9**, 1, 41–8.

Greer, H.S., Lal, S., Lewis, S.C. *et al.* (1976) Psychosocial consequences of therapeutic abortion. Kings Termination Study II, *British Journal of Psychiatry*, **128**, 74–9.

Guzick, D., Wilkes, C. and Jones, H. (1986) Cumulative pregnancy rates for in vitro fertilization. *Fertility and Sterility*, **46**, 663–7.

Halbreich, U. and Endicott, J. (1982) Classification of premenstrual syndromes, in *Behavior and the Menstrual Cycle*, (ed. R. Friedman), Marcel Dekker, New York, pp. 243–66.

Harper, R., Lenton, E.A. and Cooke, I. (1985) Prolactin and subjective reports of stress in women attending an infertility clinic. *Journal of Reproductive and Infant Psychology*, **3**, 3–8.

Haseltine, F. (1984) Psychological testing of couples in the in vitro fertilization programme suggested dysphoria among the males and high anxiety component in the couples. Paper presented at the World Congress of Infertility, Helsinki.

Hewson, S. (1979) The effects of different patterns of information given on psychological response to surgery among a sample of women undergoing surgery for sterilization. MSc Thesis, University of Manchester.

Holte, A. (1992) Influences of natural menopause on health complaints: a prospective study of healthy Norwegian women. *Maturitas*, **14**(2), 127–42.

Horney, K. (1932) The dread of women. International *Journal of Psychoanalysis*, **13**, 348–60.

Humphrey, M. (1984) Infertility and alternative parenting, in *Psychology and Gynaecological Problem*, (eds A. Broome and L. Wallace), Tavistock Publications, London, pp. 77–94.

Hunter, M. (1988) Psychological aspects of the climacteric and post-menopause, in *The Menopause*, (eds J. Studd and M. Whitehead), Blackwell Scientific Publications, Oxford, pp. 55–64.

Hunter, M.S. (1990) Emotional well-being, sexual behaviour and hormone replacement therapy. *Maturitas*, 12, 299–314.

Hunter, M.S. (1992) The south-east England longitudinal study of the climacteric and postmenopause. *Maturitas*, 14(2), 117–26.

Hunter, M.S. (1993) *Counselling in Obstetrics and Gynaecology*, BPS Books, London.

Israel, M.J. and Mood, D.W. (1982) Three media presentations for patients receiving radiation therapy. *Cancer Nursing*, 15, 57–63.

Jaszmann, L. (1973) Epidemiology of the climacteric and post-climacteric complaints, in *Ageing and Oestrogens*, (eds P.A. van Keep and C. Lauritzen), Karger, Basel.

Johnson, J.E. and Leventhal, H. (1974) Effects of accurate expectations and behavioural instructions on reactions during a noxious medical examination. *Journal of Personality and Social Psychology*, 29(5), 710–18.

Johnston, M. (1982) Recognition of patients' worries by nurses and by other patients. *British Journal of Clinical Psychology*, 21, 255–61.

Johnston, M. and Carpenter, L. (1980) Relationship between pre-operative and post-operative state. *Psychological Medicine*, 10, 361–7.

Johnston, M., Shaw, R. and Bird, D. (1987) Test tube baby procedures; stress and judgements under uncertainty. *Psychology and Health*, 1(1), 25–38.

Kaplan, H.S. (1979) *Disorders of Sexual Desire*, Brunner/Mazel, New York.

Karlsson, J.A. and Andersen, B.L. (1986) Radiation therapy and psychological distress in gynecologic oncology patients: outcomes and recommendations for enhancing adjustment. *Journal of Psychosomatic Obstetrics and Gynecology*, 5(4), 283–94.

Kaufert, P. and Syrotuik, J. (1981) Symptom reporting at the menopause. *Social Science and Medicine*, 15E, 175–84.

Kaufert, P.A., Gilbert, P. and Tate, R. (1992) The Manitoba Project: a re-examination of the link between menopause and depression. *Maturitas*, 14(2), 143–56.

Keye, W.R. (1984) The psychosocial evaluation of couples undergoing *in vitro* fertilization. Paper presented at The World Congress of Infertility, Helsinki.

Kincey, J. and McFarlane, T. (1984) Psychological aspects of hysterectomy, in *Psychology and Gynaecological Problems* (eds A. Broome and L. Wallace), Tavistock Publications, London, pp. 142–60.

King, K.B., Nail, L.M., Kreamer, K. *et al.* (1985) Patients' descriptions of the experience of receiving radiation therapy. *Oncology Nursing Forum*, 12, 55–61.

Koeske, R.D. (1983) Lifting the curse of menstruation: towards a feminist perspective of the menstrual cycle. *Women and Health*, Special issue, 1–15.

Krystal, S. and Chiriboga, D.A. (1979) The empty nest process in midlife men and women. *Maturitas*, 1, 215–22.

Lambers, K.J., Trimbos-Kemper, T. and Van Hall, E.V. (1982) Motivation of sterilization and subsequent wish for reversal in 70 women. *Journal of Psychosomatic Obstetrics and Gynecology*, 1(1), 17–21.

Lambers, K.J., Trimbos-Kemper, G.C.M. and Van Hall, E.V. (1984) Regret and reversal of sterilization, in *Psychology and Gynaecological Problems*, (eds A. Broome and L. Wallace), Tavistock Publications, London, pp. 18–39.

Lamont, J.A., Depetrillo, A.D. and Sargeant, E.J. (1978) Psychosexual rehabilitation and exenterative surgery. *Gynaecological Oncology*, 6, 236–42.

Leader, A., Galan, N., George, R. and Taylor, P.J. (1981) A comparison of the definable traits in women requesting reversal of sterilization and women satisfied with sterilization. *American Journal of Obstetrics and Gynaecology*, 145(2), 198–202.

Ley, P. (1977) Doctor – patient communications, in *Contributions to Medical Psychology*, (ed. S. Rachman), Pergamon Press, Oxford, pp. 1–29.

Ley, P. (1982) Giving information to patients, in *Social Psychology and Behavioral Science*, (ed. J.R. Eiser), John Wiley and Sons, New York, pp. 339–73.

Liao, K.L.M. and Hunter, M. (1994) The Women's Midlife Project: an evaluation of additional psychological services for mid-aged women in primary care. *Clinical Psychology Forum (BPS)*, 65, 19–22.

Lock, M. (1986) Ambiguities of aging: Japanese experience and perceptions of menopause. *Culture, Medicine and Psychiatry*, 10, 23–46.

Lopiccolo, J. and Lopiccolo, L. (1978) *Handbook of Sex Therapy*, Plenum Press, New York.

Lyles, J.N., Burish, T.G., Krozely, M.G. and Oldham, R.K. (1982) Efficacy of relaxation training and guided imagery in reducing the aversiveness of cancer chemotherapy. *Journal of Consulting and Clinical Psychology*, 50, 509–24.

McKinlay, S.M. and McKinlay, J.B. (1973) Selected studies of the menopause. *Journal of Biosocial Science*, 5, 533–55.

McKinlay, S.M., Brambilla, D.J. and Posner, J.G. (1992) The normal menopause transition. *Maturitas*, 14(2), 103–16.

Magee, J. (1975) The pelvic examination: a view from the other end of the table. *Annals of Internal Medicine*, **83**, 563–7.

Marcus, R.J. (1979) Evaluating abortion counselling. *Dimensions in Health Services*, August, 16–18.

Marteau, T.M. (1989) Psychological costs of screening. *British Medical Journal*, **299**, 527.

Marteau, T.M. (1990) Screening: reducing the psychological costs. *British Medical Journal*, **301**, 26–8.

Marteau, T.M. and Johnston, M. (1987) Health psychology: the danger of neglecting psychological models. *Bulletin of British Psychological Society*, **40**, 82–5.

Martin, R.L., Roberts, W.V., Claydon, D.J. and Wetzel, R. (1977) Psychiatric illness and non-cancer hysterectomy. *Diseases of the Nervous System*, Dec, 974–80

Matthews, A. and Ridgeway, V. (1981) Personality and surgical recovery: a review. *British Journal of Clinical Psychology*, **20**, 243–60.

Mears, E. (1978) An assessment of the work of 26 doctors trained by the Institute of Psychosexual Medicine. *Public Health*, **92**, 218–23.

Mechanic, D. (1980) The experience and reporting of common physical symptoms. *Journal of Health and Social Behaviour*, **21**, 146–55.

Miller, S.M. and Mangan, C.E. (1983) Interacting effects of information and coping style in adapting to gynaecological stress: should the doctor tell all? *Journal of Personality and Social Psychology*, **45**(1), 223–36.

Moffic, H.S. and Paykel, E.S. (1975) Depression in medical inpatients. *British Journal of Psychiatry*, **126**, 346–53.

Moore, B., Gustafson, R. and Studa, J.W.W. (1975) Experience of a National Health Service menopause clinic. *Current Medical Research and Opinion*, Suppl. 3, 42–56.

Morrow, G.R. and Morrell, C. (1982) Behavioural treatment of the anticipatory nausea and vomiting induced by cancer chemotherapy. *New England Journal of Medicine*, **307**, 1476–80.

Morse, C.A. and Dennerstein, L. (1985) Infertile couples entering an in vitro fertilization programme: a preliminary survey. *Journal of Psychosomatic Obstetrics and Gynecology*, **4**(3), 207–19.

Osborne, M. (1984) Depression at the menopause. *British Journal of Hospital Medicine*, **32**, 126–9.

Osokosky, H.J. (1967) Women's reactions to pelvic examination. *Obstetrics and Gynaecology*, **30**, 146–9.

Owens, D.J. and Read, M.W. (1984) Patients' experience with the assessment of subfertility testing and treatment. *Journal of Reproductive and Infant Psychology*, **2**, 7–17.

Parlee, M.B. (1974) Stereotypic beliefs about menstruation: a methodological note on the Moos Menstrual Distress Questionnaire and some new data. *Psychosomatic Medicine*, **36**, 229–40.

Parlee, M.B. (1983) Menstrual rhythms in sensory processes: A review of fluctuations in vision, olfaction, audition, taste and touch. *Psychological Bulletin*, **93**(3), 539–48.

Pearce, S. (1989) The concept of psychogenic pain. An investigation of psychological factors in chronic pelvic pain. *Current Psychological Research and Reviews*, **6**, 16–21.

Pearce, S., Knight, C. and Beard, R.W. (1982) Pelvic pain – a common gynecological problem. *Journal of Psychosomatic Obstetrics and Gynecology*, **1**, 12–21.

Peyser, M.R., Ayalon, D., Harell, A. *et al.* (1973) Stress induced delay of ovulation. *Obstetrics and Gynaecology*, **43**, 667–71.

Pfeffer, N. and Woollett, A. (1983) *The Experience of Infertility*, Virago Press, London.

Porter, M. (1991) Contraceptive choices: an exploration of how they are made. *Journal of Reproductive and Infant Psychology*, **9**, 227–35.

Posner, T. and Vessey, M. (1988) *Prevention of Cervical Cancer: the Patient's View*, King Edwards Hospital Fund for London, London.

Rainey, L.C. (1985) Effects of preparatory patient education for reduction oncology patients. *Cancer*, **56**, 1056–61.

Reading, A.E. (1979) The short-term effects of psychological preparation for surgery. *Social Science and Medicine*, **13A**, 641–54.

Reading, A.E. (1982) The management of fear related to vaginal examination. *Journal of Psychosomatic Obstetrics and Gynecology*, **1**(3/4), 99–102.

Redd, W.H., Andresen, G.V. and Minagawa, R.Y. (1982) Hypnotic control of anticipatory emesis in patients receiving cancer chemotherapy. *Journal of Consulting and Clinical Psychology*, **50**, 14–19.

Reid, R.L. and Yen, S.S.C. (1981) Premenstrual syndrome. *American Journal of Obstetrics and Gynecology*, **139**, 85–104.

Ridgeway, V. and Matthews, A. (1982) Psychological preparation for surgery. A comparison of methods. *British Journal of Clinical Psychology*, **21**, 271–80.

Ruble, D. (1977) Premenstrual symptoms: a reinterpretation. *Science*, **197**, 291–2.

Schwyhart, W.R. and Kutner, S.J. (1973) A reanalysis of female reactions to contraceptive sterilization. *British Medical Journal*, **3**, 220–2.

Shusterman, L.R. (1979) Predicting the psychological consequences of abortion. *Social Science and Medicine*, **96**, 683–9.

Slade, P. (1984) Premenstrual emotional changes in normal women: fact or fiction. *Journal of Psychosomatic Research*, **28**(1), 1–7.

Slade, P. (1989) Psychological therapy for premenstrual emotional symptoms. *Behavioural Psychotherapy*, **17**, 135–50.

Slade, P., Raval, H., Buck, P. and Lieberman, B.E. (1992) A three year follow-up of emotional, marital and sexual functioning in couples who were infertile. *Journal of Reproductive and Infant Psychology*, **10**, 233–43.

Smith, A.W. (1979) Psychiatric aspects of sterilization: a prospective survey. *British Journal of Psychiatry*, **135**, 304–9.

Smith, S. and Schiff, I. (1989) The premenstrual syndrome – diagnosis and management. *Fertility and Sterility*, **52**, 527–43.

Sommer, B. (1973) The effect of menstruation on cognitive and perceptual motor behaviour: a review. *Psychosomatic Medicine*, **35**, 515–34.

Steiner, M., Haskett, R.F. and Carroll, B.J. (1980) Premenstrual tension syndrome: the development of research diagnostic criteria and new rating scales. *Acta Psychiatrica Scandinavica*, **62**, 177–90.

Stephenson, L.A., Denney, D.R. and Aberger, E.W. (1983) Factor structure of the menstrual symptom questionnaire: relationship to oral contraceptives, neuroticism and life stress. *Behavioural Research and Therapy*, **21**, 129–35.

Steptoe, A. and O'Sullivan, J. (1986) Monitoring and blunting coping styles in women prior to surgery. *British Journal of Clinical Psychology*, **25**(2), 143–4.

Stevenson, D.W. and Delprato, D.J. (1983) Multiple component self-control programme for menopausal hot flushes. *Journal of Behaviour Therapy and Experimental Psychiatry*, **14**(2), 137–40.

Strauss, B. and Appelt, H. (1983) Psychological concomitants of the menstrual cycle: a prospective longitudinal approach. *Journal of Psychosomatic Obstetrics and Gynecology*, **2–4**, 215–19.

Studd, J.W.W., Chakravarti, S. and Oram, D. (1977) The climacteric, in *Clinics in Obstetrics and Gynecology*, (eds R. Greenblatt and J.W.W. Studd), WB Saunders and Co., Philadelphia, pp. 3–29

Tamburini, M., Filiberti, V., Venta Fridda, V. and DePalo, G. (1986) Quality of life and psychological state after radical vulvectomy. *Journal of Psychosomatic Obstetrics and Gynecology*, **5**(4), 263–70.

Tessler, R., Mechanic, D. and Dimond, M. (1976) The effect of psychological distress on physician utilization: a prospective study. *Journal of Health and Social Behaviour*, **16**, 353–64.

Tsoi, M.M., Poon, R.S.M. and Ho, P.C. (1983) Knowledge of reproductive organs in Chinese women: some overlooked 'common sense'. *Journal of Psychosomatic Obstetrics and Gynecology*, **2**, 70–5.

Ussher, J.M. (1992) Research and theory related to female reproduction: implications for clinical psychology. *British Journal of Clinical Psychology*, **31**, 129–51.

Van Keep, P.A., Wildermeersch, D. and Lehert, P. (1983) Hysterectomy in six European countries. *Maturitas*, **5**(2), 69–77.

Vere, M.F. and Joyce, D.N. (1979) Luteal function in patient seeking AID. *British Medical Journal*, **ii**, 100.

Voda, A.M. (1981) Climacteric hot flush. *Maturitas*, **3**, 73–90.

Walker, A. (1992) Premenstrual symptoms and ovarian hormones: a review. *Journal of Reproductive and Infant Psychology*, **10**(8), 67–82.

Wallace, L. (1983) Psychological studies of the development and evaluation of preparatory procedures for women undergoing minor gynaecological surgery. PhD Thesis, University of Birmingham.

Wallace, L. (1984) Psychological preparation for gynaecological surgery, in *Psychology and Gynaecological Problems*, (eds A. Broome and L. Wallace), Tavistock Publications, London, pp. 161–88.

Warner, P. and Bancroft, J. (1986) *PMS survey: one syndrome for 7000 respondents?* Paper presented at The Annual Conference of the Society of Reproductive and Infant Psychology, Bristol.

Watson, M. (1993) *Counselling People with Cancer*, BPS Books, London.

Webb, C. and Wilson-Barnett, J. (1983) Hysterectomy: a study of coping with recovery. *Journal of Advanced Nursing*, **8**, 311–19.

Weideger, P. (1978) *Female Cycles*, The Women's Press, London.

Whitehead, M. (1982) Menopause clinics: purpose, function and international comparisons, in *The Controversial Climacteric*, (eds P.A. Van Keep, W.H. Utian and A. Vermeulen), MTP Press Ltd, Lancaster, pp. 154–5.

Wilcoxon, L.A., Schrader, S.L. and Sherif, C.W. (1976) Daily self reports on activities, life events, moods and somatic changes during the menstrual cycle. *Psychosomatic Medicine*, **38**(6), 399–417.

Wilson, R.A. (1966) *Feminine Forever*, Evans, New York.

Wilson-Barnett, J. (1991) Providing relevant information for patients and their families, in *Developing Communication and Counselling Skills in Medicine*, (ed R. Corney), Routledge, London, pp. 25–38.

Wilson-Barnett, J., Webb, C. and Gould, D. (1982) *Recovery from Hysterectomy*, DHSS Research Report.

Worsley, A., Walters, W.A.W. and Wood, E.C. (1977) Screening for psychological disturbance amongst gynaecology patients. Australian and New Zealand *Journal of Obstetrics and Gynecology*, **17**, 214.

Chapter sixteen

Psychological aspects of neurological illness

Louise Earll

Introduction

This chapter outlines the nature of neurological illness and symptoms in a necessarily brief and selective review of the development of psychological approaches in this field. It also argues the case for the wider application of psychological models and makes specific reference to coping with chronic neurological illness and the provision of health care services. For a more comprehensive description of various neurological illnesses and psychological aspects by disease category, Table 16.1 contains key references to each of the main diagnostic groups within neurology.

The nature of neurological illness and symptoms

The population

It has been estimated that, each year in America, one person in every 100 will have a new neurological disorder and that the pre-

valence rate is 36 persons in every 10 000 under the care of a neurologist (Kurtzke, 1982). There have been no comparable UK estimates, but based on the American figures, a health district of 250 000 would yield an incidence rate of 2500 and a prevalence rate of 9000.

A variety of methods can be employed to estimate the nature and magnitude of neurological illness in the population. One method is to consult the literature available on specific neurological diseases. Neurological textbooks, for example, will give the psychologist an adequate grounding in the range of neurologic disorders and an understanding of the classification schemas used by neurologists. However, the allocation of space to various conditions does not necessarily reflect the incidence or prevalence of these disorders, either in the neurology clinic or the population as a whole. General psychology textbooks offer sparse reference to neurological conditions other than head injury, stroke and dementia, although more frequent references can now be found to conditions such as multiple sclerosis, Parkinson's disease and epilepsy in texts dealing with psychological aspects of chronic disease (Burish and Bradley, 1983; Karoly, 1986). Increasingly sophisticated and useful information on single neurological diseases is available in the literature published by the voluntary self-help societies which exist for the majority of neurological conditions. These frequently give incidence figures, major signs and symptoms and practical advice on issues relating to management and coping. Information for professionals is also produced by some societies, for example the Motor Neurone Disease Association and the Multiple Sclerosis Society.

A second method, used in the Copiah County Study (Haerer, Anderson and Schoenberg, 1986), which assesses the pre-

valence of functional disability associated with major neurological disorders, is to obtain prevalence figures from comprehensive community surveys. This method is becoming increasingly pertinent with the growing pressure from governments to plan and budget for future health care services. Such an approach provides a more accurate picture of the epidemiology of neurological signs and symptoms, and can give information about the numbers who seek medical advice, those who manage on their own and those who seek alternative advice. Equally interesting would be the choice of specialist service the patient is referred to by the general practitioner. Not all patients with tension headaches are seen in neurology clinics, and patients with strokes might be referred to a general physician equally often as to a neuro-

TABLE 16.1 References to major neurological illness

Subject	Reference	Main aspects covered
Neurology	Harrison (1983)	Contemporary neurology
Neuropsychology	McCarthy and Warrington (1990)	General neuropsychology text
	Tupper and Cicerone (1991)	The neuropsychology of every day life
	Miller (1985)	Recovery and management of neuropsychological impairments
	Wilson and Moffat (1992)	Management of memory problems
Epilepsy	Herman and Whitman (1984)	Review of behavioural personality correlates of epilepsy
	Kaplan and Wyler (1983)	Coping with epilepsy
	Thompson and Trimble (1983)	Behavioural and cognitive effects of anticonvulsant therapy
Multiple sclerosis	Rao (1986)	Review of neuropsychology of multiple sclerosis
	Vanderplate (1984)	Review of psychological aspects of multiple sclerosis
Parkinson's disease	Dakof and Mendelsohn (1986)	Psychological aspects of a chronic illness
	Boller (1980)	Mental state of patients with Parkinson's disease
Motor neurone disease	McDonald et al. (1988)	A review of the literature
Cerebrovascular disease	Wade et al. (1986)	Diagnosis, treatment and management of cerebrovascular disease
Head injury	Gronwall et al. (1990)	Head injury: the facts for families and care-givers

logist or a geriatrician. Using data from comprehensive community surveys is particularly useful for the clinician offering a population-based service.

A third method, which is more relevant in providing a clinic-based service but which does not truly reflect population figures, is to look at the incidence of neurological symptoms and diseases presenting in neurology clinics. Stevens (1989) analysed the diagnoses made over a 3-year period for all patients referred to neurology services in two health districts serving a population of 500 000. Each district is served by a district general hospital having neither neurosurgical facilities nor special rehabilitation services. One neurologist serves both districts. A total of 3714 diagnoses were made on 3020 patients over a 3-year period, with 19 diagnoses accounting for 60% of the total diagnoses made (Table 16.2).

The observation made by Fitzpatrick and Hopkins (1981a), that a considerably greater number of patients are referred with tension headaches and migraine than with multiple sclerosis, is supported by these figures.

Neurological illness and symptoms

If one considers the population of neurologically ill people seen routinely in neurology clinics, it is clear that a major concern shared by both clinical neurologists and patients is the presentation and management of symptoms. The symptoms of nervous disease are extremely varied, and interpretation is not a simple task, either for patients or neurologists. As Mathews and Miller (1972) pointed out, the patient's description, often of totally unfamiliar sensations, has to be translated by the neurologist and explained in terms of physiological

TABLE 16.2 Neurological illness in Gloucestershire 1984, population 50 000

Rank	Diagnosis	No in 3 years	%
1	Epilepsy (all types)	489	13.2
2	Migraine/tension headache	463	12.5
3	Multiple sclerosis	140	3.8
4	Head injury (all categories)	131	3.5
5	?fit/?faint	102	2.7
6	Parkinson's disease, idiopathic	96	2.6
7	Cerebral infarct	95	2.6
8	Sensory symptoms? cause (all)	81	2.2
9	Cervical spondylosis (all categories)	78	2.1
10	Transient ischaemic attacks	75	2.0
11	Vertigo (all categories)	73	1.9
12	Polyneuritis	70	1.8
13	Median nerve lesions (all types)	59	1.6
14	Ulnar nerve lesions (all types)	57	1.5
15	*Non-organic symptoms (all types)	56	1.5
16	Lumbar spondylosis (all categories)	44	1.2
17	Syncopal attacks (all types)	43	1.2
18	Postviral disorders	39	1.1
19	*Depression (all categories)	37	1.0
		2228	60

*Only listed as a diagnosis if significant
NB: Total number of diagnoses = 3714

disturbance. Determining the underlying pathology is hampered by lack of knowledge of the causes of many of the basic disease processes. Such limitations increase the importance of symptoms, for treatment is often directed at the relief of disabling symptoms and not the underlying disease cause.

The author's own research in Gloucestershire examined some of the commonly reported neurological symptoms and compared the frequency with which they were reported by both the patient and the neurologist (Figure 16.1). The patients were 50 consecutive inpatients admitted to a neurology ward for the first time for investigations and treatment and then followed up at outpatient clinic 6 weeks later. Patients were asked whether they had experienced any of a given list of symptoms; the list was also completed by the neurologist. The largest discrepancy occurred for the symptoms of dizziness, pain, concentration and forgetfulness. A study by Hawkes (1974) looked at communication between neurologists and patients and highlighted a similar issue.

Patients and doctors were given a multiple-choice questionnaire with an open-ended option, and asked to select one answer which best described the symptom. Blackout and paralysis were rated 'good' for agreement between doctor and patient, but numbness, headache and dizzy-turns received a 'poor' agreement rating.

It is clear that patients do not share the same perspectives as doctors. Fitzpatrick and Hopkins (1981a) reported on a study of patients attending neurology outpatient clinics for headache. They interviewed patients following consultation and reported that patients felt that they had not received adequate investigation, explanation or treatment. The authors commented on the lack of fit between patients' own accounts of their experiences and the assumptions about patients contained in much of the research carried out on patient satisfaction. They concluded that patients' varying concerns about their illnesses needed to be more directly considered in explaining different responses to medical consultations. This sug-

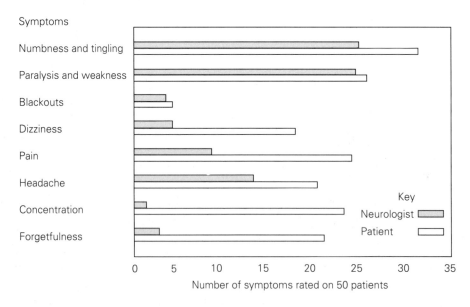

FIGURE 16.1 Frequency of symptoms assessed by neurologist and patient.

gests an argument for patient-led research as opposed to theory-led research.

Application of psychological models to neurological illness

Boll (1985), in his discussion of developing issues in neuropsychology, stated that 'it is of critical importance that neuropsychologists become aware of their psychological foundations ... psychologists have an opportunity and responsibility for the development of health care services to patients with neurological disorders and complaints'. Psychological phenomena in neurology have frequently been considered only within disease categories, rather than psychological categories. Marteau and Johnston (1987) suggest that the use of disease categories in research develops the understanding of the disease, but by contrast, where psychological schemata have been used the theoretical models have become more sophisticated and the methods of investigation more refined. Many of the models used by patients and staff working in neurology settings are indeed psychological rather than disease related. Thus, psychological similarities in the experience of neurological conditions with disparate aetiologies and symptomatologies are frequently recognized.

Perception and understanding of symptoms

To understand symptom-related behaviour one needs to consider emotions, disease labels, expectations and how people decide they are ill. The arousal of subjective emotion appears to intensify body sensations such as pain and distress, and can also generate a wide range of psychophysiological responses resulting in sensations, to which are added other non-illness sensations. Being told that one has an illness appears to increase symptomatology, also people attend more to bodily sensations to make sense of illness labels. When people notice

unexplained or unexpected bodily signs, they search for information to interpret them. This need to relate concrete symptoms and abstract disease concepts to each other can produce much bias in symptom report data (Pennebaker, 1984).

Awareness of illness may also heighten sensitivity to body changes, leading to reports of illness based on experienced bodily sensations in the absence of disease. In situations where illnesses occur on a regular or cyclic basis, people may experience symptoms simply because they expect them to occur. The need for information frequently involves talking to other people to find out if they have similar symptoms or were exposed to similar events, and typically occurs early in the process of symptom awareness. This process is short-circuited if the symptom is severe or unusual. The need for information and the tendency to seek labels is also greatly reduced if the symptoms appear familiar.

Research into symptoms and illness illustrates the importance of the labelling process. From the doctor's perspective, operating within the medical model, vague and ill-defined symptoms might not necessarily be recorded if they appear incompatible with, or surplus to, the disease label. This may explain the discrepancy noted earlier between patients and doctors on symptoms of dizziness, pain, concentration and forgetfulness. It is not unreasonable for the doctor to deduce that symptoms of forgetfulness and lack of concentration might also reflect the patient's reaction to illness, rather than the disease itself.

When looking for a framework to understand how symptoms are perceived and understood, both the Health Belief Model (Becker, 1974) and self-regulation theory (Leventhal, Nerenz and Strauss, 1980) offer interesting perspectives. The distinction in Leventhal's model (discussed in more detail later) between symptoms and label is of particular interest to chronic neurological illness. The initial symptoms of some illnesses can be very slight and perceived as relatively unimportant. For example, the early symptoms of motor neurone disease – which often consist of twitching (fasciculations) in the affected muscles – is a useful diagnostic symptom for the doctor but frequently unnoticed by the patient. Most people are not familiar with the diagnosis of motor neuron disease; the label is therefore accorded the same level of seriousness as the symptom. The seriousness of its course and consequences are not available to the patient without further information.

Motor neurone disease is a progressive muscle-weakening disease that is incurable. It has an average lifespan from diagnosis of about 4 years. It is not uncommon for a patient, given the diagnosis of motor neurone disease, to comment on how relieved they are not to have cancer or multiple sclerosis, both diseases frequently associated with the symptoms of fatigue and weakness. Thus, the disease label may even mislead the patient about the threat involved.

The Health Belief Model (see Chapter 2) assumes that people react to illness threats, including symptoms, in terms of perceived vulnerability and perceived severity. Although useful in explaining some of the variance in preventive health behaviour, it is a somewhat abstract concept, in that patients given the diagnosis of multiple sclerosis invariably see images of wheelchairs, and respond to this image rather than any estimate of their probable chances of becoming wheelchair bound. However, the perceived severity of a symptom undoubtedly has an influence on the person's decision whether or not to seek help. Furthermore, distortion of threat may influence health behaviours. If people deal with the threat of disease by changing or minimizing the nature of the threat, then they may also remove the need to act to reduce that threat, thus placing themselves at greater risk. Epileptic patients who reinterpret their diagnosis as 'faints' and not 'fits' may not see the need to take anticonvulsant medication, and also continue to drive a car, thus placing both themselves and others at risk.

Psychological sequelae and aetiology of neurological illness

One of the aims of the early psychological literature was to test the notion that patients with neurological illness showed a high degree of psychopathology. However, as Vanderplate (1984) commented in his review of psychological aspects of multiple sclerosis, most of the early studies do not conclude either that personality patterns exist unique to each disability, or that profiles reflect generalized reactions to chronic illness. In addition to attempting to categorize personality patterns, numerous studies have focused on the role of stress and depression. These earlier studies have mainly used retrospective reports and are confounded by disease variables, particularly in the case of multiple sclerosis and Parkinson's disease. Furthermore, symptoms of anxiety and depression may occur in response to the onset of symptoms, but antedate the diagnosis. These issues can only be addressed by longitudinal prospective studies.

One of the key methodological issues in this area is how to measure coping. It appears incorrect to assume that people use the same coping strategies in dealing with all aspects of a particular situation. There is now considerable evidence that different ways of coping are used in dealing with different parts of a stressful situation and at different stages. Cohen *et al.* (1986) reported on findings from their work on rheumatoid arthritis that different ways are used in dealing with the pain of the disease, compared to those used in dealing with the threats to self-esteem brought on by the disease. Similarly, it is obvious that people use different ways of coping with mobility problems and difficulties with self-care. Specific coping strategies vary depending on disease and treatment parameters, and on what the disease means to the person and the effect it has on their lives.

On the whole, the most consistent finding to arise from this research paradigm has been that people with chronic illness tend to be more depressed than healthy people. Friedman and Booth-Kewley (1989) have referred to this as the 'disease prone personality', indicating that this personality is not specifically related to particular diseases.

Current thinking views depression and stress as reactions to disease and disability. Depression and other indices of psychological problems occur fairly consistently only with chronic severe disabling disease, such as multiple sclerosis, and with advanced stages of disease, such as the latter stages of motor neurone disease. However, severity rather than type of disability is associated with psychological distress in chronic illnesses. The adaptive capacity of patients with multiple sclerosis has been seen more as a function of durable personality traits and life constructs than as specific illness variables (Counte, Bieliauskas and Pavlou, 1983).

Many investigations of chronically ill patients assume that psychological attributes are specific to particular diagnostic characteristics. Cassileth *et al.* (1984), in a study of 758 patients, each with one of six different chronic illnesses, concluded that the psychological status of these chronically ill patients reflected the population at large. He argued that an individual's adaptation represents not the demands of a particular stress, such as a specific diagnosis, but rather the manifestations of enduring personality constructs and capacities.

It can be concluded that psychological stereotyping and assumptions of diagnosis-specific emotional response are neither tenable nor clinically meaningful.

A more sophisticated analysis of the relationship between psychological factors is presented in a longitudinal study by McDonald *et al.* (1993). Patients with motor neurone disease, or amyotrophic lateral sclerosis (ALS), were classi-fied as having a positive or a negative psychological profile. A positive profile was defined following factor analysis and consisted of 'low hopelessness, depression and perceived stress; expressive of anger; well-defined purpose; internal control; and high satisfaction with life'. When followed up over 18 months, those with a positive psychological profile had a lower risk of dying and a longer survival time than those with a negative psychological profile, even allowing for length of illness, disease severity and age. It is possible that those with a positive profile cope with their condition differently from those with a negative profile.

Cognitive impairment

Psychologists working in neurological settings have tended to maintain the more traditional approaches of diagnostic assessment, in contrast to clinical psychology generally, where there is increasing concern with the issues of patient management and treatment. This is due in part to the academic research perspective from which neuropsychology is derived.

Neuropsychology has been concerned with the relationship between brain and behaviour, in both animals and humans, and with devising elaborate and multifarious ways of measuring and quantifying that relationship. An extensive literature exists dealing with this area (Tupper & Cicerone, 1991; Lezack, 1983). These findings have often been applied to the field of rehabilitation, in particular the cognitive retraining of neurological patients. Miller (1985) points out that this relatively recent development has been fuelled by two factors. The first is realization that many who suffer disease or damage to the central nervous system retain significant handicaps for the rest of their lives, and therefore need some form of rehabilitation. Cognitive retraining of neurologically impaired patients reflects an approach to psychological intervention that believes that impaired people have certain psychological defecits which must be changed if they are to function in their environment. In this approach the aim is to change people so they better fit this environment. The second, alternative, approach regards the impaired person's environment as making inappropriate demands on his or her limited cognitive capacities. The environment is therefore changed to fit these remaining capacities better. Within both these broad approaches, psychological interventions can aim to overcome different areas of deficit, for instance that of social interaction and apathy (Jorum, 1987). The second reason for an increased emphasis on rehabilitation and a decreased emphasis on cognitive assessment is the development of sophisticated radiological techniques, such as magnetic resonance imaging, which undermines the importance of neuropsychological assessment in the diagnosis.

When considering research into psychological aspects of neurological illness involving the central nervous system, the potential effects of cognitive impairments must be considered. How patients cope or respond to illness might well be influenced by personality changes brought about by cognitive impairment, as in Huntington's chorea or Alzheimer's disease.

Coping with chronic neurological illness

Understanding health-related behaviour is an important priority for health carers. As the implications of acute illness become less of a problem, the prevention of illness and the management of people with chronic illness becomes a focus for improving health. Unlike some other chronic illnesses, such as heart disease, research has not consistently indicated any lifestyle or behavioural factors which influence the onset or course of the disease process in any of the major neurological diseases. The current focus of psychological endeavour at present is to help people with chronic disease cope successfully with their impairments, so that their quality of life, both emotionally and

interpersonally and in the daily activities, is maximized.

The findings on chronic disease and distress can be interpreted using models of coping. That illness leads to distress is theoretically embedded in the context of theories of stress and coping, as is the evidence that major life events cause stress (Fisher and Reason, 1988, and see also the chapter by Cox, this volume). Being ill and having a chronic neurological illness (such as multiple sclerosis or motor neuron disease) can be seen as a stressful major life event involving loss of functional abilities and eventually the loss of life, and also as having an unpredictable course which is as yet uncontrollable by medical means.

When asking questions about chronic neurological illness, one should ask why some people become depressed and have difficulty coping, and also why, in the face of incurable disabling disease, the great majority of patients are neither depressed nor even in serious psychological distress. With respect to Parkinson's disease, but equally applicable to other chronic neurological disorders, Dakof and Mendelsohn (1986) commented that we are largely ignorant of how some people see themselves as having changed for the better and not the worse by their illness. We are largely unaware of the psychological factors that act as buffers against psychological distress, and how illness both affects and is affected by the social environment.

Work in this area has concentrated on the perception of stressors and the role of appraisal in determining whether a given person perceives an event to be stressful. Then, having appraised the event as stressful, the resources the person has to cope with the event may be appraised, indicating the likelihood of a successful outcome (Folkman and Lazarus, 1985; see also Cox, this volume).

There is growing evidence that, in chronic disease of all kinds, psychological disturbance is generally greatest in the early stages of illness

(Meyerowitz, 1980). Cassileth *et al.* (1984) found that, irrespective of diagnosis, patients with recently diagnosed illness had poorer mental health scores (as measured by the Mental Health Index) than patients diagnosed more than 4 months previously. Dakof and Mendelsohn (1986) suggest that the potential effects of increasing debility may be counteracted by patients' habituation to symptoms and their development of means to deal with them.

Towards an integrating framework

When looking for a framework to study coping with chronic illness, models that view the person as an active problem solver, and not a passive responder, are most useful. Such models include the Health Belief Model, discussed in an earlier section, social learning theory (Bandura, 1977), the theory of reasoned action (Fishbein and Ajzen, 1975) and self-regulation theory (Leventhal, Nerenz and Strauss, 1980).

Social learning theory was developed to account for human behaviour in complex situations. Much of the work of Wallston and Wallston (1984) has involved an attempt to apply this theory to understanding health behaviours. The aspect of this theory to receive most attention in the health field has been locus of control. This is generally defined as the expectancy as to whether one's own behaviour or forces external to oneself control reinforcements. Although perceived control is a very useful concept when looking at health behaviour, in chronic neurological illness, such as multiple sclerosis or motor neuron disease, perceived control may not be an effective strategy for management. Realistically, to manage the disease, shared control with others in the family and with other health professionals might arguably be better (Reid, 1983).

Fishbein and Aijzen's theory of reasoned action was developed to bridge the gap between attitudes and behaviours. They assert that not only are one's own attitudes important, but that the beliefs of significant others also contribute to taking health actions. For further discussion of these models see Wallston and Wallston (1984), and Chapter 2 of this volume.

Leventhal and his colleagues have spent several years developing a model to describe and predict how people cope with stressful health threats, and have extended the model to address the issue of coping with chronic illness (Leventhal and Nerenz, 1986). Of all the available models, this latter probably offers the widest framework to consider the many complex aspects of coping with chronic neurological illness. The basic premise is that individuals are motivated to regulate or minimize their health-related risks and to act to reduce health threats in ways consistent with their perceptions of them. This suggests that patients are actively constructing a definition or representation of their illnesses and basing or regulating their behaviour in terms of this representation. It is a complex model of an adaptive system, in which adaptation to stressful situations is viewed as the product of a system of mediating factors. Coping is the skill component.

A primary feature of the model is the idea that the underlying system is composed of a series of stages for guiding adaptive action. Any or all of these stages may be disrupted by cognitive impairment, disabling the patient's adaptive potential. The first of these stages is the representation of the illness, which includes variables that identify the presence or absence of the illness. These can be both abstract, such as labels (multiple sclerosis, Parkinson's disease) and concrete, such as signs and symptoms (double vision, fatigue, weakness). Other variables in the representation of the illness include the perceived causes of the illness, the perceived consequences (physical, social and economic) and the perceived timeframe for the development and duration of the illness. The second of these stages, action planning or coping, involves weighing up the possibilities for action, either by coping with the objective features of the illness or by dealing with the emotional reaction.

The third stage involves setting criteria for evaluating responses and appraising one's coping efforts against them. At this stage unsuccessful coping may become apparent in emotional reactions or interpersonal behaviour that has been taken as an index of psychopathology or as part of the adjustment to the stress of chronic illness. The whole system operates though a series of feedback loops.

In developing clinical treatments, there is frequently an assumption that people with these diseases and those who care for them at home view the disease in the same way as the professionals view it. There is no research to support this assumption. Earll, Johnston and Mitchell (1993), in a cross-sectional study of 50 people with motor neurone disease and their carers, examined some of the questions raised by this model, and showed that not only do individual representations vary, but that these representations do not relate to the overall objective severity or the speech and swallowing problems which are distinctive features of MND. Instead, they relate to the objective problems of daily living. Thus it is important that professionals do not assume that they can anticipate the patients' views of their condition, nor that the medical perspective is the one adopted by patients.

Health care for the chronically neurologically ill

As the distribution of illness during this century has shifted from acute infectious disease to chronic conditions traditional patterns of health care and service delivery are being put under increasing pressure to change. This pressure comes not only from the economic constraints placed on the health service, but also from the need to improve both the delivery and quality of service offered to patients. Both the structure and the pattern of health care need radical changes, particularly for the chronically physically ill.

The structure of the medical care system directs attention and coping to specific types of illness representations and self-illness linkages. The system is designed to deal with the emergencies and acute care, is orientated towards symptoms and external causes, and teaches short-term self-maintenance coping strategies. The biomedical structure reinforces the view of illness as being due to 'alien' invading forces to be destroyed by miracle drugs and surgery. The power of the medical care system in shaping illness cognitions resides in its providing an integral view: it relates labels to symptom experience, provides coping regimes for representations and ameliorates the emotional distress and fear that parallel the illness representation and the coping system.

The organization of health care services can also, arguably, contribute to psychological distress. Bosanquet and Fordham (1987) refer to information about consumer attitudes which points to outpatient services as being the most unpopular service provided by the National Health Service. In a study of 42 patients with motor neurone disease, Newrick and Langton-Hewer (1984) found 32 patients who disliked attending neurological outpatient clinics. They listed as their reasons the wait for transport, the discomfort of the journey, seeing ever-changing junior medical staff, lack of access to information, and doctors' ignorance about the disease and control of symptoms.

Chronic neurological disease requires a high level of assumed responsibility from the patient in order that day-to-day management is successful (Mazzucca, 1982). Patients both need and want more information and education about their condition, as well as advice on how to carry this information through their everyday lives. They also need and want longer consultations at which worries, needs and individual concerns can be fully aired, rather than the more usual pattern of brief, repeat visits over long periods of time. This is necessary in order for patients to test out and develop their representations and to iron out discrepancies between their views and what they see happening. Earll (1986) outlines an example of an alternative pattern of care in practice in Gloucestershire. The service was specifically designed for the management of motor neurone disease, where the patients and family are managed by a multidisciplinary clinical team in a flexible system of community and hospital care in response to patient needs. An informal 'key-worker' takes the responsibility of informing other members of the team of any developments and of ensuring that the patient and family receive the services they might need. Continuity of care is essential to maintain contact with the patients and to monitor their representation of their illness, their attempts at coping and the evaluation of their efforts. Patients are followed up from diagnosis, and bereavement counselling is made available as required by the family following the death of the patient.

The multidisciplinary clinical team is frequently advocated as a means of delivering the range of health care needed by patients with complex conditions. Some of the issues relating to the establishment and function of such teams are discussed by Furnell, Flett and Clark (1987).

Conclusion

There has been a change in demand in health care from the diagnosis and management of acute infectious disease to the management of chronic disease. Within the field of neurology, psychology has developed from the assessment of cognitive impairment to a much broader-based approach, applying developments in health and social psychology to this field. Neurological illness offers wide scope for psychologists to develop a framework within which to understand symptoms, their meaning and presentation, and the cognitive, emotional and behavioural processes patients utilize to cope with and adjust to their illness. Future research into the aetiology (including psychoimmunology) of neurological illness, and how best health care services can be organized to facilitate coping and adjustment, will be an equally valid and useful part of any future research questions posed.

References

Bandura, A. (1977) *Social Learning Theory*, Prentice Hall, Englewood Cliffs, New Jersey.
Becker, M.H. (ed) (1974) The Health Belief Model and personal health behaviour. *Health Education Monographs*, 2.
Boll, T.J. (1985) Developing issues in clinical neuropsychology. *Journal of Clinical and Experimental Neuropsychology*, 7(5), 473–85.
Boller, F. (1980) Mental status of patients with Parkinson's disease. *Journal of Clinical Neuropsychology*, 2(3), 157–72.
Bosanquet, N. and Fordham, R. (1987) Outpatient services – a case for treatment. *Health Service Journal*, 14 May, 550–1.
Burish, T.G. and Bradley, L.A. (eds) (1983) *Coping with Chronic Disease: Research and Applications*, Academic Press, London.
Cassileth, B.R., Lusk, E.J., Straus, T.B. *et al.* (1984) Psychosocial status in chronic illness – a comparative analysis of six diagnostic groups. *New England Journal of Medicine*, 311, 506–11.
Cohen, F., Reese, L.B., Kaplan, G.A. and Riggio, R.E. (1986) Coping with the stress of arthritis, in *Arthritis and the Elderly*, (eds R.W. Moskowitz and M.R. Haug), Springer, New York, pp. 47–56.
Counte, M.A., Bieliauskas, L.A. and Pavlou, M. (1983) Stress and personal attitudes in chronic illness. *Archives of Physical and Medical Rehabilitation*, 64, 272–5.
Dakof, G.A. and Mendelsohn, G.A. (1986) Parkinson's disease: The psychological aspects of a chronic illness. *Psychological Bulletin*, 99(3), 375–87.
Earll, L., Johnston, M. and Mitchell, E. (1993) Coping with motor neuron disease: an analysis using self-regulation theory. (Submitted for publication).
Earll, L. (1986) Psychological aspects of neurological illness, in *Health Psychology*, (ed A. Broome), Chapman and Hall, London.
Fishbein, M. and Aijzen (1975) *Beliefs, Attitudes, Intention and Behaviour: an Introduction to Theory and Research*, Addison Wesley, Reading, MA.

Fisher, S. and Reason, J. (1988) *Handbook of Lifestyles, Cognition and Health*, Wiley, Chichester.

Fitzpatrick, R.M. and Hopkins, A. (1981a) Patients' satisfaction with communication in neurological outpatient clinics. *Journal of Psychosomatic Research*, 25(5), 329–34.

Fitzpatrick, R.M. and Hopkins, A. (1981b) Referrals to neurologists for headaches not due to structural disease. *Journal of Neurology, Neurosurgery and Psychiatry*, 44, 1061–7.

Folkman, S. and Lazarus, R.S. (1985) If it changes it must be a process: study of emotion and coping during three stages of a college examination. *Journal of Personality and Social Psychology*, 48(1), 150–70.

Friedman, H.S. and Booth-Kewley, S. (1989) The 'disease-prone personality': a meta-analytic view of the construct. *American Psychologist*, 42, 539–55.

Furnell, J., Flett, S. and Clark, D.F. (1987) Multidisciplinary clinical teams: some issues in the establishment and function. *Hospital and Health Service Review*, January, 15–20.

Haerer, A.F., Anderson, D.W. and Schoenberg, B.S. (1986) Functional disability associated with major neurologic disorders: findings from the Copiah County Study. *Archives of Neurology*, 43, 1000–3.

Harrison, M.J. (ed) (1983) *Contemporary Neurology*, Butterworths, London.

Hawkes, C.H. (1974) Communicating with the patient – an example drawn from neurology. *British Journal of Medical Education*, 8(1), 57–63.

Herman, B.P. and Whitman, S. (1984) Behavioural and personality correlates of epilepsy: a review, methodological critique and conceptual model. *Psychological Bulletin*, 95(3), 451–97.

Jorum, A.F. (1987) *Understanding Senile Dementia*, Croom Helm, Beckenham, Kent.

Kaplan, B.J. and Wyler, A.R. (1983) Coping with epilepsy, in *Coping with Chronic Disease*, (eds T.G. Burish and L.A. Bradley), Academic Press, London, pp. 259–84.

Karoly, P. (ed) (1986) *Measurement Strategies in Health Psychology*, John Wiley and Sons, Chichester.

Kurtzke, J.F. (1982) The current neurologic burden of illness and injury in the United States. *Neurology*, 33, 1207–14.

Leventhal, H. and Nerenz, D. (1986) The assessment of illness cognition, in *Coping with Chronic Disease*, (ed) P. Karoly John Wiley and Sons, Chichester, pp. 517–54.

Leventhal, H., Nerenz, D. and Straus, A. (1980) Self-regulation and the mechanisms for symptom appraisal, in *Psychosocial Epidemiology*, (ed) D. Mechanic, Neale Watson Academic Publishers, New York, pp. 55–85.

Lezack, M. (1983) *Neuropsychological Assessment*, 2nd edn, Oxford University Press, Oxford.

McDonald, E.R., Hillell, A.D. and Weidenfeld, S.A. (1988) The psychological aspects of amyotrophic lateral sclerosis, in *Amyotrophic Lateral Sclerosis*, (eds T. Tsubaki and Y. Yase), Elsevier Science Publications (Biomedical division), Oxford, pp. 235–45.

McDonald, E.R., Weidenfeld, S.A., Hillel, A. *et al.* (1993) Differences in mortality and survival time in amyotrophic lateral sclerosis: the role of psychological factors. (Submitted for publication)

Marteau, T.M. and Johnston, J.M. (1987) Health psychology: the danger of neglecting psychological models. *Bulletin of the British Psychological Society*, 40, 82–5.

Mathews, W.B. and Miller, H. (1972) *Diseases of the Nervous System*, Blackwell Scientific Publications, Oxford.

Mazzuca, C. (1982) Does patient education in chronic disease have therapeutic value? *Journal of Chronic Disease*, 35(7), 521–9.

Meyerowitz, B. (1980) Psychosocial correlates of breast cancer and its treatment. *Psychological Bulletin*, 87(1), 108–31.

Miller, E. (1985) Cognitive retraining of neurological impairments, in *New Developments in Clinical Psychology*, (ed F.N. Watts), British Psychological Society, London, pp. 110–20.

Newrick, P.G. and Langton-Hewer, R. (1984) MND: Can we do better? A study of 42 patients. *British Medical Journal*, 289, 539–42.

Pennebaker, J. (1984) Accuracy of symptom perception, in *Handbook of Psychology and Health, IV: Social Aspects of Health*, (eds A. Baum, S. Taylor, and J.E. Singer), Lawrence Erlbaum Associates, Hillsdale, New Jersey, pp. 189–218.

Rao, S.M. (1986) Neuropsychology of multiple sclerosis: a critical review. *Journal of Clinical and Experimental Neuropsychology*, 8(50), 503–42.

Reid, D.W. (1983) Participating control and the chronic illness adjustment processs, in *Research with the Locus of Control Construct*, (ed. H.M. Lefcourt), Academic Press, London, pp. 361–89.

Stevens, D.L. (1989) Neurology in Gloucestershire: the clinical workload of an English neurologist. *Journal of Neurology, Neurosurgery and Psychiatry*, 52, 439–46.

Thompson, P.J. and Trimble, M.R. (1983) Anticonvulsant serum levels: relationship to impairments of cognitive functioning. *Journal of Neurology, Neurosurgery and Psychiatry*, 46, 227–33.

Tupper, D.E. and Cicerone, K.D. (1991) *The Neuropsychology of Everyday Life: Issues in Development and Rehabilitation*, Kluwer Academic Publishers.

Vanderplate, C. (1984) Psychological aspects of multiple sclerosis and its treatment: towards a bio-psychosocial perspective. *Health Psychology*, 3, 253–72.

Wade, D.T., Langton-Hewer, R., Skilbeck, C.E. and David, R.M. (1986) *Stroke*, Chapman and Hall, London.

Wallston, B.S. and Wallston, K.A. (1984) Social psychological models of health behaviour: an examination and integration, in *Handbook of Psychology and Health IV: Social Psychological Aspects of Health*, (eds A. Baum, S.E. Taylor and J.E. Singer), Lawrence Erlbaum Associates, Hillsdale, New Jersey, pp. 23–53.

Walsh, K. (1978) *Neuropsychology: A Clinical Approach*, Churchill Livingstone, Edinburgh.

Wilson, B.A. and Moffat, N. (eds) (1992) *Clinical Management of Memory Problems*, 2nd edn, Chapman and Hall, London.

Chapter seventeen

Emotional factors in hearing loss

Simon Jakes

Introduction

This chapter reviews the psychological literature concerning clinical issues related to abnormalities of hearing.

In particular, studies which have addressed the question of the emotional causes and consequences of these disorders and, where evidence exists, of the factors that appear to influence the emotional effects of these symptoms ('illness behaviour'). This review is not comprehensive. The most obvious omissions are the developmental effects of early-onset problems of hearing (e.g. prelingual hearing loss); the relationship between personality dimensions and auditory threshold (reviewed by Stephens, 1972); psychosomatic aspects of hearing loss (where there is a growing and exciting literature concerning the effect of personality and/or individual differences in psychophysiological dimensions on the susceptibility to noise-induced hearing loss); and the possible association between hearing loss and psychotic states and/or paranoid delusions.

The application of psychological interventions in this area is in still its infancy and the literature in this area is scanty. Most of the work to be reviewed is concerned with exploring the nature of emotional distress occasioned by malfunctions of the auditory systems.

Acquired hearing loss

Much of the research conducted on the emotional effects of acquired hearing loss has concerned itself with the proportion of those who have a hearing loss who in addition have a 'psychiatric illness'. This has limited the usefulness of these studies. Clearly, any emotional sequelae of hearing loss may well form a continuum rather than discrete 'illness', so that it may be more productive to look at the degree of disturbance rather than just its presence or absence.

It has been suggested (e.g. by Ramsdell, 1970) that hearing loss may produce adverse emotional states in several different ways. Obviously, impaired hearing can interfere with the perception of speech. This can drastically affect social interaction, particularly in groups. However, hearing loss can also distort the quality of speech that is heard: for example, the non-verbal aspects of speech, so crucial for the communication of emotion, are often less well perceived. Thus, the quality as well as the quantity of social interaction may well be affected.

Ramsdell (1970) suggested that three functions are performed by hearing, and that there are consequently three different types of deprivation in hearing loss. These functions are symbolic (perception of the spoken word); warning (shouts, automobile horns); and perception of background noise. He postulated that the last of these functions serves to keep the individual 'in touch' with the world and that deprivation of this function produces feelings of unreality and isolation (like watching a silent film). Indeed, on the basis of his clinical experience he argued that this was the most important deprivation in producing depression in the hearing impaired. He claimed that explaining this mechanism to the patient (who is much more aware of difficulties in hearing speech) was an important part of rehabilitation. This interesting hypothesis has not been tested.

Unilateral hearing loss has far fewer effects on the ability to hear than bilateral hearing loss. The major handicap associated with unilateral hearing loss is difficulty in localizing sound sources. Mahapatra (1974) utilized this fact to investigate the emotional effects of hearing loss. He compared two groups of patients awaiting surgery for otosclerosis, a degenerative condition of the middle ear involving the growth of bone which affects the ossicles. The first group had a unilateral hearing loss of at least 40 dB HL at 250 Hz; the second group had that degree of hearing loss in both ears. Both groups were given a psychiatric interview and completed the Cornell Index. Patients were assessed the day before surgery. 'Psychiatric illness' (mainly depression) was more frequent in the bilaterally hearing impaired group ($P \leq 0.005$). The bilaterally impaired group also scored significantly higher than the unilaterally impaired group on the following scales of the Cornell Index: fear, depression, sensitivity and suspiciousness, nervousness and anxiety, neurocirculatory symptoms, hypochondriasis and asthenia. Those with a severe impairment, however, were *less* impaired than those with a moderate impairment.

Thomas (1984) has pointed out that the differences between the groups could be due to the differential significance of surgery on one ear compared with two ears. This criticism does involve acknowledging that the expectation of unilateral hearing impairment differs from the expectation of bilateral hearing impairment in terms of its emotional impact. To some degree this is a paradoxical criticism, as this is the theory the criticism is aimed at.

Myklebust (1964) contrasted MMPI profiles members of a 'hard of hearing club' with those of a control group who had normal hearing, and were matched for age and class (they were friends of the subjects). He reports that the hearing impaired were rated as significantly more 'maladjusted'. Of course, these subjects were by no means a random sample of the hearing impaired, but were self-selected by joining the hard of hearing club. This may well mean that their hearing loss was particularly important to them (possibly because they were distressed by it).

Thomas and Gilhome-Herbst (1980) conducted a well-designed large-scale study to investigate these issues. The target sample was all patients seen for hearing-aid fitting at certain NHS hearing-aid centres. The control group consisted of normally hearing people matched for age, sex, occupation and geographical location. The dependent variables were scores on the Symptoms of Anxiety and Depression (SAD) scale (Bedford and Foulds, 1978). Patients also completed questionnaires concerning the effect of hearing loss on their lives. The results were analysed by categorizing subjects as 'psychiatrically disturbed' or not on the basis of the SAD scale. Of the hearing-impaired group, 19% were classified as psychiatrically disturbed on this basis; 5% of the general population are so classified. This difference is statistically significant at the 0.01% level. There was no overall relationship between pure-tone audiometry or speech audiometry and status as psychiatrically disturbed. (A small group with very poor hearing were tested using pure-tone and speech audiometry, resulting in a lack of association, but this finding was not replicated in a further study.) The presence of tinnitus and the duration of the hearing loss did not relate to 'psychiatric status'. The only variables that did discriminate between the groups were probably related to that classification (e.g. being lonely). The lack of relationship between severity of hearing loss and emotional disturbance is important, as it is evidence against any simple theory of the relationship between hearing loss and disturbance. Indeed, it weakens the case that it is hearing loss itself that produces this disturbance. However, the study had weaknesses: poor response rate (48%), the dichotomization of emotional disturbance (which excludes important data), and the lack of control for general medical status. Also, hearing-impaired individuals attending a clinic are not a random sample of the hearing-impaired population.

Singerman, Fiedner and Folstein (1980) examined the relationship between different types of hearing loss and emotional disturbance as assessed by the General Hospital Questionnaire (GHQ). All subjects were patients attending an ENT clinic. The various groups were normal hearing; unilateral hearing loss at those frequencies most important for hearing speech; bilateral hearing loss at the speech frequencies; and hearing loss outside the speech frequencies. This design controlled for the effect of having a hearing loss, and isolated the effects of particular sorts of loss. Unfortunately, such a design cannot inform us about Ramsdell's hypothesis concerning the importance of background sounds, as most of these also lie in the speech frequencies range. The most 'abnormal' group on the GHQ were those with normal hearing. This may be due to this group having 'non-organic' hearing loss or, more likely, to this group presenting in a distressed state with tinnitus or vertigo. Indeed, the authors report that the group with normal hearing did have more tinnitus and vertigo than the other groups. Those with bilateral

hearing loss had the second highest scores, followed by those with high or low-tone hearing loss (outside the speech frequencies). Patients with a unilateral hearing loss were no different from the general population. It is of interest that hearing loss outside the speech frequencies range was associated with elevated scores.

Gildston and Gildston (1972) conducted an experimental comparison of the effects of hearing loss. Patients undergoing stapedectomy (surgical removal of the stapes and replacement with a prosthesis to improve hearing in otosclerosis) were assessed pre- and postoperatively on the Guildford–Zimmerman Temperament Survey. Patients improved significantly on several scales of 'psychopathology', and became indistinguishable from population norms.

Stephens (1980) found the hearing impaired to be significantly more introverted and neurotic on the EPI, and also to obtain higher 'lie' scores.

Gilhome-Herbst and Humphrey (1980) used audiometry to assess hearing impairment in elderly people registered with one particular GP, and 69% of the target population were assessed. Those people with a hearing loss were significantly more likely to be assessed as depressed on the SAD scale. However, the severity of the hearing loss did not relate to depression. Interestingly, 'feeling different' about themselves ('closed-in', 'frustrated' or 'depressed') were all associated with onset of hearing loss before retirement. It may be that hearing loss occurring during retirement is seen as 'normal', as part of the ageing process, and therefore has less effect on mood.

The evidence from the studies reported above yields a curious picture. On the one hand, an association between depression or anxiety and hearing impairment is replicated in many studies. Gildston and Gildston's work also shows that these emotional problems seem to disappear following curative treatment. On the other hand, 'depression' or 'anxiety' have consistently been found to be uncorrelated with severity of hearing impairment (or, in one study, inversely correlated). There are several possible explanations. The 'normal' control groups used in comparative studies do not control for general medical status. Furthermore, it is rare that random samples of the hearing impaired are studied: usually, samples are based on those attending for treatment. Clearly, these patients may be self-selecting in an important way. A more important problem underlies the logic of most of these studies. Conceptualizing emotional distress along conventionally psychiatric lines by dichotomization into 'psychiatric cases' or by concentration on broad categories of distress such as 'anxiety' or 'depression', rather than looking in detail at the particular problems that individuals present, is based on a very narrow view of emotional disturbance.

The lack of relationship between severity of hearing impairment and degree of distress is intriguing. If hearing loss does predispose to depression or anxiety, it is hard to see why the probability of being distressed does not increase with the additional problems encountered with severe hearing loss. It is possible that a threshold for distress exists beyond which no additional distress is produced. Alternatively, the association between hearing loss and depression and anxiety may be illusory, or mediated through general physical health.

No real attempt has been made to try to show that hearing loss is different from any other sort of loss that people suffer. Certainly, significant losses are associated with depressed mood. It is possible that the results merely confirm that loss is associated with depression and anxiety, rather than any more specific association. It is as if 'psychiatric disturbance' is seen as being wholly different from being emotionally disturbed, so that it is treated as logically independent of the depressing event, i.e. losing one's hearing.

Silver (1988), a psychoanalytic psychotherapist who works with prelingually deaf patients and their families, suggests that a deaf child's maternal experiences are usually affected by two salient facts. First, the parents of the deaf child usually have normal hearing, and secondly deafness is not usually diagnosed until the child is 15 months old. This is of importance, Silver suggests, as it means that the child's auditory deprivation is not at first understood by his or her mother. Furthermore, when the deaf child cannot see anyone he or she feels totally alone, in contrast to a hearing child, who continues to hear while asleep. Facial expressions are particularly important to the deaf child, as quality of love – shown by tone – is not available as a means of communication.

The deaf child's handicap in these ways is not understood by his or her mother and this leads to difficulties in the normal processes of introjection and projection. Silver also suggests that later the child learns to hide the 'deaf self' and the 'real self' as it is not acceptable. This reinforces the earlier 'memories' of abandonment and isolation. She suggests that these are key issues in psychotherapy with the deaf.

As always with psychoanalytic hypotheses, it is difficult to evaluate these speculations unless one accepts the theory within which they are stated. Silver's hypotheses can be taken to be statements about the interaction of a deaf child and its mother, i.e. as historical truths. However, the evidence for these statements has come from psychotherapy sessions with deaf adults, and thus it is not clear that this is evidence about the child's early life at all. Certainly there has been no attempt to establish that these experiences relate to early infantile life.

Alternatively, these statements can be taken as a metaphor for the relation of deaf people to other people, i.e. as part of the difficulties of developing emotional relationships when there is a communication gulf.

It is possible to distinguish between the degree of hearing loss (almost always an organic question) and the degree of handicap due to hearing loss (which involves psychological and social factors). Habib and Hinchcliffe (1978) obtained an estimate of hearing handicap by asking subjects to give magnitude estimations of degree of handicap (following the method of Stevens (1955) for obtaining sensory magnitude estimations). Subjects were simply asked to use a scale of 0–100. A correlation was found between hearing threshold at 2 kHz and this handicap estimate. The correlation increased, however, when the log of the handicap ratings was used. That is to say, the relationship between handicap and hearing threshold is not linear but exponential. This finding occurred in two samples, one in London and one in Cairo. This would fit with the relationship between loudness and decibels. The contrast between these correlations and the lack of relationship in the studies reported above is probably due to the more specific assessment method. It is also clear that it is worth using the log of a handicap or distress scale, as the relationship is unlikely to be linear, that is, the physical measure (sound pressure level) is not related linearly to the loudness of sound but is curvilinear (sound pressure has to increase proportionately more at higher levels to double the loudness than it does at low levels).

Barcham and Stephens (1980) used an open-ended questionnaire to assess disability due to hearing impairment. Patients were asked to list, in order of importance, all the problems that they had as a result of their hearing loss. Most frequently reported was the inability to hear speech. Few reported emotional problems: 14% reported embarrassment, 6% nervous strain and 5% family problems. It is interesting that the vocabulary used does not match the 'psychiatric' classifications. Embarrassment has received virtually no attention in the studies reported above. Depression is not reported as

such by any of the respondents. Stephens (1980) has argued that the low incidence of reports of emotional problems may be due to the actual incidence of these problems being low, or the lack of appreciation by the patient that the emotional problems are due to the hearing loss, or the demand characteristics of the study. Whatever the reason, the disparity in the way that these problems are presented as problems is itself a fruitful area for further research.

Several studies have attempted to investigate the effects of experimentally inducing a temporary hearing loss. This is technically difficult. Occluding the ear canal will induce only a mild reduction in hearing. Eriksson-Mangold and Erlandsson (1984) occluded subjects' ear canals, inducing a hearing loss of about 30 dB, and obtained self-reports of the difficulties experienced. The problems reported were as follows (in order of the number of subjects reporting the problem): interference with hearing speech, distortion of one's own voice, not hearing non-verbal sounds of others, not hearing faint sounds and not hearing traffic sounds. Subjects were also said to have become more irritable.

Chafin and Piepher (1979) used tinnitus maskers to produce a greater degree of hearing loss. The maskers were adjusted so that they produced a speech reception threshold of 60 dB HL on free-field presentation in a sound-treated room. Subjects wore the maskers in various situations over a period of 2 weeks. This was a most interesting study, but unfortunately the way in which data were collected was not explained. Subjects apparently reported feelings of isolation, fear at night, being exploited, attracting attention and being patronized.

Although the designs of both studies were not sophisticated (no attempt was made to provide a control group, for example), the range of reports is potentially very interesting. These studies should certainly be followed up with studies using control groups and replicable methods of assessment. Obviously, having a temporary hearing loss cannot be equated to having a non-reversible hearing loss, but this method does provide a way of generating new hypotheses about the effects of hearing impairment. Ramsdell's hypothesis has not been tested, as he argued that subjects did not realize the importance of non-verbal sounds in generating their depression, and thus they would not be expected to report that this was an important loss to them.

Tinnitus

Tinnitus has not usually been regarded as psychosomatic. However, the emotional distress associated with tinnitus has for a long time been regarded as having an important psychological component to it. Fowler and Fowler (1955) argue that a reduction in the 'emotional threshold' of the patient led them to complain about their tinnitus, and that therapeutic efforts should aim to increase the emotional threshold of the patient. They suggested prescribing distracting but relaxing activity, and the ultimate aim was to: '...lessen the annoyance from tinnitus, or remove it from consciousness by making it sub-audible'. There are several lines of argument which have been used to suggest the importance of psychological factors.

Loudness matching

Loudness matching is a technique that allows estimation of the loudness of tinnitus. A tone is adjusted until it appears to the tinnitus sufferer to be of the same loudness as the tinnitus. Reed (1960) used this procedure using a tone of the frequency judged to be of the same pitch as the tinnitus: 41% of the loudness matches were under 5 dB SL, that is, 5 dB above the subject's auditory threshold. This is a typical result: 5 dB above a normal threshold is extremely quiet. This led some authors to conclude that tinnitus is actually rather quiet, but there are problems

with this interpretation. Loudness grows abnormally greater above a raised threshold when hearing loss is due to cochlear pathology (as is usually the case in acquired hearing loss). Thus, a small increment above an abnormal threshold may sound quite loud to the subject.

This problem can, however, be circumvented by using a frequency with a normal threshold. When this has been done the loudness matches certainly increase (Goodwin and Johnson, 1980). However, in the vast majority of cases the levels are still reasonably low when compared to environmental sounds that cause distress (Kryter, 1985). The loudness match of tinnitus is usually below the subject's level of most comfortable loudness (Hallam *et al.*, 1985). Additional evidence that being distressed by tinnitus involves mediating psychological processes is that not everyone with tinnitus finds it a problem. Heller and Bergmann (1953) obtained reports from normally hearing subjects in a sound-treated room. All subjects reported hearing 'noises'; the quality of these 'noises' was the same as that in clinical tinnitus. Hallam, Rachman and Hinchcliffe (1984) compared two groups of patients who experienced tinnitus and who were attending a neuro-otology clinic. Those who were attending with tinnitus as their main complaint were compared with those who were attending for some other reason, but who reported tinnitus on questioning. Self-reported loudness and the loudness match at 1 kHz were not significantly different between the two groups.

Epidemiological evidence confirms the existence of a large proportion of people who report tinnitus but who do not regard it as very annoying. The Office of Population Censuses and Surveys (1983) report that 15% of the general population have experienced tinnitus not caused by exposure to noise and of more than 5 minutes' duration; 2% of the population report continuous tinnitus; and 2% report being considerably distressed by tinnitus. Only a third of those with continuous tinnitus find it considerably annoying.

Hallam, Rachman and Hinchcliffe (1984) suggest that habituation to tinnitus usually occurs, and that persistent awareness of it and annoyance by it should be regarded as a failure of this process. Thus, therapeutic interventions should be aimed at precipitating habituation. This interesting hypothesis is based on observations that tinnitus occurs in people who do not complain of it, and that some degree of adaptation is often reported by sufferers.

The authors suggest that habituation to tinnitus can be retarded by many factors. These may include 'significance' of or 'meaning' given to the tinnitus, and general personality factors and coping style (among other things). This hypothesis (focusing on attention to the 'noise' rather than the tinnitus itself) has been the starting point for many psychological approaches to therapy.

Effects of tinnitus

Tinnitus sufferers complain of several different problems related to the 'noises'. Tyler and Baker (1983) asked members of a tinnitus self-help group to list the problems that they felt they had as a result of their tinnitus. They classified the answers as effects on hearing; effects on lifestyle; emotional problems; and effects on general health. Sleep disturbance was the most common complaint, and was reported by over half of the respondents. Depression was reported by 26% of the sample and annoyance by 25%. The length of time that the sufferer had had the tinnitus was inversely related to the number of problems reported (even when the effect of age had been partialled out). Self-help group members are not a representative sample of people who have tinnitus or people who seek medical help for it, so that proportions probably cannot be generalized to these groups. However, the range of different problems is illuminating.

Jakes *et al.* (1985) assessed the number of statistically independent complaint dimensions in a tinnitus questionnaire. Tinnitus patients attending a neuro-otology clinic with tinnitus as a main complaint rated various effects of tinnitus on them. Information on other symptoms and audiometric information (including the loudness match of the tinnitus at 1 kHz and the tinnitus frequency) was also obtained. The various scales and measures were subjected to factor analysis yielding three orthogonal main complaint factors: intrusiveness, emotional distress and insomnia. An additional factor concerned interference with listening to the television or radio. The loudness match had a rather low loading on the intrusiveness factor and did not load at all on the other factors.

Complaint about tinnitus therefore appears to be multifactorial: it is not simply a question of being more or less affected in some generalized way. None of the self-reported dimensions of complaint relate strongly to psychoacoustic measures of tinnitus. The implicit assumption of some theorists, and indeed most patients, has been that the opposite is true: that the loudness of the tinnitus is the overriding determinant of complaint, and that all the various problems experienced are closely associated to each other and to the loudness of the 'noise'.

Psychological interventions

Reduction in distress about tinnitus has been produced in placebo and control groups in various trials. This provides some indirect evidence that some psychological interventions may help tinnitus sufferers. Erlandsson *et al.* (1987) compared a masking device to an inert placebo 'electrostimulator'. The latter was a device which was worn on the ear and had several flashing lights. Subjects were told that it delivered electrical stimulation to the ear. In fact, it did not, but significant improvement occurred. Stephens and Cocoran (1985) compared the provision of masking devices to a control group which received minimal counselling. The counselling group showed significant decreases in how annoying and how loud they rated their tinnitus to be, and how worried they were about it.

Psychological interventions with tinnitus patients have aimed at three basic goals: reduction in the loudness of the tinnitus, reduction in how annoyed or distressed about the tinnitus the sufferer is, and the solution of other, unrelated psychological problems. This last may be very important, but because it is not 'tinnitus specific' it will not be discussed here.

The hypothesis that psychological interventions can reduce the loudness of tinnitus has been based on several different theories. Blood flow to the inner ear could be affected by blood pressure or blood sludging, or facial muscular tension could alter the pressure on the inner ear, for example. Hypnosis has been used to try to reduce loudness and/or annoyance due to tinnitus. Visualization of a dial which can be used to 'turn down the volume' of the tinnitus has been used. Another technique has been to suggest that the patient will feel relaxed despite the tinnitus. Marks, Karl and Onisphorou (1985) compared the induction of a hypnotic trance alone, 'ego strengthening' after induction of a trance and suggestions of active suppression of the tinnitus. No difference in the matched loudness of tinnitus occurred, and no differences between the groups were found. However, five out of the 14 patients studied reported that hypnotic induction was helpful in making the tinnitus more tolerable. Biofeedback has been used as a method of teaching relaxation, with the aim of either reducing the loudness of the tinnitus or the tinnitus distress (e.g. Wilson, 1987). Of the 41 patients treated, 33 showed improvement in diaries of tinnitus loudness. No control group was used. Borton, Moor and Clark (1981) used EEG feedback in a single-case design. EEG responded to treatment but no effect was observed on ratings of tinnitus loudness or annoyance, or on matched loudness levels.

Grecian (1976) used biofeedback with 51 patients: 40 patients apparently reported improvement, but no details of assessment are given and no control was used.

A number of authors have used relaxation training without biofeedback. Ireland et al. (1985) used relaxation training taught in groups. Ratings of the loudness of tinnitus and of insomnia pre-, mild- and post-treatment were used. Depression was assessed using the Beck Depression Inventory (BDI). Loudness matching was performed. These ratings were made pre- and post-treatment, and a waiting-list control was used. No significant differences were found between groups. Moreover, no significant change occurred across time within the groups (excepting BDI scores). In a later study by the same group (Wilson, 1987), biofeedback was used and ratings of annoyance as well as loudness were incorporated. In this study annoyance did decrease, but there was no difference between the biofeedback and waiting-list control.

In contrast, Scott et al. (1985) found that distress reduced with individually taught relaxation training combined with training in relocation of attention. The latter part of this procedure was conducted in a manner similar to imaginal desensitization. Patients imagined situations in which tinnitus would be very distressing; they then used quick relaxation and imagined a pleasant scene. This progressed to practice in vivo. Loudness ratings, discomfort ratings and depression ratings decreased significantly more than in a waiting-list control group.

Jakes et al. (1986) compared relaxation training on its own to relaxation training coupled with distraction training (similar but not identical to Scott's method). All patients received a booklet which explained a psychological approach to tinnitus and pointed out the importance of cognitions in mediating distress. There was a 2-week period for all subjects before treatment began, during which time they kept diary ratings. The dependent variables included a factor-analysed 'tinnitus effects' questionnaire. There was no difference between the two treatments, but a significant decrease in self-rated annoyance, emotional distress and insomnia occurred. Self-rated annoyance declined significantly faster once treatment had begun than during the period before treatment. There were significant improvements during the pretreatment period. Decline in self-rated loudness did occur, but was much slower and only reached significance by the end of treatment. Treatment gains were maintained at 4-month follow-up.

Jakes *et al.* (1992) randomly allocated tinnitus patients to one of five different treatments: group cognitive therapy, aural masker, group cognitive therapy *plus* masker, placebo masker and waiting-list. Outcome was assessed using a tinnitus self-report questionnaire. Only patients receiving group cognitive therapy were significantly improved at 3-month follow-up, and at 1–2-year follow-up.

How are we to reconcile these disparate results? The most obvious difference between the method of Ireland's group and those of the two other studies of relaxation training is that Scott *et al.* and Jakes *et al.* conducted the training on an individual basis, and as part of a more general psychological approach. The aim of the therapy was defined as reducing the emotional reaction to the tinnitus, rather than the perceived intensity of the noise itself. This may be crucial. Placebo-controlled trials are really needed before we can draw any definite conclusions.

These findings (improvements before the onset of relaxation training, placebo responses and the reports of the clients themselves about what was helpful in therapy) have led us to adopt a more cognitively based approach to therapy at the Royal National Throat, Nose and Ear Hospital. Sweetow (1985) has reported using cognitive–behavioural approaches with his patients, targeting the emotional sequelae of tinnitus. The authors are currently evaluating this procedure and initial results are promising.

Future directions

It seems clear that hearing loss and tinnitus are often associated with emotional distress. An important area for future work should be examining factors which increases or decreases the probability of particular types of complaint about neuro-otological symptoms. Modelling influences in early or later life seem to be a good place to start this work.

It seems important to be able to offer these clients help with their emotional distress, but several issues need to be addressed. First, it is important not to appear to dismiss the organic basis of this distress, and to be acquainted with basic information about these conditions. Secondly, it is obviously important to be able to satisfy the patient that they have been adequately medically screened. Thirdly, a method of applying psychotherapeutic techniques to clients with an acquired hearing loss needs to be developed.

Cognitive techniques offer a way of providing help to clients which makes it clear that one is not dismissing the symptoms or suggesting that they are imaginary, but that it is none the less possible to work on changing the affective response. The author routinely uses coping models as a way of concretely demonstrating that emotional adaptation is possible. These sorts of techniques could easily be applied to the other symptoms mentioned in this chapter, and probably with any medical symptom that causes distress. Thus, by setting as the target not the reduction or abolition of a symptom, but the affective and behavioural consequences of the disorder, a wide range of psychological skills become relevant.

References

Barcham, L.J. and Stephens, S.D.G. (1980) The use of an open-ended problems questionnaire in auditory rehabilitation. *British Journal of Audiology*, **14**, 49–58.

Bedford, A. and Foulds, G.A. (1978) *Delusions–Symptoms–States Inventory, State of Anxiety and*

Depression (Manual), NFER Publishing Company, Windsor, Berkshire.

Borton, T., Moor, W. and Clark, S. (1981) Electromyographic feedback for tinnitus aurium. *Journal of Speech and Hearing Disorders*, **46**, 39–45.

Chafin, P. and Piepher, R.A. (1979) Simulated hearing loss: an aid to in-service education. *American Annals of the Deaf*, **124** (4), 468–71.

Eriksson-Mangold, M.M. and Erlandsson, S.I. (1984) The psychological importance of non-verbal sounds. *Scandinavian Audiology*, **13**, 243–9.

Erlandsson, S.I. Ringdahl, A., Hutchins, T. and Carlsson, S. (1987) Treatment of tinnitus: a controlled comparison of masking and placebo. *British Journal of Audiology*, **21**(1), 37–44.

Fowler, E.P. and Fowler, E.P. Jr (1955) Somatopsychic and psychosomatic factors in tinnitus, deafness and vertigo. *Annals of Otology, Rhinology and Laryngology*, **64**, 29–37.

Gildston, H. and Gildston, P. (1972) Personality changes associated with surgically corrected hypoacusis. *Audiology*, **22**, 354–67.

Gilhome-Herbst, K. and Humphrey, C. (1980) Hearing impairment and mental state in the elderly living at home. *British Medical Journal*, **281**, 903–5.

Goodwin, P.E. and Johnson, R.M. (1980) The loudness of tinnitus. *Acta Otolaryngologica*, **90**, 353–9.

Grecian, M. (1976) Treatment of subjective tinnitus with biofeedback. *Ear, Nose and Throat Journal*, **55**, 314–18.

Habib, R.G. and Hinchcliffe, R. (1978) Subjective magnitude of auditory impairment. *Audiology*, **17**, 68–76.

Hallam, R.S., Rachman, S. and Hinchcliffe, R. (1984) Psychological aspects of tinnitus, in *Contributions to Medical Psychology*, vol. III, (ed. S. Rachman), Pergamon Press, Oxford, pp. 1–52.

Hallam, R.S., Jakes, S.C., Chambers, C. and Hinchcliffe, R. (1985) A comparison of different methods of assessing the 'intensity' of tinnitus. *Acta Otolaryngologica*, **99**, 501–8.

Heller, M.F. and Bergman, M. (1953) Tinnitus aurium in normally hearing persons. *Annals of Otology*, **62**, 73–6.

Ireland, C.E., Wilson, P.H., Tonkin, J.P. and Platt-Hepworth, S. (1985) An evaluation of relaxation training in the treatment of tinnitus. *Behaviour Research and Therapy*, **23**(4), 423–30.

Jakes, S.C., Hallam, R.S., Chambers, C. and Hinchcliffe, R. (1985) A factor analytical study of tinnitus complaint behaviour. *Audiology*, **24**, 195–206.

Jakes, S.C., Hallam, R.S., Rachman, S. and Hinchcliffe, R. (1986) Relaxation training and reassurance in the treatment of chronic tinnitus sufferers. *Behaviour Research and Therapy*, **24**, 497–507.

Jakes, S.C., Hallam, R.S. McKenna, L. and Hinchcliffe, R. (1992) *Cognitive Therapy and Research*, **16**, 67–82.

Kryter, K. (1985) *The Effects of Noise on Man*, Academic Press, New York.

Mahapatra, S.B. (1974) Deafness and mental health: psychiatric and psychosomatic illnesses in the deaf. *Acta Psychiatrica Scandinavica*, **50**, 596–611.

Marks, N.J., Karl, H. and Onisphorou, C. (1985) A controlled trial of hypnotherapy in tinnitus. *Clinical Otolaryngology*, **10**, 43–6.

Myklebust, P. (1964) *The Psychology of Deafness*, Grune and Stratton, New York.

Office of Population Censuses and Surveys (1983) *The Prevalence of Tinnitus 1981, General Household Survey*, OPCS, London.

Ramsdell, D.A. (1970) The psychology of the hard of hearing and the deafened adult, in *Hearing and Deafness*, (eds. D. Davis and A. Silverman), Holt, Rinehart and Winston, New York, pp. 78–124.

Reed, G. (1960) An audiometric study of two hundred cases of subjective tinnitus. *Archives of Otolaryngology*, **71**, 94–104.

Scott, B., Lindberg, P., Lyttkens, L. and Melin, L. (1985) Psychological treatment of tinnitus. An experimental group study. *Scandinavian Audiology*, **14**, 223–30.

Silver, J. (1988) Notes on the early development of the deaf infant. *Psychoanalytic Review* **75**, 469–71.

Singerman, B., Fiedner, E. and Folstein, M. (1980) Emotional disturbances in hearing clinic patients. *British Journal of Psychiatry*, **137**, 58–62.

Stephens, S.D.G. (1972) Hearing and personality: a review. *Journal of Sound and Vibration*, **20**(3), 287–98.

Stephens, S.D.G. (1980) Evaluating the problems of the hearing impaired. *Audiology*, **19**, 205–20.

Stephens, S.D. and Corcoran, A. (1985) A controlled study of tinnitus masking. *British Journal of Audiology*, **19**(2), 159–67.

Stevens, S.S. (1955) The measurement of loudness. *Journal of the Acoustical Society of America*, **27**, 815–29.

Sweetow, R.W. (1985) Cognitive behavioural modification in tinnitus management. *Hearing Instruments*, **35**(9), 14–52.

Thomas, A.J. (1984) *Acquired Hearing Loss: Psychological and Psychosocial Implications*, Academic Press, London.

Thomas, A. and Gilhome-Herbst, K. (1980) Social and psychological implications of acquired deafness for adults of employment age. *British Journal of Audiology*, **14**, 76–85.

Tyler, R.S. and Baker, L.J. (1983) Difficulties experienced by tinnitus sufferers. *Journal of Speech and Hearing Disorders*, **48**, 150–4.

Wilson, P. (1987) EMG biofeedback in the treatment of tinnitus. Paper given at the Third International Tinnitus Symposium, Muenster, West Germany.

Chapter eighteen

Obstetrics

Lorraine Sherr

Introduction

The overriding goal of managing childbearing experience is the wellbeing of both the mother and the baby. The maternal and neonatal risks of 100 years ago are drastically diminished. The focus is now on the quality of the experience and how the passage through the obstetric system affects the family, both medically and psychologically.

Medicine traditionally divides obstetric experience into administrative compartments which apply to caring procedures, physical buildings and health care personnel. The antenatal period starts at the point of conception and ends at the onset of labour. Labour and delivery form a second stage, and the puerperium the third. The baby is cared for by paediatric staff which generates yet another extension. However, this series of disjointed events is seen much more as a whole by the parents.

According to Birth Counts (1985), 96% of births in the UK today occur in hospitals. The pattern is widely followed in the west. Some countries (e.g. The Netherlands) maintain a comprehensive home delivery system, but this is the exception rather than the rule. In the UK, the care options within this system vary. Antenatal care can be carried out by a hospital team, a local general practitioner, midwives, or a combination of all three with the 'shared care scheme'. Deliveries can be in hospital or at home. Hospital deliveries can be in a general practitioner unit or under consultant care.

Evaluation of care and the impact of procedures on subsequent adjustment has been largely anecdotal, but has now given way to more systematic studies. There is a loud minority voice which still calls for 'the return of natural childbirth'. However, sociological and anthropological literature reveals that childbirth was never 'natural' and was always a sophisticated social event. Birth places, attenders and norms have been recounted in many cultures. The majority of women in the west today experience a hospital birth, with a small group attended by the medical profession in their own home.

Pregnancy

Society today is pronatalist and there is an inherent expectation that pregnancy and childbirth are normal and expected, with an average of 2.4 births per couple in the UK.

Some couples decided not to have children (voluntary childlessness) and some have difficulty in conceiving. Oakley (1980) and Bourne (1975) both show that over half of their samples can take up to 6 months to conceive, with 10% taking more than a year. Failure to conceive brings with it many stresses and disappointments. Such couples are faced with a threat to their ability to reproduce. Fertility options or infertility investigations available to them include fertility drugs, tubal surgery, laparoscopy, *in vitro* fertilization (IVF), gamete intrafallopian transfer (GIFT) or alternatives such as adoption or fostering. Such procedures may bring with them stress, and may affect social life, jobs and self perception. Fertility investigations and treatments can destroy or impede emotional reactions to sex. Infertility has been associated with considerable personal distress (Shaw, 1990). A large body of research has tried to differentiate factors between the infertile and others, but few attempts have been made to understand whether these differences result from infertility or contribute to it any meaningful way (Edelman and Connolly, 1986). Depressive moods are reported, and previous infertility may relate to higher anxiety if a pregnancy is achieved (Kumar and Robson, 1978).

The majority of studies focus on the role of infertility and its treatment on the female partner. Fewer studies examine the psychological impact on men who themselves may undergo extensive investigations and experience challenge and threat (Glover *et al.* 1992). Treatments for female infertility have advanced, but there are few such parallels for male infertility. The literature is typified by extensive investigations for females, males and often couples, from minor tests to surgery, all carrying with them the burdens of uncertainty, disappointment, anxiety and relatively low success rates. Psychological reactions are typified by an examination of life roles, personal life meaning, gender roles, relationship issues and life satisfaction, together with an oft-noted optimistic bias when assessing the outcome. The introduction of emotional support for such couples is following slowly – rarely comprehensively evaluated, but often seen by consumers and medical practitioners as an important aspect of care (Shaw, 1990).

Confirmation of pregnancy

Reactions to pregnancy are varied. Oakley (1979) reported that although over 50% of her UK sample were pleased, 38% had mixed feelings and 11% were upset. Most women suspect pregnancy by a missed period; others note body changes. Unplanned pregnancies were studied by Kumar and Robson (1978) who found no correlation with depression.

Termination and miscarriage

Not all pregnancies progress to full term. Some terminate spontaneously (miscarriage); others are terminated by choice for medical, social or psychological reasons, or in cases where antenatal screening reveals adverse factors such as congenital abnormality, rubella, HIV etc.

Those who considered terminations in early pregnancy were more often depressed in early pregnancy (Kumar and Robson, 1978). Previous terminations are shown to correlate with increased risk of depression in early subsequent pregnancy. There are few prospective studies examining the long-term implications of termination. The studies that do exist tend to report a range of short-term problems, but few note long-term psychological difficulties. This may reflect either reality or limitied follow-up. Psychological benefit may be present for women undergoing terminations (Greer, Lal and Lewis, 1976; Shusterman, 1979). Predictors of psychological trauma seem to relate to social support, help and approval in decision making. Thus sound counselling prior to decisions, linked with opportunities to take control and change one's mind, is important.

Not surprisingly, terminations linked to previous obstetric abnormalities correlate with increased anxiety in the first trimester of subsequent pregnancies.

A miscarriage is said to occur when a baby under 28 weeks' gestation is spontaneously aborted. This is an understudied area, but has enormous emotional impact both at the time of the miscarriage and as a factor in subsequent pregnancies. Cartwright (1984) reports that between one in six and four in six pregnancies miscarry. In one of the most comprehensive studies, she notes that women recall the experience for a long time and feel it may affect their subsequent pregnancy. The way it is handled can have implications for coping. The major deficiencies lie in staff reactions, opportunities provided to parents to talk the event over, the provision of information to them, particularly explanations about why the miscarriage occurred, and the respect couples are given for their need to grieve. Cartwright reported that some women reacted with a strong need to embark on a new pregnancy, whereas others had the opposite effect and needed to mourn and resolve their current loss before contemplating a new pregnancy. She found a wide range of individual variation, and no rules of timing ought to be proposed without consideration for individual needs. Many women expressed regret at not knowing the sex of their lost baby. In order to grieve, people need to have a memory. If this is denied, couples may find it more difficult to come to terms with their loss. Such reactions can be heightened in the circumstances of multiple or recurrent miscarriage (Gannon, 1992), where women are repeatedly exposed to these emotions which need to be acknowledged and supported.

Antenatal care

Hall and Chng (1982) reported that women attend an average of 11 antenatal clinics during one pregnancy. Garcia (1982) examined the widespread finding that women do not have uniform needs or desires. Psychological measures during pregnancy have been charted (e.g. Grimm, 1961; Gorsuch and Key, 1974; Murai and Murai, 1975; Elliott *et al.*, 1983) measuring a wide array of factors, but lack of repeated measures makes comparisons inconclusive, and workers commonly find different outcomes. Tension and anxiety, although measured differently, did not vary over the course of pregnancy in some studies (Murai and Murai, 1975; Elliott, 1984). They showed a curvilinear

relation with time (lowest levels recorded in mid-pregnancy) or a linear relationship (Grimm, 1961), with an increase at the end of pregnancy. Elliott (1984) accounts for this by noting the specific labour-related worries found at term, but this explanation would not provide understanding for the drop in anxiety shown by Lubin, Gardener and Roth (1975). Depression scores were not significantly varied over the course of pregnancy. Elliott *et al.* (1983) note the wide range of individual differences on every measure employed and caution against presumptions of pregnancy as a 'leveller': women vary in their needs and level of psychological health in pregnancy to the same extent as non-pregnant women.

Many consumer complaints of maternity care have come from minority groups (Association for Improvement of Maternity Services (AIMS) or the National Childbirth Trust (NCT)) and suffer from possible bias, as the samples are unrepresentative. Subsequent studies have been more systematic and have enlarged on the difficulties women encounter during antenatal clinics (see Garcia (1982) for a more comprehensive review). Generally, they find that women complain about poor levels of communication; there is a common lack of continuity of care; they dislike the mass approach to antenatal care, where they feel they are processed on a production line and are depersonalized; they are critical about some routine procedures and have difficulty in getting test results and feedback. Also, the efficacy and usefulness of numerous antenatal tests have been questioned (Enkin, Kierse and Chalmers 1989).

Attendance

The Spastics Society has correlated poor obstetric outcome with low antenatal attendance or late booking. Hall and Chng (1982) caution against overinterpretation, as the factors causing late booking, such as teenage pregnancy, poor socioeconomic standard etc., may account for obstetric outcome rather than absence of antenatal care itself.

Women go to considerable lengths to attend clinics, at long distances and with considerable waits. Garcia (1982) reports an average hospital wait of 156 minutes and general practitioner waits of 69 minutes. The Royal Commission's (1978) report on the health service showed that just over half of their 652 patient sample managed to arrive within 5 or 10 minutes of their appointment time, with two out of five respondents arriving earlier than that. Late arrivals were rare and were often associated with hospital transport failures. Indeed, only 1% of those making their own way to the clinic reported being late.

O'Brien and Smith (1981) showed that only four out of 200 randomly selected women had no antenatal care.

Women's views of antenatal care have been studied (MacIntyre, 1979; Graham and McKee, 1980; Oakley, 1979; Sherr, 1981, Garcia, Kilpatrick and Richards, 1990). From these large samples a discrepancy appears between expectation of care and experience. Clinic timing and organization are criticized, and although standards of medical care are acceptable to most women, the quality of communication is lacking. When questioned why they attended antenatal clinics, most felt that their pregnancy would be affected if they did not attend, but could not elaborate fully (MacIntyre, 1979). Conversely, only 17% of one group learned anything and only 31% enjoyed the visit. First visits were differentiated from subsequent visits by Oakley (1979), with 66% reporting being nervous and one-third reporting that they were given their first vaginal examination on this occasion, which frightened and embarrassed them as well as caused pain.

The Short Report (1980) concluded that dissatisfied customers made inefficient antenatal attenders. Oakley (1982) noted that it was not simply a question of educating women to appreciate the value and good intentions of antenatal provision, but that changes were needed on the part of the providers as well.

Women complain of the lack of continuity. Feedback was appreciated, even when negative (MacIntyre, 1979). Indeed, Sherr (1980) experimentally controlled for personalized feedback and explanatory information and found that subjects who were given standard feedback and explanatory information showed significantly higher satisfaction and lower anxiety levels than a control group receiving routine treatment.

Given the importance of information and feedback, it is surprising to find a reticence on the part of women to ask for it. Cartwright (1979) found a lack of correlation between the desire to ask questions and questions actually asked. Sherr (1981) found that most women want full explanations, and prefer medical sources for these, yet few asked questions and knowledge levels were low. Cartwright (1979) and Sherr (1987a) noted that subjects even requested information from the interviewer. Sherr (1987a) reported more negative comments on communication than positive.

Screening

Preventive tools available in antenatal care rely mainly on routine screening. The benefits and costs of such procedures, together with the manner in which they are carried out, has been questioned. Marteau (1989) drew attention to the fact that most testing procedures and results were associated with negative emotions.

Hall and Chng (1982) noted that the 'expectation of what can be achieved is unrealistic'. They studied 1907 women in Scotland and found that the majority of antenatal admissions arose despite routine antenatal care and were for conditions neither detected nor prevented by that care. They noted that intrauterine growth retardation was detected by the clinician in less than half of cases, and that just over half of those who selected non-hospital delivery landed up in hospital. The major problem was overdiagnosis. For every case of sustained hypertension, at least one case of inconsequential transient hypertension was diagnosed. For every accurate growth-retarded baby, 2.5 were so predicted inaccurately. This could lead to overinvestigation at high financial and psychological cost, which underlies deficiencies in a mass approach to antenatal screening.

Specific screening procedures have been examined. Farrant (1980) examined α-fetoprotein tests, and found that in those who were somehow at risk for abnormalities due to family history or previous problems, the procedure was reassuring. However, for those who never thought themselves to be at risk. the procedure raised anxiety, and they were not reassured even after results.

Reading and Cox (1982) and Campbell *et al.* (1982) showed that when women were randomly given explanations and sight of their ultrasound scan they reported more positive attitudes to their pregnancies and were more likely to heed advice about cessation of smoking and drinking.

Sherr (1989a) showed that the provision of information explaining tests and their implications, together with personalized feedback on routine blood pressure, weighting and urine tests, raised satisfaction, reduced anxiety and improved accuracy of recall and reassurance when compared to those routinely treated.

Enkin and Chalmers (1982) studied the level of diagnostic and therapeutic input from screening and revealed levels of 'irrationality in the content and process of some of the care'.

The introduction of new screening procedures (such as toxoplasmosis or HIV screening) should be viewed in the light of the growing debate on antenatal screening generally. The WHO emphasizes ground rules for screening, especially mass screening, which should centre around the 'benefit' to the individual concerned and the necessity for interventions to be available prior to the adoption of such screening. When new screening procedures are contemplated or introduced, clear policies should be worked out. These should include public information about the condition, staff training to discuss the procedure, the condition and its implications for women, and the costs of the basic test and results service. Monitoring of the procedures should be built in to all new tests.

AIDS and HIV infection in pregnancy

The human immunodeficiency virus (HIV) and acquired immunodeficiency syndrome (AIDS) present a particular problem in pregnancy (Forbes, 1986). The virus is known to cross the placenta and can infect the fetus. It has also been isolated in breast milk as a source of possible infection (Ziegler, Cooper and Johnson, 1985, Dunn *et al.* 1992). The WHO reports that over 80% of children with HIV infection are known to have been infected transplacentally (Chin, 1991).

This issue raises particular concerns about HIV screening, in pregnancy generally and HIV management specifically. At present, HIV antibody testing is inconclusive in that it takes up to 12 weeks for antibodies to the virus to be generated. Tests carried out in the interim may read negative but do not guarantee absence of the virus. In addition, testing may present false positives and false negatives. The issue of HIV testing cannot be taken lightly, and all people considering or undertaking a test need to be counselled (Green and McCreaner, 1989; Sherr, 1991). Routine testing is not advised at present, but such decisions should be based on the changing patterns of spread, the treatment options available and background infection rates. Selective testing should not be carried out without pre- and post-test counselling. Indicators for testing at present relate to high-risk behaviours of mothers or fathers, particularly where one or both have used intravenous drugs, shared needles, have had homosexual or bisexual contacts, are haemophiliac or have had sexual links over the past few years in countries with high levels of infection. Testing should not be carried out to pacify staff. The risk to staff is extremely low and invariably relates to slips in routine infection control and needlestick injuries. The universal adoption of infection control and abandonment of needle resheathing should be adopted as a matter of course in all units. This should be coupled with comprehensive staff education specifically on HIV infection control and disease management (Meadows *et al.*, 1990, 1992).

The chances of vertical (mother to infant) infection rates are now being more fully understood as the comprehensive cohort studies report (European Collaborative Study, 1992). Vertical transmission rates are reported at approximately 13% for those followed up for 2 years. Studies in Africa and South America show increased rates of vertical transmission (as high as 40% in some studies). It is unclear why this is so, but it may be linked to length of exposure to the virus, background medical factors, health status of the mother/father, virus strain or host factors (Sherr, 1991). Twin studies have shown the prevalence of dizygotic twins where one is infected and the other is not. The firstborn twin appears to be significantly more likely to be infected than the second-born.

Pregnancy is not thought to enhance disease progression, and early postulations of this possibility are now thought to have been contaminated by the passage of time. However, the exact impact of a pregnancy (or multiple pregnancies) on HIV disease progression is certainly unclear, and is still the subject of ongoing monitoring.

Treatment during pregnancy for the HIV-positive mother has been problematic in the past. A few studies are under way to examine the effects of AZT (zidovudine) treatment during pregnancy. Such effects need to be monitored on health variables of both the mother and the infant. AZT has been shown to cross the placenta, but its effects on the developing fetus are unknown. The early provision of such insight will enhance treatment options for infected women and their babies.

In the absence of clear knowledge of virus transmission rates and prevention, termination is the only option that can be offered to mothers at present. Many centres want to promote HIV testing in the belief that this is a much-sought option. International data suggest the contrary (Sherr, 1993b). Although a consistent minority of women do terminate their pregnancies, the main predictor is usually previous termination history rather than HIV status; many women proceed with their pregnancy. Indeed, the birth of an HIV-positive baby has been monitored as an impetus for a subsequent pregnancy (Temmerman *et al.*, 1990). Of those who do terminate, many go on to have a second pregnancy (Sunderland *et al.*, 1992); there is a growing group of women who conceive subsequent to HIV diagnosis (Sherr, 1993b).

Predictors of infant infection are currently being examined. Exposure to newly infected mothers (who may be viraemic) and certain biological markers appear to be associated with increased likelihood of infant infection (Van de Perre, 1991). Antibody testing of infants is inconclusive up till at least 18 months of age, and new techniques are being studied (most notably polymerase chain reaction tests) which may assist in early diagnosis. This would greatly assist in relieving the emotional burdens of uncertainty which now shroud the first 2 years of life for such children.

Staff have shown great anxiety about treating HIV-positive women (Sherr, 1987a) and the provision of accurate information about the low risk level and adequate infection control procedures can reduce such anxiety. Training in the skills of communication and front-line counselling may also help staff directly, and pregnant women indirectly (Sherr, Jefferies and Victor, 1992) .

In Africa, the virus is mainly heterosexually spread in the population, where no high-risk groups seem apparent. Drug-using mothers, who inject drugs which are contaminated by sharing dirty needles, are already indulging in self-injurious behaviours, and their antenatal attendance may be haphazard. Their babies will have the added problem of coping with drug withdrawal at birth. Mothers with contacts from high prevalence areas are also known to be disproportionately represented in those identified early on (Ades *et al.*, 1992; Peckham and Newell, 1991). As the epidemic is still in its early stages, clearer monitoring of spread patterns is possible. This is called first-generation spread and accounts for all those women who were infected by exposure to a partner indulging in high-risk behaviour. Second-generation spread is moving to the fore, and this accounts for women who were infected through heterosexual contact (Johnson, 1992).

The issue of HIV in pregnancy raises questions for all pregnant women and staff. Policy and procedure with regard to testing and handling women who are known to be seropositive need to be thought through and implemented well in advance to ensure sensitive handling of affected patients, and to preempt inappropriate reactions. Meadows *et al.* (1990) showed that the attitude of the midwives was the only predictor of whether a woman proceeded to test or not, irrespective of risk levels. In a follow-up of those who had been tested, much dissatisfaction was voiced (Meadows *et al.*, 1992). Information provision is a key element in any dialogue surrounding testing. Stevens *et al.* (1989) noted that, although most women endorsed the availability of HIV tests in pregnancy generally, less than half would undergo the procedure personally. Despite the fact that the majority of women would object if their

blood was taken for anonymous study, such studies have been ongoing in the UK (Ades *et al.*, 1992) and worldwide (Sherr, 1993a). Most such epidemiological studies have revealed alarming increases of prevalence. This is often confined to urban centres, and is often undetected during antenatal care (Ades *et al.*, 1992).

The provision of accurate information and dialogue must be seen as a priority for pregnant women and their partners in the 1990s. Written material is slowly becoming available, but is often limited and should be seen as an adjunct to counselling rather than as a substitute (Sherr and Hedge, 1990). Most studies overlook fathers, who are rarely consulted, never tested and never followed up. This is a shortcoming, given the sexually transmitted nature of the virus and the findings from many studies that the major risk factors for some women is the behaviour of their partners (Sherr, 1993a).

The use of pretest HIV counselling to address sexual behaviour change in pregnant women has received little attention, despite the fact that most pregnant women continue to have sex during pregnancy, which is rarely protected.

Mass screening of all pregnant women must be considered with extreme caution. In areas of high case prevalence, the need to screen all women must be weighed against the costs and benefits of such screening. Counselling services ought to be part of the budget. When seroprevalence and epidemiological data are needed, anonymous forms of screening have been considered. HIV tests from Guthrie data have been used widely. This raises the ethical questions of consent, as young babies are unable to give consent, mothers may not be asked and the data, although extracted from infant blood, refer to maternal antibody status.

The cost of raising the issue of AIDS and HIV infection during antenatal care must be examined. Many staff may also find this difficult and may need specialized training. Some women request tests, which may necessitate the provision of HIV counselling in obstetric units, or a system of referrals where such women can have their needs met. Once HIV has been identified in pregnancy, staff are challenged to ensure high levels of physical and psychological care for the duration of the pregnancy, the delivery and many years thereafter.

The social stigma and secrecy surrounding this condition often lead to an overdependence on formal avenues of care and support where informal avenues are simply not available. The prognosis for those with AIDS is poor, with rapid progression in infants under 1 year of age. Family-centred care can allow for adaptation to multiple illness within families and the subsequent needs of both the infected and the uninfected. AIDS will contribute to growing orphan rates, and studies in New York have also shown developmental delays in some children with HIV infection, requiring special educational input. In the absence of a cure, treatments are often symptomatic or prophylactic, and there are wide-ranging mental health requirements for those who are infected.

Pregnancy as a time to prepare

The antenatal period is not only a time of development for the fetus, but also signifies the imminent onset of labour and a new family. This time can be viewed as a preparatory period where women and their spouses may receive input.

Preparation is an oft-used tool for coping. Information and skill acquisition have been used to cope with pain. Janis (1971) examined cognitive coping strategies in the light of postoperative outcome, and proposed that preparation in the forms of rehearsal, realistic fear appraisal and thinking through coping may facilitate coping with traumatic events such as surgery or, in this case, labour.

Levels of preparedness can be assessed either by gauging information levels or by comparing input such as antenatal classes. Comparisons of women who attend classes with those who do not pose methodological considerations of self-selection which could account for any subsequent differences. A methodological advanced study would need to have random allocation and may prove unethical. However, Enkin (1982) matched 40 women who were unable to be accommodated within the classes with women of similar age, parity and delivery date within the class, and a second group of women not requesting classes.

Comparisons revealed that class attenders used significantly less analgesia during labour, needed less anaesthetic and less operative intervention than the other two control groups, and reported significantly more favourable labour experiences and lowered depression scores (Zung scale).

Enkin (1982) reviewed a number of studies on preparation and noted a consistent effect of lower use of analgesia in prepared women, although there is no corresponding evidence that these women actually felt less pain. Such women may have intended to use less medication and hence sought membership of a class; may have been persuaded against medication which was out of vogue; may have been frightened by the possible effects of medication; or been trained to accept higher pain levels. Classes may also engender expectations which, if not met, may lead to dissatisfaction.

Reid and McIlwaine (1980) reported that 42% of primiparous women in their study did not intend to go to antenatal classes, and even fewer of the multiparous intended to attend. The focus of the classes was mainly on labour and delivery itself, whereas many subjects in this study expressed a desire for information and teaching on coping with infants, crying, feeding, sleeping and childcare.

The DHSS (1978) study on breastfeeding in the UK questioned 2304 women. Over one-quarter reported not being asked by anyone about their feeding plans, and 29% who had been asked had not entered into any discussion. There does seem to be a need for more information. Retrospective interviews (Houghton, 1968) reported 92% of 600 recently delivered women criticizing the informational aspects of their experience. Cartwright (1979) reported that a fifth of the women having their first baby would have liked to know more, this figure increasing to a quarter when looking back after the baby was born. Women of lower social class turned to relatives and friends for information whereas middle-class women tended to turn to the professionals. Sherr (1981) noted that women desired information primarily from medical sources, yet were reluctant to ask. When knowledge levels were assessed, social class was a significant factor but parity was not. This was in sharp contrast to doctors, who felt that multiparous women would be more knowledgeable than primiparous women. Clearly, it seemed that the gathering of experience did not necessarily equate with the gathering of expertise.

A large group of women do not attend classes yet still have informational needs. Preparation for labour and delivery is the prime concern of most reported classes, but women feel that individual needs vary and would like to have information on a vast array of topics. Enkin (1982) notes that education not only raises information levels but results in consumer-generated questioning, which may lead to sharpening of practices and questioning of procedures. From a theoretical point of view, lack of information engenders passivity and has implications for control, fear and cognitive preparation. Health care staff may suddenly have to change their role to that of information provider. They may be ill prepared and poorly trained for such roles and these components are becoming urgent agenda items in training.

Antenatal predictors of postnatal outcomes

Anxiety has been singled out as a negative emotion in pregnancy (Read, 1944), yet Elliott (1984) finds no validated evidence to support this. Studies have attempted to locate sources of stress and implications of stress levels. Barclay and Barclay (1976) compared pregnant and non-pregnant women's knowledge and attitude towards pregnancy and labour: increased knowledge did not relate to reduced anxiety, and there were no differences in anxiety levels between the two groups. Indeed the non-pregnant group expected greater depression than was actually measured in the pregnant group. Astbury (1980) compared prepared and non-prepared pregnant women, and although he found the former significantly more knowledgeable, there was no significant difference in anxiety levels.

In order to decide whether anxiety reduction is beneficial, a definition of anxiety is necessary. Clinical anxiety states relate to irrational anxiety or anxiety out of proportion to the stressors. High antenatal anxiety has been correlated with previous obstetric abnormalities (Davids, Devault and Talmadge, 1961; McDonald, 1963; Crandon, 1979), which does not appear to be irrational. Anxiety correlated with previous miscarriage often subsides in the last trimester, when the pregnancy is obviously viable (Kumar and Robson, 1978). Moderate anxiety has been correlated with better postnatal adjustment (Pitt, 1968; Breen, 1975) and antenatal anxiety has been unrelated to labour complications (Beck et al., 1980; Astbury, 1980), Sherr (1989a) noted that anxiety related more to staff reaction than to patient experience. Klusman (1975) found that antenatal classes reduced pregnancy related anxieties, and found that one form (Lamaze) succeeded in reducing general anxiety levels, which exerted significant effects on self-ratings of pain during the transition stages of labour.

Psychological problems associated with childbirth

Depression and psychosis

A small proportion of women go on to show childbirth-related problems requiring psychiatric help (Dalton, 1971; Martin, 1977; Braverman and Roux, 1978). Postnatal depression and psychosis have received most of the attention, but there is a growing body of literature examining mood during pregnancy and trying to relate pregnancy variables to postpartum mood outcome.

The rate of mild and severe postpartum problems is low and varies from culture to culture. It is unclear whether such variation is a function of reporting, recognition, treatment or incidence. The major problems can be broadly divided into depressive and psychotic disturbance. The former can be seen as mild or severe. Mild depression is often the label given to 'postpartum blues', and there are numerous explanations for the phenomenon. There are those who seek explanations in terms of hormone fluctuations, those who view women as psychologically fragile and those who acknowledge the trauma and change that a newly delivered woman may well have faced (Phoenix, Woollett and Lloyd, 1991) often in a strange environment without the support of her familiar loved ones (visiting hours being 1–3 p.m.)!

Longer-term psychological trauma can be seen as primary or secondary. Primary problems precede the pregnancy and have a poorer prognosis. This essentially refers to women with a pre-existing psychotic or depressive condition who happen to become pregnant and have a baby. Secondary problems are identified only after the pregnancy, and are said to have a more positive prognosis. Depressive types of reactions are said to be more amenable to input than psychotic reactions. Breakdown after a subsequent pregnancy is also often noted.

Suicide

Suicide during pregnancy is a rare event (Kleiner and Greston, 1984). Most studies are case descriptions and the underlying themes usually revolve around the availability of options for the women and social pressure/support. Indeed, there is a low incidence in the west, where contraception and terminations are available and society's attitudes are more accommodating. This is in contrast to the east. Yet the trauma of a pregnancy and childrearing is a factor noted in retrospective studies of suicide completion in women particularly, and suicidal ideation is not uncommon.

Drug use

Drug use during pregnancy is widespread, and many women who are dependent on drugs proceed to have pregnancies, which are often complicated for a variety of reasons. Some of the pregnancies are desired, whereas others are not; some are identified early, whereas as others are not; unwanted and unrecognized pregnancies are often implicated in a lack of antenatal care in a group who may well benefit specifically from such input. The fear of official reprisals and the possibility of removal of the child into care may act as a disincentive for such women to seek out care or to be honest about their drug use. Few innovative approaches with these women are recorded, and many opportunities are lost when they do finally report to hospital or clinical services.

Predictors of mental health

Little *et al.* (1982) felt it would be helpful for prevention work if breakdown could be predicted. Kumar and Robson (1978) found that subsequent disturbance correlated with marital tension during pregnancy and doubts about going through with the pregnancy. Little *et al.* (1982) sought predictive use of psychiatric and psychological measures, and found that women suffering postnatal depression were not depressed before the birth.

Psychological measures during pregnancy have been compared with similar measures on non-pregnant samples or set against normative data to highlight possible pathology during pregnancy (Hooke and Marks, 1962; Murai and Murai, 1975; Elliott et al., 1983). On the whole these studies found low levels of pathology, often reaching statistical significance (neuroticism and depression; Elliott et al., 1983). These extended to the postpartum period, where the pregnant group as a whole had significantly lower depression, anxiety and neurotic scores than a normative group over time, even though a slight within-group increase of disorder was noted in the pregnant group over the course of pregnancy. Studies comparing pregnant and non-pregnant women found the latter to have a 'low incidence of pathology with lower neuroticism and depression scores than the normative group which persisted even at postnatal follow up' (Elliott et al., 1983). Elliott thus concluded that the majority of pregnant women appear to be in good psychological health and worries about labour and the health of their child seemed realistic. Anecdotal statements about whimsical and moody women were unsubstantiated. In a comprehensive review of the literature she felt that pregnancy had far less psychological effect on women than commonly assumed from the point of view of anxiety and depressive reactions. She pointed out in addition that there were aspects of positive mental health that were often not charted.

Abuse during pregnancy

Abuse of the mother is an all-too-common experience, although true prevalence has not been fully established. Some studies in the USA put the prevalence as high as 7–11% (Hilliard, 1985; Helton, McFarlane and Anderson,

1987). Similar findings were reported in Norway (Schei and Bakketeig, 1989).

Such abuse cannot be simply seen as a function of overall abuse, as an American study found an increased incidence of abusive violence of 60.6% when comparisons were made between pregnant and non-pregnant women. (Gelles, 1988). Yet some age factors may be prevalent, as younger women are more likely to be abused and more likely to be pregnant.

Abuse can be divided into physical and sexual abuse. Clearly, it is important to understand the implications for the psychological wellbeing of the mother, both short- and long-term, as well as the effects and risks on the unborn baby. Bullock and McFarlane (1989) found a higher prevalence of low birth weight where mothers had suffered abuse during pregnancy.

Women are often reluctant to report abuse, yet are more willing to divulge it if the questioning comes in a sensitive way from their carers. McFarlane et al. (1992) found that 8% of their sample self reported abuse, but the figure rose to 29% when questions from medical staff addressed the issue.

The studies on abuse pose numerous methodological problems. Many are concentrated on populations in the USA, and it is difficult to know to what extent these findings translate to other countries and other socio-cultural settings. Many of the studies focus on small samples, and there is great difficulty in differentiating levels of abuse from minor to major. Particular variables associated with the nature of the abuse may be key factors in determining outcome on the infant, and these are rarely constant. It is also unclear to what extent treatment for the abuse can ameliorate subsequent damage. No studies give a clear understanding of other cofactors of abuse, such as poor nutrition or poor emotional state, and few differentiate between single abuse events and multiple or continuous abuse.

McFarlane et al. (1992), in a study of 691 American subjects, found that one in six women had been abused, with 60% of their subjects reporting at least two occasions of abuse. Abuse was most common around the head. The perpetrator was almost always someone known to the pregnant woman, 78% being the husband or the boyfriend. Particular risks were found for teenagers who reported multiple abuse (often by both boyfriend and parents). These workers noted that abused women were highly likely to attend late for antenatal care. They also highlighted the need to keep open the avenues of dialogue on the issue of abuse for many women who were not abused during early pregnancy, but did report incidents during the course of their pregnancy.

Abuse of the pregnant woman can lead to direct and indirect effects on both mother and baby. Directly, there is a risk of trauma and physical damage; to the baby there is a similar risk, in the case of severe violence to the abdomen, of conditions such as abruptio placentae, fetal fractures, ruptures and haemorrhage (Sammons, 1981). Indirectly, the abuse may lead to emotional reactions, increased anxiety, depression or the exacerbation of any illnesses. Such a woman may also turn to alcohol, tobacco, medication or street drugs to help her cope with the trauma. All of these have documented deleterious effects on a developing fetus. (Harlap and Shiono, 1980; Simpson, 1987; Zuckerman, Frank and Hingson, 1989; Chasnoff et al., 1985) as well as on the health of the mother. If such a mother chooses to leave an abusive relationship she may suffer financial hardship, which could directly affect her nutritional status, her likelihood to seek antenatal care and the extent to which she can care for herself adequately during pregnancy. Women who are the subject of abuse often display a range of common reactions, often referred to as the 'battered woman syndrome' (Walker, 1984). Some studies have typified such women as those suffering from learned helplessness, but others (Gondolf and Fisher, 1988) have shown a high degree of

behavioural adaptation and resourcefulness in the victims of abuse.

All such women run the risk of social isolation, of detachment from social support, of shame and guilt, and they may simultaneously suffer from lowered self-esteem. There is no literature linking subsequent child abuse with the abuse of a pregnant woman, but this cannot be ruled out.

Pregnancy and age

Early work examined some of the risks and hazards associated with teenage pregnancy. More current literature is also paying attention to the growing cohort of older women who conceive. There is often an underlying assumption of normative ages for childbirth, and variation from such norms may engender puzzlement or censure (Phoenix, Woollett and Lloyd, 1991; Berryman, 1991). Many studies focus on negative outcomes for these groups, rather than describe positive outcomes or understand problems when they occur. At times poorer outcome variables with older age can be confounded because of the preponderance of those with poor outcomes still trying to conceive at such later ages. The best predictors of outcome tend to be childbirth history (Chalmers and Enkin, 1982), and in countries such as Sweden, where such statistics are kept, the findings are reassuring. Social circumstance and reasons for pregnancy may show some common themes among the teenage groups, and indeed the over-40s. Outcome may also relate to support, care, diet and desirability of the pregnancy. These may be disproportionately lacking in teenage pregnancies, which often signal specific difficulties and demands.

Consumer satisfaction

Generally, consumer satisfaction with antenatal provision is low. To summarize, reported complaints are not primarily at the level of medical expertise, but rather at the conveyor-belt mass approach which engenders a lack of perceived control, shapes up passivity, blurrs individualization and hinders the continuity of care and the formation of therapeutic relationships. Even where satisfaction is high, this often wanes when women are questioned over time (Garcia, Kilpatrick and Richards, 1990).

Labour and delivery

The culmination of pregnancy is labour and delivery of the new baby. In the British Births survey (Chamberlain, Howlett and Claireaux, 1970), only 3% of women were recorded as having had no drugs for pain in labour. A high uptake of analgesia persists. Early studies looked at the physiological effects of such chemicals on mother and baby. More recent studies look at appraisal by the mother, and show that few women have pain-free labours, despite analgesia. Many studies use the yardstick of expectation and tolerance in order to match pain level and analgesic use. The most common reported complaints with pain management seems to be lack of explanation to the mother about the effects of analgesia and lack of information.

Morgan et al. (1984) studied 1000 women of whom 536 received epidural analgesia. This group reported greater pain relief than those receiving other forms (mainly pethidine), but had longer labour and a higher incidence of assisted delivery (51% compared with 6%).

Light, Solheim and Hunter (1976) found that patients were satisfied with care during labour, but showed lowered satisfaction with doctors' explanation of medications used. These workers felt there was a communication gap between doctors and patients: 89% of women were satisfied with their doctor's competence, yet only 69% were satisfied that the doctor understood their feelings.

Surprisingly, little attention has been given to the array of psychological theories of pain management. Robinson (1980) utilized the concept of self-control. Subjects were allowed to self-administer pethidine and were compared with a group given the standard dose. The experimental group reported equal pain levels but used less pethidine; their babies were in a superior condition at birth, as measured by the APGAR score (a IO-point index measuring five major indices at birth).

Pain relief cannot be administered casually: the effects on the mother and baby need to be established. Some authors claim that babies of mothers who had been given pethidine during birth had no after-effects. Rosenblatt, Redshaw and Notarianni (1980) showed that babies with high absorption rates had reduced alertness and poorer visual and auditory responses over the first 6 weeks. There was also a relationship between higher doses of pethidine and decreased maternal interaction with the infant in the first 20 minutes after delivery. They found no relationship between drug levels and sleep patterns, yet irritability did differ. McFarlane and Turner (1978) found that sound localization in a small group of babies born to mothers who had received pethidine was depressed. Rosen et al. (1969) and Chamberlain, Howlett and Claireaux (1975) drew attention to the respiratory effects after birth, and depressed feeding has been noted (Kroh, Stein and Goddard 1966; Dubignon et al., 1969).

Special-care baby units

Not all babies arrive at the expected time. A new branch of medicine, neonatology, has evolved to care and nurture small babies, with resounding success (Kelnar and Harvey, 1987).

A fuller account of the impact of a preterm baby is given by Richards and Roberton (1983), Klaus and Fanaroff (1986), or Brimblecombe, Richards and Roberton (1978). It is necessary to note the difficulties that parents face if their baby is born early and is taken to a neonatal intensive care unit. The range and intensity of emotional reactions is broad and the structure of units may exacerbate this. Irrespective of outcome, most studies report long-term parental stress. (Minde *et al.*, 1978; Klaus and Kennell, 1983) They fear for the life of their baby, both in absolute and quality terms. Parental response is generally unrelated to the severity of the baby's problems. Mason (1963) found that high maternal anxiety, coupled with information seeking and support, was predictive of a superior relationship with the baby on discharge. Parents differ in their coping styles. Newman (1980) described parents who coped through intense commitment and those who used distance, while other researchers (Minde *et al.*, 1978) stressed the importance of models from one's own parenting experience.

The plethora of machinery and technology can inhibit parents. They grieve the loss of their expected healthy baby and often have to abandon care and control to trained staff. This can result in reluctance to handle and take over the care of their baby when the time comes. Indeed, Nicola *et al.* (1983) note that failure to visit and distancing on the part of parents may be a sign of unresolved difficulties. However, Phoenix, Woollett and Lloyd (1991) and Stacey (1992) note the role of 'experts' who take over the care of babies, and how this challenges the abilities and confidence of parents, who may distance themselves out of fear of their own inadequacies, their desire not to get too attached to a baby who may die, or simply as a reflection of the overwhelming trauma associated with special care baby units.

Small premature babies are often unresponsive and difficult to feel close to. This may add to the stress of caring for them. Smeriglio (1981) highlighted the need for sensory stimulation of young children, stressing that this was as important as physical environment.

The death of such a baby needs careful and insightful handling by all, allowing for the creation of memories and time to grieve (Sherr, 1989b). Parents need explanations and to be allowed to come to an understanding of events at their own pace. This involves the whole family, especially siblings, who are often excluded from units. It raises questions of subsequent pregnancies (Forrest, 1983) and fears and uncertainties (Klaus and Kennell, 1976). As multiple births are common in special care units, often the needs of a living baby overlap with the needs to mourn a lost baby. Parents should receive careful handling and staff ought to be aware of and trained in the skills which could facilitate coping, as well as reactive to their own personal feelings. Staff stress, support and burnout must all be issues kept under constant review.

Multiple births

The twinning rate in the population is fairly high, but the advent of fertility treatments has inflated the rates of multiple births of three or more babies. (Stacey, 1992). The chances of developmental problems increase with multiple birth, which places an additional trauma on parents, who may be coping with the overwhelming demands of three or four babies. Multiple births may account for many admissions to special-care baby units. Multiple bereavements often follow from multiple births, and there is unclear guidance on how to handle single bereavements, let alone multiple bereavement. This may be further confounded when there are survivors of the multiple birth and parents have to grieve a lost baby while adjusting to the surviving ones. The psychological trauma in the short and longer term have not been studied to a great degree, nor the sibling effects for children who comprise these networks.

Induction

In circumstances such as pregnancy progressing past expected dates, raised blood pressure in the mother, arrested fetal growth etc., the possibility of induction can be raised. Cartwright (1979) monitored attitudes towards induction, especially in relation to retrospective feelings about preparation received. Riley (1976) reported that 45% of induced patients reported that their labour was more painful than expected. Cartwright found the main advantage of induction to be the ending of tedious waiting for overdue babies, and it allowed planning. Disadvantages related to higher incidences of pain relief, uncomfortable and restricted feelings with the drips associated with induction, and an increased likelihood of assisted delivery. Induced women were more likely to be given some form of pain relief than those with spontaneous onset of labour. It is difficult to separate outcome as a result of induction or as a result of factors necessitating the induction in the first place. Chalmers (1976) examined a large group of women and failed to confirm any consistent advantages of routine induction.

Caesarean section

Caesarean section rates vary from country to country and from centre to centre. As with all major abdominal surgery (planned or emergency), there are short- and long-term effects of the procedure. Oakley and Richards (1990) point out that activities encouraged by staff in relation to the newborn baby after a caesarean section would be prohibited on a surgery ward. Trowell (1982) noted interactional differences between mothers and their babies in the presence or absence of a caesarean section, including reduced smiling, increased anger and loss of temper, and fewer play initiations. The babies in this small study showed higher birth weights and slower motor development at 1 year. Methodologically, it is always difficult to attribute causal links between observed outcome and the caesarean sections as it may relate more closely to the underlying reasons for such intervention to have occured in the

first place. In general, studies show a wide range of social variance in the willingness for the procedure to be carried out. Outcome measures vary from immediately postpartum to longer term. Many of the psychological consequences are bound up with the postsurgical demands made on a mother, and with emotional reactions to the surgery, which may have denied women the opportunity to give birth vaginally. Ameliorating factors have been noted in terms of the presence of the father (Cain, 1984; May and Sollid, 1984; Shearer, Shiono and Rhoads, 1988) and the use of epidural anaesthesia rather than general anaesthesia (Shearer, Shiono and Rhoads, 1988). No studies have looked at systematic differences between planned and emergency caesarean sections.

Medical intervention in labour

The medical management of labour involves a variety of procedures. Although there are sound reasons for implementation, in some cases individual assessment of patients is sometimes reported as lacking (Chalmers and Richards, 1977; Chard and Richards, 1977). The cost of a marginally necessary procedure is often borne by the mother. Chalmers and Enkin (1982) note that some procedures are necessary for a few, but are ill advised as general policy. The introduction of a new intervention seems to follow a pattern: initially it addresses a problem, then grows rapidly to mass utilization followed by complaints and justifications, and finally settles into a pattern of moderation, where intervention is used selectively. Examples of such a pattern of development are episiotomy, induction and fetal monitors, to mention but a few.

In 1958, 21% of primiparous women underwent episiotomy compared with 91% in 1978. Oakley (1980) reported that 98% of her sample were given an episiotomy. Moore (1977) commented that the increase in episiotomy may be related to the lack of experience in those conducting deliveries. Episiotomies are often justified on the grounds that they avoid tears, or that they will protect women against future prolapse, but these are both unsubstantiated claims.

Reading (1982) reported that episiotomy pain in recently delivered mothers was high and lasted for some time, 14% still reporting pain 3 months later. Kitzinger (1983) and Reading (1982) report on the difficulties women have with episiotomy pain, including prolonged healing, reduced subsequent sexual activity and difficulties in enduring sitting. The DHSS committee looking into breastfeeding (1978) reported that 75% of mothers who breastfed had stitches, and that 21% reported these interfering, as they found sitting down painful; 22% of mothers with painful stitches stopped breastfeeding, compared to 16% with non-painful stitches.

Delivery

The questions raised by delivery relate to the variety of roles and practices and how these affect behaviour and perceptions. The situation may engender passivity and the experience may determine long-term interaction styles. Routines such as the removal of the baby from mother and father were standard in the past, but have now been questioned and largely abandoned (Klaus and Kennell, 1976). Indeed, it took theories such as bonding and separation to reinstate parental roles in the labour ward.

Cartwright (1979) reported that almost two-thirds of women were not allowed to hold their baby immediately after delivery, although those who were allowed to do so showed great enthusiasm for the practice. The DHSS document on breastfeeding noted that mothers who were able to breastfeed babies within 4 hours of birth were less likely to give up in the first week or fortnight.

Emotional support is now recognized as a key element contributing to the wellbeing of the mother during labour. Such support is greater than mere physical presence (Enkin, Kierse and Chalmers, 1989). Controlled trials evaluating the impact of such support find that there is a universal reduction in labour length and a subsequent lowering of labour augmentation and other fetal problems. Such findings have paved the way for an examination of protocols and procedures in labour wards. The emerging norms focus heavily on the emotional needs of the labouring woman, and mark an improvement in maternity care. Position at delivery, suturing and who carries this out, water deliveries and pain management choices are all under current scrutiny. The lessons for the decade must be the need to evaluate changes and listen to the needs of the recipients before adopting routines, rather than afterwards.

The puerperium

Women can stay in hospital for anything from a few hours to 10 days, depending on their state of health, desires, and the policy of the place of birth. The effects of such a stay are variable. Although meant as a time of rest, recuperation and the acquisition of skills to cope with a new baby, Houghton (1968) noted that one-third of her sample were unable to find out all they wanted to know about their own and their baby's condition and progress, and two-fifths were given conflicting instructions. Staff were described as unwilling to explain, too busy and in a hurry, and doctors were unapproachable. The Royal Commission upholds these problems, as they reported some 90% of maternity patients not having the daily routine explained. In spite of the claim that women should have babies in hospital to rest, 68% were woken up between 5 and 6 a.m., and many experienced disturbances during the night from patient noise, night admissions, staff noise, lights and being woken by nurses checking to see whether they were asleep. Beds were too hard and too high, and the ambient temperature was too warm.

The increase in 'experts' in child care has also undermined the role of women, who are urged not to rely on their instincts and to alienate themselves from cultural knowledge (old wives' tales) (Bourne, 1975). Instead these are to be replaced by expertise and medical knowledge (old doctors' tales) (Phoenix, Woollett and Lloyds, 1991), which not only purport to have solutions to childrearing problems but are also often unavailable for consultation and dialogue. Thus women are placed in a Catch 22 situation where they are urged to 'listen to the professionals' who essentially are unavailable at the time and for the duration that women require.

Feeding

Breastfeeding is in vogue at the moment and is encouraged. Sherr (1989a) found that women who desired to bottlefeed were shunned and were often not given helpful advice. Dilemmas exist between demand and schedule feeding. Cartwright (1979) found a relation between increased breastfeeding and higher social class. The helpfulness of nurses affected feeding practices: 75% of mothers were not allowed to feed their babies when they wanted to do so, but had to adhere to hospital schedules. Fisher (1980) concluded that schedules were for the convenience of staff rather than mothers, and defeated the purpose of hospital stay.

Breastfeeding has been discussed in terms of HIV infection, and workers (Dunn *et al.*, 1992) have shown that such a route is possible for postpartum transmission of the virus. Newly infected (and thus viraemic women) are more likely to transmit HIV to their babies in this way. Few studies acknowledge the potential danger that mothers put themselves to, as HIV can also move from an infected infant to the mother via breastfeeding (Pokrovsky, 1990).

Fathers

Fathers have become the new consumer group in maternity services (Barbour 1991). They often accompany their partners to antenatal clinics and are present during labour and delivery and in the postpartum period. They are involved in childcare and are an increasing focus of attention. Barbour (1991) showed that a large proportion of her sample of fathers had attended antenatal scanning and had found the experience beneficial in forging a sense of their baby.

Non-attendance at antenatal classes is often associated with class timing (daytime to suit the staff, rather than evenings to suit the patients) or the lack of childcare provision (where fathers may tend older children to allow their partners to attend such classes). Paternal involvement is not a new phenomenon: what is new is the attention social science is now paying to it.

Thirty years ago fathers were excluded from the delivery room and now they are encouraged. Indeed, some studies have noted that paternal non-attendance is seen as problematic. Either way, pressures on fathers should be examined to accommodate their personal views as service users. Barbour notes the subtle controls exerted on attending fathers, how they are judged and selectively included or excluded from certain procedures. As 'guests' in the labour ward, the issues of control and the public expression of personal experience may need addressing before true and meaningful involvement can be achieved.

Enhancing care during pregnancy and childbirth

Knowledge of psychological factors during pregnancy and childbirth may enhance the standard of care offered. Despite the fact that they combine to form a complex experience, some of the major issues can be summarized under three headings:

- *Communications* Generally women are dissatisfied with communication aspects of their care. Communication is more than the simple provision of information: improvements relate to communication skills, understanding communication needs and appreciating the role of communication factors. This extends to front-line counselling skills which have a role to play in specific procedures (such as HIV and AIDS, antenatal screening, bereavement) or in general management (such as antenatal care, labour and delivery at one extreme, and abuse, postpartum depression/psychosis, suicide or drug use at the other).

- *Mood* Anxiety, if present in pregnancy, is not irrational. It often relates to meaningful events and therefore can be reduced with appropriate insight. Anxiety itself does not seem to provide a meaningful predictor of obstetric wellbeing. Opportunities should be provided for explanation and reassurance to minimize unnecessary anxiety. Procedures that may create anxiety ought to be scrutinized. Anxiety is often noted. It is an emotion that reflects some of the trauma of the obstetric systems through which women (and their partners) are herded, rather than pathological states within the female psyche. Anxiety reduction techniques aimed solely at the woman may fail to address the true cause, and may leave anxiety-provoking practices in place for longer than necessary. Depression is noted with varying frequency in the course of pregnancy. At times this can lead to overwhelming mood states in need of treatment and intervention. In extreme cases, clinical depression, psychosis and suicidal behaviour have been documented. Short-term mood fluctuations are more common than longer-term problems. Mood variation is most often measured from the point of view of negative mood states, and positive mood implications are rarely measured, examined or catalogued.

- *Health care models and beliefs* The medicalization of childbirth may impose a 'sick' or 'patient' role on to a mother. An understanding of such roles may go a long way to focus input, so that satisfaction can be promoted where appropriate.

The provision of unique care for any individual may be difficult as care regimes are often routine and may depersonalize women. The quality of experience may affect subsequent parenting, and therefore attention to psychological wellbeing is not a luxury but a necessity.

References

Ades, A., Parker, S., Cubitt, D. *et al.* (1992) Two methods of assessing the risk factor composition of the HIV 1 epidemic in heterosexual women in southeast England 1988–1991. *AIDS*, 6, 1031–6.

Astbury, J. (1980) Labour pain – the role of childbirth education, information expectation, in *Problems in Pain* (eds C. Peck and M. Wallace), Pergamon Press, Oxford.

Barbour, R. (1991) Fathers: the emergence of a new comsumer group, in *The Politics of Maternity Care*, (ed J. Garcia, R. Kilpatrick and M. Richards), Clarendon Press, Oxford.

Barclay, R.L. and Barclay, M.D. (1976) Aspects of the normal psychology of pregnancy – the midtrimester. *American Journal of Obstetrics and Gynecology*, 125, 207–11.

Beck, N.C., Siegel, L.S., Davidson, N.P. *et al.* (1980) The prediction of pregnancy outcome: maternal preparation, anxiety and attitudinal sets. *Journal of Psychosomatic Research*, 24, 343–52.

Berryman, J. (1991) Perspectives on later motherhood, in *Motherhood*, (ed A. Phoenix, A. Woollett and E. Lloyd), Sage Publications, London, pp. 103–22.

Birth Counts (1985) *British Birth Counts.*

Bourne, G. (1975) *Pregnancy*, Pan Books, London.

Braverman, J. and Roux, F.J. (1978) Screening for the patient at risk for postpartum depression. *Obstetrics and Gynecology*, 52, 731.

Breen, D. (1975) *The Birth of a First Child*, Tavistock Publications, London.

Brimblecombe, F.S.W., Richards, M.P.W. and Roberton, N.R.C. (1978) *Separation and Special Care Baby Units*, Spastics International Medical Publications, London.

Bullock, L. and McFarlane, J. (1989) The birthweight/battering connection. *American Journal of Nursing*, 1153–55.

Cain, R. (1984) Effects of the father's presence or absence during caesarean delivery. *Birth*, **11**, 10–15.

Campbell, S., Reading, A.E., Cox, O.N. *et al.* (1982) Ultrasound scanning in pregnancy: the short term psychological effects of early real time scans. *Journal of Psychosomatic Obstetrics and Gynecology*, **1**, 57–61.

Cartwright, A. (1979) *The Dignity of Labour*, Tavistock, London.

Cartwright, A. (1984) *Miscarriage*, Fontana, London.

Chalmers, I. (1976) Evaluation of different approaches to obstetric care. *British Journal of Obstetrics and Gynaecology*, **83**, 921.

Chalmers, I. and Enkin, M. (1982) *Effectiveness and Satisfaction in Antenatal Care*, Spastics International Medical Publications/Heinemann Medical Books, London.

Chalmers, I. and Richards, M. (1977) Intervention and causal inference in obstetric practice, in *Benefits and Hazards of the New Obstetrics*, Clinics in Developmental Medicine No 64, SIMP Heinemann Medical Books, London, pp. 34–61.

Chamberlain, G., Howlett, B. and Claireaux, C. (1975) *British Births 1970: vol 2, Obstetric Care*, Heinemann Medical Books, London.

Chard, T. and Richards, M. (1977) *Benefits and hazards of the New Obstetrics*. Clinics in Developmental Medicine 64, Heinemann Medical Books, London.

Chasnoff, I.J., Burns, W.J., Schnoll, S.H. and Burns, K.A. (1985) Cocaine use in pregnancy. *New England Journal of Medicine*, **313**, 666–9.

Chin, J. (1991) Current and future dimensions of the HIV – AIDS pandemic in women and children. *Lancet* **336**, 221–4.

Crandon, A.I. (1979) Maternal anxiety and obstetric complications. *Journal of Psychosomatic Research*, **23**, 109–11.

Dalton, K. (1971) *Depression after Childbirth*, Oxford University Press, Oxford.

Davids, A., Devault, S. and Talmadge, M. (1961) Pregnancy and childbirth abnormalities. *Journal of Clinical and Consulting Psychology*, **25**, 76–7.

Department of Health and Social Security (1975, 1978) Committee on Medical Aspects of Food Policy Panel on Child Nutrition: *Breast Feeding*, DHSS, London.

Dubignon, T., Campbell, D., Curtis, M. and Partington, M.W. (1969) The relation between laboratory measures of sucking food intake and perinatal factors during the newborn period. *Child Development*, **40**, 1107–20.

Dunn, D., Newell, M., Ades, A. and Peckham, C. (1992) Risk of HIV type 1 transmission through breastfeeding. *Lancet*, **340**, 585–8.

Edelman, R. and Connolly, K. (1986) Psychological aspects of infertility. *British Journal of Medical Psychology*, **59**, 209–19.

Elliott, S.A. (1984) Pregnancy and after, in *Contributions to Medical Psychology*, vol. 3, (ed. S. Rachman), Pergamon Press, Oxford.

Elliott, S.A., Rugg, A.J., Watson, J.P. and Brougll, D.I. (1983) Mood changes during pregnancy and after the birth of a child. *British Journal of Clinical Psychology*, **22**, 295–308.

Enkin, M. (1982) Antenatal classes, in *Effectiveness and Satisfaction in Antenatal Care*, (eds M. Enkin and I. Chalmers), SIMP, Heinemann Medical Books, London.

Enkin, M. and Chalmers, I. (1982) *Effectiveness and Satisfaction in Antenatal Care*, Spastics International Medical Publications, Heinemann Medical Books, London.

Enkin, M., Keirse, M. and Chalmers, I. (1989) *A Guide to Effective Care in Pregnancy and Childbirth*, Oxford University Press, Oxford

European Collaborative Study (1992) Risk factors for mother to child transmission of HIV 1. *Lancet*, **339**, 1007–12.

Farrant, W. (1980) Stress after amniocentesis for high serum alphafetaprotein concentrates. *British Medical Journal*, **2**, 452.

Fisher, C. (1980) *Breast Feeding*. Paper presented to The Human Relations in Obstetrics meeting, Warwick.

Forbes, P.B. (1986) The significance of AIDS in obstetric practice. *British Journal of Hospital Medicine*, **36**, 342–6.

Forrest, G.C. (1983) Mourning perinatal death, in *Care of the High Risk Neonate*, (eds M. Klaus and A.A. Fanaroff), W.B. Saunders and Co., Philadelphia.

Gannon, K. (1992) *Recurrent miscarriage*. Paper presented to the London Conference of the British Psychological Society, City University, London.

Garcia, J. (1982) Women's views of antenatal care, in *Effectiveness and Satisfaction in Antenatal Care*, (eds M. Enkin and I. Chalmers), Spastics International Medical Publications/Heinemann Medical Books, London, pp. 81–92.

Garcia, J., Kilpatrick, R. and Richards, M. (1990) *The Politics of Maternity Care*, Clarendon Paperbacks, Oxford.

Gelles, R. (1988) Violence and pregnancy: are pregnant women at greater risk of abuse? *Journal of Marriage and the Family*, August 841–47.

Glover, L., Sherr, L., Abel, P. and Gannon, K. (1992) *Male infertility*. Paper presented at the London Conference of the British Psychological Society.

Gondolf, E. and Fisher, E. (1988) *Battered Women as Survivors: an Alternative to Treating Learned Helplessness*, Lexington Mass, Lexington.

Graham, H.E. and McKee, L. (1980) *The First Months of Motherhood*, Health Education Council, London.

Green, J. and McCreaner, A. (1989) *Counselling in AIDS and HIV Infection*, Blackwell Scientific Publications, Oxford.

Greer, H., Lal, S. and Lewis, S. (1976) Psychosocial consequences of therapeutic abortion. Kings Termination Study. *British Journal of Psychiatry*, **128**, 74–9.

Grimm, E.R. (1961) Psychological tension in pregnancy. *Psychosomatic Medicine*, **23**, 520–7.

Gorsuch, R.L. and Key, M.K. (1974) Abnormalities of pregnancy as a function of anxiety and life stress. *Psychosomatic Medicine*, **36**, 352–62.

Hall, M. and Chng, P.K. (1982) Antenatal care in practice, in *Effectiveness and Satisfaction in Antenatal Care*, (eds M. Enkin and I. Chalmers), SIMP/Heinemann Medical Books, London, pp. 60–8.

Harlap, S. and Shiono, P. (1980) Alcohol smoking and incidence of spontaneous abortions in the first and second trimester. *Lancet*, **2**, 173–6.

Helton, A., McFarlane, J. and Anderson, E. (1987) Battered and pregnant: a prevalence study. *American Journal of Public Health*, **77**, 1337–9.

Hilliard, P. (1985) Physical abuse in pregnancy. *Obstetrics and Gynecology*, **66**, 185–90.

Hooke, J.F. and Marks, P.A. (1962) MMPI characteristics in pregnancy. *Journal of Clinical and Consulting Psychology*, **18**, 316–17.

Houghton, H. (1968) Problems in hospital communication, in *Problems and Progress in Medical Care*, (ed. G. McClachlan), Nuffield Provincial Hospitals Tust, London.

Janis, I. (1971) *Stress and Frustration*, Harcourt Brace Jovanovich, New York.

Johnson, A. (1992) Home-grown heterosexually acquired HIV infection. *British Medical Journal*, **304**, 1125–6.

Kelnar, C.J. and Harvey, D. (1987) *The Sick Newborn Baby*, 2nd edn, Bailliére Tindall, London.

Kitzinger, S. (1983) *The New Good Birth Guide*, Penguin, London.

Klaus, M.H. and Fanaroff, A.A. (1986) *Care of the High Risk Neonate*, 3rd edn. WB Saunders and Co., Philadelphia.

Klaus, M.H, and Kennell, J.H. (1976) *Maternal Infant Bonding*, CV Mosby and Co., St Louis.

Klaus, M.H. and Kennell, J.H. (1983) Care of the parents, in *Care of the High Risk Neonate*, (eds M.H. Klaus and A.A. Fanaroff), WB Saunders and Co., Philadelphia, pp. 146–72.

Kleiner, G.J. and Greston, W.M. (1984) *Suicide in Pregnancy*, John Wright PSG Inc, Boston.

Kline, J., Shrout, P., Stein, Z. *et al.* (1980) Drinking during pregnancy and spontaneous abortion. *Lancet*, **2**, 176–80.

Klusman, L.E. (1975) Reduction of pain in childbirth by the alleviation of anxiety during pregnancy. *Journal of Consulting and Clinical Psychology*, **43**(2), 162–5.

Kron, R.E., Stein, M. and Goddard, K.E. (1966) Newborn sucking behaviour affected by obstetric sedation. *Pediatrics*, **37**, 1012–16.

Kumar, R. and Robson, K. (1978) Neurotic disturbance during pregnancy and the puerperium, in *Mental Illness in Pregnancy and the Puerperium*, (ed. M. Sandler), Oxford University Press, Oxford.

Ligh, H.K., Solheim, J.S. and Hunter, G.W. (1976) Satisfaction with medical care during pregnancy and delivery. *American Journal Obstetrics and Gynecology*, 827–31.

Little, B, Hayworth, J., Benson, P. *et al.* (1982) Psychophysiological ante-natal predictors of postnatal depressed mood. *Journal of Psychosomatic Research*, **26**(4), 419–28.

Lubin, B., Gardener, S.H. and Roth, A. (1975) Mood and somatic symptoms during pregnancy. *Psychosomatic Medicine*, **37**, 136–46.

McDonald, R.L. (1963) The role of emotional factors in obstetric complications: a review. *Psychosomatic Medicine*, **30**, 220–240.

MacFarlane, A. and Turner, S. (1978) Localisation of human speech by the newborn baby and the effects of pethidine (meperidine). *Developmental Medicine and Neonatology*, **20**, 727–34.

MacIntyre, S. (1979) *Findings from Medical Sociological Research*. Paper given at the Scottish Home and Health Department Conference on Needs and Expectations in Obstetrics, Glasgow.

Marteau, T. (1989) Psychological costs of screening. *British Medical Journal*, **299**, 527.

Martin, M.E. (1977) A maternity hospital study of psychiatric illness associated with childbirth. *Irish Journal of Medical Science*, **146**, 239.

Mason, E.A. (1963) A method of predicting crisis outcome for mothers of premature babies. *Public Health Reports*, **78**, 1031.

May, K. and Sollid, D. (1984) Unanticipated Caesarean birth from the father's perspective. *Birth* **11**, 87–95.

McFarlane, J., Parker, B., Soeken, K. and Bullock, L. (1992) Assessing for abuse during pregnancy. *JAMA*, **267**(23), 3176–8.

Meadows, J., Jenkinson, S., Catalan, J. and Gazzard, B. (1990) Voluntary HIV testing in the antenatal clinic: differing uptake rates for individual counselling midwives. *AIDS Care*, **2**(2) 229–34.

Meadows, J., Catalan, J., Sherr, L. *et al.* (1992) Testing for HIV in the antenatal clinic the views of midwives. *AIDS Care*, **4**(2), 157–64.

Minde, K., Trehub, S., Corter, C. *et al.* (1978) Mother–child relationships in the premature nursery: an observational study. *Pediatrics*, **61**.

Moore, W.M.O. (1977) The conduct of the second stage, in *Benefits and Hazards of the New*

Obstetrics, (eds I. Chalmers and M. Richards), Spastics International Medical Publications/ Heinemann Medical Books, London.

Morgan, B.M., Clifton, P. and Lewis, P.J. (1984) The consumer's attitude to obstetrics care. *British Journal of Obstetrics and Gynaecology*, **91**(7), 624–8.

Murai, N. and Murai, M. (1975) A study of moods in pregnant women. *Tohoku Psychologia Folia*, **34**, 10–16.

Newman, L.F. (1980) Parents' perception of their low birth weight infants. *Paediatrics*, **9**, 182–90.

Nicola, C., Jacques, J.T., Amick and Richards, M.P.M. (1983) Parents and the support they need, in *Parent–Baby Attachment in Premature Infants*, (eds J.A. Davis, M.P.M. Richards and N.R.C. Roberton), Croom Helm, Beckenham.

Oakley, A. (1979) *Becoming a Mother*, Martin Robertson, Oxford.

Oakley, A. (1980) *Women Confined: Towards a Sociology of Childbirth*, Martin Robertson, Oxford.

Oakley, A. (1982) The origins and development of antenatal care, in *Effectiveness and Satisfaction in Ante-natal Care*, (eds M. Enkin and I. Chalmers), Spastics International Medical Publications/ Heineman Medical Books, London, pp. 1–21.

Oakley, A. and Richards, M. (1990) Womens' experience of caesarean delivery, in *The Politics of Maternity Care*, (eds J. Garcia, R. Kilpatrick and M. Richards), Oxford University Press, Oxford. pp. 183–202.

O'Brien, M. and Smith, C. (1981) Women's views and experiences of ante-natal care. *Practitioner*, **225**, 123–5.

Peckham, C. and Newell, M.N. (1991) Epidemiology of paediatric HIV infection, in *Caring for Children with HIV and AIDS*, (eds R. Claxton and T. Harrison), Edward Arnold, London.

Phoenix, A., Woollett, A. and Lloyd, E. (1991) *Motherhood Meanings Practices and Ideologies*, Sage Publications, London.

Pitt, B. (1968) Atypical depression following childbirth. *British Journal of Psychiatry*, **114**, 1325–35.

Pokrovsky, V. (1990) Epidemiological surveillance for HIV infection in the USSR. Paper presented to the International AIDS Conference, San Francisco.

Read, G.D.R. (1944) *Childbirth Without Fear*, Fontana, London.

Reading, A.E. (1982) Pain after birth. *British Medical Journal*, **73**, 565.

Reading, A.E. and Cox, D.N. (1982) The effects of ultrasound examination on maternal anxiety levels. *Journal of Behavioural Medicine*, **5**, 237–47.

Reid, M.E. and McIlwaine, G.M. (1980) Consumer opinion of a hospital antenatal clinic. *Social Science and Medicine*, **14a**, 363–8.

Richards, M.P.M. and Robertson, N.R.C. (1983) *Parent–Baby Attachment in Premature Babies*, Croom Helm, Beckenham.

Riley, (1976) What do women want? The question of choice in the conduct of labour, in *Benefits and Hazards of the New Obstetrics*, (eds T. Chard and M. Richards), SIMP Heinemann, London, pp. 62–71.

Robinson, J.O., Rosen, M., Evans, J.M. *et al.* (1980) Self-administered intravenons and intramuscular pethidine – a controlled trial for labour. *Anaesthesia*, **35**, 763–7.

Rosen, M. and Mushin, W.W., Jones, P.L. and Jones, E.V. (1969) Field trial of obstetric analgesics. *British Medical Journal*, **3**, 263–7.

Rosenblatt, D.B., Redshaw, M. and Notarianni, L.J. (1980) Pain relief in childbirth and its consequences for the infant. *Trends in Pharmacological Science*, **1**(13), 365–9.

Royal Commission on the National Health Service (1978) *Patients' Attitudes to the Hospital Service*, HMSO, London.

Sammons, M. (1981) Battered and pregnant. *American Journal of Maternal and Child Nursing*, **6**, 246–50.

Schei, B. and Bakketeig, L.S. (1989) Gynaecological impact of sexual and physical abuse by spouse: a study of a random sample of Norwegian women. *British Journal Obstetrics and Gynaecology*, **96**, 1379–83.

Shaw, P. (1990) Infertility counselling, in *Counselling and Communication in Health Care*, (eds H. Davis, and L. Fallowfield) John Wiley and Sons, Chichester.

Shearer, E., Shiono, P. and Rhoads, G. (1988) Recent trends in family centered maternity care for Caesarean birth families. *Birth*, **15**, 3–7.

Sherr, L. (1980) *Do Doctors Know What Women Know?* Paper presented to the Annual Conference of the British Psychological Society, Guildford.

Sherr, L. (1981) *A Smile is Not Enough – Doctor–Patient Communications in Antenatal Care*. Paper presented to the Annual Conference of the British Psychological Society, York.

Sherr, L. (1987a) *Role of Information and Feedback in Antenatal Care*. Paper presented to the annual Conference of the British Psychological Society, London.

Sherr, L. (1987b) *Communication in Obstetrics*. Paper presented to the Paediatrics Obstetrics Psychology Group, Royal Society of Medicine, London.

Sherr, L. (1987c) The impact of AIDS in obstetrics on obstetrics staff. *Journal of Reproductive and Infant Psychology* **5**, 87–96.

Sherr, L. (1989a) *Anxiety and Communication in Obstetrics*, PhD thesis, Warwick University.

Sherr, L. (1989b) *Death, Dying and Bereavement*, Blackwell Scientific Publications, Oxford.

Sherr, L. (1991) *HIV and AIDS in Mothers and Babies*, Blackwell Scientific Publications, Oxford.

Sherr, L. (1993a) HIV testing in pregnancy in women and AIDS, in *Psychological Perspectives* (ed. C. Squire) Sage, London.

Sherr, L. (1993b) Ante-natal testing, in *The Psychology of Women and AIDS*, (ed C Squire), Gender and Psychology Series, Sage, London.

Sherr, L. and Hedge, B. (1990) The impact and use of written leaflets as a counselling alternative in mass antenatal HIV screening. *AIDS Care*, 2(3), 235–45.

Sherr, L., Jefferies, S. and Victor, C. (1992) GP ante-natal care: the challenges of HIV. *AIDS Patient Care*, 6(2)

Shusterman, L. (1979) Predicting the psychological consequences of abortion. *Social Science and Medicine*, 96, 683.

Simpson, W.J. (1987) A preliminary report of cigarette smoking and the incidence of prematurity. American *Journal of Obstetrics and Gynecology*, 73, 808–15.

Smeriglio, V.L. (1981) *Newborns and Parents: Parent-Infant Contact and Newborn Sensory Stimulation*, Lawrence Erlbaum, Hillsdale, New Jersey.

Stacey, M. (1992) *Changing Human Reproduction*, Social Science Perspectives, Sage Publications, London.

Stevens, A., Victor, C. and Sherr, L. (1989) Antenatal testing for HIV. *Lancet*, Feb. 3, 292.

Sunderland, A., Minkoff, H., Handte, J. *et al.* (1992) The impact of HIV serostatus on reproductive decisions of women. *Obstetrics and Gynecology* 79(6), 1027–31.

Tappin, D., Girdwood, R., Follett, E., *et al.* (1991) Prevalence of maternal HIV infection in Scotland based on unlinked anonymous testing on newborn babies. *Lancet*, 337, 1565–7.

Temmerman, M., Moses, S., Kirau, D. *et al.* (1990) Impact of single session post partum counselling of HIV infected women on their subsequent reproductive behaviour. *AIDS Care*, 2(3), 247–52.

Trowell, J. (1982) Possible effects of emergency Caesarean section on mother-child relationship. *Early Human Development*, 7, 41–51.

Van de Perre, P., Simonson, A. and Msellan, P. (1991) Postnatal transmission of HIV type 1 from mother to infant: a prospective cohort study in Kigali, Rwanda, *New England Journal of Medicine*, 91, 593–8.

Walker, L. (1984) *The Battered Woman Syndrome*, Springer, New York Publishing Co Inc.

Ziegler, J.B., Cooper, D.A. and Johnson, R.O. (1985) Postnatal transmission of AIDS associated retrovirus from mother to infant. *Lancet*, i, 896–7.

Zuckerman, B., Frank, D. and Hingson, R. (1989) Effects of maternal marijuana and cocaine use on fetal growth. *New England Journal of Medicine*, 320, 762–8.

Chapter nineteen

Behavioural paediatrics and childhood cancer

Nicola Whitehead

This chapter gives an initial definition and overview of behavioural paediatrics. This is not an attempt at an exhaustive review but rather a 'taster' of some of the key topics, such as anxiety, therapeutic adherence, pain management and preparation for hospital. This is followed by an in-depth look at paediatric cancer which will illustrate some of the approaches used.

Behavioural paediatrics

Behavioural paediatrics involves the focusing of behavioural methodology on children with medical problems. It should also encompass an interest in the medical settings (including the medical personnel) in which the child finds him or herself. To be effective it should also focus on the wider issues that determine parents' and children's health beliefs and behaviour, described elsewhere as 'health psychology'.

Russo and Varni (1982) offer a more formalized definition of behavioural paediatrics:

> What behavioural medicine and behavioural paediatrics offer lies in their focus on learning and teaching, their emphasis on

skills training rather than the aetiology of skills deficits and their empirical assessment of treatment process and outcome (Russo and Varni, 1982).

They suggest that behavioural paediatrics should be:

- Interdisciplinary in nature;
- Concerned with the management of acute and chronic disorders, including parent training, child self-control techniques and health staff training;
- Firmly rooted in empirical methodologies;
- Concerned with long-term care, acute intervention and prevention;
- Based on assessment and treatment that are data-based;
- Interested in both community settings and inpatient care environments;
- Concerned with disease mechanisms: biochemical, physiological and biobehavioural interrelationships.

Behavioural paediatrics can be conceptualized in a number of ways. For example, following a medical model, it can be looked at in terms of specific illnesses such as asthma, diabetes and so on. From a more psychological viewpoint it can be looked at in terms of psychologically relevant concepts such as anxiety management, pain, adherence to medical advice and psychological preparation for medical procedures.

The evolution of behavioural paediatrics has followed independent developments in the fields of both clinical psychology and paediatrics. Within clinical psychology there has been an enormous growth in research into behavioural medicine and health psychology as a whole (Rachman, 1980; 1984; Prokop and Bradley, 1981; Doleys, Merideth and Ciminero, 1982; Millon, Green and Meagher, 1982; Surwit *et al.*, 1982; Steptoe and Matthews, 1984), of which behavioural paediatrics is a part. The emphasis of paediatrics has changed due to the enormous reduction in infectious diseases: the emphasis is now more on dealing with chronic illness and also the prevention of some illnesses and accidents. In this way, two quite independent developments have come together in current behavioural paediatrics.

Anxiety management is an example of one issue which cuts across much of the literature.

Anxiety management, preparation and coping strategies

Many of the signs of upset in children in medical settings, whether acting out, withdrawal or other changes in behaviour, are signs of anxiety. Anxiety management is certainly of relevance to any child and any parent who is experiencing hospitalization, outpatient appointments or investigative and treatment interventions. Preparation for hospitalization and medical procedures is well documented in the literature. The aims are to decrease overall distress levels for both parents and children, and to increase cooperation with treatment (Melamed *et al.*, 1975; Melamed and Siegel, 1975; Melamed *et al.* 1978; Ferguson, 1979; Peterson and Shigetomi, 1981; Siegel and Peterson, 1980;

Price, 1991; Adams, Gill and McDonald, 1991). Therapy is more effective with a relaxed, cooperative child and, during some tests, can avoid tissue damage (Peterson *et al.*, 1990). Most studies have been carried out on children undergoing dental treatment or minor surgery.

Children and parents can be prepared using a variety of methods, most commonly filmed modelling (Melamed and Siegel, 1975; Pinto and Hollandsworth, 1989; Karl *et al.* 1990); reading and colouring materials providing information about hospital or specific procedures (Adams, Gill and McDonald, 1991); preadmission visits, which could include question and answer sessions (Holt and Maxwell, 1991); stress-point intervention (Visintainer and Wolfer, 1975); and coping skills training (Zastowny, Kirschenbaum and Meng, 1981). Hospital tours alone have not been found to be effective (Peterson *et al.*, 1990).

Art therapy (Levinson and Ousterhout, 1980), creative writing (Lewis, 1978) and play therapy (Chan, 1980) have all been used in an attempt to prepare children for medical procedures and to prevent later problems. There are few data on the efficacy of these alone, and indeed Becker (1972) suggested that some of these procedures may actually increase anxieties and acting out in children.

Any preparation must consider the following factors:

- Previous hospital experiences;
- Level of anxiety;
- Amount and type of information;
- The involvement of parents: anxious parents are likely to induce anxiety in their child;
- Coping styles;
- The child's age and developmental level;
- The child's current health status and required interventions or surgery.

Preparatory information can be given in ways that are focused on what is going to happen (procedural) and/or how the procedure is going to feel (sensory).

Ridley-Johnson and Melamed (1986) describe the use of preparation approaches with child dental patients. They described the 'tell, show, do' (Anderson and Masur, 1983) technique where the dentist informs, demonstrates and then carries out the procedure. They highlight the additional need for:

- Sensory information about feelings, sights and sounds that will be involved in the procedure;
- Reinforcement and peer modelling to increase skills acquisition.

Siegel and Peterson (1980) found that young dental patients, both in the sensory information group and in the coping skills groups, were rated as less anxious during treatment, had lower pulse rates after treatment and showed less destructive behaviour than a no-treatment control. Johnson, Kirehhoff and Endred, (1975) found that the mean observable distress-related behaviour for children having plaster casts removed was lower for the group prepared for the expected sensations than the groups having either procedural information or no information.

A study by Rodin (1983), which looked at preparing children aged 4–7 for a routine blood test, found that children who were both told what was going to happen and allowed to play with preparatory materials, including games and books, were less anxious than a group who just sat and waited, or a second group who played with ordinary toys. Harrison (1991) found similar results using a story containing coping skills, but unfortunately this study had no control.

Adams, Gill and McDonald (1991) also found that using a preparation booklet on admissions and operating theatre procedures resulted in reduced overall anxiety in children, reduced anxiety in the theatre, fewer behaviour problems on return home and parents who were more satisfied than families who had had the usual routine and verbal preparation. A

clinically useful paper by Gross (1989) gives practical guidelines on producing a colouring booklet.

In one of the earlier studies on filmed modelling using the video 'Ethan has an operation', Melamed and Siegel (1975) compared a variety of behaviours in children who had seen the preparation film with a control group of children who had watched a non-hospital video. It was found that the experimental group showed less anxiety both prior to the operation and at their post-hospital assessment, than did the control group.

Adams, Gill and McDonald (1991) also found that using a preparation video resulted in children understanding better what was going to happen to them, and being less upset than those children who had watched a control cartoon video. It has also been suggested elsewhere (Price, 1991) that the inclusion of the postdischarge outpatient appointment should also be included in preparation materials.

There is evidence to indicate that reducing child and parent anxiety levels can have a direct impact on the child's physical status. For example, Wolfer and Visintainer (1975) found that children having minor surgery who had received an experimental nursing programme in which mothers were encouraged to care for their child in hospital, and in which mother and child received psychological preparation at six stress points (for example, blood tests on admission), had lower heart rates after blood test, lowered incidents of resistance to anaesthesia induction, increased oral fluid intake and a shorter time to first voiding than the control group.

About a third of children's admissions into hospital are as emergencies (Muller, Harris and Wattley, 1986), where advanced preparation procedures would not have been possible. One way around this difficulty are classroom educational programmes preparing children for hospital (e.g. Eiser and Hanson, 1989). However, there is little information regarding the outcomes of such work so far, and relevant here is the finding that younger children (5-year-olds) retain little information after approximately 1 week (Eiser and Patterson, 1984). It may be that stress-point intervention – preparing a child for each procedure as it happens – allows children to retain small amounts of information at a time.

More research is required into matching appropriate kinds of preparation for different child populations. Modelling procedures have been found to be more effective with naive than with experienced patients (Peterson and Harbeck, 1988). Little work has been done on the differential effects of varying coping styles in children (Melamed, Robbins and Graves, 1982; Knight *et al.*, 1979) in comparison with the wealth of literature on adult coping styles. Some children actively seek out information, whereas others deny it. The former seem to cope better, but it is not clear what is the best way of preparing denying children (Peterson *et al.*, 1990).

Age is a crucial variable affecting the child's ability to cope with processing and retaining information. The much quoted Melamed *et al.* (1976) study suggested that children under 7 are best prepared the day before an operation, and children over 7 are best prepared about a week before. There is also evidence that preparing a child for an operation on the day can increase their arousal (Faust and Melamed, 1984), particularly if done without the addition of coping skills (Klingman *et al.*, 1984; Faust, Olson and Rodriguez, 1991), although Kennedy and Riddle (1989) found no differences in anxiety in 3–6-year-olds whether they were prepared the day before or the day of the operation. Clearly, considerably more data are required regarding the best timing and type of information for each age group.

Anxiety management and coping skills

Many investigative and treatment procedures cause distress for children, for example X-rays, injections, blood tests, drips, lumbar punctures, bone marrow aspirations, plaster-cast removal, dressing changes and debridement (for burns). Some children also need to undergo medical procedures on a regular basis, for example the diabetic child or the child with cancer. Giving a child coping strategies to deal with such procedures can help increase his or her feelings of mastery and control. This can be particularly important for adolescents, so that they do not feel like passive victims of their treatment. A number of different psychological procedures have been used in the examples below, and can be a guide for future reading.

- *Hypnosis* For burns: Bernstein (1965); Wakeman and Kaplan (1978); Labaw (1973). For bone marrow aspirations: Jay *et al.* (1985).
- *Relaxation* Walker and Healey (1980) for burns and as part of Elliott and Olson's (1983) package for children with burns.
- *Attention distraction* Elliott and Olson (1983).
- *Imagery* Elliott and Ozolins (1983); Elliott and Olson (1983).
- *Desensitization* Weinstein (1976); Gale and Ayer (1969).
- *Stress inoculation* Wernick, Jaremko and Taylor (1981): Elliott and Olson (1983).
- *Reinforcement for coping* Elliott and Olson (1983).

Therapeutic adherence

The next issue which reflects current concerns in behavioural paediatrics is therapeutic adherence. Although this applies to many childhood conditions (e.g. seizure control, renal failure), this section will focus on adherence in juvenile diabetes and asthma (see also Chapters 6 and 12).

Juvenile diabetes

Juvenile diabetes exemplifies the range of issues involved in therapeutic adherence in paediatrics. Diabetes is caused by failure of the pancreas to produce insulin. Diabetic children are insulin dependent and therapy is aimed at normalizing blood glucose by injections of insulin, regulation of diet and exercise, and blood and urine testing. When the levels of glucose are exceeded, glucose is excreted in the urine and is detectable in urine and blood tests. Glucose levels are also affected by growth, illness and hormonal effects. Parents and children are largely responsible for the long-term management and are making clinical decisions daily (see Gross, 1990).

The behavioural management of diabetes is quite complex and there is not necessarily a direct relationship between behavioural adherence and diabetic control: poor adherence will result in poor control, but good adherence does not necessarily result in good control. In such a complex regimen there are many opportunities for poor adherence, and this is particularly true of blood tests, diet, correct recording of results and the rotation of injection sites. A number of studies have attempted to improve adherence in a number of these areas. Lowe and Lutzker (1979) looked at the effects of a points system verses a 'memo' condition (basically written instructions) on the compliance of a 9-year-old juvenile diabetic using a multiple baseline design. Dependent variables were urine testing, diet and foot care. The points system was found to be effective for urine testing and foot care, and the basic memo condition was sufficient to increase adherence to diet.

Epstein *et al.* (1981) looked at 19 families and attempted to increase the negative urine results by instructions in the self-management of diet, insulin and exercise, giving reinforcement in the form of points and praise for negative urine tests. The instructions were given in group form to the children and covered six topic areas. Each child had to achieve a minimum score on the quiz for that topic before he or she progressed to the next topic. There was a parallel series of programmes for the parents. This resulted in improvements in the negative

urine results immediately after the group and at a 22-week follow-up. However, the significant changes in the percentage of negative urine tests were not associated with improved diabetic control. The author suggests that this may be caused by the unreliability of urine testing, or that serum glucose may be lagging behind changes in the urine.

Gilbert *et al.* (1982) describe a study in which there were two groups of 6–9-year-old diabetics, one watching a peer modelling film for the self-injection of insulin and the other a film on diet. Among the children watching the peer modelling film, the oldest girls increased their skill in injecting themselves and made fewer errors, but unfortunately there was only a 4-day follow-up. Nurick and Johnson (1991) found that adolescents can be trained to improve their blood glucose awareness, individual symptom awareness and awareness of relevant behaviours such as exercise. Leigh (1987) looked at factors affecting poor diabetic control in adolescents, and found a relationship between poor control and stressful events in the family, such as maternal illness or divorce. This points to the need to look at wider psychosocial variables as well as the immediate issues of behavioural adherence (see also Auslander *et al.*, 1991).

Marteau and Johnston (1987) suggest that the problem may be less one of adherence but rather one of different goals between patient and physician. If the patient's glucose level is low it carries with it the danger of coma in the short term but reduces the risk of complications such as retinopathy and nephropathy. Mann and Johnston (1982) suggest that the majority of children have higher than normal blood sugar levels. Implicit in the studies aiming at increasing adherence is the belief that doctors and patients share the same goal, i.e. low blood sugar. They found that in their goals for treatment, parents differed from doctors by being more likely to find hyperglycaemia acceptable. There was also a relationship between parents' goals for treatment and diabetic control, in which parents who found hyperglycaemia more acceptable were more likely to have children less well in control. Parents who manage hyperglycaemia by testing first rather than intervening immediately also had children in better control. The parents and doctors agreed on what constituted poor control, but not on what constituted excellent, good or fair control, as doctors' goals were related to beliefs about hyperglycaemia, whereas parents' goals were related to beliefs about hypoglycaemia. The authors discuss attitudes and goals held in terms of costs and benefits of various blood sugar levels in the long and short term, which may well be based on the frequency of personal experience of various complications. It was suggested that the explicit sharing of goals, as cited by Schaefer, Glasgow and McCaul (1982), may result in improved diabetic control.

A number of studies have assessed parents' and childrens' knowledge of diabetes. There appears to be little relationship between parent and child knowledge: the length of time with diabetes does not increase the amount known about the condition, and in fact there is some evidence to show that parents' knowledge drops off over time; knowledge about diabetes management does not imply skills, nor do skills in one area predict skills in another. Auslander *et al.* (1991) found that parents of 15–18-year-olds had the poorest scores on diabetes knowledge, particularly diabetes problem solving, of all parent groups.

Health care behaviours are not intrinsically rewarding, in fact the environmental contingencies make it less likely that a child will comply. For example, some of the functions a diabetic child is expected to carry out are mildly, and in some cases strongly, aversive (Gross, 1990). There is therefore a need to increase the reinforcement value of health care behaviours. There is also evidence that parents can usefully carry out intermittent monitoring of their chil-

dren's health care behaviours. Additionally, a number of diabetic children and young people can benefit from social skills training to equip them to deal with peer pressures, for example social pressures to eat sweets, drink alcohol and smoke (see Kaplan, Chadwick and Schimmel, 1985 and Massouh *et al.*, 1989).

Although the above discussion was not intended to be a comprehensive review of adherence in diabetes, many key areas have been touched upon, such as teaching self-management skills and the disparity or otherwise of goals between physicians and patients. Many of these areas are relevant to other conditions that have not been covered here.

Behavioural paediatrics also has a role to play in modifying acute episodes in some disorders, without necessarily having an impact on the chronicity or underlying pathology involved. Work on asthma exemplifies this approach.

Asthma

> Asthma is a respiratory disorder that results in the recurrent, intermittent and variable pattern of reversible airway obstruction, ranging in intensity from a sensation of tightness in the chest accompanied by a slight wheeze to status asthmaticus (Creer, Renne and Chai, 1982).

Behavioural intervention aimed at curing asthma or improving pulmonary functioning has had disappointing results (Rakos, Grodek and Mack, 1985). More promising has been the approach of teaching children skills to prevent the occurrence of asthmatic attacks, including the appropriate use of inhalation equipment (Renne and Creer, 1976). Creer, Renne and Christian (1976) outline five goals for children with asthma:

1. To teach the family that asthma should not be the focus of attention any more than is necessary.
2. To correct any behavioural deficit, e.g. not taking medication as instructed.

3. To correct any behavioural excesses, e.g. panic during an asthma attack.
4. To teach self-management skills.
5. Normalization.

Weiss (1981) developed a package for parents and children, aimed at increased self-management skills, which included components on the internal and external triggers of asthma attacks, personal control, relaxation techniques and asthma facts. The package is designed to be totally self-administered.

Rakos, Grodek and Mack (1985) looked at the effects of the package with 43 children, on children's self-report, parents' report, school attendance and doctors' report. The impact of the package was fairly limited, with children reporting improvements in self-management skills and parents reporting improvements only in a minority of areas. The authors suggest that greater treatment effects might have occurred with more therapist input.

Fireman *et al.* (1981) investigated the possibility of reducing the severity and number of asthma attacks, absences from school and admission into hospital, through teaching self-management skills to parents and children. They used a package which included an educational programme and a self-management component, including skills on self-observation and decision making. Parents were encouraged to reinforce coping behaviour positively.

Overall, it was found that the experimental group had less absence from school, fewer hospital admissions, fewer asthma attacks and fewer wheezy days. Marion (1987) showed families that they could learn to predict the likely occurrence of an asthma attack.

In summary, as Creer, Renne and Chai (1982) point out, there appears to be a role for the psychologist in altering asthma-related behaviours, e.g. learning to attend to physical changes. They suggest a combination of an educational and a behavioural approach as being particularly hopeful. In this, as with other health problems:

> within the area of health care, it becomes increasingly clear that improvements in health status will come not from improving treatment of disease, but rather from disease prevention through lifestyle changes (Roberts and Peterson, 1984).

Pain management

Pain experienced by children can be categorized into four areas:

- Pain associated with a specific injury or trauma (e.g. burns);
- Pain caused by investigative and treatment procedures (e.g. bone marrow aspiration and burns; this will be discussed more fully in the 'Cancer' section);
- Recurrent pain not associated with a specific injury or disease (e.g. recurrent abdominal pain; Varni, 1983);
- Pain intrinsic to a disease process (e.g. arthritis).

It is important to differentiate between chronic and acute pain, which differ in their causes, functions and consequences. Further reading can be found in Gross and Drabman (1990) and also in some review papers (Jay, Elliott and Varni, 1986; Elliott and Jay, 1987). Most published work on interventions with children has concentrated on acute pain, for example bone marrow aspirations and lumbar punctures (to be discussed below) in children undergoing cancer treatment, and debridement, hydrotherapy and dressing changes in children having treatment for burns. The extreme level of distress caused by these procedures is well documented (Labaw, 1973; Hilgard and Le Baron, 1982; Walker and Healey, 1980; Elliott and Olson, 1983). There is also evidence that children do not habituate to such treatments (Katz, Kellerman and Siegel, 1980).

Pain associated with injury or trauma and treatment procedures: burns

A study by Wakeman and Kaplan (1978) still stands as one of the few systematic studies on hypnosis with burns. They found that in both the lower (0–30%) and the higher percentages (30–60%) totals of body burns, those who had learnt self-hypnosis asked for significantly less analgesic medication at all age levels (i.e. 7–18, 19–30 and 31–70) than the control group (which consisted of 'verbal support sessions'). For both levels of percentage burns, children and adolescents consistently asked for less medication than the adult group.

Elliott and Olson (1983) investigated the efficacy of a treatment package for reducing the distress of burned children undergoing stressful procedures. The package included attention distraction, relaxation breathing, the use of imagery, reinterpretation of the context of pain (using heroic imagery and a relaxing image) and reinforcement for using the coping techniques. Using a multiple baseline reversal design, it was demonstrated that children were able to reduce their levels of distress substantially as measured by the Burn Treatment Distress Scale, at three stress points: unwrapping of the bandages, the first 15 minutes of hydrotherapy, and rewrapping of the burned areas. Interestingly, the children were only able to reduce their distress successfully when they were actively coached by the therapist. It may be that the procedures are so distressing that frequent prompting is required to retain involvement in the pain anxiety management techniques. The authors suggest the need for future studies to discover the effective treatment components of such a package.

It may be, however, that it is the package that lends the strength to the treatment, so that children can switch from one technique to another as one become less effective. Wernick, Jaremko and Taylor (1981) working with adults, stressed the need for a number of coping techniques to select from; this is yet to be demonstrated for children.

The issue of prediction and control in relation to painful procedures has been highlighted by a number of authors. It has been suggested that increasing predictability and control can help children to cope with painful procedures. This can be achieved by having children involved in the actual procedures: decision making regarding the procedures and having some staff dealing with the child who never carry out the painful procedures (Kavanagh, 1983; Wright, 1984; Tarnowski et al., 1987).

If burned children and adolescents can learn an alternative method of pain relief, this has important implications for the problems of addiction, drowsiness and unwillingness to eat that can come about with frequent use of analgesic medication. Some authors do suggest, however, that in general children in pain are given too little analgesic medication for optimum pain control (Elliott and Jay, 1987).

Recurrent pain

McGrath (1987) reviewed the assessment and management of recurrent pain syndrome in children. Examples of these are recurrent headaches, either of the migraine or tension headache type, and recurrent abdominal pain and aching limb pains.

The paper by McGrath (1987) is a comprehensive review on the nature of recurrent pain syndrome, multidimensional assessment and management of recurrent pain syndrome.

Headache

Masek and Hoag (1990) subdivided behavioural treatment of headache into three categories: contingency management, cognitive behavioural therapy and self-regulation training, such as relaxation. Examples of the use of contingency management can be found in papers by Lake (1981) and Ramsden, Friedman and Williamson (1983), where children were reinforced for headache-free days. A study by Richter *et al.* (1986) is one of the few experimental studies on cognitive – behavioural methods for children with migraine headaches. They found that both cognitive coping strategies and relaxation strategies were superior to an attention control group for reducing migraine headaches.

Biofeedback and relaxation have been found to be effective for the treatment of migraine headaches. Waranch and Keenan (1985) taught relaxation and biofeedback of the frontalis muscle and digital skin temperature to 15 10–17-year-olds with headache. Counselling was also included. Out of these 15 children, 13 were either headache free or the pain was markedly reduced. This was maintained at a 6–22-month follow-up.

Other studies focusing on the efficacy of self-regulation training include Mehegan *et al.* (1987), Fentress *et al.* (1986), Olness and McDonald (1981) and Houts (1982). A review of self-regulation training for migraine is to be found in Hoelscher and Lichstein (1984), and Lascelles *et al.* (1989) detail a variety of strategies used in their treatment package for migraine, which is very useful clinically.

Recurrent abdominal pain

There are few controlled experimental studies on the treatment of recurrent abdominal pain. Some single case studies on contingency management methods are reported by Sank and Biglan (1974), Miller and Kratochwill (1979) and Wasserman (1978).

Disease-related pain

In two studies on disease-related pain, Varni (1981a,b), reported the successful self-regulation of arthritic pain perception through muscle relaxation and using meditative breathing images, such as warmth, freedom from pain and images of a gentle flow of blood to the arthritic joint. The therapeutic value of applying heat to arthritic joints has been highlighted elsewhere (Lehmann, Warren and Scham,

1974). In this study patients were instructed to imagine themselves in a place associated with warmth.

In Varni's (1981b) study it was found that the three patients significantly reduced the number of days of reported arthritic pain, and the perceived pain level reduced considerably when pain was experienced. The patients' mobility and sleep were improved, as well as the ability to increase skin temperature of the targeted site, which was maintained at follow-up.

The child suffering from haemophilia will experience both acute pain (during acute bleeding episodes) and chronic episodes of arthritic pain. The acute pain acts as an essential signal to indicate the need for Factor VIII replacement therapy (which allows blood to clot). The chronic pain caused by bleeding into the joint can lead to analgesic dependency and severe curtailment of normal activities.

Varni, Gilbert and Dietrich (1981) described the case of pain in a 9-year-old haemophiliac child. In this instance the child had developed an inhibitor to Factor VIII replacement, which meant that the bleeding could not be controlled (this occurs in about 10% of cases of haemophiliac children). Relaxation, breathing exercises and guided imagery were used to reduce both the chronic arthritic pain and the acute pain from the bleeding episodes. This treatment was significant in increasing later activity, school attendance and the number of social contacts, and in decreasing self-reported bleeding and arthritic pain. This was maintained at a 1-year follow-up. If a haemophiliac child does not have an inhibitor to Factor VIII replacement, it is essential that the child is well aware of this acute bleeding pain to use it as a functional signal for replacement therapy. For further reading on pain management in children see Russo and Varni (1982).

This first section has attempted a brief overview of behavioural paediatrics, highlighting certain processes and problems. Omissions are inevitable and some areas (e.g. neuropsychology, epilepsy, neonatology, health promotion and blood pressure) have not been discussed at all.

Much of the research has been hampered by the usual problems of single case studies, inadequate follow-ups and lack of comparative studies. Nevertheless, progress is being made:

> Meaningful contributions to behavioural health will come only out of systematic research and long term follow up that is fully sensitive to both behavioural and physical health perspectives.
> The value of contributions produced in this manner will be unlimited (Albino, 1984).

Childhood cancer

Childhood cancer has been selected for more detailed scrutiny as it encompasses many issues of relevance to health psychologists working with children in a paediatric setting, such as the control of pain and anxiety, particularly in relation to the iatrogenic effects of treatment.

Cancer is actually a lay term that encompasses many diseases with variable prognoses. Childhood cancers are very different from adult cancers, which tend to be solid tumours. Most frequent childhood cancers are leukaemias, with leukaemias and lymphomas making up about 40% of the total, intracranial tumors 25%, neuroblastomas 6%, nephroblastoma (Wilms' tumour) 5% and rhabdomyosarcoma 4%.

This medical terminology describes the site of the cancer and the cell type infected, e.g. nephroblastoma is cancer of the blast cells in the kidney. The incidence in the UK is about 100 new cases per 1 000 000 children, which averages out up to about one new case every 5 years per typical GP practice (Wheeler, 1986).

The main dramatic change in recent years which has increased the relevance of psycho-

logical input has been the improvement in outlook of many childhood cancers. The changes come about as a result of multimodal treatment, usually a combination of cranial or craniospinal radiation, chemotherapy and surgery. Of all childhood leukaemias 70% are of the acute lymphocytic type, and about 50% of these children are in remission after 6 years (Forfar and Arneil, 1984). Previously the prognosis was death within a few months; similarly, Wilms' tumour or nephroblastoma (cancer of the kidneys, which tends to affect under-8s), had a recovery rate of only 25% in the 1940s but now has a much improved prognosis.

As a result of these dramatic changes, the emphasis has shifted from the realistic and continuing concerns about how the child and family will cope with death (e.g. Vernick and Karon, 1965; Friedman et al., 1963; Binger, Ablin and Feverstein, 1969) to how the child and family can live with the disease (Kagen-Goodheart, 1977). Unfortunately, the outlook is not so favourable in all childhood cancers, e.g. neuroblastoma, central nervous system tumours and acute myeloid leukaemias.

Psychosocial issues

Families having to live with the disease face many issues, including the following:

- Disruption of schooling and subsequent reintegration. There is evidence to suggest that some of these children experience learning difficulties, perhaps partly caused by disruption of the curriculum, but also in some cases through the treatment itself, particularly CNS irradiation and some chemotherapy (Moehle et al., 1983; Berg et al., 1983; Inati et al., 1983);
- Disruption of peer and sibling relationships. (Davies et al., 1991; Sanger, Copeland and Davidson, 1991);
- Coping with the diagnosis and its implications for the future in terms of employment, marriage and fertility;

- Body image changes, e.g. those subsequent to surgery, weight loss or gain, alopecia, skeletal abnormalities and endocrine dysfunction which could lead to problems of growth, including secondary sexual characteristics;
- Frequent hospitalization, possibly involving isolation in protected environments, which are used to decrease the rate of bacterial infection. For further reading see Lesko, Kern and Hawkins, (1984), Kellerman *et al.* (1980) and Susman *et al.* (1981);
- Therapeutic and investigative procedures and their side-effects, often involving pain, anxiety and discomfort;
- Dealing with the uncertain nature of the disease and its life-threatening implications;
- Weaning families from chemotherapy and frequent medical appointments.

Sourkes (1980) found that, when asked what aspects of treatment they found most unpleasant, children cited bone marrow aspirations, X-rays, venepunctures, hair loss and nausea. For adolescents the treatments are often rated as being more disruptive than the illness itself (Zeltzer, Ellenberg and Rigler, 1980). Looking at the psychology referrals of 100 children with cancer, Kellerman, Katz and Siegel (1979) found two main categories: conditioned anxiety in relation to painful and flattening procedures, such as the acute pain from bone marrow aspirations, lumbar punctures, venepunctures, biopsies and intramuscular injections; and behavioural problems at home and difficulties in getting on with school and siblings.

The literature abounds with papers relating to the psychosocial aspects of childhood cancer (Binger, Ablin and Feverstein, 1969;Valentine, 1978; Fochtman, 1979; Nir and Maslin, 1982; Carr-Gregg and White, 1985; Van Dongen-Melman and Sanders-Woudstra, 1986).

Aaronson and Beckman's (1987) book *The Quality of Life of Cancer Patients* contains some useful papers on psychosocial issues, with a particular chapter on psychosocial research in children. Other approaches which have an important part to play with these children include play therapy (Adams, 1976), art therapy (Trent, 1986) and group discussion with a parents, for example 'We can weekend' (Johnson and Norby, 1981). These are designed for families of children with cancer so that they can have weekends away together to facilitate education and communication about issues connected with the illness (Heiney *et al.*, 1984).

Any treatment or specific problems related to cancer and its treatment must not fail to take into account the whole family and the wider social context of the child. For example, any attempt to reduce a child's distress without addressing the parents' anxiety levels is likely to be of limited therapeutic value. Sanger, Copeland and Davidson (1991) found that children's adjustment to cancer was related to parental coping. A number of papers have addressed the need for emotional support for the parents (Adams, 1976; Michielutte, Patterson and Herdun, 1981) and the giving of information and management suggestions for teachers to help reintegration into school (Ross and Scarvalone, 1982). Spinetta (1981) and Cassady (1982) point to the need for attention to the distress of siblings in the midst of the care and attention required by the sick child.

Behavioural interventions

Many of the problems encountered by children with cancer are related to exploratory procedures, e.g. X-rays, lumbar punctures, bone marrow aspirations; and therapeutic procedures and their side-effects, e.g. surgery, chemotherapy (side-effects include nausea and vomiting, hair loss, lowered resistance to infection), radiotherapy (side-effects can include nausea and vomiting, headaches, skin burns and hair loss) and venepuncture.

The fundamental aim of much psychological intervention in children with cancer is to increase their own abilities to deal with pain and anxiety while undergoing such medical procedures. This allows the child to participate in, and to some extent control, what is happening to them (Hockenberry and Bologna-Vaughan, 1985). Most studies on pain in children with cancer have focused on acute pain, but children with cancer do experience chronic pain, especially in bone, joint and soft-tissue cancer and after amputations. There are few empirical studies on children with chronic pain and cancer (Miser *et al.*, 1987).

Zeltzer, Glenberg and Rigler (1980) suggest that self-help procedures for adolescents should:

- Reduce stress, reduce treatment-related anxiety and increase the ability to relax;
- Increase tolerance of procedures and reduce non-compliance;
- Remove unnecessary symptoms;
- Be easily learnt;
- Be usable alone, without further contact to enhance feelings of self-control.

As they point out, adolescents with cancer have the same developmental issues to be concerned about as other adolescents, but they have additional problems with body image, future planning, peer relationships and sexuality.

Most of the behavioural studies on children with cancer have focused on procedure-related difficulties: reducing distress during bone marrow aspirations and reducing the side-effects of chemotherapy.

Bone marrow aspiration

Bone marrow aspiration is a diagnostic and monitoring procedure used frequently in children with leukaemia. It involves inserting a needle usually into the iliac crest of the hip bone to remove the sample of bone marrow. This procedure is extremely painful, as no local anaesthetic can alleviate the pain and repeated general anaesthetics have to be avoided.

Katz, Kellerman and Siegel (1980) and Jay *et al.* (1983) found the pain and anxiety during bone marrow aspiration to be universal, and found no evidence of habituation; in fact, if anything the reverse applied. McGrath and Deveber (1986), looking at 25 children with acute myeloid leukaemia and acute lympho-cytic leukaemia over 2 years, found that half the children reported a consistent increase in pain and anxiety over the 2 years. Interestingly, Hilgard and Le Baron (1982) found some children able to cope with bone marrow aspirations and the children's own methods of pain relief will be discussed below.

Hypnosis

Hypnotherapy has recently been 'rediscovered' as a respectable approach for dealing with a number of paediatric problems, as both primary and adjunctive therapy. As Olness (1986) pointed out, hypnotherapy was rarely mentioned in the paediatric literature between 1887 and 1978: it has really only been during the last 20 years or so that there has been an upsurge in interest in published papers. Labaw *et al.* (1975) studied the effect of self-hypnosis on 27 young people with cancer aged 4–20 years. The dependent variables were food and fluid intake, easier sleep, behaviour during administrations of intravenous medication, spinal taps and bone marrow aspirations. Groups were held twice per month, with a hypnotic trance being induced twice per session, as the authors considered that greater relaxation was found during the second repetition of the hypnosis. The suggestions included generalized relaxation and wellbeing as well as specific suggestions regarding the variables described above. This is an interesting paper with some clinically useful but anecdotal case studies. The authors make reference to calmer children, staff and parents, and weight gain in some of the children, but unfortunately there are no firmer data than these.

Ellenberg *et al.* (1980) addressed the problem of pain and anxiety during bone marrow aspiration in an adolescent girl with leukaemia who experienced multiple problems, such as anorexia, headaches, backache, nausea, vomiting, pain and anxiety during the procedure. Hypnosis was induced on six occasions beforehand, and specific suggestions were made, including dissociation, time distortion and glove anaesthesia transferred to the back. On self-report there was a reduction in pain and anxiety before, during and after bone marrow aspiration, and less pain associated with headache and backache in comparison with baseline. The authors emphasize the importance of specific symptom suggestions rather than more general suggestions. However, factors such as the placebo effect or the patient attempting to please the therapist cannot be discounted as contributory factors to these positive results. Hilgard and Le Baron (1982) described the Stanford study investigating the application of hypnosis to 24 children with a variety of cancers undergoing bone marrow aspiration. They were particularly interested in the relationship of hypnotic responsiveness to the application of hypnosis for pain relief. Hypnosis was used in a flexible way to suit the needs of the child. The book is rich in examples of case studies and detailed descriptions of how the hypnosis was actually used. For example, fantasy switchboxes to switch off the pain, or blowing out a candle, were used as distraction procedure. Of 19 of the more hypnotizable children, 14 were able to reduce their pain significantly during either their first or second session, as measured by self-rating and observation. Of the five less hypnotizable children, none were significantly able to control their pain using hypnosis. Despite the evidence cited by Katz, Kellerman and Siegel (1980) that distress during bone marrow aspiration is universal, Hilgard and Le Baron (1982) found that some children had discovered their own coping mechanism, as measured by a low self-reported pain, e.g. self-induced pressure such as gripping, squeezing, clenching hands, conversation, religion, and self-induced fantasies such as imagining eating a hamburger, having a milk shake or watching a television programme. Some of these coping behaviours could be interpreted as 'problem behaviours', for example a child was cited as constantly screaming as a distraction prior to the insertion of the needle. It is essential, then, to establish how a child is already coping rather than to substitute with a supposedly 'better' coping strategy. The authors suggest that the degree of involvement in the fantasy is important, especially since some children had induced hypnosis themselves without any specific teaching.

Hilgard and Le Baron (1984) also discuss the use of hypnosis for dysphagia, phantom limb pain, nausea and vomiting, anxiety about specific procedures such as intravenous injections, insomnia and generalized anxiety about recurrence of the disease. Studies of hypnosis and pain relief for children with cancer need more exact documentation of the procedures used, to allow for replication and comparison with other treatment approaches, such as distraction and relaxation. For a general text on hypnotherapy with children, see Gardner and Olness (1981).

Behavioural approaches

One of the best papers on behavioural management of distress during bone marrow aspiration is by Jay *et al.* (1985). The authors highlight the problem of pain and anxiety during the actual procedure, as well as that of anticipatory anxiety, producing problems such as insomnia, crying, nausea and vomiting. The paper looks at a behavioural package used with five children with leukaemia aged 3–7 years, to reduce anxiety and distress during bone marrow aspirations in lumbar punctures. The Observation Scale of Behavioural Distress (OSBD) (Jay *et al.*, 1983) was used as a measure of behavioural distress, and includes 11 operationally defined behaviours indicative of anxiety and/or pain, e.g. crying and screaming. The interventions included:

- Breathing exercises, using imagery as an attention distraction procedure;
- Reinforcement, in the form of a trophy for lying still and doing the breathing exercises;
- Imagery using heroic images to change the context of the pain;
- Behavioural rehearsal, using dolls, then the psychologist and finally the child himself or herself as a subject for the procedure. This includes a number of approaches, such as desensitization, information giving, modelling and role play;
- Filmed modelling as the child watched 'Joy gets a bone marrow and spinal tap', which describes a 6-year-old coping throughout the procedures.

All children showed a reduction in distress as measured by the OSBD, and a further four out of five had an increased reduction in distress after their second intervention session. Overall, there was a greater than 50% change from the pre- to postintervention levels. The clinical implications are important. For example, no patient required restraint during the treatment, although several had done so previously. Parents, children and medical staff likewise were all enthusiastic about the approach. However, large samples of more controlled outcome studies are required to pinpoint the effective components of the package.

Nausea and vomiting associated with chemotherapy

Chemotherapy can have a number of unpleasant side-effects, such as nausea and vomiting, lowered resistance to infection, hair loss and mouth ulcers. The treatment programme selected for the individual child depends on the type of cancer. Generally, the more complex the

treatment the more potential it has for disruption. Vomiting may also become progressively worse as the child continues treatment (Cotanch, Hockenberry and Herman, 1985). Nausea and vomiting can also cause nutritional deficits, electrolyte imbalance and weakness (Cotanch, Hockenberry and Herman, 1985), but some drugs which have an impact on emesis with adults have more side-effects in children, and therefore cannot be used (Terrin, McWilliams and Maurer, 1984).

A number of studies have been carried out on nausea and vomiting in adult cancer patients (Burish and Lyles 1979, 1981; Nesse et al., 1980; Ahles et al., 1984; Weddington, Miller and Sweet, 1984; Redd and Andrykowski, 1982; Nicholas, 1982; Andrykowski, 1986). Many of these have focused on anticipatory nausea, although child studies have tended to focus more on the nausea and vomiting experienced during chemotherapy, but see also the single case study by Gardner (1976).

Hypnosis was used in a systematic study to reduce the vomiting associated with chemotherapy in adolescents with cancer (Zeltzer et al., 1983). The authors found that the control of vomiting by pharmacological means tended to be unreliable and varied. Zeltzer, Lebaron and Zeltzer (1984) indicated that some children experience more nausea and vomiting when antiemetics were used. In Penta et al.'s (1981) study only 15% of the paediatricians found antiemetics useful, and Chang (1981) also found that antiemetics had little effect. It is worth noting at this point that a recent study (Jürgens and McQuade, 1992) has demonstrated the effectiveness of a new drug, Ondansetron, which has been found to be superior to conventional antiemetics with children.

Zeltzer et al. (1983) looked at 12 adolescents (average age 14 years) with various malignancies. A baseline study of frequency, intensity and duration of vomiting was carried out prior to hypnosis starting. Hypnosis was based on the individual's life experience (e.g. activities and situations the child has enjoyed) and focused on specific symptom control using antiemetic imagery (e.g. cooling images such as water and snow). Other dependent variables were trait anxiety, self-esteem, locus of control and illness impact, both prior to hypnosis and 6 months later. The adolescents received one to three sessions of hypnosis prior to and during chemotherapy. The results showed that eight out of the 12 children finally agreed to use the hypnosis. The reduction in the frequency of vomiting was in the range of 19–100%, with a mean of 53%. The daily mean frequency of vomiting prior to the intervention was 4.68 and changed to 2.42 during the intervention. The duration of vomiting also shortened for six out of these eight children, from a mean of 7.04 hours at baseline to a mean of 3.09 during the intervention. Of the other dependent variables, only the trait anxiety reduced. On the clinical side, only two out of eight children continued to use antiemetic medication after the intervention. Clinically, the symptomatic improvement occurred almost immediately. However, owing to the design of the study (AB design) it is not possible to say that hypnosis alone was responsible for the change in outcome: other factors may have been equally responsible, such as increased attention or distraction. Additionally, there were no adequate follow-up data.

The following year, Zeltzer, Lebaron and Zeltzer (1984) expanded on their work with adolescents receiving chemotherapy, to include a comparison group. In this study 10 patients were randomly allocated to receive hypnosis or supportive counselling for their vomiting. They were also matched for drugs.

Smith et al. (1979) showed that 33% of the paediatric population terminated their treatment as a result of nausea and vomiting. The hypnosis that was used in this study consisted of helping the children to become as intensively involved in imagery and fantasy as possible. The supportive counselling focused on distracting the children from the chemotherapy administration. The results were that both the nausea and vomiting, and the extent to which it bothered the children, were significantly reduced in both conditions. The authors point out, however, that some drugs commonly used in chemotherapy (for example cisplatin) were not used in this study, and therefore the results cannot be generalized to all chemotherapy regimens. It is suggested that it is important to know the effective intervention variable over a wide range of chemotherapeutic regimens. Interestingly, no relationship was found in this study between hypnotic susceptibility and the degree of symptom reduction with hypnosis. This is at odds with Hilgard and Le Baron's (1982) study on pain control described earlier.

Zeltzer, Lebaron and Zeltzer (1984) believe that hypnosis may not be responsible for the change, but other factors may be, for example distraction, which both the hypnotic and supportive counselling intervention had in common. The authors also highlight the difficulties in matching large numbers of children through drug regimens, as these can vary considerably between children. Another important finding was that the adolescents were able to maintain their symptom reduction without a therapist present.

In an attempt to correct some of the problems of Zeltzer et al.'s (1983) study, Le Baron and Zeltzer (1984) looked at the effect of behavioural intervention on nausea, vomiting, the extent to which chemotherapy 'bothered' the adolescents, and disruption of activities. They studied eight young people aged 10–18 years receiving chemotherapy for various cancers. They point out that many adult studies studying nausea and vomiting in relation to chemotherapy tend to look at anticipatory nausea and vomiting, whereas for adolescents the major problem is nausea and vomiting following the chemotherapy. In the Zeltzer et al. (1983) study only one course of chemotherapy was observed prior to the intervention, but as chemotherapeutically related emesis is so variable it is necessary to look at more than this. The behavioural intervention involved distraction from treatment and nausea by means of games, stories, attention distraction and relaxation. It was found that the mean self-ratings of nausea, vomiting and disruption of activities were reduced significantly. They increased slightly at follow-up (period unknown), but not to the baseline levels. There was no symptom reduction in the repeated measures prior to the intervention. Again, it only really gives us the information that some intervention is better than none. On an anecdotal level, the authors express some surprise at the adolescents' desire to be led in treatment rather than to use self-administered methods, as they had pre-supposed that they would want to achieve mastery and independence.

Dahlquist *et al.* (1985) used a behavioural approach to reduce the distress associated with chemotherapy administration, as opposed to looking at the effect of nausea and vomiting directly. They emphasized the importance of the cooperation of the child to lessen the risk of injury. The chemotherapy caused local inflammation of the veins, and therefore the subsequent use of difficult and painful veins. This study of three children aged 11–14 years used cue-controlled deep muscle relaxation, controlled breathing, pleasant imagery, positive self-talk and live coaching (as in the Elliot and Olson (1983) study). The three children were all undergoing intravenous chemotherapy. The measures included parents' rating of distress, the observation scale of behavioural distress, medical personnel ratings of distress and self-report ratings of distress. A multiple baseline was used. The observational scale of behavioural distress showed a mean reduction in distress of 46%. All three subjects reported a reduction in distress during venepuncture. There was a slight reduction in the recording of distress from medical personnel, but parents

rated no change. As found by Zeltzer, Lebaron and Zeltzer (1984), two out of the three children did not need live coaching, which is an interesting finding as it had appeared from other studies (Elliot and Olson, 1983) that children undergoing such distressing procedures might need the live coaching as a prompt, since some children find difficulty carrying out such procedures alone.

Cotanch, Hockenberry and Herman (1985), using nurses as therapists, found significant decreases in the severity, frequency, amount and duration of vomiting, and intensity and duration of the nausea. Twelve 10–18 year-olds undergoing chemotherapy and receiving a relaxation/self-hypnosis treatment were compared with the control group for frequency of vomiting. After treatment, all control group children were still vomiting, whereas eight out of 12 in the treatment group were not. The authors point out the difficulty in finding accurate assessment tools for assessing nausea and vomiting. The matching on these variables was not clear. Kolko and Richards-Figueroa (1985) found that video games were helpful in reducing self-reported, observed anticipatory, and post-chemotherapy side-effects. The potency of these games may lie in using a number of sensory modalities simultaneously.

A number of single case studies have also looked at a variety of behavioural problems in children undergoing therapy for cancer. Crasilneck and Hall (1973), for example, used hypnosis with a 4-year-old girl with brain cancer to control pain, increase food intake and decrease crying. A specific symptom-related suggestion was made and hypnosis was carried out on a daily basis to begin with, and then three times a week for the second week. They reported that the child ate better, slept better and had less pain medication and enjoyed watching the television. Cairns and Altman (1979) used social reinforcement tokens and access to play contingent on eating with an 11-year-old anorexic following surgery and radiotherapy. They reported an increase in weight and food intake.

Kellerman (1979), in another single case study, looked at a 3-year-old girl with lymphocytic leukaemia and a 1-month history of recurrent nightmares occurring approximately six times a night. Her mother was unable to stay with her during bone marrow aspirations as a result of her own anxiety. The treatment aimed at positive reinforcement for the child for restful nights in conjunction with relaxation for the mother, to enable her to stay with her daughter during the bone marrow aspirations. The girl was reported to be symptom free at a follow-up 120 days later. Finally, Elleberg *et al.* (1980) described the use of hypnosis for multiple symptoms in an adolescent girl with chronic myeloid leukaemia. They reported a reduction in self-reported pain and anxiety in relation to bone marrow aspirations, a decrease in self-reported pain from headache and backache, and some reduction in nausea and vomiting. The reduction in nausea and vomiting was particularly contaminated by the fact that the chemotherapy medication was halved during the second course.

When looking at the total needs of children undergoing such intensive therapy, Kellerman, Katz and Siegel (1979) suggested that the emotional psychological needs of children with cancer are best met by a comprehensive, multi-disciplinary psychosocial model. The alternative, they argue, is crisis intervention, which stigmatizes the individual child. This is last-resort treatment, as problems will have reached a point of severity before intervention, and it also depends on other medical staff recognizing and referring the problem. The authors suggests that their model is best considered as preventing and ameliorating psychological problems in the population of normal children under stress.

Many of the studies so far suffer from the same problems as behavioural paediatric work in general; that is, from small samples, lack of comparative groups and difficulties in obtaining homogeneous samples, particularly in relation to drug treatment. Although the behavioural literature related to the iatrogenic effects of cancer treatment and investigative procedures in children is fairly limited in output, some of the results are at least encouraging, and point towards a way forward in dealing with these distressing and painful procedures (Hilgard and Le Baron, 1982). The problems of intense pain and distress put any therapy under a severe test, and it has yet to be seen whether health psychologists can influence practice and thereby the experience of significant numbers of children and their families. It is to be hoped that Russo and Varni's (1982) prediction is proved to be correct:

> ... as medical advances continue to prolong life while concurrently subjecting the patient to treatment of growing intensity, the role of behavioural medicine in paediatric oncology can be expected to grow. (Russo and Varni, 1982).

References

Aaronson, N.K. and Beckman, N.J. (1987) *The Quality of Life of Cancer Patients*, Raven Press, New York.

Adams, J., Gill, S. and McDonald, M. (1991) Reducing fear in hospital. *Nursing Times*, 87(1), 62–4.

Adams, M.A. (1976) A hospital play programme: helping children with serious illness. *American Journal of Orthopsychiatry*, 46(3), 416–24.

Ahles, T.A., Cohen, R.E., Little, D. *et al.* (1984) Toward a behavioural assessment of anticipatory symptoms associated with cancer chemotherapy. *Journal of Behaviour Therapy and Experimental Psychiatry*, 15(2), 141–5.

Albino, J.E. (1984) Prevention by acquiring health-enhancing habits, in *Prevention of Problems in Childhood Psychology: Research and Applications*, (eds M.C. Robert and L. Peterson) Wiley, Chichester, pp. 200–31.

Anderson, K.O. and Masur, F.T. (1983) Psychological preparation for invasive medical and dental procedures. *Journal of Behavioural Medicine*, 6, 1–40.

Andrykowski, M.A. (1986) Definitional issues in the study of anticipatory nausea in cancer chemotherapy. *Journal of Behavioural Medicine*, 9(1), 33–41.

Auslander, W.F., Haire-Joshu, D., Rogge, M. and Santiago, J.V. (1991) Predictors of diabetes knowledge in newly diagnosed children and parents. *Journal of Paediatric Psychology*, **16**(2), 213–28.

Becker, R.D. (1972) Therapeutic approaches to psychopathological reactions to hospitalisation. *International Journal of Child Psychotherapy*, **1**, 65–97.

Berg, R.A., Ch'ien, L.T., Bowman, P., *et al.* (1983) The neuropsychological effects of acute lymphocytic leukemia and its treatment: a three year report. Intellectual functioning and academic achievement. *Clinical Neuropsychology*, **5**, 9–13.

Bernstein, N.R. (1965) Observations on the use of hypnosis with burned children on a paediatric ward. *International Journal of Clinical and Experimental Hypnosis*, **13**(1), 1–10.

Binger, C.M., Ablin, A.R. and Feverstein, R.C. (1969) Childhood leukemia: emotional impact in patient and family. *New England Journal of Medicine*, **280**, 414–18.

Burish, T.G. and Lyles, J.N. (1979) Effectiveness of relaxation training in reducing the aversiveness of chemotherapy in the treatment of cancer. *Journal of Behaviour Therapy and Experimental Psychiatry*, **10**, 357–61.

Burish, T.G. and Lyles, J.N. (1981) Effectiveness of relaxation training in reducing adverse reactions to cancer chemotherapy. *Journal of Behavioural Medicine* **4**(1), 65–78.

Cairns, G.F. and Altman, K. (1979) Behavioural treatment of cancer related anorexia. *Journal of Behaviour Therapy and Experimental Psychiatry*, **10**, 353–6.

Carr-Gregg, M.R.C. and White, L. (1985) The child with cancer: a psychological overview. *Medical Journal of Australia*, **143**, 25.

Cassady, L. (1982) The forgotten children: a study of the interpersonal perceptions of healthy siblings of children with a life-threatening or chronic illness. *Dissertation Abstracts International*, **32**, 1248–B2.

Chan, J.M. (1980) Preparation for procedures and surgery through play. *Paediatrician*, **9**, 210–19.

Chang, J.C. (1981) Nausea and vomiting in cancer patients: an expression of psychological mechanisms? *Psychosomatics*, **22**, 707–9.

Cotanch, P., Hockenberry, M. and Herman, S. (1985) Self-hypnosis as anti-emetic therapy in children receiving chemotherapy. *Oncology Nursing Forum*, **12**(4), 41–6.

Crasilneck, H.B. and Hall, J.A. (1973) Clinical hypnosis in problems of pain. *American Journal of Clinical Hypnosis*, **15**(3), 153–61.

Creer, T.L., Renne, C.M. and Chai, H. (1982) The application of behavioural techniques to childhood asthma, in *Behavioural Paediatrics: Research and Practice*, (eds D.C. Russo and J.W. Varni), New York, Plenum Press, pp. 27–66.

Creer, T.L., Renne, C.M. and Christian, W.P. (1976) Behavioural contributions to rehabilitation and childhood asthma. *Rehabilitation Literature*, **37**, 226–32.

Dahlquist, L.M., Gil, K.M., Armstrong, D. *et al.* (1985) Behavioural management of children's distress during chemotherapy. *Journal of Behaviour Therapy and Experimental Psychiatry*, **16**(4), 325–9.

Davies, H., Noll, R.B., Destefano, L. *et al.* (1991) Differences in the childrearing practices of parents and children with cancer and controls: the perspectives of parents and professionals. *Journal of Paediatric Psychology*, **16**(3), 295–306.

Doleys, D., Merideth, R.L. and Ciminero, A.R. (eds) (1982) *Behavioral Medicine Assessment and Treatment Strategies*, Plenum Press, New York.

Eiser, C. and Hanson, L. (1989) Preparing children for hospital: a school-based intervention. *Professional Nurse*, March, 297–300.

Eiser, C. and Patterson, D. (1984) Children's perception of hospital: a preliminary study. International *Journal of Nursing Studies*, **21**(1), 45–50.

Ellenberg, L., Kellerman, J., Dash, J. *et al.* (1980) Use of hypnosis for multiple symptoms in an adolescent girl with leukemia. *Journal of Adolescent Health Care*, **1**, 132–6.

Elliott, C.H. and Jay, S.M. (1987) Chronic pain in children. *Behaviour Research and Therapy*, **25**(4), 263–71.

Elliott, C.H. and Olson, R.A. (1983) The management of children's behavioural distress in response to painful medical treatment for burn injuries. *Behaviour Research and Therapy*, **21**, 675–83.

Elliott, C.H. and Ozolins, M. (1983) Imagery and imagination in the treatment of children, in *Handbook of Clinical Child Psychology*, (eds C.E. Walker and M. Roberts) John Wiley and Sons, New York, pp. 1026–49.

Epstein, L.H., Beck, S., Figueroa, J. *et al.* (1981) The effects of targeting improvements in urine glucose on metabolic control in children with insulin dependent diabetes. *Journal of Applied Behaviour Analysis*, **14**, 365–75.

Faust, J. and Melamed, B.G. (1984) Influence of arousal, previous experience and age on surgery preparation of same day of surgery and in-hospital paediatric patients. *Journal of Consulting and Clinical Psychology*, **54**, 359–64.

Faust, J., Olson, R. and Rodriguez, H. (1991) Same-day surgery preparation: reduction of paediatric patient arousal and distress through participant modeling. *Journal of Consulting and Clinical Psychology*, **59**(3), 475–8.

Fentress, D.W., Masek, B.J., Mehegan, J.E. and Bewson, H. (1986) Biofeedback and relaxation response training in the treatment of paediatric migraine. *Developmental Medicine and Child Neurology*, **28**, 139–146.

Ferguson, B.F. (1979) Preparing young children for hospitalization: a comparison of two methods. *Paediatrics*, **64**(5), 656–64.

Fireman, P., Friday, G.A. Gira, C. *et al.* (1981). Teaching self-management skills to asthmatic children and their parents in an ambulatory care setting. *Paediatrics*, **68**, 341–8.

Fochtman, D. (1979) How adolescents live with leukemia. *Cancer Nursing*, February, 27–31.

Forfar, J.O. and Arneil, G.L. (eds) (1984) *Textbook of Paediatrics*, 3rd ed, Churchill Livingstone, Edinburgh.

Friedman, S., Chodoff, P., Mason, J. and Hamburg, D. (1963) Behavioural observations of parents anticipating the death of a child. *Paediatrics*, **32**, 610–25.

Gale, E. and Ayer, N.M. (1969) Treatment of dental phobias. *Journal of the American Dental Association*, **73**, 1304–7.

Gardner, G.G. (1976) Childhood, death and human dignity: hypnotherapy for David. *International Journal of Clinical and Experimental Hypnosis*, **24**(2), 122–39.

Gardner, G.G. and Olness, K.N. (1981) *Hypnosis and Hypnotherapy with Children*, Grune and Stratton, New York.

Gilbert, B.O., Johnson, S.B., Spillar, R. *et al.* (1982) The efects of a peer-modelling film on children learning to self inject insulin. *Behaviour Therapy*, **13**, 186–93.

Gross, A.M. (1990) Behavioural management of the child with diabetes, in *Handbook of Clinical Behavioral Pediatrics*, (eds A.M. Gross and R.S. Drabman) Plenum Press, New York, pp. 147–63.

Gross, A.M. and Drabman, R.S. (eds) (1990) *Handbook of Clinical Behavioral Pediatrics*, Plenum Press, New York.

Gross, P.R. (1989) Preparation book for hospitalised paediatrics patients: content and design. *Journal of Biocommunication*, **16**(2), 7–10.

Harrison, A. (1991) Preparing children for venous blood sampling. *Pain*, **45**, 299–306.

Heiney, S.P., Ruffin, J., Ettinger, R. and Ettinger, S. (1984) The effects of group therapy on adolescents with cancer. *Journal of the Association of Paediatric Oncology Nurses*, **1**(4), 16.

Hilgard, J.R. and Lebaron, S. (1982) Relief of anxiety and pain in children and adolescents with cancer: quantative measures and clinical observations. *International Journal of Clinical and Experimental Hypnosis*, **30**(4), 417–42.

Hilgard, J.R. and Lebaron, S., (1984) *Hypnotherapy of Pain in Children with Cancer*, William Kaufmann, Los Altos, CA.

Hockenberry, M.J. and Bologna-Vaughan, S. (1985) Preparation for intensive procedures using non-invasive techniques in children with cancer: state of the art vs new trends. *Cancer Nursing*, **8**(2), 97–102.

Hoelscher, J.T. and Lichstein (1984) Behavioural assessment and treatment of child migraine: implications for clinical research and practice. *Headache*, **24**, 94–103.

Holt, L. and Maxwell, B. (1991) Paediatric orientation programmes. *Association of Operating Room Nurses Journal*, **54**(3), 530–40.

Houts, A.C. (1982) Relaxation and thermal feedback treatment of child migraine headaches: a case study. *American Journal of Clinical Biofeedback*, **5**, 154–157.

Inati, A. Sallan, S.E., Cassady, J.R. *et al.* (1983) Efficacy and morbidity of central nervous system 'prophylaxis' in childhood acute lymphoblastic leukemia. Eight years' experience with cranial irradiation and intrathecal methotrexate. *Blood*, **61**, 297–303.

Jay, S.M., Elliott, C.H. Ozolins, M. *et al.* (1985) Behavioural management of childrens' distress during painful medical procedures. *Behaviour, Research and Therapy*, **23**(5), 513–20.

Jay, S.M., Elliott, C. and Varni, J. (1986) Acute and chronic pain in adults and children with cancer. *Journal of Consulting and Clinical Psychology*, **54**(5), 601–7.

Jay, S.M., Ozolins, M., Elliott, C.H. and Caldwell, S. (1983) Assessment of children's distress during painful medical procedures. *Health Psychology*, **2**, 133–47.

Johnson, J.E., Kirchhoff, K.T. and Endred M.P. (1975) Altering childrens' distress behaviour during orthopaedic cast removal. *Nursing Research*, **24**(11), 404–10.

Johnson, J.L. and Norby, P.A. (1981) We can weekend. A program for cancer families. *Cancer Nursing*, **4**, 23–8.

Jürgens, H. and McQuade, B. (1992) Ondansetron as prophylaxis for chemotherapy and radiotherapy induced emesis in children. *Oncology*, **49**, 279–85.

Kagen-Goodheart, L. (1977) Re-entry: living with childhood cancer. *American Journal of Orthopsychiatry*, **47**(4), 651–8.

Kaplan, R., Chadwick, M. and Schimmel, L. (1985) Social learning intervention to promote metabolic control in type 1 diabetes mellitus: pilot experimental results. *Diabetes Care*, **8**, 152–5.

Karl, H.W., Pavza, K.J., Heyneman, N. and Tinker, D.E. (1990) Preanaesthetic preparation of paediatric outpatients: the role of a videotape for parents. *Journal of Clinical Anaesthetics*, **2**, 172–7.

Katz, E.R., Kellerman, J. and Siegel, S. (1980) Behavioural distress in children with cancer undergoing medical procedures: developmental considerations. *Journal of Consulting and Clinical Psychology*, **48**(3), 356–65.

Kavanagh, C. (1983) Psychological intervention with the severely burned child: report of an experimental comparison of two approaches and their effects on psychological sequelae. *Journal of the American Academy of Child Psychiatry*, **22**, 145–56.

Kellerman, J. (1979) Behavioural treatment of night terrors in a child with acute leukemia. *Journal of Nervous and Mental Diseases*, **167**(1), 182–5.

Kellerman, J. and Katz, E.R. (1977) The adolescent with cancer: theoretical clinical and research issues. *Journal of Paediatric Psychology*, **2**, 127–131.

Kellerman, J., Katz, E.R. and Siegel, S.E. (1979) *Psychological Problems of Children with Cancer.* Unpublished manuscript.

Kellerman, J. Zeltzer, L., Ellenberg, L. *et al.* (1980) Psychological effects of illness in adolescence-1. Anxiety, self-esteem and perception of control. *Journal of Paediatrics*, **97**, 126–31.

Kennedy, C.M. and Riddle, I.I. (1989) The influence of the timing of preparation on the anxiety of preschool children experiencing surgery. *Maternal-Child Nursing Journal*, **18**(2), 117–32.

Klingman, A., Melamed, B.G., Cuthbert, M.I., and Hermecz, D.A. (1984) Effects of participant modelling on information acquisition and skill utilization. *Journal of Consulting and Clinical Psychology*, **52**, 414–22.

Knight, R.B., Atkins, A., Eagle, C. *et al.* (1979) Psychological stress, ego defenses and cortisol production in children hospitalised for elective surgery. *Psychosomatic Medicine*, **41**, 40–9.

Kolko, D.J. and Richard-Figueroa, J.L. (1985) Effects of video games on the adverse corollaries of chemoxtherapy in paediatric oncology patients. *Journal of Consulting and Clinical Psychology*, **53**, 223–8.

Labaw, W. (1973) Adjunctive trance therapy with severely burned children. *International Journal of Child Psychotherapy*, **2**, 16–21.

Labaw, W., Holton, C., Tewell, K. and Ellies, D. (1975) The use of self-hypnosis by children with cancer. *American Journal of Clinical Hypnosis*, **17**(4), 233–8.

Lake, A.E. (1981) Behavioural assessment considerations in the management of headache. *Headache*, **21**, 170–8.

Lascelles, M.A., Cunningham, J., McGrath, P. and Sullivan, M.J.L. (1989) Teaching coping strategies to adolescents with migraine. *Journal of Pain and Symptom Management*, **4**(3), 135–45.

Lebaron, S. and Zeltzer, L. (1984) Behavioural intervention for reducing chemotherapy-related nausea and vomiting in adolescents with cancer. *Journal of Adolescent Health Care*, **5**, 178–82.

Lehmann, J.F., Warren, C.G. and Scham, S.M. (1974) Therapeutic heat and cold. *Clinical Orthopaedics and Related Research*, **99**, 207–45.

Leigh, J.M. (1987) *An Investigation of Factors Relating to Poor Glycaemic Control in Adolescents with Diabetes Mellitus.* Unpublished MSc thesis. University of Birmingham.

Lesko, L.M., Kern, J. and Hawkins, D.R. (1984) Psychological aspects of patients in germ-free isolation: a review of child, adult and patient management literature. *Medical and Paediatric Oncology*, **12**, 43–9.

Levinson, P. and Ousterhout, D.K. (1980) Art and play therapy with paediatric burn patients. *Journal of Burn Care and Rehabilitation*, **1**, 42–64.

Lewis, N. (1978) 'I probably won't have all the luxuries in the world'. *Journal of the Association for the Care of Children in Hospitals*, **7**, 28–32.

Lowe, K. and Lutzker, J.R. (1979) Increasing compliance to a medical regimen with a juvenile diabetic. *Behaviour Therapy*, **10**, 57–64.

McGrath, P.A. (1987) The multidimensional assessment and management of recurrent pain syndromes in children. *Behaviour Research and Therapy*, **25**(4), 251–62.

McGrath, P.A. and Deveber, L.L. (1986) Helping children cope with painful procedures. *American Journal of Nursing*, September, 1278–9.

Mann, N.P. and Johnston, D.J. (1982) Total glycosylated haemoglobin (HbAi) levels in diabetic children. *Archives of Disease in Childhood*, **57**, 434–7.

Marion, R.J. (1987) *Teaching Children to Predict Asthma Using an In-home Pulmometer.* Unpublished doctoral dissertation, University of Ohio, Athens, Ohio.

Marteau, T.M. and Johnston, M. (1987) Health psychology: the danger of neglecting psychological needs. *Bulletin of the British Psychological Society*, **40**, 82–5.

Masek, B.J. and Hoag, N.L. (1990) Headache, in *Handbook of Clinical Behavioural Paediatrics*, (eds A.M. Gross and R.S. Drabman), Plenum Press, New York.

Massouh, S.R., Steele, T.M.O., Alseth, E.R. and Diekmann, J.M. (1989) The effect of social learning intervention on metabolic control of insulin dependent diabetes mellitus in adolescents. *Diabetes Educator*, **15**(6), 518–21.

Mehegan, J.E. Masek, B.J., Harrison, R.H. *et al.* (1987). A multicomponent behavioural treatment for paediatric migraine. *Clinical Journal of Pain*, **2**, 191–6.

Melamed B.G., and Siegel, L.J. (1975) Reduction of anxiety in children facing hospitalisation and surgery by use of filmed modelling. *Journal of Consulting and Clinical Psychology*, **43**, 511–21.

Melamed, B.G., Meyer, R., Gee, C. and Soule, L. (1976) The influence of time and type of preparation on children's adjustment to hospitalisation. *Journal of Paediatric Psychology*, **1**, 31–7.

Melamed, B.G., Robbins, R.L. and Graves, S. (1982) Preparation for surgery and medical procedures, in Behavioural Pediatrics (eds D.C. Russo and J.W. Varni), Plenum Press, New York.

Melamed, B.G., Weinstein, D. Hawes, R. and Katin-Borland, M. (1975) Reduction of fear-related dental management problems with use of filmed modelling. *Journal of the American Dental Association*, **90**, 822–6.

Melamed, B.G., Yurcheson, R., Fleece, E.C. *et al.* (1978) Effects of film modelling on the reduction of anxiety related behaviours in individuals varying in level of previous experience in the stress situation. *Journal of Consulting and Clinical Psychology*, **46**, 1357–67.

Michielutte, R., Patterson, R.B. and Herdon, A. (1981) Evaluation of a home visitation program for families of children with cancer. *American Journal of Pediatric Hematology and Oncology*, **3**, 239–45.

Miller, A.J. and Kratochwill, T.R. (1979) Reduction of frequent stomachache complaints by time out. *Behaviour Therapy*, **10**, 211–18.

Millon, T., Green, C. and Meagher, R. (eds) (1982) *Handbook of Clinical Health Psychology*, Plenum Press, New York.

Miser, A.W., Dothage, J.A., Wesley, R.A. and Miser, J.S. (1987) The prevalence of pain in a paediatric and young cancer population. *Pain*, **29**, 73–84.

Moehle, K.B., Berg, R.A., Ch'ien, L.T. and Lancaster, W. (1983) Language-related skills in children with acute lymphocytic leukemia. *Journal of Developmental and Behavioural Pediatrics*, **4**, 257–61.

Muller, D.J., Harris, P.J. and Wattley, L. (1986) *Nursing Children. Psychology, Research and Practice*, Harper and Row, London.

Nesse, R.M., Carli, T., Curtis, G.C. and Kleinman, P.D. (1980) Pretreatment nausea in cancer chemotherapy: a conditioned response? *Psychosomatic Medicine*, **42**(1), 33–6.

Nicholas, D.R. (1982) Prevalence of anticipatory nausea and emesis in cancer chemotherapy patients. *Journal of Behavioural Medicine*, **5**(4), 461–3.

Nir, Y. and Maslin, B. (1982) Liaison psychiatry in childhood cancer – a systems approach. *Psychiatric Clinics of North America*, **5**, 379–86.

Nurick, M.A. and Johnson, S.B. (1991) Enhancing blood glucose awareness in adolescents and young adults with IDDM. *Diabetes Care*, **14**(1), 1–7.

Olness, K.N. (1986) Hypnotherapy in children. *Postgraduate Medicine*, **79**(4), 95–105.

Olness, K. and MacDonald, J. (1981) Self-hypnosis and biofeedback in the management of juvenile migraine. *Journal of Developmental Behavioural Paediatrics*, **2**, 168–70.

Penta, J.S., Poster, D.S., Bruno, S. *et al.* (1981) Cancer chemotherapy induced nausea and vomiting in adult and paediatric patients. *Proceedings from the American Society of Clinical Oncology*, **22**, 396.

Peterson, L. and Harbeck, C. (1988) *The Pediatric Psychologist: Unique Challenges and Emerging Roles*, Research Press, Champaign, Illinois.

Peterson, L. and Shigetomi, C. (1981). The use of coping techniques to minimise anxiety in hospitalised children. *Behaviour Therapy*, **12**, 1–14.

Peterson, L., Farmer, J., Harbeck, C. and Chaney, J. (1990) Preparing children for hospitalisation and threatening medical procedures, in *Handbook of Clinical Behavioural Pediatrics*, (eds A.S. Bellack, and M. Hersen), Plenum Press, New York, pp. 349–64.

Pinto, R.P. and Hollandsworth, J.G. (1989) Using videotape modelling to prepare children psychologically for surgery: influence of parents and costs versus benefits of providing preparation services. *Health Psychology*, **8**(1), 79–95.

Price, S. (1991) Preparing children for admission to hospital. *Nursing Times*, **87**(9), 46–9.

Prokop, C.K. and Bradley, L.A. (1981) *Medical Psychology Contributions to Behavioral Medicine*, Academic Press, New York.

Rachman, S. (ed) (1980) *Contributions To Medical Psychology*, Vol 2, Pergamon Press, Oxford.

Rachman, S. (ed) (1984) *Contributions To Medical Psychology*, Vol 3, Pergamon Press, Oxford.

Rakos, R.F., Grodek, M.V. and Mack, K.K. (1985). The impact of a self-administered behavioural intervention programme on paediatric asthma. *Journal of Psychosomatic Research*, **29**(1), 101–8.

Ramsden, R., Friedman, B. and Williamson, D. (1983) Treatment of childhood headache reports with contingency management procedures. *Journal of Clinical Child Psychiatry*, **12**, 202–6.

Redd, W.H. and Andrykowski, M.A. (1982) Behavioural intervention in cancer treatment: controlling aversion reaction to chemotherapy. *Journal of Consulting and Clinical Psychology*, **50**(6), 1018–29.

Renne, C.M. and Creer, T.L. (1976) Training children with asthma to use inhalation therapy equipment. *Journal of Applied Behavioural Analysis*, **9**, 1–11.

Richter, I.L., McGrath, P.J., Humphreys, P.J. *et al.* (1986) Cognitive and relaxation treatment of paediatric migraine. *Pain* **25**, 195–203.

Ridley-Johnson, R. and Melamed, B. (1986) Behavioural methods and research issues in management of child patients. *Anaesthesia Progress*, January/February, 17–21.

Roberts, M.C. and Peterson, C. (1984) Preface in *Prevention of Problems in Childhood. Psychological Research and Applications*, (eds M.C. Robert and C. Peterson) Wiley, New York.

Rodin, J. (1983) *Will This Hurt? Preparing Children for Hospital and Medical Procedures*, Royal College of Nursing, London.

Ross, J.W. and Scarvalone, S.A. (1982) Facilitating the paediatric cancer patient's return to school. *Social Work*, 27, 256–61.

Russo, D.C. and Varni, J.W. (eds) (1982) *Behavioral Pediatrics. Research and Practice*, Plenum Press, New York.

Sanger, M.S., Copeland, D.R. and Davidson, E.R. (1991) Psychosocial adjustment among paediatric cancer patients: a multidimensional assessment. *Journal of Paediatric Psychology*, 16(4), 463–74.

Sank, L.I. and Biglan, A. (1974) Operant treatment of a case of recurrent abdominal pain in a 10 year old boy. *Behaviour Therapy*, 5, 677–81.

Schaefer, L.C., Glasgow, R.E. and McCaul, K.D. (1982) Increasing the adherence of diabetic adolescents. *Journal of Behavioural Medicine*, 5, 353–62.

Siegel, L.J. and Peterson, L. (1980) Stress reduction in young dental patients through coping skills and sensory information. *Clinical Psychology*, 48, 785–7.

Smith, S.D. Rosen, D., Trueworthy, R.C. *et al.* (1979) A reliable method for evaluating drug compliance in children with cancer. *Cancer*, 43, 169–73.

Sourkes, B.M. (1980) All the things I don't like about having leukaemia. Children's lists, in *Psychological Aspects of Childhood Cancer*, (ed. J. Kellerman), Charles C Thomas, Springfield, Illinois, pp. 289–91.

Spinetta, J.J. (1981) The sibling of the child with cancer, in *Living with Childhood Cancer*, (eds J.J. Spinetta and P. Deasy-Spinetta), C.V. Mosby & Co. St. Louis, pp. 133–42.

Steptoe, A, & Matthews, A. (eds) (1984) *Health Care and Human Behaviour*, Academic Press, London.

Surwit, R.S. Williams, R.B., Steptoe, A. and Biersner, R. (eds) (1982) *Behavioral Treatment of Disease*, Plenum Press, New York.

Susman, E.J., Hollenbeck, A.R., Nannis, E.D. *et al.* (1981) A prospective naturalistic study of the impact of an intensive medical treatment on the social behaviour of child and adolescent cancer patients. *Journal of Applied Developmental Psychology*, 2, 29–47.

Tarnowski, K.J., McGrath, M., Calhoun, B. and Drabman, R.S. (1987) Self- versus therapist-mediated debridement in the treatment of paediatric burn injury. *Journal of Paediatric Psychology*, 12, 567–79.

Terrin, B.N., McWilliams, N.B. and Maurer, M.H. (1984) Side effects of metoclopromide as an antiemetic in childhood cancer chemotherapy. *Journal of Paediatrics*, 104(1), 138–40.

Trent, B. (1986) Art in the Hospital. Treating the Mind as well as the Body. *Canadian Medical Association Journal*, 135, 1198–9.

Valentine, A.S. (1978) Caring for the young adult with cancer. *Cancer Nursing*, 1, 385–95.

Van Dongen-Melman, J.E.W.M. and Sanders-Woudstra, J.A.R. (1986) Psychological aspects of childhood cancer: a review of the literature. *Journal of Child Psychology and Psychiatry*, 27(2), 145–80.

Varni, J.W. (1981a) Behavioural medicine in haemophilia arthritic pain management: two case studies. *Archives of Physical Medicine and Rehabilitation*, 62, 183–7.

Varni, J.W. (1981b) Self-regulation techniques in the management of chronic arthritic pain in haemophilia. *Behaviour Therapy*, 12, 185–94.

Varni, J.W. (1983) *Clinical Behavioural Paediatrics: An Interdisciplinary Biobehavioural Approach*, Pergamon Press, New York.

Varni, J.W., Gilbert, A. and Dietrich, S.L. (1981) Behavioural medicine in pain and analgesia management for the haemophiliac child with Factor VIII inhibitor. *Pain*, 11, 121–6.

Vernick, K.J. and Karon, M. (1965) Who's afraid of death on a leukemia ward? *American Journal of Diseases of Childhood*, 109, 393–7.

Visintainer, M.A. and Wolfer, J.A. (1975) Psychological preparation for surgical paediatric patients. The effect on childrens' and parents' stress responses and adjustment. *Paediatrics*, 56, 187–202.

Wakeman, R.J. and Kaplan, J.Z. (1978) An experimental study of hypnosis in painful burns. *American Journal of Clinical Hypnosis*, 21, 3–12.

Walker, L.J.S. and Healey, M. (1980) Psychological treatment of a burned child. *Journal of Paediatric Psychology*, 5(4), 395–404.

Waranch, H.R. and Keenan, D.M. (1985) Behavioural treatment of children with recurrent headaches. *Journal of Behavioural Therapy and Experimental Psychiatry*, 16(1), 31–8.

Wasserman, T.H. (1978) The elimination of complaints of stomach cramps in a 12 year old child by covert positive reinforcement. *Behaviour Therapy*, 1, 13–14.

Weddington, W.W., Miller, N.J. and Sweet, D.L. (1984) Anticipatory nausea and vomiting associated with cancer chemotherapy. *Journal of Psychosomatic Research*, 28(1), 73–77.

Weinstein, D.J. (1976) Imagery and relaxation with a burn patient. *Behaviour Research and Therapy*, 14, 481.

Weiss, J.B. (1981) Superstuff, in *Self-Management Educational Programmes for Childhood Asthma* (vol 2, Manuscripts). Bethesda National Institute of Allergic and Infectious Diseases, Bethesda, Maryland, pp. 273–94.

Wernick, R.L. Jaremko, M.E. and Taylor, P.W. (1981) Pain management in severely burned adults: a test of stress innoculation. *Journal of Behavioural Medicine*, 4(i), 103–10.

Wheeler, K. (1986) Caring for children with cancer. *Update*, 33, 21–32.

Wolfer, J. and Visintainer, M. (1975) Paediatric surgical patients' and parents' stress responses and adjustment as a function of psychological preparation and stress point nursing care. *Nursing Research*, 24, 244–55.

Wright, P. (1984) Fundamentals of acute burn care and physical therapy management. *Physical Therapy*, 64, 1217–31.

Zastowny, T.R., Kirschenbaum, D.S. and Meng, A.L. (1981) *Coping Skills Training for Children: Effects of Distress Before, During and After Hospitalisation for Surgery*. Paper presented at a meeting of the Association for Advancement of Behaviour Therapy, Toronto, Canada.

Zeltzer, L. Ellenberg, L. and Rigler, D. (1980) Psychological effects of illness in adolescence II. Impact of illness in adolescents – crucial issues and coping styles. *Journal of Paediatrics*, 97(1), 132–8.

Zeltzer, L. Kellerman, J, Ellenberg, L and Dash, J. (1983) Hypnosis for reduction of vomiting associated with chemotherapy and disease in adolescents with cancer. *Journal of Adolescent Health Care*, 4, 77–84.

Zeltzer, L., Lebaron, S. and Zeltzer, P.M. (1984) The effectiveness of behavioural intervention for reduction of nausea and vomiting in children and adolescents receiving chemotherapy. *Journal of Clinical Oncology*, 2(6), 683–90.

Chapter twenty

Chronic pain

Amanda C. de C. Williams and Aleda Erskine

Introduction

Psychologists have contributed more to the study of chronic pain and its management than to any other single medical specialty, yet much remains enigmatic. This chapter aims to give an overview of the area and to draw attention to many unanswered questions.

Chronic pain is most usefully defined as any pain lasting 6 months or more. Distinctions between acute and chronic pain are often made by contrasting the extent of suffering with the extent of tissue damage. Although widely used, definitions based on this distinction are unsatisfactory, for reasons discussed in this chapter. The problems of chronic pain patients are frequently much broader than the pain itself. Unremitting pain causes immense suffering and hardship, and the effects on patients' families can be devastating. It is also costly in economic terms. Each year in the UK several million working days are lost through low back pain alone (Ward, Knowelden and Sharrard, 1968). Chronic pain is the commonest cause of disability and makes endless demands on health service resources. To date, conventional medical and surgical approaches have had some success in treating terminal pain, but their effectiveness with other forms of chronic pain has overall been disappointing. This fact, together with a growing interest in the role of psychological factors in pain, has led to major developments in intervention, with physicians, psychologists and other colleagues working in collaboration.

Throughout this chapter, the authors have tried to focus on the information needs of the prospective clinician. This has meant a relatively greater emphasis on commonly practised interventions, and a relatively brief discussion of psychodynamically based approaches, or those requiring elaborate biometric technology.

Our starting point is a description of the major current models of pain, since these underpin available clinical interventions. We include consideration of patients' lay theories of pain, and the ways in which these contribute to the totality of the experience of chronic pain. Most attempts to conceptualize pain have been undermined by dualistic notions of body and mind, which can be traced back to Descartes. As a 17th century philosopher, Descartes wrote in an era when scientific discoveries about the human body and mind had to comply with religious dogma, which demanded a rigid divide between matter and pure spirit, body and mind. Three centuries later, it is still hard to find language which integrates rather than separates the physical and the psychological.

Theories of chronic pain

The lay model defines pain as a sensation arising from tissue damage: the word 'hurt' covers both pain and damage. It follows that intrapsychic, behavioural and social concomitants become reactions to the sensation. Although this appears to fit most acute pain, it sheds very little light on chronic pain. It misrepresents the experience of pain, because an intelligent being processes the painful stimulus: this involves active perception rather than passive reception. The analogy with visual perception may be a useful one: what we perceive is far more than the image on the retina or what the camera records, enriched as it is by frameworks of meaning arising from past learning, present concerns and future intentions. The common experience for most of us of difficulty in recognizing or identifying a familiar person in an unfamiliar setting remind us of the perceptual schemata that enable us to select and interpret what we see. Cortical information is integrated far earlier than the level at which we are aware of its contribution, at the stage closely preceding behaviour. For the pain experience to be otherwise than integrated in this way would imply considerable unused capacity within the nervous system: in fact, the 'hard wiring' exists for a truly multidimensional interactive system.

Until 1965, when Melzack (a psychologist) and Wall (an anatomist) published their new *gate-control theory* (Melzack and Wall, 1965), discussion of pain was dominated by the *theory of specificity*: this worked much like an alarm system, with specific receptors serving specific pathways to relay the stimulus to the brain. There was also some competition from theories describing *central summation* of the pattern of input from unspecialized peripheral receptors. However, the gate-control model proposed an integrating mechanism, the 'gate': a group of cells located in the dorsal horns of the spinal column. This receives input from two directions. Injury (or other stimulation) excites

peripheral nerve fibres which synapse at the gate; these fibres transmit messages about pain, pressure, heat and so on. From the brain, there are descending influences associated with the behavioural state of the organism, such as attention; longer-term factors, such as past experience; and inhibitory mechanisms of the brain stem. The balance of excitation and inhibition opens or closes the gate, controlling transmission of the message to various areas of the brain. This is the start of further paths and levels of processing.

> There is now compelling evidence that cognitive, motivational, judgemental and psychologic processes which result from learning, personality, past experience, culture and conditioning among other factors influence the transmission of nociceptive impulses at the very first synapse and at all subsequent levels along the neuraxis. (Bonica, 1979)

Melzack and Wall's account in their 1985 book is highly recommended. Although the 'gate' remains a model, not an identifiable mechanism, it offers the basis for creative rather than reductive attempts to understand phenomena such as 'painless pain' in some sports and war injuries and ecstatic states, and the puzzles of phantom limb pain, referred pain and chronic pain. It is a sensory–affective interactive model, incorporating cognition, and has encouraged research into psychological factors such as attention, beliefs and coping styles. The working *three-process model* which developed from this research described relatively independent physiological, subjective–affective–cognitive and behavioural components of pain.

At a less fundamental level, Fordyce (1976) focused on behaviour, such as the use of strategies, verbal and non-verbal communication and avoidance. He emphasized that this was not to deny subjective experience, but to address only the observable aspect of the patient's experience of pain (Fordyce, Roberts and Sternbach,

1985). Since the frequency of behaviour is also sensitive to its consequences, this offered a chance to modify unhelpful behaviours. At a level even further removed from primacy of neural mechanisms is the model described by Leventhal (Leventhal and Everhart, 1979). Activity at several levels takes place in parallel, with no special precedence for nociception as a first cause. The levels incorporate motor responses (innate rather than learned); encoding in memory of pain experience, with emotion as an organizing factor; and a reflexive store of experiences with the responses and their results. The flourishing development of cognitive psychology, and its extension to health psychology, is likely to build richer models and to generate testable hypotheses.

It is important not to assume that, if the cause of continuing pain cannot be understood, no other level of experience can be addressed. We should not ignore the promising developments in understanding chronic pain on a physiological level, and they are described very briefly below. However, it is clear in the accounts of these models that consideration of psychological factors is patchy. Only the gate control theory of Melzack and Wall describes the integration of psychological with physiological mechanisms.

Recent progress in neurophysiology has extended our knowledge of *altered CNS processing* immediately following an injury. The area around the injury becomes highly sensitive (hyperalgesia), and previously innocuous stimuli such as touch and temperature can become painful (allodynia) (Dubner, 1991), with increased excitability and decreased inhibition at central and peripheral levels. Although this has led to improvements in the management of postoperative pain by the early (even preoperative) delivery of analgesia, the persistence of this pain is less well understood: some structural and functional alteration in the processing of stimuli at the dorsal horn level has been confirmed, but much work remains to be done.

At a grosser level, there is very poor correlation between the persistence or disappearance of such processes and the changes visible on imaging techniques, however sophisticated. Despite long-standing and consistent evidence that radiological findings are unrelated to the complaint of pain (reviewed in Flor and Turk, 1984), many doctors initiating such investigations expect to confirm or to disconfirm the patient's subjective report.

Pain can also be produced below the level of a nerve lesion (Tasker and Dostrovsky, 1989): examples which may be familiar include phantom pain (in an amputated limb), post-stroke pain over half the body (central pain) and postherpetic neuralgia. Similarly, the sympathetic nervous system (SNS) can be disrupted by peripheral neural lesion, producing hyperactivity of the SNS and pain, usually accompanied by sympathetic changes (such as temperature and temperature regulation, skin quality, swelling and wasting) in the affected area; any or all of these may also occur without pain. The sympathetic nervous system can be considered to regulate the rest of the nervous system, so that a persistent pain problem often involves more than one system and mechanism. Pain is not an inevitable result of central or peripheral neural lesions. It may or may not be accompanied by sensory loss, and distribution of the pain may not conform to the usual dermatomal pattern, sometimes even resembling the whole-limb distributions which have been regarded as positive signs of hysterical conversion. Regrettably, there is little psychological input to the investigation of mechanisms in this area, where some part may be played by classical conditioning and by psychological effects on homoeostatic settings.

Visceral pain appears to arise from stretch, distension and local irritation of smooth muscle and organs, but the mechanisms are far from clear; even distinctions between hypersensitivity to 'normal' levels of such stimuli and painful sensitivity to 'above normal' levels are hard to make. Visceral pains tend to be diffuse, and are often felt in superficial structures (referred pain). Despite generalizations from highly selected samples about high levels of distress or disturbance, there is little systematic research. Pelvic pain is one of the few areas of visceral pain in which psychological hypotheses have been developed and tested (Beard and Pearce, 1989).

One of the areas of considerable controversy is that of muscle pain and its significance. Muscle dysfunction in patients with chronic pain has been widely accepted to be symptomatic of disuse, and distorted movement and posture secondary to the pain. However, the diagnosis of myofascial pain syndrome, in which damaged or fatigued muscles or muscle groups develop sensitive 'trigger points' and become tense, ischaemic and further fatigued, remains unacceptable to many medical personnel. Unlike all other theories outlined, no neural mechanism at spinal level is proposed, although it can be associated with other pain mechanisms.

More relevant to psychologists is the developing understanding of muscle tension in relation to psychological variables. Many chronic back pain patients react with muscle tension to perceived problems to which normal controls respond with cardiovascular change; the tension tends to be more specifically in back muscles than in normal controls, and to return to baseline more slowly. Back pain patients may also have a low awareness of changes in muscle tension of magnitudes detectable by normal controls (Flor, Turk and Birbaumer, 1985; Flor and Birbaumer, 1992). All these make for sustained tension in response to a wide range of perceived difficulties and threats, in a patient who may deny significant muscle tension.

Various attempts have been made to construct a personality profile of the 'typical chronic pain patient'. These personality models, based on retrospective data collected some years into the chronic pain problem, have

yielded few consistent data. The MMPI (Minnesota Multiphasic Personality Inventory; Dahlstrom and Welsh, 1960) has been used extensively in the USA and elsewhere, and a relationship between hypochondriasis, depression and hysteria scores of chronic pain patients has often emerged; however, there are serious criticisms about the validity of the instrument in this population (Watson, 1982; Karoly, 1985a; Main, Evans and Whitehead, 1991). Personality models are usually based on assumptions about the pain sufferer pursuing 'secondary gain', i.e. using the pain as a means of avoiding unwelcome duties, roles and demands, and achieving new forms of gratification. Such models offer little guidance on therapeutic intervention, but put the onus back on the patient, rather than the clinician or therapist, to bring about change for the better.

The most common psychiatric classification used in the diagnosis and treatment of chronic pain patients is that of depression. However, another classification of 'pain of psychological origin' has been proposed by the International Association for the Study of Pain (IASP): three syndromes of muscle tension pain, hysterical or hypochondriacal pain and the extremely rare delusional or hallucinatory pain in psychosis (IASP, 1986), any of which may be associated with depression.

Hypochondriacal pain (or similar classifications, such as somatization or somatoform disorder) is defined by reference to the absence of organic causes of pain, which assumes that all 'organic conditions' can be identified. The positive definition is of preoccupation with bodily symptoms, persistent irrational belief in the presence of illness, considerable fears about the illness, and repeated seeking of medical reassurance of the absence of severe illness. The notion of 'abnormal illness behaviour' is often used to aid such a diagnosis, and is defined by implicit and questionable reference to 'normal' illness behaviour. Abnormal illness behaviour is not a particularly helpful concept, since it is taken out of the context of the patient's beliefs and current and past experience with medical personnel (Mayou and Sharpe, 1991). This experience is nicely captured in a neglected paper concerning abnormal treatment behaviour, by Singh *et al.* (1981). It is also discussed by Pither and Nicholas (1991).

As mentioned above, depression is often invoked aetiologically in chronic pain, with some supporting hypotheses about mechanisms based on common neurotransmitters. Both case ascertainment and building and testing theories of mechanism are complicated by the inclusion of physical symptoms in all definitions of depression (House, 1988; Mayou and Sharpe, 1991); hence the usual precondition that physical illness is excluded (e.g. DSMIIIR criteria (American Psychiatric Association, 1987) require the interviewer to exclude 'symptoms which are clearly due to a physical condition', such as fatigue, insomnia and significant weight loss or gain, all of which frequently accompany the complaint of persistent or severe pain. In addition, dualistic thinking is again evident, with depression proposed as a cause when nothing organic can be found (e.g. Engel, 1959; Blumer, Heilbronn and Rosenbaum, 1984), and depression most often missed in chronic pain patients by the examining physician when there is clearly identified organic pathology related to the pain (Michie *et al.*, 1991).

Nevertheless, for the purposes of appropriate assessment and treatment of the patient's (often multiple) problems, it is important to identify depression, and to rate severity. Mayou and Hawton (1986) distinguish at least two levels, suggesting psychological distress related to current illness, often transient and responsive to discussion and advice; and psychological distress requiring more active intervention, and characterized by withdrawal, lack of interest and/or complaint of depressed mood. A similar approach, again avoiding the use of somatic symptoms in classification, is used by Goldberg *et al.* (1988) in general medical settings:

patients are asked about low energy, loss of interest, lost confidence and feeling hopeless. The patient who answers yes to two or more of these questions has a 50% risk of having a 'clinically important disturbance'. Longitudinal studies of depression in pain patients – and there are all too few (Romano and Turner, 1985) – have suggested that, most commonly, depression succeeds rather than precedes the onset of pain (Aneshensel, Frerichs and Huba, 1984; Brown, 1990; Atkinson *et al.*, 1991). The consideration of depression as an adjustment disorder in chronic illness (Mayou and Sharpe, 1991), and of the use and effect of coping strategies, moves away from aetiological theories towards the issue of exacerbating and maintaining factors; this is discussed further below.

Malingering is excluded from the IASP definitions, since it is not a pain syndrome. In practice, it is a significant achievement that the 'diagnosis' of malingering is steadily disappearing as understanding of aetiology improves, although there is still far to go before it disappears. A much more useful approach is the investigation of the relationship between the development of chronic pain and variables such as job satisfaction (Bigos *et al.*, 1991) and local socioeconomic factors (Volinn *et al.*, 1988).

Finally, it is beyond the scope of this chapter to examine psychodynamic models of pain. In the past there tended to be a rigid divide between practitioners using psychodynamic models and those using operant or cognitive–behavioural models. We welcome the new openness towards different approaches found among both psychologists and psychotherapists. For example, the emphasis in psychodynamic models on intrapsychic processes, particularly the role of unconscious fantasies and defensive mechanisms in the experience of bodily states, may well enrich theory and practice among psychologists in the pain field.

Lay models

We have already noted that for the patient, pain generally denotes damage or injury. The typical response is to seek medical help to identify the problem, in the belief that this in turn will lead to a cure (or to confirmation of the patient's worst fears, of some sinister disease). In this frame of mind, the patient is unlikely to find reassurance in repeated negative findings on investigation, as discussed above. Furthermore, many patients believe that the X-ray or more expensive investigation is only ordered if the clinician is seriously worried that a sinister finding will emerge. Lost and delayed results, or the failure to feed back results to the patient, are likely to exacerbate his or her anxiety about the condition, and arouse doubts about the honesty of clinicians. Whatever the course of failed treatments, negative investigations or waiting and hoping in vain, it is often years rather than months since the initial injury or emergence of the pain problem before the patient reaches tertiary specialists in pain. During this time, the patient has often felt confused, dismissed, disbelieved, abandoned, and ultimately blamed for the pain. It is not at all unusual for medical and nursing personnel to treat X-rays and other imaging results as 'hard' data, and the patient's experience as 'soft' data. Nor is it unusual for clinicians to feel that they can estimate the pain better than patients themselves on the basis of those data (Cleeland, 1989).

The patient's concern about the involvement of psychological factors in his or her problems usually increases as successive medical interventions fail to relieve the pain. Patients may also begin to observe how their pain varies in relation to states such as fatigue, feeling stressed, boredom or pleasant distractions. One acceptable lay model of persistent pain not associated with damage, and influenced by psychological factors ('stress'), is that of recurrent headache. However, at the point where investigations are leading nowhere, most patients feel very vulnerable about the possible role of psychological factors. Phrases such as 'all in the mind' and 'mind over matter' (as an intervention) offer little practical guidance, and imply that the patient lacks the will to get rid of the pain problem. Not surprisingly, in order to counter such suspicions, many patients emphasize their determination, both verbally and in heroic overactivity; they usually suffer considerably from the resulting exertion.

Pain can easily become the organizing schema for all unpleasant internal experiences, and a variety of psychological states may become subsumed under the label of 'not coping with' or having 'unbearable' pain. Pain may appear a more convincing reason for requiring others to help, than a complaint of depression. It is a delicate task for the clinician to work with the patient to tease out the complex interactions between pain, depressed mood, recurrent anxiety and external stressors. Once these interactions are acknowledged, most patients are able to move towards a more complex model of pain, distinguishing aetiology, exacerbation and maintenance, and focusing on current problems, of which depressed mood may be foremost.

The application of models of pain

There is, of course, no typical chronic pain patient, but there are typical problems. The most common presentation is the patient with multiple pains and other symptoms (such as persistent fatigue, dizziness, tingling), with a history of little or no relief from a range of treatments, and extensive disruption of previous lifestyle. This can be explained using several interacting models as follows, (this account is by no means exclusive of other approaches, but reflects current practice).

- Many patients present without a diagnosis, and their uncertainty about the cause and prognosis of the pain can add to their anxiety.

- Where there has been initial injury, subsequent healing has left little to detect on investigation; however, as described above, central nervous system changes do not necessarily reverse with healing. The patient, not surprisingly, seeks a diagnosis, often assuming that this will lead inevitably to a cure. However, negative findings result from almost every fresh investigation, leaving the patient confused and anxious.

- Many patients tend towards rest and avoidance of activity in order to promote healing or pain relief. Prolonged rest may be prescribed, whether in bed or by means of corsets and plaster jackets. Unfortunately, such inactivity is likely to bring about a deterioration in physical condition (Deyo, 1983; Fordyce *et al.*, 1986; Deyo, Diehl and Rosenthal, 1986). Inactivity, and the overuse of aids such as walking sticks and crutches, can promote the development of certain distorted movements and positions. All these problems can lead to the development of further symptoms. In addition, the psychological effect of avoidance is to undermine the patient's confidence, and to reduce his or her ability to find the limits of the pain (Philips, 1987).

- The patient's inactivity can lead to boredom, depression and lowered self-esteem, all of which, according to three systems theory, will tend to contribute adversely to the pain experience. Inactivity can also lead to an enhanced preoccupation with bodily symptoms, such that physical stimuli which were previously dismissed as innocuous may now be interpreted by the patient as an undetected and unresolved painful illness (Pennebaker, 1982). Injudicious prescription and use of analgesics and psychotropic drugs can also cause some of these non-specific symptoms.

- Many treatments can make matters worse. Vigorous physiotherapy applied to an unfit

and anxious patient (with whom, the physiotherapist is assured, nothing is wrong), can exacerbate the pain; this confirms patients' fears of the dangers of exertion, and leads directly to dropout from treatment. Provocation of the patient into a burst of activity by challenging the veracity of his or her complaint has the same effect.

- Lastly, the cognitive model of hypochondriasis developed by Salkovskis and Warwick (1986) suggests that the patient deals with anxiety about symptoms and illness by monitoring and checking symptoms, and by seeking reassurance from medical and paramedical practitioners. Both strategies, however, serve only to relieve anxiety for a short time. In the longer term the fears are perpetuated, and the patient's search ('doctor-shopping') continues.

Exacerbating and maintaining factors in the development of chronic pain

The understanding of chronic pain is progressing steadily with the identification (at the point of acute onset and shortly afterwards) of psychological, social, socioeconomic and occupational factors which influence the likelihood of chronicity. However, we know nothing of patients' adjustment and coping with difficulties before the onset.

Physically, the pain patient who rests more than usual is at high risk of developing further problems of disuse (Bortz, 1984; Brena and Chapman, 1985). Muscle, bone, joints and connective tissue all deteriorate in response to reduced demand, and secondary adjustments of posture and gait can lead to significant distortions that worsen the pain. Likewise, cardiovascular fitness decreases, as does respiratory function. Patients may be alarmed by the unpleasant symptoms they now feel with what used to be minor exertion, such as climbing stairs. This is worsened by anxiety-related breath-holding or hyperventilation.

Fordyce (1976) focused attention on operant behaviours of the chronic pain patient, and described their crucial role in maintaining chronic pain. In a value-free framework, he observed and defined pain-related behaviours, the activities and situations in which they occurred, their antecedents and consequences, and the related lifestyle changes. From this research came the rationale for behavioural intervention. The work of Fordyce and of others in this field places emphasis on creating opportunities for all 'well behaviours', and their systematic reinforcement. Unfortunately, the terminology of behavioural work is sometimes used to justify regimes in which patients' 'pain behaviours' are ignored, without consideration of their communicative content or of the cues eliciting the behaviour.

In the last 10 years, cognitive variables have excited increasing research and clinical interest. In the same way as in the fields of anxiety and phobia, their exploration has enabled the researcher or clinician to engage with the health beliefs, attributions and affective self-statements that guide and inform the patient's behavioural choices. The study of coping strategies began with attempts at classification into good vs bad, adaptive vs maladaptive, or active vs passive. It has moved towards more careful examination of the strategies themselves, and their role in the patient's overall coping. In particular, emotional adjustment has frequently been treated in statistical models as the outcome of coping strategies; but affect can, of course, also play an important part in the choice and the effectiveness of the strategies themselves (Keefe, Salley and Lefebvre, 1992).

It is much more helpful (for the clinician and for the patient) to treat medication use as an attempt at coping rather than as an addiction, a term still much overused in the field and a potent fear for many patients. The risk, and the incidence, of iatrogenic addiction to opiates is known to be very low (Portenoy and Payne, 1992). By contrast, the routine under-prescription of opiate analgesics (Morgan, 1989) can lead to 'pseudoaddiction' (Weissman and Haddox, 1989), an iatrogenic problem in which a patient's increasingly desperate verbal and non-verbal demands for better analgesia resemble the behaviour of the covert opiate abuser. However, much chronic pain is unresponsive to opioids (McQuay, 1989; Portenoy, 1990; Brena and Sanders, 1991). Furthermore, as with other coping strategies used in relation to pain, analgesic taking can be more a response to cognitive and affective factors than to the pain level alone, and may worsen rather than improve the situation. Irregular patterns of medication use related to overactivity and underactivity, unhelpful levels of sedation, sleep problems related to subclinical levels of withdrawal, and temporary cognitive impairment, all perpetuate the practical and emotional difficulties with which the pain sufferer is struggling. The use of psychotropic drugs in pain also requires a more critical approach (Hanks, 1984).

Reduced physical capacity does not necessarily bring about a complementary reduction in the patient's performance expectations or in the role demands by significant others. On a 'good' day, or during temporary relief from analgesics or other means, there is an effort to make up for time lost through rest. In this phase, the pain sufferer may undertake a considerable amount of physical work or an unusually strenuous task: a shopping trip, an evening out or a full day at work. Not surprisingly, this exacerbates the pain and tends to confirm the patient's fears about activity causing further damage. It is often at this point that the patient seeks emergency medical help. The patient then rests to recover, and learns to become more cautious about activity. Over time, there is a high risk of the bouts of activity becoming more infrequent, and achieving less before being abandoned, and of the rests becoming longer. With each successive failure to meet expectations and role demands, the patient loses confidence. Such pain-contingent activity and inactivity is very common on an hourly, daily or weekly level. There is a danger of focusing too much attention on the rest phase of the cycle, thereby neglecting the antecedent behaviour and the role of avoidance of increased pain.

It is these exacerbating and maintaining behaviours and beliefs that have become the main focus of treatment where the chronic pain cannot be relieved. They constitute the daily experience of pain sufferers, and are highly accessible to assessment and psychological intervention.

Assessment

The increased complexity of pain models makes assessment an ever more complicated task. Karoly (1985b) states that the object of assessment in chronic pain is ideally nothing less than the 'multilevel pain context', the interaction of 'mind', 'body' and 'setting' (all of which are interdependent). Thus any attempt to measure pain becomes part of that multilevel context, rendering impossible any non-reactive method of pain assessment: even baseline assessment constitutes an intervention. Karoly and Jensen (1987) give a full and critical account of multilevel pain assessment; Turk, Meichenbaum and Genest (1983), Chapman *et al.* (1985) and Williams (1988) on pain measurement are also recommended.

Karoly (1985b) has outlined six pain response levels which all warrant assessment. The levels may vary independently, and any response level can be examined without necessary reference to the others; they are related to one another using control (general systems) theory:

- Sensory–discriminative or somatic perception level, e.g. pain intensity, location, pain tolerance;

- Motivational–affective level, e.g. pain-related anxiety, depression, loss of reinforcers, self-efficacy;
- Neurophysiological/automatic/biochemical level, e.g. EEG, endorphin assay, heart rate change;
- Behavioural (verbal–motor) level, e.g. pain complaint, request for medication, uptime and downtime;
- Lifestyle impact, e.g. marital distress, work change, litigation;
- Information processing/central control, e.g. attention and expectation, coping style, problem-solving skills, health beliefs.

One inescapable practical consideration is the degree to which the patient is ready to be engaged in treatment and to form a therapeutic alliance. The referring doctor should always be encouraged to discuss the rationale for the referral with the patient. But patients are still likely to arrive at the appointment with any professional whose profession begins with 'psych-' feeling puzzled, ambivalent or hostile; they often fear that such a clinician disbelieves their pain and has nothing positive to offer. One way to begin is by enquiring into patients' feelings about the referral, and their beliefs about the pain. The next step will depend on the needs of the individual patient and the progress of the interview up to that point. However, without some agreement on the reality of the pain, and of a common model or models which attempt to make sense of the pain, any further effective assessment or treatment maybe impossible. Some explanation of pain theory or working models should be attempted, integrating the psychological as far as possible. The notion that pain must be proportional to the extent of damage has to be challenged, and the patient's existing understanding made explicit. For example, notions such as 'wear and tear', which provide the rationale for rest and avoidance, need discussion. In some cases, it is helpful for the psychologist to refer to a specialist medical colleague or to the patient's GP to clarify information about the condition. Fordyce (1976) and Turk, Meichenbaum and Genest (1983) have some useful accounts of ways in which the patient can be helped to reconceptualize the pain problem.

Interviews

Once some kind of shared model of pain has been established, the most acceptable starting point is often to begin a functional analysis of the pain problem. This means investigating the precipitating factors, exacerbating factors, variations in time and place of episodes of pain or illness, and the associated responses of the patient and significant others. The authors have found a schedule by Fordyce (1976) very satisfactory for the first meeting with over 500 chronic pain patients. The questions start by clarifying the patterns (if any) of pain across an average day. Then time spent in bed, asleep, trying to sleep, during the day and night, with or without hypnotics, and the strategies of the patient when he or she cannot sleep, are elicited. The patient is then asked about the activities, situations, occasions and anything else that make the pain worse. Tension, upset and 'stress' are raised as possible causes of worsening if the patient does not mention them spontaneously; many patients recognize and acknowledge the link, with occasional individuals finding that anger distracts them substantially from their pain. The patient is also asked about anything that relieves the pain, even slightly; relaxation is suggested if not mentioned.

It is important to assess the activities that have been abandoned or reduced because of pain, and to enquire into the difference the pain makes to the spouse, partner or significant others, including the quality of the relationship. Many patients report considerable guilt over their low mood, irritability and disinclination for sex; in some cases, their marriage may be in jeopardy. The patient is asked whether the

significant other can tell when the pain is bad, without being told; if so, how he or she can tell, and how he or she responds. Many patients report that their spouse can tell by expression, posture, mood or lack of interaction, that they are suffering; the response is not necessarily solicitous, nor do patients universally wish for rescue from their distress. Further questions concern the patient's perception of whether the pain is steady, worsening or improving over the last year (or appropriate timespan), and how the patient sees the next few years. This often elicits beliefs about inevitable deterioration, and the deleterious effects on lifestyle, family, social contacts and self. The schedule closes with questions about the patient's ideas about the cause of pain, current rather than aetiological, and about current or recent life events unrelated to the pain.

Only a limited and perhaps biased amount of information may be forthcoming at the first session. Patients may, for example, be unwilling to disclose environmental influences on their pain in case this throws doubt on its reality. In this case, patients may be asked to keep a diary (Fig. 20.1) of their pain before the next session, which often provides new data and opens up discussion in subsequent sessions. It may also help to normalize the patient's experience of environmental influences, by mentioning the experiences of other (anonymous) patients, or by offering an account of chronic pain written by a patient: Shone (1992) is highly recommended. The questions outlined above should be sufficient to identify the exacerbating and maintaining factors, to elicit some key cognitive distortions and to gauge the patient's beliefs about the sufficiency of his or her coping strategies to deal with the pain. This leads to consideration of expectations of treatment and possible treatment goals. It is very helpful, if possible, to interview a significant other person in the patient's life, separately or jointly, in order to gain a more complete picture of the range of behaviours, problems and associated

Day	What was I doing?	What was I thinking?	Tension rating	Pain rating
a.m.	Resting on couch	Will I ever get rid of this pain? What happens if it gets worse?	3	4
p.m.	Having tea with sister-in-law and her new baby	Thinking about my visitors	1	2
evening	Watching TV lying on couch	About TV and will I have another bad night with pain?	3	2

Pain/Tension Rating:

0 = None
1
2
3
4
5 = The worst it ever was

FIGURE 20.1 Pain diary.

variables. Lastly, but importantly, it is necessary to elicit a basic personal history in terms of previous medical history and major life events, with particular attention to past episodes of major stress.

Measures

These will be discussed in relation to each response level or component of pain (Karoly, 1985b).

Methods assessing sensory/discriminative component

Rating scales are the most common way to assess the perceived intensity of pain, and include numerical (e.g. 1–100) or verbal (e.g. no pain–mild–moderate–severe–unbearable) categorical scales, and visual analogue scales (VAS) using a ten centimetre line:

Please make a mark on this line to indicate the intensity of your pain

no   _____ extreme
pain   pain

All rating scales are problematic, mainly in their assumptions of equal distance between scale points when they are ordinal rather than interval scales, and this affects the statistical methods appropriate for their analysis. This is particularly relevant to verbal rating scales whose points are then scored (including the MPQ pain intensity score). It has not been demonstrated within or between patients that a word which scores 4 on a standard scale represents pain twice as bad as a word that scores 2 on that scale. Nevertheless, mean ratings across and between groups of patients do appear to distinguish them in a meaningful way. There is no ideal scale: it depends on the context of measurement and on the age (elderly people have difficulty with the VAS) and the population. Ratings of relief should be sampled directly, not estimated by subtracting post-treatment from pre-treatment pain ratings.

Rating scales are often incorporated into pain diaries (Fig. 20.1), which may also include assessment of other pain levels, e.g. tension ratings, activity ratings, drug use, accompanying thoughts etc. Compliance with diary-keeping can be a problem, although there is evidence that the less demanding methods are likely to improve completion and accuracy rates (Collins and Martin, 1980). A study of pain measurement in health surveys (Center for Disease Control, 1992) found recall more accurate than not, with retrospective ratings no more accurate for keeping a diary over the period of retrospection. Overestimation rather than underestimation of pain severity occurs where accuracy is poor, particularly if pain is more severe at the time of recall. This can be resolved to some extent by requesting a 'present pain intensity' rating, followed by one of 'average pain intensity' over a specified period of time. The effect of mood on pain severity ratings has been harder to establish, with investigations of mood and severity and tests of mood congruence showing no clear effect (CDC, 1992; Pearce *et al.*, 1990).

The first attempt to quantify pain intensity together with other components of the pain experience was made with the publication of the McGill Pain Questionnaire (MPQ: Melzack, 1975). The MPQ gives separate indices of sensory, affective and evaluative (i.e. cognitive) aspects of pain, and is very widely used in the field. Factor analysis of the responses of different pain populations reaches different factor solutions, with factors fairly highly correlated with one another (Holroyd *et al.*, 1992). Even the validity of the sensory and evaluative subscales has been questioned (Karoly and Jensen, 1987; Holroyd *et al.*, 1992). Graceley (1992) has suggested that pain sensation and affect can usefully be conceptualized like height and weight: although they vary together, they are by no means interchangeable, and the range of weights for a given height contains essential information.

Surprisingly, since most texts on chronic pain explicitly acknowledge the multidimensional nature of the pain experience, many attempts to measure pain make use of a single measure of 'intensity'. Intensity ratings, even when 'distress' aspects are separately sampled, inevitably incorporate pain affect (Kremer and Atkinson, 1984). Variability across single comprehensive ratings will therefore be more complex to interpret than where some attempt is made to separate intensity and distress.

Methods assessing the affective component

The MPQ, visual analogue and numerical rating scales can all be used to measure the affective component of pain, using terms such as 'pain distress'. Using pain descriptors produces much less reliable results with chronic pain patients than with experimental subjects; the problems are serious enough to warrant avoidance of these scales (Urban, Keefe and France, 1984). A study by Wade *et al.* (1990) attempted to partition the emotional unpleasantness of pain rated by chronic pain patients. Controlling for intensity, a significant effect was found for anxiety, frustration and anger, but not depressed mood, measured on a variety of mood scales. Jensen *et al.* (1991a) have developed a Pain Discomfort Scale (PDS) on chronic pain patients, with five point ratings to each of 10 items (such as 'I feel helpless about my pain'), and report it to have good reliability and validity compared with the MPQ. Its brevity recommends it, but it is too early to evaluate its performance.

Still close to the actual experience of pain are two measures of anxious preoccupation and labelling of sensory experience. The Modified Somatic Perception Questionnaire (Main, 1983) is a 13 item scale for back pain patients. It has four point ratings, from 'not at all' to 'extremely/could not have been worse', for experiences of the previous week such as dizziness and 'tense feeling across forehead'. This has recently been incorporated into a patient classification inventory (Main *et al.*, 1992). The Pain Anxiety Symptoms Scale (PASS: McCracken, Zayfert and Gross, 1992) contains 40 items covering somatic anxiety, cognitive anxiety, fear and escape/avoidance. Like the MSPQ, it has been validated against other questionnaire responses by chronic pain patients.

Although it is still very unclear how pain is related to various mood states, it is important to assess anxiety and depression. The problems with using standard forms or interview schedules developed in psychiatric populations were mentioned briefly above. This applies to DSMI-IIR interview schedules as much as to commonly used questionnaires. Nevertheless, because they are used relatively widely in chronic pain populations, certain scales should be mentioned. The Spielberger State Trait Inventory (Spielberger, 1983) is a standard measure of anxiety; the state form is used more often than the trait. The Zung Depression Inventory has been specially adapted for use with pain patients by Main and Waddell (1984), who have reduced items which might confound 'organic signs' with physical problems related to pain. The Beck Depression Inventory (BDI: Beck *et al.*, 1961) and Hamilton Rating Scale (Hamilton, 1960) are also widely used, despite the problems mentioned above in conceptualizing depression and in assigning symptoms to mood or to pain. Because it almost entirely avoids somatic symptoms, and was developed on medical patients, the Hospital Anxiety and Depression Scale (HAD: Zigmond and Snaith, 1983) is strongly recommended.

Methods assessing the neurophysiological component

There now exists a sophisticated armoury of techniques to investigate this response level. However, most clinicians have little or no access to them and there is little guidance from theories of pain on how these measures relate to presenting pain. Electromyography (EMG), however, is useful in cases where muscle tension may exacerbate the pain. Although there is mixed evidence on its contribution to the assessment of headaches, its use in back pain and myofascial pain dysfunction seems more promising. Computer technology offers considerable possibilities of integrated measures of muscle function and of dynamic measurement, and the work of Flor and colleagues (Flor, Turk and Birbaumer, 1985) has been pioneering.

Methods assessing the behavioural component

Pain behaviour is not related in any simple way to ratings of pain severity, or to lifestyle impact measures (Fordyce *et al.*, 1984). It includes all the different ways to communicate pain, such as verbal complaints, non-verbal postures and gestures, medication requests, etc.; the many adaptive and maladaptive ways of coping with pain, such as relaxation and medication use; and behaviour to prevent the onset or exacerbation of pain episodes.

Avoidance has emerged as a key behaviour, which may function in a similar way to avoidance in phobias (Philips, 1987) and is usually reported by the patient during interview. If the behavioural model is oversimplified, there is a risk of grouping all behaviour related to the pain as 'pain behaviour', and judging *a priori* that it must be deleterious to the patient's function. However, behaviour such as limping, grimacing and sighing is communicative, and is likely to be amplified when the message does not seem to have been heard. Some strategies, such as limping, which have longer-term complications, may nevertheless be reinforced by their short-term benefits in partial pain relief.

As already noted, one of the most common assessment methods is to ask the patient to complete a pain behaviour diary covering subjects such as position, medication use and type of activity at certain points during the day (Follick, Ahern and Laser-Wolston, 1984; Karoly and Jensen, 1987; CDC, 1992). Self-observation is practical and allows sampling of the whole of the patient's behavioural repertoire. Reliability can, however, be a problem, and the simplest possible form is recommended to encourage it. It is also important to think carefully about what to record, and to explain its relevance to the patient.

There are several published methods of recording observed behaviour; the most widely used is the scale devised by Keefe and Block (1982) for back pain patients, using trained raters. A recent study of the behaviour of cancer patients, notable for its methodology and for the promising approach to pain behaviour, videotaped patients in their homes. Patients then classified their behaviour according to whether it was used to express pain, to control pain, or whether it was an adaptation enforced by the pain (Wilkie *et al.*, 1992). Both observation and self-report allow the simple recording of the use of sticks, corsets, collars, crutches, wheelchairs and other aids.

Methods assessing the lifestyle impact component

Lifestyle impact refers to general psychosocial factors (such as social and family interaction, employment status, leisure activity) which may be affected by chronic pain (Turk, Flor and Rudy, 1987). Interviews with the patient and with significant other people are an important source of data. A comprehensive questionnaire such as the Sickness Impact Profile (SIP, Bergner *et al.*, 1981) can also be valuable and has been used with chronic back pain patients (Follick, Smith and Ahern, 1985); a short form of the SIP (Roland and Morris, 1983) is much more practical, containing 24 unweighted rather than 136 weighted items, and appears to perform as well as the long form (Jensen *et al.*, 1992). A widely used alternative for back pain patients is the Oswestry Low Back Pain Disability Questionnaire (Fairbank *et al.*, 1980); it consists of 60 yes/no questions on pain intensity, personal care and a range of everyday activities. The reader is referred to Fallowfield (1990) for full discussion of a range of measures. As a measure, return to work is a complicated issue, particularly in times of high unemployment rates, and is beyond the scope of this chapter. However, it is important to record the patient's past and current work history. Holidays, outings with the family (and contact with grandchildren for older patients) can also be important individual indices of change.

Methods assessing the central control component

This component includes the areas of attention to somatic state, locus of control, self-efficacy and cognitive coping strategies. Self-efficacy (Bandura, 1977) is a concept which has increasingly been linked to coping ability in a range of health problems (e.g. O'Leary, 1985; Dolce, 1987), and to outcome (Kores *et al.*, 1990; Nicholas, Wilson and Goyen, 1992). Jensen *et al.* (1991b) have made helpful distinctions between outcome efficacy – the extent to which the patient believes that the actions undertaken will bring about the expected effects on pain – and performance efficacy – the extent to which the patient believes him or herself capable of performing the action. Pain locus of control is another important concept, referring to the extent to which patients feel in control of their pain and act accordingly. Although more general measures (such as health locus of control measures developed by Wallston *et al.*, 1976) are widely used, it is the measures developed for specific populations and spheres of activity that tend to show the best relationship with actual performance. Among the most interesting cognitive measures currently are the Coping Strategies Questionnaire (CSQ: Rosenstiel and Keefe, 1983), the Pain Beliefs and Perception Inventory (Williams and Thorn, 1989; Williams and Keefe, 1991); the Pain Cognitions Questionnaire (PCQ: Boston, Pearce and Richardson, 1990); the Beliefs about Pain Control Questionnaire (Skevington, 1990); and the Pain Beliefs Questionnaire (Edwards *et al.*, 1992).

An excellent review of current literature by Jensen *et al.* (1991c), and a further editorial (Keefe, Salley and Lefebvre, 1992) provide a guide to research on coping and ways of judging the measures currently in use. Three problems are salient here: the confounding of different dimensions (such as coping strategy and outcome of coping); the advantages of specific over composite measures, particularly when the composites are based on unproven assumptions; and the poor psychometric qualities of many measures. Many of the disadvantages of coping scales are due to over-simplification of the possible associations between coping and related variables, both in terms of cause and effect and in terms of inter-actions. For instance, the effect of a strategy may differ with the rated pain intensity: Affleck *et al.* (1992) found emotional support and dis-traction as strategies to be associated with better affect at low levels of pain, but worse for higher levels of pain.

The most widely used measure is the Coping Strategies Questionnaire of Rosenstiel and Keefe (1983), a mixture of behavioural and cognitive strategies which patients endorse according to the frequency with which they use them. The strategies are grouped into seven categories, such as 'distracting attention' and 'catastrophizing', the latter emerging from a variety of studies as an important aspect of the patient's coping (see Keefe, Salley and Lefebvre, 1992; Jensen *et al.*, 1991c; Williams and Keefe, 1991).

Cultural differences in behavioural and cog-nitive coping have been sparsely addressed, and the small studies in the 1950s and 1960s which confirmed racial stereotypes have been extens-ively quoted. A recent study by Bates, Edwards and Anderson (1993) is set more in context of cognitive psychology, with attention to cultural beliefs in ideal and appropriate behaviour in pain, the extent to which this is reflected in pain ratings, and related to ethnic group membership and strength of affiliation.

In the last 10 years there have been new attempts to develop multidimensional measures of patients, with the potential to predict response to treatment and thereby to aid selec-tion for appropriate treatment. Turk and Rudy (1987) have developed the Pittsburgh Multiaxial Assessment of Pain (MAP), which incorporates the multidimensional pain inven-tory (WHYMPI) of Kerns, Turk and Rudy (1985). The MAP sets out to integrate physical, psychosocial and behavioural data and to pro-vide for a taxonomy of chronic pain patients.

Although the patient classifications are applic-able across several populations of chronic pain patients, the utility of the measure for the pre-diction of treatment response has not been demonstrated. Three more recently developed measures also wait testing in the field: the Chronic Pain Grade system (by pain severity and by disability) of von Korff *et al.* (1992), which is brief and simple to score; the Distress Risk Assessment Method (Main *et al.*, 1992), based on the modified Zung and MSPQ, which is somewhat longer but simpler than the MAP; and an incompletely developed approach using the WHO distinctions of impairment (object-ive), disability (experiential) and handicap (social) dimensions (Harper *et al.*, 1992).

Intervention

The salience of the cognitive–behavioural model of intervention brings the risk that other models, more suited to particular patients, may be overlooked. As Hanson and Gerber (1990) comment: 'It is all too easy to lose sight of the individual patient in our zeal for our preferred model and approaches. Failure to consider the relevant patient characteristics and the patients' perspective will inevitably contribute to thera-peutic failure'. Fortunately, there is a new will-ingness to entertain different or integrated treatment approaches in line with a rigorous assessment of individual patients' needs. Hanson and Gerber's text on pain management (1990) focuses mainly on the cognitive–behavioural approach, but disclaims its rigid application. They describe how, for a significant minority of patients, psychodynamic or systemic factors in the presentation need to be addressed; structured instruction in pain coping skills is then supplemented or replaced by a longer-term psychotherapeutic approach. This can be individual, couple- or family-centred. (For a family therapy systems approach, see also Roy, 1986). Similarly, the authors regularly refer certain patients on for psychotherapy of various kinds, after full assessment and discussion with the patient on the available options and what might be expected from each.

Pain management programmes can be individual or group-based. Groups have a number of advantages: therapeutic factors special to groups (Yalom, 1986), such as universality (a sense of not being alone with the problem) and altruism (being able to help others) work against the loneliness and helplessness that often accompany chronic pain. Groups give many opportunities for feedback, modelling and observational learning, and can also become powerful reinforcers of positive change. They also make multidisciplinary work cost-effective; pain clinicians (most often anaesthetists), psychologists, physiotherapists, occupational therapists, nurses and others can collaborate to target the maximum number of problems and to integrate aspects of treatment.

Multidisciplinary inpatient pain centres, largely financed by health insurance or work-based insurance, are widespread in the USA, although funders are becoming ever more selective on the basis of cost and outcome. The only published randomized controlled trial of inpatient vs outpatient treatment (Peters and Large, 1990; Peters, Large and Elkind, 1992) showed no clear advantage of one over the other. The relative advantages of inpatient and outpatient delivery of multicomponent treatment by a multidisciplinary team are similar to those in other areas of treatment, and are discussed more extensively by Williams (1993) and Pearce and Erskine (1993). These two texts contain full descriptions of an inpatient programme and an outpatient programme, respectively. In the UK there are few inpatient courses, and most intervention is carried out in the scattered multidisciplinary outpatient centres or by single-handed psychologists. A recent survey found that only 26% of pain clinics had a 'designated' psychologist, and both those with and without access to one

wanted more (College of Health, 1990). Individual work, however, is often the only option available and has the advantage that the whole of the intervention programme can be tailored to the particular needs of each patient.

Both group and individual treatments in this country use operant and cognitive methods. The patient should be engaged as an active collaborator in a joint problem-solving enterprise, with full explanation of treatment methods and written back-up of teaching material. The operant approach to treating chronic pain is described in detail by Fordyce (1976). It aims to increase 'well behaviours' which enable a return to more normal life (such as more independent activity, improve mobility, talking about subjects other than pain), and to decrease 'pain behaviours' which serve the patient poorly (such as prolonged rest, avoidance of activities, guarding, limping, excessive analgesic consumption or constant complaining). This is achieved by changing the contingencies, using in particular social reinforcement, brief rests and paced return to a range of activities. For detailed accounts of cognitive–behavioural interventions the authors recommend Turk, Meichenbaum and Genest (1983), Holzman and Turk (1986), Philips (1988); Pearce and Erskine (1989, 1993); and Williams (1993). The use of self-help texts such as Shone (1992), Broome and Jellicoe (1987) and Peck (1985) can be helpful.

Cognitive–behavioural intervention

Education

Education begun at assessment is intensified in the first phase of treatment. Patients are exposed to more complex models of pain experience, and have the opportunity to ask questions based on their own understandings. It is helpful for a doctor to take part in this process. Education about each component of treatment – for instance, learning as a part of the physiotherapy component that joints are nourished rather than damaged by using their full range of movement – plays a part in modifying catastrophic beliefs and encouraging patients to take part in the fitness programme. Learning the principles of habit change and selective reinforcement enables patients to use them in establishing and maintaining new patterns of behaviour, whether this is stopping limping or managing frustration. Discussion of the patient's current problems, which result from having chronic pain, moves the focus of treatment towards those problems and provides the rationale for the pain management approach.

Improving physical condition

Patients are taught simple exercise routines to improve strength, mobility and overall fitness. Two crucial aspects of this are first, that the starting level and the rate of increase are realistic for the patient's current physical condition; and secondly, that the exercises can be carried out with no special equipment in the patient's home. In addition to exercises, advice and information on posture and body mechanics are important, and the contribution of an occupational therapist or ergonomist can be helpful. For the single-handed psychologist, simple graded walking, stairs or swimming programmes can be planned with the patient and, if appropriate, his or her physicians.

All exercises need to be started from a realistic baseline, and increased gradually. Similarly, any activity which the patient finds increases the pain – from sitting, standing or walking to complex activities such as driving, gardening or using a keyboard – is performed repeatedly only within the limits of the baseline or current level of tolerance; breaks, rests and changes of activity between are also important. As the patient's fitness, strength and confidence improve, the time for which he or she can walk, or hoover, for instance, becomes close to the requirements of everyday life. This is called pacing: it makes activity time-contingent rather than pain-contingent, and reverses the over-activity–underactivity cycle described above.

Recovery of activities

The first step is to use the assessment data to set up long-term and short-term goals within the areas of work, leisure and domestic activity and social relationships, and to set baselines and rates of increase for the purposes of pacing. In a multidisciplinary setting, goals for physical activity and medication reduction will be negotiated in conjunction with the physiotherapist and doctor or nurse, respectively. There should be an opportunity to recognize (if not to address) obstacles to goal achievement rather than pain, which may be presented by patients as the sole reason why life is not near perfect. The next step is to negotiate some specific 'homework' targets for the week, including as far as possible some that are intrinsically enjoyable for the patient, with appropriate 'reinforcements' for chores and duties which are less so. Progress is monitored and goals are adjusted in subsequent sessions; patients thereby learn some valuable problem-solving skills.

Certain problems frequently complicate goal attainment. Patients who are demoralized at the outset may find it hard to consider the possibility of new behaviours, let alone to commit themselves to achieving them. Secondly, patients may stick to their pacing routine but diminish each achievement by comparison with what they used to be able to do, or with others' performance. These problems often provide material for cognitive work. Lastly, the contingencies operating in the patient's home and other settings can undermine their progress, either by being too cautious and solicitous or by demanding too much too soon. Ideally, significant others should be invited to attend some part of the programme, and may benefit from time devoted to their own difficulties in relation to the pain; as a minimum, patients should be encouraged to engage a significant other as an ally in their treatment.

Relaxation and sleep management

Relaxation is one of the most widely taught and versatile skills, but it is important that expectations of its use are realistic: it is not a powerful analgesic in chronic pain. Nevertheless, it is very important in countering muscular tension. Although EMG biofeedback may be useful to reduce tension in a specific muscle group directly related to the pain, there is little evidence to support its routine use, except in demonstrating to the sceptical patient the association between subjective stress and objective muscle tension. Relaxation reduces tension and improves performance; it also reduces generalized arousal and can be particularly helpful in dealing with the worst levels of pain. In this situation, cognitive pain-control strategies such as attention diversion (focusing attention away from the pain on to an external or internal stimulus) and imaginative transformation (reconstruction of the pain sensation as a non-pain sensation, such as warmth) (Pearce, 1986) are reported as helpful by patients who practise them regularly. Little is known about the efficacy of these techniques, or the processes by which they work. Nevertheless, sleep hygiene rules such as relaxing when in bed, dealing with fears and frustrations about poor sleep, not spending the day in bed or in the bedroom feeling isolated and unhappy, not napping during the day and using a 'wind-down' routine before bedtime can be helpful to patients (Lacks, 1987; Morin, Kowatch and Wade, 1989).

Medication reduction

Taking drugs which fail to produce an adequate level of analgesia, do not restore function and which may have significant adverse effects, is addressed by helping the patient to withdraw from medication while learning other strategies for pain management. In this respect, the use of analgesics and psychotropic drugs needs careful assessment. Reference to a doctor specializing in pain is recommended, for the simplification of multiple drug taking and for advice on rate of reduction. At the very least, taking analgesics time-contingently rather than pain-contingently is advisable (Fordyce, 1976; White and Sanders, 1985). Where medication is helpful in low doses, it is possible to incorporate its use into a cognitive–behavioural approach (France, Urban and Keefe, 1984).

Improving mood and confidence

Cognitive techniques aim to modify pain-related cognitions directly, to modify cognitive responses to problems and to develop effective cognitive coping strategies. The cognitive model of anxiety and panic (Clark, 1986; Blackburn and Davidson, 1990) is applicable to health-related fears (Warwick and Salkovskis, 1989), and the use of anxiety management techniques in tackling new and feared activities and situations is central to change in treatment for many patients. The use of recording forms or measures to elicit cognitive distortions is standard. Many patients report having 'lost confidence', and explanation of the relationship between success and improved confidence helps to underpin the fitness and activity schedule, which in turn serves as a graded exposure programme. For example, a patient who wakes with worse pain might think, 'By the end of the day I'll be in agony – I won't get anything done'. The objective here is to encourage the patient to challenge this thought with some realistic problem-solving, such as: 'If I do some extra relaxation after breakfast, and plan the day carefully, I shall be able to cope, as I have before'.

Standard methods of eliciting, elaborating and challenging thoughts associated with depressed mood are used (Beck et al., 1979; Blackburn and Davidson, 1990), with the emphasis on realistic re-evaluation (rather than 'positive' but unconvincing self-statements), and appreciation of the patient's demonstrated strengths, qualities and achievements. Emphasis is placed on the importance of recognizing and intervening early in such trains of thought, and thought-recording forms may be used during the programme when the patient is sleeping poorly, feels unable to exercise or at other potentially critical points. A useful example may be that of 'fighting the pain', often given by patients as a strategy but in behavioural terms consisting of overactivity to the point of collapse. The results, for the patient, are increased pain and a sense of defeat. Once patients have formulated these consequences and the antecedents of the strategy (perhaps the presence of able-bodied peers), they challenge the beliefs and perceptions involved and develop alternative self-statements or mnemonics for strategies. General stress management techniques may also be useful to patients, and assertion and negotiation techniques can help in the context of strained personal relationships or of social isolation.

Behavioural change

The whole pain management approach addresses major behavioural changes. However, it is hard to address the level of 'pain behaviour' with outpatients, since it requires consistent contingencies encouraging 'well behaviours'. This is difficult even for a well-trained inpatient team at times. Although patients may be sceptical of the extent of change possible through these methods, there is no doubt that selective attention and inattention can bring about rapid changes (Fordyce, Roberts and Sternbach, 1985). Behavioural management techniques can be empowering for the patient, who can begin to feel in control of him or herself, rather than under the control of the pain.

Generalization and skill maintenance

Discussion of relapse prevention, using the principles of Marlatt (Marlatt and Gordon, 1985), and the development of clear written plans can enable patients to learn and to recover from a setback, rather than returning to baseline levels of function. Continued access to staff

and to patient-peers can also help patients to cope with difficult patches by continuing to use the principles of pain management. Follow-up sessions can usefully combine post-treatment assessment, problem-solving sessions and celebration of achievements, preferably by the group of patients who were treated together.

The influence of spouses, family, friends and others is important during treatment as well as after discharge (Rowat and Knafl, 1985; Payne and Norfleet, 1986; Flor, Turk and Scholz, 1987; Romano, Turner and Clancy, 1989). Although involvement of the family where possible is, of course, desirable, it may be ambitious to hope to change long-standing patterns of interaction in a few sessions, unless the patient is equipped with techniques to continue this task. In addition, employers and workmates may be powerful adverse influences, but are much harder to address directly.

Outcome

The results of treatment depend in part on the selectivity of the programme and the population on which follow-up is reported: these are not always explicit in publications (Turk and Rudy, 1990). One of the most common selection criteria is that of current litigation, although the evidence is at best equivocal on its predictive power (Turk, Meichenbaum and Genest, 1983; Benjamin, 1989). The discretionary nature of many welfare benefits is similar in financially rewarding increased disability, but has not been a major focus of research. There are not yet any consistent predictors of performance in treatment or afterwards, and at present exclusion criteria are best kept to the practical minimum. Programmes in the UK tend to treat patients somewhat older and more disabled than many of those in the USA, but both outpatient (Skinner et al., 1990) and inpatient programmes (Fisher, 1988; Williams et al., 1993) have produced significant improvement in these patients.

In the last few years, the previous picture of rather modest changes evident from pain management programmes (Linton, 1986; Turk, Meichenbaum and Genest, 1983; Malone and Strube, 1988) has become more impressive. A meta-analysis of 65 treatment studies (Flor, Fydrich and Turk, 1992) showed improvements not only in the direct effects of treatment, such as pain ratings, mood and interference of pain with daily life, but also in work and health care use. Multidisciplinary treatments showed a lasting effect not shown by control groups or medical or physical treatments alone. Component research is also beginning to show the advantage of including psychological components (Kerns, Turk and Rudy, 1985; Nicholas, Wilson and Goyen, 1992; Fydrich et al., 1992).

Many fundamental questions remain. We still know very little about who is likely to benefit from cognitive–behavioural intervention, in what ways and from which components of the programmes. After discharge, what factors external to the programmes, such as spouse interaction or workplace health care policy, help or hinder the process of change? The complexity and diversity of cognitive–behaviour interventions make process research difficult; the mechanisms of both treatment success and failure remain obscure. It is not clear whether treatment failures would be better helped by entirely different models of intervention. Could self-efficacy and health beliefs be more important for outcome than the specific methods adopted (Weisenberg, 1987)? And how can we help prevent acute pain turning into the misery of chronic pain? Psychologists have a major role to play in addressing these and other similar questions.

References

Affleck, G., Urrows, S., Tennen, H. and Higgins, P. (1992) Daily coping with pain from rheumatoid arthritis: patterns and correlates. *Pain*, 51, 221–9.

American Psychiatric Association (1987) *Diagnostic and Statistical Manual of Mental Disorders*, 3rd rev edn, American Psychiatric Association, Washington DC.

Aneshensel, C.S., Frerichs, R.R. and Huba G.J. (1984) Depression and physical illness: a multiwave, nonrecursive causal model. *Journal of Health and Social Behaviour*, 25, 350–71.

Atkinson, J.H., Slater, M.A., Patterson, T.L. et al. (1991) Prevalence, onset, and risk of psychiatric disorders in men with chronic low back pain: a controlled study. *Pain*, 45, 111–21.

Bandura, A. (1977) Self-efficacy: towards a unifying theory of behavior change. *Psychological Review*, 84, 191.

Bates, M.S., Edwards, W.T. and Anderson, K.O. (1993) Ethnocultural influences on variation in chronic pain perception. *Pain*, 52, 101–12.

Beard, R.W. and Pearce, S. (1989) Gynaecological pain, in *Textbook of Pain*, (eds P.D. Wall and R. Melzack), Churchill Livingstone, Edinburgh, pp. 467–81.

Beck, A.T., Rush, A.J., Shaw, B.S. and Emery, G. (1979) *Cognitive Therapy of Depression*, Guilford Press, New York.

Beck, A.T., Ward, C.H., Mendelson, M. et al. (1961) An inventory for measuring depression. *Archives of General Psychiatry*, 4, 561–71.

Benjamin, S. (1989) Psychological treatment of chronic pain: a selective review. *Journal of Psychosomatic Research*, 33, 121–31.

Bergner, M., Babbit, R.A., Carter, W.B. and Gilson, B.S. (1981) The Sickness Impact Profile: developmental and final revision of a health status measure. *Medical Care*, 19, 787.

Bigos, S.J. Battie, M.C., Spengler, D.M. et al. (1991) A prospective study of work perceptions and psychosocial factors affecting the report of back injury. *Spine*, 16, 1–6.

Blackburn, I-M. and Davidson, K. (1990) *Cognitive Therapy for Depression and Anxiety*, Blackwell, Oxford.

Blumer, D., Heilbronn, M. and Rosenbaum, A.H. (1984) Antidepressant treatment of the pain-prone disorder. *Psychopharmacology Bulletin*, 20, 531–5.

Bonica, J.J. (1979) Letter. *Pain*, 7, 203.

Bortz, W.M. (1984) The disuse syndrome. *Western Journal of Medicine*, 141, 691–4.

Boston, K., Pearce, S. and Richardson, P.H. (1990) The Pain Cognitions Questionnaire. *Journal of Psychosomatic Research*, 34, 103–9.

Brena, S.F. and Chapman, S.L. (1985) Acute versus chronic pain states: the 'learned pain syndrome'. *Clinics in Anesthesiology*, 3, 41–55.

Brena, S.F. and Sanders, S.H. (1991) Opioids in nonmalignant pain: questions in search of answers. *Clinical Journal of Pain*, 7, 342–5.

Broome, A. and Jellicoe, H. (1987) *Living with Your Pain*, British Psychological Society, Leicester, in association with Methuen and Co. Ltd., London.

Brown, G.K. (1990) A causal analysis of chronic pain and depression. *Journal of Abnormal Psychology*, 99, 127–37.

Centers for Disease Control/National Center for Health Statistics (1992) *Reporting Chronic Pain Episodes on Health Surveys*, US Department of Health and Human Services, Hyattsville, Maryland.

Chapman, C.R., Casey, K.L., Dubner, R. *et al.* (1985) Pain measurement: an overview. *Pain*, 22, 1–31.

Clark, D.M. (1986) A cognitive approach to panic. *Behaviour Research and Therapy*, 24, 461–70.

Cleeland, C.S. (1989) Pain control: public and physician's attitudes, in *Advances in Pain Research and Therapy*, Vol 11, (eds C.S. Hill and W.S. Fields), Raven Press Ltd, New York, pp. 81–9.

College of Health (1990) *Pain Relief Clinics in the UK*, unpublished.

Collins, F.L. and Martin, J.E. (1980) Assessing self report of pain: a comparison of two recording processes. *Journal of Behavioral Assessment*, 1, 73.

Dahlstrom, W.G. and Welsh, G.S. (1960) *An MMPI Handbook*, University of Minnesota Press, Minnesota.

Deyo, R.A. (1983) Conservative therapy for low back pain: distinguishing useful from useless therapy. *Journal of the American Medical Association*, 250, 1057–62.

Deyo, R.A., Diehl, A.K. and Rosenthal, M. (1986) How many days of bed rest for acute low back pain? A randomized clinical trial. *New England Journal of Medicine*, 315, 1064–70.

Dolce, J.J. (1987) Self-efficacy and disability beliefs in behavioural treatment of pain. *Behaviour Research and Therapy*, 25, 289.

Dubner, R. (1991) Neuronal plasticity and pain following peripheral tissue inflammation or nerve injury, in *Proceedings of the VIth World Congress on Pain* (eds M.R. Bond, J.E. Charlton and C.J. Woolf), Elsevier, Amsterdam, pp. 263–76.

Edwards, L.C., Pearce, S.A., Turner-Stokes, L. and Jones, A. (1992) The Pain Beliefs Questionnaire: an investigation of beliefs in the causes and consequences of pain. *Pain*, 51, 267–72.

Engel, G.L. (1959) 'Psychogenic' pain and the pain-prone patient. *American Journal of Medicine*, 26, 900–18.

Fairbank, J.C.T., Couper, J., Davies, J.B. and O'Brien, J.P. (1980) The Oswestry Low Back Pain Disability Questionnaire. *Physiotherapy*, 66, 271–3.

Fallowfield, L. (1990) *The Quality of Life: the Missing Measurement in Health Care*, Souvenir Press, London

Fisher, K. (1988) Early experiences of a multi-disciplinary pain management programme. *Holistic Medicine*, 3, 47–56.

Flor, H. and Birbaumer, N. (1992) *The Psychobiology of Chronic Back Pain*. Paper presented at the Second International Congress of Behavioural Medicine, Hamburg.

Flor, H. and Turk, D.C. (1984) Etiological theories and treatments for chronic back pain. I. Somatic models and interventions. *Pain*, 19, 105–21.

Flor, H., Fydrich, T. and Turk, D.C. (1992) Efficacy of multidisciplinary pain treatment centers: a meta-analytic review. *Pain*, 49, 221–30.

Flor, H., Turk, D.C. and Birbaumer, N. (1985) Assessment of stress-related psychophysiological reaction in chronic back pain patients. *Journal of Consulting and Clinical Psychology*, 53, 354–64.

Flor, H., Turk, D.C. and Scholz, O.B. (1987) Impact of chronic pain on the spouse: marital, emotional and physical consequences. *Journal of Psychosomatic Research*, 31, 63–71.

Follick, M.J., Ahern, D.K. and Laser-Wolston, N. (1984) Evaluation of a daily activity diary for chronic low back pain patients. *Pain*, 19, 373.

Follick, M.J., Smith, P.W. and Ahern, D.K. (1985) The Sickness Impact Profile: a global measure of disability in chronic low back pain. *Pain*, 21, 67.

Fordyce, W.E. (1976) *Behavioural Methods for Chronic Pain and Illness*, CV Mosby and Co., St Louis, Missouri.

Fordyce, W.E., Brockway, J.A., Bergman, J.A. and Spengler, D. (1986) Acute back pain: a control-group comparison of behavioral vs traditional management methods. *Journal of Behavioral Medicine*, 9, 127–40.

Fordyce, W.E., Lansky, D., Calsyn, D.A. *et al.* (1984) Pain measurement and pain behaviour. *Pain*, 18, 53–69.

Fordyce, W.E., Roberts, A.H. and Sternbach, R.A. (1985) The behavioural management of chronic pain: a response to critics. *Pain*, 22, 113–25.

France, R.D., Urban, B.J. and Keefe, F.J. (1984) Long-term use of narcotic analgesics in chronic pain. *Social Science and Medicine*, 19, 1379–82.

Fydrich, T., Ferber, U., Flor, H. and Turk, D.C. (1992) *Efficacy of Psychological Intervention for Chronic Back Pain: a Meta-analysis*. Paper presented at the Second International Congress of Behavioural Medicine, Hamburg.

Goldberg, D., Bridges, K., Duncan-Jones, P. and Grayson, D. (1988) Detecting anxiety and depression in general medical settings. *British Medical Journal*, 297, 897–9.

Graceley, R.H. (1992) Evaluation of multi-dimensional pain scales. *Pain*, 48, 297–301.

Hamilton, M. (1960) A rating scale for depression. *Journal of Neurology, Neurosurgery and Psychiatry*, 23, 56–61.

Hanks, G, W. (1984) Psychotropic drugs. *Postgraduate Medical Journal*, 60, 881.

Hanson, R.W. and Gerber, K.E. (1990) *Coping with Chronic Pain*, Guilford Press, New York.

Harper, A.C., Harper, D.A., Lambert, L.J. *et al.* (1992) Symptoms of impairment, disability and handicap in low back pain: a taxonomy. *Pain*, 50, 189–95.

Holroyd, A., Holm, J.E., Keefe, F.J. *et al.* (1992) A multi-center evaluation of the McGill Pain Questionnaire: results from more than 1700 chronic pain patients. *Pain*, 48, 301–11.

Holzman, A.D. and Turk, D.C. (eds) (1986) *Pain Management: a Handbook of Psychological Treatment Approaches*, Pergamon Press, New York.

House, A. (1988) Mood disorders in the physically ill – problems of definition and measurement. *Journal of Psychosomatic Research*, 32, 345–53.

International Association for the Study of Pain Subcommittee on Taxonomy (1986) *Classification of Chronic Pain*, Elsevier, Amsterdam.

Jensen, M.P., Karoly, P. and Harris, P. (1991a) Assessing the affective component of chronic pain: development of the pain discomfort scale. *Journal of Psychosomatic Research*, 35, 149–54.

Jensen, M.P., Turner, J.A. and Romano, J.M. (1991b) Self-efficacy and outcome expectancies: relationship to chronic pain coping strategies and adjustment. *Pain*, 44, 263–9.

Jensen, M.P., Turner, J.A., Romano, J.M. and Karoly, P. (1991c) Coping with chronic pain: a critical review of the literature. *Pain*, 47, 249–83.

Jensen, M.P., Strom, S.E., Turner, J.A. and Romano, J.M. (1992) Validity of the Sickness Impact Profile Roland scale as a measure of dysfunction in chronic pain patients. *Pain*, 50, 157–62.

Karoly, P. (1985a) The logic and character of assessment in health psychology: perspectives and possibilities, in *Measurement Strategies in Health Psychology*, (ed. P. Karoly), John Wiley and Sons, New York, pp. 3–45.

Karoly, P. (1985b) The assessment of pain: concepts and procedures, in *Measurement Strategies in Health Psychology*, (ed. P. Karoly), John Wiley and Sons, New York, pp. 461–515.

Karoly, P. and Jensen, M.P. (1987) *Multimethod Assessment of Chronic Pain*, Pergamon Press, New York.

Keefe, F.J. and Block, A.R. (1982) Development of an observation method for assessing pain behavior in chronic low back pain patients. *Behavior Therapy*, 13, 363.

Keefe, F.J., Salley, A.N. and Lefebvre, J.C. (1992) Coping with pain: conceptual concerns and future directions. *Pain*, 51, 131–4.

Kerns, R.D., Turk, D.C. and Rudy, T.E. (1985) The West-Haven, Yale, Multi-Dimensional Pain Inventory (WHYMPI). *Pain*, 23, 345.

Kores, R.C., Murphy, W.D., Rosenthal, T.L. *et al.* (1990) Predicting outcome of chronic pain treatment via a modified self-efficacy scale. *Behaviour Research and Therapy*, 28, 165–9.

Kremer, E.F. and Atkinson, J.H. (1984) Pain language: affect. *Journal of Psychosomatic Research*, 28, 125–32.

Lacks, P. (1987) *Behavioural Treatment for Persistent Insomnia*, Pergamon Press, New York.

Leventhal, H. and Everhart, D. (1979) Emotion, pain, and physical illness, in *Emotions in Personality and Psychopathology* (ed. C.E. Izard), Plenum Press, New York, pp. 263–99.

Linton, S.J. (1986) The relationship between activity and chronic back pain: a status report. *Pain*, 24, 125.

McCracken, L.M., Zayfert, C. and Gross, R.T. (1992) The Pain Anxiety Symptoms Scale: development and validation of a scale to measure fear of pain. *Pain*, 50, 67–73.

McQuay, H.J. (1989). Opioids in chronic pain. *British Journal of Anaesthesia*, 63, 213–26.

Main, C.J. (1983) The modified somatic perception questionnaire (MSPQ). *Journal of Psychosomatic Research*, 27, 503–14.

Main, C.J. and Waddell, G. (1984) The detection of psychological abnormality using four simple scales. *Current Concepts in Pain*, 2, 10.

Main, C.J., Evans, P.J.D. and Whitehead, R.C. (1991) An investigation of personality structure and other psychological features in patients presenting with low back pain: a critique of the MMPI, in *Proceedings of the VIth World Congress on Pain*, (eds M.R. Bond, J.E. Charlton and C.J. Woolf), Elsevier, Amsterdam, pp. 207–17.

Main, C.J., Wood, P.L.R., Hollis, S. *et al.* (1992) The Distress and Risk Assessment Method. A simple patient classification to identify distress and evaluate the risk of poor outcome. *Spine*, 17, 42–51.

Malone, M.D. and Strube, M.J. (1988) Meta-analysis of non-medical treatments for chronic pain. *Pain*, 34, 231–44.

Marlatt, G.A. and Gordon, J.R. (1985) *Relapse Prevention: Maintenance Strategies in the Treatment of Addictive Behaviours*, Guilford Press, New York.

Mayou, R. and Hawton, K. (1986) Psychiatric disorder in the general hospital. *British Journal of Psychiatry*, 149, 172–90.

Mayou, R. and Sharpe, M. (1991) Psychiatric problems in the general hospital, in *Handbook of Studies on General Hospital Psychiatry*, (eds. F.K. Judd, G.D. Burrows and D.R. Lipsitt), Elsevier, Amsterdam, pp. 11–28.

Melzack, R. (1975) The McGill Pain Questionnaire: major properties and scoring methods. *Pain*, 1, 275.

Melzack, R. and Wall, P.D. (1965) Pain mechanisms: a new theory. *Science*, 150, 971.

Melzack, R. and Wall, P.D. (1985) *The Challenge of Pain*, Penguin, Harmondsworth.

Michie, M.H., Tyrer, S.P., Charlton, J.E. and Thompson, J.W. (1991) The assessment of psychiatric illness by physicians in patients with chronic pain, in *Proceedings of the VIth World Congress on Pain*, (eds M.R. Bond, J.E. Charlton and C.J. Woolf), Elsevier, Amsterdam, pp. 235–40.

Morgan, J.P. (1989) American opiophobia: customary underutilization of opioid analgesics, in *Advances in Pain Research and Therapy*, Vol 11, (eds. C.S. Hill and W.S. Fields), Raven Press, New York, pp. 181–9.

Morin, C.M., Kowatch, R.A. and Wade, J.B. (1989) Behavioral management of sleep disturbances secondary to chronic pain. *Journal of Behaviour Therapy and Experimental Psychiatry*, 20, 295–302.

Nicholas, M.K., Wilson, P.H. and Goyen, J. (1992) Comparison of cognitive–behavioural group treatment and an alternative non-psychological treatment for chronic low back pain. *Pain*, 48, 339–47.

O'Leary, A. (1985) Self-efficacy and health. *Behaviour Research and Therapy*, 23, 437.

Payne, B. and Norfleet, M.A. (1986) Chronic pain and the family: a review. *Pain*, 26, 1–22.

Pearce, S. (1986) A biobehavioural approach to chronic pain, in *The Psychosomatic Approach: Contemporary Practice of Whole Person Care*, (eds M.J. Christie and P.G. Mellett), John Wiley and Sons, Chichester, pp. 217–39.

Pearce, S. and Erskine, A. (1989) Chronic pain, in *The Practice of Behavioural Medicine* (eds S. Pearce and J. Wardle), British Psychological Society, Leicester/Oxford University Press, Oxford, pp. 83–111.

Pearce, S. and Erskine, A. (1993) Outpatient management of chronic pain, in *Psychological Treatment in Disease and Illnesses*, (eds M. Hodes and S. Moorey), Gaskell Press, London, pp. 140–56.

Pearce, S.A., Isherwood, S., Hrouda, D. *et al.* (1990) Pain: tests of mood congruity and state-dependent learning in experimentally induced and clinical pain. *Pain*, 43, 187–93.

Peck, C. (1985) *Controlling Chronic Pain*, Fontana, London.

Pennebaker, J.W. (1982) *The Psychology of Physical Symptoms*, Springer-Verlag, New York.

Peters, J.L. and Large, R.G. (1990) A randomized control trial evaluating in- and out-patient pain management programs. *Pain*, 41, 283–93.

Peters, J., Large, R.G. and Elkind, G. (1992) Follow-up results from a randomised controlled trial evaluating in- and outpatient pain management programmes. *Pain*, 50, 41–50.

Philips, H.C. (1987) Avoidance behaviour and its role in sustaining chronic pain. *Behaviour Research and Therapy*, 25, 273.

Philips, H.C. (1988) *The Psychological Management of Chronic Pain: a Treatment Manual*, Springer, New York.

Pither, C.E. and Nicholas, M.K. (1991) The identification of iatrogenic factors in the development of chronic pain syndromes: abnormal treatment behaviour? in *Proceedings of the VIth World Congress on Pain*, (eds M.R. Bond, J.E. Charlton and C.J. Woolf), Elsevier, Amsterdam, pp. 429–34.

Portenoy, R.K. (1990). Chronic opioid therapy in nonmalignant pain. *Journal of Pain and Symptom Management*, 5 (Suppl.), S46–S62.

Portenoy, R.K. and Payne, R. (1992) Acute and chronic pain, in *Comprehensive Textbook of Substance Abuse*, (eds. J.H. Lowinson, P. Ruiz and R.B. Millman), Williams and Wilkins, Baltimore, pp. 691–721.

Roland, M. and Morris, R. (1983) A study of the natural history of back pain Part I. Development of a reliable and sensitive measure of disability in low-back pain. *Spine*, 8, 141–44.

Romano, J.M. and Turner, J.A. (1985) Chronic pain and depression: does the evidence support a relationship? *Psychological Bulletin*, 97, 18–34.

Romano, J.M., Turner, J.A. and Clancy, S.L. (1989) Sex differences in the relationship of pain patient dysfunction to spouse adjustment. *Pain*, 39, 289–95.

Rosenstiel, A.K. and Keefe, F.J. (1983) The use of coping strategies in chronic low back pain patients; relationship to patient characteristics and current adjustment. *Pain*, 17, 33–44.

Rowat, K.M. and Knafl, K.A. (1985) Living with chronic pain: the spouse's perspective. *Pain*, 23, 259–71.

Roy, R. (1986) A problem-centred family systems approach in treating chronic pain, in *Pain Management: a Handbook of Psychological Treatment Approaches* (eds A.D. Holzman and D.C. Turk), Pergamon Press, New York.

Salkovskis, P.M. and Warwick, H.M.C. (1986) Morbid preoccupations, health anxiety and reassurance: a cognitive–behavioural approach to hypochondriasis. *Behaviour Research and Therapy*, 24, 597–602.

Shone, N. (1992) *Coping Successfully with Pain*, Sheldon Press, London.

Singh, R., Nunn, K., Martin, J. and Yates, J. (1981) Abnormal treatment behaviour. *British Journal of Medical Psychology*, 54, 67–73.

Skevington, S.M. (1990) A standardised scale to measure beliefs about controlling pain: a preliminary study. *Psychology and Health*, 4, 221–32.

Skinner, J.B., Erskine, A., Pearce, S. *et al.* (1990) The evaluation of a cognitive behavioural treatment programme in outpatients with chronic pain. *Journal of Psychosomatic Research*, 34, 13–19.

Spielberger, C.D. (1983) *Manual for the State–Trait Anxiety Inventory (Form 1)*, Consulting Psychologists Press Inc., Palo Alto, California.

Tasker, R.R. and Dostrovsky, J.O. (1989) Deafferentation and central pain, in *Textbook of Pain*, (eds P.D. Wall and R. Melzack), Churchill Livingstone, Edinburgh, pp. 154–80.

Turk, D.C. and Rudy, T.E. (1987) Towards a comprehensive assessment of chronic pain patients: a multiaxial approach. *Behaviour Research and Therapy*, **25**, 237.

Turk, D.C. and Rudy, T.E. (1990) Neglected factors in chronic pain treatment outcome studies – referral pattern, failure to enter treatment, and attrition. *Pain*, **43**, 7–25.

Turk, D.C., Meichenbaum, D. and Genest, M. (1983) *Pain and Behavioral Medicine*, Guilford Press, New York.

Turk, D.C., Flor, H. and Rudy, T.E. (1987) Pain in families. 1. Etiology, maintenance and psychosocial impact. *Pain*, **30**, 3–27.

Urban, B.J., Keefe, F.J. and France, R.D. (1984) A study of psychophysical scaling in chronic pain patients. *Pain*, **20**, 157–68.

Volinn, E., Lai, D., McKinney, S. and Loeser, J.D. (1988) When back pain becomes disabling: a regional analysis. *Pain*, **33**, 33–9.

von Korff, M., Ormel, J., Keefe, F.J. and Dworkin, S.F. (1992) Grading the severity of chronic pain. *Pain*, **50**, 133–49.

Wade, J.B., Price, D.D. Hamer, R.M. *et al.* (1990) An emotional component analysis of chronic pain. *Pain*, **40**, 303–10.

Wallston, B.S., Wallston, K.A., Kaplan, C.D. and Maides, S.A. (1976) Development and validation of the health locus of control scale. *Journal of Consulting and Clinical Psychology*, **44**, 580–5.

Ward, T., Knowelden, J. and Sharrard, W.J.W. (1968) Low back pain. *Journal of the Royal College of General Practitioners*, **15**, 128.

Warwick, H.M.C. and Salkovskis, P.M. (1989) Hypochondriasis, in *Cognitive Therapy: A Clinical Casebook*, (eds J. Scott, J.M.G. Williams and A.T. Beck) Routledge, London, pp. 78–102.

Watson, D. (1982) Neurotic tendencies among chronic pain patients: an MMPI item analysis. *Pain*, **14**, 365–85.

Weisenberg, M. (1987) Psychological intervention for the control of pain. *Behaviour Research and Therapy*, **25**, 401.

Weissman, D.E. and Haddox, J.D. (1989) Opioid pseudoaddiction – an iatrogenic syndrome. *Pain*, **36**, 363–6.

White, B. and Sanders, S.H. (1985) Differential effects on pain and mood in chronic pain patients with time- versus pain-contingent medication delivery. *Behaviour Therapy*, **16**, 28–38.

Wilkie, D.J., Keefe, F.J., Dodd, M.J. and Copp, L.A. (1992) Behaviour of patients with lung cancer: description and associations with oncologic and pain variables. *Pain*, **51**, 231–40.

Williams, A.C.de C. (1993) Inpatient management of chronic pain, in *Psychological treatment in human diseases and illnesses* (eds M. Hodes and S. Moorey), Gaskell Press, London, pp. 114–39.

Williams, A.C. de C., Nicholas, M.K., Richardson, P.H., *et al.* (1993) Evaluation of a cognitive behavioural programme for rehabilitating patients with chronic pain. *British Journal of General Practice,* **43**, 513–18.

Williams, D.A. and Keefe, F.J. (1991) Pain beliefs and the use of cognitive–behavioural coping strategies. *Pain*, **46**, 185–90.

Williams, D.A. and Thorn, B.E. (1989) An empirical assessment of pain beliefs. *Pain*, **36**, 351–8.

Williams, R.C. (1988) Toward a set of reliable and valid measures for chronic pain assessment and outcome research. *Pain*, **35**, 239–51.

Yalom, I.D. (1986) *Theory and Practice of Group Psychotherapy*, 3rd edn, Basic Books Inc., New York.

Zigmond, A.S. and Snaith, R.P. (1983) The hospital anxiety and depression scale. *Acta Psychiatrica Scandinavica*, **67**, 361–70.

Chapter twenty one

Renal care

Clive G. Long

Introduction

The technological advances in the treatment of end-stage renal disease (ESRD) have both increased the life expectations of patients and highlighted the psychological aspects of adaption to a changed existence. In 1960 the longest reported maintenance of life with intermittent haemodialysis was 181 days (Maher, Schreiner and Waters, 1960), but such treatment today imposes psychosocial stressors upon patients and their families for a period that may exceed a decade. This chapter is concerned with the nature and effects of these stressors and their treatment and care by psychological means. The text is concerned with all forms of renal treatment other than transplantation (i.e. intermittent and continuous ambulatory peritoneal dialysis (CAPD) and unit, minimal-care and home dialysis), unless specifically mentioned.

The numerous studies of psychological functioning have provided a patchwork of divergent findings. All have been beset with the difficulty of separating the relative contributions of organic factors, situation-appropriate and maladaptive responses. Also, characteristics associated with dialysis populations limit the validity of many established psychological tests (Yanagida and Streltzer, 1979). However, estimates of the incidence of psychiatric disturbance that are severe enough to warrant psychological intervention generally exceed those found in the general population,

and may exceed those found in patients with other chronic diseases (Simmons, Klein and Simmons, 1977). In a review of studies, excluding case reports and earlier studies, Armstrong (1978) found that the median incidence of emotional maladjustment was 40%. Petrie's (1989) more recent survey found that 43% of CAPD and dialysis patients fell within the probable psychiatric case range. This indicates a rate of psychiatric symptomatology between three and five times that of the general population. Although surveys of home dialysis patients suggest a prevalence of psychiatric illness equivalent to those attending a GP surgery (Farmer, Snowden and Parsons, 1979), it seems likely these represent a psychological elite who are able to deal more effectively with problems than unit-based patients (Schreiber and Huber, 1985).

Psychological correlates of ESRD

The most frequently cited psychological reactions to haemodialysis are phobic and anxiety responses, depression, suicidal reactions, passive non-compliance with medical demands, depressive equivalents such as anorexia and sleep disturbance, sexual dysfunction and psychosocial problems (Salmon, 1980). A 2-year British prospective study (House, 1989) found that a diagnosis of mood disorder was most common among renal patients referred for psychological help, although major mental illness was rare.

Anxiety

It is likely that the majority of dialysis patients experience episodes of anxiety and depression at some stage in their treatment (Salmon, 1980). For some, a pre-existing high level of anxiety is exacerbated by the stress of dialysis: some develop phobias about components of the haemodialysis procedure, such as needling, and yet others exhibit concurrent symptoms such as tension headaches. Generalized anxiety disorders predominate (Levy, 1985), with anxiety more commonly manifested during treatment and during the earlier phase of training and home dialysis. In the Exeter study (Nichols and Springford, 1984), 37.5% of the dialysands were rated as experiencing episodes of at least moderate anxiety in their first year of treatment, with some 6% at mild phobic levels. This accords with the finding by De Nour (1981), who found 30 of her 100 subjects to suffer episodes of moderate to severe anxiety.

Depression, suicidal reactions and non-compliance

Depression is considered to be the most common psychiatric complication of dialysis treatment, although its incidence may be overestimated due to the misidentification of 'depressive' symptoms of uraemic origin (Devins et al., 1986) and differences in the definitions and criteria used for depression across studies (Streltzer, 1983; Levenson and Glocheski, 1991). However, reliable studies show this to reach clinical proportions in as many as 45–53% of all ESRD patients (Czaczkes and De Nour, 1978; Levy, 1981; Smith, Hong and Robson, 1985). The majority of such patients display reactive disorders (Salmon, 1980) that require psychotherapeutic support (Streltzer, 1983). This may be most apparent in the first year of treatment, when 50% of the Exeter dialysands showed moderate depression (Nichols and Springford, 1984),

and in dialysands experiencing an unsuccessful transplant (Christensen et al., 1989). Increased depression has also been found to predict earlier death from the complications of ESRD (Burton et al., 1986).

There is a high incidence of suicide among patients, and many readily available avenues for suicidal behaviour (Levy, 1985). Abram, Moore and Westvelt (1971) claimed the suicide rate to be more than 100 times that of the general population, a figure that rises to 400 times the normal rate when it includes deaths that occur through overt non-compliance with the medical regimens. The proportion of patients whose withdrawal from dialysis represents suicide is unknown, but may have been underestimated (Levenson and Glocheski, 1991). Roberts and Kjellstrand (1988) found that 1.5% of 1766 patients preferred death to the stress of dialysis, and that these patients were more likely to be on home dialysis.

Most patients are torn between the fear of jeopardizing their own lives and the need to reduce the number of restrictions that successful management of a chronic illness imposes. The strict control of diet and fluid is difficult to tolerate. Fluid compliance is a widespread problem for more than one-third of ESRD patients (Cummings et al., 1981; Streltzer and Hassell, 1988). Patients report being persistently preoccupied with thirst (Britton, Will and Davison, 1982; Rosenbaum and Ben-Ari Smira, 1986) and rank fluid compliance as the most stressful of 30 physiological and psychological stressors (Baldree, Murphy and Powers, 1981). Dietary abuse is a problem for up to 58% of adult dialysis patients (Brown and Fitzpatrick, 1988), and non-adherence to the treatment regimen is a significant problem in the management of children on dialysis (Hudson et al., 1987).

Factors that appear to predict noncompliance include a low tolerance of frustration, reinforcement for maintaining the sick role (De Nour and Czaczkes, 1972), family problems (Cummings *et al.*, 1982) and cognitive variables such as locus of control, self-evaluations of past compliance and self-efficacy to resist fluid intake (Schneider *et al.*, 1991). These responses are understandable: the chronic patient finds that what was 'normal' once is 'normal' no longer. He or she may no longer be healthy, independent, active, physically attractive to others, capable of long work hours and sexually potent. Indeed, sexual difficulties are frequently rated as being among the most common psychological complications for both male and female patients (Milne, Golden and Fibus, 1978; Degen, Strain and Zumoff, 1983).

Sexual problems

The types of sexual dysfunction encountered by ESRD patients are decrease or loss of libido in men and women; partial or total impotence (erectile dysfunction) in 28–88% of males, in which organic factors play a major causal role; and difficulty in ejaculating in males and insufficient or absent lubrication in females, with either less frequent orgasm or loss of the orgasmic response. Although the specific aetiology of these problems remains to be firmly established, organic factors (e.g. hormonal changes, low plasma levels of zinc), treatment (e.g. antihypertensive drugs) and psychosocial factors may contribute to their development following the initiation of dialysis. Many individual patients feel they are no longer sexually attractive people. There are often major changes in appearance which may be perceived as a loss in gender identity by both sexes, such as scarring of skin following vascular access surgery, the unsightly swelling of the fistula arm, changes in skin colour associated with uraemia and the siting of the catheter for peritoneal dialysis. The relationship between depressed mood and loss of sexual interest or overt sexual difficulties is well recognized (Degen, Strain and Zumoff, 1983). However, anxiety, feelings of low self-esteem due to loss

of employment and, finally, a preoccupation with illness may also affect the individual's capacity to function sexually. Dependence on machine and/or partner and the shift in the balance of the relationship between partners may also have strong repercussions on the sexual relationship. The role of the male partner, for example, may shift from breadwinner and partner to that of another child to be cared for (Salmon, 1980).

Social consequences

The psychosocial consequences of chronic renal failure include family and marital problems, financial burdens and severe role disruption in work and social spheres. The practical demands of renal failure can strain even the most stable of families. Most patients exercise a disproportionate amount of control in the family, with an attendant restriction of family activities to patient-centred concerns (Maurin and Schenkel, 1976). High levels of anxiety, depression and psychosomatic problems have recently been found in one-quarter to one-third of the parents of children with renal failure (Fielding *et al.*, 1985).

Although some couples are drawn closer together with the start of the dialysis, many patients become increasingly isolated within the family. This can result in a situation where their dependency is resented, but the feelings are not voiced (Salmon, 1980). Psychological difficulties for couples have been consistently reported, with feelings of depression, frustration, hostility, anxiety and pervasive insecurity being most frequently noted (Chowanec and Binik, 1982). The burden of home dialysis, for example, may fall most heavily on the spouse and they may consider themselves to be under greater stress than the dialysands themselves (Speidel *et al.*, 1979). Nichols and Springford (1984) found that the number of partners experiencing moderate anxiety increased with time on dialysis. The stress of coping with the changes in dialysands' health and personality was represented in the 61% of partners, who felt depressed at how their partner had changed during the first year of dialysis: 54% were 'exhausted' with the effort of coping.

The partner's individual adjustment appears to be strongly influenced by the patient's reactions to illness. In a study by Rideout, Rodin and Littlefield (1990), it was found that social support from the ill partner was the most significant predictor of spouse level of depression. In Czackes and De Nour's (1978) formulation the stress effect of dialysis depends on the match between the partner's dependency needs and their respective roles in the illness situation: whether their role within the marital dyad is dependent or dominant, whether this role has been assumed by choice or forced upon them, and whether they are the afflicted or the non-afflicted party.

Stress of being a renal patient

There are numerous causes of stress on the patient whose life is maintained by dialysis. The major sources of stress are:

● Consciousness of the life threat in kidney failure. The mortality rate in renal patients is high, there are many possibly physical complications and patients treated in group settings may witness other patients dying.

● Impaired bodily and cognitive functioning. Kidney failure is a urological, nephrological and endocrinological disease, and people on dialysis vary greatly in their sense of well-being. Fluctuating uraemia causes a severe reduction in physical energy, and constant feelings of illness include nausea, dizziness, fatigue, restlessness, sleep difficulties, itching, inability to concentrate and deterioration of bones and nerves. Those on haemodialysis treatment may also have a consistently less efficient level of cognitive functioning (Wolcott, Nissenson and Lausberk, 1988).

● Secondary consequences of kidney failure and dialysis. Loss of employment, financial stringencies and restrictions on travel and leisure may reduce the individual's coping resources and give rise to stress. In a study of 102 patients, De Nour (1982) found a severe decrease of interest in social life and an even greater decrease in actual participation in leisure activities: 50% reported having no social life at all and only 38% reported maintaining an interest in family leisure activities. Another investigation of 195 patients (Ferrans and Powers, 1985) found that only 23% were responding well to dialysis and judged able to work by their physicians. The dialysis patient becomes a 'marginal' person who has lost full integration into society.

● The exigencies of the dialysis regimen, i.e. adherence to salt-free diets, fluid restrictions and attendance at time-consuming treatments.

● Dialysis treatment. In the early stages of dialysis patients contribute little to their own management and exist in a state of helpless dependency that involves the loss of adult status and power (Nichols, 1983). Later, the 'dialysis double bind' (Alexander, 1976) – being required to be compliant and dependent on the medical processes while actively pursuing a normal lifestyle – becomes apparent to the patient. Further, although the provision of information by unit staff is a most important aid to adaptation, it is apparent that many patients lack information, having erroneous or conflicting ideas and feeling confused (Nichols, 1983). This factual confusion may reinforce patients' beliefs that they cannot control the situation, increase their dependency on staff and interfere with successful conversion to home dialysis (Lowery and Aitchison, 1980).

● Interpersonal confusion. Nichols (1983) cites interpersonal confusion resulting from high staff turnover and inconsistencies in self-care tuition as causing stress. Also stressful is the fact that the setting in which extreme pressures have to be dealt with requires separation from known security-giving places, people and roles, leading to separation anxiety (Strain, 1981).

Clearly, the effects of these stressors are mediated by a number of factors, including mode of treatment, premorbid adjustment, length of time on dialysis and the patient's characteristic styles of stress management or psychological defence. Although a number of studies have compared psychosocial quality of life with type of dialysis treatment versus transplant (Levenson and Glocheski, 1991), the results are confounded by bias in treatment assignments (Smith, Hong and Michelman, 1983). Recent studies that have attempted to correct for this statistically (Tucker *et al.*, 1991; Julius, Hawthorne and Carpenter-Altin, 1989) have found few significant differences in quality of life between haemodialysis, CAPD and transplant patients. Further, there are no clear differences across treatment modalities in terms of the incidence of psychological disturbance among patients (Morris and Jones, 1989). Adaptability to previous life changes is significantly related to positive dialysis adjustment (Malmquist *et al.*, 1972) and adjustment improves for most patients as time progresses (Blodgett, 1981). Denial (those defensive behaviours that lead to a failure to incorporate emotionally significant external information into consciousness) has often been cited as an effective coping mechanism for mediating the impact of dialysis-related stress, especially at critical milestones in a renal career (Devins *et al.*, 1986). However, the denial hypothesis has typically been proposed *post hoc*, and as yet no standardized objectively validated instrument has been developed to measure defence mechanisms such as this (Weisman, 1972).

Whatever coping mechanisms are used, it is apparent that continuing personal, familial and vocational responsibilities is often done at a price to the individual. De Nour and Czaczkes (1972) concluded that personality restriction (shallowness of affect, concrete thinking, little flexibility in response to stress) was a consequence of living with dialysis, for the majority of patients. Shanan, De Nour and Garty (1976) found that the coping style of dialysis patients was marked by a high degree of passive behaviour and little inclination to deal actively with a problem situation.

Such findings suggest that dialysis patients generally exhibit an external locus of control, which could be a product of the illness. It is negatively correlated with dietary compliance, vocational rehabilitation and acceptance of disability (Poll and De Nour, 1980). The myriad of stressors impinging on the dialysis patient make predictions about adjustment a complex business. However, the research to date makes it possible to identify in broad terms 'high-risk' patients. Acute presentation of ESRD is associated with a greater incidence of emotional problems than in those who have attended predialysis clinics and thus made better psychological and practical preparations for treatment (Auer, 1982). The absence of a confiding relationship (House, 1989) is associated with psychological referral, whereas the presence of a coping partner is associated with an improved outcome in terms of how long patients survive on home dialysis (Farmer, Snowden and Parsons, 1979). Nichols and Springford (1984) found that those who had the highest number of problems and were most emotionally disturbed were the younger patients who had been on dialysis 1 year or less, with low fluid allowance and who were living well away from the kidney unit. Older age (over 51 years), male sex and vocational inactivity have also been found to be associated with poorer dialysis adaptation (Wolcott, Nissenson and Lansberk, 1988). Further, it is likely that patients with previous or current psychiatric illness and prominent anxiety reactions to treatment will be at risk of dropping out of home treatment (Lowry and Aitchison, 1980).

Obstacles to psychological care

Despite the incidence of psychosocial problems there are many impediments to the delivery of psychological care, including the resistance of staff and patients (Kalman, 1983) and the treatment setting itself (Bader, 1982). In contrast to traditional psychotherapy, where the client has usually accepted that he or she has a (psychological) problem, many dialysis patients bristle at the suggestion that they should receive psychological help. Typically, patients do not interpret their behaviour as indicative of psychological disability. With some justification, they think of themselves as being understandably upset, anxious and disturbed, and baulk at the psychiatric label. The practical and psychological adaptations that dialysis necessitates leave many with a feeling of resentment and displacement towards the psychologist, or hostility towards the nephrologist or dialysis nurse. Many are afraid to express even minimally negative feelings towards someone on whom they feel dependent, and whose affections they are frightened of alienating. The patient may resist open discussion with the psychologist, if they are seen as acting in a liaison capacity to help nursing and medical staff understand individual reactions more clearly. 'Agreeing' with the staff diagnosis of psychological difficulties may lead to questions about their stability/suitability for desired alternative treatments (transplantation, CAPD). Finally, there is a general atmosphere of no 'permission' for patients to be overtly anxious, depressed and to express strong feelings (Nichols, 1983).

Studies of psychological treatment

Studies of psychological guidance and intervention have begun to appear more frequently in the literature. They can be differentiated according to their emphasis on individual or group work, and according to whether they are problem or insight oriented. However, there are few controlled-outcome studies and most represent either the opinions of authors or are confined to case studies.

There is broad agreement that individual psychodynamic psychotherapy has only a limited place among renal patients. Although Levy (1985) reports success with 'several' clients, these were 'carefully screened and well motivated'. In most cases this work is limited by the sense renal patients have of being 'over-doctored' and their propensity for denying psychological problems (Reichsman and Levy, 1972). De Nour's (1970) attempts to resolve the psychological conflicts of the dialysis experience and improve adjustment by individual psychotherapy was largely ineffective. This was mainly because of difficulties in establishing a relationship with patients.

There is a similar paucity of evidence that emotional insight through group work is helpful to patients. Wilson *et al.* (1974) found no difference after 1 year between patients who had received time-limited group therapy and those who had not. Campbell and Sinha (1980) selected 11 chronic haemodialysis patients for group therapy based on high depression scored on the MMPI, anger and hostility towards treatment staff and the absence of psychosis. The fortnightly sessions were conducted while patients dialysed, with the aim of changing their perceptions. Sessions were intended to help patients to view their illness as a challenge rather than an enemy. Although nine patients had a 'good' or a 'fair' outcome as measured by therapist ratings in 10 areas of functioning (e.g. diet and fluid control), they failed to develop group trust and cohesiveness.

Overall reviews, however, suggest that traditional insight-oriented interpretive psychotherapy groups for dialysis patients are 'unsuccessful', since patients fail to 'identify' with their illness and since insight may be 'too threatening' (Buchanan, 1981). Accordingly, group patient education and self-help groups that depend on patient observations, education and cognitive learning are advocated.

The usefulness of behavioural and cognitive therapies to deal with dialysis-related problems in a direct practical way has been reported in the literature (Nichols, 1983; Agashura *et al.*, 1981). To date, these interventions have addressed the following problems:

- Anxiety reactions related to dialysis treatment and the responsibilities entailed. Interventions have highlighted the usefulness of progressive and deep muscle relaxation (Salmon, 1980; Alarcon *et al.*, 1982) and biofeedback (Budzynski, 1979) to control panic attacks, generalized anxiety and tension headache in dialysis populations. Katz (1974) has described the brief and successful treatment of a haemodialysis phobia using the combined techniques of systematic desensitization, fading of stimulus control and social reinforcement. Another case study (Cooley *et al.*, 1985) has shown that it is possible to lessen the frequency of vomiting behaviours accompanying dialysis treatment by attacking the accompanying anxiety and contingencies (e.g. staff attention) that surround and maintain it. These methods inhibited the habitual snorting/gagging that preceded vomiting by relaxation training, aversive conditioning, contingency management, goal setting and systematic desensitization.
- Non-compliance with dietary and fluid restrictions. A number of investigators have described the use of token economy procedures to reduce intersession weight gain for both adults (Barnes, 1976; Hart, 1979) and children (Magrab and Papadopoulou, 1977; Wysocki *et al.*, 1990). Behavioural contracting has also been used, but whereas Keene, Prue and Collins (1981) reported long-term maintenance of treatment effects,

Cummings *et al.* (1981) reported a lack of effect. Contingency management strategies however, in contrast to patient education, have been recommended as a potentially cost-effective treatment for non-compliance by Mosley *et al.* (1993). Hypnotherapy has been used to help patients overcome excessive thirst (Frater, Dani and Gallo, 1986). Although the treated group showed a significant improvement in terms of fluid restrictions after 2 months, compared with controls, no follow-up data are presented. Most recently the work of Schneider *et al.* (1991) has highlighted the importance of increasing the motivations and attributions of success, since cognitive rather than emotional variables are related to non-compliance.

- Sexual dysfunction. Although there is a paucity of literature on the psychological treatment of sexual dysfunction in dialysis patients, applications of modifications of Masters and Johnson's (1970) techniques have been advocated by many, and would seem to have an important role among selected patients (Watts, 1983; Levy, 1985). This method of treatment enables patients to re-enter sexual functioning, if not by engaging in sexual intercourse, then by other orgasmic pleasures and/or by enjoying non-orgasmic sexual intimacy. Problems in reporting on this area include the low rate of requests for help, the avoidance of the subject by renal unit staff and the absence of controlled trials of therapy (Milne, Golden and Fibus, 1978).
- Depression. Patients with mainly reactive disorders may benefit from supportive counselling (Salmon, 1980) and the use of cognitive–behavioural treatment using Beck's approach (Beck *et al.*, 1979). This has recently been described by Marcus (1983) and Shaw and Harris (1985).
- Compliance with treatment procedures. Brantley *et al.*'s (1990) study of treatment conditions found that a behavioural pro-

gramme using visual cues and a monetary incentive was the most effective in enhancing compliance with vascular access cleansing procedures in 56 patients.

Finally, a multifaceted ecological and behavioural approach to outpatient dialysis has been reported by Tucker *et al.* (1982). Part of the rationale for this was the finding that targeting specific problems (e.g. sexual dysfunction) requires general improvement in the quality of life of these patients. Tucker *et al.*'s programme was directed at haemodialysis patients, their families and friends and renal unit staff. In addition to the individual counselling of patients, five group sessions addressed marital happiness, sexual satisfaction, anxiety-related problems (e.g. fear of needling), personal happiness (dealing effectively with depression) and self-improvement (to improve social skills, self-concept and weight control). Adjunctive and indirective treatment strategies included training nurses in behaviour management techniques, a workshop for families and friends of dialysis patients to demonstrate self-control techniques, and peer facilitation training in which nurses and well-adjusted patients were taught empathic listening skills and psychological support strategies. Although data were collected on only eight patients, the indices used (pre- and post-measures of patients' and nurses' self-esteem and level of hope, behaviour changes and programme evaluations by patients and staff) suggest that the programme resulted in positive psychosocial consequences for patients and nurses.

Psychological care in renal units

The very scarce treatment literature (most of which is American or Israeli) highlights both the complexity of therapeutic tissues involved and the slow development of psychological care in renal units. This is particularly true in the UK, where few units are served by clinical psychologists and where differing practices makes comparative research between units difficult. Nichols, whose work in Exeter is the exception to this rule, suggests that the role of the clinical psychologist must be aimed at the individual psychological needs and difficulties of dialysands and their partners, and particular organizational approaches to training and communication of staff (Nichols and Springford, 1984; see also Nichols, this volume).

Prophylaxis is the first order of psychological management, since 70% of patients who experience major depression do so as a reaction to the diagnosis of ESRD (Hong *et al.*, 1987) and because problems with fluid compliance begin early in the course of treatment and stabilize over time (Streltzer and Hassell, 1988). Therefore, psychological intervention must begin at the predialysis clinic stage. The time between diagnosis and dialysis treatment should be used for a comprehensive psychosocial assessment, which gives frequent opportunities for patient support and education and which may be of help in tailoring the specific modality of the renal treatment to the personality type of the patient. In the author's work in Coventry, patients at the renal unit were routinely introduced to the clinical psychologist as early as possible before dialysis was begun. The aim of this consultation was to demystify the psychologist's role and to prime the patient regarding common emotional feelings that may be experienced. In this respect it is important to acknowledge that establishing some understanding of the 'normality' of certain responses, such as sexual dysfunction, may be as useful as techniques to correct them. Another function is to create a 'permission-giving atmosphere' in which patients feel they can discuss these problems, since many are ashamed of their feelings of anxiety and depression (Nichols and Springford, 1984). Many may benefit from information-based interventions. Katz (1974), in an early paper, noted that much of the fear provided by the dialysis situation could be prevented by thorough predialysis preparation to remove misconceptions. The provision of care-fully worded and 'readable' (Flesch, 1948) education material and an introduction to well-adjusted dialysands as models is useful. In this report the timing of information is as import-ant as the content: a patient's anxiety level may, for example, significantly impede his ability to absorb information if he is given a guided tour of a haemodialysis unit on the day he has been told that he is to begin dialysis. Further, although the dialysis period is a convenient and popular time for patient education, it may be unsuitable because of decreased cognitive func-tioning at this time (Smith and Winslow, 1990).

Although experience and evidence would suggest a limited role for long-term psychother-apy with those on dialysis, a specific problem-oriented therapy service for dialysands and their partners is often required. Typical prob-lems that may be dealt with in this way include anxiety reactions to needling and the respons-ibility of dialysis, sexual and relationship difficulties arising from renal failure, grief and depressive reactions and self-control difficulties in relation to fluid and dietary restrictions. On occasions, advice is needed on more effective methods of learning. Working with staff to reduce the burden of training, by the use of videotape-assisted learning modules, as in the Coventry unit, is another aspect of the liaison psychologist's role. The provision of such a psychological service must be knowledgeable and sensitive to the following:

- The likely critical stages in a dialysand and his or her partner's chronic illness career, namely, diagnosis and pretreatment, the ini-tial entry into treatment, phases in training such as self-needling and learning emergency treatment procedures, the transition from unit to home dialysis or from one treatment mode to another (e.g. haemodialysis to CAPD), and the failure of a transplanted kidney or CAPD.
- Psychological help is often hindered by the

instability of the complex medical condition of renal failure.

- Psychological input may be brief, but it may often be required intermittently throughout the illness. Over time, the major focus of help may shift from an emphasis on the indi-vidual to an emphasis on the family. Nichols and Springford (1984) found that, although home dialysis might increase feelings of per-sonal control, isolation from the unit was associated with rising levels of anxiety in partners, who were reluctant to call for help. Further, since an inevitable decline in the dialysand's health may lead to a withdrawal from home dialysis, partners may need help to cope with feelings of guilt or failure that can accompany a readmission for short- or long-term treatment.
- Rehabilitation is not equivalent to a return to predialysis levels of functioning (Richardson, 1986). In the multidisciplinary renal team the psychologist is responsible for identifying the psychological, emotional and environmental strengths that will enhance the attainment of goals established with the context of the patient's post-ESRD capabili-ties. An important part of this process is helping the patient and their family to fit dialysis into their daily routine as much as possible, rather than organizing their lives around treatment.

It is clear, however, that not every patient issue that is not primarily medical requires expert psychological help, and that monitoring for emotional distress is a team rather than an individual responsibility. The need for greater emphasis on this point is highlighted by the finding that staff overestimated the adjustment of their patients against objective criteria (De Nour, 1981), and by studies showing that the 'ward atmosphere' of renal units is charac-terized by low scores on relationship dimen-sions (Herron, 1985). This may well account for the finding that half of patients with major depression concurrent with their renal disease remain untreated (Hong *et al.*, 1987). Consequently, training to sensitize staff to psychological aspects of renal failure and in basic counselling techniques is an important aspect of the psychologist's role. It should be recognized, however, that the amount of counselling nursing staff can engage in is limited as much by the practical demands of their work as by their willingness to employ these techniques. In addition, in an area in which burnout is common, and in which there is a relationship between staff stress and years of work (De Nour, 1984), staff needs must be considered. The value of staff rotation and regular staff support group meetings to deal with intra-professional conflicts and problems with patients is attested in many dialysis centres (Banthien, 1982).

Conclusions

It might be thought that, in a health care system that purports to profess holistic care, and in a medical specialty where the incidence of emotional disturbance and staff stress is so patently high, psychological input in renal units in the UK would be routine. It is not, and this sorry state of affairs is made even more surprising when such a service may pay for itself in terms of a decrease in unit dialysis and other treatments and reduced pressure on unit facilities (Nichols, 1981). Such care might best be provided if renal patients were viewed as normal people confronted with often overwhelming stress, whose need for psychological support begins at the point of diagnosis. In this way a preventive rather than a reactive service can be provided which is informed by an understanding of coping strategies used by the chronically ill and which is sensitive to the needs of a highly trained and committed staff group. Ultimately, a comprehensive psychobiosocial service must aim to transform the renal patient's natural environment into a sup-port system, and evolve it into a community with resources conducive to optimal overall adjustment.

References

Abram, H.S., Moore, G.L. and Westvelt, F.B. (1971) Suicidal behaviour in chronic dialysis patients. *American Journal of Psychiatry*, 127, 1199.

Agashura, P.A., Lyle, R.C., Liversley, J.W. *et al.* (1981) Predicting dietary noncompliance of patients on intermittent haemodialysis. *Journal of Psychosomatic Research*, 15, 289–301.

Alarcon, R.D., Jenkins, C.S., Heestand, D.E. *et al.* (1982) The effectiveness of progressive relaxation in chronic haemodialysis patients. *Journal of Chronic Diseases*, 35, 797–802.

Alexander, L. (1976) The double-bind theory and haemodialysis. *Archives of General Psychiatry*, 33, 1353.

Armstrong, S.H. (1978) Psychological maladjustment in renal dialysis patients. *Psychosomatic Medicine*, 19, 169–71.

Auer, J. (1982) Social and psychological implications of acute presentation in ESRF. *European Dialysis and Transplant Nurse's Journal* 1, 56–9.

Bader, M.J. (1982) Renal dialysis: problems and advantages of on-site psychiatric intervention. *Psychosomatics*, 23(4), 377–80.

Baldree, K.S., Murphy, S.P. and Powers, M.J. (1981) Stress identification and coping patterns in patients on haemodialysis. *Nursing Research*, 31, 107–12.

Banthien, V. (1982) Staff stress in renal units – who helps the helpers? in *Proceedings of the European Dialysis and Transplant Nurses Association*, vol. 10, (eds. M. Selsby and E. Stevens), Pitman, London, pp. 76–80.

Barnes, M.R. (1976) Token economy control of fluid overload in a patient receiving haemodialysis. *Journal of Behaviour Therapy and Experimental Psychiatry*, 7, 305–6.

Beck, A.T., Rush, A.J., Shaw, B.F. and Emery, G. (1979) *Cognitive Therapy of Depression*, Guilford Press, New York.

Blodgett, C. (1981) A selected review of the literature of adjustment to haemodialysis. *International Journal of Psychiatry in Medicine*, 11(2), 97–124.

Brantley, P.J., Mosley, T.H., Bruce, B.K. *et al.* (1990) Efficacy of behavioural management and patient education on vascular access cleansing compliance in haemodialysis patients. *Health Psychology*, 9, 103–13.

Britton, C., Will, E.J. and Davison, A.M. (1982) The 'alternative' dialysis diet, in *Proceedings of the European Dialysis and Transplant Nurses*

Association, vol. 10, (eds. M. Selsby and E. Stevens), Pitman, London, pp. 21–4.

Brown, J. and Fitzpatrick, R. (1988) Factors influencing compliance with dietary restrictions in dialysis patients. *Journal of Psychosomatic Research*, 32, 191–6.

Buchanan, D.C. (1981) Psychotherapeutic intervention in the kidney transplant service, in *Psychonephrology 1*, (ed. N.B. Levy), Plenum Press, New York, pp. 265–79.

Budzynski, T.K. (1979) *Biofeedback Principles and Practice for Clinicians*, Williams & Wilkins, Baltimore.

Burton, H.J., Kline, S.A., Lindsay, R.M. and Heidenheim, A.P. (1986) The relationship of depression to survival in chronic renal failure. *Psychosomatic Medicine*, 48, 261–9.

Campbell, D.R. and Sinha, B.K. (1980) Brief group psychotherapy with chronic haemodialysis patients. *American Journal of Psychiatry*, 137, 1234–7.

Chowanec, G.D. and Binik, Y.M. (1982) End-stage renal disease (ESRD) and the marital dyad. *Social Science Medicine*, 16, 1551–8.

Christensen, A.J., Holman, J.M., Turner, C.W. and Slaughter, J.R. (1989) The quality of life in-end-stage renal disease: influence of renal transplantation. *Clinical Transplantation*, 3, 46–53.

Cooley, S.G., Sutton, E.P., Melamed, B.G. and Privette, R.M. (1985) Behavioural intervention in vomiting associated with haemodialysis. *Dialysis and Transplantation*, 14(9), 529–33.

Cummings, K.M., Becker, M.H., Kirscht, J.P. and Levin, N.W. (1981) Intervention strategies to improve compliance with medical regimens by ambulatory haemodialysis patients. *Journal of Behavioural Medicine*, 4(1), 111–27.

Cummings, K.M., Becker, M.H., Kirscht, J.P. and Levin, N.W. (1982) Psychosocial factors affecting adherence to medical regimens in a group of haemodialysis patients. *Medical Care*, 20, 567–80.

Czaczkes, J.W. and De Nour, A.K. (1978) *Chronic Haemodialysis as a Way of Life*, Brunner/Mazel, New York.

Degen, K., Strain, J.J. and Zumoff, B. (1983) Biopsychosocial evaluation of sexual function in end-stage renal disease, in *Psychonephrology 2*, (ed. N.B. Levy), Plenum Press, New York, pp. 223–35.

De Nour, A.K. (1970). Psychotherapy with patients on chronic haemodialysis. *British Journal of Psychiatry*, 115, 207–15.

De Nour, A.K. (1981) Prediction of adjustment to haemodialysis, in *Psychonephrology 1*, (ed. N.B. Levy), Plenum Press, New York, pp. 117–33.

De Nour, A.K. (1982) Psychosocial adjustment to illness scale (PAIS): a study of chronic dialysis patients. *Journal of Psychosomatic Research*, 26, 11–22.

De Nour, A.K. (1984) Stresses and reactions of professional haemodialysis staff. *Dialysis and Transplantation*, 12(3), 137–49.

De Nour, A.K. and Czaczkes, J.W. (1972) Personality factors in chronic haemodialysis causing non-compliance with the medical regime. *Psychosomatic Medicine*, 34, 353.

Devins, G.M., Binik, Y.M., Mandin, H. *et al.* (1986) Denial as a defence against depression in end-stage renal disease: an empirical test. *International Journal of Psychiatry in Medicine*, 16(2), 151–63.

Farmer, C.J., Snowden, S.A. and Parsons, V. (1979) The prevalence of psychiatric illness among patients on home dialysis. *Psychological Medicine*, 9, 509–14.

Ferrans, C.E. and Powers, M.J. (1985) The employment potential of haemodialysis patients. *Nursing Research*, 34(5), 273–7.

Fielding, D., Moore, B., Dewey, M. *et al.* (1985) Children with end-stage renal failure: psychological effects on patients, siblings and parents. *Journal of Psychosomatic Research*, 29(5), 457–65.

Flesch, R. (1948) A new readability yardstick. *Journal of Applied Psychology*, 32, 221–33.

Frater, J., Dani, E. and Gallo, R. (1986) Group hypnotherapy for chronic haemodialysis patients, in *Aspects of Renal Care 1*, (eds. E. Stevens and P. Monkhouse), Baillière Tindall, London, pp. 223–71.

Hart, R.R. (1979) Utilisation of token economy within a chronic dialysis unit. *Journal of Consulting and Clinical Psychology*, 47, 646–8.

Herron, R.I. (1985) The atmosphere of a chronic haemodialysis unit. *Dialysis and Transplantation*, 14(9), 524–8.

Hong, B.A., Smith, M.D., Robson, A.M. and Wetzel, R.D. (1987) Depressive symptomatology and treatment in patients with end-stage renal disease. *Psychological Medicine*, 17, 185–90.

House, A. (1989) Psychiatric referrals from a renal unit: a study of clinical practice in a British hospital. *Journal of Psychosomatic Research*, 33, 363–72.

Hudson, J., Fielding, D., Jones, S. and McKendrick, H. (1987) Adherence to medical regime and related factors in youngsters on dialysis. *British Journal of Clinical Psychology*, 26(1), 61–3.

Julius, M., Hawthorne, V.M. and Carpenter-Altin, P. (1989) Independence in activities of daily living for end-stage renal disease patients: biomedical and demographic correlates. *American Journal of Kidney Disease*, 13, 61–9.

Kalman, T. (1983) Obstacles to the delivery of psychiatric care to transplant recipients and dialysis patients. *Clinical Experience in Dialysis and Apheresis*, 7(4), 335–48.

Katz, R.C. (1974) Single session recovery from a haemodialysis phobia: a case study. *Journal of*

Behaviour Therapy and Experimental Psychiatry, 5, 205–6.

Keene, T.M., Prue, D.M. and Collins, F.L. (1981) Behavioural contracting to improve dietary compliance in chronic renal dialysis patients. *Journal of Behaviour Therapy and Experimental Psychiatry*, 123, 63–7.

Levenson, J.L. and Glocheski, S. (1991) Psychological factors affecting end-stage renal disease: a review. *Psychosomatics*, 32, 382–9.

Levy, N.B. (ed) (1981) *Psychonephrology 1*, Plenum Press, New York.

Levy, N.B. (1985) Psychological problems of patients on dialysis, in *Proceedings of the European Dialysis and Transplant Nurses Association – European Renal Care Association*, vol. 14, (eds. E. Stevens and P. Monkhouse), Baillière Tindall, London, pp. 177–84.

Lowry, M.R. and Aitchison, E. (1980) Home dialysis dropouts. *Journal of Psychosomatic Research*, 24, 173–8.

Magrab, P.R. and Papadopoulou, S.L. (1977) The effects of a token economy on dietary compliance for children on haemodialysis. *Journal of Applied Behavioural Analysis*, 10(4), 573–8.

Maher, J.F., Schreiner, G.E. and Waters, T.J. (1960) Successful intermittent haemodialysis – longest reported maintenance of life in true oliguria (181 days). *Transactions of the American Society of Artificial Internal Organs*, 6, 123–33.

Malmquist, A., Kopfstein, J.H., Frank, E.G. *et al.* (1972) Factors in psychiatric prediction of patients beginning haemodialysis: a follow-up of 13 patients. *Journal of Psychosomatic Research*, 16, 19–23.

Marcus, M. (1983) Behavioural treatment of depressed mood in dialysis patients. *Dissertation Abstracts International*, 44, 5A, 1578.

Masters, W.H. and Johnson, V.E. (1970) *Human Sexual Inadequacy*, Little Brown, Boston.

Maurin, J. and Schenkel, J. (1976) A study of the family unit's response to haemodialysis. *Journal of Psychosomatic Research*, 20, 163–8.

Milne, J.F., Golden, S.J. and Fibus, L. (1978) Sexual dysfunction in renal failure: a survey of chronic haemodialysis patients. *International Journal of Psychiatry in Medicine*, 8(4), 335–45.

Morris, P.L. and Jones, B. (1989) Life satisfaction across treatment methods for patients with end-stage renal failure. *Medical Journal of Australia*, 150, 428–32.

Mosley, T.H., Eisen, A.R., Bruce, B.K., Brantley, P.J. and Cocke, T.B. (1993) Contingent social reinforcement for fluid compliance in a hemodialysis patient. *Journal of Behavior Therapy and Experimental Psychology*, 24, 77–81.

Nichols, K.A. (1983) Psychological therapy and personal crisis: the care of physically in people, in *Psychology and Psychotherapy: Current Issues*, (ed D. Pilgrim), Routledge & Kegan Paul, London, pp. 83–203.

Nichols, K.A. and Springford B. (1984) The psychosocial stressors associated with survival in dialysis. *Behaviour Research and Therapy*, 22(5), 563–74.

Petrie, K. (1989) Psychological well-being and psychiatric disturbance in dialysis and renal transplant patients. *British Journal of Medical Psychology*, 62, 91–6.

Poll, I.B., and De Nour, A.K. (1980) Locus of control and adjustment to chronic haemodialysis. *Psychological Medicine*, 10, 153–7.

Reichsman, F. and Levy, N.B. (1972) Problems in adaptation to maintenance haemodialysis. *Archives of Internal Medicine*, 130, 859–65.

Richardson, Y.W. (1986) How can more dialysis and transplant patients be fully rehabilitated? *Dialysis and Transplantation*, 15(11), 607–8.

Rideout, E.M. Rodin, G.M. and Littlefield, C.H. (1990) Stress, social support, and symptoms of depression in spouses of the medically ill. *International Journal of Psychiatry and Medicine*, 201, 37–48.

Roberts, J.C. and Kjellstrand, C.M. (1988) Choosing death. Withdrawal from chronic dialysis without medical reason. *Acta Medica Scandinavica*, 223, 181–6.

Rosenbaum, M. and Ben-Ari-Smira, K.B. (1986) Cognitive and personality factors in the delay of gratification of haemodialysis patients. *Journal of Personality and Social Psychology*, 51, 357–64.

Salmon, P.H. (1980) Psychosocial aspects of chronic renal failure. *British Journal of Hospital Medicine*, 23, 617–22.

Schneider, M.S., Friend, R. and Whitaker, P. (1991) Fluid noncompliance and symptomatology in end-stage renal disease: cognitive and emotional variables. *Health Psychology*, 10(3), 209–15.

Schreiber, W.K. and Huber, W. (1985) Psychological situation of dialysis patients and their families. *Dialysis and Transplantation*, 14(12), 696–8.

Shanan, J., De Nour, A.K. and Garty, I. (1976) Effects of prolonged stress on coping style in terminal renal failure patients. *Journal of Human Stress*, 12, 19–27.

Shaw, B.F. and Harris, G. (1985) Affective disorders, in *Practice of Inpatient Behaviour Therapy: A Clinical Guide*, (ed. M. Hersen), Grune and Stratton, New York, pp. 93–112.

Simmons, R.G., Klein, S.D. and Simmons, R.L. (1977) *Gift of Life: the Social and Psychological Impact of Organ Transplantation*, Wiley Interscience, New York.

Smith, B.C. and Winslow, E.H. (1990) Cognitive changes in chronic renal patients during haemodialysis. *American Nephrology Nurses Association Journal*, 17, 283–6.

Smith, M.D., Hong, B.A. and Michelman, J.E. (1983) Treatment bias in the management of end-stage renal disease. *American Journal of Kidney Disease*, **3**, 21–6.

Smith, M.D., Hong, B.A. and Robson, A.M. (1985) Diagnosis of depression with end-stage renal disease. *American Journal of Medicine*, **79**, 160–6.

Speidel, H., Koch, U., Balck, F. and Kneiss, J. (1979) Problems in interactions between patients undergoing long term haemodialysis and their partners. *Psychotherapy and Psychosomatics*, **31**, 240–5.

Strain, J.J. (1981) Impediments to psychological care of the chronic renal patient, in *Psychonephrology 1*, (ed. N.B. Levy), Plenum Press, New York, pp. 47–58.

Streltzer, J. (1983) Diagnostic and treatment considerations in depressed dialysis patients. *Clinical and Experimental Dialysis and Apheresis*, **7**(4), 257–74..

Streltzer, J. and Hassell, L.H. (1988) Non-compliant haemodialysis patients: a biosocial approach. *General Hospital Psychiatry*, **10**, 255–9.

Tucker, C.M., Mulkerne, D.J. and Ziller, R.C. (1982) An ecological and behavioural approach to outpatient dialysis treatment. *Journal of Chronic Diseases*, **35**, 21–7.

Tucker, C.M., Ziller, R.C., Smith, W.R. *et al.* (1991) Quality of life of patients on in-centre haemodialysis versus continuous ambulatory peritoneal dialysis. *Peritoneal International*, **11**, 341–6.

Watts, R.J. (1983) The patient on renal dialysis: strategies for sexual counselling, in *Psychonephrology 2*, (ed. N.B. Levy), Plenum Press, New York, pp. 107–17.

Weisman, A.D. (1972) *On Dying and Denying: a Psychiatric Study of Terminality*, Behavioural Publications, New York.

Wilson, C.J., Muzekam, L.H. Schne, S.A. and Wilson, D.M. (1974) Time-limited group counselling for chronic home haemodialysis patients. *Journal of Consulting and Clinical Psychology*, **77**, 473–7.

Wolcott, D.L., Nissenson, A.R. and Lansberk, J. (1988) Quality of life in chronic dialysis patients. Factors unrelated to dialysis modality. *General Hospital Psychiatry*, **10**, 267–77.

Wysocki, T., Herr, R., Fryar, M. *et al.* (1990) Behaviour modification in paediatric haemodialysis. *American Nephrology Nurses Association Journal*, **17**, 250–4.

Yanagida, R.H. and Streltzer, J. (1979) Limitations of psychological tests in a dialysis population. *Psychosomatic Medicine*, **41**(7), 557–67.

Chapter twenty two

Surgery

John Kincey

Introduction

In the comparatively harsh economic realities of current health care provision there is a significant risk that health service managers, surgeons and other clinicians might dismiss concerns about the psychological welfare of the surgical patient as something of a luxury, compared with the need to maximize throughput and reduce waiting lists. This phenomenon has become even more recognizable since the first edition of this book was published, exemplified by the clinical and managerial pressures to ensure that no patients wait more that 2 years for non-emergency hospital surgery, while costs are contained and clinical outcomes improved. A major aim of this chapter is to suggest that the concerns of the patient, surgeon, manager and health psychologist in fact overlap and interact in important ways. Identifying the psychological needs of surgical patients and attempting to influence their psychological reactions to surgery may potentially have any or all of the following benefits:

- Patients may be more satisfied with and less distressed by the process and outcome of surgery.
- Patients may show higher levels of understanding, memory and 'compliance' with relevant surgical health care advice.
- Consequently, they may make faster and less complicated physical recoveries from their

surgery and show fewer significant post-operative psychological complications.
- Following from this, they may make fewer subsequent demands on surgical and other health care resources, thus making more cost-effective and efficient use of those resources, enabling better use of the surgeon's time and the available operating theatre and other inpatient facilities.

To achieve these effects, what is needed is the application of psychological principles in ways capable of practicable implementation, based on empirical data and ideally with a validated theoretical rationale. The aim is to meet, as far as possible, the unique psychological needs of the individual patient. Such psychological principles can, however, also be used prospectively in the planning and operational policy making for new or revised surgical services. With rapid technological developments leading to increasing use of day-care and 'keyhole' surgery, this is becoming an even more important issue.

This chapter does not provide a comprehensive review of published studies concerning psychological reactions to surgery. Several detailed such reviews exist, including those of Kendall and Watson (1981), Ray (1982), Anderson and Masur (1983), Gil (1984), Johnson (1984), Mathews and Ridgway (1984), Wilson-Barnett (1984), Kincey and Saltmore (1990) and Salmon (1992. Certain categories of surgery or specific surgical procedures have been the focus of reviews, such as those concerning gynaecological surgery (Wallace, 1984), hysterectomy (Kincey and McFarlane, 1984) or mastectomy (Maguire, 1985). Other reviews, for example that of Mumford, Schlesinger and Glass (1982) have examined psychological factors relevant to both the surgical and the medical care of particular problems, such as cardiovascular disorders. In addition, the present chapter does not focus on specific conditions or surgical procedures directly but instead will use illustrative studies to consider a number of questions which the patient, care staff or manager might wish to ask when attempting to meet the psychological needs of surgical patients.

Psychological responses to surgery

This is usually considered in terms of the subjective feelings of the individual before and after surgery. Most published research focuses on the negative emotional reactions to such an event, usually measured in terms of levels of anxiety, depression or other negative mood states or self-perceptions. It is important, however, to remember that assessments of positive subjective outcomes, such as increased confidence, hope or self-esteem, need equally close study.

There have been two major strategies to examine the subjective psychological aspects of surgery. The first has involved the assessment of mood states over time, usually preoperatively and at one or more postoperative stages. This immediately focuses attention on the temporal process of surgery. The tempting but simplistic model of raised anticipatory preoperative anxiety, followed by a steady linear decrease in such anxiety postoperatively has been shown by Johnston (1980) not to apply in all situations. In the context of breast cancer, Morris, Greer and White (1977) demonstrated that the proportion of patients showing

significant levels of depression varied in a non-linear fashion at different times over the 2 years after simple mastectomy. Gath (1980) and Kincey and McFarlane (1984), among others, have addressed the problem of whether postoperative psychological reactions can be objectively attributed to the effects of the surgery, or whether they may relate to pre-existing psychological or psychiatric disorders. In the context of hysterectomy there is clear evidence that negative psychological outcomes and the incidence of diagnosed psychiatric depressive disorders are much higher where such problems exist prior to surgery. The above studies illustrate the problems of survey methodology in this field, even where good pre- and post surgical measures of subjective emotional response concerning surgery are taken.

The second major strategy has been to compare the emotional responses of individuals who have undergone surgery without specific psychological preparation, with individuals who have been exposed to such interventions. Types of intervention are examined more closely later in the chapter. A considerable number of such studies (e.g. Anderson and Masur, 1983; Wallace, 1984) have shown significant reductions in reported anxiety among patients in the psychological intervention groups compared with controls. Equally, however, a number of studies have failed to show significant positive effects.

Another category of psychological responses to surgery comprises reactions which have overt behavioural components. In the preoperative stage, the most obvious of these is the identified response of some individuals not to seek medical opinion in a setting where they may suspect illness, but fear either the diagnosis and its implications or the prospect of surgery, a phenomenon identified by Andrew (1972). Postoperatively, the speed and accuracy with which individuals take up appropriate physical and social activities again seems clearly to be determined not only by physical outcome factors but by the psychological characteristics of the person and the setting. Ley (1977; 1988 see also Ley and Llewelyn, this volume) has reviewed studies in which psychological intervention led to both earlier discharge from hospital and reduced analgesia usage in patients receiving such preparation than in no-intervention controls. Ley has also very clearly documented the complexity of relationships between such outcomes and other communication variables concerning comprehension, memory, satisfaction and compliance in health care.

A further category of psychological reactions to surgery comprises those physiological responses which may be affected by psychological variables. It is not the aim of this chapter to explore these in depth, but again there is evidence that these influences can operate on both intraoperative and postoperative physical complications, as exemplified by Williams *et al.* (1975), Wilson (1981) and Krantz *et al.* (1982). It should be emphasized that different individuals show very different psychophysiological responses to seemingly identical stressors, and that the same individual may show similar psychophysiological stress responses to different physical stimuli. Consequently, it is difficult to generalize across different surgical procedures in making predictions about psychophysiological responses, let alone about cognitive or emotional responses. It is also important to acknowledge the multiple determinants of post surgical pain and analgesia usage. Finally, it is important for the clinician to bear in mind the phenomenon of 'desynchrony', which has been clearly identified in the context of anxiety by Rachman and Hodgson (1974), and similarly in the context of chronic pain behaviour by Kincey and Benjamin (1984). 'Desynchrony' acknowledges that the correlations between subjective experience, overt behaviour and psychophysiology may often be low. Clinicians must therefore take care not to draw conclusions about one of these three categories of reaction on the basis of the others.

Of particular interest and potential importance is the recent suggestion from the work of Manyande *et al.* (1992) that there is an inverse relationship between subjective anxiety levels and postoperative hormonal stress responses. If further confirmed, this could imply that interventions successful in reducing subjective anxiety might do so at the cost of some delay in physical healing. This hypothesis depends upon the assumption that such hormonal disturbances have been proved to delay physical recovery. It also raises the important 'consumer' issue that patients may eventually be able to choose between preoperative psychological preparation strategies which either reduce their subjective emotional distress or speed up their physical healing rate, but do not do both. It is also again unclear whether improvements in one or both of these 'domains' of surgical outcome will be accompanied by improvements in the behavioural or social outcomes of surgery.

Do patients differ in their psychological responses to surgery, and if so, how and why?

The simple, global answer to the above question is yes. A more complicated question asks which factors are responsible for these differences, and to what extent they lie within the characteristics of an individual or the characteristics of the particular form of surgery, or within the organizational structure of the health care system. Each of these areas has been examined in the literature, although to differing degrees. One obvious intraindividual variable of relevance is that of age, in that the cognitive, perceptual and emotional characteristics of the very young child obviously differ dramatically from those of an adult. However, as Melamed (1977) has shown, the provision of information based on peer modelling can significantly reduce children's surgical anxiety in ways similar to those used with adults (see also Whitehead, this volume). This suggests that similar principles may be relevant across most of the age span beyond early childhood, and that children should be viewed as information consumers just as adults are. There appears to be little published experimental evidence concerning ways in which repeated experience of different forms of surgery, or repeated experience of the same surgical procedure within the same individual, affects reactions to future surgery. The tempting assumption that previous experience of surgery will typically improve the quality of future psychological post surgical outcome seems not to be automatically justified.

Several personality variables have been fairly intensively studied as potential predictors of psychological outcomes or response to psychological intervention in the surgical setting. On a group basis, the personality characteristic of high neuroticism (Eysenck and Eysenck, 1968) has been put forward as a predictor of increased postoperative pain and medical complications by, for example, Haywood (1975). Researchers recognize the weak power of such a variable to predict accurately an individual's response. The related measure of trait anxiety has been shown also to be only a weak predictor of adjustment to and recovery from surgery (Wallace, 1987). Measures of state anxiety in the surgical setting are not clearly predicted by trait anxiety, and do not themselves clearly predict pain or postoperative stress (Boeke *et al.* 1991; Boeke, Jelicic and Bouke, 1992). When considering preoperative psychological interventions it is unclear whether high-anxiety patients do (Johnson *et al.*, 1978; Wilson, 1981) or do not (Wallace, 1986) benefit most from such interventions.

The locus of control concept, derived originally from the work of Rotter (1966), and in the health care setting particularly developed by Wallston *et al.* (1976), has also been studied in the surgical context (Johnson, Leventhal and Dabbs, 1971; Levesque and Charlebois, 1977; Wise, Hall and Wong, 1978; Phillips and Bee, 1980). Where significant correlations do occur between locus of control orientation and surgical outcome, which is by no means consistent, it seems that these effects may be due to interactions between perceived control and other preoperative variables. For more detailed examination of the relationships between personality and surgical outcome, the reader is referred to Mathews and Ridgway (1981) and to Kincey and Saltmore (1990).

Increasing attention is being paid to the relationship between 'coping responses' and surgical outcome, although again the literature is still incomplete and confusing. Perhaps the major conceptual concern is that of whether coping styles are predominantly trait characteristics of an individual, consistent across times and settings, or are more specific patterns of response, unique to one situation at one time. In either case, the extent to which individuals can be taught appropriate coping strategies and the extent to which different individuals will differentially benefit from different types of strategy, remain important questions. There has emerged a broad consensus that one relevant dimension of coping is that of whether individuals 'approach' or 'avoid' information relevant to potentially stressful situations. The repression–sensitization dimension of Byrne (1961), and the distinction between 'monitors' and 'blunters' made by Miller (1987), are variations on this theme. There are suggestions that those who use a monitoring or approach strategy both possess and seek more information about health-related behaviours (Steptoe and O'Sullivan, 1986), and that those using blunting or avoiding strategies may actually be harmed by the presentation of 'unwanted' information (Andrew, 1970), although methodological criticisms of both of these conclusions have been put forward.

In addition to the personality and coping variables outlined above, increasing relevance is being attributed to the presence or absence of social support mechanisms for patients undergoing surgery. Kincey and Saltmore (1990) highlighted particularly the need to distinguish between social, professional and financial support, as identified by Funch and Mettlin (1982), and the importance of considering the source of different types of support or information giving as emphasized by Ray and Fitzgibbon (1979). The timing, as well as the nature and source of support, may well also be of critical importance.

From the above, it can be seen that there are no simple ways to predict the psychological outcome of surgery on the basis of intra-individual variables, and certainly not at a sufficient level of accuracy to be absolutely certain whether one individual will or will not experience psychological difficulties before or after an operation.

Do different types of surgery typically produce different psychological consequences?

In both medical and lay terminology a distinction is made between 'major' and 'minor' surgery. From the surgeon's perspective this distinction can be made on the basis of objective data concerning postsurgical mortality rates or the incidence of postsurgical complications or residual problems. From the patient's viewpoint, these data, where they are available to the patient, are very likely to influence psychological reactions to surgery. However, there is still insufficient information in the literature to identify which characteristics of surgery, rather than of the individual patient, most affect psychological outcome. Data do exist concerning a number of surgical procedures to give indications of the proportion of patients who may experience serious postoperative psychological or psychiatric problems, particularly for those

undergoing oncological (Maguire, 1985) or cardiovascular (Mumford, Schlesinger and Glass, 1982) surgery. The incidence of long-term and severe psychological problems does seem to be higher for these patients than for those undergoing surgery of minor objective complexity, such as hernia or cholecystectomy operations. What is missing, however, is a proper psychological taxonomy of surgical operations. The extent to which surgery may restore or remove function, increase or decrease life expectancy, increase or decrease the incidence of pain, produce or remove visible evidence of mutilation, and increase or decrease the demands of self-care, may represent a number of dimensions of importance in predicting psychological outcome. Some operations may result in a mixture of positive and negative outcomes on these dimensions to complicate prediction even further.

Kincey and Saltmore (1990) have produced a tentative taxonomy based on the above logic, and discuss a number of methodological questions to test out which dimensions are important. In the same way that individuals will differ in their responses, it seems likely that some of the variance in outcome will be specific to particular operations and some of more general relevance across different types of surgery. One task for the clinician in advising an individual about potential surgery, and in helping the individual to cope with it subsequently, may be to consider the balance of outcomes and the extent to which they will influence that individual's life in the future.

Decision making as to whether the individual wishes to undergo specific surgical treatment, and predictions as to how the individual will view this decision in the longer term, may well be assisted by attempts to assess changes in perceived quality of life, both in the short-term postsurgical phase and in the longer term. It is not the purpose of this chapter to review the full range of such quality of life measures now available, or the conceptual difficulties in defining the term. It is suggested, however, that in such decision making, individualized as well as more generic quality of life methodologies may be important. The relative values placed by individuals on improvements in different dimensions, such as pain experience, social interaction problems, self-care abilities and limitations of physical mobility, will almost certainly vary considerably. The effects of specific operations, such as hip replacement, plastic surgery for facial disfigurement, surgery for weight reduction in massive obesity, or heart valve replacement, may have very different values on these dimensions for different individuals. O'Boyle et al. (1992) illustrate a methodology for evaluating the individualized quality of life in patients undergoing hip replacement, suggesting that individuality of outcome can be highlighted while still being assessed scientifically. Variations on this methodology and comparisons with other approaches could usefully be applied in other surgical settings, such as those examined by Bardsley and Coles (1992).

Psychological procedures in preparation for surgery

The general reviews cited in the introduction to this chapter pay particular attention to this issue. Types of psychological intervention have been classified in several different ways, none of which is definitively better than the alternatives. A major distinction is usually made, however, between procedures that stress information giving and those that attempt to teach individuals particular combinations of behavioural, cognitive or psychophysiological stress management procedures. Clearly, however, these latter also depend upon accurate, comprehensible and relevant information giving. Studies are of varied sophistication and stringency, with varied outcomes, but predominantly suggesting that preoperative psychological interventions can help to reduce postopera-

tive distress. Several issues deserve particular mention. First, the provision of information must be considered as containing several components. Johnson (1984) summarizes her important distinction between the giving of information about the procedures involved in preparation for surgery and postsurgical care on the one hand, and information concerning the psychophysiological and cognitive reactions to the surgery which the individual might expect to experience, on the other hand. The clinician may need to check carefully with the individual patient which, if either, of these areas of information they would wish to acquire. The positive effect of providing such information occurs probably because it enables the patient to predict and understand events and experiences, even if not always actively to control them.

A number of studies have demonstrated that teaching patients preoperatively how to use psychophysiological relaxation training procedures, or to successfully distract themselves from worries concerning their surgery, may significantly improve postoperative psychological response. Anderson and Masur (1983) review outcome studies involving these various interventions and several smaller subdivisions of them. Schultheis, Peterson and Selby (1987) take the next important step by reviewing the interaction between these intervention procedures and the personal characteristics of patients. They demonstrate a number of interesting interactions, particularly, as outlined earlier in this chapter, with coping styles. One conclusion of this work is that clinical and organizational planning of surgical services should provide opportunities for individuals to obtain information and/or advice, both before and after surgery, but should not 'force' these in blanket fashion at all individuals. Organizational changes will be necessary to provide information when patients wish for it and can best use it (pre- or postoperative), from the individuals whom they consider the best source of information (surgeon, GP, nurse, fellow patients), and in the most appropriate modality (written, verbal, audiovisual, computerized self-teaching).

Important steps in this direction are being made, initially in the US health care system, via the development of an interactive video system to which patients have access before making the decision as to whether or not to proceed with prostate surgery. A pilot project in Denver involving 250 patients saw the rate of uptake of surgery drop by 44% during the first year of availability of this system (MacLachlan, 1992). Data on clinical outcomes and subsequent patient satisfaction with the surgical care process will be fascinating. An evaluation of this system in a number of UK health care settings is now under way, with reference both to prostate surgery and to other health care topics (Darkins, 1992, personal communication).

Issues of cost-effectiveness can also be examined by addressing these questions. Young and Humphrey (1985) demonstrated that a booklet providing written information about the cognitive control of anxiety in women about to undergo hysterectomy was equally psychologically effective but more cost-effective than the oral provision of such information, and significantly more successful than a standard preparation not involving this information. In similar vein, Kincey and McFarlane (1984) reported that detailed verbal discussion with posthysterectomy patients several days after surgery did not produce significant improvements in consumer satisfaction or relevant knowledge, when compared with a control group receiving standard reassurance about operative success. However, the same group of researchers were able to demonstrate that preoperative written information produced significant increases in satisfaction with communications and knowledge, compared with patients in a control group not receiving this intervention (Redman *et al.* 1986).

Another possible organizational strategy is the regular screening for psychological or psychiatric problems of individuals wishing to undergo or having undergone surgery. This would almost certainly produce evidence of considerably more psychopathology than is currently recognized by clinicians. The problem would remain of how to identify which distress was caused by surgery, as distinct from the illness or injury for which surgery was recommended, and which was caused by other extraneous factors. The ethical and practical question of how to deal with such an increase in identified psychological morbidity would also have to be confronted.

Model for the psychological care of surgical patients

Based on the concepts and data referred to above, the following is a simple model suggested for the psychological care of surgical patients. It is based around a series of issues which involved clinicians might usefully consider at each of three stages during the process of surgical care, namely, the preoperative period, the immediate postoperative inpatient period and the longer-term postoperative recovery stage. This model has most relevance to the situation in which there is some advance warning of the need for surgery. In the situation in which emergency surgery is required, the preoperative period is clearly truncated or even non-existent. The general postoperative principles still apply however, and may be particularly important for the psychological care of relatives where there is a high risk of patient mortality.

Preoperative stage

1. In the situation involving planned potential surgery, it may be the GP or the surgical team who first raises the possibility. At this

initial stage it should be recognized that the cognitive and emotional reactions of individuals will vary considerably. It should also be acknowledged that high levels of anxiety, engendered by possible psychological threat to self or body, may interfere with the capacity to understand and remember, or make decisions about, relevant information. The extent to which surgery is considered 'essential' rather 'optional' by the clinical team involved needs to be clarified with the patient. Distinctions between surgery aimed at improving physical functioning, reducing chronic pain or increasing life expectancy may differentially affect the reactions of the individual. However, the likely 'multidimensional' psychological nature of surgery needs to be recognized.

2. Some check on the level of the patient's knowledge and understanding of the proposed surgery should be made. This may reveal either gaps in knowledge or active misconceptions by the patient. The latter should probably be explored and corrected, but care should be taken to assess how much the patient wishes to know at this point, particularly about the procedural details.

3. There should be an acknowledgement that most patients experience anticipatory anxiety before surgery, whether this is objectively 'minor' or major'. This anxiety may be partly, although not entirely, reduced by acknowledging that unpredictability tends to increase perceived stress and subsequent anxiety. Recognition that a long waiting period, followed perhaps by short notice of availability of a surgical bed, may lead to approach-avoidance thinking by the patient, may help the individual to cope with this phenomenon. Clarification of whether surgery will be solely exploratory, specifically as a treatment intervention or possibly both, depending upon findings, increases uncertainty in one sense but may also prepare the individual for the various outcomes of surgery.

4. The clinician should recognize that discussions about risk involve both objective and subjective probabilities from the patient's perspective, and that communication in this field is fraught with psychological complexity. The clinician's use of verbal probability expressions may convey to the patient very different probability values from those the clinician intended. This issue is very effectively explored by O'Brien (1986). Not only the probabilities, but also the relative values of various outcomes for the individual patient, should be carefully considered. The values attached to different health states by the individual patient should be incorporated into clinical thinking, as they are now being incorporated into health service planning at the organizational level. Comparisons of methodologies, as illustrated by Buxton, Ashby and O'Hanlon (1986), should be developed for decision-making with individual patients.

5. The clinician should attempt to assess whether the individual's predominant coping style in the situation is based upon an 'approach' or an 'avoidance' strategy. Where individuals are actively seeking information or advice, they should be pointed in the right direction for this. This might involve detailed verbal discussion with a clinician and/or the provision of relevant written, audiovisual or computerized information. Where the individual tends to avoid issues which must be addressed, the clinician may need to prime or actively prompt the patient to consider these, possibly by initiating specific appointments. However, where information is optional the patient should know that it is available, but only at the point when he or she wishes for it. The extent to which the individual wishes to leave responsibility for information giving and clinical decision making

entirely with the clinician, or to retain maximum possible psychological responsibility, should be considered and used in joint decision making.

6. Where possible, preoperative admission information should not only give patients relevant factual information about hospital policy and self-preparation (e.g. restrictions on eating or drinking) prior to surgery, but also should prime patients to feel confident in asking questions about pre- and post-operative procedures on admission to hospital.

Postoperative hospitalization stage

1. In the immediate postoperative stage, after waking from general anaesthesia, simple verbal feedback confirming that the surgical procedure carried out was the one anticipated (provided that this was the case) may be important. Where surgery is undertaken using local anaesthesia, the clinician's comments should recognize that the patient's attention and thinking will be focused on what verbal comments are being made, and that these can easily be misconstrued.

2. Immediate postoperative nursing and medical care should recognize that the pattern of pain experience will vary considerably between patients undergoing the same objective surgical procedure, that some patients more than others will communicate this verbally or non-verbally, and that this may not correlate very highly with requests for analgesia. Ward staff should recognize that patients are assessing their own recovery in terms of comparisons with other patients whom they perceive as undergoing a similar process, and in terms of their own expectations of how rapidly they should recover after surgery. Correcting misconceptions and pointing out appropriate comparisons concerning progress may be very important.

3. Prior to discharge it is essential that relevant self-care information is given to the patient, in a comprehensible, behaviourally specific, and above all consistent way. It should be clear who is giving such information, and where information is given by or sought from several sources those sources should be mutually reinforcing. Where it is possible to be exact about when certain behaviours can be undertaken again (e.g. lifting, walking, sexual activity, driving) this should be stressed, but where exact timing is imposs- ible to predict, this should also be acknowledged. Patients should then be given a definite prompt to re-enquire at follow-up.

Post discharge stage

1. It should be considered essential to build in some assessment of psychological progress as well as physical progress at postoperative review. This psychological review may be undertaken either by the surgeon, if time permits, or by the GP. One possible approach is for the individual to clarify with the GP after surgery which questions, if any, need further discussion with the surgeon at the subsequent hospital outpatient clinic. This process is probably equally important in both 'minor' and 'major' surgery, in order to maximize rate of return to appropriate activities while minimizing the risks of complications caused by inappropriate postoperative activity.

2. Following major surgery, with its possible implications of uncertainty of prognosis, loss of physical function or negative effects on body image, psychosexual functioning or self-concept, the clinician should be prepared to look for significant instances of anger, depression, anxiety or even hopelessness, while recognizing that the time at which these phenomena become salient may vary considerably. The message should be

given that such phenomena are 'allowable' and valid, and that help can be sought.

3. At this point the opinion of specialist services and/or of relevant lay support groups should be considered, but again not forced upon the individual. Where the individual is uncertain about whether to pursue such help, effective initial contact may often be best made in the primary care setting which is well known to the individual, or via someone already known to the person concerned. Exploratory discussions about types of help without initially implying subsequent commitment, may be necessary. Subsequent involvement may then be easier and will frequently need to involve other key family members, either as therapeutic agents themselves or to help them to cope with the psychological effects on relationships produced by the response of the patient to surgery. In the situation where repeated surgery may be necessary, continuity of such support may be important and enhanced by direct links with the surgical team in the hospital.

There is an important distinction between the application of psychological principles in the surgical health care setting and the roles the psychologist can usefully fulfil in working directly with patients, surgeons or others in this situation. Many of the recommendations outlined in the above model can and should be undertaken by the non-psychologist team members involved in patient care. However, there may be specific instances, at each of the three stages outlined above, in which direct referral of an individual patient to the psychologist may be of value.

Referral to specialist psychologists

In the preoperative stage this may be necessary where an individual defined as needing surgery has such a high level of anxiety and behav-

ioural avoidance that he or she does not feel able to accept and cope with the proposed hospital admission. This may seem to the GP or surgeon to be a 'phobic' reaction, out of proportion to the objective risk in the situation, and it may indeed share some of the characteristics of phobic responses. Whether the reaction seems disproportionate or objectively understandable, it may be helped by the use of cognitive and behavioural techniques to familiarize the patient with the relevant hospital setting and to teach anxiety management techniques, perhaps using appropriate combinations of cognitive distraction, physical relaxation and habituation training. The health psychologist may usefully act as the 'bridge' between the community and the hospital setting in this treatment approach (Kincey, 1988). A second variant of this situation might involve referral to the psychologist at the preoperative stage, to help the individual understand and use psychological decision making approaches to clarify whether he or she wishes to pursue elective surgery. The use of such models might help the patient to make a clearer, more confident and committed decision, and perhaps, therefore, to cope more effectively with mixed negative and positive surgical outcomes.

In the immediate postsurgical stage referral to the psychologist may be appropriate on occasions where the patient's psychological recovery does not appear to be progressing as expected and where psychological factors appear to be interfering with physical recovery. Opinion and possible psychological intervention concerning mood or pain management may be useful. These situations will typically necessitate a careful cognitive–behavioural analysis of the individual's coping strategies and information needs.

In the postdischarge stage, the use of appropriate behavioural target setting and cognitive therapy approaches to improve the self-perception of the patient who is making slow progress may help to reduce subjective distress, increase recovery rate and reduce the demands on other aspects of the health care system. Other problems relating to interpersonal, sexual or occupational issues may also be identified and helped by these approaches, either alone or, on occasions, in conjunction with psychiatric pharmacological advice or social case work approaches.

Another contribution of the psychologist will be at the broader organizational level, where a surgical team or unit may request a psychological opinion in analysing systems of service provision. Here the psychologist would be helping to analyse the psychological needs of patients for information, the optimal timing, modality and sources to provide these, and possibly working with other staff to improve the monitoring of psychological reactions to surgery, the detection of significant difficulties, and the decision making as to whether or not to refer individuals for specialist psychological opinion. Outcome criteria to assess such interventions can include those outlined at the beginning of this chapter, in order to evaluate not only clinical changes but also consumer views and economic factors in the service, thereby addressing two of the major considerations identified by Griffiths (1983). These criteria, and the relationships between them, should now be central to the development of audit and quality assurance systems concerning surgical as well as all other health care provision.

References

Anderson, K.O. and Masur, F.T. (1983) Psychological preparation for invasive medical and dental procedures. *Journal of Behavioural Medicine*, 6(1), 1–41.

Andrew, J.M. (1970) Recovery from surgery, with and without preparatory instruction for three coping styles. *Journal of Personality and Social Psychology*, 15, 223–6.

Andrew, J.M. (1972) Delay of surgery. *Psychosomatic Medicine*, 34(4), 345–54.

Bardsley M. and Coles J. (1992) Practical experiences in auditing patient outcomes. *Quality in Health Care*, 1, 124–30.

Boeke S., Duivenvoorden H, Verhage, F. and Zwaveling, A. (1991) Prediction of post-operative pain and duration of hospitalisation using two anxiety measures. *Pain*, 45, 293–7.

Boeke, S., Jelicic, M. and Bouke, B. (1992) Pre-operative anxiety variables as possible predictors of postoperative stay in hospital. B*ritish Journal of Clinical Psychology*, 31, 366–8.

Buxton, H., Ashby, J. and O'Hanlon, M. (1986) *Valuation of Health States Using the Time-Trade-off Approach: Report of a Pilot Study Relating to Health States One Year After Treatment for Breast Cancer.* Health Economics Research Group, Brunel University.

Byrne, D. (1961) The repression–sensitisation scale: rationale, reliability and validity. *Journal of Personality*, 29, 334–49.

Eysenck, H.J. and Eysenck, S.B.G. (1986) *Manual of the Eysenck Personality Inventory*, Educational and Industrial Testing Service, San Diego, California.

Funch, D.P. and Mettlin, C. (1982) The role of support in relation to recovery from breast surgery. *Social Science and Medicine*, 16, 91–8.

Gath, D. (1980) Psychiatric aspects of hysterectomy, in *The Social Consequences of Psychiatric Illness*, (eds L. Robins, P. Clayton and J. Wing), Brunner/Mazel, New York, pp. 33–45.

Gil, K.M. (1984) Coping effectively with invasive medical procedures: a descriptive model. *Clinical Psychology Review*, 4, 339–62.

Griffiths, F.R. (1983) *NHS Management Inquiry Report*, DHSS, London.

Haywood, J. (1975) *Information – A Prescription Against Pain*, The Study of Nursing Care Project Reports, Series 2, No. 2, No. 5, Royal College of Nursing, London.

Johnson, J.E. (1984) Psychological interventions and coping with surgery, in *Handbook of Psychology and Health, vol. 4, Social Psychological Aspects of Health* (Eds A. Baum, S. Taylor and J. Singer), Lawrence Earlbaum Associates, Hillsdale, New Jersey, pp. 167–87.

Johnson, J.E., Leventhal, H. and Dabbs, J.M. (1971) Contributions of emotional and instrumental response processes in adaptation to surgery. *Journal of Personality and Social Psychology*, 20 (55), 64.

Johnson, J.E., Rice, V.H., Fuller, S.S. and Endress, M.P. (1978) Sensory information, instruction in a coping strategy and recovery from surgery. *Research in Nursing and Health*, 1, 4–17.

Johnston, M. (1980) Anxiety in surgical patients. *Psychological Medicine*, 10, 145–52.

Kendall, P.C. and Watson, D. (1981) Psychological preparation for stressful medical procedures, in *Medical Psychology: Contributions to Behavioural Medicine*, (eds C.K. Prokop and L.A. Bradley), Academic Press, New York, pp. 198–223.

Kincey J. (1988) A case of anxiety management in a general hospital surgical setting, in *Clinical Psychology in Action*, (eds J. West and P. Spinks), John Wright and Sons, Bristol, pp. 206–10.

Kincey, J. and Benjamin, S. (1984) Desynchrony following the treatment of pain behaviour. *Behaviour Research and Therapy*, 22(1), 85–6.

Kincey J. and McFarlane, T. (1984) Psychological aspects of hysterectomy, in *Psychology and Gynaecological Problems*, (eds A.K. Broome and L.M. Wallace), Tavistock Publications, London, pp. 142–61.

Kincey, J. and Saltmore, S. (1990) Stress and surgical treatments, in *Stress and Medical Procedures*, (eds M. Johnston and L. Wallace), Oxford University Press, Oxford, pp. 120–37.

Krantz, D., Arabian, J., Davia, J. and Parker, J.S. (1982) Type A behaviour and coronary artery bypass surgery: intraoperative blood pressure and perioperative complications. *Psychosomatic Medicine*, 44(3), 273–84.

Levesque, L. and Charlebois, M. (1977) Anxiety, locus of control and the effect of pre-operative teaching on patients' physical and emotional state. *Nursing Papers*, 8, 11–26.

Ley, P. (1977) Psychological studies of doctor–patient communication, in *Contributions to Medical Psychology*, vol. 1, (ed S. Rachman), Pergamon Press, Oxford, pp. 9–41.

Ley P. (1988) *Communicating with Patients: Improving Communication, Satisfaction and Compliance*, Croom Helm, London.

MacLachlan R. (1992) Out and art success? Would outcomes management make doctors accountable to patients and purchasers? *Health Service Journal*, 19 November, 26–27.

Maguire, P. (1985) Psychological morbidity associated with cancer and cancer treatment. *Clinics in Oncology*, 4(3), 559–75.

Manyande, A., Chayen, S., Priyakumar, *et al.* (1992) Anxiety and endocrine responses to surgery: paradoxical effects of preventative relaxation training. *Psychosomatic Medicine*, 54, 225–87.

Mathews, A. and Ridgeway, V. (1981) Personality and surgical recovery: a review. *British Journal of Clinical Psychology*, 20, 243–60.

Mathews, A. and Ridgeway, V. (1984) Psychological preparation for surgery, in *Health Care and Human Behaviour*, (eds A. Steptoe and A. Mathews), Academic Press, London, pp. 231–59.

Melamed, B. (1977) Psychological Preparation for hospitalisation, in *Contributions to Medical Psychology*, vol. 1, (ed S. Rachman), Pergamon Press, Oxford, pp. 43–74.

Miller S.M. (1987) Monitoring and blunting: validation of a questionnaire to assess styles of information

seeking under threat. *Journal of Personality and Social Psychology*, 52, 345–53.

Morris, T., Greer, S.H. and White, P. (1977) Psychological and social adjustment to mastectomy. *Cancer*, 40, 2381–7.

Mumford, E., Schlesinger, H.J. and Glass, G.V. (1982) The effects of psychological intervention of recovery from surgery and hearty attacks: an analysis of the literature. *American Journal of Public Health*, 72, 141–51.

O'Boyle, C., McGee, H., Hickey, A. *et al.* (1992) Individual quality of life in patients undergoing hip replacement. *Lancet*, 339, 1088–91.

O'Brien, B./Office of Health Economics (1986) *What Are My Chances Doctor? A Review of Clinical Risks*, Health Economics Research Group, Brunel University.

Philips, B.U. and Bee, D.E. (1980) Determinants of post-operative recovery in elective orthopaedic surgery. *Social Science and Medicine*, 14, 325–30.

Rachman, S. and Hodgson, R. (1974) Synchrony and desynchrony in fear and avoidance. *Behaviour Research and Therapy*, 12, 311–18.

Ray, C. (1982) The surgical patient: psychological stress and coping resources, in *Social Psychology and Behavioural Medicine*, (ed J.R. Eiser), John Wiley and Sons, Chichester, pp. 483–508.

Ray, C. and Fitzgibbon, C. (1979) The socially mediated reduction of stress in surgical patients, in *Research in Psychology and Medicine*, vol. 2, (eds D.J. Osborne, M.M. Gruneberg and J.R. Eiser), Academic Press, London, pp. 321–7.

Redman, C., McFarlane, T., Cottrell, D. and Kincey, J. (1986) Improving communication between doctors and patients having a hysterectomy. *Journal of Obstetrics and Gynaecology*, 6, 275–6.

Rotter, J.B. (1966) Generalised expectances for internal versus external control of reinforcement. *Psychological Monographs*, 80 (1, Whole no. 609).

Salmon P. (1992) Psychological factors in surgical stress: implications for management. *Clinical Psychology Review*, 12, 681–704.

Schultheis, K., Peterson, L. and Selby, V. (1987) Preparation for stressful medical procedures and person–treatment interactions. *Clinical Psychology Review*, 7, 329–52

Steptoe, A. and O'Sullivan, J. (1986) Monitoring and blunting coping styles in women prior to surgery. *British Journal of Clinical Psychology*, 25, 143–4.

Wallace, L.M. (1984) Psychological preparation for gynaecological surgery, in *Psychology and Gynaecological Problems*, (eds A.K. Broome and L.M. Wallace), Tavistock Publications, London, pp. 162–88.

Wallace, L.M. (1986) Pre-operative state anxiety as a mediator of psychological adjustment to and recovery from surgery. *British Journal of Medical Psychology*, **59**, 253–61.

Wallace, L.M. (1987) Trait anxiety as a predictor of adjustment to and recovery from surgery. *British Journal of Clinical Psychology*, **26**, 73–4.

Wallston, B.S., Wallston, K.A.Kaplan, G.D. and Mades, S.A. (1976) Development and validation of the health locus of control scale. *Journal of Consulting and Clinical Psychology*, **44**, 580–5.

Williams, J.L., Jones, J.R., Workhoven, M.N. and Williams, B. (1975) The psychological control of pre-operative anxiety. *Psychophysiology*, **12**(1), 50–4.

Wilson, J.F. (1981) Behavioural preparation for surgery: benefit or harm? *Journal of Behavioural Medicine*, **4**, 79–102.

Wilson-Barnett, J. (1984) Interventions to alleviate patients' stress: a review. *Journal of Psychosomatic Research*, **28** (1), 63–72.

Wise, T.N., Hall, W.A. and Wong, O. (1978) The relationship of cognitive styles and affective status to post-operative analgesic utilisation. *Journal of Psychosomatic Research*, **22**, 513–18.

Young, L. and Humphrey, M. (1985) Cognitive methods of preparing women for hysterectomy: does a booklet help? *British Journal of Clinical Psychology*, **24**, 303–4.

Chapter twenty three

Terminal care

Christine Wilson

Introduction

This chapter will review what the author considers to be the most relevant and helpful literature on the psychological reactions of the terminally ill to impending death, the management of their emotional responses, the psychological management of distressing emotional, behavioural and physical symptoms in the terminally ill, and psychotherapeutic interventions intended to ease the individual through the dying process.

In recent years there has been a tremendous growth of literature focusing on the individual's reaction to diagnosis of a fatal illness, and dealing with such treatments as radiotherapy and chemotherapy. The following will be concerned with people who have reached the stage in their illness when it is realized that they will not recover. The focus is particularly on the terminally ill cancer patient, where dying is often a gradual process. There is a wealth of relevant literature, although some of it is humanistic, descriptive and anecdotal in nature. Recently there have been more systematic studies, which have helped to pinpoint a particular place for psychological skills (Spiegel *et al.*, 1989, Black and Morrow, 1991). However, most importantly, the needs of the terminally ill are multifaceted and are best met by many different caring groups working together.

Psychological reactions to impending death

Do people want to know if they are dying?

Many studies have indicated that the terminally ill and people in general desire knowledge of their own impending deaths, although such information is not always forthcoming. In a study of 434 members of the general public, Kalish and Reynolds (1976) reported that 55% of the whole group thought that someone should be told if they were dying. Younger people put forward this view more often than older subjects in the study. More that 70% of the group also said that they personally would like to be told if they were dying. Studies of the terminally ill show that they too would like to know their fate. Crammond (1970) reported that 80% of dying patients know that they are dying, and would wish to talk about it. Annas (1974) gave similar findings, reporting that 90% of patients wanted to know they were dying, but 60–90% of physicians questioned telling them. Further, it is not only the communication of information between the doctor and the patient that is important, but also the way in which the information is given (Payne, 1991). Terminally ill cancer patients receiving information about their prognosis from doctors in one study (Miller, 1987) felt uncomfortable about asking questions, and described the doctors involved as abrupt and lacking in empathy. In another study (Lock, 1990), patients complained not about the information that they were given but rather that doctors failed to communicate to them that they cared about them. Finally, Slevin (1992), in a study by Maguire and Faulkner (1988), observed that when breaking news to a patient it was most important to convey to the patient a sense of control over the situation and the continuance of hope.

Any reluctance among carers to acknowledge the patient's impending death may interfere with the patient's awareness of this fact. Glaser and Strauss (1966) reported different levels of patient awareness, depending on the willingness of carers to inform patients. These workers describe closed awareness, in which the patient is suspicious, enquiring but never informed; mutual pretence, where staff and patient both know but do not openly acknowledge it; and finally, open awareness, when both staff and patients know and acknowledge impending death. Other research findings indicate that people may well be aware that they are dying, despite lack of open expression of this information, and not surprisingly, as the terminal illness progresses, more people show open awareness. Cartwright, Hockey and Anderson (1973), interviewing cancer patients within a year before their deaths, found that 47% of the groups had some awareness that they would not recover from their present illness. Hinton (1963), reviewing groups of terminally ill patients referred for psychiatric consultation, reported at the first interview that 49% believed they were dying. As death approached, 75% of the group eventually expressed this idea. Further, Kubler-Ross (1970) found that only three out of 200 patients she studied did not acknowledge that they were dying.

Levels of awareness of approaching death will vary among the terminally ill, according to the patient's willingness to accept or deny the situation. Such willingness will be related to the particular circumstances of the individual's illness and personality factors. Saunders (1966) reported that terminally ill patients in her care were likely to enquire more that once about their own deaths, with varying levels of acceptance of the idea.

Acceptance of death can be a problem for the carers of the terminally ill. In our culture death is viewed as failure by many health professionals: the health care system is geared up to do battle with death, and death is considered a fearful and frightening experience.

Many doctors and nurses find it difficult to talk to dying patients: antidepressants and tranquillizers are often prescribed to deal with the emotional response to dying. It is still not acceptable to place emphasis on dying, choosing and achieving the sort of death that one wants (Pietroni, 1991). Also, people vary in the way they might try to cope with impending death. Some just try to deny the threat, but others may try and obtain as much knowledge as possible about their illness, in order to maintain some control over the situation (Hinton, 1984). In addition, it is worth pointing out that very few people absolutely accept or deny their own deaths. They are in an ambivalent state, moving between acceptance and denial. Throughout the dying process, individuals will deny the reality of their situation from time to time, as it is only natural that people do not want to think about their own deaths all the time (Schneidman, 1978).

Models of psychological reactions to knowledge of personal death

Many different models have been proposed to explain how dying people's awareness and acceptance of their impending death change during the course of a terminal illness. The best known model is that propounded by Kubler-Ross (1970), whose theory was based on observations of over 200 terminally ill people, and put forward the idea that the dying person progresses in awareness through a particular pattern of emotional responses as the illness progresses. Initially, Kubler-Ross states, the individual experiences shock and numbness, then passes through a stage of denying the situation and feeling isolated, then becomes angry about what is happening. After this, individuals will attempt to bargain for goals they wish to achieve before death overtakes them.

Eventually, the person comes to some acceptance of impending death. During this progress through the stages of gradual awareness the individual maintains hope that death is not a certainty. Further, Kubler-Ross did not regard these stages as discrete, nor propose that they should occur in the order in which they are set out here, and she observed that people move backwards and forwards between these stages. However, the idea of discrete stages is the main point on which the model has been criticized. Hinton (1984) indicated that individuals fluctuate to the fro in their reactions to impending death, and Schneidman (1978) commented that dying individuals experience a wide range of emotions, which appear and reappear, and rejects the idea that many people reach the stage of acceptance described by Kubler-Ross.

In contrast, Garfield (1978) suggested that Kubler-Ross's approach could be helpful if dying people could use progress through the stage model to complete unfinished business, and recognize aspects of their lives as fulfilled and successful. Kastenbaum (1975) points out that Kubler-Ross's model does not take sufficient account of the nature of various diseases, sex and age differences, cultural background and many other personal variables. Further, there is very little actual systematic clinical research to substantiate the model. In one attempt at verification, Shultz and Aderman (1974) could find only depression to be uniformly present in the dying. Other workers have also put forward the idea that there may be stages through which the dying person progresses. For example, Crammond (1970) described stages of fear of death, followed by depression about loss of life. He also talked about the person becoming angry about the illness, and the use of denial and regression as defence mechanisms.

At the present time, it is generally agreed that the dying person often experiences the emotional responses described by Kubler-Ross and others, but the list is not exhaustive, nor is every element necessary. Further, dying people's response to their own death is not unique: it is thought to be similar to that experienced when the individual is under threat of loss of any kind (Holland, 1977). In addition, many researchers have related dying people's response to death to their response to past experiences (Crammond, 1970; Hinton, 1976, 1984; Schniedman, 1978). Thus, depending on the individual's past experience of stress and the circumstances of the terminal illness, one could expect a whole range of emotional responses and coping strategies from the dying individual. Some struggle and fight, others are passive and accepting, some cling to independence, others take to their beds, give up and become depressed, and some achieve a more positive acceptance of their situation (Hinton, 1984). Kalish (1978) doubts that such a model is helpful to the dying, and sees it rather as manufactured to give a framework for carers of the dying.

Incidence of psychological disturbance in the terminally ill

Given the well documented, if anecdotal, reports of dying people's gradual awareness of their predicament, it is worth giving attention to evidence of clinical levels of psychological disturbance in the terminally ill, and also some consideration of means to help individuals deal with this emotional disturbance.

A substantial weight of evidence demonstrates that individuals suffer from high levels of anxiety and depression before they reach the terminal phase of their illness. Some studies suggest that treatments such as radiotherapy and chemotherapy, which often precede the terminal phase, actually cause this emotional disturbance. For example, Peck and Boland (1977) reported a higher incidence of anxiety and depression in 50 patients following radiotherapy than with pretreatment measures. Forester, Kornfeld and Fleiss (1978), looking at anxiety and depression levels among 200 patients receiving radiotherapy, also found high levels of anxiety and depression, although these were lower that those found in psychiatric inpatients. Greer (1984), studying the effects of cancer treatment on the quality of patients' lives, found it to be the main source of emotional disturbance. Palmer *et al.* (1980) looked at the impact of chemotherapy on cancer patients, and found not only physical side-effects but also severe anxiety, depression and sexual difficulties. Finally, Morris (1979) reported that 25–33% of women having a simple mastectomy were still experiencing problems a year later, including sexual and relationship problems, disrupted working lives and depression. Although all these studies indicate psychological disturbance associated with treatment and its impact, some would dispute this. Weisman (1976), investigating 163 new patients with cancer, found emotional distress to be more related to situational factors, such as home support and other stresses, rather than the illness. One would assume that the terminally ill would show higher levels of anxiety and depression than those at an earlier stage in their illness; however, Silberfarb, Maurer and Crowthamel (1980), investigating 146 breast cancer patients through the course of their illness and treatment, reported that those at the first recurrence of their illness were more anxious and depressed than the terminally ill patients studied.

Hinton (1972) compared a group of 50 terminally ill patients referred for psychological problems to 50 terminally ill patients not referred for psychiatric help, and found that only two of the latter group were psychiatrically anxious or depressed. This suggests differences in the way individuals respond to terminal illness, and several workers have put forward reasons for these apparent differences. Hinton (1972) suggested that people respond to terminal illness in the way that mirrors their response to previous stresses: in fact, five of the depressed people in his referred group had received psychiatric treatment for depression before their terminal illness. Holland (1977) also made a similar point about patients with a previous psychiatric history.

Nevertheless, many studies have reported high levels of depression among the terminally ill. Rees (1972), looking at those cared for in the community and in hospital, found that 40% of the community group were depressed, 26% to a moderate or severe degree. Out of the latter group of 50, six expressed a wish to die. Seagar and Flood (1965) reviewed cases of self-poisoning and found a certain proportion of the group already suffering from terminal illness. In a hospital-based study (Hinton, 1963), 17% of the terminally ill were judged as depressed by nurses and 28% admitted depression.

Anxiety is also a commonly found reaction among the terminally ill. In Rees' study, 13 of his 15 community patients were anxious, and in the hospital group 26 out of 50 were anxious. In Hinton's (1984) study 13% of hospitalized patients showed observable anxiety. Frequently, anxiety and depression are both present in the terminally ill (Hinton, 1976). Further, the longer the illness the greater degree of emotional disturbance to be expected (Hinton, 1984).

More recently, it has been shown that it is not necessarily the direct effect of treatment but rather the impact of that treatment and the illness on the individual that is of greatest importance. Slevin (1992) showed that more intensive therapy did not necessarily lead to reduced quality of life. For example, the side-effects of therapy may be less important to the individual than the fact that therapy may control the course of the disease. Increasingly, the term 'quality of life' has been introduced to the relevant literature. This term represents what the illness means in individual terms to a particular person, and encompasses psychological, social, occupational and physical aspects (Fallowfield, 1991). There have been a number of new questionnaires and checklists introduced in order to measure quality of life for the seriously ill person. Among the most commonly used is the Rotterdam Symptom Checklist (de Haes, Van Knipperham and Neijt, 1990), which has 30 items, each measured on a four-point scale. Another measure frequently used in relevant studies is the PAIS scale assessing the patient's psychosocial adjustment to medical illness (Morrow, Chiarello and Derogatis, 1978). This scale has seven domains of psychosocial adjustment, again using a four-point scale.

Also of relevance here is the issue of awareness of psychological morbidity among the terminally ill. Some workers have drawn attention to the fact that the incidence of psychological problems may be underestimated (Maguire, 1985). Maguire (1984) found that 25% of cancer patients had psychiatric difficulties but only 10% of these were recognized and treated by their GPS. GPS assumed that patients would let them know about their emotional difficulties, and did not see that they had much to offer their patients, and patients did not disclose their difficulties because their doctor was busy and they did not know what the doctor could do to help them.

Watson (1988) also thought that psychological morbidity among cancer patients was underestimated, and put the incidence as high as 89%. She advocated specialist training for nurses to identify these problems and to look for 'at-risk' individuals in order to prevent psychological disturbance occurring. She listed 11 'at-risk' categories, including diagnosis of cancers associated with visible deformities, and lack of support from family and friends. Maguire (1984) also suggested the use of specially trained doctors or nurses to help identify those at risk and those already suffering from psychological disturbance associated with serious illness. This has led to the development of two further measurement tools to limit the necessity for specially trained staff. These measures are the Hospital Anxiety and Depression Scale (HADS), which was developed specifically for use with medical patients: it largely excludes somatic features and is easy to score; and the Mental Adjustment to Cancer (MAC) scale, which assesses feelings of helplessness or positive fighting spirit towards the disease (Zigmond and Snaith, 1983, Watson et al., 1988).

Psychological interventions to treat anxiety and depression

Hinton (1984) proposed that symptoms such as anxiety can be relieved by dealing with their source, and warned against preoccupation with symptoms in isolation. He emphasized the need to relate these to the individual's circumstances. Holland (1977) proposed drug control of psychiatric symptoms caused by terminal illness, and Plumb and Holland (1977) suggested psychiatric referral to deal with emotional disturbance in the terminally ill.

Hinton (1972), in his work with 50 terminally ill patients referred for psychiatric help, found that 31 of the group were helped by psychotropic medication, and he reported that after two to three psychiatric interviews, 21 were not improved, 12 were slightly improved and 17 definitely improved. Hinton (1972) also recommended psychotherapeutic intervention, and consideration of this approach will be detailed below.

Physical symptoms in the terminally ill

Obviously, the kind of physical symptoms experienced depends partly on the disease process and partly on how well the illness is managed. Cartwright, Hockey and Anderson (1973) reported the following symptoms among cancer sufferers in their study: in the last year of life, 42% suffered pain to a very distressing degree: 28% had breathing difficulties, 17% vomiting and 17% sleeplessness, 12% had loss of bowel and bladder control, 11% loss of appetite, 10% mental confusion, 10% had no symptoms and 5% had symptoms only in the last month. It is difficult to judge how many also suffered symptoms they did not report, perhaps because they did not realize that they could be relieved (Hinton, 1984). Even when patients received help from a home visiting service attached to a hospice, over 20% still suffered unrelieved pain and breathlessness (Parkes, 1980). Cartwright, Hockey and Anderson (1973) also reported behavioural changes in their study, which could be the result of physical or emotional effects of the illness. They found that two-thirds of the dying people in their study restricted their activities in their last 3 months of life, 20% were confined to bed, many more stayed inside the house and needed help with basic tasks of washing, dressing and toileting.

More recent studies have shown that physical weakness is a large problem for the terminally ill (Wilkes, 1985). Also of relevance here is the development of quality of life measures such as PAIS and the Rotterdam Symptom Checklist, which are able to highlight particular physical symptoms for the individual.

Holland (1977) commented on confusional states which resulted from the physical disease process in the terminally ill. These included confusion, delirium, mental disturbance, personality change and psychotic symptoms. Hinton (1976) noted similar symptoms resulting from disease processes and the effects of drugs. However, a good proportion of the terminally ill remain alert even in the last days of their illness. Rees (1972) reported that 20% of patients at home were alert on the last day of life, and Cartwright, Hockey and Anderson (1973) reported obvious confusion in only 36% of their group.

Pain management

Twycross (1975) reported that 40% of the terminally ill suffered severe pain, 10% less intense pain and 50% no real pain or discomfort. Such pain is usually chronic and constant, although it may vary in intensity. Twycross pointed out that it is important to deal with the meaning of pain for the patient, and to separate physical from psychological aspects of pain. Twycross recommends pain control with 4-hourly medication to prevent pain re-emerging. Woodford and Fielding (1970) also emphasized the psychological aspects of pain experienced by the terminally ill, and noted that patients referred to their clinic for pain control were more psychologically disturbed than patients not referred. Weisman (1972) suggested that pain in terminal illness is often difficult to tolerate because it is meaningless and unrelenting.

However, most of the work concerning psychological techniques for pain control with the terminally ill focuses on pain sensation and its management. Melzack and Perry (1975) looked at the effectiveness of biofeedback and hypnotic training in 24 patients with chronic pain, including those with terminal cancer. They found the most effective treatment to be a combined procedure, although pain relief was only achieved during the actual training. Fotopoulos, Graham and Cook (1979) attempted biofeedback training with seven cancer patients. They achieved a significant reduction in pain level ratings in four; however, only two subjects were able to generalize this pain relief to their own environment.

Finer (1979) taught hypnosis to achieve pain reduction in groups of terminally ill cancer patients. Once patients had practised in groups they were each given a tape and encouraged to practise at any time. Finer reported that sleeping patterns and appetite were improved by this training, and patients became more active and independent. Barber (1980) also reported successful alleviation of cancer pain using self-hypnosis with three individuals.

A different approach to pain control was taken by Turk and Rennert (1981), who taught patients new patterns of thinking to enable them to take control of their situation. In their treatment patients were given a multidimensional concept of pain, involving affective, cognitive and sensory elements. Patients were asked to describe their feelings when they experienced pain and to monitor these feelings. They were then taught a variety of coping skills, such as relaxation, attention diversion and the use of imagery. Patients were then asked to practise these skills. Unfortunately, the effectiveness of the treatment in controlling pain for terminally ill cancer patients was not reported. (See Chapter 20 for a fuller discussion of general pain management.)

Management of other symptoms

There is little information on the use of psychological techniques in the management of other symptoms experienced by the terminally ill. However, it is possible that some of the approaches used to control symptoms related to cancer treatment, such as nausea and vomiting, may also be helpful in the terminally ill. Morrow and Morrell (1982) reported the successful use of systematic desensitization to control conditioned anticipatory nausea in 60 chemotherapy patients, compared to counselling alone for this problem. Burish and Lyles (1981) also had success with 16 chemotherapy patients suffering from conditioned nausea, reducing signs of arousal measured by blood pressure and pulse rates, and vomiting rates, by using progressive muscle relaxation and guided relaxing imagery. Many more systematic and larger studies of behaviour therapies to control nausea and vomiting have recently taken place. It has also to be noted that new drugs have now been introduced which are more effective at controlling the side-effects of chemotherapy. Black and Morrow (1991) conducted a review of 34 studies using such techniques as progressive muscle relaxation, systematic desensitization, hypnosis, stress inoculation training, biofeedback and relaxation and cognitive diversion. They concluded that there was no systematic evidence in favour of these techniques; it was rather that different techniques worked for different individuals, just as there are individual differences in reactions to chemotherapy.

Management of sick role behaviour

Much work has been done in the management of sick role behaviour for those with chronic pain problems, particularly low back pain (Fordyce, 1976); although there is little research into the use of this approach with the terminally ill, there is some indication that it may be helpful for this group. Hinton (1972) and Stedeford (1980) both report sick role behaviour among the terminally ill. Stedeford in particular reports that the terminally ill may use sick role behaviour to gain attention, although this may make them unpopular with those caring for them. Stedeford suggested many people who responded in this way may not have received much care in the past, and reassurance that they are cared for can often reduce the problem.

Sobel (1981) carried out a study to help terminally ill patients to maintain daily activities. Patients initiated forms of activity and kept records of these. The object was to redirect the person to take part again and rediscover pleasure previously associated with engaging in such activities. An attempt was also made to restructure cognitions by making the patients aware of their negative thoughts and their effect on mood. Information was also given about the illness so that patients did not place the wrong construction on events. For instance, patients might inaccurately believe that the present illness was the consequence of some misconduct in the past. No data were supplied on the effectiveness of this approach.

Finally, a second study by Redd (1982) successfully controlled some sick role behaviour displayed by a 64-year-old terminally ill man, using behavioural techniques. The person was often crying, yelling and moaning, particularly in the presence of others, notably his family. Redd used 'time out', so that when crying behaviour began staff left the patient's room, returning when he stopped. If the patient was quiet staff would pay him attention. As a result the patient cried less and slept better.

Psychotherapeutic interventions

There has recently been a change in orientation in the psychotherapeutic supportive work carried out with the long-term cancer patient. People with cancer are now surviving longer because of improved treatments and emphasis is increasingly being placed on the quality of that remaining life as evidenced by the development of measures of quality of life (de Haes, Van Knippenham and Neijt, 1990; Morrow, Chiarello and Derogatis, 1978). Now more that ever it has become important to offer support for a longer lifespan, and to make sure that remaining life is as fulfilling as possible for the terminally ill person (Fallowfield, 1991). Fortunately there are now a number of large and systematic studies which have evaluated the usefulness of adjuvant psychological therapy for this group.

Group work

Some of the more systematic studies available are concerned with group therapy for termin-

ally ill individuals. In one well known study (Ferlic, Goldman and Kennedy, 1979), the value of a counselling programme for 30 patients was compared with the progress of 30 similar patients who did not receive counselling. Counselling groups met for 90 minutes three times a week for a total of six sessions. There were eight patients in each group and topics included individual adjustment to hospital and illness, staff-patient communication and patient knowledge of cancer. Compared to controls, counselling group members were helped because increased knowledge enabled them to take an active part in their treatment, gave them a sense of control and allowed them to live their remaining lives to the full.

In another study, Yalom and Greaves (1977) ran support groups for 4 years with patients with metastatic carcinoma. Pre-meeting training was given in meditation and hypnosis for pain control, and groups met once a week for 90 minutes, usually six or seven individuals at each meeting. Yalom and Greaves reported that patients were helped because the groups enabled them to support one another, and gave them the opportunity to express their needs and fears openly.

In a more systematic study, Spiegel, Bloom and Yalom (1981) looked at the effects of weekly supportive group meetings for women with metastatic carcinoma in a 1-year randomized prospective outcome study. The groups focused on the problems of terminal illness, including improving relationships with family and physicians and living as full a life as possible in the face of death; 86 patients were evaluated at 4-month intervals. The treatment groups had significantly lower mood disturbance scores on the Profile of Mood State Scale, fewer maladaptive coping strategies and fewer phobic symptoms than the control group. Recently, Spiegel was able to review this study at a 10-year follow-up (Spiegel et al., 1989). This showed that on average the treatment group survived twice as long (mean 6–36 months) as the control group (mean 9–18 months), demonstrating an effect for psychotherapeutic support in terms of longevity as well as increased quality of life.

Other recent studies include one by Moorey (1990), which offered adjuvant psychological therapy to 44 cancer patients referred for anxiety and depression. Treatment involved looked at the personal meaning to individuals of their illnesses, and looking at their resources to cope based on the Lazarus model (Lazarus, 1984), as well as fostering a positive attitude towards their disease developed from Beck's approach (Beck, 1976). In the group sessions people were also encouraged to improve communication within their family and with close friends, and to vent their feelings (Moorey and Freer, 1989). Success was assessed through initial assessment and at an 8-week follow-up. Those in treatment showed improvements in anxiety and depression measured on the HADS and on the MAC scale; measures of fighting spirit increased and hopelessness and helplessness decreased.

Finally, Greer (1992) reported a study in which 1974 patients aged 18–74 with a life expectancy of at least 12 months were given psychological therapy in a randomized prospective study. The measures used were the Hospital Anxiety and Depression Scale (HADS), the Mental Attitudes to Cancer Scale (MAC), the Rotterdam Symptom Checklist and the Psychosocial Adjustment to Illness Scale (PAIS), administered before therapy and at 8 weeks and 4 months follow-up. The results showed that the therapy group did better at 8 weeks and some gains were maintained at 4 months, even though patients only attended an average of five sessions each.

Generally, support groups for the terminally ill emphasize such processes as coping with a shared problem, open ventilation of feelings, enhancing knowledge about illness to increase the individual's sense of control, and making the most of remaining life. The studies reviewed here indicate that such interventions are helpful and effective. Group interventions may be more effective than work with individuals, because group members can share common problems and solutions to these. It is an opportunity for individuals to give to one another, at a time when they may feel isolated from those not sharing their situation. Additionally, the group may offer the chance to meet people at different stages of their illness and with different responses to dying (Spiegel, Bloom and Yalom, 1981). Some medical staff fear that letting people talk openly in groups about death may increase their fears; however, the opposite seems true, and patients in fact seem to be 'desensitized' to their fear by sharing it with others (Weisman, 1978). Le Shan (1992) raises another point of relevance here: reviewing the success of adjuvant psychological therapy for groups of patients suffering from cancer, he points out that there is an ethical dilemma here because the effect of such treatment is so strong that can it be right, for whatever reason, to exclude individuals for the sake of conducting a randomized trial? This view is especially well highlighted in the study by Spiegel et al., (1989), which reported that those receiving supportive psychological therapy survived twice as long as the control group.

Individual psychotherapeutic interventions

Some writers have suggested that talking with the dying person about death may actually hasten it, and that therapeutic support is of no value (Weisman, 1978). Nevertheless, there are many accounts in the literature of the needs of the dying person for psychotherapeutic help, and advice as to how interventions should be carried out.

Garfield (1980), for example, has stressed the need for psychotherapeutic support of terminally ill cancer patients, who often become increasingly isolated because of social and emotional withdrawal from those around them.

Individuals may also feel a lack of control over their situation because their illness causes a gradual loss of control over bodily functions, and loss of identity as they become increasingly less able to fulfil familiar roles.

Schneidman (1978) indicated that the psychotherapist should focus on topics initiated by the dying person. Topics likely to be raised by patients include wanting to know what is happening to them, expressing hope and despair about what is going to happen, wanting to live and die, being angry about the situation, revolting against it and submitting to it, and worrying that they may be rejected by those close to them as they deteriorate physically and become outwardly less appealing (Feigenberg, 1987).

Mansell-Pattison (1978) outlined the sort of fears dying individuals experienced, including fear of loneliness, loss of friends and family, fear of loss of body and self control, fear of pain and suffering and fear of regression due to physical deterioration.

Feigenberg (1987) advised therapists that a background knowledge of the problems of the dying is an essential requirement for working with the terminally ill, as is sufficient empathy and self-awareness. Feigenberg also points out the differences between work with the terminally ill and other kinds of psychotherapeutic interventions. For example, the aim of treatment is not cure and the course of the therapeutic relationship is governed by the individual's illness. He also stresses the need to carry the relationship, once initiated, to its conclusion.

Schneidman (1978) also notes different goals in therapy with the terminally ill. Therapeutic relationships are usually quickly and deeply established with the terminally ill, and the aims of treatment must be changed according to the level of the patient's deterioration. The goal of treatment is likely to be psychological comfort and stability for the patient, rather than achieving a 'state of psychoanalytic grace'.

Allied to psychotherapeutic approaches are some studies exploring the use of LSD as an adjunct to psychotherapy (Pahnke, 1969). It is not clear what value such approaches have had: although patients apparently benefited, it is suggested that those benefits accrued because of the amount of time spent with the patient during therapy, rather than the specific effects of LSD itself.

Using a more behavioural approach, a study by Hillier and Lunt (1980) applied a goal-setting approach to helping the terminally ill which also incorporated some of the elements encouraged in psychotherapeutic group interventions. They proposed looking in detail at individuals' problems, strengths and abilities, the resources available and past successful coping strategies. Problems and necessary changes were identified and prioritized with the patient, and specific goals were set to achieve these aims.

There is little systematic evaluation of individual psychotherapeutic interventions with the terminally ill, but there are strong advocates of commonsense approaches. Hinton (1984) points out that this sort of support enables individuals to reach a more positive acceptance of their situation. Stedeford (1981) indicated that support and open communication with a professional figure can be helpful for the terminally ill.

Finally, Weismann and Worden (1975) noted that people who react to their illness with pessimism and depression are likely to die sooner that those who feel more positive, suggesting that psychotherapeutic support may be of value in prolonging life, and this view is certainly upheld by the long-term follow-up conducted by Spiegel *et al.* (1989).

Anticipatory grief

Dying people have to come to terms with many losses and changes during the last phase of their lives which in some ways mirror the response of their families to losing them

(Hinton, 1972). Patients and relatives alike experience denial in the early stages of the illness, and bereaved people, like the terminally ill, commonly have feelings of anger and depression as they experience grief.

There is evidence to suggest that working through feelings together about the forthcoming loss can be helpful. Obviously, open awareness between patients and their families is essential for such anticipatory grief. Garfield (1980), Hinton (1972) and Stedeford (1980) showed that shared grieving about the patient's loss of independence can prevent resentment towards carers building up.

Patients who have always been care-givers in the family may find it difficult to accept being cared for, and working through this with the family can make it possible to give patients maximal choice about how they are cared for, so that they can continue to live with some independence, doing as many everyday tasks as possible (Stedeford, 1980).

Being terminally ill means relinquishing roles. Anticipating and working through this with dying people can prevent them giving these up too early, letting them continue with as many as they can manage without being made to feel guilty when some tasks are finally beyond them (Kastenbaum, 1975). Worden (1986) suggests that patients' and their families can work together, finding others to fill the patients' roles in life as they need to relinquish them. This may lessen the feelings of loss for patients as they hand over roles, and also for the family, who will not feel the acute loss and helplessness created when such roles are suddenly unfilled. Anticipatory grief allows the dying person and their relatives to reminisce about all the good things they have done together, to mourn experiences that were less successful and to express their disappointment about events that will never now occur because of the impending death. There may be unfinished business to complete, a chance to express their feelings about one another and

make their goodbyes (Garfield, 1980; Worden, 1986). Families may need professional guidance with this work, and Pincus (1974) has outlined how such work may be done through the process of family therapy.

There is also evidence that anticipatory grieving is beneficial for relatives, because it is easier to accept a loss occurring gradually over a long period as they have more opportunity to come to terms with it. Natterson and Knudson (1960) and Worden (1986) compared people with a short-term unanticipated dying period with those having a longer anticipated dying period, and found that relatives' grief was more severe in the absence of anticipation. However, there are times when a prolonged wait for death can be disadvantageous. Riley and Foner (1968) noticed families cutting off from the patient before death, indicated by a decrease in visiting once the ill person was admitted to an institution for terminal care. Weisman and Hackett (1961) point out that some relatives' premature acceptance of the individual's death go to the point of behaving as though the person is actually dead, speaking in hushed tones and drawing the curtains. Patients may similarly detach themselves from the family when they feel prepared for death. When the terminal illness goes on for a long time this response is more likely, and the opportunity for prolonged anticipatory grieving may not be beneficial. Clayton, Halikas and Maurice (1973) found that when the length of illness exceeded 6 months there were more likely to be negative effects, such as increased irritability among surviving relatives.

Conclusion

In this review it can be seen that personal awareness and understanding of the predicament of the terminally ill are prerequisites for work in this area (Feigenberg, 1987). It has been repeatedly noted that much of the relevant literature is subjective and anecdotal: this is precisely because it seeks to explore individuals' personal experiences with those who are dying and relay these to those people who wish to offer professional help to the terminally ill.

From the psychologist's point of view, many mainstream techniques are appropriate for work with the dying, for example the management of anxiety and depression and the ability to facilitate open expression of feeling in the patient (Schneidman, 1978; Miller, 1986; Beck 1976). Further, the skills necessary for building a therapeutic relationship are also important, such as the ability to show empathy, warmth and openness (Rogers, 1958). Finally, techniques developed for psychological aspects of other problems, such as the management of chronic pain (Finer, 1979), unpleasant physical symptoms (Burish and Lyles, 1981) and sick role behaviour (Fordyce, 1976), can be useful to help both dying people and those close to them. The psychologist with a broad base in the above skills areas, together with a good understanding of the problems facing the terminally ill, should be able to offer helpful service, to be interwoven with those skills of other professional groups essential to the proper care of the dying.

References

Annas, G. (1974) Rights of the terminally ill patient. *Journal of Nursing Administration*, **4**, 403.

Barber, J. (1980) Cancer pain: psychological management using hypnosis. *Cancer Journal for Clinicians*, **30**(3), 130–6.

Beck, A.T. (1976) *Cognitive Therapy and Emotional Disorders*, International Universities Press, New York.

Black, P.M. and Morrow, G.R. (1991) Anticipatory nausea and emesis – behavioural interventions, in *Cancer Patient Care: Psychosocial Treatment Methods*, (ed M. Watson), Cambridge University Press, Cambridge.

Burish, T.G. and Lyles, J.N. (1981) Effectiveness of relaxation training in reducing adverse reactions to cancer chemotherapy. *Journal of Behavioural Medicine*, **4**(4), 65–78.

Cartwright, A., Hockey, L. and Anderson, J. (1973) *Life Before Death*, Routledge and Kegan Paul, London.

Clayton, P.J. Halikas, J.A. and Maurice, W.L. (1973) Anticipatory grief and widowhood. *British Journal of Psychiatry*, **122**, 47–51.

Crammond, W.A. (1970) Psychotherapy of the dying patient. *British Medical Journal*, **15**(4), 389–93.

de Haes, J.C.J.M., Van Knippenham, F.C.E. and Neijt, J.P. (1990) Measuring psychological and physical distress in cancer patients: structure and applications of the Rotterdam Symptom Checklist. *British Journal of Cancer*, **62**, 1034–8.

Fallowfield, L. (1991) *The Quality of Life – the Missing Measurement in Health*, Human Horizons Series.

Feigenberg, L. (1987) Care of the dying, in *The Quality of Life of Cancer Patients*, (eds N.K. Aaroman and J. Beckmann), European Organisation for Research and Treatment of Cancer, pp. 255.

Ferlic, M., Goldman, A. and Kennedy, B.J. (1979) Group counselling in adult patients with advanced cancer. *Cancer*, **43**, 760.

Finer, B. (1979) Hypnotherapy of pain in advanced cancer, in *Advances in Pain Research and Therapy*, vol. 2 (eds J.J. Bonica and V. Ventrafridda), Raven Press, New York.

Fordyce, W.E. (1976) Behavioural methods for chronic pain and illness, in *Behavioural Management of Anxiety, Depression and Pain*, (ed. P.O. Davidson), Mosby, St Louis.

Forester, B.M., Kornfeld, M.S. and Fleiss, J. (1978) Psychiatric aspects of radiotherapy. *American Journal of Psychiatry*, **135**(8), 960–3.

Fotopoulos, S.B., Graham, C. and Cook, M.R. (1979) Psycho-physiological control in cancer pain, in *Advances in Pain Research and Therapy*, vol. 2 (eds J.J. Bonica and V. Ventrafridda), Raven Press, New York.

Garfield, C.A. (1978) Psychosocial oncology: doctor–patient relationships in terminal illness, in *Psychosocial Care of the Dying Patient*, (ed. C.A. Garfield), McGraw-Hill, New York.

Garfield, C.A. (1980) Emotional aspects of death and dying, in *The Continuing Care of Terminal Cancer Patients*, (eds R.G. Twycross and V. Ventrafridda), Pergamon Press, Oxford, pp. 43–56.

Glaser, B.G. and Strauss, A.L. (1966) *Awareness of Dying*, Aldine Press, Chicago.

Greer, S. (1984) The psychological dimensions of cancer treatment. *Social Sciences and Medicine*, **18**(4), 345–9.

Greer, S. (1992) Adjuvant psychological therapy for patients with cancer: a prospective randomised trial. *British Medical Journal*, **304**, 675–80.

Hillier, E.R. and Lunt, B. (1980) Goal setting in terminal cancer, in *The Continuing Care of Terminal Cancer Patients*, (eds R.G. Twycross and V. Ventrafridda), Pergamon Press, Oxford.

Hinton, J.M. (1963) The physical and mental distress of the dying. *Quarterly Journal of Medicine*, **32**, 1–21.

Hinton, J.M. (1972) The psychiatry of terminal illness in adults and children. *Proceedings of the Royal Society of Medicine*, **65**, 1035–40.

Hinton, J.M. (1976) Approaching death, in *Modern Trends in Psychosomatic Medicine*, vol. 3, (ed. O. Hill), pp. 471–97.

Hinton, J.M. (1984) Coping with terminal illness, in *The Experience of Illness* (eds R. Fitzpatrick, J.M. Hinton, S. Newman *et al.*), Tavistock Publications, London, pp. 227–45.

Holland, J. (1977) Psychological aspects of oncology. *Medical Clinics of North America*, **61**(4) 737–48.

Kalish, R.A. (1978) A little myth is a dangerous thing: research in the service of the dying, in *Psychological Care of the Dying Patient*, (ed. C.A. Garfield), McGraw Hill, New York, pp. 218–27.

Kalish, R.A. and Reynolds, D.K. (1976) *Death and Ethnicity: A Psychocultural Study*, University of South California, Los Angeles (unpublished manuscript).

Kastenbaum, R. (1975) Is death a life crisis? On the confrontation with death in theory and practice, in *Life-Span Development Psychology Normative Life Crisis*, (eds N. Datan and L.H. Einsberg), Academic Press, New York, pp. 19–50.

Kubler-Ross, E. (1970) *On Death and Dying*, Macmillan, London and New York.

Lazarus, R.S. (1984) *Stress Appraisal and Coping*, Springer, New York.

Le Shan, L. (1992) A new question in studying psychosocial intervention and cancer. *Holistic Health – The British Holistic Medical Association Newsletter*, N.34, 1–4.

Lock, S. (1990) Chasms in communication *British Medical Journal*, **301**, 1407–8.

Maguire, P. (1984) Doctor patient communication, in *Health Care and Human Behaviour*, (eds A. Matthews and A. Steptoe), Academic Press, London.

Maguire, P. (1985) Improving the detection of psychiatric problems in cancer patients. *Social Science and Medicine*, **20**(8), 819–23.

Maguire, P. and Faulkner, A. (1988) How to communicate with cancer patients: handling bad news and difficult questions. *British Medical Journal*, **297**, 907–9.

Mansell-Pattison, E. (1978) The living/dying process, in *Psychosocial Care of the Dying Patient*, (ed. C.A. Garfield), McGraw-Hill, New York, pp. 133–68.

Melzack, R. and Perry, C. (1975) Self-regulation of pain: the use of alpha feedback and hypnotic training for the control of chronic pain. *Experimental Neurology*, **46**, 452–69.

Miller, D. (1986) Psychology, AIDS, ARC and PGL, in *The Management of AIDS Patients*, (eds D. Miller, J. Weber and J. Green), Macmillan Press, London, pp. 131–51.

Miller, S.M. (1987) Monitoring and blunting: validation of a questionnaire to assess styles of information seeking under treat. *Journal of Personality and Social Psychology*, **52**(2), 345–53.

Moorey, S. (1990) Cognitive therapy for cancer patients. *British Journal of Hospital Medicine*, Suppl, 35–7.

Moorey, S. and Greer S. (1989) *Psychological Therapy for Patients with Cancer. A New Approach*, Oxford, Heinemann Medical Books.

Morris, T. (1979) Psychological adjustment to mastectomy. *Cancer Treatment Review*, **6**, 41–6.

Morrow, G.R. and Morrell, C. (1982) Behavioural treatment for anticipated nausea and vomiting induced by cancer chemotherapy. *New England Journal of Medicine*, **307**, 1476–80.

Morrow, G.R., Chiarello, R.J. and Derogatis, L.R. (1978) A new scale for assessing patients' psychosocial adjustment to medical illness. *Psychological Medicine*, **8**, 605–10.

Natterson, J.W. and Knudson, A.G. (1960) Observations concerning fear of death in fatally ill children and their mothers. *Psychosomatic Medicine*, **22** (6), 456–63.

Pahnke, V.N. (1969) The psychedelic mystical experience in the human encounter. *Harvard Theological Review*, **62**, 1–32.

Palmer, V., Walsh, G.A., Mckinna, J.A. and Greening, W.P. (1980) Adjuvant chemotherapy for breast cancer: side effects and quality of life. *British Medical Journal*, **281**, 1594–7.

Parkes, C.M. (1980) Terminal care: an evaluation of advisory domiciliary service at St Christopher's Hospice. *Postgraduate Medical Journal*, **56**, 685–9.

Payne, S. (1991) Cancer patients' perceptions of health. *Senior Nurse*, **II**(2), 29–32.

Peck, A. and Boland, J. (1977) Emotional reactions to radiation treatment. *Cancer*, **40**, 180–4.

Pietroni, P. (1991) *The Greening of Medicine*, Victor Gollancz, London.

Pincus, L. (1974) *Death and the Family*, Pantheon, New York.

Plumb, M. and Holland, J. (1977) Comparative studies of psychological function in patients with advanced cancer: self-reported depressive symptoms. *Psychosomatic Medicine*, **39**(4), 264–76.

Redd, W.H. (1982) Behavioural analysis and control of psychosomatic symptoms in patients receiving intensive cancer treatment. *British Journal of Clinical Psychology*, **21**, 351–8.

Rees, D. (1972) The distress of the dying. *British Medical Journal*, **3**, 105.

Riley, M. and Foner, A. (1968) *Ageing and Society*, Russell-Sage Foundation, New York.

Rogers, C.R. (1958) The characteristics of a helping relationship. *Personal and Guidance Journal*, 37, 6–16.

Saunders, C. (1966) Management of terminal illness. *Hospital Medicine*, 5(8), 22.

Schneidman, E.S. (1978) Some aspects of psychotherapy with dying persons, in *Psychological Care of the Dying Patient*, (ed. C.A. Garfield), McGraw-Hill, New York, pp. 201–18.

Seagar, C.P. and Flood, R.A. (1965) Suicide in Bristol. *British Journal Psychiatry*, 111, 919.

Shultz, R. and Aderman, D. (1974) Clinical research and the stages of dying. *Omega*, 5, 137–44.

Silberfarb, P.M., Maurer, H. and Crowthamel, C.S. (1980) Psychosocial aspects of neoplastic disease. I. Functional status of breast cancer patients during different treatment regimes. *American Journal of Psychiatry*, 137(4), 450–5.

Slevin, L. (1992) Current issues in cancer: quality of life: philosophical question of clinical reality? *British Medical Journal*, 305, 466–9.

Sobel, W.K. (1981) Behavioural treatment of depression, in *Behavioural Therapy in Terminal Care*, (ed. H. Sobel), Balinger, USA.

Spiegel, D., Bloom, J. and Yalom, I. (1981) Group support for patients with metastatic cancer. *Archives of General Psychiatry*, 38, 527–33.

Spiegel, D., Kraemar, H.C., Bloom, J.R. and Gottheil, E. (1989) The effects of psychosocial treatment on survival of patients with metastic breast cancer. *Lancet*, ii 888–91.

Stedeford, A. (1980) Common psychological problems, in *The Continuing Care of Terminal Cancer Patients*, (eds R.G. Twycross and V. Ventrafridda), Pergamon Press, Oxford, pp. 57–62.

Stedeford, A. (1981) Couples facing death. *British Medical Journal*, 283, 1033–6.

Turk, D. and Rennert, K. (1981) Pain and the terminally ill cancer patient: a cognitive social learning perspective, in *Journal of Behaviour Therapy in Terminal Care*, (ed. H. Sobel), Ballinger, USA.

Twycross, R.G. (1975) Disease of the central nervous system: relief of terminal pain. *British Medical Journal*, 212–14.

Watson, M. (1988) Screening for psychological morbidity cancer patients. *Cancer Journal*, 2(6), 195–6.

Watson, M., Greer, S and Young. J. (1988) Development of questionnaire. Measure of Adjustment to Cancer, the MAC Scale. *Psychological Medicine*, 18, 203–9.

Weisman, A.D. (1972) Psychosocial considerations in terminal care, in *Psychosocial Aspects of Terminal Care*, (eds B.Schoenberg, A.Carr and A.H.Kutscher), Columbia University Press, New York, pp. 162–72.

Weisman, A.D. (1976) Early diagnosis of vulnerability in cancer patients. *American Journal of Medical Science*, 27, 187.

Weisman, A.D. (1978) Misgivings and misconceptions in the psychiatric care of terminally ill patients, in *Psychosocial Care of the Dying Patient*, (ed. C.A. Garfield), McGraw-Hill, New York, 185–200.

Weisman, A.D. and Hackett, T.P. (1961) Predilection to Death. *Psychosomatic Medicine*, 23, 232–55.

Weisman, A.D. and Worden, J.W. (1975) *Psychosocial Analysis of Cancer Deaths*, Omega Project, Department of Psychiatry, Harvard Medical School, Boston, MA.

Wilkes, P. (1985) *A Source Book on Terminal Care*, University of Sheffield, Sheffield.

Woodford, J.M. and Fielding, J.R. (1970) Pain and Cancer. *Journal of Psychosomatic Research*, 14, 365–75.

Worden, I.W. (1986) *Grief Counselling and Grief Therapy*, Tavistock, London.

Yalom, I.D. and Greaves, C. (1977) Group therapy with the terminally ill. *American Journal of Psychiatry*, 134(4), 396–400.

Zigmond, A.S., and Snaith, R.P. (1983) The Hospital Anxiety and Depression Scale., *Acta Psychiatrica Scandinavica*, 67, 361–70.

Index

Page numbers in **bold type** refer to figures; those in italics refer to tables.